Chinese Economic Dev

This book outlines and analyzes the economic development of China between 1949 and 2007. Avoiding a narrowly economic approach, it addresses many of the broader aspects of development, including literacy, mortality, demographics and the environment. The book also discusses the Great Leap Forward, the Cultural Revolution, the aims of Maoism and the introduction of an outward-looking market economy since 1978.

The distinctive features of this book are its sweep and its engagement with controversial issues. For example, there is no question that aspects of Maoism were disastrous, but Bramall argues that there was another side to the programme taken as a whole. He urges that China's Cultural Revolution of the 1960s and late Maoism more generally (1964–78) need to be seen as a coherent plan for development, rather than the genocidal programme of vengeance portrayed in some quarters. The current system of government in China has presided over three decades of very rapid economic growth. However, the author shows that this growth has come at a price. One of the most unequal countries in the world, China is rife with inequalities in income and in access to health and education. Bramall makes it clear that unless radical change takes place, Chinese growth will not be sustainable.

This wide-ranging text is relevant to all those studying the economic history of China as well as its contemporary economy. It is also useful more generally for students and researchers in the fields of international and development economics.

Chris Bramall is Professor of Chinese Political Economy at the School of East Asian Studies, Sheffield University, UK.

Chinese Economic Development

Chris Bramall

LONDON AND NEW YORK

First published 2009
by Routledge
2 Park Square, Milton Park, Abingdon, Oxon OX14 4RN

Simultaneously published in the USA and Canada
by Routledge
270 Madison Ave, New York, NY 10016

Routledge is an imprint of the Taylor & Francis Group, an informa business

© 2009 Chris Bramall

Typeset in Times New Roman by
Bookcraft Ltd, Stroud, Gloucestershire
Printed and bound in Great Britain by
TJ International Ltd, Padstow, Cornwall

All rights reserved. No part of this book may be reprinted or reproduced or utilised in any form or by any electronic, mechanical, or other means, now known or hereafter invented, including photocopying and recording, or in any information storage or retrieval system, without permission in writing from the publishers.

British Library Cataloguing in Publication Data
A catalogue record for this book is available from the British Library

Library of Congress Cataloging in Publication Data
Bramall, Chris.
Chinese economic development / Chris Bramall.
   p. cm.
   Includes bibliographical references and index.
   1. Economic development—China—History.
   2. China—Economic conditions—1949- I. Title.
HC427.9.B64 2008
338.951—dc22   2008012563

ISBN10: 0-415-37347-6 (hbk)
ISBN10: 0-415-37348-4 (pbk)
ISBN10: 0-203-89082-5 (ebk)

ISBN13: 978-0-415-37347-0 (hbk)
ISBN13: 978-0-415-37348-7 (pbk)
ISBN13: 978-0-203-89082-0 (ebk)

For Sophie, Rosa, Alexandra and Kay

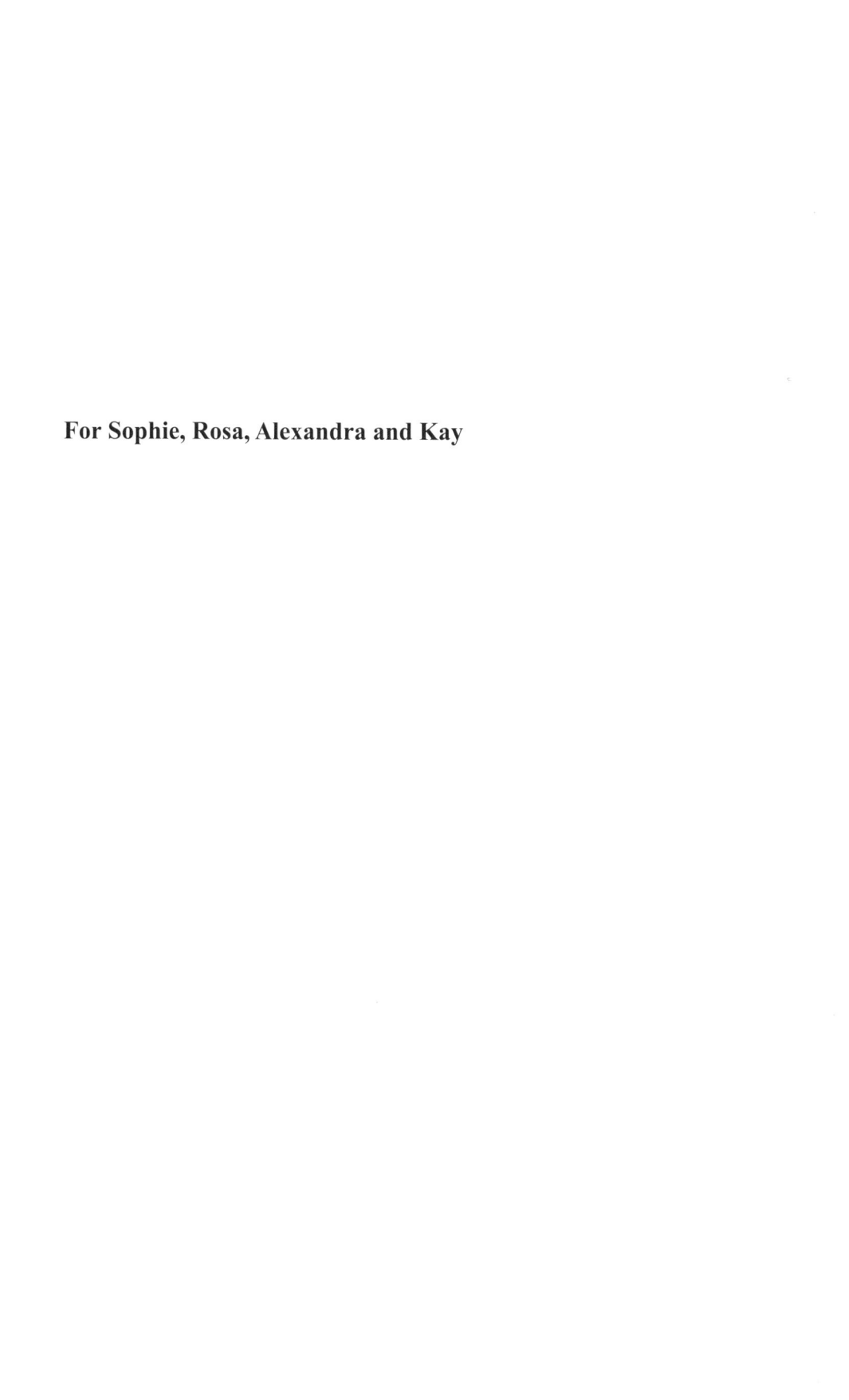

Contents

List of boxes   ix
List of figures   x
List of tables   xiii
Glossary   xv
Introduction   xxi

PART 1
Starting points   1

1 Measuring development   3
2 The Chinese economy on the eve of revolution   44

PART 2
The transition to socialism, 1949–1963   77

3 Early Maoism, 1949–1955   79
4 The Great Famine, 1955–1963   118

PART 3
The late Maoist era, 1963–1978   143

5 The late Maoist development strategy   145
6 The revolution in education   174
7 Collective farming   213

8	The Third Front and rural industrialization	261
9	Late Maoism: an assessment	286

PART 4
Market socialism, 1978–1996 — 323

10	The era of market socialism, 1978–1996	325
11	Foreign trade and inward investment since 1971	360
12	Industrial development since 1978	394
13	China's developmental record in the era of Deng Xiaoping	435

PART 5
The transition to capitalism, 1996–2007 — 467

14	Chinese capitalism since 1996	469
15	The Revolution betrayed?	497
16	Summary and conclusions	544

Bibliography	555
Index	594

Boxes

1.1	The determinants of economic potential	29
3.1	The Marxian theory of history	81
3.2	Pivotal moments in Chinese development during the early 1950s	86
4.1	The key speeches and initiatives of the Great Leap Forward	120
5.1	Phases of late Maoism	146
5.2	The evolution of Maoist thought	149
5.3	The logic of the late Maoist development strategy	155
5.4	A political chronology of late Maoism	159
6.1	Summary effects of late Maoism on years of education by class	207
7.1	Chinese agricultural institutions, 1949–2007	215
10.1	Chinese economic policy, 1978–1996	330
10.2	Agricultural institutions, 1976–1984	338
12.1	Strategies designed to improve SOE performance, 1978–1996	408
14.1	Key events of the post-1996 era	476

Figures

1.1	The Gini coefficient	17
2.1	Modern cotton spindles in China, 1890–1936	47
2.2	Chinese geographical regions	59
2.3	Average annual rainfall in northern Chinese cities	60
2.4	Average annual rainfall in southern Chinese cities	61
2.5	Per capita GDP by province, 1953	64
2.6	Chinese crude death rates, 1953	67
3.1	The growth of light and heavy industrial output, 1952–1957	90
3.2	Growth of industrial GVA and gross fixed capital formation (GFCF), 1952–1957	92
3.3	The dispersion of provincial GDP per capita, 1952–1957	109
4.1	Share of fixed investment in GDP	122
4.2	Mortality rates by province, 1960	127
4.3	Grain output, procurements and rural availability during the Leap	133
4.4	Trends in gross value-added in agriculture and industry	136
4.5	Coefficients of variation for provincial per capita GDP	138
5.1	Population growth, 1949–1978	157
5.2	Share of gross fixed investment in GDP	157
5.3	Industrial value-added during late Maoism	162
6.1	School enrolments, 1949–1965	178
6.2.	Primary school gross enrolment rates	179
6.3	The enrolment gap, 1949–1965	183
6.4	Primary enrolment rates and number of graduates, 1962–1978	192
6.5	Promotion rates to junior and senior middle schools, 1964–1978	193
6.6	Illiteracy rates in 1982 by year of birth	194
6.7	The gap between progression rates in urban and rural areas, 1962–1978	203
6.8	Literacy rates by county and city, 1982	205
7.1	Net grain exports	214
7.2	Distribution of idle time in agriculture by month in the early 1930s	223
7.3	Growth of agricultural output, 1952–2006	229
7.4	Rice yields in Asia and the USA, 1961–2004	231

Figures   xi

7.5	Trends in labour productivity under collective farming, 1955–1981	233
7.6	Cultivated and sown area, 1949–2006	244
7.7	The internal terms of trade, 1950–1984	246
7.8	Production and imports of chemical fertilizer	248
8.1	The share of the secondary sector in GDP at Panzhihua, 1952–1978	268
8.2	Growth of commune and brigade industrial output, 1962–1978	271
8.3	Coefficients of variation for per capita industrial output	279
8.4	Share of accumulation in national income in fast and slow-growing provinces	280
8.5	Industrial employment in 1982 by county and city	282
9.1	Food consumption in China, 1963–1978	294
9.2	Chinese infant mortality rates, 1963–1978	297
9.3	The dispersion of per capita GDP by province and municipality	301
9.4	The urban–rural gap in terms of per capita GDP, 1963–1978	302
9.5	Regional variations in infant mortality at the time of the 1982 census	307
9.6	The urban–rural infant mortality gap, 1963–1978	309
10.1	The impact of Readjustment	334
10.2	Annual growth rate of GNI during Readjustment	335
10.3	The growth of agricultural value-added, 1963–2006	340
10.4	The internal terms of trade, 1978–2006	347
10.5	Growth of gross national income and the consumer price index, 1982–1991	351
10.6	Growth of government consumption and capital construction expenditure	354
11.1	The share of exports in Chinese GDP, 1931–2006	360
11.2	The changing composition of Chinese imports, 1950–1978	364
11.3	Exports of crude oil and refined petroleum, 1971–1982	366
11.4	Trends in foreign direct investment and the share of exports in GDP, 1996–2006	370
11.5	Ratio of the value of exports from Jiangsu and Shanghai to those of Guangdong, 1991–2005	377
12.1	Trends in labour productivity in Chinese industry, 1965–1978	403
12.2	Trends in defence spending	410
12.3	Rates of profit in the SOE sector, 1978–1996	415
12.4	Value-added per worker in manufacturing in China as a percentage of value-added in other countries, 1978–1994	417
12.5	Industrial employment by sector	422
12.6	The rate of profit in the SOE sector since 1996	425
12.7	Growth of industrial GVA, 1996–2006	426
12.8	Urban unemployment after 1993	428
13.1	Indices of per capita GDP in transition economies	439
13.2	Fluctuations in GNI and the retail price index, 1978–1996	442
13.3	Junior and middle school enrolment rates, 1968–1996	443

xii *Figures*

13.4	Poverty in rural China, 1978–1996	448
13.5	Estimated rates of urban poverty	453
13.6	Coefficients of variation for per capita GDP at the provincial level, 1978–1996	457
14.1	Growth of real GDP and the consumer price index, 1996–2007	471
14.2	The western region of China, 1997	482
14.3	The ratio of per capita GDP in Guizhou to per capita GDP in Guangdong	486
15.1	Particulate matter concentrations in Panzhihua	500
15.2	Average life expectancy at birth, 1977–2005	507
15.3	Numbers living below the rural poverty line in five provinces, 1996–2004	511
15.4	The growth of farm and rural income, 1996–2005	512
15.5	Poor counties in China (map)	513
15.6	Official urban unemployment rates, 1996–2006	515
15.7	Urban–rural illiteracy rates in 2004	519
15.8	Migration and the Chinese labour market	523
15.9	Progression rates to junior and senior middle school	538

Tables

1.1	Estimates of GDP per person using national and US prices in 2005 ($US)	7
1.2	Mismatch between trends in life expectancy and per capita GDP	10
1.3	HDI and per capita GDP rankings: some country examples	12
1.4	Gini coefficients for a range of countries	17
1.5	Ratio of black to white mortality rates in the USA, late 1980s (for men and women aged 35–54)	23
2.1	GDP per capita on the eve of modernization	54
2.2	The share of agriculture in GDP and employment in poor countries	56
2.3	Industrial production, 1952	66
3.1	Shares of gross industrial output value by ownership	90
3.2	Growth of industrial production, 1949–1955	92
3.3	The growth of agricultural cooperatives in China, 1950–1955	96
3.4	Alternative estimates of grain production in the early 1950s	98
3.5	Estimates of GDP growth, 1914–1955	102
3.6	Human development indicators, 1949–1955	104
3.7	Differentials in the Chinese countryside, 1954	107
3.8	The distribution of income by class and by region, 1951–1952	111
4.1	Collectivization in China, 1955–1956	121
4.2	The famine in Sichuan province	128
4.3	Famine mortality and participation in communal canteens	129
4.4	Trends in economic aggregates during the Leap and its aftermath	131
4.5	Population trends, 1957–1964	138
6.1	Total JMS enrolment by place of residence, 1962–1965	185
6.2	School enrolment rates for children aged 7–12 in 1964	186
6.3	Number of senior and junior middle schools, 1964–1978	188
6.4	Provinces with illiteracy rates of over 60 per cent in 1964	201
7.1	The size of collective farms, 1959–1981	217
7.2	Trends in irrigated area, 1952–1978	225
7.3	Chinese agriculture under collective and family farming	228
7.4	The growth of land productivity, 1952–2005	230
7.5	The decollectivization of Chinese agriculture	251
7.6	Output and conditions of agricultural production, 1974–1984	254

8.1	Growth of industrial output in Third Front centres, 1965–1978	267
8.2	The share of industry in employment and GDP, 1952 and 1978	272
8.3	Growth of commune and brigade industrial output by province, 1962–1989	278
9.1	Estimates of GDP growth, 1963–1978	292
9.2	Life expectancy	295
9.3	Provincial deviations in life expectancy and literacy from the national average in 1982	296
9.4	Trends in GDP per capita by province and municipality, 1964–1978	303
9.5	Poor counties in China, 1977–1979	310
9.6	Per capita GDP growth during the East Asian miracles	315
10.1	Agricultural growth rates, 1963–2006	340
11.1	Chinese imports by country of origin, 1963–1971	362
11.2	Trade shares and growth rates in selected provinces, 1978–1988	373
11.3	International evidence on export shares, 2005	381
12.1	Profit rates in the state industrial sector at the end of the Maoist era	402
12.2	The readjustment of the commune and brigade enterprises, 1978–1983	405
12.3	Employment in the TVE sector since 1978	406
12.4	Growth rates of light and heavy industry	409
12.5	The structure of Chinese industrial output, 1980–1996	412
12.6	Total factor productivity growth in independent-accounting industrial enterprises, 1980–1996	416
12.7	Growth of industrial output and employment, 1965–1996	418
12.8	Sectoral shares in total employment	427
13.1	Chinese GDP growth after 1978 in historical perspective	438
13.2	Chinese life expectancy, 1973–2000	445
13.3	Official estimates of rural poverty	447
13.4	SSB Estimates of Chinese income inequality	454
13.5	Alternative estimates of the Chinese income distribution, 1978–1995	455
13.6	Rural daily calorie consumption per capita, 1990	460
13.7	China's growth rate in comparative perspective, 1978–1996	461
14.1	Variation in growth rates across plan periods	473
14.2	The floating population in 2000	478
14.3	Fiscal surpluses as a share of GDP, 1978–1989	484
14.4	Budgetary revenue and expenditure in a sample of western provinces	490
15.1	Growth of Chinese GDP since 1996	498
15.2	GDP growth rates during economic miracles in large countries	499
15.3	Water quality in China's most polluted river basins	501
15.4	Educational attainment in China	507
15.5	Human development levels in China and India, 2004	509
15.6	Official estimates of rural poverty	510
15.7	SSB and other estimates of Chinese income inequality	517
15.8	Public spending on health and education	533

Glossary

Abbreviations and key concepts

CBEs   commune and brigade enterprises. Renamed TVEs in 1984

CCP   Chinese Communist Party

collective farming   the three-tier structure of farming in operation in China between 1955 and 1983. Under it, most land was managed by the collective rather than by private households (which directly managed about 5 per cent of arable area). The three tiers of collective farming were communes (*renmin gongshe*), production brigades (*shengchan dadui*) and production teams (*shengchan dui*)

collectively owned enterprises   notionally distinct from SOEs in that COEs retain profits rather than remitting them to the state, but in terms of their actual mode of operation, SOEs and COEs are virtually indistinguishable

Cultural Revolution   the term is used in this book to refer to the period 1966–8 when Red Guard (university and middle school students) launched an unprecedented attack upon China's educational system, its cultural artefacts, many of the institutions of state and leading members of the CCP seen as trying to restore capitalism. Much of the literature uses the term to refer to the whole period between 1966 and 1976

CV   coefficient of variation

EEFSU   Eastern Europe and the Former Soviet Union

FAD   food availability decline. This is the view that famine is caused by a decline in the amount of food available per person. As Sen has shown, and as also illustrated by the case of China in 1958, famine conditions can also be caused by changes in the distribution of income, which may lead to a decline in 'entitlements' (the ability to buy food) and hence to starvation – even if average food availability is unchanged

FAO   Food and Agriculture Organization of the UN

FDI   foreign direct investment

five small industries   rural industries set up to produce cement, chemical fertilizer, iron and steel, machinery and power in the 1960s and 1970s

GDP   gross domestic product

GDP measured at purchasing power parity a method of adjusting GDP to allow more accurately for differences in prices between countries and hence to measure 'true' differences in purchasing power between countries

***geti* enterprises** individual enterprises. These are best thought of as small household or family enterprises, officially defined as an enterprise employing fewer than seven workers. Larger non-enterprises are classified as private

Gini coefficient the standard international measure of income inequality. Varies between 0 (absolute equality) and 1 (all income accrues to one person)

Great Leap Forward an ambitious (and ultimately disastrous) programme of rapid economic growth launched in 1958 which centred around the creation of communes and the diversion of the rural workforce from farming into iron and steel production

GNI gross national income (previously known as GNP)

GVA gross value-added. The standard measure of output net of material inputs consumed in the production process ('gross' because it does not allow for the depreciation of machinery)

GVIO and GVAO gross value of industrial and agricultural output respectively. These were key output indicators in the Chinese statistical system before 1992 and even now are widely calculated and published. However, they are not measures of value-added, because the value of intermediate inputs is included

***hukou* system** the system of household registration, whereby Chinese citizens have an official place of residence. The system still operates; for instance, unofficial migrants to urban areas still find it hard to find schools for their children. However, the development of markets after 1978 (which allow unofficial migrants to buy food, education, etc.), means that it is far less effective a means of control than it was during the Maoist era

HYVs high-yielding crop varieties introduced in China during the 1970s. The package of improved irrigation, HYVs and chemical fertilizer is usually called the Green Revolution

ICP International Comparison Project designed to adjust GDP estimates across countries for differences in prices

infant mortality rate deaths per thousand of the population amongst infants aged up to one year old

internal terms of trade the ratio of agricultural to industrial prices

JMS junior middle school

KMT Kuomintang (or Guomindang). The Chinese Nationalist Party

MPS the material product system of national accounting developed in the Soviet Union and used in China between 1949 and 1992. Its key concepts include NDMP, GVIO and GVAO

NDMP net domestic material product. A narrower measure of economic activity than GDP because it excludes 'non-productive' economic activities such as advertising

NDP gross domestic product minus depreciation

NEP New Economic Policy. The development strategy pursued in the USSR between 1921 and 1928. It combined elements of capitalism (such as private farming) and socialism (such as state ownership of the key industries)

NICs newly industrializing countries. Typically applied to Taiwan, Singapore, South Korea, Singapore and to parts of Latin America and South Asia in the second half of the twentieth century to distinguish them from LDCs (less developed countries)

PLA People's Liberation Army

progression rate enrolment in a given level of education as a percentage of graduates from the previous level

SEM Socialist Education Movement (1963–6)

SEZs special economic zones. Set up after 1979 to attract foreign investment

shangshan xiaxiang the programme whereby urban youth were sent down to the countryside. Most of the 'sending down' occurred between 1968 and 1972. Often abbreviated as *xiafang*

social formation a Marxist concept developed by Althusser. Refers to the combination of the forces of production (roughly technology and labour), relations of production (economic organization and incentives) and the superstructure (culture, government and the legal system). The relationship between these three remains a controversial issue amongst Marxists

SOE state-owned enterprises. 'State' here includes county governments and higher, but excludes enterprises owned by town and village governments

SSB China's State Statistical Bureau. Now likes to call itself the National Bureau of Statistics

SMS senior middle school

Third Front the programme of defence industrialization initiated in western China after 1964 (and later extended to central China and to mountainous areas within the coastal provinces). Halted in the early 1980s

TFP total factor productivity: output per unit of total input (labour, capital and land combined)

TVEs township and village enterprises

xiafang see *shangshan xiaxiang*

Chinese slogans

gaige kaifang reform and opening up
liangge fanshi the two whatevers
mo shitou guohe crossing the river by touching the stones
pinqiong bushi shehui zhuyi poverty is not socialism
xian fuqilai to get rich is glorious
yiliang weigang take grain as the key link
zai nongye xue Dazhai in agriculture study Dazhai

Main political figures

Chen Yun (1905–95) The architect of the market socialist economy introduced after 1978. Much more sympathetic towards the notion of traditional (Leninist) socialism than Deng Xiaoping.

Deng Xiaoping (1904–97) A staunch follower of Mao in the 1950s and an advocate of the Great Leap Forward. Purged in the 1960s for being a close ally of Liu Shaoqi. *De facto* ruler of China between 1978 and 1997. Responsible for introducing the policy of *gaige kaifang* and for the liberalization of the economy in the 1980s and 1990s.

Gang of Four Jiang Qing (Mao's wife), Zhang Chunqiao, Yao Wenyuan and Wang Hongwen. All four continue to be characterized as 'evil' in official CCP accounts, but we lack a proper evaluation of their true role during the Cultural Revolution and the 1970s.

Hu Jintao (1942–) Party Secretary, October 2002–.

Hu Yaobang (1915–89) Party Secretary, 1980-19–87. Purged for his failure to check student protests.

Hua Guofeng (1921–) Mao's rather ineffectual successor. Chairman of the CCP, 1976–81; Prime Minister 1976–80.

Jiang Qing (1914–91) Mao's third wife. A brilliant actress before her marriage to Mao, Jiang became a politically important figure during the 1960s and the leader of the Gang of Four. Arrested in 1976 and imprisoned until her death. An object of much sexist hatred in the 1970s, and since. Probably better seen as a puppet of Mao than as an independent political actor.

Jiang Zemin (1929–) Party Secretary, June 1989–October 2002. Largely responsible for the abandonment of market socialism and the creation of a capitalist economy in China.

Lin Biao (1906–1971) The PLA's most brilliant general. Never really recovered from serious wounds suffered in 1938, which limited his political and military role after 1949. Named as Mao's successor in 1966. Killed fleeing China in a plane crash in September 1971.

Liu Shaoqi (1898–1969) The leading advocate of greater use of markets in the Maoist era, and hence identified as a 'revisionist' and 'capitalist roader'. Persecuted to death during the Cultural Revolution.

Mao Zedong (1893–1976) Leader of the CCP between 1943 (some would say 1935) and 1976. All the most recent research shows that his authority was unchallenged from the early 1940s until his death.

Peng Dehuai (1898–1974) Famously opposed the Great Leap Forward at the Lushan plenum in 1959. As a result, purged, and persecuted to death in 1974.

Wen Jiabao (1942–) Prime Minister, March 2003–.

Zhao Ziyang (1919–2005) Party Secretary, January 1987; purged May 1989 for his weak efforts to suppress the Tian'anmen democracy movement.

Zhou Enlai (1898–1976) China's Foreign Minister during much of the Maoist era. Prime Minister, 1949–76. Often praised in China and the West for mitigating the excesses of Maoism, but much of the evidence suggests he was little more than a cipher.

Zhu Rongji (1928–)   Prime Minister 1998–2003. The architect of China's WTO entry.

Note

Some of the judgements in this list are controversial. For example, I follow Kampen's (2000) view that the famous Zunyi conference of January 1935 was less important in signalling the accession of Mao than CCP hagiography suggests, and that Mao only really became CCP leader in 1943. The characterization of Lin Biao follows Teiwes and Sun (1996).

Introduction

This is a work of political economy. By that, I mean that this book discusses political questions as well as more narrowly economic issues. I have taken this approach because I do not believe that that we can separate the economics from the politics in explaining, or assessing, the Chinese road to development. The very commitment of the Party to some notion of socialism has translated into pervasive state intervention across the economy. During the 1980s and early 1990s, the role of the state actually expanded in the industrial realm, as new rural industries were established by township and village governments across China. Even now, despite the massive privatizations of the late 1990s, about a third of all industrial output is the product of state-owned industries, a much greater proportion even than in other state capitalist economies across the developing world. The Chinese state is withering away, but it has dominated Chinese economy and society for many years. It is an integral part of China's story of development.

Perhaps more importantly, politics, education and culture cannot be ignored in any discussion of Chinese development, because Mao saw all as instruments by means of which the economy could be transformed. In more Marxian language, Mao regarded superstructural change as an independent causal factor; social outcomes were not merely the product of changes within the economic base but were significant in their own right. Mao's approach to the problem of development therefore differed from the economic determinism of Lenin, Stalin and Mao's successors, and this is one of the reasons why Maoism is of great interest as a developmental strategy. Some scholars (such as Lin Kang) have argued that Mao was a cultural determinist. I would not go so far. To my mind, the Maoist approach is better seen as one of over-determination – that is, base and superstructure interact to determine economic and social outcomes rather than one being more important than the other. That was not true of the 1950s, when Mao followed a relatively orthodox Leninist approach in believing that changes in the forces of production – though increasingly the relations of production as well – were the only way to accelerate the pace of growth. By 1963, however, Mao had come to the conclusion that modernization could be achieved in China only if economic change was supplemented by fundamental cultural change brought about by the exercise of state power and mass mobilization. Superstructure and economic base needed to be transformed simultaneously in order to achieve modernity. Out of this analysis was born the Cultural Revolution.

Accordingly, precisely because Mao gave such importance to state, culture and superstructure, it makes no sense to assess the course of Chinese development in narrowly economic terms. The mature Mao was many things, but he was not an economic determinist: culture was no superstructural epiphenomenon which responded passively to changes in the economic base. On the contrary, cultural change was a necessary precondition for economic modernization. We will never understand the purpose – still less appreciate the significance – of late Maoism for the Chinese countryside unless we recognize that point. Furthermore, as we shall see, it is state and cultural failure over the last decade which is beginning to undermine China's economic and social progress. Unless reversed, this failure may ensure that it is India, not China, which becomes the next Asian giant. The modernization of China is not only an economic enterprise but also a project which requires a fundamental reshaping of society and a reordering of priorities. Mao understood that very well. His successors may understand it too, but they baulk at what it means.

This book also differs from much of the recent literature in that it provides an extension discussion of the Maoist era. It is not fashionable to do this any more. Very little has been written in recent years about the economics of either the 1950s, or the 1960s and 1970s. Instead, most of the scholarly literature on Chinese political economy published over the last two decades (it is less true of the narrowly political literature; the Culture Revolution itself has attracted renewed attention) has restricted its compass to the years after Mao's death. True, such works often start with a background chapter in which the Chinese economy has been brought to the brink of collapse by the mid-1970s. But it is readily apparent that the interest of the author lies elsewhere; it is the post-1978 years, so the subtext proclaims, which demand our attention, not the wasted years of Mao. Maoism is an unfortunate interlude in the pages of contemporary scholarship, a period best forgotten.

This neglect of Maoist era is unfortunate for two reasons. First, a great deal of information has been released on the Maoist era over the last two decades, yet very little of this has been properly assessed. If we are to appreciate what has happened in China over the last half century, we have to understand what happened before 1978. Second, the Maoist era is a fascinating one, much more so than the decades after Mao's death. This is because the development strategy pursued over the last thirty years has been remarkably orthodox. To be sure, as we will see, it has not been a model of capitalist economic development, at least until 1997. Nevertheless, the focus of policy has been on promoting economic growth, and on doing so by exclusively economic means. It is hard to get very excited about this; capitalist economies are two a penny. The same cannot be said about Maoism, which was a unique attempt at social and economic transformation. Moreover, whatever one may feel about the Maoist strategy, it was nothing if not ambitious in intent and breathtaking in scope. Few leaders have sought to remake their country in the way that Mao did. To be sure, it was an era of catastrophe as well as triumph. But Mao at least recognized the scale of the challenge, and the need to address it in a distinctive way. By comparison, everything that has happened since 1978 speaks of the prosaic, and of a poverty of ambition on the part of China's leaders. Such timidity – it amounts to that – will not serve the Chinese people well in the long run. 'Catching up' is a remarkably difficult task, and few countries have succeeded. China will not do so unless the ambition of its leaders exceeds their grasp.

The significance and importance of Maoism for an understanding of contemporary Chinese development is so great that the period which I consider spans the years between 1931 and 2007, and within that temporal compass I give full weight to the Maoist era. I should have liked to have said more about the Republican period. However, an abbreviated treatment is mandated in my judgement by limited data availability. We have no usable macroeconomic data before 1931 (the year which marks the launch of a proper crop reporting system by the National Agricultural Research Bureau) and therefore it is little more than speculation to consider the Chinese economy before that time. Moreover, despite the heroic efforts of a number of Western and Chinese scholars to come up with usable estimates of GDP growth, the only period about which we can be reasonably confident is 1931–6, and even then grave doubts hang over the estimates of farm production.

This book also starts from the premise that we will not understand very much about either the Chinese revolution, or Chinese economic development, unless we recognize the extent and the significance of spatial variation. Of course this point about spatial variation should not be overemphasized. China has long been a nation-state, and there is a strong sense of nationalism across the People's Republic. Moreover, China is not likely to go the same way as the Soviet Union. Indeed, the extent of provincial deviation in key policy areas has generally been rather modest since 1949. To be sure, there have been variations in the pace of change; some provinces abandoned collective farming earlier than others at the start of the 1980s. But these deviations have lasted for only short periods of time, and have typically been sanctioned as experiments by central government. Chinese structures and institutions are remarkably uniform across the length and breadth of the country.

Nevertheless, economic and social outcomes are not. The centres of Chinese industry have long been Manchuria and the Yangzi delta, and little has changed in that respect over the last century. By contrast, the main concentrations of poverty are in the provinces of western China such as Gansu, Ningxia and Shaanxi to the north, and Sichuan, Guizhou and Yunnan to the south. This persistence of the patterns of the past has not been for want of trying on the part of the Chinese state, and in some respects the history of Chinese development since 1949 can be read as a search for solutions to the problem of spatial inequality. Even now the Hu Jintao regime pays at least lip-service to the need to develop western China. These spatial variations not only tell us a story but provide an analytical compass. For by investigating spatial variation, and making use of the cross-sectional data which are available, we can tease out answers to many of the puzzles of Chinese development. Accordingly, there is considerable emphasis throughout this book on spatial inequalities, and on differences in socio-economic outcomes. To give one example, the impact of the Great Famine was much greater in some provinces than in others. To give another, an important element in rural poverty is its spatial dimension; many of China's poorest people live in the western provinces, whereas its wealthiest citizens are to be found in the great metropolitan cities along the east coast

The central questions which this book tries to answer are twofold. The first question is a descriptive one: what development strategy has China pursued? There is no simple answer to this; the strategy has varied over time. For that reason we need to distinguish between the strategies pursued in different eras. I adopt a fourfold categorization here: early Maoism (1949–63); late Maoism (1963–78); market socialism (1978–96); and Chinese capitalism (1996–2008).

In dividing up Chinese development into four periods, it is probably fair to say that 1978 is an uncontroversial climacteric, marking as it does the close of the Maoist era. There is much to be said for choosing 1972 (the year of China's rapprochement with the USA, with all that implied for Chinese trade policy), or 1976 (the year of Mao's death). In all truth, however, the policy changes implemented between 1972 and 1978 were modest. Sino-American trade grew only slowly, and economic policy under Hua Guofeng between 1976 and 1978 was little different from that which preceded it. There are certainly important continuities across the 1978 divide, not least in respect of the process of rural industrialization. Even there, however, I think it hard to argue that rural industrial take-off began before the late 1970s. I have therefore stuck with the orthodox chronology.

The other climacterics I have chosen – 1963 and 1996 – are more controversial. I have distinguished between early and late Maoism, with 1963 as the turning-point, because that was the year of the Socialist Education Movement (SEM). That movement ultimately evolved into the Cultural Revolution, and it marks a watershed in Maoist thinking. This is because it signalled the abandonment of the Leninist orthodoxy in favour of a development strategy which gave as much emphasis to superstructural transformation as it did to the modernization of the economic base. The SEM was followed in 1964 by the initiation of the programme of Third Front construction, by some way the defining economic feature of the 1960s and 1970s. My choice of 1996 is dictated primarily by the fact that it was the last full year of economic activity prior to Deng's death. That was, I think, an event of great significance, because it led to the abandonment of any attempt to maintain a market socialist economy. The mass privatizations of the late 1990s, the decision to join the WTO and the rapid removal of many controls on labour migration together ensured that the Chinese economy of 2007 was capitalist in all but name. By contrast, 1991–2 is much less important as a turning-point, even though some scholars have chosen to adopt that as a climacteric. To be sure, the pace of growth accelerated, and so too the inflow of foreign capital. In its fundamentals, however, the Chinese economy of early 1997 was little different from the Chinese economy of 1991–2.

The second question which I try to answer in the pages which follow is that of whether the development strategies have been successful. Accordingly, we need both a definition of success (my approach to this is outlined in Chapter 1), and concrete discussions of developmental outcomes. Chapters 9, 10 and 15 focus specifically on answering this question of success in the respective eras of development. The record of the early Maoist era is assessed within Chapters 3 and 4; the performance of the economy between 1955 and 1963 needs to be distinguished from that of 1949–55.

More concretely, the book begins by sketching the background. Chapter 1 sets out the criteria by which developmental success should be judged. Chapter 2 then goes on to set the scene by discussing the level of development that had been attained by 1949. We then turn to the substance of the book. Part 2 begins the story proper by focusing on the early Maoist era, by which I mean the years between 1949 and 1963. I treat the Great Leap Forward as a part of early Maoism, because, during the entire period between 1949 and 1963, Mao remained true to his Marxian heritage: he and the CCP sought to transform Chinese society by developing the economic base. Changes in the forces and relations of production were perceived to be the drivers of modernization; by contrast, superstructural and cultural change was strictly subordinate to the transformation of the economic base. In that sense, there are clear parallels between China's Great Leap Forward and First Soviet Five Year Plan (1928–32). Moreover, although the planners sought to accelerate the pace of growth after 1955, the development strategy pursued during 1955–63 was little different in a *qualitative* sense from that pursued between 1949 and 1955.

The late Maoist period was very different. In the fifteen years between 1963 and 1978, the aim was develop Chinese society as much by political and cultural change as by economic means. As the approach pursued was unique, I devote a whole chapter to outlining and explaining the late Maoist strategy (Chapter 5). Moreover, late Maoism was a remarkably ambitious project. For that reason, I discuss its aims and effects in three separate thematic chapters, focusing on education, collective farming and rural industrialization respectively. These were the three integral components of late Maoism, and they merit chapters in their own right. They mark out the era as utterly distinct from anything which had preceded it in Chinese history, or anything pursued in other developing countries. Other countries had established collective farms, but Maoist China was the first country to mobilize labour for infrastructural construction on such a scale. I then assess whether late Maoism should be regarded as a successful strategy by bringing these threads together in Chapter 9.

Part 4 of the book outlines the way in which the structures and institutions of late Maoism were abandoned in an attempt by Deng Xiaoping to create an economic system which combined elements of capitalism and socialism. This market socialist strategy was very unusual by international standards in that it marked a break with both traditional socialism (which focused on state ownership) and capitalism. This last point deserves to be emphasized, because, at the time of Deng's death in early 1997, China was still recognizably different from capitalist economies across the world. The broad aims and intent of Deng's strategy are set out in Chapter 10. Chapters 11 and 12 focus on two of the most distinctive components of the Dengist strategy, namely the open-door policy and the way in which industrial development was promoted by means of a mixture of public ownership and private-sector growth. In fact, and it is point rarely recognized, the reach of the Chinese state in terms of industrial ownership actually *extended* in rural areas during the Dengist era. Chapter 13 brings the discussion together and offers an assessment of economic performance in the years of Deng Xiaoping.

Deng's death signalled the end of any attempt to forge an alternative path to modernity. Over the last decade, and as discussed in Part 5, socialism has to all intents and purposes been abandoned in China. To be sure, some of the rhetoric remains, and the role of the state in the industrial sphere remains quite large. Indeed industrial policy has not yet been entirely abandoned. However, this merely marks China out as being an example of state capitalism: the market does not have the free rein that it has in (say) the USA, but there is nothing about contemporary China that marks it out as a socialist. These issues are discussed in Chapter 14. Chapter 15 concludes the analysis by offering a rather negative appraisal of China's development record over the last decade. I am not sure that we should necessarily lament what has been abandoned since 1996, but it seems blindingly obvious to me that there is little in China's contemporary developmental model to admire. This is capitalism at its most brutal. It may ultimately deliver the goods, but I rather doubt even that.

This account of Chinese development since 1949 offers a mixture of chronology and thematic discussion and analysis. I make no apology about offering an essentially chronological skeleton. Precisely because the Chinese development strategy has changed so markedly from one era to another, we cannot generalize about (say) industrial development. Moreover, it is hard to comprehend – let alone appreciate – the full scope of Maoism, or the scale of the changes introduced since 1978, if one focuses on themes. By the same token, the economic structures which have evolved, and the strategies which have been pursued, are so complex that they defy simple generalization. For that reason, some thematic chapters are essential. In picking themes for more in-depth discussion, I have selected the issues which define the eras. Collective farming, educational reform (the centrepiece of the Cultural Revolution) and rural industrialization were the features which made Maoism unique. And it has been the open-door policy and the unusual approach to industrial reform that stand out during the period after 1978.

Inevitably some subjects have been omitted. The most obvious area of omission is that of finance. Tax policy has also been touched upon only in passing. In my judgement, it is more useful to focus on macroeconomic policy and on developmental outcomes than these more technical issues. By that I do not mean to suggest either that money is a veil, or that the rates and structure of taxation are unimportant. But choices have to be made if a book like this is ever to be concluded, and in my judgement the broader questions of political economy are much more important if we are to understand China's development path.

It is a great pleasure to be able to acknowledge here a number of intellectual debts built up over the course of twenty-five years of studying China's political economy. Mine are principally to the people who taught me to think, provoked my interest in China and have provided support over the years. Peter Nolan and I have long since moved in different directions, but it was he who first inspired my interest in both development economics and China. Bob Ash has always been a great source of encouragement and good cheer, as well as a mine of information on Chinese agriculture. Terry Byres did much to provoke my interest in Marx and in issues of class differentiation in the countryside; he has never been less than unfailingly encouraging. And Tim Wright has been immensely supportive over the last few years.

I have also greatly enjoyed and profited from discussions of various kinds over the years with Stuart Corbridge, Jane Duckett, Marion E. Jones, Liu Minquan, Mushtaq Khan, Gao Mobo, Mark Blecher, Rachel Murphy, Vivienne Shue and Christopher Howe. I have been encouraged by the many kind words of Brian Turner, Walt Byers, Satya Gabriel and Daniel F. Vukovich. And I am happy to acknowledge the influence of the scholarship of Carl Riskin, Ellen Meiksins Wood, Amartya Sen and Jon Unger, and hope that they will forgive me if I include their names in the same sentence as Louis Althusser's. I have benefited from discussions with Zhang Yanbing on Chinese politics. And I am indebted to Kerstin Lehr for sharing some of her ideas on education and for her invaluable comments on parts of the manuscript.

I owe much also to Rob Langham: it was he who encouraged me to write this book in the first place, and I am grateful for his many contributions to its evolution. I am also grateful to Sarah Hastings and to the staff at Routledge and at Bookcraft for speeding the book through the production process; I am especially appreciative of the skilful copy-editing of Christopher Feeney. Diane Palmer, based at the Informatics Collaboratory of the Social Sciences at Sheffield University, has been an invaluable source of advice and wisdom on the application of Arc Map to Chinese data. Finally, the School of East Asian Studies at Sheffield University continues to provide a congenial environment for scholarship, and I am grateful to all my colleagues for their encouragement and support.

Sheffield
March 2008

Part 1
Starting points

1 Measuring development

Before considering China's developmental record over the last half century, we need to answer a fundamental question: what do we mean by a successful developmental record? The answer is contested terrain, not just in the case of China but for all countries. However, there are two main issues: which indicator should we use, and what should a country's record be compared with?

As far as indicators are concerned, the approach favoured by economists emphasizes measures of affluence such as GDP per head. It is therefore axiomatic in some circles that Maoist China 'failed' because its GDP per person grew only slowly, whereas China since 1978 has 'succeeded' because there has been very rapid growth. In the wider development community, however, the approach pioneered by Amartya Sen – that policy should aim to expand the capabilities or freedom of the population, and that an increase in the supply of goods is only one factor in that calculus – has won much favour. Again this is of great relevance to assessing China, because its record under Mao was much better in terms of life expectancy than in terms of GDP per head. More recently, the focus has shifted to more subjective measures of welfare, an approach in which persons are asked about their perceived level of happiness. The relevant question to be asked here is therefore whether the happiness of China's people has risen since the 1980s. This approach is thus unusual, because it relies on direct measures of development. Earlier approaches, whether focused on GDP per head (the opulence approach) or on life expectancy (the capability approach), sought to measure development by looking at proxy indicators, but one can see the attraction (at least in principle) of looking at well-being in a more direct way.

The second issue in assessing development centres on the appropriate comparison to make. If we believe that China's performance is best assessed using (say) life expectancy, how do we decide whether China has done well or badly in any given time period? This subject is much less explored in development textbooks than the subject of development indicators, and this is undoubtedly because the issue is especially difficult. One answer is to rely on temporal comparisons; how has a country performed in a given period relative to its performance during a previous time period? For example, we can assess the developmental record of Maoist China by comparing it against China's record in the 1930s. These sorts of historical comparisons are attractive because they normalize for country-specific factors. However, the historical approach runs headlong into the problem of how to normalize for differences in technology or for the performance of the world economy. This is one reason why many economists prefer to rely more on international comparisons. We might, for example, compare China's record during the 1990s with that of another large poor country such as India during the same decade. However, this approach is also problematic, because of differences in country size, differences in the degree of religious or ethnic fragmentation, differences in the availability of natural resources, etc. A third possibility is to compare actual performance against potential; we might deem a country successful if it fulfilled its potential, even if that potential was low. Self-evidently, however, the biggest problem with this sort of methodology is that it is hard to construct a plausible counterfactual against which actual performance can be compared. A fourth issue is making comparisons is that of how much weight to give to short-run fluctuations as opposed to long-run trends, and how much significance should be attached to policies which expand the potential of the economy even if their short-run effects are small (or perhaps even negative). This is one of the key issues when it comes to assessing Maoism. Even if we conclude that China's record was poor between 1949 and 1976 (for example, many believe that actual consumption levels fell short of potential), can we still argue that Maoism was a developmental success because it laid the foundations for the growth of the 1980s and 1990s?

Development indicators

Much of the discussion on how to measure development during the last twenty years has focused on the respective merits of opulence and capability indicators. The opulence approach, first developed during the Second World War as a way of making systematic international comparisons, has focused on trends in GDP (or GNI) per capita. The second, or human development approach is often associated with the work of Amartya Sen (1983, 1985, 1999; Hawthorn 1987), Mahbub ul Haq (1995) and the United Nations Development Programme (UNDP) (1990). In the human development approach, close attention is paid to trends in mortality and education.[1]

In one sense, this debate about opulence versus capability is philosophical, because in most instances capability and opulence indicators tell the same sort of story: most obviously, the OECD countries are developed in terms of both opulence and capability. However, there may be a real policy dilemma here for the governments of developing countries if opulence and capability measures diverge. For the governments of developing countries, the issue is about which strategy to follow; spending on basic health care may lead to big improvements in longevity, but if this delays industrialization is it a wise strategy? The only sensible way to resolve these dilemmas is via a democratic form of government. The populations of developing countries must decide for themselves which strategy to pursue.

Donors with limited aid budgets face in some respects an even more difficult decision in that they have to decide which country is most needy. At the most basic level, this is about whether opulence is a better measure of development than capability. Is a country with a high level of life expectancy but a low level of per capita GDP more in need than a country with low life expectancy but comparatively high GDP per head?[2]

The opulence approach

The most commonly used opulence criterion is GDP per capita. Unless a country is a large net recipient of income from abroad (e.g. property income; migrant remittances), GNI and GDP measures produce very similar results and therefore it matters little which one is used for measuring development. That is certainly so for China. I therefore use the two terms interchangeably.

GDP can be measured in one of three ways: as the sum of all expenditure (investment, consumption, net exports and government spending); as the sum of domestic incomes (wages, profits, rents and dividends); and as the sum of the value of all types of goods produced in the economy. In principle, these three should give the same figure, but in practice the data on expenditure tend to be more reliable than those on income and production; the former are distorted by tax evasion, and the latter by under-reporting of production in family businesses.[3] GDP per head provides an attractive way to assess development. It is value-free in the sense that all types of marketed goods and services are included. International comparisons can easily be made by converting the value of national GDPs into a common currency (usually the US dollar) using current exchange rates. Furthermore, data on GDP for most countries are now available. Calculated originally by national statistical offices, these figures have been brought together by the World Bank going back to 1960, and these have been published in the Bank's annual *World Development Report* (more detailed data are published in its *World Development Indicators*). More recently, thanks to the work of Angus Maddison, consistent data on GDP per head have been compiled for most countries going back to 1500 (Maddison 2006b: 294). We therefore now have a vast amount of data which allow far more systematic analysis of development trends going back all the way to the Renaissance.

Nevertheless, GDP is problematic as a measure of development even on its own terms.[4] For one thing, there are big measurement difficulties. Most of the pre-1945 data are not very reliable by any standard, partly because of data collection problems, and partly because national income accounting was not developed until after the Second World War. The work done by Maddison is therefore (well-informed) speculation for many countries

There are also big conceptual problems. The GDP approach assumes that an extra dollar earned by a rich woman increases national well-being by as much as an extra dollar earned by a poor man, an assumption with which most would take issue. Second, a range of outputs which typically do not have a well-defined market price (externalities) are difficult to incorporate into GDP: environmental damage is one example. Some non-marketed output is usually included in estimates of GDP. For example, the value of farm products which are produced and consumed by farm households without entering the market is estimated using the market price multiplied by the volume of production (itself calculated as the yield of rice in any given year multiplied by the area sown). The main problem from a national accounting point of view is how to deal with the value of housework, leisure and urban disamenities. As all three are large, the results are very sensitive to the method of valuation.[5] Third, many would disagree with the notion that certain types of goods and services (such as crime, drugs, telephone marketing and advertising) are as valuable to society as education or health care products. For this reason, the Soviet Union used a much narrower measure of opulence (material product) which excluded a range of 'social bads' to assess its developmental progress. China adopted the same approach after the Revolution, and this continued until the early 1990s, when it reverted to using the GDP approach.[6] The difference between the two measures is quite considerable. In 1978, for example, Chinese GDP (calculated retrospectively) was 359 billion *yuan* whereas its net material product or national income (*guomin shouru*) was only 301 billion *yuan* (SSB 1990a: 4–5).[7]

At least as problematic is the question of which set of relative prices to use to value output. In practice GDP is measured using a fixed set of market prices, or constant prices. For example, we might value Chinese GDP in 1952 by using data on the volume of goods produced in 1952 multiplied by the prices of 2007, and compare it with the value of GDP in 2007 (calculated again using 2007 prices but this time applied to the volume of goods produced in 2007). This approach thus factors out the impact of inflation, because the same prices are used to value output in both 1952 and 2007. Although this approach is elegant and makes sense, it does presuppose that the relative prices which existed in 2007 provide a true measure of the value of goods. This is by no means obviously correct. Even where markets do exist, they invariably function badly because of a range of imperfections (such as monopoly power and imperfect information); only in economics textbooks are markets in equilibrium. Furthermore, relative prices can fluctuate dramatically from year to year. For example, the price of oil was quite low in the late 1980s compared with other goods; by contrast, it was much higher in 2006. Should we therefore use the relative prices of 2006 or those of the late 1980s to value output? Unfortunately there is no easy answer to this question, and the set of prices used can make a considerable difference to estimates of GDP growth.

Comparisons of GDP across countries are also difficult. Aside from a lack of consistency in the way production is measured, the main problem is that the exchange rates used to convert GDP from national currencies into dollars are heavily distorted by capital movements, speculation and by barriers to trade in goods and services. As a result, actual exchange rates are not equilibrium rates. But the problem is not merely one of market imperfections. Rather, price distortions arise primarily because of the existence of non-tradable goods. The prices of labour-intensive non-tradables in poor countries are typically much lower than in rich countries; labour productivity differences between countries in these sectors are relatively small (because little capital is employed), yet wage differentials are very large because national wages are driven by trends in the high wage – high productivity sector. In principle, the exchange rate should adjust to reflect these price differences, but the exchange rate cannot adjust to reflect the implicit competitive advantage of poor countries if the goods are not traded.[8]

A way to circumvent this problem is in effect to revalue production in all countries using world or international prices. This is the purchasing power parity (PPP) approach.[9] It makes a very big difference to international comparisons of GDP per head, as Table 1.1 shows. The GDP per capita of poor countries is increased, whereas that of relatively rich but high-price countries – Switzerland is a good example – is cut.

These sorts of adjustments are not enough to make either China or Ethiopia rich, but they do lead to a significant narrowing of the gap between rich and poor countries. In China's case, per capita GDP increases by a factor of nearly 2.5. The adjustment also has the effect of making China the second-largest economy in the world in absolute terms, which emphasizes the fact that China is increasingly becoming a global rival to the USA.

Nevertheless, the PPP approach remains an inexact science, because of the pricing problem previously discussed. We can all agree that the prices used by poor countries should not be their own prices, and intuitively the case for using US prices to value production in all countries makes sense because the US economy is the largest in the world. However, significant problems remain. World market prices are themselves heavily distorted, and the same is true of those which prevail across America. In any case, it is not obvious that US consumer preferences – which play a key role in determining US prices – should be used to value production in China or indeed in any other country.

The capability approach

The main criticism of the opulence approach is that it takes a materialistic view of living standards, focusing exclusively on the ownership and consumption of goods. Much of the criticism derives from the work of Amartya Sen (Nobel

Table 1.1 Estimates of GDP per person using national and US prices in 2005 ($US)

	Unadjusted	PPP	Ratio
Switzerland	49,675	35,520	0.7
USA	41,674	41,674	1.0
Japan	35,604	30,290	0.9
UK	37,266	31,580	0.8
India	707	2,126	3.0
Taiwan	15,674	26,068	1.7
Ethiopia	154	591	3.8
China	1,721	4,091	2.4

Source: World Bank (2007b).

Note
Unadjusted GNI per capita is the per capita GNI of the country converted to $US using the current exchange rate. PPP uses US prices to value directly the output produced in all countries. These estimates are preliminary results from the latest round of the International Comparison Project (ICP) and differ significantly from the estimates in World Bank (2007a).

Laureate in 1998). Sen's argument is that goods are only a means towards achieving happiness, rather than an end in themselves. We also need to consider other factors, of which probably the most important are health and education. In other words, a person cannot make full use of his or her ownership of commodities without good health and without an education (for example, participation in a democracy depends on education, as does avoidance of illness). From this, Sen infers that a much better indicator of living standards is life expectancy at birth (measured in years). Life expectancy is obviously influenced by the ownership and consumption of goods but it also depends upon health and upon education. In some sense, therefore, life expectancy is a broader measure of well-being than commodity ownership and consumption of goods because it is influenced by other factors; for an especially clear discussion of the case for using mortality data, see Sen (1998). Of course a person may choose not to live as long as is possible, perhaps by following an unhealthy lifestyle. Accordingly, our real interest is in what Sen calls capabilities (the range of choices available) rather than what he calls functionings (the actual choices made). More precisely:

> A person's 'capability' refers to the alternative combinations of functionings that are feasible for her to achieve ... While the combination of a person's functionings reflects her actual *achievements*, the capability set represents the *freedom* to achieve: the alternative functioning combinations from which this person can choose. (Sen 1999: 75; original emphasis)

Thus for Sen the aim of development should be to expand the freedom to achieve, or what he calls the capability set. We should focus much more on ends (capabilities) than on means (the possession of goods) in measuring development. Sen and others have also argued that capability measures tend to do a much better job of incorporating information on inequalities in well-being. It is rare to find examples of countries where high average life expectancy coincides with high levels of human poverty, but extensive income poverty is commonplace in countries with medium or high average GDP per capita; oil-exporting countries are often in this category. In other words, because the distribution of life expectancy is more equal than that of income, life expectancy provides a broader measure of development than GDP per head.

In practice, of course, we cannot easily measure capabilities. We have to rely on data on functionings (actual achievements or choices made) instead. Nevertheless, for societies as a whole, we would expect to see a close correspondence between the two. Measured life expectancy (which is calculated from actual age-specific mortality rates) is likely to correspond to the capability for life. We can thus evaluate the record of developing countries by looking at the extent to which they have been able to improve average life expectancy at birth over time.

To be sure, the record in terms of opulence and capability is very similar in many countries. We can think of Japan, Western Europe and North America, regions which are developed in terms of both opulence and capabilities. China before 1949 was underdeveloped in terms of both GDP per head and life expectancy.

In fact, there is a clear relationship between per capita GDP and life expectancy across countries, the so-called Preston curve (Cutler *et al.* 2006: 98; Anand and Ravallion 1993: 139). This relationship is not surprising: opulence helps to provide the base for improvements in capabilities. Thus greater GDP per head allows more expenditure on health and education and better nutrition. Conversely, improvements in life expectancy, especially in so far as they imply a healthier workforce, will raise GDP. So too will improvements in education (Ranis *et al.* 2000). For example, Russia's mortality record since the early 1970s is especially poor; there, life expectancy fell from about seventy years in the early 1970s to sixty-seven years by 2000. However, GDP per capita also shows a sharp decline – it therefore matters comparatively little whether we use GDP per head or mortality to chart its decline. The same is true for Zambia, where HIV/AIDS has taken its toll. As a result, average life expectancy fell from fifty to thirty-two years between 1970 and 2000 (UNDP 2003: 262–5). Again, however, the GDP per capita data (which show an average annual decline of 2.2 per cent per year between 1975 and 2001) tell a similar story (UNDP 2003: 281).

Yet there are many countries whose experience does not correspond to that implied by the Preston curve. There are in fact four main groups of outliers. Southern Africa (notably Swaziland, Lesotho, Zambia, Botswana and South Africa) is mineral-rich and has a relatively high level of GDP per head, but HIV/AIDS means that it has a low life expectancy. A number of oil-rich economies have lower life expectancy than is to be expected from their material living standards. For example, Saudi Arabia's life expectancy in 2001 was seventy-two years, a respectable figure but well below the seventy-eight years achieved in countries like Malta or Barbados with an equivalent purchasing power parity GNI per head. Thirdly, those countries or regions which have pursued a basic needs strategy (Costa Rica, Sri Lanka and the Indian state of Kerala) do better in terms of life expectancy than GDP per capita would predict.

Finally, and perhaps most interestingly, current or former 'communist' countries (such as Cuba, the former Soviet Union and China) have also tended to do better in terms of life expectancy than in terms of GDP per head.[10] Admittedly, the move away from socialism has had adverse effects. Russian life expectancy in 2005 was around four years lower than it had been in the early 1970s, and a marked decline was registered both in Ukraine and in most of the other states (UNDP 2007: 262). And, as we will see, China's record on life expectancy deteriorated during the 1980s as it moved away from socialism (though it picked up again the 1990s). Nevertheless, even now, most of the countries of the former Soviet Union do much better than the norm in terms of average life expectancy and educational attainment. And in Cuba, where the economic system has changed little in recent decades, life expectancy now stands at around seventy-seven years at birth, some six years higher than in the early 1970s, and well ahead of both China and Russia. Accordingly, and as Sen (1981: 293) says, it seems that we can conclude that 'communism is good for poverty removal', at least as measured in terms of mortality.

Trends over time in life expectancy and GDP per head diverge as much as levels of life expectancy and GDP per capita across countries (Table 1.2).[11] The record

Table 1.2 Mismatch between trends in life expectancy and per capita GDP

Country	Change in life expectancy 1970–2005 (years)	Growth of GDP per capita 1975–2005 (per cent per year)
Mali	+11.8	+0.2
Malawi	+3.2	–0.2
Lesotho	–5.2	+2.7
Nigeria	+4.4	–0.1
Moldova	+3.1	–4.4
Botswana	–9.4	+5.9
Nicaragua	+15.6	–2.1
China	+8.8	+8.4

Source: UNDP (2007: 263–4 and 278–80).

Note
The data on life expectancy in some of these countries are rather suspect. Recent UNAIDS/WHO (2007) work suggests that the prevalence of HIV amongst the population is considerably lower (perhaps 16 per cent lower worldwide) than was thought at the end of 2006. This lowering of the estimate reflects changes in the survey methodology used. As HIV-AIDS, and associated complications, is a key factor in driving up mortality in recent years, it may well be that the records of countries such as Botswana are less bad than they appears. Note too that even under the old methodology, HIV prevalence seems to be stabilizing or even declining in southern Africa.

of Botswana, which has a large diamond industry, is extraordinary. Although GDP per capita rose annually by nearly 6 per cent between 1970 and 2005, life expectancy declined by more than nine years. Sen (1998: 6) also gives the telling example of England and Wales between 1901 and 1960, where the change in life expectancy was the opposite of the change in GDP per capita on a decade-by-decade basis. These are not just isolated examples. More generally, 'the cross-country data show almost no relationship between changes in life expectancy and economic growth over 10-, 20-, or 40-year periods between 1960 and 2000' (Cutler *et al.* 2006: 110). In China, by contrast, the correlation is much closer. One might have expected a bigger rise in life expectancy given the sustained period of rapid economic growth that has occurred; I will return to this subject later in the book. Nevertheless, when seen in global perspective, China's record is good according to both indicators.

None of this is to suggest that life expectancy or other functionings are without their limitations as measures of development. One issue is whether the anomalies emphasized so much by Sen and others – many mineral-rich African countries, Kerala, Sri Lanka, Cuba and (as we shall see) Maoist China – are so important that we need either to abandon GDP per capita or at the very least supplement it with life expectancy data. Second, the most reliable estimates of life expectancy are usually derived from mortality data collected during population censuses. However, there is often a ten-year interval between censuses, and for these years life expectancy has to be estimated by interpolation or by using (typically much less reliable) annual registration data on mortality. Inter-censual data on life expectancy are therefore not very reliable.

A third problem in using life expectancy as an indicator of development is that the measure has an upper bound of around eighty years on average, and therefore it is increasingly more difficult to increase life expectancy as countries come close to that bound. Thus a country which achieves a very big initial rise in life expectancy but then, after twenty or thirty years, is able to achieve only small increases is not necessarily experiencing a decline in performance. Changes in life expectancy therefore do not serve as a very good measure of performance when a country has surpassed the threshold of about seventy. Similarly, life expectancy is not very responsive to short-run fluctuations in economic fortune (unless there is some sort of acute crisis, such as famine). Korean life expectancy, for example, rose from seventy-four in 1996 to seventy-five in 1998 and seventy-six in 1999 (NSO 2006) despite the devastating impact of the Asian crisis, which led to a fall in GDP of 6.7 per cent in 1998 (OECD 2000: 211). Finally, life expectancy measures need to be adjusted for morbidity to reflect quality of life issues; a country's population might be long-lived but its elderly may be experiencing a very low quality of life. One way of expressing this is in terms of DALYs (disability-adjusted life years), but nobody would pretend that this is a straightforward business. For what it is worth, 'expert opinion' assigns a value of around 0.5 to a person with AIDS and 0.14 to HIV on a scale where 0 is healthy and 1 near death (Canning 2006: 123). That is, a year of life with AIDS counts as only half a year of life expectancy.

Synthesis: the HDI

There are thus two very different approaches to measuring development. The opulence approach focuses on GDP or GNI per capita as the best measure, whereas the capability approach regards measures such as life expectancy as being far preferable. Which, then, is the best measure? Given that both opulence and capability measures have their limitations, an obvious solution is to average them in some way. And this is precisely the approach taken by the UNDP, which in 1990 published for the first time estimates of what it called the human development index (HDI).[12]

The UNDP's conceptualization of human development has always been very broad – 'Human development is a process of enlarging people's choices' (UNDP 1990: 10) – and Sen's emphasis on 'development as freedom' offers much the same perspective.[13] In practice (and perhaps realistically), however, the UNDP has adopted a rather reductionist approach in measuring human development in terms of its HDI. Although the human development index has changed somewhat in its detail over time, it has always incorporated three key elements. First, the HDI includes life expectancy. Second, and in deference to the opulence approach, it includes a measure of purchasing power parity GDP per head. Third, the HDI also includes a measure of knowledge, which is itself an average of the adult literacy rate and the enrolment rate at primary, secondary and tertiary levels (UNDP 2003: 341). In each case, a country's achievement is expressed in relation to the maximum and minimum possible. Each of the three elements is assigned a weight of a third, and the HDI is scaled so that it varies between 0 and 1, where 1 represents an exceptionally high level of human development.

The HDI leans rather more towards the capability than towards the opulence approach. First, it incorporates two capability measures (knowledge and life expectancy). Second, GDP is expressed on a logarithmic scale. The logic here is that, once a country has attained a high level of per capita GDP, increases in opulence have very little effect on well-being. This logarithmic approach means that big increases in GDP at the top end of the scale produce only a small rise in the GDP index. For example, Norway's per capita GDP in 2001 was four times larger than Brazil's but that translated into an increase in the GDP index of only 32 per cent. By contrast, life expectancy in Norway was only about a decade longer (15 per cent), yet this translated into a life expectancy index which was 27 per cent greater.

The dominance of the capability approach in its construction means that the development ranking of countries changes very considerably if they are assessed using the HDI instead of GDP per head (Table 1.3).

The general pattern is clear. For OECD countries, there is typically little difference between their HDI and GDP ranking; they are typically developed on both counts. Australia is a little unusual; its HDI ranking (3) is far better than its GDP per capita ranking (16). And Luxembourg and Hong Kong are unusual amongst high income countries in having quite poor human development records, but we should not read much into this because the two are little more than cities. But the concordance between the HDI and GDP per capita ranking is much less true of other groups of countries. The oil-rich states of the Middle East like the United Arab Emirates do well if their development is assessed in terms of GDP per head, but much less so using the HDI, although the mismatch between the two has narrowed over the last two decades as a result of progress in human development.

Table 1.3 HDI and per capita GDP rankings: some country examples

Country	GDP per capita rank	HDI rank	Difference
Iceland	5	1	+4
Australia	16	3	−13
Cuba	94	51	+43
Tajikistan	154	122	+32
United Arab Emirates	27	39	−12
Botswana	54	124	−70
South Africa	56	121	−65
China	86	81	+5

Source: UNDP (2007: 230–2).

Note
A rank of 1 is best. A positive number in the final column indicates that a country does better in terms of human development than in terms of GDP per head. The 2007 *Human Development Report* gives an HDI for 177 countries.

In 1987, for instance, the UAE was ranked 50 places higher in terms of GDP per head than it was in terms of the HDI (UNDP 1990: 128–9). The same mismatch between human development and GDP per head is true of resource-rich sub-Saharan African countries such as South Africa or Botswana. In both cases, and in contrast to trends in the Middle East, the gap between human development and GDP per head has widened since the late 1980s of the decline in life expectancy due to HIV-AIDS.

By contrast, socialist countries like Cuba and former socialist countries (such as Tajikistan) do badly in terms of GDP but appear much more developed if the HDI is used. In China's case, its GDP ranking has caught up with its HDI ranking over the last two decades. In 1987, the Chinese HDI rank was forty-four places higher than its per capita GDP rank, reflecting the combination of rapid human development but slow GDP growth in the Maoist era (UNDP 1990: 128). By contrast, China's HDI ranking was only five places higher in 2005. In effect, its rapid growth has meant that its GDP ranking has virtually caught up with its HDI ranking.

Conceptually, however, the HDI leaves much to be desired. For example, it is not obvious that enrolment rates should be included in the index if we are interested primarily in ends. We can all agree that education has intrinsic as well as instrumental value, but on any sensible calculation, education is far more important for instrumental (improved life expectancy, high worker productivity and greater 'happiness') reasons than for intrinsic reasons. More importantly, the privileging of capability over opulence indicators within the HDI shows that the index is by no means a true compromise. Moreover, the very fact that GDP per capita enters the index in logarithmic fashion is also a source of bias. One could, for example, reasonably argue that the returns to increases in education are diminishing at the margin and therefore that the knowledge component of the HDI should also be treated in logarithmic fashion (Noorbakhsh 1998). One might also make the same point about longevity; additional years beyond the age of (say) ninety have comparatively little worth because of the steeply diminishing quality of life, though (as Noorbakhsh notes) that is at best a highly controversial proposition. Perhaps the most fundamental objection, however, is that the index assigns arbitrary weights of one third to each of life expectancy, knowledge and opulence. Of course this is not objectionable *per se* but it is hard to make any philosophical case for this type of approach. My own view is that the HDI obscures more than it reveals, and that one does better to assess trends in GDP per capita and life expectancy separately for policy and analytical purposes.

Subjective measures of well-being

An alternative approach to the use of proxies like GDP per head or life expectancy is to measure welfare directly using subjective measures of well-being. In practical terms, this means the use of survey data based on responses to questions asking about levels of personal happiness.[14] Indeed, there is an emerging literature which advocates the direct measurement of happiness by means of interviews, questionnaires and brain scans as an alternative to the use of proxies such as GDP per capita or the HDI; see for example Oswald (1997), Layard (2005), Offer (2006) or Kahneman and Krueger (2006).

Some of the results obtained are markedly at odds with what is implied by GDP per capita and HDI indicators. In particular, the big postwar rise in GDP per head in the USA, Japan and Europe has not been matched by any rise in happiness (Offer 2006: 30). Some of the countries which do well in terms of the HDI do far less well in terms of happiness. Australia is one example. It is third from the top in terms of country HDIs, but its happiness ranking is much lower and it is close to the bottom of the list in terms of reported levels of job satisfaction (Blanchflower and Oswald 2005). In China, too, big increases in per capita income between 1994 and 2005 have not led to increases in happiness; the proportion of those surveyed reporting themselves dissatisfied actually increased over the period (Kahneman and Kruger 2006: 15–16).

This evidence suggests the conclusion that happiness rises with per capita income up to a certain point, but thereafter increases in income generate sharply diminishing returns. There are several reasons why this might be the case. One interesting finding is that that relative income is much more important in determining happiness than absolute income in affluent societies. The increase in inequality that has occurred in countries such as the USA and the UK in the last twenty-five years has therefore offset their per capita income gains. The same is probably true of China. A second possibility is that happiness is increased by the decline in corruption, by trust and by the development of effective social and political institutions. Such outcomes may be attainable at comparatively low levels of per capita GDP, and therefore increases beyond that income threshold generate few additional gains.

A third possibility is that happiness may be increased by a range of economic and social factors, but that the overwhelming influence at work is simply genetic; some people have more of a predisposition to be happy than others and these states are largely invariant to social change. By implication, increased prosperity will lead to little by way of a happiness payoff. Cultural factors may also be important: reported levels of happiness are much lower in Japan and in Catholic countries than amongst the English-speaking peoples or in Nordic countries (Offer 2006: 33).

Whatever the true explanation for such temporal and cross-sectional variation, the happiness approach is problematic as a way of measuring well-being. Aside from the problems inherent in using questionnaires and interviews to illicit information, the approach is questionable because those who are clearly disadvantaged (by some form of disability or other) often classify themselves as no less happy than persons without disability. This suggests that personal happiness depends as much upon expectations as external criteria, and by implication that development can be increased by 'expectation management'. If true, this finding points to the conclusion that the metric of happiness is much less useful as a way of measuring development than either GDP per head or life expectancy.

The issue of distribution

The measures of development discussed in the previous section are national averages. These averages say nothing about the personal distribution of income, or the impact of growth on the extent of poverty. Indeed many would argue that a country cannot be considered truly 'developed' if its society is characterized by a high degree of poverty, or by extensive inequality. However, there is much here which is controversial. Does, for example, inequality matter? And if inequality does matter, how should it, or indeed the degree of poverty, be measured?[15]

Income inequality

All societies are characterized by income inequality. The workforce is typically segmented along gender lines such that women are employed disproportionately in low wage sectors. Within sectors, women doing the same work are typically paid less than men. Discrimination against ethnic groups is also pervasive. By contrast, most Marxists see class-based inequality as the most salient characteristic of capitalist societies. But others reject this perspective entirely, pointing to the failure of avowedly socialist countries to prevent the emergence of 'new' classes. Indeed neo-populists see the state as the problem, rather than the solution. For writers such as Lipton (1977) and Bates (1989), the most obvious form of inequality in poor countries is the urban–rural divide. The same has been said of China, especially in the late Maoist era (Oi 1993). Such bias arises as a result of the 'capture' of the state by a metropolitan elite, which used state power to shift prices against the rural sector and to impose restrictions on migration (thus ensuring that the urban wage remains much higher than the rural wage).[16] For Lipton (1977: 13) in particular, such inequality constitutes a much greater evil than the dominance of capital:

> The most important class conflict in the poor countries of the world today is not between labour and capital. Nor is it between foreign and national interests. It is between the rural classes and the urban classes.

Still others argue that the low level of market integration means that regional inequality is the most pervasive form of inequality in developing countries. In China, for example, the contemporary income gap between coast and interior is attributed to restrictions on labour migration from low-wage interior provinces to high-wage coastal provinces. A variant on this theme is to focus on the role played by physical geography in creating regional differences. The 'tyranny of distance' imposed by high transport costs, shortages of raw materials and being land-locked all condemn ill-favoured regions – like Tibet – to poverty. This is especially so for economies characterized by decentralized fiscal systems, because there successful regions are able to retain the bulk of their tax revenue, hence setting up a process of cumulative causation.

It is an easy step from here to conclude that what we need is some aggregate measure of inequality which takes all these various different types of inequality into account. The best-known measure, and the one most commonly used, is the Gini coefficient. A diagrammatic explanation of the Gini is provided in Figure 1.1, which shows the percentage share of income which accrues to each decile of the population. If income were to be equally distributed, we could represent the income distribution using the line labelled 'Equality'. It is called a line of equality because it means that everybody is receiving an equal share of national income, i.e. the bottom 10 per cent of the population is receiving 10 per cent of income, and so on.

In all economies, however, income is unequally distributed. In other words, the bottom 10 per cent of the population typically achieves much less than 10 per cent of national income. In practice, therefore, the income distribution of a country describes a curve which is more like the line labelled 'Inequality'. Basically, the further the curve is away from the line of perfect equality, the more unequal is the income distribution. The Gini coefficient provides a statistical measure of the divergence of the Lorenz curve from the line of perfect equality. More precisely, the Gini is area A divided by the sum of area A and area B.

In theory, the value of the Gini coefficient varies between 0 (perfect equality) and 1 (all income accrues to one person). In practice, however, the range is much less than that. Table 1.4 brings together Gini coefficients for a number of different countries. The figure for Lesotho is indicative of the top end of the range (though that estimate is now rather dated, figures of around 0.6 are very much at the top end of the range), whereas the figure for Norway delineates the bottom end. The Chinese figure of 0.47 is towards the top end of the range, and there is little doubt that the Gini is growing over time, and an underestimate of the true level of inequality. One of the reasons for the high figure in China and for the comparatively low figure usually found in OECD countries is the impact of the tax and benefit system. In the UK, for example, the Gini coefficient for original income in 2005–6 was 0.52 before the impact of progressive income taxes and cash benefits reduced it to the figure of 0.34 given in Table 1.4.

However, we should be wary of the deceptive simplicity of the Gini coefficient. For one thing, international definitions and concepts of income vary quite considerably. Another problem is that the measurement of income inequality is fraught with peril. Even for a country as prosperous as Japan, the data on inequality are so unreliable that one of the world's leading experts on income inequality chose not to include Japan in his survey of income inequality in OECD countries (Atkinson 1995). In poorer countries, the problems are much worse. It is often said that East Asia has combined growth with equity since 1950, but this conclusion rests on flimsy empirical foundations. In fact, it is clear from close examination of the data that income inequality in East Asia only appears to be lower than in other countries because the income surveys typically ignore the rich and the poor. Two quotations give a flavour of the limitations of the surveys:

Table 1.4 Gini coefficients for a range of countries

	Year	Concept	Gini
Lesotho	1995	expenditure	0.63
Brazil	2004	income	0.57
USA	2000	income	0.41
Russia	2002	expenditure	0.40
India	2004–5	expenditure	0.37
UK	2005–6	income	0.34
Norway	2000	income	0.26
China	2004	income	0.47

Sources: World Bank (2007d: 66–8); Jones (2007: 39).

Note
Expenditure is invariably more equally distributed than income because households typically borrow to finance consumption where necessary.

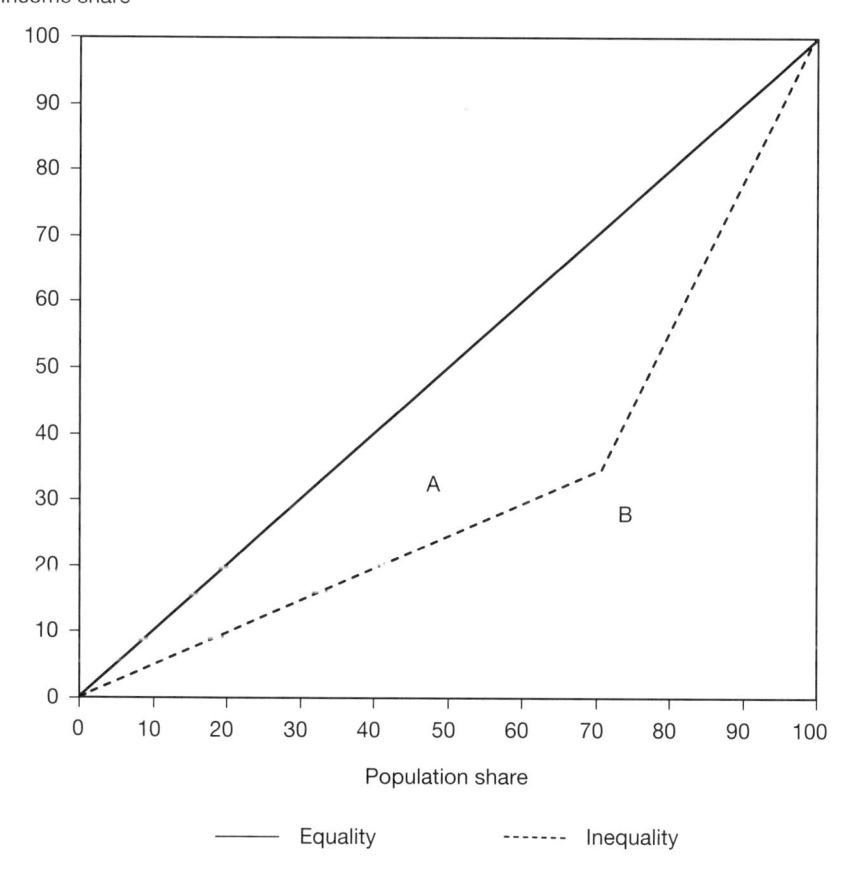

Figure 1.1 The Gini coefficient

[Japanese data] exclude households engaged in agriculture, forestry or fishing, one-person households, foreigner households, households which manage restaurants, hotels or similar establishments, households with 4 or more live-in employees and households where the head is absent long term. (Atkinson 1995: 69–70)

[South Korean data exclude] wealthy households, single-person households, non-farm households in rural areas, and small farmers. (Hart-Landsberg 1993: 199)

A further area of concern centres on the measurement of regional inequalities. For one thing, there are big regional price differences within large developing economies, and these need to be allowed for in measuring true inequality. In addition, migration causes problems, because migrants are often excluded from the populations of destination regions (population figures are usually based on the number of permanent residents) and because remittance flows can make a significant difference to per capita income levels in rich and poor regions alike.

More fundamentally, contrasting Gini coefficients across countries does not really tell us very much about comparative levels of development because it simply ducks the fact that some forms of inequality matter more, whether for good or ill, than others. A country might have a high Gini coefficient, but that in itself tells us nothing. We need much more information before rushing to judgement. Most obviously, the United States has long been a society characterized by considerable inequality, and it has often been condemned on such grounds. Yet there is very little evidence that American society considers such inequality to be a matter of grave concern, at least in so far as preferences are demonstrated by voting behaviour. Why is that?

One issue affecting perceptions is whether observed inequality is permanent or largely transient. If the latter, it is less likely to be a concern. This argument is of particular relevance to developing countries, because it has long been argued that inequality follows an inverted U shape – that is, it rises in the initial stages of development before falling back as a country becomes more prosperous. This is the famous Kuznets (1955, 1963) hypothesis, and it is easy to show that labour migration from the low-income rural sector to the high-income urban sector will cause the Gini coefficient to follow such a pattern over time in a market-orientated economy (Fields 1980). However, the empirical evidence suggests that the Kuznets hypothesis does not hold (Anand and Kanbur 1993), and this undercuts attempts to argue that inequality is a short-term problem and therefore of little real concern. Moreover, the evidence points overwhelmingly to the conclusion that market-based economies like the UK and the USA are characterized by low and declining levels of social mobility (Glyn 2006). Indeed few societies are more class-ridden (in the sense that parental income is the most decisive influence on the income of children) than the USA. The American dream is just that, even if it continues to hold in its thrall the hearts and minds of so many of the US population.

This absence of temporal mobility of social groups leads on to a second issue. Even if inequality is not a transient phenomenon, does it matter in a moral or philosophical sense? In practical terms, the answer is clearly that inequalities which serve some social purpose are likely to be more widely accepted than those which do not. Here there is widespread agreement that some types of income inequality are desirable in order to provide incentives, and that it may even be desirable to transfer resources to growth-promoting groups within society; entrepreneurship, for instance, is encouraged in many societies by a variety of tax concessions. Conversely, it is hard to justify income inequalities which derive from inherited wealth; there is no reason why we should allow children to benefit from the talent of their parents. However, we should be under no illusion as to the radical nature of that type of proposition. True equality of opportunity is about far more than equal access to health or education. The creation of a meritocratic society requires radical and far-reaching redistribution of wealth to prevent parental advantage being passed on to children in the form of income and assets. Even then, policies of positive discrimination within the educational system will be needed to overcome the effects of differences in inherited levels of cultural capital, at least where access to education is rationed on the basis of exam-based merit (such as university education).

It is equally hard to justify gender discrimination or discrimination against ethnic minorities, because neither serves much of a social purpose. That said, neither gender nor ethnic inequality has a big effect on the Gini coefficient in many societies.[17] Ethnic minorities typically comprise only a small fraction of the population in many countries. And per capita female income usually depends less upon female wages than male income depends on male wages; marriage and income-sharing with higher-wage men means that many women are less disadvantaged than implied by the distribution of wages. To put this another way, the gender distribution of per capita income is more equal than that of wages. Furthermore, whilst many women are poor, the real reason for their poverty is much more likely to be their class status than their gender. Many women are affluent, but not when they are members of the working class: an affluent female worker is an oxymoron. Of course working-class women are disadvantaged on the grounds of both class and gender, but it is their class rather than their gender status which is usually crucial. We also need to recognize, as argued by Becker and other members of the Chicago–Columbia school, that low female wages are in part a consequence of voluntary decisions to have children (it makes no sense to see fertility as uncontrolled in most societies). The result of having children is of course that women are less likely to be promoted and more likely to have part-time jobs than men. But the voluntary dimension to childbearing means that we should be less concerned about this type of inequality than others. Many feminists argue that the social benefits from children justify state subsidies for child care, but the argument is not supported by the evidence; even aging societies would do better to encourage immigration than subsidize child care. None of this is to justify gender discrimination, but considerations such as these suggest that we should be worried much less about gender inequality than other forms of inequality. And if action is to be taken on behalf of women, public policy should focus on the needs of working-class single women, rather than women as a whole.

Inequalities between capital and labour (the main contributory factor to the Gini coefficient in most societies) are defensible on functional grounds.[18] Rawls (1972) famously argued that inequality was justifiable in so far as (a) the inequality promoted growth (and thereby poverty reduction) and (b) the society in question was characterized by *de facto* equality of opportunity. Still more famously, Marx (1875: 213–15) argued that inequalities were necessary in the early stages of communism, and only in the later stages could distribution be according to need:

> Here we are dealing with a communist society, not as it has developed from first principles, but, on the contrary, just as it emerges from capitalist society, hence in every respect – economically, morally, intellectually – as it comes forth from the womb, it is stamped with the birthmarks of the old society. The individual producer retains proportionately, after deductions, exactly what he put into it. What he has put into it is a quantity of his individual labour … In a higher phase of communist society, after the subjection of individuals to the division of labour, and thereby the antithesis between mental and physical labour, has disappeared; after labour has become not only a means of life but life's prime want; after the productive forces have also increased with the all-round development of the individual, and all the springs of co-operative wealth flow more abundantly – only then can the narrow horizon of bourgeois right be crossed in its entirety and society inscribe on its banner: From each according to his ability, to each according to his needs!

These sorts of arguments are of course the mainstay of neoliberal agendas: inequality is argued to be necessary to promote risk-taking and hence technical progress. One can go further and argue that even corruption can be growth-promoting (Khan and Jomo 2000; Rock and Bonnett 2004). Corruption does lead to a deadweight loss because resources are used up in the process of rent-seeking (such as lobbying for government favours) which would be better used in promoting innovation and accumulation. However, if corruption has the effect of transferring resources to a growth-promoting class – as it seems to have done in (say) South Korea – the net effect will be strongly positive. Or, to put this another way, everything depends on the use to which the rents from corruption are put. It is certainly arguable that corruption in China is not growth-promoting, but the possibility cannot be dismissed a priori.

For all that, we need to recognize that the case for inequality on growth-promoting grounds is far from unambiguous. For example, if there are diminishing returns to investment in education, it follows that a redistribution of income from the rich to the poor will lead to a higher overall level of education and hence to more rapid growth. In so far as low productivity in developing countries reflects under-nutrition, a redistribution of income to the poor will raise labour productivity (Dasgupta and Ray 1986). Thus Maoist redistribution of land in the early 1950s may well have increased farm productivity by improving levels of human nutrition. It is well known too that the impact of very high levels of income on work incentives is likely to be adverse; the income effect (higher income makes work less necessary) outweighs the substitution effect (a higher wage per hour encourages more hours of work) at high level of income, such that tax rises for the rich are likely to have a more positive effect on productivity than tax cuts.[19] In addition, the evidence suggests that it is inequality which is leading to falls in happiness despite rises in per capita income (Offer 2006). Finally, there is considerable evidence that high levels of wealth inequality are harmful to growth in the short run because an incoming regime is forced to pursue redistributive policies, which in turn harm growth (Persson and Tabellini 1994). For example, land reform may cause the fragmentation of farms and penal rates of taxation may harm incentives. That said, once redistribution is completed, the country is likely to gain a growth reward. This appears to be the lesson from East Asia. Initial inequality, and the policies needed to tackle it, hampered growth in Taiwan and South Korea in the 1950s. However, once wealth had been redistributed by means of land reform, growth was rapid (Alesina and Rodrik 1994). Part of the argument here is that the absence of powerful interest groups made it much easier for East Asian states to be 'hard' and hence pursue properly selective industrial policy.

In any case, even if the end (economic growth) can be argued to justify the means (inequality), societies may not see inequality in such a favourable light.[20] Inequality may be growth-promoting, but it may also have adverse social consequences. For example, there is considerable evidence that income inequality reduces life expectancy; social standing affects psychic health, and hence well-being (Wilkinson 2005). More starkly, income inequalities may lead to revolution if they are perceived to be unjust.[21] However, the causes of revolution are hard to pin down. As Collier (2007) rightly argues, revolutionary groups may proclaim to the world that their armed struggle is motivated by redistributional aims, but the truth may be much more prosaic. To be sure, revolutions often take place against a backcloth of inequality – one thinks of France in 1789, Russia in 1917, China in 1949 and Iran in 1979 – but causality is very hard to establish. In the Chinese case, for example, it has often been claimed that nationalism (Johnson 1962) or poverty were much more important factors in creating a revolutionary peasantry than any commitment by the CCP to equality. Moreover, some types of inequality may not lead to social action because they are widely seen as in some sense inevitable. Inequalities which derive from physical geography provide one example. It is hard to deny the existence of geographically determined spatial inequalities in large countries such as the USSR, Brazil, China and India. It is even harder to believe that the land-locked countries of central Asia – whether Tibet or the Asian republics of the former Soviet Union – have promising economic futures as independent states. To sure, there is a powerful Tibetan independence movement, but that clamour is driven far more by fears of colonization and cultural obliteration than it is by income inequality. Still, we have to be very careful here before accepting that geography makes inequality inevitable. As Krugman's (1991) work has shown, the location of manufacturing in countries typically owes more to chance and to population concentrations than to resource availability, elevation or the proximity of rivers. Moreover, regional inequalities can be reduced by means of fiscal transfers, or perhaps by encouraging out-migration. Geography is not destiny, and governments which seek to justify underdevelopment in peripheral regions on grounds of geographical determinism are pursuing a dangerous course.

In sum, it is hard to make judgements about whether one country is doing 'better' in terms of income inequality than another. The Gini coefficient is a superficially attractive way of making such comparisons, but in reality an informed judgement requires far more information about the nature of inequality and its consequences than the Gini allows. Some forms of inequality are much more growth-promoting than others, and on that matter the Gini coefficient is silent.

Poverty

For many economists, however, poverty is much more of an evil than inequality (Rawls 1972; Fields 1980). Inequality produces envy, but absolute poverty can kill. It follows that the primary aim of development – especially in a very poor country – should be absolute poverty reduction rather than redistribution *per se*. Moreover, there can be no easy presumption that growth will trickle down automatically to the poorest in society. The type of growth matters; growth which is employment-creating and disproportionately benefits the rural population is more likely to reduce poverty than other types of growth. Even so, state intervention will still usually be necessary to eliminate absolute poverty. But if poverty is hard to eliminate, it is also very hard to measure. And it is with the question of measurement that our discussion starts.

(a) Relative versus absolute poverty

An important distinction needs to be drawn between absolute and relative poverty. The absolute poverty approach compares the status of a household (or person) against a poverty line, usually set at subsistence. In other words, we ask whether the household has enough food or enough clothing for survival. Absolute poverty measures are commonly employed in assessing the degree of poverty in poor countries precisely because such countries have sizeable populations living below subsistence. By contrast, the relative poverty approach compares the status of the poor with the national mean or median; it is in this sense that poverty is relative. In Western countries, poverty is usually measured in relative terms because hardly any of their populations have a below-subsistence level of income. For example, according to the EU (European Union) definition, a person is deemed to be living in poverty if his/her income is less than 60 per cent of the EU median. By contrast, Chinese poverty lines are usually based upon the income needed for subsistence; estimates of poverty are therefore measures of absolute poverty.

Notice that trends in absolute poverty need not mirror trends in relative poverty. Consider a situation in which the real income of a poor person is increasing by

5 per cent per year but average and median real income for the country is rising by 10 per cent. In this example, absolute poverty is falling (the poor person is better off in real terms), but relative poverty is rising (the income of the poor person is increasing less quickly than the average). This is likely to be a source of concern even in a poor country, because it shows that the fruits of growth are being unequally shared; such an outcome may well lead to widespread social discontent. Policymakers in poor countries such as China are therefore typically concerned about trends in both absolute and relative poverty. We cannot define a country as truly developed unless it scores well in terms of both relative and absolute poverty, though it is probably reasonable to conclude that absolute poverty alleviation should be the key short-term priority.

(b) Income versus human poverty

The second problem in assessing poverty lies in deciding whether we should measure poverty in terms of income, or in terms of some other indicator. For a long time, economists and social scientists have concentrated on what is now called income poverty – that is, poverty has been defined in terms of how much income the poorest members of the population have. More recently, however, it has been argued (especially by the United Nations) that we should look at what is called human poverty. The idea is that we should try to measure poverty by using an indicator which is more general than income. For example, a person might be well off in monetary terms and yet disabled or working in a highly polluted environment. Should not such a person be categorized as poor?

The debate here parallels than on GDP per head (income) versus capability (human poverty), and as in that case, there is no reason to expect human and income measures of poverty to tell the same story. To give an example, consider the mortality rate of blacks in the USA in the late 1980s relative to those of whites. Table 1.5 shows what is well recognized: even after adjusting for income, there are big differences in mortality rates for blacks and whites in America. To put this another way, even if a black woman has the same income as a white woman, she is still twice as likely to die between the ages of 35 and 54. One might therefore argue that black women who are well off in terms of income are nevertheless living in poverty. Similarly, ethnic minorities living in geographically disadvantaged areas of China are much more likely to die prematurely than Han Chinese living in the same area.

Table 1.5. Ratio of black to white mortality rates in the USA, late 1980s (for men and women aged 35–54)

	Men	Women
Unadjusted ratio	1.8	2.9
Ratio adjusted for differences in income	1.2	2.2

Source: Sen (1999: 97).

As with the capability versus opulence debate, there is no right answer to the question of whether human or income poverty provides the better measure. We can be clear, however, on the point that the two measures may tell different stories. Policymakers therefore need to pay attention to both types of measure in promoting development. If the eradication of human poverty is the main priority, then communism appears to be hard to beat. However, the Cuban path will not appeal to those who see that country as one in which most members of society enjoy a level of per capita income which is barely above the poverty line. And many would argue that the Maoist regime was unpopular in the late 1970s precisely because it failed to bring about significant increases in material living standards across China.

Assessing development: the problem of comparison

The choice of indicators has received, as we have seen, a great deal of attention. Much less extensively discussed is the question of what the pace of development – however defined – should be compared against. Does a country with a 3 per cent GDP per capita growth rate classify as successful or not?

Historical comparisons

One way to proceed is to make a historical comparison. We could look at the performance of a country over a given time period, and then compare this performance against that of the same country in a period during its recent past. The attraction of this sort of approach is that it normalizes for country-specific factors such as culture, country size and geography. Some of these factors change over time, but they do so very slowly. Accordingly, a comparison of (say) India's human development record before and after its independence in 1947 makes much more sense than comparing India with a small and very different country such as Lebanon.

However, historical comparisons necessarily cannot normalize for changes in the global environment, and this is their great weakness. A particular difficulty here is caused by the extent of technological progress since Britain began its Industrial Revolution in the late eighteenth century. Britain's growth rate certainly accelerated during its Industrial Revolution (Crafts 1985: 45) – but the change was rather modest and its per capita growth rate (of about 0.5 per cent per year between 1801 and 1831) appears very low compared with contemporary developing countries. This of course was because Britain was the first country to experience sustained per capita growth: it was therefore operating at close to the world technological frontier and the scope for learning from other countries was limited. By contrast, contemporary developing countries can in principle grow very quickly by importing and applying the backlog of technology which has accumulated since Britain's Industrial Revolution. This is the process of 'industrialization by learning', to use Alice Amsden's (1989) famous phrase. It is this scope for catch-up which explains why the growth rates of developing countries have exhibited trend acceleration over time; whereas Britain achieved barely 0.5 per cent, Germany and America achieved over 1.5 per cent per capita GDP growth per year between 1870 and 1913 and Japan around 8 per cent per annum between 1950 and 1973 (Maddison 2001: 265).

Technical progress thus means that it is hard to make a valid comparison across time periods for the same country; the scope for growth is so much more extensive now than it was in the early nineteenth century. Britain's growth rate now is considerably faster than it was during its Industrial Revolution, but to argue that Britain failed during its Industrial Revolution makes little sense. Similarly, the scope for China in terms of technological catch-up was far greater in the 1980s than it was in the 1930s. The China of the 1930s certainly failed, but at best (at least to judge by other countries successfully undergoing industrialization at the same time) it could not have generated per capita GDP increases of more than 5 per cent a year. To compare China in the 1980s with China in the 1930s is therefore a biased comparison.

Similar sorts of technological considerations apply to life expectancy. Medical improvements occurred very rapidly during the Second World War, especially in respect of inoculation. Therefore, it was much easier for developing countries to achieve big reductions in mortality by the application of comparatively simple medical technology after 1945 than it had been during the 1930s. Accordingly, it makes little sense to compare (say) South Korea's record on life expectancy before and after the Second World War; we need to normalize for technological change if the comparison is to be a fair one.

Normalization problems for historical comparisons are also caused by fluctuations in the performance of the world economy. The 1930s, it is universally recognized, was an extremely disturbed period. International trade grew very slowly because of the Great Depression and therefore it was hard for any country to achieve rapid growth. By contrast, international conditions were much more favourable during the period between 1870 and 1913, the era of the operation of the Gold Standard. And between 1945 and 1973, the year of the first big oil price rise, conditions were better still (Glyn 2006). This was the Golden Age, the era of *pax Americana*, during which international trade grew at an unprecedented rate. Any country that began to develop successfully during these decades, and was relatively open to international trade, was at a great advantage over countries which attempted to follow them during the much more disturbed period of 1973–90. In other words, if we compare the performance of Japan between 1950 and 1973 with Japan between 1918 and 1941, we end up with a very biased comparison. Most would agree that Japan did perform better after 1945, but there is no question that its path was eased by the Golden Age.

Nor can we ignore political considerations, which also varied over time. The isolated Japan of the 1930s was very much at a disadvantage when compared with the satellite state that was integral to *pax Americana* in the Pacific after 1945. More generally, for any developing country that was fortunate enough to be an American satellite during the Golden Age – compare the situation of Hong Kong, South Korea, Singapore and Taiwan with that of Cuba, North Korea or

Albania – conditions were benign indeed. Not all countries were able to take advantage, as is clear from the example of the Philippines, but an alliance with the USA brought clear advantages for many countries. Even sub-Saharan Africa benefited from the Cold War, because the continent was contested terrain; indeed its poor record since 1990 has much to do with the way in which it has fallen off the political agenda in both Washington and Moscow.[22] As for China, it obviously lost out as a result of its isolation in the Maoist era, whereas its ability to trade has been far greater since the late 1970s.

International comparisons

An apparent way around these problems is to make an international comparison. Instead of comparing the performance of a country with itself during some previous time period, we can compare it with a similar country during the same epoch. Such a procedure has great appeal because it normalizes for variations over time in the world economy. For example, we might compare Indian and Chinese development during the postwar era, as Drèze and Sen (2002) have done. Both countries became *de facto* independent at the same time, both are large countries and the initial level of development in the two (whether measured in terms of GDP per head or mortality) was very similar. Or we might compare two small landlocked countries with each other – Bolivia and Nepal over the post-1990 period, for example.

Nevertheless, cross-country comparisons are very difficult to make because it can reasonably be objected that some countries enjoy much more favourable circumstances than others. Indeed one cannot but acknowledge the severity of the problems involved in making international comparisons. Can we really compare China and India? Not only do we need to normalize for country size, natural resources and climate but we also need to allow for differences in the degree of ethno-linguistic fragmentation and the very different histories of the countries involved. Economic growth and human development may not be path-dependent in a literal sense (countries can jump off an inefficient equilibrium path – that, after all, is what development is all about) but history nevertheless casts a dark shadow in all corners of the globe. And in saying that country characteristics do not change much, we have to recognize the potency of asymmetric shocks. That is, change in the globally environment (broadly defined) can produce very big country-specific effects – we can think of a natural resource discovery, severe weather (especially drought, because it can affect a very large area, unlike flooding) or some sort of industry-specific shock. For example, a big change in the world oil price will have very large effect on those countries which are big net importers or exporters of oil. China is a case in point. As a net importer, the Chinese empire is becoming increasingly vulnerable to oil price shocks, and this helps to explain its desire to carve out new colonies for itself in Angola and Sudan and to continue the exploitation of its own internal colonies of Xinjiang and Tibet.

It is also fair to argue that some cultures are much more inimical to development than others. Many neoclassical and Marxist writers have treated culture as essentially superstructural, meaning that it is determined by economic factors rather than vice versa. However, this is not very convincing. Many scholars, notably Weber (1905) and Tawney (1926), have rightly argued that culture helps to explain the rise of the West, and recent writers have sought in culture an explanation for what they perceive to be the decline of the United States (Putnam 2000). Others, like Morishima (1982), have argued that Japanese Confucianism was much more growth-promoting than Chinese Confucianism. Fukuyama (1995) has sought to explain differences in the size of firms between Taiwan and South Korea in terms of different levels of societal trust; and for Lal (1998) the slow growth of India is because of its culture (it has long been trapped in the 'the Hindu equilibrium'). Moreover, Althusserian Marxists – following, as we shall see, in the footsteps of Mao – have argued that superstructural change has an independent effect on the economic base. Some of these arguments are not very convincing, and at best difficult to test; how precisely does one measure things such as culture or social capital? However, that is no good reason to conclude that culture is a superstructural epiphenomenon. That is economic determinism at its worst.

Yet even if we accept that culture matters and that cultures differ across countries, we can make too much of the cultural objection to cross-country comparisons. Country specialists are prone to object that their country is unique and that this makes any form of cross-country comparison an impossibility; this line of argument is what one might call the area studies fallacy. Its main weakness is that it often fails to distinguish between conditions which are given, and conditions which are amenable to policy change. Culture, for example, does not change quickly, but it can change. For example, many have argued that Japanese culture altered as a result of the Second World War and that Mao remade Chinese culture during the 1960s and 1970s. To argue therefore that a comparison between (say) Japan and Nigeria is unfair because Japan was lucky in having a more growth-promoting culture has more than an element of fatalism about it. If Japan was able to remake its culture in the aftermath of the Second World War, why not Nigeria in the aftermath of independence? Similarly, it is not unreasonable to ask whether we should regard Cuba's economic isolation as given, or a consequence of internal policy decisions which in principle could be changed. Some countries do have limited economic potential, and we need to bear that in mind when making cross-country comparisons. But at the same time, we need to recognize that some types of cross-country comparisons are perfectly reasonable.

Comparing actual performance with potential

It has been suggested in the previous sections that a country's developmental record can sometimes be assessed by employing an international or historical yardstick. Nevertheless, my own view is that we are usually best served by an approach which assesses performance by comparing actual performance against economic potential, because this approach explicitly attempts to normalize for the constraints faced and opportunities enjoyed by the country in question. It is certainly not easy to assess economic potential, because it requires the formulation of a proper counterfactual, but that does not mean we should shy away from the attempt. What then determines economic potential?

In answering that question, we may group together the variables for consideration under the headings of initial conditions and environmental factors (in the widest sense). It is easy enough to list the sorts of factors we need to consider. Much less straightforward – and highly controversial – is the determination of whether (and how) the factors in question promote development.[23] Are (for example) natural resources a help or a handicap when it comes to economic development? Box 1.1 summarizes my approach.

(a) Environmental variables

The environmental variables are comparatively easy to assess. There is little doubt that a country will benefit (via rapid export growth) if it attempts to industrialize at a time when the world economy is growing rapidly.[24] Thus Taiwan and South Korea benefited enormously because the opening up of their economies in the 1960s coincided with the long postwar boom or Golden Age. Similarly, China has benefited from the globalization of the 1990s, whereas it was hampered by world depression during the 1930s. In other words, its growth potential was higher in the 1990s than in the 1930s. Nevertheless, the evidence suggests that only in the smallest countries does growth tend to be export-led. For most countries, it is the domestic market and therefore domestic growth which is the key factor. Trade matters, but its impact is secondary in both developed and underdeveloped countries alike (Rodrik 1995). As Krugman persuasively argues, it is productivity which is decisive for living standards, and the impact of trade on that is usually small:

> Productivity isn't everything, but in the long run it is almost everything. A country's ability to improve its standard of living over time depends almost entirely on its ability to raise its output per worker. (Krugman 1994: 13)

Krugman's argument was outlined with reference to the USA, but it applies to China too. For large economies, growth is driven by internal rather than by external factors, and so it is with China.

As for economic and political isolation, its effects are usually adverse. The catch-up possibilities for countries which are isolated are fewer (though the Soviet Union was able to access US technology via a range of illicit channels and by third-country dealings during the Cold War) and they will be forced to spend far more on indigenous R&D than more open countries. Perhaps more importantly, isolation typically forces the country affected to spend far more on defence in an attempt to secure itself against attack. This in turn constrains its ability to invest in civilian industry. There will be some spillovers from military R&D, but it is far better to invest directly in the civilian sector. Ultimately, the need to spend increasing sums on defence may even undermine the entire economy. It is surely no accident that the acceleration in Japan's growth rate after the Second World War

Box 1.1 **The determinants of economic potential**

	Variable	Assumed impact on GDP growth
Initial conditions ('history')	Ethno-linguistic fragmentation	Adverse
	Low level of GDP per capita (scope for catch-up)	Positive
	Infrastructure	Positive but slight
	Human capital	
	• educational attainment	Positive, but more so for skills and primary education than other types of education
	• the skills base	
	• health and morbidity	Positive
	Industrial capital	Adverse
	Inequality of wealth	Adverse
Environment	Geography	
	• rainfall	Positive, but slight
	• extent of coastline	Positive, but slight
	• arable area per head	Positive, but slight
	• natural resources per head	Usually adverse
	Country size	Positive
	Growth of the world economy	Positive, but slight (for a large economy)
	Political isolation	Adverse

Note
A factor classified here as an environmental variable is one which is outside the control of the country in question. Initial conditions are a product of history and are in principle amenable to policy-induced change.

coincided with vastly reduced levels of military spending. And many American neoconservatives have contended that the Cold War was won under Reagan by increasing US defence spending to the point where the Soviet Union, in order to compete, was forced to allocate an unsustainable proportion of its (much lower) GDP to defence. These arguments are contentious; Castro, for example, has long argued that corruption was the decisive factor behind the collapse of the USSR. Nevertheless, even if it is difficult to determine just how adverse defence spending can be, there is little evidence that military spending is growth-promoting. In that sense, isolation imposes a cost.

To be sure, an external threat can be a unifying force. Isolation acts as a spur to nationalism and patriotism, as does war. This in turn helps to hold consumption in check, making possible higher investment. Furthermore, isolation guards a country against external shocks. And the evidence suggests that isolation is rarely disastrous; Cuba and North Korea have been able to improve their living standards significantly despite the US trade boycott, the former (at least in terms of human development) remarkably so. Nevertheless, it is hard to see isolation as a factor which has helped development; the debate is only about the seriousness of its adverse consequences. And so it is for China. Its response to its isolation in the 1960s was a massive programme of defence industrialization which cost it dear in many ways, but primarily because it was financed by squeezing agricultural incomes. There were collateral benefits in terms of industrialization in backward regions and import legacies. On balance, however, its effects were harmful; isolation depressed China's economic potential in the 1960s and 1970s.

As for country size, both theory and evidence are ambivalent. Small countries can in principle sell on world markets and therefore the size of their domestic market may not be an issue. Access to world capital markets can also provide a vital source of investment finance. Singapore and Hong Kong provide obvious examples of how a small country can thrive. However, integration into the world economy increases political and economic risk; a boycott of export products initiated for political/military reasons or because of protectionist pressure from interest groups will have devastating effects on small countries reliant on external trade. As previously noted, the prices of primary commodities are notoriously volatile. And reliance on foreign capital makes a country vulnerable to capital flight. A large domestic market and an abundant supply of domestic finance effectively insulate a country against much of this risk. Keynes (1933: 236) summarized the dangers associated with international economic integration thus:

> Advisable domestic policies might often be easier to compass, if, for example, the phenomenon known as 'the flight of capital' could be ruled out ... I sympathise, therefore, with those who would minimise rather than maximise economic entanglement between nations. Ideas, knowledge, art, hospitality and travel – these are the things which should of their nature be international. But let goods be homespun whenever it is reasonably and conveniently possible; above all let finance be primarily national.

Country size confers other advantages and disadvantages. Large countries are much better able to develop nuclear arsenals and this will protect them against strategic blackmail or invasion; India is much less vulnerable than was Iraq. More generally, there are economies of scale in the production of public goods and this gives the large country an advantage. However, large countries are much more likely to suffer from heterogeneity of preferences driven by linguistic, ethnic and religious factors – that is, their population is likely to be much less united in what it demands of governments, and therefore precious resources will need to be expended on meeting the rival demands of different groups (Alesina and Spolaore 2003). But on balance, size probably confers benefits by allowing countries to engage more strategically with the world economy; large countries have much more policy autonomy. This is surely the case with China. It suffers little from ethno-religious fragmentation (though it is unfortunate that its ethnic minorities live in important border provinces), and its large domestic market allows the exploitation of economies of scale in production. More importantly, it can largely dictate the terms of its engagement with the world economy.

Nevertheless, the significance of some of the factors associated with large country size is hard to assess. Take, for example, ethno-linguistic fragmentation. It is easy to see both the advantages (the pace of learning and innovation tends to be greater in diverse societies such as that of the UK) and disadvantages (differences in preferences and tastes, leading to disputes and rent-seeking), but the balance of empirical evidence is not easy to sift. India has not fared badly since 1947 – but one might argue that the less fragmented East Asian countries have done better still, and that both sub-Saharan Africa and Iraq have suffered enormously. This last conclusion is borne out by the more systematic work of Easterly and Levine (1997); however, we should also note that Collier and Gunning (1999) concluded that fragmentation was only a problem in the absence of democracy. While it is true that innovation-driven growth is probably less important than extensive (or investment driven) growth for most *poor* countries given the scope for catch-up, it is probably fair to include that the disadvantages of fragmentation outweigh the advantages. Wealth inequality, however, seems easier to judge. It is hard to justify inherited wealth, especially land, in terms of positive incentive effects. Moreover, as noted earlier, the Persson–Tabellini (1994) argument that inequality in effect forces a state to engage in redistribution, usually at the expense of growth-promotion, has a compelling force to it. A degree of income inequality may be good for growth, but wealth inequality is much less so.

Assessing the significance of geography for China and for other countries is more difficult. It is not difficult to argue that economic development in Tibet and Qinghai province is fatally hampered by their location on the high Himalayan plateau far from the coast. And some, notably Sachs *et al.* (2004, 2005), have argued that geography has played a decisive role in determining the poor growth record of sub-Saharan Africa (SSA). Much of SSA is tropical and this brings with it high levels of infant mortality as a result of malaria (Sachs and Gallup 2001). But all this is controversial. One difficulty is that deaths from malaria amongst adults in SSA are not especially high (seemingly because of acquired immunity – Acemoglu *et al.* 2001: 1380–1), and high infant mortality may actually promote economic growth by holding down the dependency rate (Evans 2004: 118). However, the main problem with the Sachs line of argument is that many geographical variables – soil quality, irrigation networks and even the incidence of malaria – are not exogenous but are functions of economic policy. Second, it is often difficult to generalize. Being land-locked is not a disadvantage if one has a large and prosperous neighbour across the border, or if relations with neighbours are so good that overland trade presents few difficulties. For example, Bolivia's fortunes are inextricably tied to its relations with Chile and Argentina. Land-locked countries are of course more vulnerable to trade interdiction, and therefore on balance a large coastline is probably an advantage (Collier 2007). The vast majority of land-locked countries are poor; one thinks especially of central Asian countries such as Tibet, Mongolia and the central Asian republics of the former Soviet Union. But even here the evidence is not uniform. One land-locked success story is Switzerland, and some have acclaimed Botswana as 'An African Success Story' (Acemoglu et al. 2003).[25] Moreover, it is far from obvious that Tibet's economic prospects would be transformed were it to be independent. Its status as an integral part of the Chinese empire allows it to compensate for geographical disadvantage. As an independent sovereign state it would need to negotiate access to the coast with China from a position of relative weakness.

As for mineral resources, majority opinion is that these are a curse rather a blessing (Collier 2007). There are number of well-documented studies demonstrating that resource discoveries typically lead to exchange rate appreciation and thence to deindustrialization via loss of export competitiveness. If it is assumed that manufacturing industry once lost is hard to recreate, these 'Dutch disease' effects have long-run consequences as well as short-run distributional costs (in terms of higher unemployment). However, the evidence is hard to decipher. Britain in the early 1980s is often used as the classic example; manufacturing was crowded out by an appreciation of sterling driven by the extraction of North Sea oil. But monetary contraction (which drove up the interest rate and thereby attracted short-run capital inflows) was probably even more important. More generally, unless an economy is at full employment, exchange rate appreciation can always be offset by monetary expansion. Moreover, if natural resources per capita truly are vast (as in the case of Saudi Arabia or Kuwait), the country may be able to live in perpetuity off the rents. More generally, a recent study concluded that natural resource abundance was growth-promoting across the globe over the period 1970–2000 (Brunnschweiler 2008).

Nevertheless, it is certainly clear that natural resource discovery is a mixed blessing; governments will need to respond with relatively sophisticated macroeconomic policy change if the fruits are not to be lost. And much the same can be said of having a large volume of arable land per capita. It will help to raise agricultural production (Brazil is a good example of a country with a large arable area characterized by low yields), but this in turn may actually discourage the development of manufacturing industry, where the scope for long-run productivity growth is greater. For all these reasons, most economists have rejected the notion that 'geography is destiny', preferring instead to argue that endogenously determined institutional structures are decisive (Rodrik 2003; Acemoglu et al. 2001, 2002). Geographical advantage yields potential benefits, but these are difficult to harness and are rarely crucial in driving developmental success. Botswana's problems, despite its vast inheritance of diamonds, offers a cautionary tale to those who think in terms of geographical determinism. The very fact that China has comparatively few natural resources per head has arguably meant that it has been forced to concentrate on the development of manufacturing much more than might otherwise have been the case.

(b) Initial conditions: history

Assessing the impact of initial conditions ('history') on a country's developmental potential is more difficult. Take the effect of a low level of GDP per head at the start of the development process. Does it help or hinder growth? Was China helped by the fact that it was (allegedly) 'poor and blank' even in 1978?

The answer here is almost certainly that a low level of per capita GDP is helpful to growth. A poor country enjoys 'the advantages of backwardness' in the sense that a combination of a high investment rate and low initial GDP per head can generate very rapid growth based around the application of technology developed abroad, and its embodiment in the form of new capital. If a country starts at higher levels of income, however, its scope for catch-up is diminished because (by assumption) it has already applied some of the available world stock of technology, and therefore its growth rate will slow down. Alternatively, and to use a more neoclassical methodology, richer countries are apt to be on a flatter section of their production function, such that the marginal productivity of new capital is lower. Within this framework, all countries converge on their equilibrium level of output but, because these equilibria differ across countries (as a result of differences in preferences, etc.), convergence is conditional. There is no reason to expect absolute convergence of per capita income across the world.

To be sure, there are several critiques of this approach. One is that countries may find themselves in a poverty trap, or on a low-level equilibrium growth trajectory, because of path dependency (David 1985). Low initial per capita income offers them the *possibility* of rapid growth but they may not be able to mobilize the investment and savings needed to shift the equilibrium to a higher point; this is Sachs's (2005) argument applied to Africa. Here low per capita income is a hindrance because it makes saving very difficult: consumption has to have priority. In such circumstances, foreign aid may be a necessary condition for take-off. But that said, it can reasonably be objected that it is very rare to find a country without the surplus needed to finance investment; the problem for developing countries is more that they are unwilling to redistribute that surplus to growth-promoting classes. Aid in such circumstances is likely to be pointless.

A second critique of the 'advantages of backwardness' approach is that offered by endogenous growth theorists. Models of this sort hold out the possibility that growth will not be brought to a halt by diminishing returns, because some types of investment generate externalities. If true, this implies that being poor offers little advantage. Moreover, rich countries will have no trouble in maintaining relatively high growth rates, at least in principle, because of constant returns to spending on research and development (Romer 1986, 1990), or education (Lucas 1988). As a result, not even conditional convergence will take place (per capita incomes in countries with the same preference set, or in the same 'club', will not converge). In essence, this type of approach resurrects the earlier insights offered by Myrdal (1957) and by Kaldor (1970): growth is better characterized as a process of cumulative causation rather than one dominated by diminishing returns to physical and human capital.

Nevertheless, the empirical evidence is rather thin for endogenous growth theory. Cumulative processes do seem to operate at a regional level; for example, there is little evidence of convergence between London and the rest of the UK. However, even here we do well recognize that the growth of London is only possible because it is able to increase its land area, and in that sense the process is not truly endogenous. At a national level, the evidence is even less compelling, though there is some evidence of accelerating growth in the US over the last decade, driven by technologies (especially computer software) which are in some respects akin to public goods; shared use is possible without loss of value to any of the users. If the argument is true, it implies that rich countries will enjoy a longer-run growth advantage over middle-income countries which have exhausted much of the scope for catch-up. In general, however, the evidence supports the notion that poor countries can grow quickly via learning and catch-up, and that a process of slowdown is inevitable once the country reaches middle-income status. Arguably this is what has happened to China. It enjoyed rapid catch-up growth in the 1980s and 1990s, but its growth rate is likely to slow down over the next ten years.

Having said all this, we need to recognize that favourable preconditions – in other words, prior economic development – is likely to provide a springboard for future growth. In a sense, a country is likely to grow most quickly if it starts from a low base but only if it already has in place both infrastructure and a skilled workforce. The well-known Lewis model views development as a simple progress requiring no more than the transfer of labour from agriculture to industry. In practice, however, countries need much more than a large unskilled workforce to grow.

For example, the effect of initial levels of infrastructure on growth appears relatively clear. It is hard to believe that India's inheritance of railways and irrigation networks from British colonial rule were anything other than beneficial. Western China was hampered by the absence of railways in 1949. The issue is more whether such infrastructural legacies *significantly* raise the growth rate. In India's case, the railway network built by the British served military rather than economic ends and therefore its utility was less than it might have been. The construction of railways in western China as part of the Third Front programme during the 1960s did not suddenly transform the region's economic prospects. In fact, estimates of the 'social savings' generated by railways in most countries are typically small relative to GDP, largely because they substituted for canals and waterways which worked relatively well already.[26] The impact of the railway was thus quantitative rather than qualitative even in America, where the distances are great (Fishlow 1965; Fogel 1964). Of course estimates of social savings are subject to wide margins of error; for example, it is not easy to measure the impact of railway construction on (say) the development of financial markets (which were undoubtedly given a boost by the need to raise large sums of capital). But for all that, the gains from infrastructural construction appear to have been disappointingly small.

The desirability of an extensive inheritance of physical capital is also difficult to establish. One advantage is that a well-favoured country would be able to produce a wide range of outputs even in the short term, whereas a country with negligible industrial capacity would have to go through a long gestation period. To put this another way, the consumption share of GDP would have to be depressed in order to raise the investment share. Inherited industrial capacity thus offers a particular advantage if there is limited scope for international trade. In order, for example, to increase the production of grain, an isolated country would not be able to import grain directly, or import chemical fertilizer, or import machinery capable of producing chemical fertilizer. It would have to itself produce machines which produce chemical fertilizer – which, for a largely agricultural economy, would tend to imply producing machines which produce machines which produce chemical fertilizer. In other words, the degree of 'roundaboutness' in production would be very great for a country starting with limited industrial capital and few opportunities for trade.[27]

Nevertheless, an industrial inheritance confers disadvantage as well as advantage. It has, for example, often been argued that the UK's relative decline after 1870 was a legacy of its early start (Crafts 1985). Its factories and machinery were not well suited to the market conditions and technologies of the late nineteenth century, and such inputs could not easily be redeployed from one sector of the economy to another. Britain's factories were still profitable – it therefore made little sense to close them – but they were much less so than the new plants being established in America or Germany. Similarly, the impact of the Second World War was paradoxically very positive for the Japanese and German economies. Institutional effects aside, the destruction of so much German and Japanese capital effectively forced them to start afresh using the best available technology and practice, and thus giving them an advantage over the UK and the USA (Olson 1982, 1983). In other words, periods of creative destruction are necessary if a market-orientated economy is to flourish, and a large initial capital stock can stand in the way of that sort of process. Only if the inherited capital stock 'fits' market conditions does a physical capital inheritance provide advantages. In other words, it is not evident that an inheritance of mining or forestry infrastructure confers many long-run advantages; as Kaldor argued on many occasions, it is manufacturing that it crucial because of the scope there for static and dynamic economies of scale. Western China had a substantial inheritance of industrial capital at the end of the Maoist era, but this did not raise its growth potential very much because much of the industry was either defence-orientated or extractive. Defence industries were inefficient, and located with military rather than economic considerations in mind. Factories, for example, were small, dispersed and often located underground. And the growth of the timber industry was hampered by the fact that much of the best quality timber had already been cut by the end of the 1970s.

These sorts of ideas are controversial. It is easy to argue that resource allocation in any given country is sub-optimal and to suggest a counterfactual reallocation of resources which would have led to faster growth. However, this begs the question of why contemporaries did not make such reallocations if the gains are so obvious in hindsight. This is the essence of the famous question put by McCloskey (1970) to his fellow economic historians: if you are so smart, why aren't you rich? Nevertheless, McCloskey's argument is at root based upon the notion that market forces always work, and by implication that economies are rarely far removed from equilibrium (and therefore operating efficiently). Given the obstacles to factor mobility which are the norm in all economies – the notion, for example, that modern America is a society characterized by spatial and inter-generational mobility is no more than a myth, and physical capital is far less mobile than labour – it is hard to accept McCloskey's view that Britain was not hampered by its early start.[28] In China's case, of course, pre-1978 industrialization was not dictated by market forces and therefore resource allocation was inevitably suboptimal. A different configuration of industrial capital would have raised China's growth potential. In short, it is probably fair to assume that an extensive physical capital legacy is as likely to be a constraint as a springboard.

An inherited stock of human capital is by contrast more likely to be an advantage than a disadvantage. This is because general education confers a *range* of competencies – analytical, critical and organizational skills – which are not specific to any type of manufacturing process. It is the flexibility of a general education which is its great advantage. By contrast, a more vocational education provides the same disadvantages as physical capital: the skills are only of value if they fit in with market demand. It therefore follows that the type of inherited human capital is as important as its size. The other dimension of human capital which appears to be important is experience. Wages in almost all countries are strongly correlated with experience, because manufacturing processes are typically characterized by learning-by-doing. There is also a good deal of evidence that the making of an industrial workplace is a painful and protracted process. This is because of the brutal and alienating nature of the transition from farm to factory, and it is a challenge which confronts all developing countries. Peasant workers are not usually unproductive even early on in a factory setting, but much time must elapse before they are able to match the productivity of the established workforce. Thus the Lewis (1954) model, the workforce of much development economics, is very simplistic in the way that it assumes that surplus labour can be readily transferred from agriculture to industry without adverse effects on industrial productivity. It follows that a country which inherits a significant industrial workforce will have a great advantage over a country which does not.

For all that, the evidence on the causal link running from education to economic growth needs to be interpreted carefully, and there is certainly evidence of diminishing returns to years of education. In a developed country like Britain, for example, the evidence suggests that the average private rate of return to a degree in arts or humanities had fallen to zero by 2002; workers would have been better off leaving school at 18 (Machin and Vignoles 2005: 182). And when we take into account state subsidies for tertiary education, the social return to education is negative. Even in developing countries, the pay-off to education in terms of increased output appears to have been comparatively small (Easterly 2001; Barro 1997; Pritchett 2001). Various reasons have been put forward. One is that education involves opportunity costs in the sense that the teenage years are more directly productive if spent in learning-by-doing in industry. An alternative possibility is that it is not education *per se* that is 'bad' but rather that the same institutional structures which support educational expansion (i.e. substantial state subsidies for education) make for distorted incentives – such that more education simply leads to more effective and more time-consuming rent-seeking behaviour.

None of this is to argue that the expansion of education is undesirable: few would challenge the Bowman and Anderson (1963) notion that a literacy rate of at least 30 per cent is a necessary condition for modern economic growth. More generally, educational attainment is included in the HDI because it is seen as good in itself, irrespective of whether it generates a pay-off in terms of higher levels of GDP. Nevertheless the evidence here is such that the case for investment in some types of education has to be made on intrinsic rather than instrumental grounds.

In summary, it appears that country size; the level of GDP per head; the initial level of inequality (partly manifested in the form of ethno-linguistic fragmentation); the extent of basic education and skills; and the extent of isolation all exert a powerful effect upon growth. The impact of other initial conditions and environmental variables seems, however, to be less important. From this perspective, we can probably conclude that China was relatively disadvantaged in 1949: that is, its developmental potential was quite limited. Per capita income was low and China is a big country, but these advantages were more than offset by inequality, its international isolation and its underdeveloped human capital. By contrast, China in 1978 was in a much better position. Per capita GDP was still low by world standards, and by then its human capital and infrastructure was much more developed. Moreover, income inequality was relatively low and China was no longer isolated. Accordingly, its developmental potential was much higher than it had been thirty years earlier, and we need to bear this in mind when assessing the country's record after 1978.

The time period

A final complication in assessing the development record of a country concerns the relevant time horizon over which economic performance should be assessed. Is it short-term performance that matters, or should we also take into account the extent to which a regime is successful in expanding economic potential?

Here it is tempting to say that only the long-run trend in a variable matters. We are therefore attempting to answer the question of whether there has been a sustained increase in the level of development. From this sort of perspective, a short-run rise in the growth rate or in human development would be regarded sceptically. For example, the impressive growth rates achieved under Stalin in the USSR need to be set against the marked slowdown that occurred during the 1960s and 1970s. We might therefore conclude that the development of the Stalinist era was a failure because it did not establish the foundations for a sustained process of catch-up in the USSR. Conversely, it might be argued that Japanese colonial rule in Taiwan, Korea and Manchuria was a long-run success because it made possible rapid postwar growth – even though the short-run effect on levels of food consumption was not very positive because of the diversion of food products to Japan itself. This whole question of legacies is an important one when it comes to assessing Maoist China, as we will see.

However, we need to judge a country's developmental record as much by its success in avoiding sharp short-run fluctuations as by its long-run achievements. An intense famine, or a financial crisis which causes big increases in unemployment and poverty, cannot simply be ignored just because a country achieves great long-run success. For example, one of the most powerful criticisms of the Stalinist model in the Soviet Union is that, in trying to accelerate the growth rate by increasing the investment share during 1928–32, the regime caused one of the largest famines in history. One can argue that the rise in the investment share was necessary to ensure Soviet survival in the Second World War, but it is hard to justify the famine; in fact, the famine made Soviet victory more difficult because the rise in mortality in Ukraine (and the perception that it was part of a deliberate war on the *kulaks*) further alienated large sections of Ukrainian society. Similarly, the postwar developmental records of South Korea, Thailand and Indonesia have been tarnished by the sharp increases in poverty and unemployment which occurred in the aftermath of the Asian financial crisis of 1997. Thus the ability to avoid crises is as important a yardstick by which to judge regime performance as long-run trends in opulence and human development indicators. Development requires growth, but it also requires the avoidance of fluctuation. It has to be about the achievement of short-run, as well as long-run goals.

Conclusion

There is no easy answer to the question of how to measure development. It is clear that the metric of GDP comparison typically used by the World Bank and the IMF is far too limiting. However, it is not so obvious what should be put in its place. Tempting though it is to argue that 'everything matters', that does not really get us very far when development indicators move in different directions for any particular country.

My own view is that life expectancy is the best measure of development, at least until OECD-type levels of life expectancy have been attained (when GDP per head is likely to offer a better assessment of development in the short and medium term). Opulence indicators are far too narrow a proxy for well-being (as Sen has argued), and an indicator like education is more of a means to an end than an end in itself. Not that one can ignore distributional issues, and I would not suggest that we do. However, reliance on Gini coefficients measuring the distribution of income will tell us very little about a country's developmental record. We need a much more disaggregated analysis than that allows, and we need to accept that assessing the distributional record of a country is not amenable to easy generalization. To my mind, the regional and the urban–rural dimension of inequality has been overemphasized in recent years, and that of class-based inequality downplayed. This is mainly because acceptance of the latter as the major type of inequality has unpalatable policy implications for neoclassical economists and neoliberal thinkers. It is much easier to think of inequality as mainly geographical in origin and therefore unavoidable, but that is far too Panglossian a view. And to argue that the major fissure is the urban–rural divide is in effect to argue that what is needed is redistribution from workers to peasants – thus sidestepping the entire issue of class conflict and ensuring endemic social unrest.

As for the issue of comparison, it makes far more sense to judge the actual record of a country in terms of life expectancy against its potential rather than by making historical or international comparisons. I do not for a moment believe that positing a plausible counterfactual is either easy or uncontentious. However, that approach is the least bad of the options available to us – and the only way to evaluate the record of countries which face a binding external constraint of some form, such as Cuba or Maoist China.

When it comes to the question of short-run achievements versus long-run capacity building, it is indisputable that there are great dangers in ignoring the short run. Keynes's view on this is justly famous: to advocate increased saving at a time of endemic unemployment was, he argued, both economically illiterate (as his celebrated *General Theory* made clear) and a further manifestation of the threadbare Victorian morality that the Bloomsbury set was so keen to expose and to ridicule.[29] Of course the lifestyles of Keynes, Lydia Lopokova, Duncan Grant, Virginia Woolf and Lytton Strachey were far removed from those which are the norm in developing countries. Nevertheless, it is not hard to see that a doctrine which advocates the suppression of consumption in favour of savings and investment may be especially misguided. The very nature of underdevelopment – low life expectancy and low levels of consumption – calls out for a rapid short-term response. To argue that a developing country should sacrifice consumption in favour of investment – the classic Stalinist approach – is a notion which at the very least demands careful scrutiny.

Yet the extent of the trade-off here can easily be exaggerated. To be sure, there is a trade-off between short-run consumption and savings; it cannot be otherwise. However, as the evidence of the second half of the twentieth century so amply demonstrates, it is quite possible to bring about sharp reductions in mortality by simple, low-cost measures designed to improve water quality and sanitation, by mass vaccination programmes and by income redistribution. In this way, human development can be enhanced and at the same time savings can be used to finance increases in investment – and hence the expansion of economic potential.

Not that any of this is easy to accomplish. A number of countries have performed well in terms of enhancing human development in the short and medium run; Sri Lanka, Taiwan, Costa Rica and Cuba all come to mind. Indeed Costa Rica's record is one of the best in the world. Its GDP grew at around 5 per cent per annum during the 1990s and by 2005 male life expectancy at birth had reached seventy-seven years (World Bank 2007d). Its environmental record is a good one; so too its record on female participation in public life. To be sure, Costa Rica has been out-performed in terms of GDP growth by Taiwan in the postwar era; Costa Rica's per capita income was double that of Taiwan in the mid-1950s, whereas per capita GDP was three times greater in Taiwan by 2003 (Maddison 2006b). However, Taiwan's critical role in the containment of China gave it a place of privilege in the formation of US foreign policy, and that undoubtedly has helped its development (the contrasting fortunes of Cuba make for a striking comparison). Accordingly, we should not be too ready to conclude that Taiwan (rather than Costa Rica) offers a model for other countries to follow.

The real question that needs to be asked about the record of all these countries (and the Indian state of Kerala for that matter) is whether short-run gains in human development have bought at the expense of the expansion of long-run economic capacity and potential. A case can certainly be made along these lines for Sri Lanka and Kerala, and doubts hang over the sustainability of the Taiwanese economic miracle. Its relations with China remain a source of great uncertainty, and it remains to be seen whether the sexism and disregard for the environment that characterize Taiwan's development strategy provide the basis for sustainable development. Self-evidently, however, the question of sustainability is the right one to pose. Modernization is necessarily a long-run project, and a development strategy which privileges the short run at the expense of long-run capacity building will not succeed.

These, then, are the criteria by which China's record needs to be judged: To what extent has it managed to increase life expectancy? Has China's development record lived up to or fallen short of its potential? Did the Maoist development model lay the foundations for the rapid growth of the 1980s and beyond?

Notes

1 See Little (1982), Todaro and Smith (2006) or Ray (1998: ch. 2) for more general discussions of development.
2 In addition, donors must necessarily make some sort of judgement about a country's development strategy in the widest sense. One might argue that countries have an inalienable right to decide their own course of development, and that donors have no right to question it. That of course is very much the position of the Chinese government whenever the subjects of Tibet and human rights abuse are raised. However, as aid budgets are limited, some sort of judgement has to be made by donors, and many would argue that donors have the right to impose conditions on aid that is provided. One might, for example, insist that no aid will be provided unless some forms of gender, ethnic or religious discrimination are done away with. Of course implicit in this sort of approach is the proposition that some types of human rights are universal – and that 'cultural differences' cannot be used a pretext for the denial of such rights if a country wishes to receive aid. These are important questions, and my own view is that the cultural relativism that the Chinese government seeks to use as a defence of its actions is abhorrent. In essence, however, these are questions concerning the distribution of income, power and status within a country and are therefore discussed under that section below.

Measuring development 41

3 A more direct way to measure living standards would be assess nutrition using data on food consumption or anthropometric data (average population height and weight). Both approaches have their merits. Food consumption data provide a good guide to short-run living standards; unlike GDP, this measure excludes investment. Anthropometric measures tell us little about the short run, but there is some evidence that they provide rather more reliable data (because height and weight are easy to calculate) than other opulence measures. For that reason they have been widely used to analyze trends in living standards during the industrialization process in many countries (Floud *et al.* 1990; Mosk 1996; Steckel and Floud 1997). The main limitation of anthropometric data is that of sample bias; most of the datasets used are unrepresentative – for example, data on convicts transported to Australia or army recruits. For all its limitations, GDP per head is the most general measure of well-being from an opulence perspective.

4 It is sometimes said that GDP per head is problematic because it ignores distributional questions. In fact, of course, it implicitly assumes that a $1 increase in income for a poor person has exactly the same effect on welfare as a $1 increase in income for a rich person because both have the same effect on GDP. See Fields (1980) for a discussion of some of the general issues, and Daly and Cobb (1994) for an attempt to develop an index of sustainable economic welfare (ISEW) which takes inequality into account.

5 For a discussion of measures of economic welfare – such as that developed by Nordhaus and Tobin in the early 1970s – which attempt to account for leisure, disamenities and other non-marketed output, see Daly and Cobb (1994: ch. 3).

6 A useful discussion of China's material product system and how the methodology compares with the UN System of National Accounts (SNA) can be found in Hsueh and Li (1999).

7 The problem with using material product is that some sort of judgement has to be made about which types of goods and services are bad. Prostitution may be a social evil but it generates income for the men and women involved; they would arguably be even worse off without it. Using material product also makes international comparisons next to impossible because countries will take a different view of what constitutes material product.

8 One of the areas in which prices are especially low in poor countries is services (which are highly labour intensive). However, many service outputs are non-traded goods: haircuts are obviously not the same as manufactured goods. Furthermore, many agricultural products are not really tradable, because of limited market integration in many poor countries, high transport costs and perishability. Globalization and falling transport costs (for example, the cost of air freight) will reduce but not solve these problems.

9 The main problem in calculating purchasing power parity GDP for comparative purposes is that a vast amount of quality-adjusted price data is needed. For many countries, in fact, 'benchmark' studies had not even been carried out before the mid-1990s, and therefore corrections could only be made by using average deviations for entire groups of countries (Heston and Summers 1996). A useful discussion of some of the problems involved is offered in Lancieri (1990).

10 Whether these countries really were communist is moot. To be sure, they were/are governed by communist parties but their economic systems were quite different from the model envisaged by Marx, especially in terms of income distribution. That was usually according to work done rather than need, except during brief periods (in Cultural Revolution China, for example, work-point allocation often owed little to work done. Similarly, there was a system of free food supply in the communes during the Great Leap Forward in 1958–9.). It is probably more sensible to call these countries socialist, and that is the terminology I use here.

11 For a discussion of the role played by income, nutrition, education and psycho-social factors in determining life expectancy, see Cutler *et al.* (2006). The general conclusion is

that public health is a key factor. Health 'gradients' in rich countries do exist. However, these gradients are not closely tied to income. In many poor countries the level of disease and public health trumps per capita income; we can think of the slight difference in life expectancy between aristocrats and the labouring poor in the premodern era in Europe, and the way in which life expectancy increased in Cuba, Sri Lanka and Maoist China against a background of very modest per capita income rises. Thus the view expressed by Pritchett and Summers (1996) – that 'wealthier is healthier' – is not really supported by the data. Even in so far as the evidence does lend it support, the direction of causality is as much from health to income as the reverse.

12 The HDI was by no means the first attempt at the construction of an index. For a discussion of its antecedents, including Morris's famous PQLI (physical quality of life index) – which was an average of infant mortality, life expectancy and literacy – see Streeten (1981: 85–90) and Daly and Cobb (1994). For the literature on the merits and limitations of the HDI, see UNDP (1990), Kelley (1991), Anand and Ravallion (1993), Streeten (1994), Srinivasan (1994) and Noorbakhsh (1998).

13 Paradoxically, the case made for expanding GDP per head in the 1950s was that it too expanded freedom. According to W. A. Lewis: 'The case for economic growth is that it gives man greater control over his environment, and thereby increases his freedom' (Lewis 1955, cited in Little 1982: 8).

14 Bhutan has even set itself the objective of maximizing gross national happiness instead of GDP. However, gross national happiness there has been defined in vague terms to encompass human development, self-reliance and cultural preservation. It is therefore more an aspiration than a concrete goal of policy.

15 A useful discussion of the literature and the evidence (from a neoliberal perspective) is provided by Fields (2001). I focus here on income inequalities. However, inequalities in social status exert at least as great an influence on measures of happiness and on health indicators as inequalities in income; for a useful discussion, see Offer (2006: ch. 12). For example, mortality rates are higher amongst black American males than white American males even when income differentials are controlled for.

16 This 'retreat from class' in favour of an emphasis on rural bias is very controversial (Byres 1979). Marxists have objected to Lipton's misuse of the word 'class' to describe the rural and urban population, and no wonder. The very notion of a unified urban elite able to extract surplus is decidedly problematic; that sort of approach effectively rules out any possibility of a class divide within urban (and rural) communities. Moreover, measurement of all types of spatial inequality is highly sensitive to the choice of jurisdictional boundaries. It is easy, for example, to place small but dynamic and rich metropolitan centres in a separate category; this generates a high degree of spatial inequality. But if the metropolitan centres are amalgamated for statistical purposes with their rural hinterland, much of the supposed spatial inequality disappears. Similarly, one can easily create spatial inequality by creating separate jurisdictions out of mineral- and timber-rich areas which have small populations. In consequence, the notion of urban bias is a useful analytical device, but it is built upon foundations of shifting sand.

17 It should be noted here that another one of the limitations of the Gini coefficient is that it is not easily disaggregated, and that makes it difficult to determine which types of inequality are most important in any given society. More precisely, certain types of disaggregation are possible, but additive decomposition is not. For example, the overall Gini coefficient is not some average of the Gini coefficients of the urban and rural sectors, except in the very special case where subgroups are non-overlapping, i.e. the highest rural income is less than the lowest urban income. Indeed, it is quite possible for the Gini coefficient to fall even though inequality within each subgroup of the population increases. The Theil coefficient is much more amenable to decomposition, and is for that reason preferred by many economists. However, comparative international

17 ...Theil coefficients do not exist in the way that Gini coefficients do. For a discussion of some of these issues, see Cowell (1995).
18 For some of the literature, see Deininger and Squire (1998), Tanzi and Chu (1998) and Persson and Tabellini (1994).
19 Arguments against this are either special pleading or based upon the notion that high incomes make tax avoidance a simple matter and therefore penal rates of taxation are unlikely to raise total tax revenue.
20 For a withering attack on the foundation of inequality, the account by Tawney (1931) retains its moral force even today.
21 The notion of fairness is itself of course very controversial. Most statistical measures of income inequality like the Gini coefficient assume that a 'fair' distribution is one in which each person receives the same amount. However, this ignores questions of justice: should distribution be according to need or according to work done?
22 Maddison's (2006b) estimates have African per capita GDP growing at only 0.7 per cent per annum between 1990 and 2003, compared with 1.4 per cent per year between 1950 and 1990, and over 2 per cent during the Golden Age of 1950–73.
23 A full discussion is impossible here. Some of the key initial conditions thought to influence GDP growth are summarized in standard texts on growth theory such as Barro and Sala-i-Martin (1995), Barro (1997), Easterly (2001) and Bosworth and Collins (2003).
24 Industrialization here is the key word. A growth strategy based around primary commodity exports is unlikely to succeed because of price volatility, and possible terms of trade deterioration or so called immiserizing growth (increased commodity supply reduces global commodity prices). In its most extreme form, it is argued that the prices of primary commodities show a secular decline (the Prebisch–Singer hypothesis). This assessment is over-stated; there is not very much evidence to support Prebisch–Singer. Nevertheless, there is no doubt that the price of manufactured goods is much less responsive to changes in supply. For this reason, those who see agricultural exports and fair trade as the solution to the problems of many sub-Saharan African countries are almost certainly wrong.
25 A claim which can be sustained in terms of GDP growth but not in terms of mortality; as we saw above, life expectancy fell by sixteen years between 1970 and 2000.
26 An excellent and accessible summary of the issues involved is offered by McCloskey (1987: ch. 4).
27 This type of strategy has been implemented in a number of countries; the classic examples are the USSR in the 1930s and India during its First Five Year Plan. In India's case it was more out of choice than necessity, and it is very debatable whether it made sense as a development strategy, given that imports were feasible. The models developed by Feldman and Mahalanobis offer a theoretical rationale, but it will only make sense if a country's population has a very long-term time horizon. Per capita output will be higher in the long run, but it is not clear that a poor country can disregard the short run in the cavalier fashion implied by these models. For an introduction to the theory, see Ellman (1979).
28 That there is more inter-generational mobility in Scandinavia than in the US shows, in fact, that it is education and state led income redistribution which raises mobility, not market forces (Glyn 2006).
29 His most famous quotation on the subject comes from his under-read *Tract on Monetary Reform*: 'In the long run we are all dead. Economists set themselves too easy, too useless a task if in tempestuous seasons they can only tell us that when the storm is long past the ocean is flat again' (Keynes 1924).

2 The Chinese economy on the eve of revolution

One of the most intensely contested debates in Chinese studies is the question of continuity versus change across the 1949 divide. The current fashion is to emphasize continuity over change, to take issue with the idea of a revolutionary climacteric. Take the following example:

> [T]hese glorious artifacts of Chinese civilization are gone, if not torn down by mindless modernizers then destroyed by Maoist radicals in their zeal to discard the old, combat religious superstition, and free the socialist present from its feudal past. (Skinner 1999: 63)

Skinner is writing here on the specific subject of the impact of urban reconstruction, and its impact on traditional Chinese buildings. However, his view is indicative of a mindset that longs for a return to a lost golden age.[1] This issue – how should we see the Chinese past? – is important because any assessment of the impact of Maoism depends very much on how we view the socio-economic system that it displaced. If the late Imperial and Republican economy was on the brink of take-off, it follows almost as a matter of course that the Maoist path to modernity was at best unnecessary and at worst a fatal detour – and that we should see the Dengist regime as resuming in 1978 where Chiang Kaishek left off in 1937.

Chinese economic development, 1839–1949

The trajectory of the Chinese economy in the prewar period remains controversial.[2] For the period before 1912, the estimates we have are at best informed conjectures. To be sure, the work of Maddison (2001: 265) suggests a decline of 0.25 per cent per year in per capita GDP between 1820 and 1870 (reflecting in the main the devastating impact of the Taiping rebellion), and a rise of 0.1 per cent annually between 1887 and 1913. Estimates made by Wang Yuru (2004: 104) show a decline of 3 per cent per annum between 1850 and 1887, and a rise of 0.3 per cent between 1870 and 1914. But as we have no reliable data on indicators as basic as agricultural productivity or population, all this is little more than speculation.

Things are only a little better for the Republican era (1912–49). The pioneering work of K. C. Yeh (1979: 104) put per capita growth at barely 0.3 per cent per year between 1914 and 1936. Wang (2004: 104) estimates an annual increase of 1 per cent between 1914 and 1936, and a decline of 3 per cent per year between 1936 and 1949. Maddison's (2003: 180 and 182) more recent estimates show per capita China GDP rising at 0.2 per cent per year between 1913 and 1937, but *contracting* at a rate of 0.6 per year between 1913 and 1950 as a result of the devastating impact of the Second Sino-Japanese War and the subsequent civil war in eastern and central China between 1937 and 1949.[3] The most optimistic figures are those of Rawski (1989: 330), who, by taking a more positive view of agricultural performance, suggests that GDP per head grew by around 2 per cent per year between 1914 and 1936.[4]

Yet even for the Republican period, these estimates are still highly conjectural. Indeed, the first year for which we have remotely plausible estimates is 1933. That year saw China's first proper industrial census, and by then comprehensive crop data were being collected by the National Agricultural Research Bureau. Nevertheless, any analysis of economic trends in the 1930s is hampered by the absence of any modern population census; the first was not carried out until 1953. Much of the debate on pre-1949 Chinese demography focuses in fact on whether society is best characterized as one of a high birth rate and a high death rate (Barclay *et al.* 1976) or of low birth rates and low death rates (Lee and Wang 1999). However, this has not taken us very far towards establishing the total size of the population. Part of the problem is that it is impossible to arrive at reliable estimates of China's pre-1949 population because back-projection from the 1953 census beyond 1949 is little more than guesswork given the unknown impact of war with Japan (1937–45) and civil war (1945–9) on both birth and death rates. Maddison (2001: 241) assumes a growth rate of 0.6 per cent per year between 1870 and 1950, based on the estimates of Schran (1978) and this is almost certainly of the right sort of order of magnitude. Liu and Yeh (1965) put the rate at close to 1 per cent, but the difference between these two is slight, and in any case, as Schran argues, the lower estimate is more plausible because it is entirely likely that population growth after 1933 was negligible in the face of demographic disaster.

Nevertheless, three conclusions about the performance of the prewar Chinese economy seem well founded. First, there is little to suggest that imperialism fatally undermined Chinese development. Second, there is abundant evidence to support the contention that some economic modernization was occurring during the Republican era but that it was limited in scale because of pervasive institutional weakness. Third, and crucially, the performance of the agricultural sector was extremely poor; this was the main constraint on economic development. The next sections discuss these issues in more detail.

Imperialism, institutional structures and the development of modern industry

Any notion that Western imperialism led to the wholesale destruction of Chinese industry is not supported by the evidence. Given that the share of imports in GDP was only around 5 per cent and changed little over time, it is hard to make a compelling argument for either deindustrialization or export-led growth. Moreover, the notion that imports produced powerful spillovers (in this case so-called backwash effects) is weak. The resilience of the handicraft sector is clear from the data on the composition of GDP. In 1933, the value of handicraft production was around 2 billion *yuan* (1933 prices), more than three times larger than that of the factory sector (Liu and Yeh 1965: 66). In short, the deindustrialization hypothesis simply does not hold up in China's case.

In fact, the impact of imports may well have been positive in some respects. To see this, consider cotton. For many years it was widely believed that China's experience was similar to that of India's Gangetic Bihar, where the native textile industry was allegedly wiped out by British imports. However, the work of Feuerwerker (1970) and the new estimates of Xu Xinwu (1988) paint a very different picture for China. To be sure, the traditional cotton *spinning* industry was largely destroyed in the late nineteenth and early twentieth century, in no small measure because of the introduction of the machine-spun yarn produced in Britain and in Japan. By 1894, the share of imported yarn was about 23 per cent of the total (Xu 1988: 35) and in the first decade of the twentieth century, yarn imports accounted for 41 per cent of total supply (Rawski 1989: 93). However, much of the destruction in the native cotton spinning sector was wrought by machine-spun yarn produced in mills located in China, mainly in Shanghai and Wuxi, rather than by imports. The growth of modern cotton spinning in China in turn owed much to political developments. The Treaty of Shimonoseiki (1895) legalized foreign-owned manufacturing enterprises, and a number of firms were established in China – especially by Britain and Japan – over the next twenty years (Hou 1965: 86). However, the real growth of domestic machine-spun yarn began during the First World War – the golden age of the Chinese bourgeoisie, as Bergère (1989a) calls it – when imports dwindled. Between 1914 and 1922, the total number of spindles rose from fewer than 900,000 to 3 million (Eastman 1988: 177). By 1923/4, imports accounted for only 5 per cent of the domestic market, and the process continued thereafter, such that yarn imports were almost negligible by 1936 (Rawski 1989: 93; Xu 1988: 35 and 37).

Of course, this evidence does suggest that it was foreign contact that precipitated deindustrialization, albeit indirectly. But such a conclusion reckons without the positive impact of the modernization of cotton spinning on China's traditional cotton *weaving* industry. For although native cotton spinning was destroyed, cotton-weaving flourished, and it flourished precisely because the modernization of the cotton spinning sector ensured an abundant supply of cheap, high quality cotton yarn (Xu 1988). As a result, native hand-weaving, confined in the early nineteenth century to cotton-growing provinces, actually expanded into regions where previously there had been no tradition of weaving. The net effect of all this was that the gains in employment in native cotton weaving and in modern cotton spinning offset the loss of jobs in native cotton spinning.

Integral to the process of industrialization in the cotton sector was the Chinese, rather than the foreign entrepreneur. The first modern factory in China was the

Shanghai cotton cloth mill, which began operation in 1890, and of the twenty-nine mills established between 1890 and 1911, only five were foreign-owned. There were 500,000 Chinese-owned spindles in 1911 compared with 230,000 foreign-owned (Feuerwerker 1970: 346).

The sector grew explosively in the immediate aftermath of the First World War. Japanese-owned mills were a key part of this, and they increasingly displaced European and American producers (Figure 2.1). By 1936, there were 2.7 million foreign-owned spindles in China (mainly Japanese-owned). Nevertheless, the growth of the capacity of the foreign sector was matched by that of Chinese-owned firms, so that total indigenous capacity (2.9 million) exceeded that of the foreign sector. And there are many examples of dynamic Chinese entrepreneurs; one such is Zhang Jian, who was responsible for the creation of a modern cotton industry in Nantong, close to Shanghai (Köll 2003). Still more famous was the Rong family (notably Rong Zongjin and Rong Desheng), which owned and controlled an empire of flour and cotton enterprises by the 1930s.

The data on the manufacturing sector as a whole tell the same story about the sources of entrepreneurship. To be sure, foreign firms were important. However, domestic firms made up 75 per cent of the gross value added of the modern manufacturing sector by 1933 (Liu and Yeh 1965: 426–8; Rawski 1989: 74). Chinese enterprises supplied 65 per cent of the output value of cotton cloth and yarn, almost all modern silk production, all wheat flour and well over 90 per cent of machine-produced garments. Xue Shouxuan, for example, played a key role in restructuring the silk industry in Wuxi in the 1930s (Bell 1999). Cigarette manufacture, where the domestic share was about 52 per cent, was the only major sector where the foreign share came close to parity.[5] All this evidence suggests that Chinese entrepreneurs were more than capable of taking advantage of the opportunities that presented themselves in and around the Treaty Port economy.

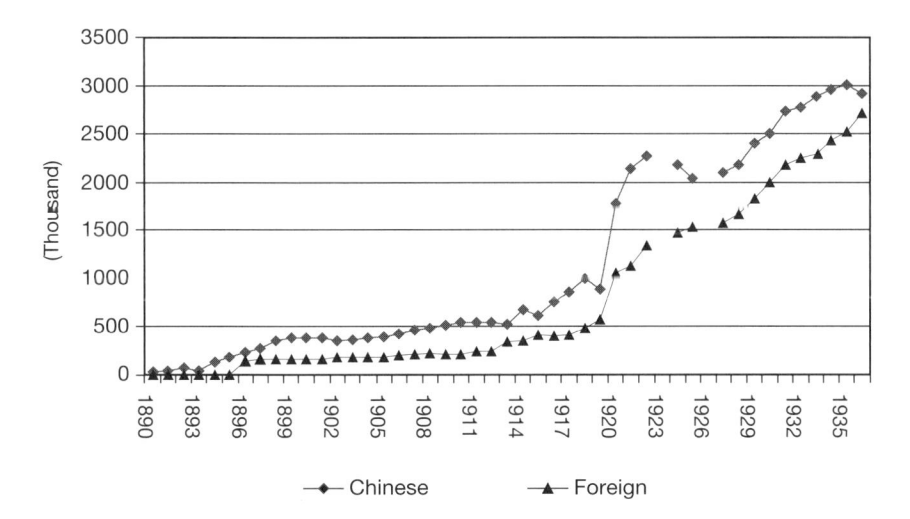

Figure 2.1 Modern cotton spindles in China, 1890–1936 (Source: Chao (1977: 301–2).)

At no time was this more evident than during and immediately after the First World War, when Chinese industrial production soared in the absence of competition from imports (Bergère 1989b). In the Treaty Port economy at least, foreign impact was met by a positive Chinese response.

Nevertheless, the overall impact of technology transfers on the Chinese economy is difficult to assess. Manufacturing may have gained, but the impact elsewhere is less certain. Railways are a case in point. China's first line was constructed in 1876, fifty-one years after the beginning of the railway age in Britain. By 1895, 150 million ton-kms of freight were moved by rail, and this figure climbed to 12,800 million by 1933. However, the cost of transporting goods by rail was not very much lower than shipping costs, whether by steamboat or junk, on many routes (Huenemann 1984: 222–4). Thus the main advantage of (say) the Shanghai–Nanjing railway was in terms of speed rather than cost. This was not a trivial gain; the very fact that freight volume carried on that line grew rapidly testifies to the significance of speed. Nevertheless, the net gain to the economy was comparatively small. China's experience with railway construction in fact seems similar to that elsewhere; studies of the impact of the railway in many countries have come up with comparatively low figures for the social savings generated (Fogel 1964; Hawke 1970). The impact of the railway may well have been qualitative only in north China. The riverine system in the north was much more limited than in the south, and railway construction arguably played an important role in famine relief in that region. According to Li (2007: 299): 'The railways were seen as the main factor in limiting the loss of life [during the famine of 1920–1]. For North China as a whole, the estimated mortality was half a million victims, a terrible human toll, but far less than the estimated 9–11 million victims of the 1876–79 famine.' The case of railways illustrates the more general point: outside the Treaty Port economy, the effects of technology transfer were limited. The reason for this was in part the underdeveloped nature of internal trade and commerce, which restricted the ability of the rural sector to gain access to advanced technology. For example, the survival of cotton weaving owed much to high transport costs in the Chinese interior (as well as the fact that native cloth was more durable than imported cloth).

However, we need to recognize that China's developmental 'problem' went far beyond restricted access to modern technology, and for this very reason the impact of foreign technology was only ever going to be marginal. To be sure, the notion that China's failure to develop before 1949 was primarily technological has been put forward.[6] According to Elvin (1973):

> It is quite unwarranted to assume … that China was heading towards an industrial revolution. There was less technological progress during this time than at almost any other previous moment in two thousand years of Chinese history [p. 284] … It was the historic contribution of the West to ease and then break the high-level equilibrium trap in China [p. 315].

In essence Elvin's argument is that China's surplus had been eroded over the centuries by a combination of limited innovation and population pressure, and therefore investment was low. A technological solution was needed to create an investible surplus and break out of the poverty trap. There is some *prima facie* evidence to support such a view: there was, after all, only limited innovation outside the Treaty Port economy.

Yet this type of technological hypothesis does not get to the heart of the matter. *Pace* Elvin, the evidence suggest that the surplus may well have amounted to no less than 30 per cent of GDP in the early 1930s (Riskin 1975). The crux of China's problem was surely that it was incapable either of generating invention or diffusing any technology that was available. Foreign technology might solve the first problem, but it would not address the second. Contact with the West made accessible a whole range of inventions, but China could not close the ideas gap except in a handful of sectors because the incentives to adopt and to adapt the new technologies were lacking. The surplus existed; it was the adequacy of the Chinese response to the opportunities presented that was lacking. Why?

One answer is to blame imperialism itself. It has been argued that China was generating a wave of indigenous innovation prior to Western contact in 1839 and that imperialism undermined the late Qing state. This created a range of socio-economic obstacles which prevented both innovation and diffusion of technology during the 1930s.[7] There are two possible strands to this sort of argument. One is that economic modernization requires a state-led programme of industrialization, and that China was unable to follow in the footsteps of Japan during the late nineteenth century because the Western powers fatally undermined the late Qing state. The second strand suggests that the key role for the state in the modernization process is to provide a secure system of property rights such that private sector investment can flourish. Again, the impact of imperialism was to create political and social instability, and thus to undermine the mainsprings of domestic entrepreneurship. The Boxer indemnity, for example, deprived the Qing state of a key source of tax revenue.

However, alternative explanations for China's lack of technological capability abound. Neoclassicals blame the failure on ill-defined and insecure property rights, which discouraged investment and risk-taking. For Marxists, the lack of a capitalist class in the countryside was the main problem. For neo-Weberians, the root cause of China's difficulties was that the state was too weak to mobilize the resources necessary to invest in irrigation, transport infrastructure and new industries. The very failure of the agricultural sector to generate sustained growth in labour productivity even in the 1930s hints at the underlying socio-economic failure in the countryside, namely the absence of a genuine capitalist class. The presence of foreign capitalists in the Treaty Ports gave would-be domestic entrepreneurs a role model, but there was no comparable process at work in the Chinese countryside.

Explaining Chinese underdevelopment is a big task indeed. It cannot be undertaken properly without at the very least a detailed discussion of Qing economic history, and that is well beyond the scope of this book. To my mind, however, most of the explanations of Chinese stasis are not very compelling.

For one thing, I think we do better to regard early nineteenth-century China as technologically stagnant rather than on the verge of take-off. Despite the efforts of Chinese scholars to identify the 'sprouts of capitalism', and those of revisionist Western scholars to argue that China's level of development was on a par with that of the West in 1839 (Pomeranz 2000), there is little to suggest that late Qing China was on the verge of take-off prior to Western intervention.

Despite the work of Pomeranz and others, the evidence still points to the conclusion that Western Europe, and England in particular, was well ahead of China before the First Opium War (1839–42).[8] Maddison's estimates of per capita GDP put the UK slightly ahead of China in 1500 at $714 compared with $600. By 1820, however, Chinese GDP per head was unchanged, whereas Britain's had leapt to $1,706 (Maddison 2006b). Furthermore, labour productivity in agriculture in the Yangzi delta almost halved between 1500 and 1800, whereas it rose by 50 per cent in England between 1500 and 1759 (Brenner and Isset 2002: 625). These estimates are of course subject to large margins of error, but it is hard to deny the conclusion that something was amiss in late Qing China on the eve of the First Opium War (Landes 2006). Marx's assessment in a piece published in the *New York Herald Tribune* of 20 September 1858 is particularly apt:

> a giant empire, containing almost one-third of the human race, vegetating in the teeth of time, insulated by the forced exclusion of general intercourse and thus contriving to dupe itself with delusions of Celestial perfection.

I think there is something to be said for the view that imperialism accelerated the demise of the Qing state. Military defeat undermined its credibility and deprived it of tax revenue. Nevertheless, the seeds of destruction were planted well before the late nineteenth century, when the external explanation of Chinese failure is at its most potent.

If this analysis suggests that we cannot explain China's failures in terms of external forces, what of internal factors? There certainly is some force to Elvin's quasi-Malthusian hypothesis. Indeed the evidence increasingly suggests an environmental crisis in China by the middle of the nineteenth century, as population pressure led to deforestation, soil degradation and species destruction (Marks 1998). However, as I have argued, the real question is why was there no technological response to this crisis, which takes us back to our original question. And any notion that underdevelopment was caused by an impressive (or Asiatic) Qing state falters in the face of the evidence suggesting that the state's impact on the economy and society was far too limited to explain the absence of per capita growth in the long run. Its sins were more those omission than commission. The other possibility is to argue that the divergence of China and Europe was driven by accident. The Yangzi delta, it is said, was unable to develop because of the absence of coal deposits, whereas Europe escaped the 'proto-industrial cul de sac' by exploiting New World resources (Pomeranz 2000). But again none of this is very convincing. If coal was the real constraint on the development of Sunan, why were transport links to the Shanxi coalfields or to the Pingxiang coalfield via the Yangzi and Xiang rivers (see Huang 2002: 533) not developed earlier? And what made possible the English conquest and exploitation of the New World? This takes us back to some other more fundamental cause (such as culture).

My own view is that the explanation of China's failure is the obverse of the explanation of England's rise, namely the absence of a capitalist class in the former. The most convincing explanation of the origins of the Industrial Revolution in England focuses on changing class relations, and in particular the emergence of a class of capitalist landowners, who, after the twin revolutions of the seventeenth century, took advantage of the opportunities offered by the New World and revolutionized English agriculture (Brenner 1986, 1994; Wood 1991; Allen 1992, 1999). The failure of such a class to emerge in China explains its inability to pioneer the industrial revolution. Such a class could have developed the frontier regions of the south-west and Manchuria; China after all had its own colonies, so to argue that English growth was based on empire begs more questions than it answers. And in the absence of a class of Chinese capitalists, foreign technology was powerless to bring about economic modernization in China. The emergence of capitalism in England in turn owed much to the Enlightenment. To be sure, this sort of cultural argument is necessarily vague. Evidently the Enlightenment itself is not enough to explain why England, rather than some other part of Western Europe, was first. The First Industrial Revolution must at root have its origins in the peculiar nature of English Protestantism and the nature of the twin English Revolutions of 1649 and 1688 (Weber 1905; Tawney 1926). Although it is hard to be more precise than that, the very fact that there was no process remotely comparable occurring in China suggests that this is the crux of an explanation of the divergent paths of England and China.

In sum, there is no doubt that the impact of Western contact on the Treaty Port economy was very considerable indeed. As new technology became available in the Treaty Ports, so the pace of development accelerated – so much so that industrial output in the modern manufacturing sector was running at over 8 per cent per year in the 1930s (Rawski 1989: Appendix A). The impact of the foreign sector was thus far greater than the share of trade in GDP suggests. Nevertheless, the Treaty Port economy was weakly integrated with the Chinese economy; the macroeconomic data, the existence of high transport costs and the limited impact of the great depression in the 1930s all point in that direction. However, China's socio-economic structures were an even more formidable obstacle to technological diffusion. It was already far behind Europe in 1840. We are left with the conclusion that the impact of Western contact was ultimately rather limited. It was not modern technology but an adequate Chinese response which was lacking. Only in the sphere of ideas – Marxism gained an increasingly wide range of adherents in the 1930s and paved the way for the 1949 Revolution – was its impact decisive.

Agricultural weakness

Nowhere was Chinese economic weakness more evident than in the countryside. There is little doubt that China's modern sector was growing quickly in the 1930s.

Rawski (1989: 330) concludes that the growth of the modern sector was 8.1 per cent per year between 1914 and 1936. Most other economic historians are of like mind; for example, Wang (2004: 106) has the modern sector growing at 7.7 per cent over the same period, a rate which was much faster than that achieved by handicrafts (1 per cent).

The real constraint on Chinese development in the 1930s was the poor performance of the agricultural sector.[9] Agriculture's central problem stemmed from the fact that China had, to all intents and purposes, reached its arable frontier by the 1930s. There was still some scope for expanding the cultivated area in the north-east, but elsewhere the limits had been reached. The only way to increase output was by increasing sown area (raising the multiple cropping index) or by increasing yields. Both these avenues were closed off by the rural institutions of the 1930s. Only about 20 per cent of arable land was irrigated, and this affected yields directly. It also limited the expansion of sown area: in order to ensure adequate supplies of water for critical spring planting of rice, fields were often left flooded during the winter with the rains of the previous summer and autumn. The elimination of this system of winter flooding (*dongshuitian*) had clear advantages, but it could be accomplished only by guaranteeing irrigation during the spring. That in turn required the mobilization of labour for irrigation projects, a task beyond the capacity of small-scale peasant farmers. Institutional reform was evidently needed to resolve this coordination problem, and cooperation offered one possible solution.

Agriculture was also constrained by the size of Chinese farms, which were not large enough to maximize either yields or profits. Buck (1947: 7), for example, was of the view that some 80 per cent of farms were too small and no wonder: 50 per cent of farms in south China were of less than 10 *mu* in size, and 50 per cent of farms in north China were of less than 20 *mu* in size (Bramall 2000: 40).[10] Larger farms would certainly have led to an increase in yields. Admittedly, Buck's own data (as reaggregated by Arrigo 1986) show that yields were lower on Buck's category of 'very large farms' (averaging 68 *mu* in size) than on the category of large farms (averaging 24 *mu* in size). However, there was much scope for increases in yields at the bottom end of the scale as farm size increased; in Sichuan, the yield on large farms was 4,651 kg of grain per *mu*, well above the 2,012 kg recorded for small farms and which averaged 7 *mu* in size (Arrigo 1986: 351). In addition, the creation of larger farms would have led to substantial increases in labour productivity, at least if accompanied by mechanization. That in turn would have made possible a release of labour for use in the industrial sector, which was the key contribution of agriculture to England's industrial revolution (Allen 1992; Crafts 1985).

The best evidence for the poor performance of agriculture comes from the data on growth in the 1930s. Rawski (1989: 330) and Brandt (1989) have argued that agricultural output was growing at around 1.5 per cent per year between 1914 and 1936, which would represent an impressive rate of growth by any international or historical standard. However, these estimates are very much at the top of the range. Wang (2004: 103) has agriculture growing at about 1.2 per cent per year, and

Rawski's figure of 1.5 per cent per year is approximately double the rate estimated by Yeh (1979), and it needs to be recognized – as Rawski himself does – that the basis for these sorts of estimates is very fragile. Data on agricultural output were collected in a systematic way only after the creation of the National Agricultural Research Bureau (NARB) in 1931, and therefore estimates for before that date are little more than conjecture. However, even the estimates for the 1930s are themselves very problematic, because, as is universally recognized, the figures for cultivated area used by the NARB underestimate true area, which was under-reported for tax reasons (Liu and Yeh 1965; Bramall 1993). It is therefore very difficult to assess trends in productivity directly from the macroeconomic data.

Rawski attempts to circumvent these problems by using an indirect method, namely deriving trends in agricultural output from data on trends in real wages in a handful of locations. However, the survey data used by Rawski are not very representative; he relies on the monumental survey presided over by Buck (1937), the results of which are problematic in many respects (Arrigo 1986; Stross 1986). Furthermore, some strong assumptions are needed before we can infer (as he does) that trends in real wages in a handful of unrepresentative locations provide a reasonable proxy for trends in nationwide agricultural productivity (Bramall 1992; Huang 1990). Accordingly, the most plausible conclusion remains that, even if agriculture was not stagnant in the 1930s, agricultural output was increasing no faster than the rate of population growth. As a result, industrialization was constrained by agricultural weakness. Limited supplies of raw materials and high food prices (which forced up nominal wages) depressed industrial profits and hence investment; it was poor agricultural performance more than anything else which brought the boom of the 1920s to an end and exposed the underlying fragility of Chinese economic performance (Bergère 1989a, 1989b). There is therefore every reason to suppose that, in the absence of the Japanese onslaught of 1937, the industrialization of the 1930s would still have run out of steam.[11]

The Chinese macroeconomy in the early 1950s

The weaknesses that pervaded the Chinese economy in the 1930s were exacerbated by the Japanese invasion of 1937 and the civil war of 1945–9. The Chinese economy did not collapse (Bramall 1993); indeed the pace of industrialization in and around Chongqing (the wartime nationalist capital), and at Yan'an (the centre of CCP developmental activities) accelerated. Nevertheless, economic growth was checked by the events of 1937–49.

To be sure, some of the worst ravages of these years were quickly put right after 1949. The hyperinflation of the late 1940s was brought to an end by increasing output and reducing government spending. Instrumental to this process was the policy of 'new democracy' which was designed to co-opt China's private sector entrepreneurs ('the national bourgeoisie' in Maoist language) and rich peasants. This stabilized the position of the new regime by guaranteeing private-sector profits, thus encouraging increased private-sector investment and production.

The view expressed to Stalin by Mao in their talks during December 1949 that

China needed 'three to five years ... to bring the economy back to pre-war levels' may well have been over-optimistic.[12] In no small measure, this was because of Mao's decision to intervene in the Korean War; Chinese troops crossed the Yalu river in October 1950. Stalin secretly encouraged North Korea's invasion in early 1950, but there was no expectation that China would come in on the side of the North, and most of Mao's advisers counselled him against intervention. Mao undoubtedly had a point in arguing that war in Korea would help to solidify China's borders and strengthen the People's Republic by promoting a spirit of nationalism. However, Lin Biao strongly advised against it. Fighting the Guomindang, he argued, was one thing; taking on the American Army in a conventional war quite another (Teiwes and Sun 1996: 171–2). It is also arguable that Chinese intervention in Korea prevented the recovery of Taiwan by inducing Truman to adopt a more belligerent approach across East and South-East Asia. Moreover, intervention was ill-advised in economic terms because it increased military spending and distorted the pattern of civilian production. For example, official military spending increased from 2.8 billion *yuan* in 1950 to 7.5 billion *yuan* in 1953. As a percentage of government spending, this represented a fall from 41 to 34 per cent, but these sorts of shares were nevertheless well above the average of 16 per cent for the 1950–2004 period (ZGTJNJ 2005: 273; ZGTJNJ 1985: 524; ZGTJNJ 1983: 448). These data demonstrate the extent of the distortion caused by China's decision to commit ground troops in South Korea.

GDP, material living standards and Chinese economic structure

One clear consequence of Chinese involvement in Korea was that economic recovery was by no means complete in 1952. But it also meant that the development of the Chinese economy was further delayed, a matter of no small consequence given the country's poverty in the early 1950s. One way to see the extent of Chinese underdevelopment is to compare levels of per capita GDP across countries in 1952 using the consistent estimates produced by Angus Maddison (Table 2.1).

These sorts of figures should not be taken too literally. There are great uncertainties surrounding the underlying data in all these cases. Second, Maddison's

Table 2.1 GDP per capita on the eve of modernization

Country	Year	*GDP per capita (1990 US$)*
China	1952	537
India	1952	629
Japan	1870	737
England and Wales	1801	2006
Former USSR	1913	1488
Africa	1950	852

Source: Maddison (2001: 247, 264, 304).

adjustments to the sources he has used are in many cases problematic. And it is far from clear that it makes much sense to value eighteenth-century English or Japanese GDP at 1990 prices.[13] Nevertheless, it is very clear that China's level of development was lower than that of all these other countries and regions at the beginning of their modern economic development. The contrast between China on the one hand and England and Wales on the other is especially striking; per capita income in the former was barely one quarter of that in England some 150 years earlier.

All this suggests that, in material terms, China was very poor in the early 1950s, and other indicators point to a similar conclusion. The most obvious sign of underdevelopment was the dominance of the agricultural sector, which provided the bulk of both output and employment. This meant that China faced the extremely difficult task of making the transition to an industrial economy; industrial capacity had to be created, and a peasant workforce had to be transformed into an industrial proletariat. This farm-to-factory transition is one of the greatest challenges for any developing country. Many economic models, most famously that of Lewis (1954), see this as a simple process. However, these models ignore the alienation suffered by the peasantry during the process of becoming habituated to a factory environment in which the rhythms and routines are so very different from those of farming. Even when the workforce does become accustomed to the factory environment, many years of learning-by-doing are needed before productivity levels will match those of the existing industrial workforce. In this regard, China had far to go in 1952.

The scale of the challenge is further apparent from Table 2.2. In the China of the early 1950s agriculture provided about half of GDP and over 80 per cent of employment.[14] In both respects, China was as underdeveloped as post-Independence India. More strikingly still (but in line with the evidence in Table 2.1), the China of the 1950s was not only behind the Europe of two centuries earlier but markedly inferior to Britain even before that country had embarked upon its own Industrial Revolution. It also interesting to observe that structure of the Chinese economy in the early 1950s was remarkably similar to that of Russia prior to its Revolution; the share of GDP accounted for by Russian agriculture in 1913 was identical to that for China in 1952, and the 1926 employment share (the first year for which we have plausible data) is also identical to China's 1952 figure.

The similarity between the level of developments attained in China and Russia on the eve of Revolution is striking. It can be read in two ways. One reading is that because China was no worse off in 1949 than the Soviet Union in 1917 and because the USSR was able to industrialize very rapidly, China could follow the Soviet path. Certainly the view offered by Soviet advisers to the CCP in the 1920s and 1930s – that any attempt at revolution and modern economic development in China was doomed to failure because the country was even more backward than Russia at the time of the First World War – seems in retrospect to have been unduly pessimistic.

The second reading, of course, is that socialist transition was premature in the Soviet case, and therefore it was equally premature in the China of the early

56 *Chinese Economic Development*

Table 2.2 The share of agriculture in GDP and employment in poor countries (percentages)

	GDP	Employment
China, 1952		
Official	51	84
Liu and Yeh	46	77
Britain, 1760	38	50
Europe, 1760	47	64
Russia, 1913	51	84
India, 1951	56	72
All developing countries, 1965	31	72
Sub-Saharan Africa, 1965	43	78

Sources: SSB (1997: 31); SSB (1990: 3); Liu and Yeh (66 and 69); Crafts (1985: 62–3); UNDP (1990: 157); World Bank (1990: 183) Bhagwati (1993: 102); Patel *et al.* (2002: 153); Davies *et al.* (1994: 277); Gregory (1982: 73 and 185).

Note
Most scholars assess the state of the Chinese economy at the start of the Maoist era using the 1952 data. This is because the 1949 data are both unreliable and misleading; output in that year was reduced by continuing civil war between the Guomindang and the CCP. By 1952, the economy had largely recovered but few economic policy changes had been introduced by the new government. 1952 was in effect the first normal post-Revolutionary year. Note that the employment figure for Russia is for 1926, but there is little reason to suppose it was very different in 1913; the agricultural share in GDP, for example, had fallen to only 48 per cent by 1928. The agricultural output share for Russia in 1913 is as a percentage of net national product.

1950s. Most early twentieth-century Marxists had dismissed the possibility of revolution in Russia on the grounds that the country had still to make a complete transition to the capitalist mode of production. Russia lacked a suitably motivated proletariat, and transition to socialism was premature because of the inadequate development of the forces of production. So too with China. Neoclassicals offer a similar view: modernization was fraught with difficulty in both countries because they lacked the key prerequisites for modern economic growth. Development was still possible, but it needed to be built around the development of light industry and the gradual modernization of agriculture – rather than by means of the growth of heavy industry.

To argue, therefore, that the China of 1952 was no more underdeveloped than the Soviet Union in the early 1920s is hardly enough to make the case that the People's Republic was 'ready' for modern economic growth. Of course countries have to start somewhere, but China's situation in 1952 was hardly auspicious, and it inevitably conditioned what was possible in the decade which lay ahead.

Human development

Measures of human development also suggest that China was very backward in the early 1950s. Some progress was certainly made during the 1930s. According to Buck's data (1937: 375–7), the literacy rate was about 30 per cent for men and barely 1 per cent for women in the early 1930s. China's own post-1949 population censuses, which collected data for literacy rates for every age group, point to a similar conclusion. The 1982 census, for example, found that literacy rates amongst women born before 1922 (and still alive in 1982) was less than 5 per cent (RKNJ 1985: 618). But the trend was upward; the 1982 census, for example, gives a literacy figure of about 25 per cent for women born between 1933 and 1937. This reflected the expansion of education during the Republican era. In fact, according to Ministry of Education data, the number enrolled in primary school rose from 3.8 million in 1916 to 12.4 million in 1933 (Yeh 1979: 118). Nowhere was this more true than in Jiangsu: the records available for each of the counties in that province show that primary-school enrolment rates of over 30 per cent were by no means uncommon in the mid-1930s. By 1952, some 3.4 million Jiangsu children were enrolled in primary schools (JSZ 2000: 1301–4).

But such figures were hardly impressive even by early twentieth-century Asian standards. Literacy was practically universal amongst the soldiers conscripted into the Japanese Imperial Army in 1941 (Honda 1997: 263), far higher than the figure of 40 per cent for Chinese males of the same age (RKNJ 1985: 618). Comparisons with Industrial Revolution England are equally unfavourable. Although literacy dipped between 1780 and 1810, literacy rates of around 50 per cent were the norm by 1850 (Floud and Harris 1997: 99). Even in a relatively advanced Chinese province like Jiangsu, only about 100,000 children were enrolled in secondary schools in the whole of the province in 1952, out of a population of about 37 million (JSZ 2000: 1301–4).

The argument of Chapter 1 was that life expectancy is the best single measure of development. And here there is evidence which suggests progress during the Republican era.[15] As Campbell (1997) has shown, life expectancy was rising in several of China's cities in the 1920s and 1930s. In Beijing, for example, life expectancy at birth was forty-one and thirty-six years for men and women respectively in the early 1930s. This reflected programmes aimed at improving public health, such as vaccination, the supply of treated tap water (Beijing began to develop a municipal water supply system during 1908–10) and improved methods of nightsoil collection. Improvements in material living standards appeared to have played little role (Campbell 1997: 201).

Nevertheless, Beijing was not representative of China, and especially not the Chinese countryside. According to Notestein and Chao (1937: 391), life expectancy at birth was only thirty-five years for men and women during 1929–31. Moreover, even Notestein and Chao (19937: 390) thought this exaggerated the true position: 'The data gathered during the relatively uneventful three year period of the present study yield life tables which present a somewhat over-optimistic picture of conditions as they would have been if such events had not occurred.' In any case, the Notestein–Chao study underestimated true infant mortality. Once corrected, true life expectancy even in the 'good' years of 1929–31 was only around twenty-five years at birth (Barclay *et al.* 1976).

In short, for all the progress which may have been occurring in the cities – and it needs to be said that serious questions have to be asked about the reliability of the surveys used by Campbell and others – China's pre-1949 mortality record was abysmal. The most obvious comparison is with England at the start of its Industrial Revolution, and in a sense that says it all. As early as 1801, English life expectancy was around thirty-six years at birth, and by the middle of the century it was running at around forty years (Wrigley and Schofield 1981: 231). In other words, China in the late 1940s was about a century behind Britain. A direct comparison of infant mortality rates in the middle of the twentieth century is even more revealing. Banister's (1987: 352) estimates put the Chinese infant mortality rate at 152 per 1,000 in the early 1950s. By comparison, the rate was 107 in Japan during 1936–40 (Japan Statistical Association 1987: 205) and only 55 per 1,000 on average in Britain between 1926 and 1950, war notwithstanding (Woods 1992: 29).

Spatial variation

The prewar life expectancy data discussed in the previous section illustrate the dangers of all-China generalization: Beijing then, as now, is not China. Of course, it does makes sense to think of China as a unified whole for some purposes. The People's Republic of 1949 was far less politically and culturally diverse than the modern European Union in terms of language, and China had been a nation-state for many centuries. Its ethnic minority population was small and relatively localized. The contrast between the China of the second half of the twentieth century and the polyglot Soviet Union is stark, so much so that there is no reason to expect China to disintegrate along ethnic lines and to follow the USSR into oblivion. Nevertheless, it is important to recognize the extent of spatial variation at the beginning of the 1950s.

Physical geography

One fissure is an east–west geographical divide (Figure 2.2).[16] We can think of China as rising in three broad steps from the Pacific seaboard to the inner Asian frontier. The North China plain and the low hills of the south-east comprise the first tier. The second tier comprises the bulk of China. Here agricultural conditions are less good than along the coast, but there is still an abundance of alluvial plain and high quality agricultural land in provinces such as Shaanxi, Hunan and Sichuan. The third tier comprises the high Himalayan plateau, which runs from just outside Chengdu in the east to the frontier, and the Gobi desert. The mineral wealth of this third region is enormous, but distances are great and agricultural conditions are poor. However, although the divide between the western region and the rest of China is striking, such a small proportion of China's population live in the far western provinces that the Himalayan plateau and Gobi desert are of limited functional significance in thinking about Chinese prosperity and development.

Note that the regional categorization adopted here differs markedly from the usual Chinese division of the People's Republic into eastern, central and western

Figure 2.2 Chinese geographical regions

Note: This map is a simplification because the new municipality of Chongqing (created from eastern Sichuan) is included within Sichuan. Moreover, as noted in the main text, much of western Sichuan properly falls within the western region; again that is not shown.

regions. This latter includes the south-western provinces of Sichuan, Guizhou and Yunnan in the western region. However, this makes little sense in geographical terms. The physical geography of the Chinese south-west is not as favourable to economic development as the Pacific seaboard, but – with the exception of the territory included in Sichuan's three western prefectures – it is far more conducive than the high Himalayan plateau, the Gobi desert or the Inner Mongolian steppe. The Chinese south-west is a poor region, but it is very far from clear that physical geography is the main reason. There are, to be sure, geographical differences between (say) the provinces of the south-west and the south-east, but the similarities are much greater than the differences. Very little of Guangdong province is flat. Conversely, the hills of Guizhou and Yunnan offer few barriers to economic development. The only real difference between these two regions is access to the sea, a difference which, as we shall see, has assumed increasing significance since the late 1970s.[17]

In some ways, however, the north–south geographical divide is more significant than that between east and west, at least for agriculture. The main problem faced by north China is lack of water. The average amount of water available across the whole of China in 2005 was 2,152 cubic metres per person. In Hebei province, however, the figure was only 197 cubic metres per person, far worse even than in the desert province of Gansu (1,042 cubic metres per person) and only a little better than the exceptionally dry province of Ningxia, where only 144 cubic metres of water were available per person. By contrast, water-rich Guangxi had 3,704 cubic metres of water per person at its disposal (SSB 2006d: 15). The water-table in north China has been falling by one metre per year for several decades, and there is now serious talk of moving the Chinese capital from Beijing. Such talk is not surprising; some estimates suggest there is more water in the Middle East than in north China. The underlying problem is limited rainfall in the north (Figures 2.3 and 2.4), and this lack of rainfall inevitably hampers both industrial and agricultural development.

The interesting question in all this is not so much whether geographical variation exists across China. Manifestly it does. Rather, we want to know whether geography can help to explain differences in economic development. Was the impact of physical geography more important than that of other factors, whether trade, the state or some other constellation of factors?

Theory: Skinner's macroregional analysis

The principal advocate of the view that physical geography has had a major impact upon the pace and pattern of Chinese development has long been G. William Skinner (1977, 1999.[18] The concept at the heart of Skinner's work is the macroregion, and he argues that China divides up into nine macroregions. These macroregions cut across provincial boundaries; for example, Shantou prefecture in northern Guangdong is not part of the same macroregion as Guangzhou and the Pearl River delta. More importantly, Skinner offers a systematic assessment of the pattern of trade within and between macroregions.

As far as the former is concerned, Skinner argues that each macroregion exhibits a clear structure of core and periphery, and that this has changed little over time. For example, Sichuan's central riverine zone has retained its position

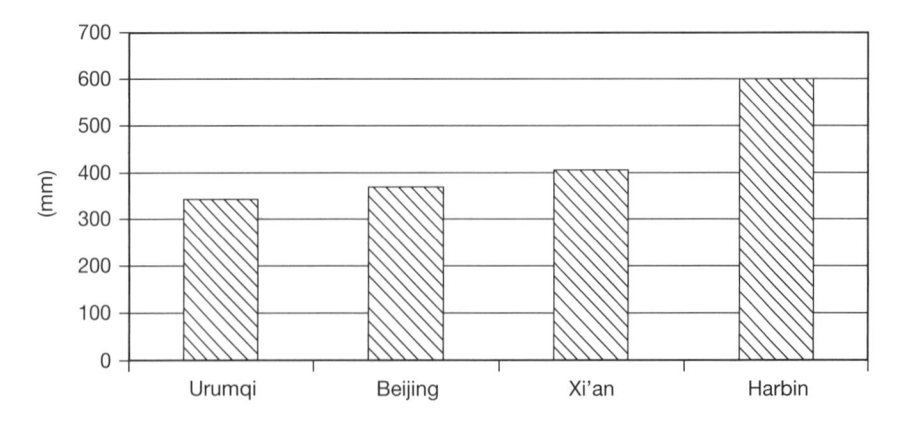

Figure 2.3 Average annual rainfall in northern Chinese cities (Source: SSB (2003: 14).)

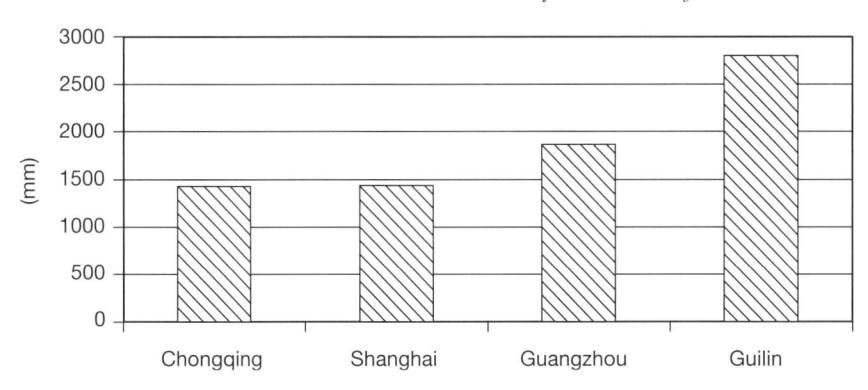

Figure 2.4 Average annual rainfall in southern Chinese cities (Source: SSB (2003: 14).)

of dominance despite industrialization and transport modernization. However, the core–periphery dichotomy within each macroregion does not rest on any assumption of limited trade or migration. Rather, trade within macroregions is extensive. In effect, the Skinnerian macroregion is a neoclassical world of low transaction costs and competitive markets; for example, Skinner assumes that living standards can be proxied by population density, implying a highly efficient labour market. However, this type of assumption can produce a core–periphery dichotomy; the new economic geography has done precisely that by developing models in which population density, transport costs and external economies of scale interact to determine spatial trends. If core and periphery have different equilibria (underpinned by differences in preferences or savings), then there is no reason to expect absolute convergence of per capita incomes over time despite low transaction costs.

Skinner's model also posits that trade *between* macroregions (long-distance trade) – in contrast to trade *within* macroregions – is limited because of high transport costs. As a result, the history of Chinese macroregions is very different, making it difficult to talk about national patterns of development. Moreover, transport improvement over the last century has not made the concept of the macroregion any less useful:

> Macroregional systems of cities are far more tightly integrated today than they were a century ago, and in at least some macroregions the internal transport net has been greatly expanded and upgraded, whereas interregional routes, despite mechanization and upgrading, have not been appreciably intensified.
> (Skinner 1999: 61).

Skinner recognizes that long-distance trade certainly did occur, especially along the Yangzi river even during the Qing dynasty. Nevertheless, its importance was comparatively small compared to trade within macroregions because of the lack of a proper long-distance transport infrastructure.

Not surprisingly, Skinner's striking analysis has attracted a good deal of criticism.

That offered by Sands and Myers (1986) is essentially empirical. The allocation of counties to macroregions, they argue, is arbitrary; the extent of long-distance trade was underestimated by Skinner; and there is considerable evidence from movements in commodity prices that the markets of the Chinese mainland were comparatively well integrated. This last argument has been buttressed by the work of a number of writers in recent years (Brandt 1989; Rawski and Li 1992; Li 2007). And scholarship has firmly documented the extent of long-distance trade along the Yangzi and the Grand Canal (Rowe 1984; Xu and Wu 2000).

Some of these criticisms seem soundly based. The characterization of macroregions is indeed arbitrary. For example, some recent research suggests a high degree of correlation between (say) grain prices in the Beijing region and prices in the lower Yangzi region even in the early nineteenth century. At the same time, however, the degree of price integration within regions was limited (Li 2007: 217 and 219). This suggests that coastal shipping and trade along China's major river routes integrated the cities and Treaty Ports quite well in the 1930s, but that the absence of transport modernization within supposed macroregions ensured that the extent of intra-regional trade and migration was much less than Skinner alleges. One reason for this was the existence of cultural and social obstacles to migration. This was true even in the lower Yangzi region; for example, migrants from Subei were treated as outsiders and widely discriminated against in Shanghai and Sunan (Honig 1992, 1996). But whatever the reason, these considerations suggest that the core–periphery divide within regions was much greater than that between regions – thus reversing Skinner's position and suggesting that the very concept of a macroregion is doubtful.

The notion of an essentially unchanging core–periphery structure over time is equally problematic. Assumptions aside, the prediction of spatial stasis sits uneasily with what we know of the impact of the state in the Republican and Maoist eras. Warlordism brought about marked changes in the spatial pattern of economic activity, as did state-led industrialization during the Second World War. Take the case of Chengdu in Sichuan, a province extensively studied by Skinner. The most visible change in the long run has been the rise of Chengdu to a status equal to that of Chongqing, the historic centre of the Upper Yangzi region. The very fact that Chengdu has developed so rapidly flatly contradicts any notion of spatial stasis.[19] Moreover, the rise of Chengdu was driven not by riverine transport – it is essentially disconnected from Sichuan's riverine system – but by warlord-led industrialization in the late 1920s and early 1930s and wartime industrialization under Nationalist rule in the early 1940.[20] In ignoring the role played by the state, Skinner offers a theory which has more than a hint of geographical determinism about it.

Evidence: spatial inequalities in the early 1950s

Nevertheless, the notion that geography played an important role in configuring the pattern of spatial development in China before 1949 has an important element of truth about it. Skinner is undoubtedly right in pointing out the limited extent of long-distance trade in the Qing and Republican periods; it did exist, but scholars such as Sands and Myers exaggerate its extent. The macroregion may be an arbitrary construct, but Skinner is surely correct to emphasize the limited degree of integration between China's regions – and by implication the limited interaction between the foreign sector and the Chinese hinterland emphasized by *inter alia* Murphey (1970). As Feuerwerker (1970: 377) concluded: 'Anyone who would claim that the Hunan or Szechwan peasant in the 1930s dressed in Naigaiwata cottons, smoked BAT cigarettes, and used Meiji sugar has a big case to prove.' The central problem was that of high transport costs. The cost of moving goods by water was low: the cost per tonne-mile of moving goods by junk was around a quarter of the cost of transport by mule or cart (Buck 1937: 354). However, few parts of northern and western China were accessible in this way; even the Treaty Port of Chongqing could only be reached by ships of shallow draught because of the obstacles posed by the Yangzi gorges. Railways offered, of course, a useful alternative, but the network in western China was almost non-existent before 1949. The main east–west Longhai line ran no further than Xi'an, and there were no railways in Sichuan (except for a short coal-carrying line running out of Chongqing), Yunnan, Guizhou, Guangxi or Fujian in 1937. Rawski (1989) is right to point out that China's transport infrastructure was in the process of transformation in the Republican era, but the process demonstrably had far still to go before one could talk of an integrated national market.

One good indicator of this lack of integration was the limited impact of the Great Depression (Wright 2000).[21] Unless one makes the implausible new classical assumptions of Rawski and Brandt – that money is neutral and that the economy is always at the natural rate because markets work efficiently – Wright's finding that the Depression had little impact on the economies of Yunnan, Guizhou and Sichuan in the 1930s can only be taken as showing that China's international economic integration was comparatively slight. Sichuan was by no means self-sufficient – there was an extensive trade in opium and wood oil along the Yangzi – but these commodity flows constituted only a small part of economic activity. Bergère (1989b) makes the same point about the depression of the early 1920s, which devastated the Western economies. In China's case, and despite problems in the export sector, the domestic sector was largely unaffected and hence economic growth continued.

However, the real test of the geographical approach is whether it is systematically supported by the empirical evidence for China at the dawn of the 1950s. Were spatial inequalities in per capita GDP and human development widespread? And if so, was the pattern of inequality dictated by physical geography?

(a) Inequalities in GDP per capita

Of course, a provincial set of data cannot be decisive when it comes to assessing either spatial inequality in general or Skinner's hypothesis in particular. As China's post-1949 provincial boundaries are not contiguous with Skinner's macroregions – part of eastern Guangdong province, for example, falls outside the Lingnan macroeconomic region – the provincial data do not allow of any decisive evaluation of the hypothesis.

Nevertheless, the data certainly do suggest that geography exercised a key influence on levels of prosperity at the start of the 1950s. The extent of disparities in GDP per head is displayed in Figure 2.5. The per capita level of GDP in the People's Republic of China was 142 *yuan* in 1953. The richest parts of the country were the big metropolitan centres; Shanghai was by some way the most developed part of China, with a per capita GDP of almost 600 *yuan*. Those provinces which were rich were in general resource-rich with relatively low populations (Gansu and Inner Mongolia), or provinces where considerable pre-1952 industrialization had occurred.[22] The most obvious illustration of the latter is provided by the Manchurian provinces, which had developed a large industrial base whilst Japanese colonies (Chao 1983; Myers and Peattie 1984).

Two parts of China were especially poor. The most impoverished region was the south-west; the bottom five provinces (Sichuan, Guizhou, Hunan, Guangxi and Yunnan) were all to be found there. These provinces had large populations but, more importantly, they had experienced very limited industrial development. The clearest demonstration of this is provided by Chongqing, which was considerably

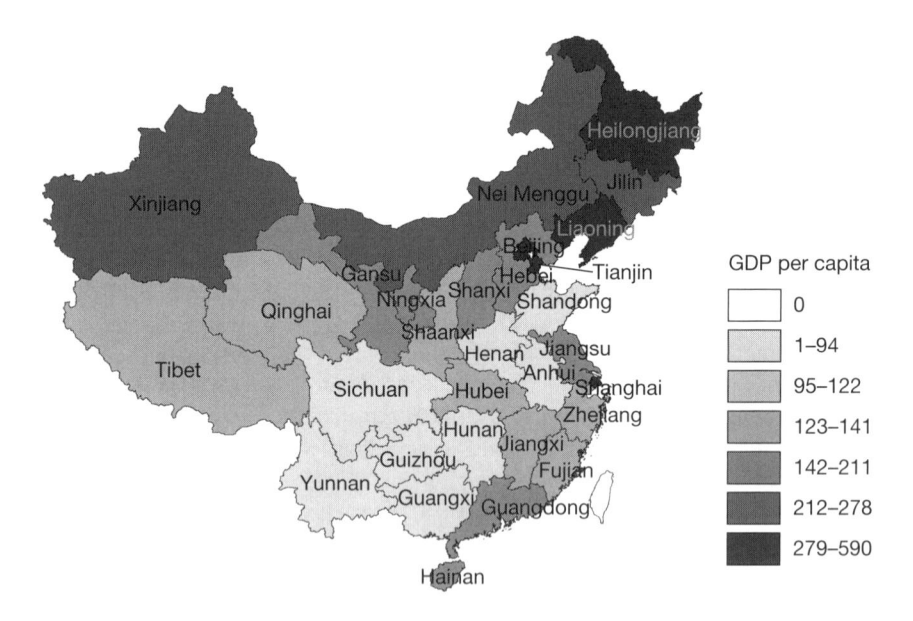

Figure 2.5 Per capita GDP by province, 1953 (Source: SSB (2005a).)

Note: I have used the data for 1953, even though it is more conventional to use those for 1952. There are two reasons. First, 1953 was a population census year and therefore the population figures for that year are more reliable than for 1952. Second, recovery from the civil war trough was not really complete until 1953 (and perhaps not even then). Recovery was especially slow in the big cities; Beijing's GDP per head more than doubled between 1952 and 1953, whereas national GDP per head rose by only 19 per cent. The 1953 data thus give a less distorted picture. However, I have used the 1952 data for Ningxia because GDP per head in 1953 was actually lower than in both 1952 and 1954.

more affluent than the rest of Sichuan because of wartime industrialization. China's other poor provinces were located on the north China plain (Anhui, Shandong and Henan). Their physical geography was a little better than that faced by the south-western provinces; however, they too were industrially underdeveloped and their agriculture vulnerable to drought.

One striking feature of the data is the absence of any marked division between coast and interior. It is true that none of China's poorest provinces were coastal (except Guangxi, and that province has very little coastline). However, provinces such as Zhejiang, Fujian and Guangdong – all of which are very affluent in 2007 – were all rather average by Chinese standards in 1952. Jiangsu was something of an exception, reflecting both the considerable degree of industrialization which had occurred in Sunan around the textile centres of Wuxi and Suzhou, and Nanjing's status as national capital in the 1930s. And, as has already been noted, some of the interior provinces – Gansu and Xinjiang – were quite affluent. Even Tibet, little more than Stone Age in 1952 in terms of its institutions and system of government, had a respectable level of GDP because of its small population and considerable natural resources.

We do well of course to remember the fragility of the data which underlie apparent regional inequality. The figures for Tibet and for the western provinces must be seen as conjectural, given that the statistical system was barely functioning in China until the mid-1950s and therefore the estimates for 1953 involve a considerable degree of back-projection. On the other hand, the very fact that Tibet was not the poorest of China's provinces in 1953 tends to suggest that these data reflect an honest attempt to accurately assess levels of economic development in the early 1950s. There is no especially good reason to reject these data, and they certainly fit in with most subjective assessments of levels of prosperity in China at the time. No amount of statistical legerdemain is going to alter the fact that Shanghai, the other cities and Manchuria were pockets of prosperity, and that grinding poverty was the norm in the south-west and in a swathe of provinces running south from Beijing across the north China plain and the Yangzi into Hunan province.

It is particularly worth underscoring the extent to which there were spatial differences in the level of industrial production. Table 2.3 shows the gulf between the most and the least industrialized provinces in 1952. The staggering differential in industrial production between Shanghai and Sichuan – production per head was around 100 times higher in the great metropolitan centre – goes far towards explaining levels of relative prosperity. Even on the Chengdu plain, the most industrially developed part of Sichuan in 1952, per capita gross industrial output value was little higher than in the poorest part of Jiangsu, and well below the levels of production being recorded in Sunan (Bramall 2007: 283). These data also point to the real dilemma that the CCP faced in formulating its economic strategy in the 1950s. Should China build on its well-established industrial base in Liaoning and Shanghai, or should it attempt to redress the underdevelopment of the western provinces?

What does all this tell us about the determinants of spatial inequality across the

66 *Chinese Economic Development*

Table 2.3 Industrial production, 1952 (current *yuan*; top and bottom four provinces)

	Industrial output per capita (yuan)	Total industrial production (million yuan)
Shanghai	318	1822
Tianjin	139	612
Liaoning	94	1810
Heilongjiang	63	700
Qinghai	6	10
Anhui	6	180
Ningxia	5	7
Sichuan	3	360

Source: SSB (2005a).

Note
Data here are for gross value-added. Industrial production in Tibet is given as negligible for the early 1950s and therefore it is excluded from this table.

Chinese mainland? For one thing, trade was not a significant factor. That much is evident from the lack of any systematic per capita income gap between the coast and the interior. And this result is not surprising. The war with Japan and civil war had curtailed China's international trade, and internal trade was underdeveloped for much the same reason. It is also likely that geography did exert some influence. Although we saw in the previous chapter that natural resources are often a curse rather than a boon, it does appear that the relatively high levels of GDP per head in some of China's western and central provinces owed something to their natural resource base, in particular mineral, timber and pastureland. It is, for example, at least arguable that Shanxi was more prosperous than its neighbours because of its extensive coal reserves.[23] By contrast, the south-west provinces were poor because they lacked an extensive resource base and the transport network to access the mineral resources available in other parts of China; there was not a single functioning mile of railway in the entire region in 1952.

To be sure, geography was not destiny. Nothing for example could trump a legacy of industrialization; Liaoning, Shanghai and the port city of Tianjin were proof of that. So too, admittedly on a smaller scale, was Chongqing. Indeed the absence of natural resources in Shanghai's hinterland demonstrates rather vividly that external trade could overcome mineral and agricultural shortages. In other words, history mattered. Of course historical patterns of industrialization themselves owed something to natural resource availability and population, and one can hardly claim that coastal cities such as Shanghai and Tianjin were hampered by their geography. Nevertheless, accident and state agency exerted an important influence. Manchuria's relative prosperity reflected the impact of Japanese colonial rule and Shanghai's elevated position was not unrelated to its Treaty Port status in the late nineteenth century. After all, Shanghai's harbour *per se* has little to recommend it, in contrast to Hong Kong, Sydney or Rio de Janeiro – which suggests that the effects of pure geography were far from decisive. Moreover, Chongqing enjoyed rapid growth in the 1940s not because of its geography, but because it was the wartime capital of the KMT. In other words, history and state agency could trump geography. That they did not do so more often says more about the weakness of the Chinese state than it does about the decisive impact of geography on economic development.

(b) Spatial inequalities in human development

Variations in levels of human development aplenty also existed in the early 1950s. We are not able to document this with any great precision, because life expectancy data are either unavailable or unreliable for the early 1950s. Nevertheless, data on provincial crude death rates, calculated from the data collected during the 1953 census, offer some insight into the regional picture (Figure 2.6).

It is evident from this figure that the spatial patterns of human development were very similar to those for GDP per head. The south-west of China did poorly in terms of human development, just as it had done in terms of GDP per capita. The same is true of much of the north China plain (Henan, Anhui and Shandong). Conversely, just as Hebei and Shanxi did better than other parts of the north China plain in terms of GDP per head, so they also did better in terms of mortality. And the Manchurian provinces also did well on both criteria. The only real divergence evident in these data is that the provinces located along China's inner Asian frontier did much less well in terms of human development than they did using the criterion of GDP per head. The mortality rate in Inner Mongolia, for example, was especially high, and Xinjiang's crude death rate was by no means low. In

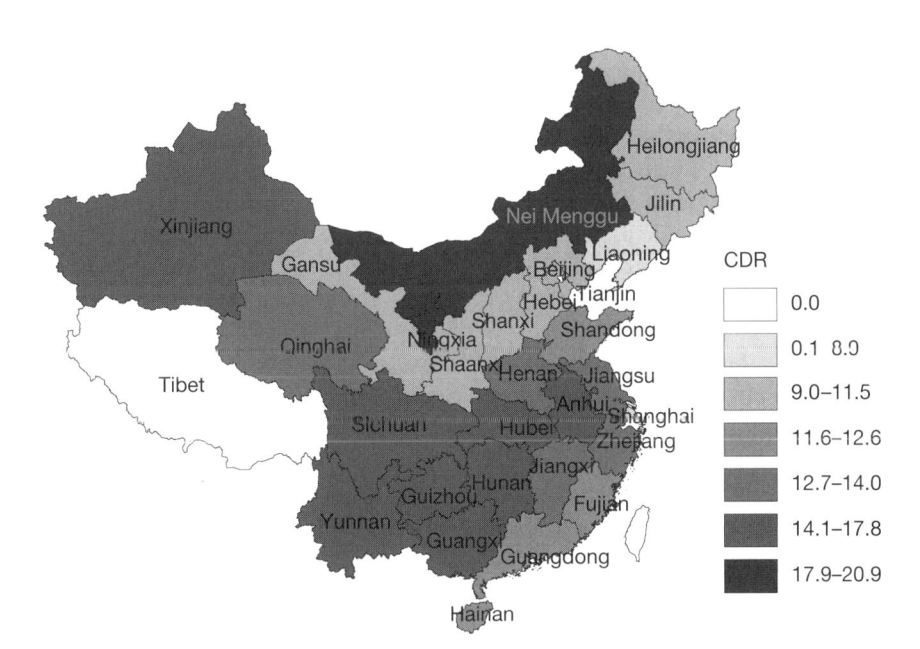

Figure 2.6 Chinese crude death rates, 1953 (Source: SSB (2005a).)

other words, the abundant raw materials in these provinces did not translate into low rates of mortality.

This broad correlation between levels of material development and human development is as one would expect. The Chinese state had been historically weak, and in any case human development was not one of its primary goals in the century before 1949. It is therefore not surprising that the sort of state-led divergence between human development and GDP per head observed in countries such as Sri Lanka or post-revolutionary Cuba did not exist in China. The Chinese state was simply too weak to drive such a wedge between the two. As with GDP per head, geography does appear to have exerted a decisive influence over human development levels precisely because of the absence of any countervailing force.

Inequalities within the Chinese countryside

Inequality within Chinese communities was at least as significant as inequalities within regions. Admittedly the extent of inequality within China's cities and countryside (intra-local inequality, for short) in 1949 cannot be documented with any degree of certainty. Nevertheless, there is little doubt that it was extreme.[24] Tawney provides the most evocative description:

> There are districts in which the position of the rural population is that of a man standing permanently up to the neck in water, so that even a ripple is sufficient to drown him. (Tawney 1932: 77)

Some of this inequality reflected short-run factors: the devastation caused to the countryside and to infrastructure by war, unemployment caused by industrial disruption and the effects of hyperinflation. None of this is in doubt. The controversial issue is the extent of intra-local inequality in 1937, for if the China of the 1930s was characterized by a relatively equitable distribution of income, it follows that the redistributive programmes launched by the CCP in the early 1950s were not necessary. All that was required in 1949 was the restoration of peace and political stability

Few scholars doubt that land ownership was unequal. The data collected by the National Land Commission for 1934 show a Gini coefficient of 0.72, which rises to 0.60 if absentee landlordism is included (Brandt and Sands 1992: 181 and 205). Alternatively, we can use the data collected by the CCP on the extent of inequality on the eve of land reform; these figures were collected at various times (depending on the location) between 1947 and 1952. Esherick concludes from them that the landlord class – which accounted for around 5 per cent of the rural population – owned about 39 per cent of arable land, very close to the official CCP estimate of 37 per cent (Esherick 1981: 404–5; Li 1959: 119). In the south-west the figure was higher; in Sichuan, based on an analysis of the distribution of land in thirteen counties, I estimate the landlord share at around 44 per cent (Bramall 1997: 557).

These CCP surveys were subject to biases of their own. There was a great deal of pressure on cadres to ensure that 5 per cent of the population of each village was classified as 'landlord'. The results also depend upon whether temple land is classified as landlord-controlled land (which it ought to be) and whether landless labourers are included in the population figures (again as they ought to be). Nevertheless, the very fact that the CCP estimate of the landlord share in cultivated land ownership was strikingly similar to the National Land Commission estimate for 1934 – the top 5 per cent of the rural population owned 39 per cent of land (Brandt and Sands 1992: 182) – suggests that the extent of bias was not so great as to render meaningless these data.

The effects of unequal land ownership on the distribution of income were mitigated by the operation of rural markets Even though the rental market in land was far from perfect, its existence did at least provide access to this key asset for the bulk of the rural population. The very fact, therefore, that around 20 per cent of the farm population in north China and 40 per cent of the farm population in the south during mid-1930s (Feuerwerker 1977: 58; NARB 1934: 62) were tenants should be seen in a positive rather than a negative light. Similarly, a lack of capital could be circumvented by borrowing. Landless labourers, and farm households with excess labour, could boost their income by taking up employment in the non-farm sector. Moreover, at least for the villages studied by Brandt and Sands (1992), labour power and ownership of draught animals was not correlated with land ownership; land-deficient households were able to make up for their lack of land by utilizing these other assets. In other words, land, capital and labour markets went some way towards equalizing incomes in the countryside, and it is therefore misleading to focus exclusively on land ownership in thinking about the prewar distribution of income in the Chinese countryside.

Of course nobody pretends that these markets functioned so well as to eliminate inequality; in many cases, markets were either missing or functioned badly. Nevertheless, it is the contention of a number of scholars that rural factor markets worked in such a way that income inequality was modest in the Chinese countryside during the Republican era (Myers 1970; Brandt 1997). According to Brandt and Sands (1992: 180):

> income inequality was much lower in rural early twentieth century China than has been previously inferred on the basis of data on land distribution alone; in fact, when compared with other low-income countries, China actually appears to be on the moderate side.

From this perspective, the 1949 Revolution was a result of poverty and peasant nationalism, not a product of inequality, and this view is supported by some of the available estimates of inequality. Buck's (1937) survey of conditions in 1929–33 suggests a Gini coefficient for per capita income of 0.33 (Roll 1980: 48–50). The National Land Commission survey of 1934 suggests a Gini for household income of 0.44, but the per capita distribution was more equal because the richer households tended to be larger. On the basis of these data, and their own estimates

Brandt and Sands (1992: 202 and 205) conclude that the rural Gini coefficient was probably around 0.38 and certainly no larger than 0.40. As they say, this is not an especially high figure; many parts of postwar sub-Saharan African and Latin America have recorded Ginis close to 0.60.

For many other academics, however, there is a Panglossian quality to this type of analysis (Riskin 1987; Esherick 1981; Little 1989). One of the problems with the neoclassical approach is that the Buck and National Land Commission surveys understate the true extent of inequality (Bramall 2004: 110). Buck's survey made extensive use of untrained survey staff (his own students) and his averaging techniques for farm size tended to reduce the level of inequality. In the case of Sichuan, for example, Buck concluded that the top 10 per cent of farms owned 24 per cent of land, but proper averaging shows that they owned 39 per cent (Arrigo 1986: 280). Moreover, Buck was determined to prove that inequality was low, irrespective of what the evidence suggested. For him, 'The great pressing need of China is Christianity and education' (Buck 1916, cited in Stross 1986: 111) and China's agriculture needed a technocratic solution rather than extensive land redistribution. As Stross (1986: 187) says: 'Buck was blind to rural problems that were being discussed in his own time. And that blindness sometimes seemed to be almost wilful, in that he ignored problems simply because they did not fit into the models of ideal farm management or land utilization that he had brought with him from the United States.' The National Land Commission survey was little better, carried out as it was by an organ of the government that had concurrently embarked upon a series of military campaigns designed to wipe out the Chinese Communist Party, the only political force in China serious about land reform (Esherick 1981: 407–8). Nor did it help that the 1934 survey excluded the very part of China (the south-west) where the problem of tenancy was most extreme. A much more plausible statement of Chinese realties is that offered by R. H. Tawney (1932: 69).

The theory that agitation is produced by agitators, not agitators by agitation, is among the western doctrines which certain circles in China have absorbed without difficulty. But no reference to communist propaganda is required to explain the no-rent campaigns and peasants' revolts which have taken place in parts of the country. It is surprising, indeed, that they have not been more frequent.

Equally telling is what we know of the operation of Chinese factor markets. There are two problems here, one theoretical and the other empirical. As far as the former is concerned, even if factor markets did work as well as Brandt and others claim, efficient markets in themselves offer no solution to the problem of inequality.[25] As is well known, a continuum of seriatim contingent future markets is needed to ensure the existence of a Pareto efficient allocation of resources. Of course the China of the 1930s fell well short of this ideal, but even if it had not, a Pareto-efficient general competitive equilibrium is compatible with a vast range of distributional outcomes. That is, Pareto-efficient is not the same as socially desirable. This is because inequalities in asset ownership necessarily translate into inequalities of income, no matter how efficient market operation. To put the point more bluntly, the labour power at the disposal of poor rural households was not enough to offset their lack of land and shortage of capital, except in special circumstances.

This theoretical objection is no mere quibble. For although the Chinese land-rental market produced a distribution of farms that was more equal than the distribution of land, the income inequalities that remained were still profound. Even Buck, whose pro-nationalist sympathies are well known, thought that Chinese farms were on average too small and that rents were on average too high. The evidence on rents tends to support this interpretation. The data for 1934 suggest that they averaged around 43 per cent of the value of crops, well above the 37.5 per cent that the Kuomintang deemed to be acceptable when it promulgated the 1930 Land Law (Feuerwerker 1977: 59 and 62). Still, these data are hard to interpret. For example, the 37.5 per cent figure – and many of the other data bandied around in the literature for rental levels – applied only to the main crop. More significantly, the terms of the rental contract varied dramatically and these have a great bearing on how we assess class relations in the Republican countryside. Some tenants were forced to pay a rent deposit (which entailed borrowing), notionally fixed rents were anything but, and it was common practice to expect tenants to pay their rent before the harvest could be collected (which again forced them into debt). Yet other tenants had *de facto* security of tenure, enjoyed rent reductions in years of poor harvests and even received interest from their landlord on their rental deposits (Bramall 1993: 224–32).

The greater burden was probably that imposed by high interest rates. Economic theory tells us that high interest rates in peasant agriculture are in part a reflection of high risk. However, a range of studies on developing countries show that rates owe far more to usurious behaviour than to risk, and that high rates were used by lenders as a means of forcing borrowers to default so that land put up as collateral could be seized (Bhaduri 1973; 1977). Many scholars have concluded that this was very much the case in rural China as well. NARB estimates suggest that 56 per cent of farmers were in debt in 1933, and even Buck cites a figure of 39 per cent. The overwhelming majority of these loans were distress loans: they were used for consumption rather than for investment purposes. Most annual rates of interest varied between 20 and 40 per cent during the 1930s, but rates of up to 200 per cent were by no means uncommon and collateral was routinely undervalued (Feuerwerker 1977: 63–4; Tawney 1932: 62). A 1934 NARB survey found that interest rates above 50 per cent applied to around 13 per cent of loans (NARB 1936. 71). Again, however, we do need to be careful. The rampant inflation experienced in China after 1937 mean that interest rates which appeared to be high were anything but, as inflation depressed the real value of debt very quickly. Many of the loans were supplied by friends and relatives rather than by usurious landlords or moneylenders. Hyperinflation in particular meant that indebtedness was far *less* of a problem during the years after 1937 than during the previous decade. But Tawney's (1932) conclusion is probably the right one for the 1930s:

> No statistics exist as to the indebtedness of Chinese farmers, but all observers are agreed that it is always extensive and sometimes crushing. The peasant's capital is tiny, and his income too small to enable him to save. Towards the

end of the winter, when last year's grain is exhausted, he is often on the verge of starvation, and any unexpected emergency drives his head under water [p. 58] ... It is not open to question ... that rural indebtedness is among the curses of China [p. 62].

To compound the problems faced by Chinese farmers, prices in commodity markets were routinely manipulated by traders with monopsony and monopoly power. Thus the prices paid were low at the time the harvest was collected, but far higher in the run-up to the next harvest. Of course a degree of seasonality was inevitable and was partly indicative of a well-functioning market economy. In rural China, however, seasonal price fluctuation was a device to extract surplus from the peasantry (Tawney 1932: 57). Even at harvest time, the price received by tenants was much lower than that obtained by owners; one Sichuan survey shows a price differential of 22 per cent in 1941 (Buck 1943: 45).

Ultimately, however, it is the enthusiasm with which the rural population greeted land reform and the elimination of usurious interest rates in the 1950s that provides the most compelling support for the view that inequality in the Republican countryside was very high. There is an abundance of evidence – not least in the accounts of the land reform process – pointing to the conclusion that the elimination of the landlord class was wildly popular. In a very real sense, the Chinese peasantry voted with its feet in the early 1950s to reject the structures and institutions which had prevailed in the Republican countryside.

Conclusion

The Chinese economy experienced some development during the Republican period, especially in the Treaty Port economy. A modern industrial sector of sorts had been established by the 1930s, and its output was growing at a rate which was impressive by most standards.

For all that, China was an extremely poor country in 1949, and the economic inheritance of the CCP was severely impoverished. Per capita income was low, and had barely increased over the previous half century. Worse, the growth of modern industry was constrained by the abject performance of an agricultural sector incapable of supplying the wage goods and raw materials required. Indicators of human development gave no cause for satisfaction either. Life expectancy at birth was no better than the figures recorded in Britain in the middle of the previous century, and the overwhelming majority of the Chinese population could neither read nor write. The China of the early 1950s was a land riven by a range of socio-economic inequalities along ethnic, geographical and class lines. And although China had a long coastline, the scope for international trade was to be limited by the American trade embargo.

It was not a very auspicious inheritance, and it inevitably limited what was possible in the short term. That is not to say that China was without economic potential. On the contrary. Its large population provided a vast market which made it possible to exploit economies of scale. And China's per capita natural resource base, whilst undoubtedly inferior to that of many other countries, was by no means small. However, low levels of human capital, the underdeveloped state of infrastructure, the extent of poverty and inequality (which demanded immediate action) and low productivity in agriculture inevitably constrained the pace of economic growth in the 1950s. Of these constraints, it was perhaps inequality of income and wealth that was the greatest, because it forced the new CCP to move quickly and decisively towards a thoroughgoing programme of land reform. This succeeded in addressing the clamour for redistribution but, as we will see below, the creation of a sea of small-scale peasant farms during the 1950s in itself did little to promote the cause of agricultural modernization or industrial development.

Notes

1 Rawski's revisionist economic history is rather similar in its premises. He rightly documents the extent of modern sector development, but the tone and language of the book convey an unmistakable message: the Maoist era was an unfortunate aberration.
2 For an introduction to the Republican economy, see Feuerwerker (1977), Eastman (1988) and Richardson (1999). Great pleasure and profit is to be had from Tawney (1932). For estimates of agricultural output and national income, see Buck (1937) and Liu and Yeh (1965) respectively. For studies of economic growth, see Liu and Yeh (1965), Yeh (1979), Rawski (1989), and Maddison (2001). Useful starting-points for the debates on the link between the socio-economic conditions and the 1949 Revolution are Johnson (1962) and Bianco (1971).
3 The consensus amongst scholars is that the Great Depression of the early 1930s had little real effect on China. However, there is no agreement as to why this was the case. Some, like Brandt (1997), Myers (1989) and Rawski (1989), rule it out by assumption. The monetary shock led to no more than a small and temporary deviation from the equilibrium; prices adjusted very quickly and, as a result, pre-crisis output and employment levels were quickly restored. The monetary shock therefore had no long-run real effects. A variant on this theme is simpler: the shock was too small to have powerful effects. The alternative interpretation sees the Chinese economy as dualistic, comprising a small Treaty Port sector integrated with the world economy, and a much larger unintegrated interior. The external shock badly affected the Treaty Port sector, but not the rest of the economy precisely because of a lack of market integration. See, for example, Wright's (2000) work on the impact of the Depression on the Chinese south-west.
4 Whatever the plausibility of Rawski's all-China estimates, regional studies show that stagnation was by no means universal. For example, the lower Yangzi delta region appears to have done well between 1914 and 1936, enjoying per capita GDP growth over 1 per cent per annum according to one recent estimate (Ma 2006). This was mainly because the delta's economy was increasingly based around industry, which we know was a rapidly developing sector in the Republican era. Manchuria was also little affected by the Depression. There, GDP was growing by 2 per cent per year between 1924 and 1937, and in no small measure this was because Manchuria was a Japanese colony. Fiscal policy in Japan and in many parts of the empire was broadly Keynesian with Prime Minister Takahashi at the helm. The increase in government spending focused on the military sector, but it did have the effect of stimulating economic growth in Manchuria and elsewhere (Wright 2007). Thus overall growth across China was undoubtedly hampered by poor agricultural performance, but those parts of the mainland subject to colonial governance or where modern industry was a large component of the economy undoubtedly fared better than the average. Even some of China's warlords engaged in defence-driven industrialization. Sichuan offers one such example (Kapp 1973).

5 These figures exclude Manchurian production. They were collected in the survey carried out by D. K. Lieu. They exclude much of western China but, as there was little modern industry located there, this is not a significant omission. The general consensus is that these data are reliable (Liu and Yeh 1965: 429).
 6 For a summary of the issues, see Riskin (1987: 18–19).
 7 This type of argument has been famously articulated by Paul Bairoch (1993) as a general explanation for underdevelopment across the Third World.
 8 Maddison (2003: 249–51) offers a good summary of the limitations of the Pomeranz hypothesis.
 9 The best introduction to Chinese rural issues in the 1930s is Feuerwerker (1977); see also Riskin (1987) and Eastman (1988). For a more detailed discussion, see Perkins (1969). For neoclassical treatments, see Myers (1970), Rawksi (1989) and Brandt (1989). For a more heterodox perspective, see Huang (1985, 1990).
10 There were 15 *mu* to the hectare. Note that farms were in general larger in north China because of lower soil fertility, which in turn owed much to differences in rainfall.
11 Conversely, where the industrial sector was both large and vibrant, the overall rate of growth of GDP was quite impressive. The Yangzi delta region around Shanghai provides a good example (Ma 2006). In a sense, the instance of Shanghai reinforces the more general point. It was able to grow rapidly only by relying on external markets and external supplies of raw materials: Chinese agriculture could not meet its needs.
12 We can now be fairly certain about the content of Mao's discussion with Stalin because of the release of the Soviet version of the documents following the collapse of the USSR.
13 The figure for the USSR in 1913 seems particularly high, especially in the light of the data on the structure of the economy revealed in Table 2.2, below.
14 In China's case, I give both the official estimates (published in the 1990s) and the detailed estimates made by Liu and Yeh (1965) on behalf of the US Air Force. The two sets are very similar.
15 For a useful collection of materials on Chinese life expectancy and mortality in the long run, see Lee and Wang (1999: ch. 4).
16 For an up-to-date treatment of Chinese geography, see Veeck *et al.* (2007).
17 The significance of coastal access is thrown into sharp relief by the fact that, even now, there is little real difference in living standards between counties located in the poorest parts of Guangdong (around Meizhou) and counties located in much of upland Guizhou. Provincial boundaries are not as helpful in delineating physical geography as they might be.
18 For a useful introduction to this debate see Little (1989) and Cartier (2002). Two of the leading critics of the Skinnerian approach from a neoclassical perspective are Sands and Myers (1986, 1990). Many scholars have sought to explain the relative underdevelopment of western China in similar geographical fashion, albeit without reference to the Skinnerian macroregional framework (Démurger *et al.* 2002; Bao *et al.* 2002).
19 Over the same period, Sichuan's old industrial centres – such as Nanchong, Neijiang and Suining – deindustrialized as trade along the Yangzi river became much less important. Note that Skinner is only able to reach his core–periphery conclusion by assuming that living standards can be proxied by population density. This produces the result that Chengdu was already prosperous in the 1930s, a finding which is contradicted by much of the evidence. The region had a high population density, but its industrial underdevelopment meant that living standards were comparatively low (Bramall 1993, 2007).
20 The rise of Chengdu continued after 1949 (Bramall 2007). Third Front investment and the construction of railways linking Chengdu and Chongqing, and Chengdu with Baoji

The Chinese economy on the eve of revolution 75

to the north and Kunming to the south changed Sichuan's economic geography for ever, and the Chinese state was instrumental in this process.
21 For a range of perspectives on the impact of the Great Depression, see Brown (1989).
22 Gansu is often thought of as a desert province, but its (relative) prosperity in 1952 owed much to the fact that it had much more arable land per head than the national average. It is agricultural production per head, rather than industry, that explains its relatively lofty position in Figure 2.5.
23 Shanghai of course reinforces the point. Despite the absence of any indigenous resource base, it was a great trading centre and therefore able to satisfy the needs of its industries by means of imports.
24 We have no useful data on inequality within urban China and therefore it is not discussed here.
25 Note that Brandt's work is based upon a handful of surveys carried out by the Japanese in North China. The very fact that they were conducted by the Japanese invaders must call into question their reliability: was inequality after conquest really the same as beforehand?

Part 2
The transition to socialism, 1949–1963

3 Early Maoism, 1949–1955

The Chinese civil war was brought to an end in 1949–50 by the military successes of the PLA (People's Liberation Army) under Lin Biao's brilliant leadership.[1] Beijing surrendered in January 1949, Chengdu (China's last major unconquered city) fell in December and Hainan Island was recaptured in April 1950. PLA troops entered Lhasa in October 1951; it is one of the many ironies of the CCP 'project' that a party committed to eliminating any imperial presence within China was nevertheless determined to preserve its own internal colonies in Tibet, Qinghai, Xinjiang and Inner Mongolia. To be sure, the Chinese empire had still to be completed; Hong Kong, Macau and Taiwan remained to be conquered. Nevertheless, the Han heartland had been regained. And to mark that process, the founding of the People's Republic was declared on 1 October 1949, well before the conclusion of the civil war.[2]

Although military triumph solved one problem, it opened up a more daunting challenge: that of how to develop the economy. In meeting that challenge, the CCP was handicapped in several respects. Many of its veteran cadres had perished in the revolutionary struggle; of those who remained, few had experience of economic management or of government. The Party's base in the populous provinces of south-western China was weak; the heartland of the Revolution during the 1940s was in the north and north-west. This weakness held out the real possibility of provincial separatism. And the very seizure of power by the CCP had won it the enmity of the USA; with that came real limits on China's opportunities for foreign trade.

Nevertheless, the CCP's position in 1949 was one of considerable strength. By completing the nationalist project begun in the 1890s, the Party had won the support of China's middle classes and its revolutionary youth. Industrialists saw in CCP rule the hope of an end to the feckless incompetence and endemic corruption of the Kuomintang. The leaders of the CCP had some experience of economic management from the time they had spent in the Communist base area around Yan'an during the 1940s. They could also turn for advice to Soviet experts, who were available because of China's close alliance with the Soviet Union during the 1950s. And though land reform had won little affection from either landlord or rich peasants, the programme was nevertheless very popular across the Chinese countryside.

Three questions arise out of all this. First, what use did the CCP make of its newly won power? More precisely, what development strategy did the Party pursue in the early 1950s? Second, did economic performance live up the hopes and expectations of the CCP and its supporters? Third, and perhaps most interestingly of all, was the development strategy of the earliest Maoist era sustainable? What might China's destiny have been if the policies of the early 1950s not been cast aside so speedily after the summer of 1955?

Marxist theory and Chinese practice

The CCP viewed the task of developing the backward Chinese economy in the early 1950s through a Marxian lens. But Chinese policy-making was influenced not only by readings of Marx but also by practice in the Soviet Union in the 1920s.

Marx's theory of history

The Marxian theory of history has three distinct strands to it: a description of the nature of society, a description of the evolution of society over time and a theory of transition from one type of society to another.

Society, or what Marx called the social formation, comprised three elements: the forces of production (the sum of technology, capital and the labour force), the relations of production (the pattern of ownership and the structure of incentives) and the superstructure (politics, ideology, culture and law). The base, or economic structure of society, comprised the forces and relations of production, and it in turn determined the nature of the superstructure:

> In the social production which men carry on, they enter into definite relations that are indispensable and independent of their will; these relations of production correspond to a definite stage of development of their material powers of production. The sum total of these relations of production constitutes the economic structure of society – the real foundation on which rise legal and political superstructures and to which correspond definite forms of social consciousness. The mode of production in material life determines the general character of the social, political and spiritual processes of life. (Marx 1859)

Social formations changed over time. Indeed Marx conceived of the evolution of economic systems in a teleological way: all economies would pass from one mode of production to another over time (Box 3.1). Each of these modes of production was characterized by distinctive forces of production (the level of technology) and relations of production (the way in which employment was organized).[3] Slavery was the starting-point, and feudalism, capitalism and socialism were all phases through which the economy would inevitably pass. And these modes of production were distinctive. Although there is a tendency in much of the literature blithely to equate socialism with communism, Marx

Box 3.1 **The Marxian theory of history**

Mode	Forces of production	Relations of production
Slavery	Primitive; little use of capital	Extraction of surplus via slavery. Labour bought and sold at will by slave owners
Feudalism	Under-developed, but increasing use of capital. Agricultural strip farms too small to be efficient	Slow emergence of a mobile urban workforce no longer involved in agriculture. But most peasants tied to the land and under the control of their lord. Peasants and workers made to work by use of force if necessary
Capitalism	Rapid growth of capital. Most forms of production in agriculture and industry mechanized	Workers legally free to move from job to job and no longer coerced into working by force. Incentive systems put in place to motivate workforce. Property privately owned
Socialism	Continued growth of capital stock and technological development	Incentive structures gradually become weaker; wage structure much more egalitarian. Private ownership replaced by collective and state ownership
Communism	Highly-developed technology and an abundance of capital	Private ownership abolished and replaced by public ownership. Income incentives virtually eliminated – incomes distributed according to need rather than work done

himself was careful to distinguish between the two. The distinction is especially clear in his *Critique of the Gotha Programme* (Marx 1875), in which he argued that incentives needed to be maintained in the immediate aftermath of the Revolution and that only in the 'higher phase of communist society' could distribution be on the basis of need rather than work done. Communism was of course the 'end of history'; once communism had been achieved, no further evolution was either necessary or desirable.

Much more controversial was the question of how transition from one social formation to another occurred. It was controversial because this is the most pressing matter of concern for revolutionary parties across the world, and because Marx's writings were rather contradictory on this point. However, the orthodox interpretation on the eve of the Russian Revolution was as follows. The development trajectory of a society, and especially the transition from one social formation to another, was driven by changes in the forces of production. For example, new technologies imported from abroad would bring about changes in the forces of production. That in turn would produce a contradiction between the forces of production and the relations of production. The resolution of this contradiction would ultimately require a process of revolution, whereby the relations of production would change to accommodate the prior change in the forces of production. The superstructure would in turn accommodate itself to the changes in the economic base. In a famous passage, Marx outlined the process of transition as follows:

> At a certain stage of their development, the material forces of production in society come into conflict with the *existing* [emphasis added] relations of production, or – what is but a legal expression of the same thing – with the property relations within which they had been at work before. From forms of development of the forces of production, these relations turn into their fetters. Then comes the period of social revolution. (Marx 1859)

The conventional wisdom amongst Marxist practitioners in the 1920s adhered closely to this interpretation of Marx. Changes within the economic base (the forces and relations of production combined) provided the crucial causal factor in a process of social change, and the nature of the superstructure was determined by the economic base. If the economic base was capitalist, then the state would be controlled by the capitalist class and culture would be geared towards meeting the needs of capitalism; in the words of the Marx of the *Communist Manifesto*, 'all that is solid melts into air'.[4] Marxist orthodoxy thus assumed that, if the economic base could be transformed, then a transformation of the superstructure would be inevitable.

By the 1920s, however, this Marxist orthodoxy was far less compelling to those on the left and to the Soviet leadership than it had been before the Russian Revolution. For one thing, the 1917 Revolution had evidently been brought about by a change in the relations, rather than the forces, of production. Tsarist Russia was far less technologically advanced than (say) Germany, which rather gave the lie to the notion that technological modernization was the motor of history. It was Germany where the Revolution should have occurred. That it did not testified both to the capitulationism of the German Social Democratic Party – which was as eager for war in 1914 as the Kaiser – and to the weakness of any Marxist theory based around the dynamic of the forces of production. Moreover, there were many passages in Marx's own writings that seemed to accept the idea of the primacy of the relations of production in causing social change. The famous sentence in the *Communist Manifesto* declaring that 'The history of all hitherto existing society is the history of class struggles' (Marx and Engels 1848: 34) encapsulates the view that it is this – not trade, population growth or scientific change – which is the decisive engine of social change.[5]

Second, and perhaps most importantly, Marx's writings were practically silent on what to do after the Revolution in circumstances where the forces of production were plainly backward. Should the attention of the Party-State focus on the modernization of the forces of production, or the relations of production? This was in essence the nature of the debate in the Soviet Union in the 1920s. Most economists argued that the forces of production needed to be developed first; this meant that the conditions for agriculture mechanization had to be created, which in turn required the development of industrial capacity. It would be pointless to create large collective farms (and thus abolish private ownership) unless mechanization could be carried out. Transformation of the relations of production would be premature until a transformation of the forces of production had been accomplished.

New economic policy in the Soviet Union, 1921–1928

The answer arrived at by Lenin in the early 1920s was that the modernization of the forces of production should take precedence over changes in the relations of production. In practical terms this led to the implementation of New Economic Policy (NEP) in the Soviet Union between 1921 and 1928. NEP was in essence a compromise between private and state ownership. Farmland remained in private hands, and private trade was encouraged. However, the 'commanding heights' – modern industry and infrastructure – were taken into state ownership.

Soviet NEP was in many respects successful, and it has sometimes been portrayed as a Bukharinist alternative to Stalinism (Cohen 1971).[6] There is admittedly much about Soviet performance in the 1920s which remains uncertain. It is for example very difficult to construct time series data from GDP for the 1920s. However, the critical question is that of how the level of output in 1928 compares with that of 1913. On this matter, Western scholarship has been in full cry for many years; according to the latest estimates, per capita national income had been restored to its 1913 level by 1928, and total national income was around 10 per cent higher (Davies *et al.* 1994: 42; Maddison 2003: 100). In other words, NEP served to pull the Soviet economy out of the nadir of 1921, and virtually succeeded in restoring prewar levels of per capita output. As importantly, the growth of the 1920s had not been bought at a prohibitive social cost.

Stalin held an altogether less positive view of Soviet NEP. Stalin's focus (and that of the planners) was on the inadequate supply of grain being made available to the urban population; there was a widespread perception of hoarding by rich peasants, and official Gosplan estimates suggested that the amount of grain which was marketed outside the villages was only 50 per cent of the prewar norm in 1926–7. But the underlying problem was that of production. Total agricultural production was higher in 1928 than it had been at the prewar peak, but grain production was actually lower (Davies *et al.* 1994: 111 and 285). Whether this was true or not, there is much to suggest that Soviet performance was rather poor. Even official Soviet data put per capita in income in 1928 at only 9 per cent greater than it had been in 1909–13, and a recent Western estimate suggests that there was no increase at all (Davies *et al.* 1994: 41–2).

These factors led to the abandonment of the gradualist NEP approach. Instead, the Soviet Union pressed ahead with collectivization during its Second Five Year Plan (1928–32). The hope was that collectives would allow the exploitation of economies of scale in agriculture and facilitate early mechanization. This in turn would both release labour for use in industry and raise the level of agricultural production. Collective farming would also make it easier to extract surplus from the agricultural sector. At the same time, the planners aimed to accelerate the rate of overall growth by raising the share of investment in GDP.

Chinese practice: gradual transition

China's challenge in 1949 was to decide upon the most appropriate development strategy. In principle, there were three paths open to it. First, it could follow the path taken by American and Britain, and create a genuinely capitalist economy. Second, it could emulate Soviet New Economy Policy as implemented in the 1920s. Third, it could make a more rapid transition to socialism by following the post-1928 Stalinist path taken by the USSR.

The first of these alternatives was never really considered. To be sure, the creation of a capitalist economy would have been true to the spirit of Marx in many ways precisely because the Chinese social formation in 1949 was so primitive. Chinese agriculture was very unsophisticated and could be best characterized as feudal; in fact, slavery persisted in parts of western Sichuan into the mid-1950s.[7] The 'traditional' industry found in urban and rural areas was scarcely less backward. However, China also boasted a modern industrial sector, found principally in Shanghai and in Manchuria. Part, therefore, of its industrial sector was capitalist. The general conclusion reached by the leadership and by scholars was that the Chinese mode of production was characterized by capitalist and feudal elements. In other words, China needed to modernize its technology, expand its capitalist stock and create a free labour market. The implications for economic policy from a strict Marxian perspective were therefore clear: the China of 1949 needed to complete the transition to capitalism before there could be any thought of socialism.[8]

However, the very idea of a protracted transition to socialism was anathema to the Chinese leadership.[9] Capitalism was seen to have failed China in the Republican era. In any case, even if capitalism was capable of generating rapid economic growth, the inequalities which would inevitably occur were antithetical to the entire CCP project. The Revolution had not been won merely to enhance the power of the landlord and capitalist classes. Indeed any attempt to renege on the Party's commitment to land reform and public ownership would have swept the CCP from power before it had even had a chance to accelerate the pace of growth. These considerations made the CCP reluctant to accept Marx's teleology in which capitalism had to precede socialism. Instead, China looked to the Soviet Union, which in 1917 was in some ways similar to China in 1949 in respect of its economic structure. It too was an economy comprising feudal and capitalist elements. Nevertheless, the USSR had still been able to make the transition to socialism by 1932, suggesting that it was possible for China also to make a fairly rapid transition. Indeed the very fact that China had experienced a peasant-led 'revolution from below' – instead of the proletarian-based movement expected by Marx – suggested to Mao and others that the case for a slavish adherence to the teachings of Marx was even less compelling in the Chinese context.

But that conclusion in itself did not resolve the question. The issue for China in 1949 was to decide on which Soviet model to follow: would the cause of Chinese development be served best by adopting the NEP model of 1921–8, or by adopting the post-1928 Stalinist approach?

In fact, the question was easily answered: the case for adopting some form of New Economic Policy in 1949 was overwhelming. For one thing, it was recognized that China, even after the recovery of 1949–52, was much less developed than the Soviet Union in 1913, let alone in 1928. Although the size of the agricultural sector was comparable in the two, Soviet GDP per head was much higher. According to Maddison (2001: 264; 2003: 182 and 184), per capita Chinese GDP in 1952 was only $537 (it was $580 in 1937), compared with the $1,488 recorded in the territories which were to become the Soviet Union in 1913.[10] This meant that the USSR was better able to generate the savings needed to finance the level of investment required to accelerate the pace of growth, and implied that if anything China needed a longer period of transition (and hence slower growth) than the Soviet Union. Second, the CCP leadership was mindful that the Soviet decision to accelerate the pace of transition in 1928 led to a devastating famine and as many as 10 million deaths (Conquest 1986).

The policy conclusion drawn from all this was that China would be best served in the 1950s by copying Soviet NEP.[11] There was in fact a high degree of unanimity within the CCP as to the need for a gradualist 'general line' during the transition period. As has been convincingly demonstrated in the writings of Teiwes (1993; Teiwes and Sun 1999; Teiwes and Sun 1993), the notion that China during the 1950s was characterized by a 'two-line' struggle between the radicals centred around Mao and conservatives led by Liu Shaoqi, Deng Xiaoping and Deng Zihui (head of the Central Rural Work Department) is not supported by the evidence.[12] To be sure, there were shifts in policy-making. The most noteworthy was the decision to abandon gradualism in July 1955 and press ahead with rapid collectivization. But all this occurred simply because Mao changed his mind. Even in March 1955, he was calling only for 33 per cent of cooperatives to form collectives under the slogan 'stop, shrink and develop', which amounted to a reduction in the number of collectives (Teiwes and Sun 1993: 9). To be sure, there were local conflicts, but elite agreement was the norm (Selden 1988: 67). Only after the summer of 1955 was there disagreement, and even then Deng Zihui was very much in a minority.

Emblematic of this commitment to gradualism was Mao's declaration that transition would not be completed until the end of the Third Five Year Plan, a view he reiterated as late as the March conference of the CCP in 1955:

86 *Chinese Economic Development*

> Our general objective is to strive to build a great socialist country. Ours is a big country of 600 million people. How long will it really take to accomplish socialist industrialization and the socialist transformation and mechanization of agriculture and make China a great socialist country? We won't set a rigid time-limit now. It will probably take a period of three five-year plans, or fifteen years, to lay the foundation. (Mao 1954)

So it transpired: the hallmark of Chinese economic policy-making before 1955 was gradualism. Early collectivization was ruled out. The nationalization of industrial assets proceeded slowly. Material incentives were retained in order to motivate the workforce. Even the preamble to the 1954 constitution emphasized gradualism:

> From the founding of the People's Republic of China to the attainment of socialist society is a period of transition. During the transition, the fundamental task of the state is to bring about, step by step, the socialist industrialization of the country and to accomplish, step by step, the socialist transformation of agriculture, handicrafts, and capitalist industry and commerce. (Central Committee 1954)

In fact, there were even significant continuities between the pre- and post-1949 regimes. The Nationalists had drawn up three-, four- and ten-year plans in the 1930s and had committed themselves to a postwar development strategy based around extensive state ownership of the industrial sector and an expansion of

---

Box 3.2 **Pivotal moments in Chinese development during the early 1950s**

	Event	Significance
1950	Agrarian Reform Law	Set out the principles to be adopted in carrying out land reform
1953	First Five Year Plan	Outlined the main aims of economic development (only formally adopted in 1955)
1954	Constitution of the People's Republic of China drawn up	Explicit commitment to gradual transition
1955	'On the Question of Agricultural Cooperation' (speech by Mao Zedong, 31 July 1955)	Launch of rapid collectivization. Marks abandonment of gradualism

heavy industrial production modelled on the approach adopted in Germany (Kirby 1990).[13] Moreover, many of the planners engaged in drawing up the First Five Year Plan had gained much of their knowledge and experience whilst working for the National Resources Commission during the 1930s and 1940s. To be sure, 1949 was a climacteric, and the programme of land reform carried out between 1947 and 1953 marked a sharp break with China's Nationalist past. But these changes such not blind us to the continuities across the 1949 divide.

Industrial development

A hallmark of the industrialization of Britain and Japan was the early development of light industry; only later did heavy industry start to grow. It was for this reason that Rostow famously advised developing countries during the 1960s to follow the path of 'textiles first' in formulating their industrialization strategies.

By contrast, China (along with India) followed the Soviet approach in giving early priority to heavy industry. Chinese industrial policy in the 1950s was unusual in two other respects. First, there was a definite commitment to the nationalization of private enterprises. Part of this was ideological, but it was also rooted in a belief that state enterprises would invest more than those owned by the private sector. Second, some attempt was made to alter the geography of Chinese industrial production, and in particular to shift it away from the coast and towards the interior.

The prioritization of heavy industry

Chinese industrial production in the early 1950s was underdeveloped. The industry that China possessed in the early 1950s was orientated towards the production of consumer goods; only 26 per cent of factory output was made up of producer goods, and consumer good production dominated the handicrafts sector (Liu and Yeh 1965: 66). Admittedly the structure of Chinese industrial output had changed very considerably in the 1930s and 1940s, reflecting Kuomintang-initiated modernization programmes, the impact of war and the development of Manchuria under Japanese colonial rule. In 1933, net value-added in Chinese factories accounted for 24 per cent of manufacturing production, but by 1952 the share was up to 34 per cent. Over the same period, the share of producer goods in factory output had climbed to 42 per cent (Liu and Yeh 1965: 66). The port city of Tianjin had the highest share of secondary sector output in GDP of any provincial-level administrative jurisdiction in 1952 (54 per cent). However, Shanghai and Liaoning province dominated industrial production; the two together accounted for about 28 per cent of national secondary sector value-added (SSB 2005a).

Nevertheless, the industrial foundations of the Chinese economy were weak in 1952. Only in Manchuria, the coal-producing province of Shanxi and in Chongqing (because of wartime industrialization) were producer good industries important.[14] Net value-added in Chinese manufacturing stood at about 11 billion *yuan* in 1952, but of this only about 3.2 billion *yuan* (28 per cent) constituted output of producer goods. Outside the main cities and Manchuria, modern industry barely existed; the industrial towns of Wuxi and Suzhou were very much the exception rather than the rule. Provinces such as Jiangsu and Guangdong, now centres of Chinese industry, were dominated by agriculture and by commerce, not by industrial production. And away from the enclave of Chongqing, the centre of Kuomintang resistance to the Japanese invading forces and which experienced a degree of defence industrialization as a result, modern industry in western China was conspicuous by its absence. It could hardly be otherwise given the underdevelopment of the railway network in the western provinces in 1949; a short coal-carrying line in Chongqing aside, there was not a single railway in Sichuan – a province the size of France.

The case, then, for industrial development was overwhelming. The issue for the planners was whether to follow the Rostowian 'textiles first' strategy or to copy the Soviet Union and to give priority to heavy industry. Two factors came into play here: economic and military.[15] As far as the economics was concerned, there certainly was a case for focusing on light industry. The data on relative labour productivity by industrial sector make this clear (Wu 2001). In 1952, labour productivity in Chinese manufacturing (measured using purchasing power parity GVA) stood at about 3 per cent of that in the USA. In heavy industry, the ratios were even lower – 1 per cent in metal products and 1 per cent in machinery. However, productivity in China's clothing and apparel sector was 8 per cent of that of the USA, and it was much higher still in tobacco (31 per cent) and textile products (93 per cent). The emphasis that the First Five Year Plan placed on heavy industry therefore amounted to a very substantial resource misallocation in the short term.

Nevertheless, there is a case for investment in heavy industry in the early stages of development. This is because the pay-off to investment in producer goods ('machines producing machines') in terms of GDP growth can be demonstrated under certain assumptions to be higher in the long run than investment in the production of consumer goods.[16] Moreover, the case for giving priority to heavy industry is more than just theoretical. Japan had been advised to take the 'textiles first' path in the 1950s by the World Bank, but that advice was ignored. Taiwan and South Korea also deviated from the 'textiles first' development strategy in the 1960s and 1970s. It is by no means fanciful to argue that the successful development of all three reflects their deviance (Johnson 1985; Amsden 1989; Wade 1990). These theoretical issues are discussed further in Chapter 12.

However, defence considerations were far more important than economic factors in dictating a shift in the pattern of investment towards heavy industry during the early Maoist period. The experience of the PLA in fighting against the Kuomintang in the later stages of the civil war, and the stunning display of US firepower directed against Chinese troops during the war in Korea made it plain that military security required the creation of a heavy industrial base capable of supplying the weaponry required for modern warfare. In this regard, China's industrial base was doubly deficient. For one thing, it was simply too small. The secondary sector contributed only 21 per cent of GDP and 7 per cent of employment in 1952 (SSB 2005a: 7 and 10). And second, as we have seen, too much industry was geared to the production of consumer goods.

These economic and defence imperatives mandated that, although China's First Five Year Plan emphasized the importance of a *gradual* transition to socialist ownership, it focused on the *rapid* development of heavy industry: 'To implement socialist industrialization is the central task of our transition period and the road to socialist industrialization is the development of heavy industry' (Wang 1955: 11).[17] China's strategy was thus about building dynamic comparative advantage – just as it was in Japan and South Korea during the 1960s. Industrialization built around the expansion of the textile, food processing and garment industries, no matter that it accorded with the 'textiles first' strategy later to be extolled by Rostow, was simply not a viable option. The development of heavy industry had to be the priority.

This desire to develop heavy industry was given concrete expression in the First Five Year Plan in two ways. First, consumption was squeezed in order to make resources available for investment. In the early 1930s, the investment share stood at about 5 per cent of GDP but by the mid-1950s this had gone up to 14 per cent (Yeh 1968: 510).[18] This was not a remarkably high figure, either by late Maoist standards (as we shall see) or by the standards of many countries in the postwar era; investment rates of over 30 per cent were normal across East Asia in the 1950s and 1960s. It suggests that the CCP strategy squeezed consumption, but not by an alarming amount. The very fact that consumption and calorie intake both rose during the early 1950s suggests that the type of strategy implemented in China was certainly sustainable.

Second, the composition of output shifted firmly away from agriculture and towards heavy industry. The share of modern producer goods in net domestic product (1952 prices) had risen from 1.4 per cent of net domestic product in 1933 to 4.4 per cent by 1952. By 1955, it had gone up to 7.6 per cent, and it reached 11.6 per cent by 1957 (Liu and Yeh 1965: 66). The official data show the post-1949 trend even more clearly (Figure 3.1): heavy industrial production grew at about double the rate of the light industrial sector (24.8 per cent compared to 12 per cent per year) between 1952 and 1957.

Of course China still had far to go in the mid-1950s in terms of restructuring its industrial sector. Not only was the producer goods sector still comparatively weak, but the process of rural industrialization had barely begun. Nevertheless, rapid expansion had taken place and the foundations of modern industry had been laid in many parts of central and western China.

Nationalization

The nature of industrial ownership – often seen as the hallmark of a socialist economic system – changed only slowly after 1949, but the rising share of the state is nevertheless apparent. As Table 3.1 shows, the share of state-owned industry in gross output value stood at about 26 per cent in 1949. Most of this industry had been confiscated from the Japanese government in 1945, and in turn inherited

90 Chinese Economic Development

Table 3.1 Shares of gross industrial output value by ownership

	State	Collective	Joint State – private	Private	Individual
1949	26	1	2	49	23
1950	33	1	2	38	26
1951	35	1	3	38	23
1952	42	3	4	31	21
1953	43	4	5	29	19
1954	47	5	10	20	18
1955	51	8	13	13	15
1956	55	17	27	neg	1
1957	54	19	26	neg	1

Source: ZGTJNJ (1984: 194).

Note
Per cent; the figures may not add to 100 in some cases because of rounding. GVIO measured at 1952 prices. The meanings of state and private ownership need little explanation, but the nomenclature is otherwise confusing. Individual (geti) is a term often used in Chinese publications; it refers to small-scale private enterprises. As for collective enterprises, these were originally handicraft industries which rarely made use of mechanical power and which were taken into state ownership. In terms of their method of operation, they became increasingly similar to state-owned enterprises. Note that the Chinese data on both the handicraft and the collective sector in the 1950s are fraught with ambiguities (Donnithorne 1967: ch. 8). Finally, joint state – private (gongsi heying) companies were 'capitalist enterprises working with raw materials supplied by the government and selling the manufactured goods to the latter or acting as dealers in state goods' (Xue 1981: 27).

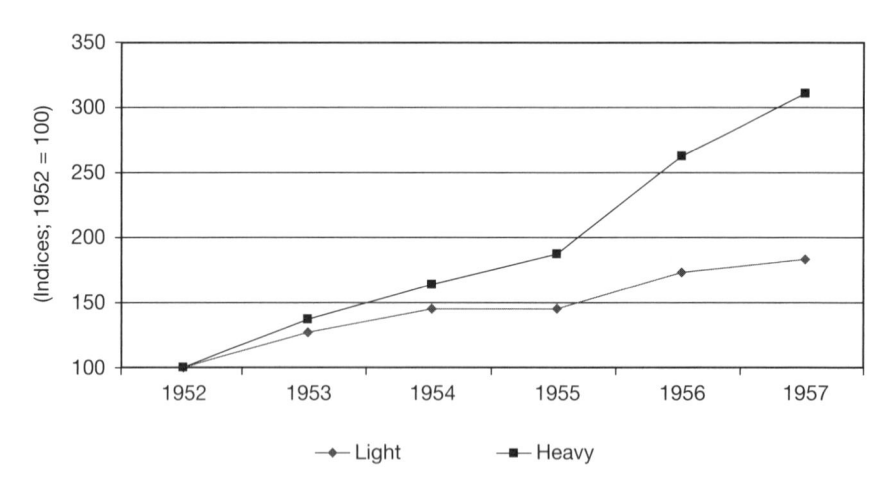

Figure 3.1 The growth of light and heavy industrial output, 1952–1957 (Source: SSB (1990a: 10).)

Note: Data are for gross industrial output value at 1952 prices.

from the KMT by the CCP. If collective and joint enterprises are included in the state total, that gives a state share of only around 30 per cent.[19]

However, the trend is the most interesting aspect of these data. Although the share controlled by the state climbed, the private and individual sector together still accounted for close to 40 per cent of output in 1954. Even if it is agreed that the state sector was more modern and generated more value-added per unit of output than the other sectors (implying that GVIO data understate its true importance), it is still apparent that state enterprises constituted only one component – albeit the largest – of the industrial sector. In fact, the total output of both private and individual enterprises more than doubled between 1949 and 1953, so that the rising share of the state sector was due more to a faster rate of growth than it was to asset seizure (ZGTJNJ 1984: 194). Indeed, as Donnithorne points out, a woollen mill continued to operate under British management until 1959, and those private owners whose assets were acquired by the Chinese state continued to receive dividend payments (and then interest paid at a rate of between 3.5 and 5 per cent) during the late 1950s and into the early 1960s as compensation. Perhaps as many as 250,000 former capitalists were in receipt of such payments in the mid-1960s (Donnithorne 1967: 146–7). Whatever else it was, the expansion of state ownership in China fell well short of a policy of nationalization without compensation.

Industrial outcomes

There is no doubt that China's industrial policy drive led to significant increases in production; gross value-added in the industrial sector grew by around 19 per cent in real terms between 1952 and 1957.[20] Not surprisingly, the output of producer goods like steel, coal and cement grew very swiftly; steel production, for example, grew at the remarkable rate of 28 per cent per year between 1952 and 1955. But the output of consumer goods – like cigarettes, cloth and sugar – also grew quickly by pre-1949 Chinese standards (Table 3.2). Of course the 1949 base level of output for all these goods was low because of the ravages of war, but the pace of recovery and the expansion of output beyond its previous peak testify to the scale and effectiveness of the industrialization programme.

However, as Figure 3.2 shows, the process of industrial advance was deficient in several respects. First, the rate of expansion was anything but smooth. Although Chen Yun and other CCP members looked back on the 1950s as a Leninist golden age from their vantage point of the early 1980s, Chinese industrialization was fitful. Although growth was rapid in 1952, much of this was merely recovery from the trough of war and civil war. Moreover, the impressive growth rates of 1954 and 1956 were offset by the rather unimpressive rates recorded in 1955 and 1957. The problem was that Chinese growth in the 1950s was very unbalanced, and therefore marked year-on-year fluctuations were inevitable. The reason for this was variation in rates of investment; as Figure 3.2 shows, the slow growth of industrial output in 1955 and 1957 was directly associated with much slower growth of investment in those years. These investment fluctuations in turn reflected concerns over consumption, which was being squeezed by high investment rates. In trying

Table 3.2. Growth of industrial production, 1949–1955

	Cloth	Sugar	Cigarettes	Coal	Electricity	Steel	Cement
1949	1890	200	1600	32	4300	158	660
1950	2520	240	1850	43	4600	610	1410
1951	3060	300	2000	53	5700	900	2490
1952	3830	450	2650	66	7300	1350	2860
1953	4690	640	3550	70	9200	1770	3880
1954	5230	690	3730	84	11000	2230	4600
1955	4360	720	3570	93	12300	2850	4500
Growth rates:							
1949–5	17	27	17	19	21	53	36
1952–5	5	16	10	13	19	28	17

Source: SSB (1985: 43–50).

Note
Growth rates are per cent per annum. Data are in thousand tonnes except for cloth (million metres), cigarettes (thousand cases) and electricity (million kwh).

to balance the twin imperatives of consumption and rapid growth, policymakers veered between conservatism and rashness during the 1950s and so industrial output fluctuated markedly.

Second, and despite the industrial growth of the early 1950s, China was still very far from being industrially developed even in 1957. In that year, secondary sector output accounted for only 30 per cent of GDP, and the employment share

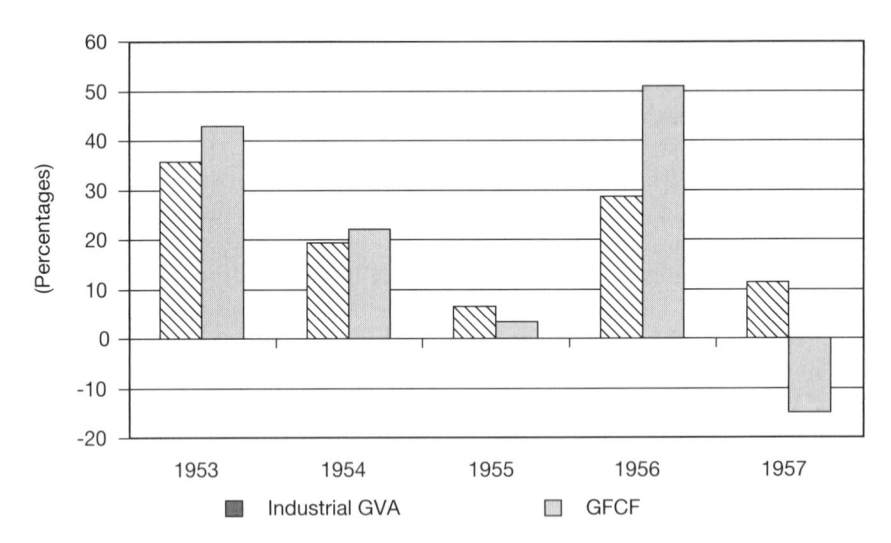

Figure 3.2 Growth of industrial GVA and gross fixed capital formation (GFCF), 1952–1957 (Source: SSB (2005a: 7, 12 and 13).)

Note: Industrial GVA growth is measured at current prices; changes in gross fixed capital formation are measured at current prices.

was much lower at a mere 9 per cent (SSB 2005a: 7 and 9). By comparison, well over 50 per cent of Britain's workforce was employed in industry in the mid-1950s. Britain of course needed to export manufacturing products in vast quantities to service its wartime debts and to finance agricultural imports. For all that it is a remarkable fact that around 30 per cent of Britain's male workforce was employed in industry as early as 1800 (Crafts 1985: 62–3). By postwar British standards, China had barely begun to industrialize in 1955.

One further qualification is important. Although light industrial output did rise during the 1950s, it is clear that the production of consumption goods was indeed squeezed by the emphasis given to the producer good sector in investment allocation. The most obvious indicator of this is the supply side crisis of 1955, when light industrial output was no higher than it had been in 1954. In fact, the production of key consumption items such as cloth and cigarettes actually declined. This stagnation meant of course a decline in per capita light industrial output because of continuing population growth. The CCP's response was to try to engineer an acceleration in the growth rate. Buoyed by the success of collectivization, the first (or small) leap forward was launched; this aimed to achieve the First Five Year Plan targets by the end of 1956, a year ahead of schedule. Mao's own role in all this was crucial; he pressed in the autumn of 1955 for an acceleration in the pace of growth, and he seems to have been supported in this by other leading figures in the CCP (Teiwes and Sun 1999: 21–3). But it quickly became clear that this was not feasible, and in April 1956 Zhou Enlai and Chen Yun initiated a campaign to 'oppose rash advance' (*fanmaojin*).[21] As a result, industrial growth was more balanced during 1956 and 1957 than it had been in 1955 – or was to be in 1958.

In retrospect, the First Five Year Plan was relatively successful in terms of achieving its objectives. The rate of industrial growth was very fast, and (as will be discussed below) the geographical distribution of Chinese industry became less uneven. Nevertheless, industrial development was not smooth, and in following the Soviet model, China's industrialization neglected rural areas. All this was recognized in two of Mao's key speeches: 'On the Ten Great Relationships' (25 April 1956) and 'On the Correct Handling of Contradictions among the People' (27 February 1957). These heralded a much more ambitious attempt to accelerate the growth rate and to deal with the contradictions in industrial development during the 1960s, which focused on rural industrialization.

Agricultural policy

Despite the emphasis on industrialization that was the hallmark of the 1950s, the difference between the prewar Nationalist vision of economic development and that realized during the First Five Year Plan during 1953–7 was much more in terms of agriculture than in terms of industry.

Before 1949, both CCP and Nationalists had agreed on the importance of state ownership of key industries and the need to accelerate the pace of growth via higher investment. On the means by which agricultural development was to be promoted, there was no such agreement.[22] The KMT strategy was one of modernization of technology and rationalization of farm management.[23] The CCP did not disagree with either imperative, but saw the redistribution of land ownership as the necessary first step. Accordingly, land reform was swiftly implemented in regions conquered by the CCP after 1947, and by 1953 the process has extended across the whole of China.[24]

Land reform

Land reform centred around the seizure of the property of landlords by newly-created Peasants' Associations and adhered to the principles codified in the Agrarian Reform Law of 1950 (Bramall 2000b). The first step was to assign class status to every family in the village. Once this had been done, 'surplus' land and property was transferred from landlords, lineage associations and rich peasants to the middle peasants, the poor peasants and to landless labourers. The Party's aim was to create an agricultural sector characterized by small-scale family farming, to end the exploitation (via rents, high interest rates and low wages) which it saw as endemic during the Republican period, and to raise farm output by putting a halt to absentee landlordism. Article 1 of the 1950 Law set out the general principles:

> The land ownership system of feudal exploitation by the landlord class shall be abolished and the system of peasant land ownership shall be introduced in order to set free the rural productive forces, develop agricultural production and thus pave the way for new China's industrialization.

Three general points need to be made about this process. First, the land reform of 1947–53 was rather more moderate than the earlier land reforms presided over by the CCP. It was not intended to be an egalitarian redistribution of land. Land reform had been extremely radical in 1946–7, when the aim was to achieve an egalitarian distribution of land. This 'left adventurism' was led by Liu Shaoqi and Bo Yibo; it provides an example of the type of opportunistic behaviour that has characterized the behaviour of the right within the CCP since 1949. Liu, for example, advocated radical land reform in 1946–7 and was an ardent promoter of the Leap in 1958, before becoming a convert to family farming in the early 1960s. Liu and his supporters have long tried to cloak such opportunism in theoretical robes, but Liu's very vacillation from the extreme left to the extreme right exposes his opportunism for what it was. Deng's behaviour was similarly unprincipled. He too was a powerful advocate of the Great Leap Forward before coming over to family farming in the late 1970s and early 1980s. In fact, it was Mao who put an end to the extreme egalitarianism of 1945–6 on the eminently sensible grounds that redistribution alone would not solve the problem of poverty, because the level of production was too low.

By the late 1940s, CCP policy had moved on. As Liu Shaoqi explained in a speech in May 1950, the purpose of land reform was to redistribute land and property but simultaneously to preserve the rich peasant economy. In fact, the explicit aim of CCP policy was to create a rich peasant economy, the argument being that a rich peasantry was needed to spearhead growth. Equalization of land holdings, it was argued, would both destroy incentives and lead to the creation of farms that were too small to be viable. Mao set out this approach in June 1950:

> [T]here should be a change in our policy towards the rich peasants, a change from a policy of requisitioning their surplus land and property to one of maintaining the rich peasant economy in order to facilitate the early rehabilitation of rural production. (Mao 1950: 29)

Thus the Chinese land reform was 'a wager on the strong', rather than a policy designed to guarantee an equal per capita level of landownership. The Party was conscious of the need to raise output during the transition era and egalitarian redistribution was not seen as a viable solution. Land reform was therefore very much in accord with Marx's analysis of what was possible in the early stages of transition. The 1950 Agrarian Reform Law was in fact less radical than that of 1947. To be sure, extensive redistribution took place, but the rich peasant economy was left largely untouched so as to ensure that those economies of scale which did exist in agriculture could be exploited, and to avoid alienating the key group of farmers (Hinton 2006: 62–5). The ultimate aim was of course to create collective farming, but in the early 1950s the necessity of a long transition period was recognized. One result of this determination to preserve the rich peasant economy was that neither money-lending nor the leasing out of land was banned. Furthermore, less than half of all arable land was redistributed, and in the main the rich and middle peasants lost very little. In fact, the amount of land held by the average rich peasant was at least twice the amount held by the average poor peasant after the reform. More generally, the effect of land reform was to reduce the share of the top 10 per cent of the rural population in income only marginally; its share fell from 24.4 per cent in the 1930s to 21.6 per cent in 1952 (Roll 1980; Selden 1988).

Second, the process of land reform was bloody. Mao himself admitted that around 700,000 counter-revolutionaries were either executed or beaten to death during 1950–2 (MacFarquhar *et al.* 1989: 142). The total may well have been higher because it is not clear that landlords were included in this total. Furthermore, those who were classified as landlords (and their families) retained this class status until the late 1970s and were discriminated against in terms of educational opportunity and numerous other ways. For all that – indeed to some extent because of that – land reform and everything that went along with it was remarkably popular in the Chinese countryside.[25]

Third, the newly established rich peasant economy was seen as a transitional stage on the road to full-scale collective farming. In order to raise farm productivity, it was widely believed that mechanization was essential, and that it in turn would require the creation of large farms. As such farms could not be privately owned – such a step would amount to a recreation of the pre-1949 system – collective farms would have to be created, and that was regarded as a step too far in the early 1950s because of the likely adverse incentive effects attendant upon the abolition of private property. Policy in the aftermath of the land reform therefore focused on the promotion of voluntary cooperation between households, rather than compulsory collectivization. Thus the early 1950s saw the growth of mutual aid teams and lower stage agricultural producer cooperatives. The main aim here was to raise agricultural output by pooling tools, livestock and land.[26] And the emphasis was on voluntarism as far as possible. One indication that this was in fact the case is the slow growth in the number of lower stage cooperatives (Table 3.3). Even in July 1955, well after the completion of land reform, only 14 per cent of rural households were members of a cooperative.

Nevertheless, the Party was largely happy with this slow pace of transition towards collectivization in the early 1950s. In fact, under the banner of *fanmaojin* (oppose rash advance), the pace of transformation was deliberately slowed on a number of occasions between 1952 and 1955, and indeed cooperatives were even dissolved where their formation were felt to be premature. Even as late as the spring of 1955, there was a consensus in the upper echelons of the Party that the pace of institutional transformation was fast enough (Teiwes and Sun 1993: 6).

Agricultural performance

Assessments of the impact of land reform, and of agricultural performance in the early 1950s more generally, vary considerably. Some have argued that land reform was largely unnecessary on the grounds that landlordism (in the sense of exploitation of the rural poor) was virtually non-existent, and that traditional rural institutions were progressive and growth-promoting. One such account is that offered in the context of Hebei province by Friedman *et al.* (1991).[27] However, it is difficult to take seriously this sort of idealization of the Republican village. In fact, the majority of scholars have argued that land reform both improved the distribution of income, and accelerated the pace of agricultural growth. One of the most optimistic appraisals is that offered by Griffin *et al.* (2002: 310) who claim that 'Radical land confiscation and redistribution did not slow the pace of

Table 3.3 The growth of agricultural cooperatives in China, 1950–1955 (percentage of peasant households by membership)

	Mutual aid teams	*Cooperatives*
December 1950	10.7	neg
December 1951	19.2	neg
December 1952	39.9	0.1
December 1953	39.3	0.2
June 1954	n/a	2.0
December 1954	58.3	10.9
June 1955	50.7	14.2

Sources: Walker (1966: 17 and 35); SSB (1959: 29); Su (1980).

Note
Much of the secondary Chinese literature uses inconsistent months, especially when making comparisons between 1955 and 1956.

agricultural growth. On the contrary.' For Griffin and his collaborators, small-scale family farming was the ideal solution to China's agricultural problems; one of Mao's biggest mistakes, they argue, was to press ahead with collective farming after 1955 instead of simply preserving family farming.

However, the evidence does not really support the notion that agricultural performance was impressive in the early Maoist era. To be sure, there is some support for the notion that the land reform had a positive impact. The data on agricultural value-added show the growth rate rising from 0.8 per cent per annum between 1914 and 1936 (or 1.6 per cent if Rawski's optimistic estimate is accepted) to 3.6 per cent per year between 1952 and 1955 (Bramall 2004: 114). As the agricultural growth rate also accelerated after the completion of decollectivization in the early 1980s, it is not hard to see the basis for the Griffin *et al.* claims about advantages of small-scale peasant farming.

It is hard to draw clear causal inferences from the Chinese data. First, there is considerable evidence of output underreporting in the early 1950s, when the new statistical system was still in the process of being set up. Thus Liu and Yeh (1965) question the reliability of the official data for the early 1950s on the grounds that the CCP simply relied upon the reporting system which had been devised before 1949 by the NARB. It is generally accepted that the pre-1949 NARB estimates substantially underestimate true output; C. C. Chang (1936), who created the system, admitted as much.[28] In part this was because they were based upon sown area data which were unreported for tax avoidance purposes. But the NARB data were also problematic because they understated rice yields, the key farm product. Given that the CCP did little to change the system of crop reporting during 1949–52, there can be little doubt that the official data understate true production, and therefore overstate the growth rate that was achieved between 1952 and 1957. As the data for 1955–7 are relatively reliable, the effect of comparing output in 1952 with output in 1955 or 1957 is to set up a wholly invalid trough-to-peak comparison which exaggerates the true rate of growth. Liu and Yeh (1965) attempt to correct for these underreporting problems by producing a revised series for grain production of their own (Table 3.4).[29] It shows a much more modest rate of growth of grain production, and this in turn implies a slower overall rate of growth of agricultural production. According to Liu and Yeh (1965: 54, 132 and 140), the true overall growth rate between 1952 and 1955 was only about 1.6 per cent – well below the official SSB estimate of 3.6 per cent per annum.[30]

Second, it is not very clear as to why the creation of small-scale family farms in the wake of land reform would have increased output. The idea that family farming is growth-promoting rests heavily on the notion of an inverse relationship between farm size and land productivity. This is the theoretical basis for the claims made by Griffin *et al.* (2002), and by many others. However, the evidence to support this claim is very doubtful in the Chinese case, and the theory itself is also extremely dubious.[31] Redistributing land in a poor agricultural economy may be egalitarian, but it is far from obvious that it is growth-promoting (Bramall 2000b, 2004). Even if we accept that the growth rate accelerated, some of the growth of the 1950s was simply recovery from a low base rather than a consequence of land reform.

Table 3.4. Alternative estimates of grain production in the early 1950s (million tonnes; grain includes soya and tubers)

	Original NBS estimate	Revised/current NBS estimate	Liu and Yeh estimate	Weather
1949	113.2	113.2	n/a	–
1950	132.1	132.1	n/a	–
1951	143.7	143.7	n/a	–
1952	154.4	163.9	176.7	good
1953	156.9	166.8	180.4	average
1954	160.5	169.5	184.5	bad
1955	174.8	183.9	186.4	good
Growth, 1952–5 (per cent per annum)	4.0	3.7	1.8	

Sources: NBS (1959); SSB (2000: 37); Liu and Yeh (1965).

Agricultural policy debates in the mid-1950s

Perhaps the most important piece of evidence to support the view that agricultural performance in the 1950s was poor was the CCP's decision to accelerate the pace of institutional change in 1955. The apparent inability of the rural economy to generate rapid growth was blamed by Mao (and many others in the CCP) on the slow pace of institutional development, as exemplified by the very low numbers of peasants living in cooperatives in the mid-1950s (Table 3.3).[32] This paucity of large farm units (cooperatives) prevented the exploitation of economies of scale, hampered the mobilization of the workforce and delayed farm mechanization. By July 1955, Mao had had enough.[33] He argued that the pace of growth in rural China had to be accelerated by moving rapidly towards full collectivization, and that rural conditions were ripe for such an advance:

> A new upsurge in the socialist mass movement is imminent throughout the countryside. But some of our comrades are tottering along like a woman with bound feet and constantly complaining, 'You're going too fast.' … [p. 389] … On the question of developing the co-operatives, the problem now is not one of having to criticize rashness. It is wrong to say that the present development of the cooperatives has 'gone beyond the real possibilities' or 'gone beyond the level of political consciousness of the masses' … although the standard of living of the peasant masses since the land reform has improved or has even improved a good deal, many are still in difficulty or are still not well off, there being relatively few who are well off, and hence most of the peasants show enthusiasm for taking the socialist road [p. 402]. (Mao 1955)

More than anything, Mao argued, an acceleration of agricultural growth was needed to make possible an adequate pace of industrialization. According to him (Mao 1955: 404–7), agricultural modernization was needed in order to supply necessary raw materials to industry, to raise peasant living standards directly and to provide the surplus necessary for industrialization; it was wrong to treat agriculture and industry as independent sectors.[34] And there was general agreement within the Party that collectivization was the right vehicle for agricultural modernization. Deng Zihui disagreed with Mao over the pace of transition, but not with the notion that collectivization was a necessary precondition for mechanization and modernization (Howe and Walker 1989: 204–6). The stage was therefore set for the rapid transition to collective farming which occurred during 1955–6 (see Chapter 4, below).

Trade policy

The pattern of China's trade during the 1950s was dominated by its poor relations with the United States, and its close relationship with the Soviet Union. The US imposed a trade embargo on China in December 1950 which was even tougher than that imposed on the USSR: 'it placed a total embargo on its trade with the PRC; controlled all of Beijing's foreign assets; prohibited US carriers from calling at PRC ports, and all US-flag, air, or sea carriers from loading or in any way transporting goods destined for the country. It also denied bunkering facilities to all vessels that had called at Chinese ports' (Foot 1995: 53). Not surprisingly, trade rapidly dwindled and the trade returns show a figure of precisely zero for imports from the USA in every year between 1953 and 1971. China's involvement in the Korean War intensified the problem because it led to the imposition of a UN trade embargo on strategic exports in May 1951. Despite US pressure, however, trade between Western Europe and China never entirely ceased. It began to rise again after the trough of 1952, and by 1957 the UK, France and West Germany were together supplying some 9 per cent of Chinese imports (ZGTJNJ 1981: 355–67). Nevertheless, China's poor international relations meant that total imports accounted for about 5 per cent of GDP in the early 1950s, little different from the figure in the 1930s (Yeh 1979: 98; SSB 1999: 3 and 60), though by no means an unusually low figure for such a large country.

Close relations with the Soviet Union were the central feature of Chinese trade in the 1950s; imports from the USSR contributed 65 per cent of all imports at their 1955 peak. A one-year trade agreement was signed in July 1949, and a $US300 million loan was agreed, to start from January 1950. A further loan of $130 million was agreed in 1954 (Eckstein 1964: 138–39 and 149). Most importantly of all, contracts were signed whereby the Soviet Union agreed to build 156 industrial projects; the first 50 were agreed during 1949–1952, 91 more followed in May 1953 and a further 15 in October 1954. As Reardon (2002: 55) rightly notes, this made possible 'one of the largest transfers of technology in history'. These projects were to provide the foundation for China's new programme of industrial development, which had as its long-run aim economic independence from both the USA and the USSR (a resolve strengthened by Khrushchev's denunciation of Stalin in 1956). This approach did not lead to any marked rise in the trade share in GDP, but the pattern of trade altered significantly towards the importation of producer goods. Many of the 156 Soviet-led projects focused on the production of producer goods; there were 25 new coal mines, 25 new power stations and 24 new machine-building plants. Revealingly, only three of the 156 were geared towards the production of light industrial goods (Wang 1994: 550–8). In fact, means of production accounted for over 90 per cent of all imports in every year between 1953 and 1960 (ZGTJNJ 1981: 354). And these imports were crucial. As Eckstein (1964: 137) says: 'the single most important statistic is the statement that 50 per cent of Mainland China's machinery and equipment requirements for the First Five Year Plan had to be imported.'

China's post-1949 trade strategy yielded two sets of benefits. First, the very fact that trade was much more geared towards meeting the needs of industry rather than consumption – trade after all was an integral part of the Plan – meant that the multiplier effects were considerably greater than during the 1930s, when imports were either of consumer goods or machinery used for the production of consumer goods (such as cotton looms and spindles). The pace of technological diffusion therefore accelerated. In addition, and second, the process of technological diffusion was greatly assisted by the location of a significant number of the new plants in the Chinese interior (Wang 1994: 550–8). The spatial impact of China's foreign trade during the 1950s was therefore altogether greater than it had been in the 1930s.

For all that, the positive effects of foreign trade on the Chinese economy were less than they might have been. The central problem was that the Soviet Union was providing loans, rather than aid. These loans therefore had to be repaid. The People's Republic did receive substantial inflows from overseas Chinese; the total inflow amounted to $600 million in total between 1950 and 1954 (Reardon 2002: 59–60). However, these dwindled during the 1950s (partly because of US pressure). Accordingly, Soviet loans had to be repaid by Chinese commodity exports, principally food and raw materials. And therein lay China's problem. The development of rubber production in Hainan and in Yunnan was not perhaps a course that China would have chosen, not least because of the environmental damage caused and the fact that conditions were far less suitable than in (say) Malaysia (Shapiro 2001). Moreover, the diversion of a significant fraction of food production to the USSR intensified the consumption squeeze on the Chinese peasantry (Walker 1984). The USSR helped China during the 1950s, but the cost of its assistance was considerable.

Assessing China's development record in the early 1950s

Chinese economic policy in the 1950s was, as we have seen, designed to achieve a gradual transition to socialism. Land reform preserved the rich peasant economy, early collectivization was avoided, the process of nationalization proceeded slowly and trade with 'capitalist' countries was welcomed when it was possible. As such, it represents something of a middle way between a capitalist development strategy and Soviet-style socialism practised between 1928 and the end of the 1980s. Indeed the parallels between China's development course in the 1950s and Soviet New Economic Policy in the 1920s are striking. How successful then was the Chinese strategy?

Data problems

In answering this question, we are hampered by the quality of the data for both the early 1950s and the Republican period (which makes it hard to make proper comparisons). As far as agriculture is concerned, the first usable data we have date from the early 1930s in the form of the massive *Land Utilization* survey carried out by J. L. Buck and his team during 1929–33, and the systematic *Crop Reports* collected by the National Agricultural Research Bureau from 1931 onwards.[35] The industrial data are rather more sporadic, but the 1933 industrial census provides a useful starting-point (Feuerwerker 1977; Rawski 1989). A great deal of data was also collected on parts of western China during the Second World War, when Sichuan province was the centre of Nationalist resistance; many of these sources are given in Bramall (1993). Population data before the (relatively reliable) 1953 census are, however, almost wholly unreliable, and the devastating impact of the period of war and civil war between 1937 and 1949 make backward projection from 1953 very problematic. All this makes it very difficult to estimate prewar GDP, though a number of attempts have been made (Liu and Yeh 1965; Yeh 1979; Rawski 1989; Brandt 1989; Maddison 2003; Wang Yuru 2004).

After 1949, the process of statistical collection began to improve, but it was a slow process (Liu and Yeh 1965: 40–2; Yue 1990). A new State Statistical Bureau (SSB) was established in August 1952 (Yue 1990: 38) and, crucially, China's first modern population census was carried out in 1953.[36] However, it was a number of years before reasonably good quality data on agriculture were being collected. As Xue Muqiao (the head of the SSB) and Zhou Enlai (the Prime Minister) both admitted, the quality of the agricultural data as late as 1954–5 was very poor (Liu and Yeh 1965: 46). Moreover, as Liu and Yeh rightly point out, the tendency in much of the Western literature to regard the 1957 data as especially reliable is open to question. The process of *collection* was by then relatively good, but there was increasing pressure on cadres to use the data to show that China was making excellent progress.

The difficulties involved in creating a new statistical system meant that the data available for the 1950s are much less complete than we should like. One consequence is that we have no proper GDP or national income data for pre-1952, giving only a three-year interval of data on which to assess early Maoist economic performance.[37] More significantly, it also made it extremely difficult for the leadership of the CCP to assess the development strategy adopted during the 1950s – which in turn made it easier for Mao to argue in 1955 that the strategy needed to be changed.

Economic growth and material living standards

The official GDP data suggest an overall growth rate of close to 9 per cent per year (at 1952 prices) between 1952 and 1955, or about 6 per cent per head when adjusted for population growth (SSB 1999: 1 and 4). Other estimates of GDP suggest a considerably lower growth rate (Table 3.5). Nevertheless, the GDP data

102 Chinese Economic Development

Table 3.5 Estimates of GDP growth, 1914–1955

Period	Real growth rate (per cent per year)	Constant price set used
1914/18–31/6		
Yeh	1.1	1933
Rawski (preferred)	1.9	1933
Rawski (high)	2.5	1933
1952–5		
Official	8.6	1952
Official	6.9	1978
Liu and Yeh	4.0	1933
Liu and Yeh	5.1	1952
Maddison	4.5	1987

Sources: Rawski (1987: 330); Yeh (1979: 126); Liu and Yeh (1965: 82); SSB (1999: 4); Maddison (1998: 157).

Note
Rawski provides three sets of estimates which he refers to as low, preferred and high, reflecting different sets of assumptions.

suggest that China's performance during the first few years of Communist rule was much superior to its record during the Republican era. Even if we accept the most optimistic estimates of growth suggested by Rawski for 1914/18–1931/6, there is no doubt that the growth rate was higher between 1952 and 1955.

International comparisons are a little less clear, but largely in China's favour. To be sure, its growth rate was less fast than that achieved in Japan during the 1950s. Furthermore, China did no better than the USSR under NEP between 1921 and 1928, which is in some ways the best comparison. Just as Soviet per capita output in 1928 had barely regained its 1913 peak, so Chinese per capita GDP was still a little below its 1937 level in 1955 (Davies *et al.* 1994: 42; Maddison 2003: 100, 182, and 184). But early Maoist China outperformed both Taiwan and South Korea. Its performance in terms of both GDP growth and human development was significantly better than that of India. And compared with sub-Saharan Africa, China was in an altogether different league.

More difficult to assess is how China performed relative to its potential in the early Maoist years. In one respect, China certainly handicapped itself; the war in Korea not only cost lives but diverted investment away from the civilian sector at a time when capital was extremely scarce. Moreover, Chinese support for North Korea led to the imposition of trade sanctions by the very European powers which could have eased China's development path. Had China avoided its Korean entanglement, the growth rate and human development record would both have been considerably better.

As for more direct measures of short-run living standards, the scattered data which are available point to a clear increase in per capita living standards. If we consider first the period 1949 and 1954, data for Zhejiang province, for example, peasant consumption (unadjusted for inflation) increased from 51 *yuan* in 1949 to

91 yuan in 1955 (ZJJ 1997: 354). As Vermeer (1982) rightly notes, the surveys on which these data are based are decidedly problematic in terms of both their spatial coverage and sampling procedures; the first semi-plausible national survey did not even take place until 1954. It therefore makes more sense to rely on production data to measure income, and these data show a definite increase. Data on this indicator published by the Central Rural Work Department in 1957 show a rise from 55 yuan in 1949 to 85 yuan in 1955 (Zhongguo shehui kexueyuan 1998: 1145–6). Schran (1969) also reaches a positive conclusion.

More interesting is the direct evidence on the long-run trend – that is, the change in material living standards between the 1930s and the mid-1950s. Here the evidence is difficult to assess, but it certainly does not point to any significant rise. Some of the evidence is admittedly positive. Rawski (1989: 336), for example, estimates that per capita GDP in 1952 was already about 18 per cent higher than it was in 1931–6. Although the Liu and Yeh (1965: 82) estimates using 1933 prices show a slight decline down to 1952, the data for the mid-1950s show a clear rise over the 1930s irrespective of which set of prices one uses. Some of the provincial-level data also show an increase in material living standards over time. According to the survey data used by Reynolds (1981: 228), the incomes of Shanghai workers rose by between 16 per cent (1930 prices) and 37 per cent (1956 prices) between 1936 and 1956. Over the same period, the average number of hours worked per day fell, suggesting an even more substantial increase in income per hour worked. As for the rural sector, the average income (at constant prices and after tax and production costs) of Hunan's peasants rose by 19 per cent. Grain availability per person (after procurements and sales, and including grain needed for seed and animal feed) rose from 238 kg in 1936 to 268 kg even in the poor harvest year of 1954 (HNNY 1959: 70 and 93).

But Hunan was by no means the norm. As previously noted, Maddison (2003: 182 and 184) has Chinese per capita GDP in 1955 below its level in 1937. As for the data on per capita consumption, the trend is even less positive. In Shanxi, peasant consumption levels changed very little between 1936 and the mid-1950s; consumption of grain and pork appears to have been lower (Vermeer 1982: 8).[38] Liu and Yeh's data show that per capita consumption even in 1957 was lower than in 1933, irrespective of which prices are used to value it. This, for them, was 'the real cost of the Communist investment program' (Liu and Yeh 1965: 79). The rise in the investment share was simply crowding-out consumption.

Human development

China's record on human development was rather better than its record on GDP growth (Table 3.6). Banister (1987: 80–3) argues, no doubt correctly, that the official population data understate mortality especially amongst infants. Yet the mortality picture changes little whether one uses her estimates of the crude death rate or the official figures; the fall in the rate between 1949 and 1955 is a massive 40 per cent. Much of the decline was brought about by the reduction in infant mortality. To be sure, some of the mortality decline was simply a reflection of

Table 3.6. Human development indicators, 1949–1955

	Crude death rate (official) (per 1,000)	Crude death rate (banister) (per 1,000)	Official infant mortality rate (per 1,000 live births)	Primary school enrolments (million)
1949	20.0	38.0	177	24.4
1950	18.0	35.0	175	28.9
1951	17.8	32.0	154	43.2
1952	17.0	29.0	133	51.1
1953	14.0	25.8	122	51.7
1954	13.2	24.2	112	51.2
1955	12.3	22.3	105	53.1

Sources: SSB (1999: 1); Banister (1987: 352); RKTJNJ (1991: 537); ZGJYNJ (1985: 1021).

the ending of the civil war. Nevertheless, the very fact that the rate continued to fall after 1952 indicates that genuine progress was being made. Much of this was because of improvements in preventive medicine: inoculation against infectious diseases, public health campaigns and the training of midwives all played crucial roles. Better nutrition also played a role. Piazza's (1986: 77) estimates of calorie intake show a rise from 1,742 kcals per day in 1950 to 2,232 kcals in 1955. This upward trend is probably misleading for the same reasons that the trend in grain production is misleading. Food production in 1950 is underestimated in the official data; it is hard to see how the population could have survived with per capita food availability of only 1,742 kcals per day. In fact, the fall in mortality was due more to the redistribution of food consumption from the rich to the poor as a result of land reform than to any rise in the average.

Still, we should not exaggerate China's achievement in terms of mortality during the early Maoist era. Most of the mortality reduction occurred during 1949–52 and reflected little more than the effects of the restoration of political stability. Progress thereafter was very slow. In fact, life expectancy at birth in 1955 was still only forty-five years (Banister 1957: 352), much higher than the twenty-five-year norm recorded in the 1930s but still well short of what might be called impressive.[39]

The Chinese educational system also expanded in the early Maoist era. By 1955, primary-school enrolments had reached over 50 million, double the 1949 figure, and around 3 million students were being graduated every year, compared with barely half a million in 1949. Over the same period, the number enrolled in lower middle schools rose from 800,000 to 3.3 million, and from 200,000 to 580,000 at upper-middle-school level (ZGJYNJ 1985: 1001 and 1021).

However, these were not spectacular increases. Primary-school enrolments stagnated after 1952, and the very fact that the illiteracy rate was still as high as 78 per cent in 1956 (Pepper 1996: 212) shows just how far China still had to travel. Much of the problem resulted from the reluctance of educational officials to sacrifice quality in favour of quantity, as we will see in Chapter 6. And the State Council contributed to slow enrolment growth with its 1953 instruction to slow down the pace of expansion (Han 2000: 24). Thus low numbers of students per class, small numbers of classes per school and restrictions on overaged children enrolling all worked to hold down the rate of expansion (Pepper 1996: 192–7). So too did entrance tests and tuition fees (Han 2000: 25–6). Furthermore, it was argued that the needs of industry placed a premium on the provision of educated urban workers; this meant that the expansion of education in the countryside needed to be carefully controlled. One consequence was an actual fall in educational spending in many counties. In Jimo county (Shandong), spending declined from 789,000 *yuan* in 1953 to 721,000 *yuan* in 1956 (Han 2000: 24).[40] As Han (2000: 34) says, policymakers had a clear choice between expanding rural education and increasing the quality of urban schools still further; in the early 1950s, they chose the latter: 'The lack of will to improve the rural education was the problem, as the education reform during the Cultural Revolution was to demonstrate.'

In short, the early Maoist development model delivered only fitful progress in terms of educational expansion and mortality reduction. Achievements there certainly were, and China's record was by no means a bad one. Nevertheless, these were wasted years, and a growing perception thereof on the left of the Party set the stage for the more radical solutions which were to be delivered in the late 1960s.

The distribution of income

The CCP assumed power in 1949 committed to reducing the disfiguring social and economic inequalities of the Republican era. It had made progress along these lines by actively implementing rent-reduction programmes in Communist base areas during the 1930s and 1940s. To what extent was it successful on the national stage?

Land reform and income inequality

We saw in Chapter 2 that the prewar level of income inequality is a matter of conjecture. It is, however, beyond question that the 1947–53 land reform led to a significant reduction in inequality. A direct comparison between inequality in 1951–2 (when the bulk of land reform had been completed) and the early 1930s (based on Buck's data) shows the rural Gini falling from 0.33 to 0.22 (Roll 1980). In the process, the share of the top 20 per cent of the population in rural income declined from 42 per cent in the 1930s to 35 per cent in 1952, whereas the share of the bottom 20 per cent rose from 6 to 11.3 per cent (Roll 1980: 76). Admittedly the source from which the 1951–52 Gini is derived is problematic (Li 1959). We are forced to draw inferences about total income from data that cover crop income only, and the survey was published in the middle of the Great Leap Forward, a fact sufficient in itself to make us doubt its reliability.

Nevertheless, the notion of a sharp decline in inequality brought about by land reform is so amply confirmed by village-level studies and provincial data that only the magnitude of the decline is really in doubt. The data given for Zhejiang

Economic Development

situation before and after land reform are typical. The landholdord class were reduced from about 8 *mu* per head to a little over hereas the average holding of landless peasants rose from 0.2 to rich peasant holdings declined only slightly (Zhongguo shehui 1992: 412).[41] This was the pattern across the whole of China, and it testifies to the way in which the land reform process worked to redistribute land from landlord to poor peasant whilst preserving the essence of the rich peasant economy.[42] One clear result was improved nutritional levels for the rural poor, and this undoubtedly contributed to the decline in mortality that occurred during the early 1950s.

Much more controversial, both then and since, is the trajectory of income inequality after the completion of land reform. The land reform process itself did not eliminate inequality: far from it. As we have seen, it preserved the rich peasant economy, and no attempt was made to grapple with the thorny issue of spatial inequality. However, the real concern for the CCP was not so much the static distribution of income in 1952 but the evolution of rural income over time. Was land reform no more than a once and for all redistributive process which left in its wake the conditions which would ensure that the polarization of the pre-land reform era was all but certain to re-emerge?

Mao's view on this is well known:

> As is clear to everyone, the spontaneous forces of capitalism have been steadily growing in the countryside in recent years, with new rich peasants springing up everywhere and many well-to-do middle peasants striving to become rich peasants. On the other hand, many poor peasants are still living in poverty for lack of sufficient means of production, with some in debt and others selling or renting out their land. If this tendency goes unchecked, the polarization in the countryside will inevitably be aggravated day by day. (Mao 1955: 411–12)

In essence, Mao's assessment was the traditional Leninist position; in a market economy, the differentiation of the peasantry was bound to proceed apace. As such, Mao's stance needs to be distinguished from the Chayanovian view of peasant agriculture, which has it that differentiation is demographic: incomes fluctuate in line with changes in household labour power, and households are able to avoid permanent poverty by having more or fewer children, and by intensifying their labour inputs in a process sometimes described as self-exploitation. From a Chayanovian perspective, therefore, inequalities in traditional agriculture reflect not entrenched class positions but temporary demographic factors (demographic differentiation).[43]

By contrast, much of the literature has accepted the findings of the 1954 national survey, which was published in 1957 (Nolan 1988; Selden 1988). This survey shows that the gap between rich and poor peasants in terms of consumption was still considerable in 1954. For example, rich peasants were on average consuming about 50 per cent more pork per head than poor peasants. However, the *time* trend in terms of land cultivated showed an unambiguous narrowing of differentials (Table 3.7). Most significantly of all, there is no evidence of any re-emergence of landlord power. Even the data on 'distress' sales of land collected by Chen Boda – Mao's own secretary and the man charged with 'cleansing' the Party's Rural Work Department of its capitalist tendencies in the late summer of 1955 – suggested a decline rather than an increase during the early and mid-1950s. For Nolan and Selden, this lack of any tendency towards polarization reflected the policies implemented in the aftermath of land reform – rent controls, access to subsidized credit via credit cooperatives, restrictions on private sales of both land and agricultural produce and the unified purchase and supply system of grain quotas and fixed prices introduced in November 1953. One also might argue that the very fact that such an anti-Maoist set of results was published in the middle of the 1957 anti-rightist movements testified strongly to the veracity of this report.

However, these results are open to a variety of interpretations. For example, the sharp increase in the differential between rich and poor peasants in terms of draught animal use is marked, and the same is true for many other agricultural implements, e.g. carts. Given that access to these inputs was as important as access to land, it is certainly not impossible to take a more Maoist view of these results. Moreover, even if we accept that the data show a decline in differentials, it is moot as to whether quite so much faith should be placed in the results of a single survey. Although it was comparatively large in scale (covering 15,432 households – SSB 2000: 3), the survey was highly selective in terms of the villages which were chosen for inclusion.[44] Moreover, as Vermeer (1982: 5–11) points out, the primary purpose of the 1954 survey was to show that the living standards of poor peasants had improved since 1950, and therefore it is not entirely surprising that the survey

Table 3.7 Differentials in the Chinese countryside, 1954

	Consumption per head, 1954		Use of agricultural inputs			
	Grain (kg)	Pork (kg)	Arable land (mu per household)		Draught animals (per 100 households)	
			Land reform	1954	Land reform	1954
Poor peasants	177	3.7	12.5	15.9	46.7	50.0
Middle peasants	169	4.9	19.0	23.7	90.9	110.4
Rich peasants	206	4.7	25.1	31.1	114.9	184.1
Former landlords	181	3.6	12.2	12.8	23.2	51.3
Average	187	4.6	15.3	15.8	64.0	75.5

Source: Zhang (1987: 160–1).

Note

All the data are taken from the 1954 rural income survey carried out by the SSB. The figures for arable land refer to land managed (not owned) per household in *mu*. Draught animal data refer to animals used per 100 households. Grain consumption data seem to exclude grain used for animal feed and seeds.

supplied precisely this evidence. More generally, it also needs to be said that it is hardly surprising that the rich peasant class does not emerge as especially rich. They had been stigmatized almost as much as former landlords during the land reform process – most were seen as a necessary evil which would disappear once transition was complete – and it would have taken a remarkable act of bravado to declare to a income surveyor a high per capita income level. Given that the 1954 survey was based around self-reporting of income from memory, such underreporting was almost bound to go unchecked.

The other point to note is that the 'high tide' of 1955 did not reflect some deliberate decision to ignore the findings of the 1954 survey. For one thing, only preliminary results from the 1954 survey were available to the CCP leadership before July 1955, because the survey was only completed in August of that year. And even if the full report had been available, the situation in 1954–5 was very fluid. In fact, Mao perceived the rural situation to have changed quite considerably between 1954 and July 1955 (when he called for the pace of collectivization to be accelerated); even as late as early 1955, as we have seen, Mao's vision was not especially radical. One factor at work here in influencing Mao was the evidence showing the emergence of a new class of upper middle peasants who by 1955 had an average income which actually exceeded that of rich peasants.[45]

Perhaps more importantly, there were political considerations to take into account. For if collectivization was to be achieved, the circumstances had to be right. Even if inequality was not yet extreme in the summer of 1955, there was a case for acting if political conditions were ripe. And there is much to suggest that they were. Although 1954 had been marked by extensive flooding in Hunan, Hubei and Anhui, the state had been slow to respond to the crisis by reducing grain procurements (Walker 1984: 59–60). By contrast, the weather was altogether better in 1955, and it may have been this above all else that made the peasantry much more favourably disposed to collectivization – as the reports reaching Mao certainly attested – than they had been in 1954. There were also rural opinions to consider, and on this point the evidence suggests a hardening of attitudes towards the rich peasant economy in 1955. As Shue (1980: 214) says, the raft of post-land reform policies made it impossible to become truly rich in the countryside, but there was nevertheless growing hostility towards a rich peasantry which, by the mid-1950s, was perceived to have outlived its usefulness. As a result, the 1955 drive for collectivization was far from unpopular. According to Shue (1980: 332):

> Some analysts have regarded the 'high tide' as a betrayal of the peasantry, which had been promised a gradual transition ... As it is analyzed here, however, Mao accurately perceived the precariousness of the shifting balance of power in the villages. The peasant constituency for a swifter transition was clearly in place; the demand for it was voiced by a restless village cadre force. ... The undignified speed of the 'high tide' is not proof of what one visionary could do to disorient a whole national economy. It indicates rather that many cadres at the bottom found in Mao's go-ahead an answer, if only a temporary one, to their most vexing problems.

The likelihood is therefore that Mao and other members of the CCP thought of polarization much more in terms of peasant attitudes – and in particular their attitude towards the survival of the rich peasant class and emergence of well-to-do middle peasants – than in terms of 'objective' economic conditions as measured by income inequalities.

In sum, the evidence suggests that the early Maoist period was one marked by considerable success in reducing intra-local inequalities across China. Land reform had not led to the elimination of inequalities in China's villages, and there is considerable evidence that inequality was increasing in the mid-1950s. Ultimately, however, collectivization was driven by political considerations rather than by any notion of income stratification; there is nothing to suggest polarization in the Chinese countryside in 1955.

Spatial inequality

The CCP also attempted to reduce spatial inequality during the early 1950s, and in this sphere it seems to have met with modest success (Figure 3.3). To be sure, the population-weighted coefficient of variation for per capita GDP at the provincial level was a little higher in 1957 (0.68) than it had been in 1952 (0.62). However, the data for 1952 provide a distorted picture, because economic recovery from the civil war was much more incomplete in the cities than in the provinces. If

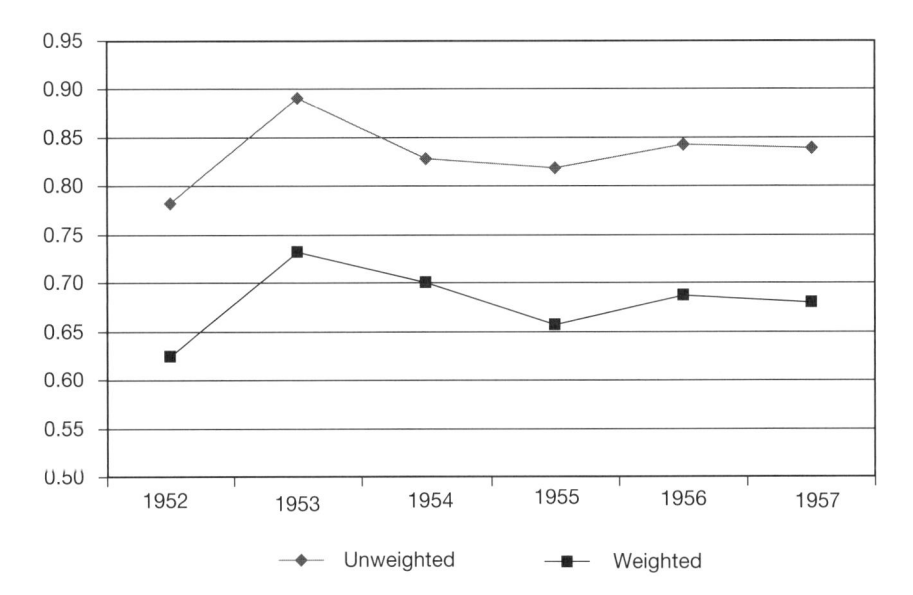

Figure 3.3 The dispersion of provincial GDP per capita, 1952–1957 (Source: SSB (2005a).)

Note: The weighted coefficient of variation is calculated using the population of each province and metropolis as a weight. Accordingly, the high per capita GDP of (say) Shanghai has less impact on the weighted coefficient because its population was comparatively small. This results in the weighted coefficient of variation being smaller in every year than the unweighted coefficient.

instead we compare 1953 with 1957 (or with 1955), the trend in both weighted and unweighted coefficients of variation was downwards.

Two factors were at work in preventing any rise in spatial inequality. First, agricultural performance was much better than it had been in the 1930s; accordingly, China's (predominantly rural) provinces were less disadvantaged. Second, the First Five Year Plan deliberately emphasized the industrial development of central China as much as it did the modernization of China's traditional industrial centre in Manchuria. Liu and Wu (1986: 209) summarized the logic:

> With due consideration for the possibility that the imperialist countries might unleash a war of aggression against our country, and with a view to changing the uneven development of China's industries, energetic efforts were made to build industries in the inland provinces during the First Five Year Plan period.

Take the example of the 156 industrial plants built with Soviet assistance. To be sure, Manchuria claimed the lion's share, receiving 50 of the 104 civilian projects (Wang 1994: 550–8). Of these, three were particularly large: the Number 1 Automotive Works at Changchun (production started in 1956), the steel plant at Wuhan (where production finally began in 1962) and the massive new steel complex at Anshan (which began production in 1960). Nevertheless, many of these plants were built inland rather than in the coastal provinces; the cities of Wuhan, Baotou, Luoyang, Lanzhou and Taiyuan emerged as important industrial centres as a result. And although central China benefited most, the western provinces were not neglected.[46] Sichuan, for example, received two electricity generating stations. Gansu received no less than seven plants, as the CCP determined to develop it as a centre for steel and chemical production. Shaanxi also received seven; four machine-building plants were started in Xi'an. To facilitate this process of industrialization, a number of new railway lines were constructed, of which the most important were the Longhai east–west line linking Jiangsu and Gansu, and the two lines in Sichuan, linking Chengdu with the Longhai line and connecting Chengdu with Chongqing (China Handbook Committee 1984). But most significant was the neglect of the coastal region in the First Five Year Plan. Shandong, Jiangsu, Shanghai, Zhejiang, Fujian and Guangdong received not a single plant between them, a clear signal that the former Treaty Port economy was to be subordinated to wider developmental goals. The decision also made sense in that these provinces had few raw materials, and were strategically much more vulnerable.

Nevertheless, spatial inequalities persisted, nowhere more so than in rural China. The data on differences in per capita income in the aftermath of land reform show this very clearly. To be sure, there were class-based inequalities aplenty; the average rich peasant in any given Chinese region was earning at least double the income of the average poor peasant. However, as Table 3.8 shows, spatial inequalities were considerably greater; the gap in average income between regions was in the order of six to one, far greater than the gap within any given region.

The case, therefore, for a more thoroughgoing attempt to narrow spatial

Table 3.8 The distribution of income by class and by region, 1951–1952 (income per capita; kg of grain equivalent)

Region	Average	Rich peasants	Middle peasants	Poor peasants	Landlords
1	900	1650	1000	750	750
2	625	1150	700	500	500
3	450	800	500	380	380
4	350	625	385	300	300
5	250	450	275	210	210
6	150	270	165	125	125

Source: Li (1959: 136).

Note
This spatial categorization was drawn up for tax purposes; the 'regions' identified here had in common only their average level of income.

inequalities in the Chinese countryside was strong. The First Five Year Plan had done something to check the growth of the coastal provinces, but more was needed. This persistent inequality was to be one of the motivating forces behind Mao's speech 'On the Ten Great Relationships' (1957), which set out the desirability of closing the income gap between China's regions.

An assessment of economic performance, 1949–1955

China's economic record between 1949 and 1955 was impressive in many respects. GDP growth was much faster than during the 1930s and 1940s. The worst of the inequalities which had disfigured the Republican countryside had been eliminated by means of land reform. And, though Mao was articulating a widely held view within the Party in July 1955 in contending that polarization was a genuine problem in many of China's villages, it is evident that inequality was much lower than it had been in the 1930s.

Nevertheless, China's development record in the early 1950s was by no means outstanding. Inequality had been sharply reduced, but rural poverty remained extensive. In essence, the problem here was low agricultural productivity, which both constrained farm incomes and prevented the development of rural industry. At root, the problem here was that China had reached its arable frontier (in contrast to say much of Latin America). By dint of a tremendous effort and the expansion of multiple cropping, China was able to increase its cultivated area from 98 million hectares in 1949 to 110 million hectares in 1955 (SSB 2000a: 21). But this was more or less the limit. Cultivated area peaked in 1957 at 112 million hectares and thereafter declined; the only place where there was significant scope for expansion of cultivated area was in Heilongjiang, and this was offset by losses (as a result of erosion, transport and urban construction) elsewhere. Even with increases in multiple cropping, it proved impossible to increase sown area beyond the level of 159 million hectares reached in 1956 (MOA 1989: 34). The scope for traditional agricultural growth was thus almost at an end.

Furthermore, China's record in terms of human development was rather disappointing. To be sure, mortality rates were considerably lower than they had been in the early 1930s, but this reduction owed far more to the one-off effects of income redistribution and the restoration of peace than to improvements in the system of preventive health care. As noted in the Introduction, it is certainly arguable that life expectancy is the best single criterion by which to measure development, and by this measure the China of the 1950s fared quite poorly.

The other issue is of course whether China before 1955 was living up to, or falling short of, its potential. In one sense, the CCP faced fewer challenges in the early Maoist era than it did after the Great Leap Forward. For one thing, it had a great deal of popular support, much of which evaporated after the great famine of 1958–62. Given that level of support, policy-making could have been more radical than it turned out to be. For another, China's close relations with the USSR blessed it with considerable scope for trade, and facilitated technology transfer in a way which was not possible after the Sino-Soviet split.

On the other side of the coin, however, we should not understate the constraints on Chinese development. For one thing, China was a very poor country. According to Maddison's (2006b) estimates, per capita real GDP in China in 1953 was only $552, less than half the figures for South Korea ($1,072) and Taiwan ($1,142). That limited the scope for investment, and also meant that much of its investment had to go into basic infrastructure. It would not have been easy for China to emulate the development strategies pursued in the 1960s in these two countries. In addition, skilled manpower in 1949 was very limited, making it hard to develop industry at a faster pace than that which had already been achieved; rapid rural industrialization was especially difficult in the absence of skilled workers. Moreover, many of China's mineral resources were only beginning to be explored, much less exploited, the early 1950s. The scope for breakneck industrial expansion based around the use of these resources was simply not there in the early 1950s – not least because of the underdevelopment of China's transport infrastructure. China in principle enjoyed the advantages of backwardness in 1952, but it lacked the crucial social capabilities needed to exploit that notional advantage. Furthermore, there is no doubt that it was hard to raise agricultural productivity in the short run given the constraints previously noted. China could have improved its economic performance by avoiding involvement in the Korean War. But the economy was probably operating at close to its potential during the years between 1949 and 1955. It is hard to imagine an alternative development strategy which would have led to a big improvement. If we ask the question 'Was the Great Leap Forward really necessary?', the answer must surely be no.[47]

Yet in accepting that Chinese short-run economic performance was close to potential, it needs also to be recognized that the CCP did little to expand that potential in the short run. It is in that sense that questions remain as to the wisdom of the early Maoist development strategy. For one thing, the limits to extensive growth in agriculture could have been circumvented by a combination of labour mobilization (to build irrigation networks) and technological modernization. To be sure, the use of chemical fertilizer was uncommon even in the West in the

1950s and China lacked the industrial capacity to produce it. Moreover, the mechanization of farming would have done little to increase yields, and, though it would have freed labour for use in irrigation projects and in the development of rural industry, the mechanization of agriculture was simply not a realistic proposition in the early 1950s given the other claims upon industry.

Early collectivization is another matter. Much debate continues in the context of China as to the effects of collective farming (see Chapter 8). The debate is unlikely to be resolved, not least because the debate on Soviet collectivization – which has been going on for much longer – continues unabated. For example, Hunter and Szyrmer (1992) claim that it reduced GDP in 1940 by around 30 per cent, whereas Allen (2003: 164 and 166) argues that it brought about a small net increase. Nevertheless, it is worth pointing out that the case for collective farming was much stronger in China than in the Soviet Union because of the potential for increasing rice yields and rice sown area by means of the expansion of irrigation. Collectivization in China would have allowed a much more effective mobilization of female labour, and farm labour more generally during the winter slack period. This labour could have been used both to expand the irrigated area and to create the rural industries needed to supply modern inputs.[48] Had collectives been created earlier – it surely would have been possible to have extended the land reform campaign in this direction given the experience already acquired before 1949 – it would have brought forward the date on which both mechanization and irrigation would have been possible. Of course the gains from collectivization would have been long run; there was no easy short-run solution to the problem of slow agricultural growth. The scope for extensive growth was almost at an end, but the preconditions for intensive growth based around the modern technological package of water, chemical fertilizer and high-yielding varieties – irrigation networks and modern industry – would not be in place until the mid-1970s. Nevertheless, the failure to collectivize early was a missed opportunity.

Second, it is also arguable that more could have been done to expand human capital, reduce mortality and to develop infrastructure. The CCP could, for example, have made more of an effort to expand rural education. The intrinsic gains from literacy are self-evident, but there were big instrumental advantages to be had in the 1950s as well. A more literate and better educated workforce would have been healthier. More education for women would have brought down fertility rates in China's more prosperous provinces (though perhaps not in poorer regions). Rural industry could have been developed more quickly in the presence of a larger pool of skilled labour. And rural income inequalities would have been reduced still further. All this could have been achieved by raising the overall investment rate. The official data show that fixed investment accounted for only 15 per cent of GDP on average during 1953–5 compared with 21 per cent during 1964–6, when per capita GDP was little different (SSB 2005a: 13). Had the investment rate of the mid-1960s been achieved during the early Maoist era, there is no doubt that growth of output and capability expansion would have been faster.[49]

In short, and for all the progress made across China during the early 1950s, it is clear in retrospect that the development strategy of the early Maoist era was not ambitious enough. The Great Leap Forward was certainly not the answer, as the next chapter will show, but the fact remains that the First Five Year Plan was not the route to prosperity. The early 1950s were not a Leninist golden age but rather a missed opportunity.

Notes

1. Lin was undoubtedly China's most brilliant general; he was recognized as such even by those who castigated him during the late 1960s and early 1970s. For a fine recent study of Lin's role in the Cultural Revolution and his earlier life, see Teiwes and Sun (1996).
2. There is a case for dating the beginning of the early Maoist period from 1947, which saw the start of land reform in those parts of north China controlled by the CCP. However, that chronology assigns too much significance to land reform. 1949 is the real climacteric because the founding of the PRC meant that it was possible for the CCP to pursue a proper macroeconomic strategy for the first time.
3. The best introduction to Marxian economic theory is that of Wolff and Resnick (1987). A more general introduction to Marx is that offered by Elster (1986). For an introduction to concepts, see Bottomore (1991). It needs, however, to be stressed that there is a vast literature debating the meaning of Marx's writings and that any interpretation of Marx is controversial.
4. Many have argued that this is increasingly what has happened to culture and cultural production in Western Europe and North America during the era of 'late capitalism' since the 1960s (Jameson 1991).
5. The key role of class struggle in producing social change is emphasized in the interpretations of Marx offered in Brenner (1986) and Wood (1991).
6. For discussions of Soviet NEP, see Cohen (1971), Gregory and Stuart (1974), Allen (2003) and Davies *et al.* (1994).
7. I use 'feudal' here advisedly. Classical feudalism after all involved the granting of titles to land in return for military service, a practice which was very uncommon even in Imperial China. Landlordism is perhaps a better description, though that term fails to convey the problems caused by parcellization of land management, which afflicted both China and medieval Europe. The extent of slavery is also very controversial. Traditional Han accounts have characterized the Yi (or Nuosu) of Liangshan in southwestern Sichuan as constituting a society based on slavery. However, more recent work by Western and Yi scholars (Heberer 2007) suggests that, although slavery did exist, social mobility was considerable. More importantly, at least from a Marxist view point, there is little evidence to suggest that the prosperity of the affluent members of the Yi population was based upon slave production; in other words, it seems wrong to talk about a slave mode of production.
8. Note, however, that some of Marx's writings suggest that it was possible to build socialism without first creating a capitalist social formation. Of these, the most famous is Marx's letter to Vera Zasulich (1884), in which he perceived the primitive Russian *obschina* as an embryonic collective farm. There was therefore a precedent for omitting the capitalist stage of development.
9. Probably the best introduction to the debates on transition in China during the 1950s is Selden (1988). The classic study of transition in agricultural economies remains that of Moore (1967).
10. These estimates are in $US and measured using 1990 prices.
11. The analysis here is something of a simplification. CCP policy in the 1940s was formulated under the slogan 'New Democracy', and in fact New Democracy was in some ways less radical than the policies adopted between 1952 and 1955. This is because its focus – at least in the early 1940s – was more on rent reduction (rather than

land reform), and on uniting with those Chinese industrialists who were nationalistic (rather than expropriating their assets). However, New Democracy never amounted to a coherent economic programme, and the notion that it was less radical than the policies put in place after 1952 (a claim made by Li 2006) is rather contradicted by the fact that land reform was carried out very bloodily in north-western China during 1947–52. To my mind, we do better to regard the whole period between 1947 (the beginning of land reform) and 1955 (collectivization) as a coherent whole.

12 This notion of a split in the Chinese leadership has been often used by the CCP since 1978 to try to distinguish the 'correct' strategy of gradual transition supposedly advocated by Deng Xiaoping and Liu Shaoqi from the 'incorrect' strategy pushed by Mao. In fact, as was also true of the Great Leap Forward, Deng and Liu fully supported Mao in July 1955 (Teiwes and Sun 1993). Deng Zihui, however, was required to write a self-criticism and was labelled a 'right opportunist' at the 7th Central Committee in October 1955. Much of the reinterpretation of the events of the 1950s is based upon analysis of the reflections of Bo Yibo, which were published in 1991.

13 As Kirby (1990: 124) says: 'The CCP, after all, was not the only Chinese party to be influenced by the Soviet Union.'

14 The share of producer good output in GVIO exceeded 40 per cent in only five provinces in 1952 (SSB 1990a). The five were Liaoning (70 per cent), Heilongjiang (60 per cent), Shanxi (58 per cent), Jilin (44 per cent) and Sichuan (43 per cent; Sichuan here includes Chongqing).

15 For some of the literature on Chinese industrialization in the 1950s, see Liu and Wu (1986), Donnithorne (1967) and Riskin (1987).

16 This is one key result of the model developed by G. A. Feldman, and which informed the Soviet industrialization debate of the 1920s. However, this result is sensitive to the assumptions made about gestation periods and the scope for international trade. If one assumes that gestation periods are shorter for the production of consumption goods, or that there is scope for importing producer goods, Feldman's conclusions no longer hold. A useful introduction to many of the theoretical issues involved is provided in Ellman (1979).

17 A useful overview of economic development before 1957 is provided by Lardy (1987). For a discussion of policy-making in the 1950s from a Chinese perspective, see Liu and Wu (1986) and Xue (1981); Xue was Director of the State Statistical Bureau and Vice-Chairman of the State Planning Commission during the early 1950s. For English translations of some of the key documents, see Howe and Walker (1989) and Selden (1979). The most detailed account of the structure of the Chinese economy is that of Donnithorne (1967).

18 These data are for gross domestic capital formation as a percentage of GDP, both at 1933 prices. If valued at 1952 prices, the increase in the investment share would be much higher, because the 1952 relative price set inflates the value of capital goods. Rawski (1989: 260) puts the prewar investment rate at least 10 per cent, almost double the Yeh estimate. In essence this is because he assumes a higher rate of agricultural output growth, which in turn implies that overall investment must have been much higher than assumed by Yeh.

19 A higher figure of 34.7 per cent for the (pure) state sector is given in Xue (1981: 22); it also appears in Riskin (1987: 47). This 34.7 figure is in fact the state share in the factory, or non-handicraft, industry, rather than in total industrial production (SSB 1960: 38).

20 Maddison's (1998: 157) revised series for industrial output shows a somewhat slower growth rate (14 per cent), but the difference is quantitative rather than qualitative.

21 This retrenchment was accepted as necessary by Mao at the time, but the conservatism of many CCP officials was later to be heavily criticized by Mao (Teiwes and Sun 1999).

22 For discussions of general agricultural policy issues in China, see Brown (1995), Findlay and Watson (1999), Huang *et al.* (1999), Carter and Rozelle (2001), OECD (2001) and Dong *et al.* (2006). For useful summaries and analysis of the Maoist era, see

Walker (1984), Perkins and Yusuf (1984), Nolan (1988), Unger (2002) and Ash (2006). Schran (1969) remains an invaluable source for the 1950s.
23 With the benefit of hindsight, the KMT recognized that its opposition to land reform in China had been a mistake and it sought to put that right; one of its first major policy initiatives in Taiwan was to carry out land reform.
24 Areas where land reform was not initially carried out were Xinjiang, Greater Tibet (Tibet, Qinghai and western Sichuan). Land reform was implemented here during 1955–7; one consequence was armed rebellion in the Tibetan areas of Sichuan.
25 Land reform at a village level in north China features prominently in Hinton (1966), Crook and Crook (1979) and Friedman *et al.* (1991). For land reform in south China, see Potter and Potter (1990) and Ruf (1998).
26 By cooperative – lower stage or elementary agricultural producer cooperatives to give them their full title – is meant an organizational unit in which management of land was jointly conducted by all members of the coop, but land remained under private ownership. The CCP classified these as semi-socialist organizations. Members received income partly on the basis of how much land they contributed (their dividend) and partly on the basis of the amount of work done (work points). The higher stage cooperatives established in late 1955 and 1956 were collectives proper. Land was no longer privately owned, income was distributed purely on the basis of work done and households no longer had the right to withdraw from the cooperative.
27 For a withering critique, see Hinton (2006).
28 For a detailed discussion of Chinese agricultural data in the 1930s see Liu and Yeh (1965) and Perkins (1969).
29 Liu and Yeh's estimates are obtained partly by revising upward the sown area data. They also assume that yields at the start of the 1950s must have approximated those of the early 1930s. Yield data for the early 1930s are then obtained by averaging Buck's estimates (which were too high) and the NARB data (which were too low). This procedure is carried out at a provincial level for rice yields (Liu and Yeh 1965: 287).
30 But note that Walker, who compiled the most detailed assessment of Chinese grain data for the 1950s, came up with estimates of production very similar to the revised SSB data (Walker 1984: 202). Schran (1969: 90–1 and 100–1) has taken a similar view, arguing that the NARB yield estimates for the early 1950s are much closer to the truth than those compiled by Liu and Yeh. However, as Liu and Yeh (1965: 45) say, the official data for the early 1950s do seem to imply a level of calorie consumption well below subsistence (only 1,800 kcals in 1952, a very low figure for a predominantly agricultural population with a high activity rate), and therefore it is hard to accept the official CCP data at face value.
31 See the discussion in the special issue of the *Journal of Agrarian Change* (volume 4, numbers 1 and 2, January and April 2004).
32 For the literature see Walker (1966), Shue (1980) and Teiwes and Sun (1999). An excellent collection of documents is that contained in Teiwes and Sun (1993).
33 Chinese concerns about slow agricultural performance and the attendant difficulties associated with a recalcitrant peasantry paralleled those in the Soviet Union in the mid-1920s. In both case, collectivization was adopted as the solution (Selden 1988).
34 Similar arguments appear in many of Mao's writings after the mid-1950s. See for example Mao's *A Critique of Soviet Economics* (Mao 1977).
35 For the primary data, see Buck (1937). The *Crop Reports* are available in many Western libraries but the results are also summarized in various sources such as Ministry of Information (1945; 1947) and Xu (1983). For useful discussions of these data, see Perkins (1969), Liu and Yeh (1965), Feuerwerker (1977) and Rawski (1989).
36 The SSB now prefers to be called the National Bureau of Statistics, just as the Propaganda Department of the CCP prefers to be called its Publicity Department. In neither case has the Chinese changed, and there is no question that 'state' is a far better translation

of *guojia* than 'national' (this latter is the usual English translation of *guomin*). This Orwellian manipulation of language by the Chinese state does its cause few favours.
37 Data on gross output value and national income have been published, but the official data make no attempt to adjust for inflation during 1949–52. Note too that Liu and Yeh (1965) make no attempt to estimate national income for 1949–52 in their detailed study because of the data problems.
38 The Shanxi survey data also show a clear increase in the consumption of industrial goods such as cigarettes, coal and cotton cloth (Vermeer 1982: 8).
39 In fairness, note that Chinese life expectancy was certainly above India's, which averaged only about forty years at birth during the 1950s (World Bank 1989: 198; Drèze and Sen 2002: 127).
40 Across Shandong as a whole, the number enrolled in primary schools declined from 4.5 million in 1952 to 4.3 million in 1955 – and this after enrolments more than doubled between 1949 and 1952 (ZSDSWY 1989: 724).
41 An alternative source is ZJJ (1997: 372–3).
42 For the impact of land reform see Roll (1980), Selden (1988), Du (1996) and Bramall (2000, 2004).
43 The debate between Lenin and A. V. Chayanov arose in the context of the development of capitalism in the Russian countryside in the late nineteenth century. It is fair to note that China's situation in the 1950s was rather different from the classic Chayanovian case in that the Chinese state was playing a key role in reducing differentiation via low interest rates and the promotion of cooperation amongst farm households. For a useful summary of the debates and the Chinese context, see Huang (1990: ch. 1) and Little (1989: ch. 2). For more recent restatements of an essentially Chayanovian perspective on peasant agriculture, see Scott (1976) and Shanin (1986). For a critique of Scott, see Popkin (1979).
44 A useful discussion of the 1954 survey is provided by Matsuda (1990). The survey was actually carried out between May and August of 1955, and relied upon the memories of informants in order to gather data for February 1954 to January 1955. The work was carried out by provincial statistical bureaux, and this ensured a lack of consistency.
45 Su's (1980: 125) data from the 1955 rural income survey have average incomes for upper middle peasants at 93 *yuan* per head compared with 91 *yuan* for rich peasants and 66 *yuan* for poor peasants. However, Su's book was little more than an extended defence of collectivization and we therefore need to treat these data with caution.
46 The geographical focus of the First Five Year Plan was therefore very different to that of the Third Front during the 1960s in that the latter concentrated on the development of western China.
47 E. H. Carr famously posed the question many years ago in the context of the Soviet Union's change of direction after 1928: Was Stalin really necessary?, a phrase which later became the title of an essay by Alec Nove. The debate on the Soviet Union remains unresolved; see the contribution by Allen (2003). The same is true of the debate about the abandonment of the early Maoist strategy in favour of the Leap, though here the debate is altogether less well developed.
48 About 40 per cent of the population was employed in 1964 compared with 36 per cent in 1953, even though the proportion of the population aged between fifteen and sixty-four actually declined because of rising fertility rates (ZGTJNJ 2001: 93; SSB 2005a: 6–7). In other words, and as collectivization was to show, there was considerable scope for increasing the participation rate in the 1950s.
49 Allen's (2003: 164) simulation for the USSR shows that had NEP continued but been combined with a higher rate of investment in producer goods, the rate of growth in the 1930s would have been nearly as rapid as it actually was. In other words, it was more investment in heavy industry – rather than collectivization – which was the decisive factor in raising the Soviet growth rate after 1928. Collective farming made a contribution, but only a small one.

4 The Great Famine, 1955–1963

China's strategy of gradual transition to socialism was abandoned in 1955. Instead, an attempt was made to accelerate the growth rate by the adoption of an altogether more radical development strategy which centred on the suppression of material incentives, public ownership of land and economic assets, the mass mobilization of labour and an overwhelming emphasis on defence industrialization. That year marks the launch of this strategy, characterized as it was by the rapid establishment of producer cooperatives in Chinese agriculture and the nationalization of the last remnants of private industry. It culminated in the Great Leap Forward of 1958, and the disastrous famine of the late 1950s and early 1960s.

Towards the Great Leap Forward: policy debates in the 1950s

In retrospect, and as we saw in the previous chapter, it is evident that early Maoism adhered to the Soviet approach of the 1920s.[1] In fact, early Maoism was little more than a sinified form of NEP. To be sure, the relations of production were not left untouched; land reform is the most obvious example of a policy designed to raise output by means of institutional change. Nevertheless, the focus of Chinese policy during the early 1950s was on economic modernization and the transformation of the forces of production using Soviet technology and based on a high (but not extreme) rate of investment.

Many within the Chinese leadership, notably Liu Shaoqi, advocated a continuation of this strategy during the late 1950s. Most of these officials were afraid that an attempt at acceleration would fail because China simply lacked the capacity to mechanize its agriculture in the 1950s, something which was widely seen as a necessary condition for rapid agricultural development and the release of labour for rural industrialization. In the absence of mechanization, agriculture would flounder and China would risk a repeat of the famine which afflicted the Soviet Union after 1929, when it too tried to accelerate agricultural growth in defiance of 'objective' conditions. Moreover, the performance of the Chinese economy appears to have been better in the 1950s than that of the Soviet Union in the 1920s. Maddison's (2003: 182–4) estimates show that per capita GDP in 1957 was about 7 per cent higher than it had been in 1936. That certainly suggested that there was no need to abandon the early Maoist development strategy.[2]

This perspective on China was shared by Khrushchev and other members of the Soviet leadership. Economic development was progressing encouragingly in China during the 1950s, but any attempt to accelerate its pace would be premature. In particular, any comparison with the Soviet Union was foolish. Tsarist Russia had experienced much more rapid development before 1914 than China before 1949, and was therefore in a much better position to make an early transition to socialism. China needed a much longer period of transition before collective farming could be successfully introduced. This assessment is supported by Maddison's (2003: 100 and 184) estimates of GDP per capita in China and the USSR. According to him, GDP per head in 1913 in what was to become the USSR was $1,488 at 1990 prices. This had fallen so much as a result of war and civil war that even the growth of the 1920s had not restored this output level; per capita GDP by 1928 was only $1,370. Nevertheless, even this 1928 level was well above that achieved by China by 1957, which was a mere $637. In other words, if transition was premature in the USSR in 1928, it was doubly so in China in 1958.

Mao, however, was unmoved by these sorts of arguments. By the mid-1950s, he had moved away from the Soviet orthodoxy, and for much the same reasons that had motivated Stalin in 1928. He was, for example, very far from convinced that it was premature to attempt to transform China's relations of production. More than anything else, Mao seems to have taken the view that there was no alternative to an accelerated pace of transition. The plain facts of the matter were that the growth rate achieved between 1949 and 1955 was not fast enough either to bring about a big increase in living standards or to ensure military security. At root, as we saw in the previous chapter, the problem was seen to be poor rural performance, and because this was largest single sector, it dragged down overall economic growth. The Great Leap Forward was therefore first and foremost geared towards improving rural performance by means of collectivization. Thus collective farms (late called communes) were established in order to exploit economies of scale and to provide an institutional framework within which mass mobilization of labour for infrastructural projects could take place.

In two respects, however, the Maoist conception of the Leap diverged from Stalin's Second Five Year Plan. First, the importance of material incentives within the new communes was downplayed. This emphasis on the role for ideology foreshadowed the approach later to be adopted during the Cultural Revolution. Second, the Leap strategy stressed the need for rural industrialization, primarily as a way of modernizing agriculture (by supplying farm machinery, chemical fertilizer and the steel and concrete needed for irrigation systems). Thus China would 'walk on two legs': rural industrialization and modernization would complement what was already talking place in the urban sector.

High tide and hundred flowers, 1955–1958

The year 1955 was a climacteric in Chinese economic development because it marked the abandonment of the gradualist transition strategy pursued in the early 1950s. In fact, this was the year in which the Chinese economy became socialist to all intents and purposes. There are two reasons for drawing such a conclusion. First, the remaining privately owned industrial companies were taken into state control. In 1954, these companies still accounted for 38 per cent of gross industrial output value and therefore one might still argue that the industrial sector was more like that typically found in a state capitalist economy (such as South Korea or Taiwan in the 1960s) than the industrial sector typical of a socialist economy. But this figure dropped to 28 per cent by the end of 1955 and stood at barely 1 per cent by the end of 1956. Although many of these newly nationalized enterprises were classified as joint

Box 4.1 **The key speeches and initiatives of the Great Leap Forward**

31 July 1955	'On the Question of Agricultural Cooperation' (speech by Mao Zedong)	Launched rapid collectivization. Marks abandonment of gradualism
January 1956	Adoption of 'The Forty Articles' (Twelve Year Plan for Agriculture)	Outlined the Maoist vision of rural development
25 April 1956	'The Ten Major Relationships' (speech by Mao Zedong)	A further statement of Maoist economic policy. Seemingly a manifesto for balanced development, but less so in practice. Launches the 'Hundred Flowers'
27 February 1957	'On the Correct Handling of Contradictions Among the People' (speech by Mao Zedong)	Another seemingly conservative Maoist statement accepting the existence of rifts ('contradictions') within the Party
13 November 1957	Renmin Ribao editorial	First use of phrase 'Great Leap Forward'
July 1959	Lushan Plenum of the CCP	Letter critical of the Leap circulated by Peng Dehuai; Peng and allies purged
September 1962	Adoption of the 'Sixty Articles on Agriculture'	The articles (first drafted in June 1961) regulated the operation of communes and thus signalled the official end to the Leap

state–private enterprises (because their former owners were paid fixed interest payments as compensation for their loss of control), they were *de facto* state-owned enterprises. A private industrial sector was not to reappear in China until 1980.

As noted in the previous chapter, 1955 was also a turning-point because Mao's speech of late July signalled a massive acceleration in the process of creating collective farms. The initial step was to push peasant households into producer cooperatives. As Table 4.1 shows, the proportion of households in cooperatives increased very rapidly after Mao's July speech. In the sense that land ownership was still vested in the hands of those peasants who had joined the cooperatives, and that peasants notionally enjoyed the right to withdraw from the cooperatives, one might argue that Chinese agriculture was still not socialist at the end of 1955. However, with the withdrawal right much more notional than real by the end of that year and with commerce firmly under the control of the state, the Chinese countryside was far removed from a market economy by that time. The events of 1956, during which land ownership was transferred from peasant households to the collective, merely completed the process. The very pace of the transformation during 1955–6 is aptly captured in the phrase 'socialist high tide'. Whereas it had been envisaged in 1953 that 'complete socialization' of agriculture would not take place until 1967, collectivization was in fact achieved by the end of 1956 (Yeh 1973: 493).

Nevertheless, although collectivization had been achieved far earlier than originally planned, one would be hard put to argue that it was a policy disaster. The contrast between Chinese collectivization in 1955–6 and Soviet collectivization during 1928–32 is especially sharp (Nolan 1976). In the latter, collectivization resulted in a gigantic famine; mortality was especially high in Ukraine. In China, however, there was no such increase in mortality. On the contrary: the crude death rate fell from 12.3 per thousand in 1955 to 10.8 per thousand in 1957 (SSB 2005a: 6).

Table 4.1 Collectivization in China, 1955–1956 (per cent of peasant households by membership)

	In cooperatives	In collectives	Other
1955			
June	14	0	86
December	59	4	37
1956			
January	50	31	19
March	34	55	11
June	29	63	8
December	9	88	3

Sources: Walker (1966: 35); Su (1980: 160).

Note
The 'Other' figure (i.e. households which were neither members of coops or collectives) is the residual. The figures are for the end of each month.

Given the momentum that had built up during 1955–6, it is not surprising that many of those on the left within the Party pushed for still further radicalization at the end of 1956.[3] Mao was amongst them. The upshot was a whole raft of policies which were implemented under the slogans 'small leap forward' and 'more, faster, better and more economical' (*duo, kuai, hao, sheng*) between July 1955 and April 1956. In concrete terms, this period saw *inter alia* the adoption of the Twelve Year Plan for Agriculture (usually called the Forty Articles) in January 1956 and an escalation of investment targets. The significance of the Forty Articles cannot be overstated, because it provides the blueprint for the Maoist vision of rural development. The Plan called not only for big increases in grain yields but also for rapid mechanization, the mass mobilization of the rural workforce, the elimination of key infectious diseases and the wiping out of illiteracy within five to seven years (Selden 1979). All this was hugely ambitious. The grain yield targets implied total production of over 500 million tonnes by 1967, a figure which China did not attain until 1996.

In the short term, however, the most destabilizing feature of the little leap was the surge in investment that occurred in 1956. Figure 4.1 shows this very clearly, using the official data on fixed investment as a percentage of GDP. As the trend line shows, the investment share increased over time as the Chinese economy became more capital- and less labour-intensive. More interesting, however, are the deviations from that trend, the earliest of which occurred in 1956, when fixed investment surged above its level during the early 1950s to exceed 20 per cent of GDP. The aim was to accelerate the rate of industrialization, and in fact industrial production increased by nearly 29 per cent in 1956, compared with only 7 per cent in 1955 (SSB 1999: 5).

Yet no sooner had the Forty Articles been announced and investment begun to surge than the process was thrown into reverse – seemingly with Mao's acquiescence. Under the slogan of *fanmaojin* ('oppose rash advance'), a coalition of CCP leaders and planners – notably Zhou Enlai, Liu Shaoqi, Chen Yun, Bo Yibo

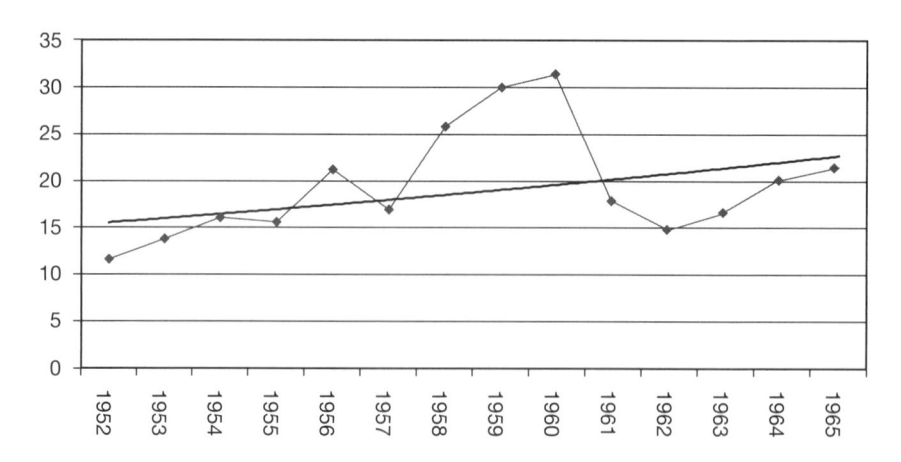

Figure 4.1 Share of fixed investment in GDP (Source: SSB (1999: 6).)

and Li Xiannian – sought to cut back on investment and to slow down the rate of economic growth. In part, their concern was over the impact of higher investment on consumption; in the short run, there could not be anything other than a direct trade-off between the two. In addition, they were concerned by events in the countryside. As we have seen, the 'high tide' was successful in the sense that there was no repeat of the Soviet famine of 1928–32. In part, this was because rich and middle peasants were often compensated for the loss of animals and equipment that they incurred in joining the collective (Potter and Potter 1990: 65). Nevertheless, the immediate economic consequences of rapid collectivization in China were mixed. Agricultural value-added in 1955 was 8 per cent up on 1954 in real terms, and the increase in 1956 was 4 per cent (MOA 1989: 66). But most of this was due to growth in the crop subsector. The value of livestock production was almost 10 per cent down in 1955 on the level of the previous year, and even though it rose the next year, the value of production in 1956 was still lower than it had been in 1954 (MOA 1989: 106). More significantly, the number of large draught animals declined from 87.7 million head in 1955 to 83.8 million in 1957. This was important because animal power was crucial for ploughing; the loss of animals therefore hampered attempts to increase sown area (MOA 1989: 242). In part, the problems in the animal husbandry sector occurred because a considerable proportion of the Chinese peasantry resented the process of *de facto* coercive collective formation, and responded by widespread slaughter of animals. The decline in numbers also reflected teething problems; many of the animals were overworked or simply neglected in the new collectives (Shue 1980: 310–11). The pig stock was also affected, declining to 88 million by the end of 1955, well down on the figure of 102 million recorded at the end of 1954 (MOA 1989: 244). These problems were not new; they had occurred in 1954, when an attempt had been made to push cooperatives (Walker 1966; Teiwes and Sun 1993). But the decline was much more acute in 1955–6.

Mao's role in *fanmaojin* remains rather uncertain. The chief advocates of the programme were all forced to write self-criticisms in 1958, and Mao insisted on 1956 being referred to as a 'leap forward' rather than a 'rash advance' after the summer of 1957. Nevertheless, all the evidence suggests that Mao's policy outlook was actually rather conservative between April 1956 and June 1957, and that there was little real disagreement between him and the planners at the time over the need to curb some of the excesses.[4] He may, for example, have been a strong advocate of the Twelve Year Plan in January 1956, but this advocacy seems to have dwindled as the year progressed. At the 2nd Plenum of the Eighth Central Committee in November, his message was a little different from that of Zhou Enlai in that he defended imbalance as inevitable and cautioned against cooling the enthusiasm of the masses (Teiwes and Sun 1999: 26–41). Nevertheless, Mao appears to have favoured a slowdown in the pace of growth. In all this, it is hard to believe that Khrushchev's speech of February 1956 denouncing Stalinism did not have a considerable effect in tempering his enthusiasm, and the turmoil in Poland and Hungary during 1956 also no doubt gave him pause. Whatever the reason, the Party's Eighth Congress (September 1956) was notably restrained in its policy outlook. 'Rash advance' and 'right opportunism' were both criticized, investment targets were scaled down and the class struggle between bourgeoisie and proletariat was declared to be essentially over. For the CCP, reviewing its history in the early 1980s, the 8th Congress epitomized the Chinese road to socialism at its best: 'The line laid down by the eighth National Congress of the Party was correct' (Liu and Wu 1986: 592).

Mao's stance between April 1956 and June 1957 – the period during which he was at his most conservative – is most apparent from his speeches during these months, many of which are amongst his most famous. This is certainly true of 'On the Ten Major Relationships'. This speech seemed in many respects to represent a break with the Soviet model, in that Mao emphasized the need for balance in economic development, and in particular for more weight to be placed on the needs of the rural sector than was allowed for under the Soviet model. More precisely, Mao called for the allocation of more investment in light industry, agriculture, the coastal region and the civilian sector in general – and less investment in defence, heavy industry and the interior. The speech also called for a decentralization of power from the centre to the provinces and to the counties, a policy which was implemented in late 1957 and early 1958 (Riskin 1987: 100–9; Lardy 1978).

His speech 'On the Correct Handling of Contradictions among the People' of February 1957 went much further, and seemed at the time to herald a break with classical (Stalinist) socialism. Mao's central argument was that public ownership by itself did not ensure the triumph of socialism, because of the survival of non-Marxist attitudes:

> The class struggle is by no means over ... The proletariat seeks to transform the world according to its own world outlook, and so does the bourgeoisie. In this respect, the question of which will win out, socialism or capitalism, is still not really settled ... It will take a fairly long period of time to decide the issue in the ideological struggle between socialism and capitalism in our country. The reason is that the influence of the bourgeoisie and of the intellectuals who come from the old society will remain in our country for a long time to come, and so will their class ideology. (Mao 1957: 463–4)

In order to identify and root out these influences, Mao encouraged artists ('flowers') and intellectuals and academics ('schools') to criticize; hence the celebrated phrase 'Let a Hundred Flowers Bloom, Let a Hundred Schools of Thought Contend.'[5] Admittedly Mao made clear his view that criticism of 'the socialist path and the leadership of the Party' (Mao 1957: 468) was not legitimate. But this was very much softened by his statement that the criteria he advocated for deciding between 'poisonous weeds' and 'fragrant flowers' were themselves open to debate. This left open the possibility of criticism of the Party, and of Mao himself.[6] For many, all this seemed to herald a real break with the Soviet model and the beginning of a new approach to the attainment of modernity within a communist system.

The Great Leap Forward and recovery, 1958–1966

It was not to be. China's seeming flirtation with the notion of an alternative path to modernity, at least in the political sphere, was abruptly abandoned with the launch of the Anti-Rightist movement in June 1957 and the initiation of the Great Leap Forward in 1958. The Anti-Rightist movement was undoubtedly a precursor to the Cultural Revolution.[7] It was sparked by the way in which the Hundred Flowers became a wave of criticism directed not just at many members of the Party but at Mao himself. As it developed, the Anti-Rightist movement was both an attack on artists and intellectuals and also an assault on those elements within the CCP who had advocated the policy of *fanmaojin* in late 1956 and early 1957. The key moment here was not so much the beginning of the anti-rightist campaign in June 1957 but the Third Plenum of September–October 1957 when, in his closing speech, Mao launched a furious attack on *fanmaojin* and the rejection of both the Twelve Year Plan and *duo, kuai, hao, sheng* by majority opinion within the Party.[8]

The Leap strategy

The Third Plenum of 1957 heralded the beginnings of the Great Leap Forward.[9] The Leap comprised several elements. Perhaps the most important in macroeconomic terms was the surge in investment. As Figure 4.1 (above) shows, fixed investment as a percentage of GDP surged in 1958 to a figure well in advance of its trend, and the surge continued until 1960, when the fixed investment share peaked at over 31 per cent, the highest figure recorded during the entire Maoist era. As China was still a desperately poor country, this constituted a massive diversion of resources away from consumption, and by implication risked famine. In microeconomic terms, the Leap involved a transfer of labour (the key input) away from the production of consumer goods – especially grain – towards the production of producer goods, notably iron and steel, but also water conservancy projects. The emphasis on iron and steel production in the Chinese countryside was the hallmark of the Leap as 'backyard furnaces' sprung up everywhere.

The other key aspect of the Leap was the establishment of people's communes in the countryside during the autumn of 1958. These differed from collectives in two main respects. First, they were much larger; the purpose of enlargement was to exploit further the scope for economies of scale. Second, the communes incorporated canteens at which the population were expected to eat. A large proportion of the food supplied was provided free of charge (typically 70 per cent) and only 30 per cent distributed according to work done. This did much to sever the link between consumption and work done; the peasantry could eat their fill, irrespective of their output. It was also hoped that canteens would free more women from domestic chores and thus enable the workforce to be further expanded. It remains a little unclear whether the canteens were popular or not; Han (2000: 35) notes that they were seen as comparable to the special dining rooms provided for cadres, and therefore highly regarded by the rural population.[10]

The mortality toll

The scale and pattern of mortality during the Chinese famine of the late 1950s and early 1960s remains relatively unresearched. Nevertheless, we can be sure of several things. For one, the total number of lives lost as a result of the famine make it the worst in human history.[11] Many attempts have been made to estimate total mortality, and the lower bound (based on the official data) for total excess deaths across the People's Republic is around 15 million. However, during the course of the retrospective 1982 fertility survey, Chinese women reported having had more children over the course of their lifetime than reported in the 1982 population census, and most Western demographers have interpreted this as suggesting that considerable underreporting of births (and by implication infant deaths) occurred during the famine period. Thus Ashton et al. (1984) suggest that only about 30 per cent of all deaths amongst children aged under ten were actually reported. On this basis, it has been estimated by both Ashton et al. (1984: 619) and Banister (1987: 85) that around 30 million excess deaths occurred. Many Chinese scholars have suggested that the total was even higher. Chang and Halliday (2005: 456) put the total at around 38 million, based upon revisions to the official demographic data.[12] Although some have attempted to argue that these figures vastly overstate mortality (Patnaik 2002), these contentions are not very convincing.[13] After all, acceptance of Patnaik's lower estimate still implies over 12 million deaths, and whether 30 million or 12 million died, the *qualitative* conclusion is surely still the same.

We also know that the impact of the famine was spatially uneven. Visitors to China during these years typically reported that they had seen no signs of famine, and for that reason even the existence of a famine was doubted until the release of the 1982 Population Census data, which showed a massive shortfall of people aged around 20, the very cohort most affected by fewer births and very high infant mortality during the Leap. The visitors who failed to find evidence of famine have often been decried as being wilfully blind, but the very extent of spatial variation (and the fact that the cities, where most of the foreign visitors were to be found, were little affected) suggests that it was entirely possible not to have come across evidence of mass starvation.

Figure 4.2 shows famine mortality by province during the 1960, the worst single year. The provinces worst affected by the famine were Anhui, Sichuan, Guizhou and Gansu. Anhui's average death rate was almost 69 per thousand in 1960, but the rate was a mere 6.9 in Shanghai and 9.4 in Nei Menggu. Within provinces, the variation was even greater. Some of the worst-affected counties in Sichuan and Anhui recorded crude death rates of well over 100 per 1,000, exceptionally high figures by any standard. Yet in parts of these provinces, the crude death rate was low; death rates of 20 per thousand or less were by no means uncommon in some of Sichuan's countries, higher than in the mid-1950s but not so alarmingly high as to be obvious to a casual observer. In Chengdu city, the rate was lower still. For all that, in emphasizing the point that the Great Famine was far more intense in some provinces than others, it is worth emphasizing too that high mortality rates were

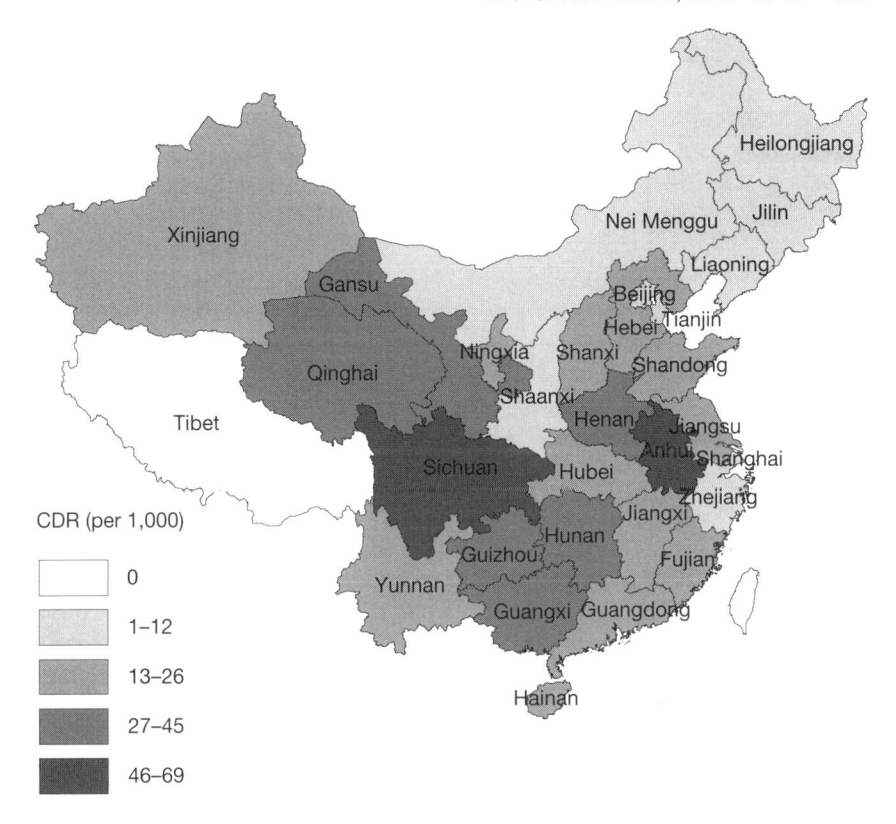

Figure 4.2 Mortality rates by province, 1960 (deaths per thousand) (Source: Bramall (1993: 292).)

Note: No data are available for Tibet or Hainan. I have used the Guangdong figure to proxy that in Hainan.

recorded even in provinces where the average mortality rate was quite low by Chinese standards. Take the case of Shandong. Although the overall crude death rate was only around 24 per thousand in 1960, death rates of between 70 and 90 per 1,000 were recorded in several counties.

The data in Table 4.2 go far towards showing why a province like Sichuan was so badly affected. They show that food availability per person was on average only about 1,400 calories, compared with the 2,200 calories needed given the height and weight of the population. As result, perhaps 10 million people died in Sichuan alone, and my own research suggests that the figure may well have been higher (Bramall 1993).

Conditions were often little better elsewhere. Events in parts of Henan province have been extensively publicized; in Xinyang prefecture, cannibalism was apparently rife (Becker 1996). In Anhui too, mortality rose sharply; the data show the crude death rate rising from 17 per 1,000 in 1959 to 69 per 1,000 in 1960 (SSB 1990: 405). These Anhui data are admittedly a little odd. It seems rather unlikely

Table 4.2 The famine in Sichuan province

	Food availability per head (calories per day)	Crude death rate (per 1,000)
1957	1,955	12.1
1958	2,176	25.2
1959	1,641	47.0
1960	1,422	54.0
1961	1,354	29.4
1962	1,684	14.6
1963	1,827	12.8

Source: Bramall (1993: 296 and 317).

Note
1957 was not an unusual year in terms of mortality.

that the death rate would rise quite so abruptly and, for that matter, decline so quickly to only 8 per 1,000 in 1961. I suspect that mortality was spread over the three-year period 1959–61, and that the excess mortality was simply attributed to 1961 for statistical convenience. But what is not in doubt is the extent of the mortality. This emerges very clear from both the Anhui literature (for example Wang 1988) and the mortality data; in some of Anhui's counties mortality rates were far above the (high) provincial average. We can also be fairly confident that the impact of the famine was much less severe elsewhere. In at least ten of China's provinces and municipalities, the 1958–61 mortality rate was 'only' about 10 per cent higher than the 1957 figure (Bramall 1993: 293). Indeed the 1959 nutrition survey – biased towards urban centres – put average calorie intake at no less than 2,060 kcals (MOH 2003).

Causal factors

The conventional wisdom on the Great Famine assigns special causal significance to the creation of people's communes. Some have argued that the elimination of the right of households to leave the communes and return to family farming played a key role in affecting producer incentives – thus leading to the collapse in food production and thence to famine (Lin and Yang 2000). When collectives were set up in the mid-1950s, argues Lin (1990), peasants were highly self-motivated. They realized that there were significant gains to be made from cooperation with other households. There were economies of scale in marketing, input purchase, credit and bulky capital inputs, and cooperation inevitably ensured a degree of risk pooling: the collective would subsidize a household handicapped by the death or illness of a key able-bodied member. More importantly, Lin suggests, membership of the cooperatives was voluntary. In other words, there was a possibility that high-productivity households might leave the cooperative (thus leading to its collapse) in the event of shirking by low-productivity households. The threat of exit therefore acted as a disciplinary device; it forced all households to be productive and not to shirk. In the worst-case scenario, the collective might simply collapse and that possibility served to encourage all households to maximize their productivity. This all changed in 1958, argues Lin, when the right to exit the commune was removed. Households with a low level of productivity, or a tendency to shirk, no longer feared the prospect of exiting by high-productivity households. The removal of the exit right thus encouraged free riding and therefore a collapse in productivity.

It has also been contended that 'overeating' led to the rapid depletion of stocks and contributed to famine (Chang and Wen 1997). For example, it is surely no accident that the famine was most intense in Sichuan, where the leadership of Li Jingquan gave the Leap an especially radical dimension. And Shanghai's Ke Qingshi was only saved from the worst consequences of his radicalism by Shanghai's very prosperity – and the fact that it was not a significant grain producer (and therefore not vulnerable to the effect of adverse incentive effects in agriculture).

These incentive problems were compounded by the tendency of poor brigades (and teams) to annex the assets and property of richer brigades (teams) within the same commune, without compensation, in the name of egalitarianism. This caused a great deal of resentment amongst the peasantry, as some of the leaders of the CCP discovered for themselves during inspection tours in 1961 (MacFarquhar 1997: 45–7).

On the face of it, these arguments have some plausibility about them. The most obvious piece of supporting evidence is the correlation at the provincial level between mortality and participation rates in canteens (Yang 1996). Some provincial leaders were much more enthusiastic about setting up communal dining arrangements than others, and this spatial variation is matched by spatial variation in mortality (Table 4.3).

Table 4.3 Famine mortality and participation in communal canteens (bottom and top five provinces by participation rate)

Province	Mortality rate in 1960 (per 1,000)	Canteen participation rate (per cent of households)
Bottom five		
Inner Mongolia	9.5	16.7
Liaoning	11.5	23.0
Heilongjiang	10.5	26.5
Jilin	10.1	29.4
Qinghai	40.7	29.9
Top five		
Guizhou	52.3	92.6
Yunnan	26.3	96.5
Sichuan	54.0	96.7
Hunan	29.4	97.6
Henan	39.6	97.8

Source: Yang (1996: 57).

However, closer analysis suggests that this provincial pattern reflects correlation but not causality. In fact, interesting though many of these arguments about canteens are, they are not particularly convincing. The Chang–Wen overconsumption argument is implausible because the numbers simply do not add up. Sichuan's mortality crisis actually began in 1958; the crude death rate in 1957 was 12.2 per thousand but climbed to 26 per thousand in 1958 (SCTJNJ 1990: 58). However, canteens were not set up until the autumn of that year. Given that the main harvest was not even collected until the early autumn (and therefore was not available to be eaten), it is hard to see how overconsumption could have caused so many deaths in 1958. The depletion of grain stock in Sichuan may help to explain mortality in 1959 (though even then the decline in output is a far more plausible and logical explanation), but not in 1958.

Nor is Lin's argument about exit rights very convincing. Its main weakness is that membership of a farming collective became compulsory for the vast majority of farmers in 1955/6.[14] However, the collapse in output did not occur until 1959. In other words, the timing of Lin's argument is wrong; if he is correct, the output decline ought to have occurred in 1956 and 1957. In fact, output increased in both years and the 1958 harvest was a record. Furthermore, the right to withdraw from the commune was not restored even after 1960. Yet output and productivity recovered and there was no other significant famine in the Maoist period. In fact, the very notion that incentive failure explains the famine is flatly contradicted by all the evidence pointing to a rise in yields in 1958, the very year in which communes were introduced. Even in 1959, grain yields were no lower than they had been in 1957. As Kueh (1995: 212) concludes: 'there is no evidence of a consistent decline in grain yield across the various crops to suggest that peasants' incentives were drastically impaired by the rural upheaval of 1958.' All this suggests that the exit right argument is a red herring. We therefore probably need to look beyond canteens to explain the mortality crisis.

A far more plausible argument is that the emphasis on iron and steel production in the countryside was critical because it led to the wholesale diversion of labour from farming to industry, thus bringing about a collapse in production because of labour shortages.[15] The extent of this diversion of resources emerges very clear in the data (Table 4.4). Grain sown area was cut in 1958, and again in 1959, and this translated directly into lower output despite high yields. More remarkable, however, is the employment trend. Primary-sector employment fell by almost 40 million workers in 1959, almost a fifth of the agricultural workforce, because farmers were moved into rural industry. The exceptionally volatile rural non-agricultural employment data show extremely clearly the scale of the rural industrialization undertaken. The total quadrupled between 1957 and 1958 as iron and steel production commenced. It then collapsed after 1960 as the extent of the famine became increasingly apparent; by then, all available labour was being transferred into farming in a desperate attempt to mitigate the famine conditions. This diversion of labour led directly to a fall in food output after 1958, as is very clear from the data in Table 4.4.

The impact of the fall in food production was compounded by Chinese trade

Table 4.4 Trends in economic aggregates during the Leap and its aftermath

	Grain output (m tonnes)	Grain sown area (m ha)	Rural household consumption (index; 1952 = 100)	Rural non-agricultural employment (millions)	Primary sector employment (millions)
1956	192.8	136.3	115	14.8	185.9
1957	195.1	133.6	117	12.6	185.4
1958	197.7	127.6	120	58.1	193.1
1959	169.7	116.0	97	45.1	154.9
1960	143.9	122.4	92	27.5	162.7
1961	136.5	121.4	94	5.1	170.2
1962	154.4	121.6	100	1.0	197.5

Sources and notes
1 The grain data are the revised figures given in SSB (2000a: 37). These are for unhusked grain and differ quite considerably from those published in MOA (1989: 410) or SSB (1999: 33).
2 Sown area from MOA (1989: 130). These figures have not been revised in the 1990s.
3 The figure for rural household consumption excludes government consumption and is calculated on a GDP basis; the index is at comparable prices, i.e. inflation-adjusted. From SSB (1999: 23).
4 Employment data are from LDTJ (2005: 7). The figure given for rural non-agricultural employment is total rural employment minus primary sector employment (which include some mining but is mainly agriculture). The figures are year-end.

policy. For despite the cuts in production, China remained a net food exporter (principally to repay its debts to the Soviet Union), reducing grain availability further. And to compound the difficulties of the situation, there was a distributional problem within China in that those provinces which produced surplus grain in the early 1950s (notably Sichuan and Heilongjiang) were expected to continue to supply grain to deficit regions (such as Shanghai), even though their production had fallen. Sichuan, for example, exported 2.9 million tonnes of trade grain to other provinces and abroad in 1957, and the province was still exporting 1.4 million tonnes in 1960 – even though grain production had fallen from 21 million tonnes to only 13 million tonnes (SCTJNJ 1990: 135).[16] The net grain procurement rate (gross procurements minus resales) thus fluctuated between 25 per cent and 20 per cent during 1958–60 (Walker in Ash 1998: 138), staggering figures for a province suffering from a massive collapse in output.[17]

The problems afflicting agriculture were exacerbated by three additional problems. First, there was widespread overreporting of output by cadres, largely in response to the purges of 1957 (the Anti-Rightist movement) and 1959 (after Lushan). In this climate no cadre wished to run the risk of being labelled a 'right opportunist' by suggesting that the Leap had failed, and therefore production was routinely exaggerated. For example, grain output in 1958 was reported to be 375 million tonnes in December 1958, and that was the figure Zhou Enlai gave to the April 1959 People's Congress. By the autumn, however, it was clear that the figure was wrong; it was revised down to 250 million. Actual output in 1958 according to the post-1978 figures was only 200 million tonnes (Yeh 1973: 511–12). This overreporting contributed very significantly to the failure on the part of the CCP leadership to reduce procurements and import grain before it was too late. The very fact that there was widespread population migration – some of it deliberately designed to open up new areas (such as migration to Heilongjiang and Yunnan) and some of it distress migration in response to famine conditions – exacerbated the planning problem of ensuring adequate supplies of grain in every Chinese region.

Second, the problem of inadequate grain supply was intensified by increases in food demand caused by the high activity rates inherent in mobilizing the entire population. For example, a typical Chinese woman aged between eighteen and forty-nine needs around 3,200 calories per day if engaged in heavy physical work, as opposed to a requirement of 2,200 if essentially sedentary; the requirement for Chinese men engaged in very heavy work is around 4,000 (Chen *et al.* 1990: 17).[18] This surge in demand may help to explain why, in Sichuan, food availability in rural areas was higher in 1958 than it had been in 1957 yet mortality rose. The onset of famine there can therefore only be explained in terms of the sort of entitlement failure approach advocated by Sen. In Sichuan's case, very high levels of grain procurements in some of the province's most affluent counties left them with totally inadequate supplies.[19] In other words, a decline in food availability offers only an incomplete explanation of famine mortality in China, and in this sense Sen's view that we need a broader explanation of famine is undoubtedly correct. The food availability decline argument does not hold for Sichuan in 1958.

Finally, the impact of poor weather needs to be mentioned. It was argued for many years in the West that any notion that the fall in production was caused by poor weather was little more than a CCP excuse for policy failure. However, the work of Kueh (1995) has demonstrated the true extent of the drought which affected many parts of China during these years. The problem faced by China in the late 1950s and early 1960s is shown most clearly by his weather index, which measures annual deviation from the 1952–84 average (Kueh 1995: 299). The index shows that the weather in 1958 was nearly 30 per cent better than average, whereas it was 86 and 96 per cent worse in 1960 and 1961 respectively.[20] Nevertheless, there is no suggestion here that weather provides the main explanation. As Kueh points out, weather-related factors go far towards explaining the fall in *yields* in 1960 and 1961, but they cannot explain either the deliberate reduction in grain sown area, nor the high rates of procurement. These last two were policy-induced failures and of great importance. As Kueh (1995: 207) says: 'even without bad weather, the peasants could not possibly have survived, purely on account of the unwarranted sown area contraction and excessive state farm procurement.' Furthermore, it is worth noting the view of the Chinese peasantry on these matters; the typical response seems to have been that only around a third of the fall in output could be attributed to the weather. In short, poor weather played a much more important role in causing the famine than is allowed for in much of the literature, but in the final analysis policy failure was the primary culprit.

The net effect of these various factors was a catastrophic fall in grain output, compounded by a range of distributional failures – across provinces, between the cities and the countryside, and within rural areas. As Figure 4.3 shows, the effect of falling output and rising net grain procurements was to squeeze rural grain availability to a dramatic extent as early as 1958 and 1959. By 1961, the worst year, availability per head was down to 207 kg, almost 100 kg lower than the figure in 1956. With some of this grain required for feed and for seed, the amount available for direct consumption was low indeed and famine was inevitable.

The failure of the CCP to act in response to widespread famine conditions is one of the most powerful indictments of Party rule in China. Several factors seem to explain its slow response to famine conditions. Probably most important was the deterioration in China's relations with the Soviet Union. Khrushchev's attempts to improve Soviet relations with the USA and his open criticism of Chinese communes in July 1959 led to a rapid deterioration in Sino-Soviet relations; Soviet advisers and assistance were withdrawn in 1960. This had two consequences. For one thing, it mean that much of the attention of the CCP during these years was given over to Sino-Soviet relations, and as a result less attention was paid to the unfolding crisis in the Chinese countryside (Bernstein 2006). Second, it coincided with the sending of a letter by Peng Dehuai – then China's Minister of Defence – to Mao which was critical of the Leap and which urged its

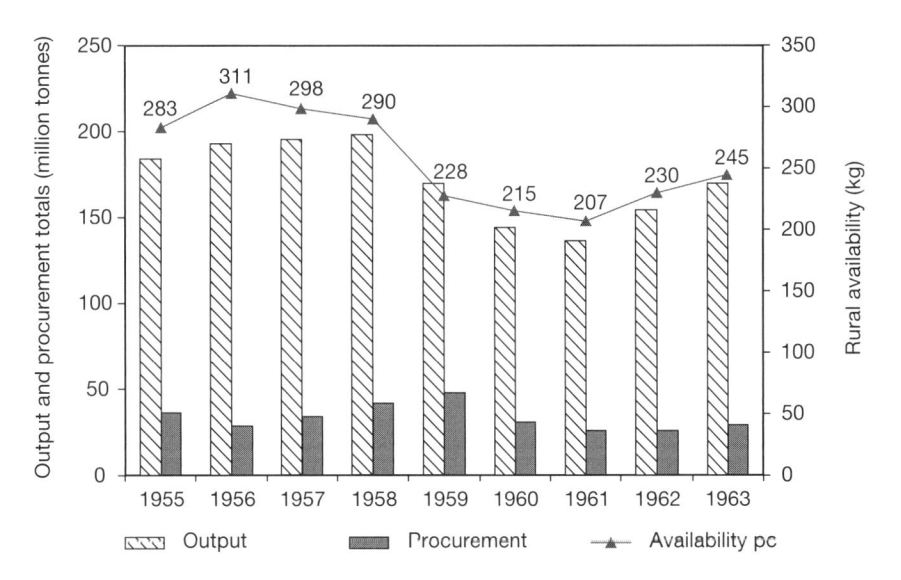

Figure 4.3 Grain output, procurements and rural availability during the Leap (Sources: MOA (1989: 6, 410–11); SSB (2000a: 37).)

Note: Data are for unhusked grain and are taken from SSB (2000a: 37), which provides revised estimates of output compared with MOA (1989: 410–11). These revised figures show that the per capita trough occurred in 1961, rather than 1960 (as suggested by the MOA estimates), implying a longer period of crisis. Procurements are net of rural resales and from MOA (1989). The population denominator used to calculate grain availability per head is the agricultural population (nongye renkou). For grain availability in terms of husked (trade) grain, see Walker (in Ash 1998: 136). Walker's data show that urban grain availability was some 60–80 kg of husked grain higher than for the rural population during 1959–61.

abandonment. Peng's relations with Mao were poor by this time. Peng's military tactics had been criticized by Mao before 1949; Mao's son had died in Korea whilst serving under Peng; and Peng had close ties with the Soviet Union, and indeed wished to modernize the Chinese army along Soviet lines. Mao seems to have interpreted Peng's letter as an attempt by the Soviet Union to interfere in Chinese affairs and as part of a wider conspiracy to marginalize China. In consequence, Mao responded with a full-blown attack on Peng at the Lushan Plenum in July 1959 and this developed into a purge of the Party on an even bigger scale than in 1957. In order to properly discredit Peng, his views on the Leap needed to be discredited as well – and this meant that any criticism of the Leap or attempt to modify its excesses was impossible for other prominent CCP members. The Leap therefore continued, and if anything intensified in 1959 and 1960.

Two other factors are worth noting. First, and as Bernstein (2006) argues, there is some evidence that Mao was ignorant of the true extent of famine conditions in the countryside. Mao's ignorance stemmed partly from a lack of willingness to consider even the possibility of famine, but it also reflected the nature of the Chinese political system: it was hard for subordinates to question the direction of policy, still less to bring to Mao's notice the scale of the unfolding crisis. In fact, as Bernstein (2006: 444) rightly notes, Mao did act in 1960 when he finally understood what was happening in China. Second, and relatedly, there is surely no doubt that the Chinese famine would have been lessened if China had been democratic and its economy more market-orientated. As Sen (1989) properly points out, Indian democracy – for all its faults – guaranteed some sort of speedy response to famine precisely because of its free press and because of the inevitable price-based response that occurs in an economy where private markets do exist; if the food price rises, it becomes profitable for importers to acquire food from abroad. None of this should be taken to mean that market forces *always* ensure an absence of famine – that implies perfectly functioning markets – but it remains the case that market forces will tend to mitigate famine. The very fact that private markets had been so fully suppressed by the late 1950s compounded China's difficulties and contributed to the scale of mortality.

Recovery

The famine conditions which prevailed in many parts of rural China were brought to an end by the abandonment of the Leap.[21] This began in September 1960, when the slogan 'readjusting, consolidating, filling out and raising standards' first appeared. Mao seems to have recognized the scale of the crisis only in October (Bernstein 2006; Teiwes and Sun 1999: 215), but thereafter he too pushed for the Leap to be halted. The Party's 9th Plenum (January 1961) made the policy more concrete. However, real momentum only seems to have developed in the aftermath of a series of inspection tours by CCP leaders in the spring of 1961; Liu Shaoqi, for example, spent forty-four days touring Hunan in April and May (MacFarquhar 1997: ch. 3). This brought home to all of them the dire state of food supplies in the countryside, and led to a veritable barrage of regulations designed to prevent any repetition of the excesses of the Leap. In particular, the Sixty Articles (produced in draft form in May 1961 and continually revised until the final version was accepted by the Party in September 1962) were drawn up to regularize the operation and management of people's communes.[22] The reversal of policy was given further momentum by the 7,000 Cadre Conference organized by the Central Committee and held in January 1962. This whole process of policy reversal was presided over by Liu Shaoqi. However, as Teiwes has convincingly shown (Teiwes and Sun 1999), the evidence suggests not that Mao was marginalized, but rather that he deliberately refrained from playing a more active role during the recovery from the Leap. That his true power was undiminished appears clearly from the manner in which he was able to launch the Cultural Revolution

The policies developed during 1960–2 involved the virtual cessation of rural iron and steel production (which returned labour to farming), the abolition of communal canteens (which had a broadly positive effect upon peasant producer incentives), the restoration of some private markets, a sharp reduction in procurement quotas and even the restoration of family farming in some parts of China.[23] The most famous example of this latter occurred in Anhui, one of the provinces most severely hit by the famine (Lu 1992; Wang 1988). By the end of 1961, almost 90 per cent of production teams had adopted family farming across the province – with Mao's undoubted blessing (Teiwes and Sun 1999: 219–21). By mid-1962, perhaps as many as 40 per cent of teams were using the system. But that was its high-water mark. By then, Mao seems to have concluded that its spread threatened the entire system of collective farming. Its growth was stopped and the process thrown into reverse; at the same time, Chen Yun and Deng Zihui (both regarded by Mao as being strong advocates of private farming) were dismissed. From late 1962 until the late 1970s, Chinese agriculture remained fully collectivized.[24]

The scale of the recovery is apparent from the data. Grain production reached its nadir in 1961 at 137 million tonnes, well down on the 1957 figure of 195 million tonnes. Thereafter, production pushed upwards, though it was not until 1965 that it was back to its pre-Leap level (SSB 2000a: 37). The recovery of overall agricultural production was also largely complete by 1965. However, the restoration of per capita output – China's population rose by 80 million people, famine notwithstanding, between 1957 and 1965 – took even longer. In these parlous circumstances, the very fact that China imported 5.8 million tonnes of grain in 1961 – compared to a mere 66,000 tonnes in 1960 – made a substantial difference to rural food consumption levels (MOA 1989: 534).

The collapse of output during the Great Leap Forward was by some way the biggest fluctuation in output in the entire post-1949 period. As is clear from the data (Figure 4.4), the trough in agriculture was far deeper than anything caused by the Cultural Revolution; in other years, the decline took agriculture barely below the trend line. However, the Leap was much more of a disaster for agriculture than for industry. It is true that industrial output did boom in the late 1950s and then fell back rather quickly. But in the early 1960s, industrial production was only a little below its long-run trend because urban-based industry was barely affected by the

136 *Chinese Economic Development*

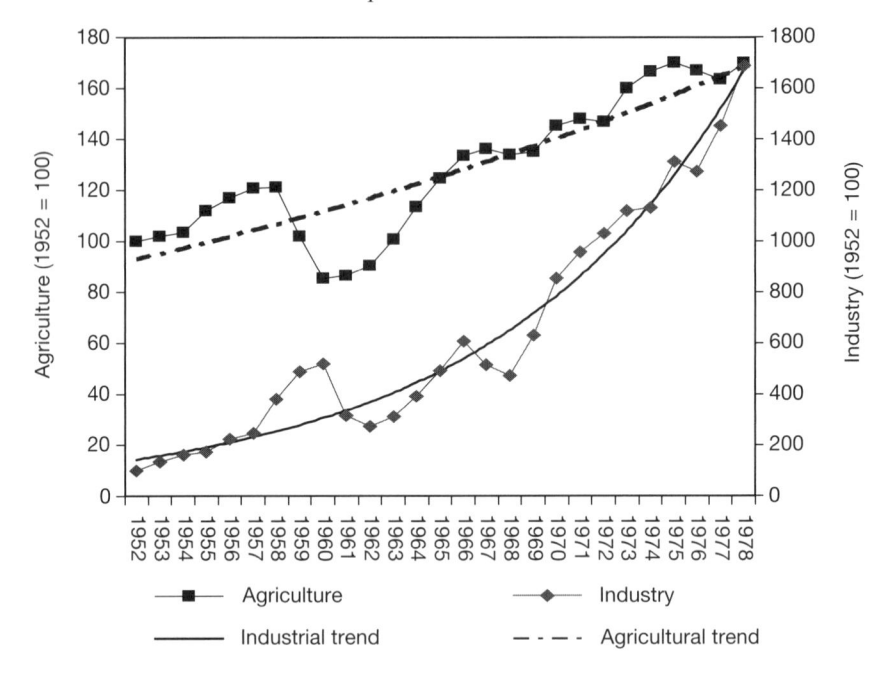

Figure 4.4 Trends in gross value-added in agriculture and industry (comparable price indices; 1952 = 100) (Source: SSB (2000a: 4).)

Leap. The boom was primarily an iron- and steel-based rural phenomenon, and similarly the collapse. China's main industrial producers, based in the large cities, suffered little from food shortages, and, because of their heavy industry orientation, were not reliant upon raw materials produced in the farm sector.

During the early 1960s, the climate of opinion had changed so much that the CCP leadership even toyed with idea of adopting a more outward-orientated development strategy. This was Zhou Enlai's famous 'Four Modernizations' strategy, first outlined as early as January 1960, and fully articulated in 1963. It proposed a policy of import substitution instead of self-reliance, and was designed to modernize Chinese agriculture, industry, scientific culture and defence. It was ultimately rejected because of the military implications of relying heavily on imports from the US at a time of deteriorating Sino-American relations over Vietnam. This strategy was briefly revived in 1971–4 as relations with the USA improved, but was only really implemented during 1978–82. We can only speculate on what might have happened but for US involvement in Vietnam.

The evolution of spatial inequality

Although the main purpose of the Great Leap Forward was to boost output, one of its subsidiary objectives was to reduce regional inequality. One particular aim was to narrow the urban–rural gap by means of rural modernization, as we have seen.

The strategy outlined in Mao's (1956) speech 'On the Ten Great Relationships' was more ambitious in that it also called for a narrowing of the gap between the coastal provinces and the Chinese interior by means of rural industrialization. Nevertheless, this speech was primarily about balanced growth. As the text makes clear, the interior provinces were to be developed but the coastal provinces were not to be neglected. In fact, Mao (1956) even argued that the strategy pursued in the early 1950s gave too much weight to the interior:

> About 70 per cent of all our industry, both light and heavy, is to be found in the coastal regions and only 30 per cent in the interior. This irrational situation is a product of history. The coastal industrial base must be put to full use, but to even out the distribution of industry as it develops we must strive to promote industry in the interior. We have not made any major mistakes on the relationship between the two. However, in recent years we have underestimated coastal industry to some extent and have not given great enough attention to its development. This must change. ... It does not follow that all new factories should be built in the coastal regions. Without doubt, the greater part of the new industry should be located in the interior so that industry may gradually become evenly distributed; moreover, this will help our preparations against war. But a number of new factories and mines, even some large ones, may also be built in the coastal regions.

The evidence suggests that this goal of reducing spatial inequality was achieved. On the eve of the Third Front in 1964, the unweighted coefficient of variation stood at 0.70, well down on the levels of both 1952 (0.78) and 1957 (0.84). One might be forgiven for concluding from this that the spatial processes at work in the 1950s were benign, and indicative of the redistributive impact of Maoism. And the trajectory of some of the key jurisdictions seems to support this happy conclusion. For example, Shanghai's per capita GDP rose substantially between 1952 and 1964, but the rise (from 640 to 927 *yuan*) was smaller in percentage terms than elsewhere. In Guizhou, for instance, per capita GDP doubled, and in Sichuan the rise was no less than 150 per cent. The rapid rural industrialization of the initial years of the Leap tended to help those provinces which already had a well-established industrial base, but this increase in the dispersion was short-lived, and the trend after 1964 was firmly downwards. In short, the raw data show a clear process of catch-up at work.

In reality, however, the processes at work were much less favourable than this interpretation suggests. For one thing, although inequality had declined, the provincial rankings had not changed very much; the top seven provinces and cities in 1964 were the same seven as in 1952, and six of the bottom seven of 1964 had been there in 1952. In other words, the gap had narrowed between rich and poor provinces, but we can hardly talk about transformation. More importantly, much of the narrowing that had taken place was as a result of the Great Famine, which had the unintended effect of reducing population (and hence raising GDP per head) in poor provinces much more than in rich provinces.

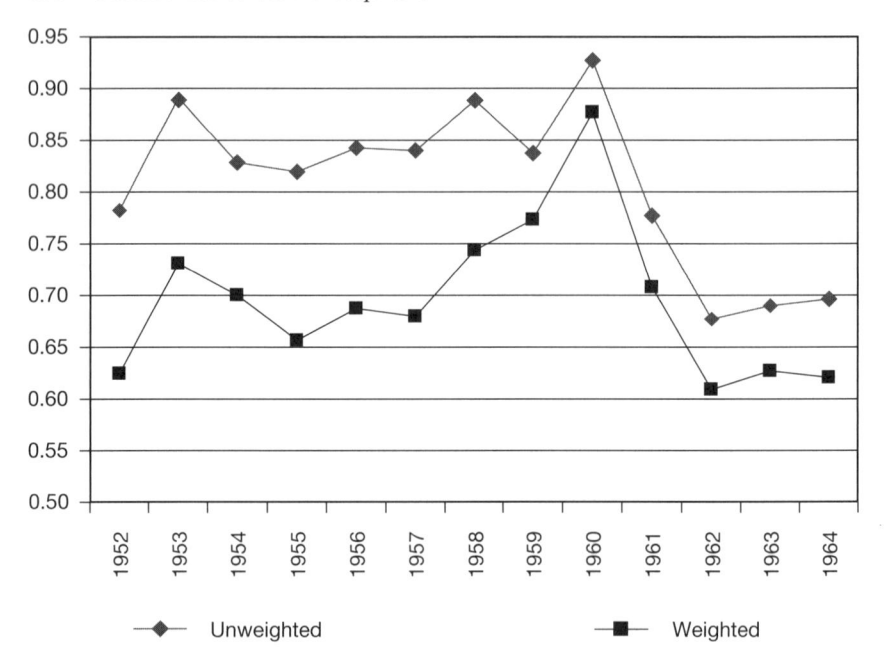

Figure 4.5 Coefficients of variation for provincial per capita GDP (current prices) (Source: SSB (2000a).)

Note: The weighted coefficient of variation is calculated by weighting the per capita GDP of each province and municipality by the size of its population.

Table 4.5 shows this very clearly. Anhui and Sichuan enjoyed above-average income growth because, as the population data show, they experienced mortality rates which were far above the average. Slow population growth thus translated into big GDP per capita growth. Thus Anhui's population in 1964 was 5 per cent lower than it had been in 1957, and Sichuan's population was 2 per cent lower. By contrast, Tianjin's population was 19 per cent higher and the rise for Beijing was

Table 4.5 Population trends, 1957–1964

	Total population (million)		Change (per cent)	Peak mortality rate (per 1,000)
	1957	1964	1957–1964	
Shanghai	6.90	10.86	+57	7.7 (1961)
Beijing	6.33	7.76	+23	10.8 (1961)
Tianjin	5.30	6.30	+19	10.3 (1960)
Henan	48.40	50.99	+5	39.6 (1960)
Sichuan	50.89	49.81	−2	54.0 (1960)
Anhui	33.37	31.81	−5	68.6 (1960)

Source: SSB (2005a).

23 per cent. In Shanghai, the rise was a colossal 57 per cent. These trends reflected both the absence of any demographic disaster in the big cities, and massive in-migration. In short, the narrowing of spatial inequality between 1955 and 1964 was simply an unintended by-product of the horrendous mortality toll in some parts of China during the late 1950s and early 1960s.

Assessment

There were some gains from the Leap, especially in terms of learning-by-doing in rural industry; many Chinese peasants had barely seen steel before 1958, let alone attempted to make it. The skills acquired in the learning process helped in the development of rural industry in the 1970s, and especially after 1978. We may also note the important point that famine in China was hardly unusual; the death tolls in the famines of late Qing and Republican periods were also extremely high. During the North China famine of 1876–9 between 9 and 14 million died. Shandong suffered around half a million deaths, 2.5 million died in Zhili province (which covered the modern province of Hebei and the cities of Beijing and Tianjin) and perhaps 5.5 million died in Shanxi. Even the coming of railways did not put an end to famine. True, famine relief kept the death toll in the North China famine of 1920–1 down to 0.5 million, but the famine of 1928–30 claimed perhaps as many as 10 million dead. Some estimates suggest that 3 million died in Gansu (its population was only about 6 million) and 3 million died in Shaanxi (Li 2007: 272, 299 and 303–4; Bohr 1972: 16 and 65). And perhaps as many as 10 million died during the famine of 1896–1900 which played an important role in precipitating the Boxer rebellion (Davis 2001: 7, 64–79 and 177–88).

For all that, the Great Leap Forward was a policy disaster. The famine which it precipitated was on a vast scale. It constitutes the single greatest failure of the Maoist era, and it did much to erode the CCP's fund of goodwill within rural China. Moreover, it is hard to avoid the conclusion that the blame for the failure of the Leap and the extent of the famine must be shared across the CCP leadership. To be sure, much of the impetus for the Leap came from Mao himself. Nevertheless, other prominent members of the Party – including Deng Xiaoping, Bo Yibo, Liu Shaoqi, Zhou Enlai and Chen Yun – went along with the programme. In a very real sense, they were Mao's willing executioners. The culpability of those on the right of the Party goes far towards explaining why discussions of the famine have been largely expunged from the numerous 'histories of the victors' which have published since 1978.

Notes

1 For the Chinese debates on economic strategy in the 1950s, see Lardy and Lieberthal (1983), Selden (1988) and Teiwes and Sun (1993, 1999).
2 The estimates made by Liu and Yeh (1965: 66) suggest that total Chinese GDP in 1957 was between 40 and 60 per cent higher (depending on the prices used) than it had been in 1933. Maddison's estimate is at the bottom end of this range.

3 The best discussion of the politics of the period 1955–8 is provided by Teiwes and Sun (1999), much of which is based upon newly published Chinese sources, including the memoirs of Bo Yibo (who was Chairman of the State Economic Commission in the late 1950s). Much of the older literature on this period is now rather dated. However, Selden (1979) remains a very useful collection of documents and commentary, whilst the works of MacFarquhar *et al.* (1989) and Cheek and Saich (1997) have done much to broaden our understanding.

4 Here I accept Teiwes's view that Chinese politics in the 1950s is best thought of in terms of a dominant Mao (who was at times conservative and other times radical), rather than in terms of a two-line struggle between radicals (led by Mao) and conservatives (led by Liu Shaoqi and Chen Yun) which was only eventually 'won' by Mao in the mid-1960s. The Teiwes version makes more sense, because there is no example of a policy dispute where Mao was *forced* to give ground to the opposition.

5 The phrase itself was first used by Mao in May 1956 (MacFarquhar *et al.* 1989: 162fn).

6 This excerpt comes from the edited version of the speech which originally appeared in *People's Daily in* June 1957. A much more detailed (but far more rambling) version of Mao's view is given in the 'Speaking Notes' to the 1957 speech; see MacFarquhar *et al.* (1989) for the full text.

7 By way of comparison, criticism of the Party was led by intellectuals, academics and artists in 1957, whereas it was led by Red Guards during the Cultural Revolution. The level of violence was much greater in 1966 than in 1957.

8 For some of the extensive literature on the politics of the Leap, see MacFarquhar (1983), Teiwes and Sun (1999), Chan (2001) and Bernstein (2006). For the impact on the agricultural sector, see Bramall (1993), Walker (in Ash 1998), Chang and Wen (1997), Lin and Yang (2000) and Yang (1996, 1997). For a flavour of the intensity of some of the debates about the famine, see Nolan (1993a) and the reply by Sen in the same issue of the *Journal of Peasant Studies*.

9 It deserves to be noted that both Deng Xiaoping and Liu Shaoqi were strong supporters of the Leap, though since 1978 the Party has sought to play down its own culpability in the events of 1958–62. Instead, the burden of responsibility has been shifted entirely – but wrongly – to Mao and to the Gang of Four. The only coherent alternative vision was that sketched by Chen Yun (Lardy and Lieberthal 1983); neither Deng nor Liu had much useful to say.

10 See also the evocative description of eating in communal canteens given in Potter and Potter (1990: 71–3).

11 Whether that is true in terms of the percentage of the population who died is more questionable, but it does not alter the qualitative point that the Chinese famine was a tragedy of catastrophic proportions.

12 For example, the official death rate given nationally for 1960 is 25 per 1,000, but these revised data assume a rate of 43 per 1,000 (Chang and Halliday 2005: 456fn). This revision is close to Banister's (1984: 254) estimate of 44 per 1,000 for that year. The difference between the Banister and Chang–Halliday estimates is largely explained by Chang–Halliday's use of a mortality figure of 28 per 1,000 in 1961, compared with Banister's 23 per 1,000.

13 Even Patnaik (2002: 52) think that a figure of 12 million excess deaths is plausible, though she hedges her bets by saying that mortality 'may be overestimated' and that there was a 'fairly adequate level of per capita food grain output even in the worst year'. She is, I think, rather optimistic about food availability; the national figure for calorie availability according to the FAO (2006) was only 1,641 kcals in 1961, and that was not the worst year; Piazza's (1986) estimates put the 1960 figure at only 1,578 kcals. In any case, the shortfall was concentrated in a few provinces, and that was the real problem; above-average availability in some provinces could not compensate for

14 Some households may still have been able to withdraw from collectives after 1956, as Lin (1990: 1240) himself rightly observes. However, few did so, and certainly not in numbers sufficient to lead to the collapse of collectives. It therefore makes sense to date the *de facto* removal of the exit right to 1956 rather than to 1958. This chronology undermines Lin's argument that the removal of the right caused the famine.
15 The reduction in the number of draught animals caused by collectivization in 1955–6 must also have contributed to this crisis.
16 Trade (or husked) grain is grain after processing; in China this typically reduces grain weight by about 30 per cent. Chinese output data are typically in terms of unhusked grain (*yuanliang*), whereas internal and external trade data for grain are usually given in terms of husked grain (*maoyiliang*).
17 It is important to emphasize here that Sichuan's problem during 1959–61 was primarily as a result of the fall in output. The procurement rate rose because of the fall in output, not because the total *volume* of procurements rose. Note, however, that Sichuan's experience was unusual; the national net procurement volume in 1959 was nearly 48 million tonnes, about 6 million tonnes higher than in 1958 (MOA 1989: 410).
18 These estimates are for the 1980s. Chinese men and women were of smaller stature in the early 1960s and therefore the food requirement would have been a little less.
19 There was thus an FAD during 1958 in the counties affected, but not in rural Sichuan as a whole.
20 Kueh's index is based on official Chinese estimates of area affected by natural disaster. However, as he points out (Kueh 1995: Appendix A), these trends are largely confirmed by the rainfall data collected by the State Meteorological Bureau. Note that not all the local studies pick up the existence of drought conditions (partly because of local variations). For example, Endicott's (1988: 229) account of rural trends in Shifang county – the heart of Sichuan's Chengdu plan and a county where famine conditions were widespread – presents data showing July rainfall in 1961 to have been well *above* the 1960–70 average. By contrast, Kueh (1995: 283) states that 'the July precipitation in 1961 throughout … the Sichuan basin was over 50 percent lower than the long-term mean.' This type of discrepancy may reflect abnormal local conditions in Shifang county, but it may also reflect data collection problems; some of Endicott's informants (his study was based on interviews conducted in the early 1980s and therefore was reliant upon the memories of his informants) apparently did speak of a drought during the planting season (Endicott 1988: 56).
21 Useful discussions of the policy reversal are those offered by MacFarquhar (1997), Teiwes and Sun (1999) and Chan (2001).
22 Commerce was regulated by the Forty Articles, handicrafts by the Thirty-Five Articles, and so on. For a full discussion, see MacFarquhar (1997: ch. 4)
23 Strictly speaking, the system was one of *baochan daohu* (contracting production to households). Land remained under collective ownership (and could not be sold) but management was placed in the hands of households. There was considerable debate in China during the early 1960s as to whether this was collective farming or not.
24 The organization of communes was also regularized. Communes themselves remained, but decision-making powers were delegated in the main to production brigades and production teams. A production team typically consisted of about thirty households (150 people) in the early 1970s. The production brigade comprised on average some seven production teams and is best thought of as being a village community. There were about twelve brigades to each commune in the early 1970s. For the fluctuating size of teams, brigades and communes, see SSB (1983: 147).

Part 3
The late Maoist era, 1963–1978

5 The late Maoist development strategy

The launch of the Socialist Education Movement (SEM) in 1963 marks a distinct turning-point in Mao's approach to economic development and heralded the beginning of a fifteen-year period which I shall call the late Maoist era.

In adopting this periodization, I am suggesting that we should regard the fifteen-year period between 1963 and 1978 as an era in which policy-making was coherent. This is not an uncontroversial approach. After all, many have seen chaos and random violence as the leitmotifs of this period. Indeed it is not without reason that Chinese officialdom has styled the period between 1966 and 1976 as the 'ten years of chaos' ever since the end of the 1970s (Central Committee 1981). In the political realm at least, there was much in the 1960s that was unplanned, decentralized and perhaps even spontaneous. I will consider the question of how we should view this period in rather more detail below, but it is worth emphasizing here that there was certainly a coherence to economic policy-making during these years. To be sure, there were changes in emphasis across this period; for example, the economy became more open to foreign trade after 1971. However, the key structures and policies – collective farming, the emphasis on state-led rural modernization ('walking on two legs'), the suppression of the private sector – changed very little. Moreover, and perhaps more importantly than anything, the level and allocation of investment was determined by defence considerations; the shadow of the Third Front hangs across the entire period between its inception in 1964 and the end of the 1970s, when it was scaled back.

Nor is it unreasonable to regard 1963 and 1978 as turning-points. 1963 marks the end of the Great Famine; by then, the crude death rate had returned to its 1957 level. More importantly, 1963 marked the first real attempt to transform Chinese society and its economy by means of cultural change.[1] The instrument of change here was the SEM, which evolved into the far better-known policies of the Cultural Revolution of 1966–8. The choice of 1978 as the end-date of late Maoism is less controversial; despite the death of Mao (9h September) and the arrest of the Gang of Four (6 October) during 1976, there was little real change in economic policy until after the Third Plenum of 1978.

Nevertheless, although the fifteen years from 1963 to 1978 are viewed as a coherent whole, it make sense to distinguish between the different phases of the late Maoist era (Box 5.1). The best-known of these phases was 1966–8, years

Box 5.1 Phases of late Maoism

Period	Phase	Themes
1963–6	First things	The Socialist Education Movement and the beginning of the Third Front
1966–8	The Cultural Revolution	The Red Guard movement; the attack on urban cadres and officials; urban violence and factional street fighting
1968–71	The Army in command	Suppression of the Red Guard movement; dominance of Lin Biao
1971–6	Disillusion and opening up	Growing popular disillusion over class struggle; the gradual decline and death of Mao; expanding international trade
1976–8	The struggle for the succession	The gradual assumption of power by Deng Xiaoping

which I shall refer to as the Cultural Revolution. In this regard, my approach is at variance with that of other Chinese and Western scholars, many of whom use Cultural Revolution to refer to the entire period between 1966 and 1976. However, this is not a very helpful label to my mind, because the phase 1966–8 was qualitatively different from the rest.[2] That is because they were years of mass mobilization, during which newly established Red Guard groups were mobilized by Mao to restructure the CCP itself. In other words, this was a period during which there developed a grassroots movement directed against the Party itself. This phase of late Maoism only came to an end when most Red Guards were rusticated in 1968. After 1968, factional fights were mainly within the Party itself, and therefore of a very different character from those of 1966–8.

In fairness, it is worth noting that the phrase 'second cultural revolution' was also used to describe the process of rectification that occurred after the death of Lin Biao. That lends credence to the notion of a continuing Cultural Revolution for the entire 1966–76 period. However, the most radical period in policy terms – and one which saw protracted street fighting between rival factions which were made up mainly of university and, even more prominently, middle-school students, in many of China's cities – was 1966–8. The street fighting in Nanning, which continued into the summer of 1968, is perhaps the most extreme example (MacFarquhar and Schoenhals 2006: 244–5). However, the decision to recommence classes in middle schools and at universities in the autumn of 1967 (using PLA troops to restore order where necessary), as well as the 'sending down' programme (whereby much urban youth was sent to live in the countryside), put paid to the worst of the Red Guard activism by the end of the summer of 1968. Although 1968 was an exceptionally bad year for violence – the "cleansing of class ranks' in that year led to an unprecedented wave of murders and executions, with cannibalism reported in parts of Yunnan and Guangxi (Macfarquhar and Schoenhals 2006: 258–9) – the scale of persecution diminished thereafter. As a result, much of the literature uses the term 'Cultural Revolution' to refer exclusively to the period between 1966 and 1968, and that is the approach adopted here.[3]

The late Maoist era (and especially the Cultural Revolution phase) is widely seen as being little more than a period of acute political upheaval which inflicted immense damage on Chinese society, and on the Chinese economy. However, I shall argue that this conventional wisdom is inaccurate. There can be no doubting the violence which pervaded these years. However, late Maoism was first and foremost intended to be a programme of rural economic development which would be driven by ideological and cultural change.[4] The only way forward for China, argued Mao, was make a decisive ideological break with the traditional interpretation of Marx, and to cast off in particular the economic determinism associated with Stalinism, in which the superstructure is simply derivative and of no independent causal importance. For Mao, economic modernization could only be achieved by cultural and ideological transformation – in other words, by means of a Cultural Revolution. To put this in Marxian terminology, superstructural change was needed to transform the economic base. I will suggest that Mao took these theoretical concepts very seriously, and that we can only really understand the Chinese political economy during the late Maoist era Revolution if we follow in his footsteps.

This chapter outlines the politics, policy-making and economic trends of the late Maoist era. The chapters which follow discuss the programme of rural modernization in more detail. Chapters 6, 7 and 8 each discuss the principal development strategies adopted during the late Maoist era: education, rural industrialization and collective farming. Chapter 9 assesses the overall impact of late Maoism on Chinese development. We begin by outlining the ideas at the heart of the late Maoist development strategy.

Superstructural change as an instrument of policy

At the most general level, the key to understanding the late Maoist development strategy is to recognize that it represented a repudiation by Mao of several aspects of the very Marxist orthodoxy that he himself espoused in the 1950s (and discussed in the previous chapter).[5] As conceived by Mao, the development strategy was a programme designed not merely to develop the forces of production or alter the relations of production, but to transform the superstructure of Chinese society.[6] The Cultural Revolution was thus a key component of the overall development strategy.

The role of the superstructure in Maoist thought

The relegation of the superstructure to a subordinate role in Marxist theory had long been questioned by Mao.[7] The insight dates as far back as his essay 'On Contradiction' of 1937:

When the superstructure (politics, culture, etc.) obstructs the development of the economic base, political and cultural changes become principal and decisive. Are we going against materialism when we say this? No. The reason is that while we recognize that in the general development of history the material determines the mental, and social being determines social consciousness, we also – and indeed must – recognize the reaction of mental on material things, of social consciousness on social being and of the superstructure on the economic base. (Mao 1937a: 116)

During the 1950s (and as discussed in Chapter 3), Mao adhered in terms of practical policy quite closely to the Marxian orthodoxy, rather than to the views expressed in 'On Contradiction'. To be sure, he increasingly emphasized the need to transform the relations of production – the introduction of collective farming was the embodiment of that – but nevertheless this type of approach was rather orthodox. Even the Great Leap Forward was in many ways (not in all, as we have seen) a copy of the Soviet Second Five Year Plan. However, the Cultural Revolution in particular, and late Maoism more generally, amounted to a decisive break with the orthodoxy and a reversion to the analysis outlined in his 1937 text.

The idea that superstructural transformation is a decisive causal factor in bringing about social change is Mao's major theoretical contribution to the development of Marxist thought, as well as his principal contribution to Marxian practice.[8] Marx himself wrote a considerable amount about the superstructure and its role in his theory of social change, but there is little agreement amongst Marxist scholars about what Marx really meant. One interpretation is that Marx believed that economic factors are crucial in the 'final instance', but that there will be times when the superstructure will exercise an autonomous influence on the economy. The superstructure is thus 'relatively autonomous'. As Larrain (1991) puts it, we need to distinguish between determinant and dominant. The economy determines social change in the last instance, but the superstructure will sometimes dominate the relations and forces of production.

An alternative and much more plausible approach is that offered by Mao and by Althusser. For them, there will never be an instance where only economic factors, or only superstructural factors are important. It simply will not do to replace one form of determinism (economic determinism) with another (superstructural determinism).[9] As Althusser (1969: 113) put it:

[I]n History, these instances, the superstructures, etc. – are never seen to step respectfully aside when their work is done or, when the Time comes, as his pure phenomena, to scatter before His Majesty the Economy as he strides along the royal road of the Dialectic. From the first moment to the last, the lonely hour of the 'last instance' never comes.

Instead, events are overdetermined in the Althusserian scheme of things. Social change therefore requires a simultaneous transformation of the superstructure, the forces of production and the relations of production. There is no sense in which any of these three are independent variables, and the others dependent. On the contrary: all three are both independent and dependent.

Box 5.2 shows the unfolding logic of Mao's approach. Transformation failed in the early 1950s because it focused on changing the forces of production. The strategy of 1955–63 was also flawed because it focused exclusively on changing the relations of production by establishing first collectives and then communes. The purpose of late Maoism was to transform both relations and forces of production – and to change the superstructure as well.

That Mao saw superstructural change as a key element in the broader process of social transformation that he wished to achieve in China is evident from both policy statements and from practice during the late 1960s and the 1970s. Consider Lin Biao's justification for the Cultural Revolution (Lin 1966: 14–15).[10] The argument was put forward with particular clarity in the 'Sixteen Points' written by the Central Cultural Revolution Group and adopted by the 11th Plenum of the Central Committee on 8 August 1966:

> The proletariat must ... change the mental outlook of the whole of society. At present, our objective is to struggle against and overthrow those persons in authority who are taking the capitalist road, to criticize and repudiate the reactionary bourgeois academic authorities and the ideology of the bourgeoisie and all other exploiting classes and to transform education, literature and art and all other parts of the superstructure not in correspondence with the socialist economic base, so as to facilitate the consolidation and development of the socialist system. ... The aim of the Great Proletarian Cultural Revolution is to revolutionize people's ideology and as a consequence to achieve greater, faster, better and more economical results in all fields of work. If the masses are fully

---

Box 5.2 The evolution of Maoist thought

1949–55	Accelerate economic growth by developing the forces of production and limited changes to the relations of production (land reform)
1955–63	Accelerate economic growth by a radical transformation of the relations of production (collectivization and nationalization)
1963–78	Accelerate economic growth by changing the superstructure (the Cultural Revolution) and by the continuing development of the rural forces of production (labour mobilization, rural education and rural industrialization)

aroused and proper arrangements are made, it is possible to carry on both the Cultural Revolution and production without one hampering the other, while guaranteeing high quality in all our work. The Great Proletarian Cultural Revolution is a powerful motive force for the development of the social productive forces in our country. Any idea of counter posing the Great Cultural Revolution to the development of production is incorrect. (Rojas 1968)

Another illustration of Mao's rethinking of Marxism is provided by his attitude towards material incentives. In the 1950s, China followed the Soviet pattern of establishing rigid pay scales for state employees, and attempting to link pay and work done in a 'scientific' way. By the mid-1960s, however, it seems to have become clear to Mao that China needed to change this approach to incentives. Instead of the 'scientific' approach which was the hallmark of Taylorism (which been very influential in the Soviet Union), it was necessary to abandon material incentives if the agricultural workforce was ever to be sufficiently motivated. This was extremely radical but it gained expression in several ways. As we have seen, communal canteens were established during the Great Leap Forward and in them households could eat free of charge. This effectively broke the link between consumption and work done; even if output was low, households would still be fed. The result was disastrous. But Mao's faith in non-material incentives was undiminished and this led to his wholehearted support for the Dazhai system of payments, which was introduced across much of rural China in the 1960s. Under the Dazhai system, peasants were awarded work points and these determined their income. However, work points were awarded as much on the basis of the ideological fervour ('virtue', as Shirk (1982) calls it) of the worker as on the amount of work done. The radicalism of such a system is transparent, and its implementation in many parts of rural China signalled a profound break with the Soviet 'scientific' approach

Changing the Chinese superstructure

Acceptance of an important role for the superstructure in driving the process of modernization in turn required Mao to supply answers to two distinct questions. First, which aspects of the Chinese superstructure needed to be changed? Second, how was such change to be accomplished?

As far as the first question is concerned, Mao's primary targets in the mid-1960s were the middle classes and intellectuals who continued to dominate China's universities and schools, and those cadres within the Party itself who were bent upon restoring capitalism in one form or other. For Mao, the elite structures and institutions of the Chinese state were acting both as a barrier to socio-economic mobility and to suppress the creativity and enthusiasm of the mass of the population; those structures therefore need to be destroyed, or at the very least thoroughly reformed. Qinghua University was a classic example (Hinton 1972; Andreas 2002). Its leadership was made up of Qinghua graduates from the 1930s who had gone on to study together abroad and then returned to take up faculty and leadership positions; in a very real sense, it was run by a self-perpetuating clique. Furthermore, its approach to education focused entirely on academic performance, an approach very much out of line with that pioneered at the Resistance University in Yan'an, which sought to combine manual work and the study of politics with academic work. Moreover, its practices tended to be discriminatory;[11] Not surprisingly, therefore, the initial targets of the Cultural Revolution were the intellectuals who were in positions of power in China's universities and schools, and their children.

As to the instruments of change, Mao's answer in 1956 had been to co-opt intellectuals. The Socialist Education Movement adopted a different approach by employing CCP work teams to cleanse villages of corrupt practices. However, as noted above, this was a revolution from above, of cadres criticizing other cadres. It was not a mass movement. Moreover, it was too local in its focus; the SEM did not target the central ministries, universities or Party organizations. The alternative adopted in the mid-1960s was to create extra-Party organizations, and that was the rationale behind the green light given to the Red Guard movements of 1966 and 1967.[12]

There were echoes of Rosa Luxemburg (1918) in all this. She recognized the usefulness of the worker-led strike – a mass movement if ever there was one – in bringing about social change and even revolution itself. Luxemburg argued passionately (in the immediate aftermath of the 1917 Russian Revolution) for a process of cultural change as a precondition for the successful transition to socialism. She also argued that genuine democracy was a necessary condition for the realization of socialism. Not only did it offer the means by which mass culture could be developed but it was also of immense instrumental significance in offering a mechanism whereby Party rule could be checked and controlled:

> [S]ocialism by its very nature cannot be decreed or introduced by *ukase*. ... The whole mass of the people must take part in it. Otherwise, socialism will be decreed from behind a few official desks by a dozen intellectuals. ... Socialism in life demands a complete spiritual transformation in the masses degraded by centuries of bourgeois rule. Social instincts in place of egotistical ones, mass initiative in place of inertia, idealism which conquers all suffering, etc., etc. No one knows this better, describes it more penetratingly; repeats it more stubbornly than Lenin. But he is completely mistaken in the means he employs. Decree, dictatorial force of the factory overseer, draconian penalties, rule by terror – all these things are but palliatives. The only way to a rebirth is the school of public life itself, the most unlimited, the broadest democracy and public opinion. It is rule by terror which demoralizes.

Whatever the provenance of the Red Guard movement, and whatever else one might say about the Cultural Revolution, it was not a movement orchestrated by a small number of desk-bound individuals. Mao, the Gang of Four, Liu Shaoqi and Zhou Enlai all sought to control the Red Guard movement, but none succeeded. It really was a mass movement in a way that was entirely lacking after 1968, when conflict revolved around intra-party factional fighting over the succession.

The late Maoist development strategy

Late Maoism broke with Stalinism in assuming that the superstructure – the system of law, government, cultural production and ideology – was a key determinant of the pace of modernization. It was not enough, Mao argued, to attempt to change the economic basis directly; that was mere economic determinism. Rather, it was necessary to change the superstructure as well.

But what then? When the old superstructure had been torn down, what was to be erected in its place? What type of development strategy was China to pursue? The answer to that question was an alternative path to modernity that was neither capitalist nor Stalinist. On the one hand, Mao had long recognized that capitalism was no more than a *cul-de-sac*. Free trade offered no basis for economic development in a China faced by an overwhelming military threat. US involvement in Vietnam and deteriorating relations with the USSR made state-led defence industrialization a priority if other developmental goals were not to be compromised. And the mass internal migration and uneven development that would inevitably result from the adoption of a market-orientated development strategy would undercut the very promise of the Revolution that had attracted the Chinese peasantry to the cause of the CCP in the first place. At the same time, and as is evident from Mao's own critique of Stalin's writings on economics, the Soviet road was not the answer. Not only had the Soviet bureaucracy ossified but also the Soviet development strategy was flawed because it overemphasized urban industrial growth at the expense of the development of the countryside, and had also neglected the possibilities inherent in small-scale industrial development

The alternative pioneered in China during the 1960s and 1970s was a strategy of 'walking on two legs': the balanced development of the urban and rural sectors. In terms of Marxist theory, China would combine a programme of superstructural change with a transformation of the economic base. In terms of practical policy, the late Maoist development strategy aimed first and foremost at the modernization of the Chinese countryside by means of the expansion of education, rural industrialization and collective farming. The aim was to put the countryside on a par with the level of development already achieved in the urban sector. The transformation of the superstructure would underpin all three of these rural modernization strategies.

Late Maoism was thus an ambitious attempt to change Chinese society by bringing about a simultaneous transformation of the forces of production, the relations of production and the superstructure. Superstructural transformation was to be brought about by educational reform in the urban sector, and by using urban youth as teachers to bring about a vast expansion of schooling in the Chinese countryside. Relations of production were to be based on public ownership of agricultural and industrial assets. There was to be no going back on the transformation of property rights which had been accomplished during the 1950s. Production in the countryside would be carried out by collectives and in border regions by quasi-military state farms. By enabling the mobilization of surplus labour, these institutions would prepare farmland for mechanization and would greatly expand the irrigated area. The expansion of industrial production would be carried out by state and collectively owned firms operating at different levels within the Chinese administrative hierarchy. The largest and most modern industries would be under the control of China's central ministries. Less significant industrial enterprises would be run by provincial, prefectural, municipal and county governments. And the communes and brigades would take responsibility for the creation and management of small-scale rural industry. None of this could be accomplished on the basis of private ownership, and therefore the private sector – in agriculture, industry and commerce – was to be suppressed as much as possible.

However, this emphasis on the transformation of the relations of production in the late Maoist strategy did not mean that technology and the modernization of the forces of production was to be neglected. On the contrary. The transformation of the relations of production was to go hand-in-hand with a massive programme of defence industrialization (the Third Front); and the development of rural industry would be accomplished by means of state subsidies and by using whatever imported technology was available. Research and development expenditure on new high-yielding crop varieties would be expanded. This willingness to use foreign technology suggests, rightly I think, that late Maoism was not envisaged as a programme of self-reliance. Of course some of the policies of the 1960s and 1970s certainly encouraged local communities to develop their economy using local resources; the case of Dazhai offers the classic example. Nevertheless, the idea that self-reliance was pursued to an extreme is contradicted by the subsidies provided to rural industry and to the Third Front (financed by resource extraction from agriculture via the internal terms of trade), and by Mao's willingness to expand international trade wherever possible. As we will see, it was the international environment rather than any ideological hostility which conditioned the extent of China's engagement with the world economy.

It is also fair to say that egalitarianism was not pursued to extremes during the late Maoist era. There was no attempt to abolish the elaborate pay scales for cadres and industrial workers that had been established in urban areas. Gender inequality was accepted and even promoted; it was a rare commune where even the most productive woman was paid more work points than the least productive male. Nevertheless, a reduction in inequality was one of the main purposes of the post-1963 development strategy. The principles of balance and 'walking on two legs' had been set out in Mao's 1956 speech 'On the Ten Great Relationships' and the late Maoist strategy did not deviate from these goals. Even a cursory reading of the text makes clear that Mao by no means envisaged that urban industrialization would come to a halt, or that the development of the coastal provinces would come to an end. Nevertheless, it is clear that he hoped that an acceleration in the pace of development in the Chinese interior would reduce spatial inequality. As Mao (1956) pointed out:

> About 70 per cent of all our industry, both light and heavy, is to be found in the coastal regions and only 30 per cent in the interior. This irrational situation is a product of history. The coastal industrial base must be put to full use,

but to even out the distribution of industry as it develops we must strive to promote industry in the interior.

Given the coherence of the development strategy which unfolded in the 1960s and 1970s, it seems right to conclude that late Maoism should not be seen as a moment of madness.[13] Nor should it be viewed as a programme which grew out of a misinterpretation of Marxist theory – which is the essence of the verdict delivered by the Party on Mao in 1981 and echoed in the writings of Western political scientists who have tended to write off late Maoist ideas as 'Utopian' and 'voluntarist'.[14] And it makes little sense to characterize Maoism as some desperate attempt to retain power, the usual interpretation of late Maoism in the West. As Teiwes (1993) has shown, Mao's hold on power was never in serious doubt at any point after the early 1940s, and certainly not from Liu Shaoqi. Furthermore, it is not very convincing to portray Maoism as indistinguishable from Stalinism, as many have done. Rather, the late Maoist strategy represents a decisive rupture with Marxist–Leninist thought. It was conceived as a thoroughgoing programme of superstructural change designed to make possible a simultaneous restructuring of the economic base, and to render impossible any capitalist restoration.

The underlying vision behind the late Maoist strategy is set out in tabular form in Box 5.3. Late Maoism thus involved a simultaneous transformation of the Chinese superstructure and economic base to effect economic modernization. What was unusual about it from a Marxist point of view was that it placed such emphasis on the superstructure at all.

Late Maoism can also be seen as crystallizing around three specific economic initiatives designed to transform both superstructure and the economic basis, namely collective farming, rural industrialization and expansion of rural education. Collective ownership and the development of new crop varieties would make possible the modernization of farming and the expansion of yields. State and collective ownership, the development of a rural skills base and industrial subsidies would promote the expansion of rural industry. The expansion of rural education was conceived as being both good in itself and as a means towards the end of developing rural industry and raising agricultural production. The significance of these policy initiatives is such that they each deserve a chapter. I therefore discuss education, collective farming and rural industrialization in Chapters 6, 7 and 8 respectively.

However, before looking at these policy initiatives in detail, we need to outline the way in which late Maoism unfolded in practice after 1963 in both the economic and political spheres. The remainder of this chapter therefore charts the course of economic policy and Chinese political change over the years between 1963 and 1978.

Economic structures and macroeconomic policy

The ideas articulated in the previous section amounted to much more than mere talk. Indeed their implementation in practice meant that China's economic structure

Box 5.3 The logic of the late Maoist development strategy

Marxist Category	Maoist Instruments

Superstructure	1 **Education**
	  a Abolition of examination-based progression
	  b The introduction of work and study across the whole educational system
	  c The *xiafang* programme
	  d The expansion of rural schooling
	2 **Purge of the party and institutions of state**
	  a The Socialist Education Movement
	  b The Cultural Revolution
	  c 'Cleansing of class ranks' (1968)
	  d Learning from the Army, 1968–71

Relations of production	3 **Public ownership**
	  a State and collective industries
	  b Collective and state farms

Forces of production	4 **Imported technology**
	  a Modernization of urban industry
	  b Modernization of agriculture
	5 **Industrial subsidies to:**
	  a The Third Front
	  b Commune and brigade industry
	6 **Research and development spending**

during the late Maoist period was unusual by the standards of other developing countries. Private ownership was virtually non-existent. Instead, China followed the Soviet model in combining collective farming in agriculture with state and collective ownership of industry. However, Chinese macroeconomic policy in the late Maoist era was in some respects relatively conventional. It emphasized the achievement of a high rate of investment, and the mobilization of surplus labour, in order to achieve rapid economic growth. The non-superstructural aspects of the late Maoist strategy therefore something much in common with the development policies being pursued at that time in Latin American and across East Asia

The structure of ownership

In the Chinese countryside, farmland was owned and managed by the collective farms set up in 1955–6. These collectives had been merged to form communes during the Great Leap Forward, but the famine resulted ultimately in a reversion to smaller units of agricultural organization. Communes remained, but the key units of production were the production brigade (usually a group of villages) and the production team (a village). During the most radical years of the late Maoist era, private plots were eliminated entirely in many parts of China, but for the most part households were allowed to manage a small amount of land, typically amounting to around 5 per cent of cultivated area ('private plots'). This land was often used to grow vegetables and to provide the feed to rear a pig.

Industrial production was carried out by state – and collectively owned enterprises; there was no private industry to speak of during the late Maoist era. Though notionally distinct – collective industrial enterprises in principle retained full control over the disposal of post-tax profits – SOEs and COEs operated in a way that was virtually indistinguishable in both urban and rural areas. Most of them were to be found in the larger urban conurbations, but, as we will see, a feature of the late Maoist era was the development of rural industry and the urbanization of parts of the countryside.

Macroeconomic policy

The main policy challenges faced by the Maoist regime were both internal and external. The dissolution of China's alliance with the Soviet Union in the early 1960s left it strategically isolated, and growing US involvement in Vietnam triggered what was to become the famous programme of defence industrialization carried out mainly in western China (the Third Front). The main internal constraint was imposed by accelerating population growth. Banister's (1987) estimates show the growth rate accelerating from around 0.5 per cent in 1949 to about 2.5 per cent by the late 1950s. After the demographic disaster of the famine, the growth rate accelerated still further, rising to close to 3 per cent per year during the late 1960s. Thereafter, under the influence of the two-child policy, the promotion of late marriage and the expansion of female education, the rate fell back.[15] By the late 1970s, the growth rate was down to about 1.5 per cent per year. Nevertheless, the net effect was that China's population grew significantly. By 1978 the total stood at 959 million, over 300 million more than the figure recorded in 1962.

Together, rapid population growth and limited scope for international trade meant that the first task for the planners was to ensure an adequate supply of food for the Chinese population. That translated into the overwhelming emphasis placed on the expansion of agricultural production during the 1960s and 1970s, which in turn limited the rural labour which could be safely redeployed for the expansion of rural industrial production.

In broad macroeconomic terms, the strategy adopted to resolve these dilemmas was to import technology from abroad wherever possible, to intensify spending on domestic research and development (a programme which eventually produced superb high-yielding seed varieties and artemisinin, a spectacularly successful treatment for malaria) but principally by maintaining an exceptionally high rate

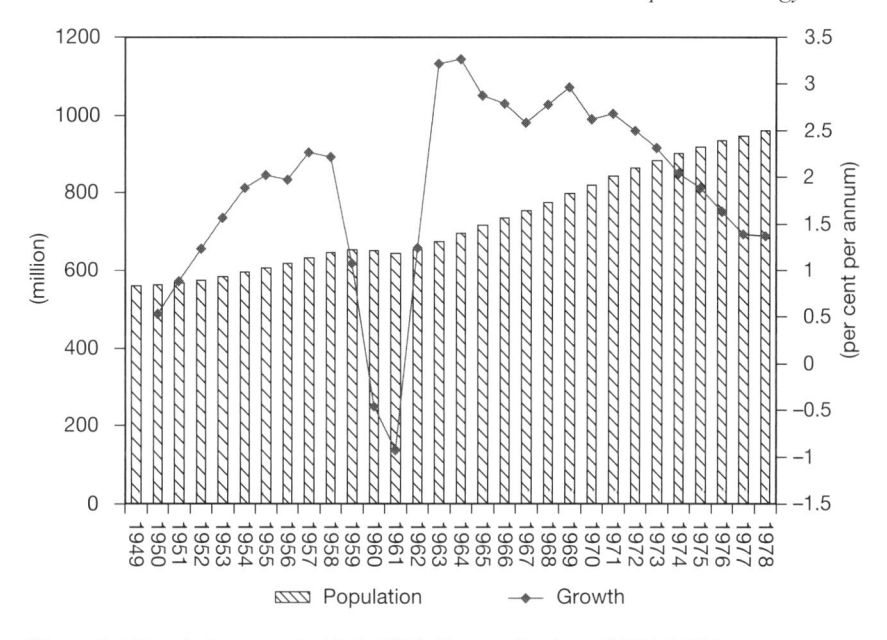

Figure 5.1 Population growth, 1949–1978 (Source: Banister (1987: 352).)

of investment. In this sense at least, the Maoist strategy had strong similarities to those pursued by Stalin in the 1930s and by Lee Kuan Yew in Singapore during much of the postwar era. The scale of the investment drive is shown in Figure 5.2. On the eve of the Leap, the investment share was about 20 per cent, a figure which was reattained by 1964. By the end of the Maoist era, however, that share had risen to 30 per cent, a very high figure for such a poor country.

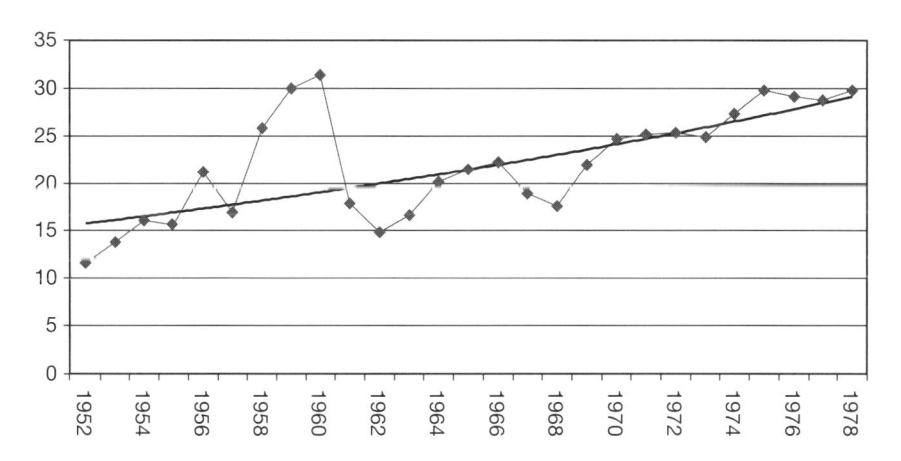

Figure 5.2 Share of gross fixed investment in GDP (per cent; current prices) (Source: SSB (2005a: 13).)

158 *Chinese Economic Development*

The late Maoist programme of superstructural change

Nevertheless, and as already noted, there was far more to the late Maoist era than public ownership and high rates of investment. A central element was the programme of political and ideological change, which began with the Socialist Education Movement and culminated in the Cultural Revolution.

The Socialist Education Movement[16]

The Maoist attempt to transform the superstructure of Chinese society began in earnest in 1963. The first shot was the campaign to 'learn from Comrade Lei Feng'; the slogan first appeared in March 1963 (MacFarquhar 1997: 338). Much more important, however, was the commencement of the Socialist Education Movement (SEM) in May 1963.[17] The aims of the SEM were set out initially in the form of a ten-point CCP resolution detailing a range of problems which needed to be overcome, especially in rural areas. The centrepiece was initially the 'Small Four Clean Ups' campaign, which aimed to rid the countryside of cadre corruption in relation to accounts, warehouses, housing and work points.[18] It was supplemented by the 'Five Antis', which focused on urban corruption.

The SEM was significant because it was the first major attempt to purge Chinese cadres since the 1949 Revolution. It was designed first and foremost to rid the Chinese countryside of the nepotism and corruption which had developed during the previous decade, as well as to put an end to re-emergence of private farming, business and commerce which had occurred in the immediate aftermath of the Great Famine. Precisely because the Socialist Education Movement focused on political change, it was very different from the campaigns of the 1950s, such as collectivization (1955–6) and the Great Leap Forward (1958), which had focused on changing the economic base. And the manner in which the SEM had evolved by 1965 meant that it was much more comparable in scope and scale to the Cultural Revolution which was to follow, and it therefore should be seen as part of the same programme of superstructural change – even though not part of the Cultural Revolution itself.[19]

The Cultural Revolution, 1966–1968

The Cultural Revolution began in the late spring of 1966. It started as an elite conflict over how to interpret Wu Han's play *Hai Rui Dismissed from Office*, which had been heavily criticized by Yao Wenyuan, one of Jiang Qing's coterie, in November 1965. Peng Zhen and officials in the Ministry of Culture regarded the play as unexceptionable, but Jiang Qing and her Shanghai forum took issue with its premise that the masses were not the motive force of history. This argument escalated into a wider debate over cultural production, and student groups started to become involved. Mao himself had derided the Ministry as the 'Ministry of Foreign Mummies' and that was sufficient encouragement in the initial stages. Campus disruption steadily increased during the early of 1966, before work teams

Box 5.4 **A political chronology of late Maoism**

March 1963	Mao calls on the nation to 'Learn from Lei Feng'
May 1963	Socialist Education Campaign launched
1964	Third Front programme begins
May 1966	Start of the Cultural Revolution. Peng Zhen, Yang Shangkun and Luo Ruiqing removed from office. 'May 16th' circular setting out aims of the Cultural Revolution
25 October 1966	Lin Biao's speech at the Central Work Conference setting out the logic of the Cultural Revolution
August 1967	Ministry of Foreign Affairs seized by the Red Guards. Burning of the British mission
October 1968	End of the Red Guard phase; Mao calls for cadres and educated youth to go down into the countryside. Army used to purge cadres and Red Guards alike
late 1968	Exceptionally violent 'Cleansing of class ranks' campaign
March 1969	Border clashes in Manchuria between PLA and Soviet troops
1970–1	'One hit, three antis' campaign marked by a high level of violence
13 September 1971	Death of Lin Biao; end of the 'Army in command' phase of late Maoism
October 1971	China resumes its seat at the UN
February 1972	Nixon visits China
1972	Normalization of relations with Japan Restoration of diplomatic relations with the UK and West Germany
1974	Campaign to criticize Lin Biao and Confucius
9 September 1976	Death of Mao
6 October 1976	Arrest of the Gang of Four

were dispatched by Liu Shaoqi to quell the disturbances. At this point Mao intervened, defending the right of students to rebel. Buoyed by this encouragement, organizations developed which were dedicated to defending the ideas and the writings of the Chairman. And so, at Qinghua University in May 1966, the Red Guard movement was born.

At around the same time, Mao saw the possibilities inherent in using a mass student movement to transform China's elite institutions and structures. He therefore encouraged the Red Guard movement to flourish, and so it did.[20] A series of mass rallies were held in Tian'anmen square in the autumn, during which the Guards were reviewed by Mao, and Red Guard groups from across the country travelled to Beijing to participate. Many of these groups subsequently went on to travel across China, some of them making it to ethnic minority regions and to Tibet. The most enthusiastic Red Guards were often middle-school rather than university students, and as a result the violence was usually greater in China's schools than in its universities.

Several sociological factors played a key role in motivating participation in the Red Guard movement in Chinese middle schools.[21] Perhaps the most important factor was resentment directed towards the operation of China's educational system. Many of the middle-school children who joined the movement seem to have been disaffected at the growing competition for university entrance in the early 1960s and the obstacles thus placed in the way of socio-economic mobility. By that time, there was an enormous imbalance between the supply of would-be university students (as a result of school expansion) and university demand. Only around 30 per cent of upper middle-school graduates were able to enter university by that time, a very different situation from that which had been the norm in the mid-1950s.

By August 1966, the Red Guard movement was directing its energies towards destroying the 'four olds' (ideas, culture, customs and habits). Schools and universities started to close down. The homes of well-to-do families were looted, and many of their possessions were confiscated or destroyed. Public property was an even more obvious target, and many monasteries and temples across China were destroyed; examples include the Confucian temple at Qufu (in Shandong), Uighur mosques across Xinjiang and Buddhist temples on Mount Wutai in Shanxi. Nevertheless, it is said that Zhou Enlai was able to protect some sites such as the Forbidden City and the Dunhuang grottoes. More generally, all manner of strategies of resistance were adopted to protect historical relics. Sometimes it was enough simply to argue that a temple had been built by the sweat of the masses. But more innovative strategies were usually required. Thus custodians often claimed that Mao had liked and visited a particular site (such as Du Fu's cottage in Chengdu), or protected priceless murals by painting them over in advance of the arrival of Red Guards. Other cultural treasures were buried, or so festooned with pictures of the Chairman that any attack on the relic necessarily involved damaging a picture of Mao himself, a very serious crime. The Forbidden City was protected by letting it be known that Peng Zhen, the hated mayor of the city, had himself planned to raze it to the ground in order to construct a new Beijing. As no Red Guard wish to be associated with a plan of Peng's, the site was saved. More ignobly, Kang Sheng protected treasures by adding them to his own private collection (Ho 2006). But whatever the motivation, and irrespective of the truth of many of these accounts (for example the true role played by Zhou Enlai remains obscure), it is plain that many of China's cultural relics survived the despoliations of the Red Guards.

Throughout the autumn of 1966, a Red Guard terror took hold. By that time, most schools and universities had closed to allow students to participate in the Red Guard movement. In fact, most Chinese middle schools remained closed between June 1966 and October 1967, and most universities did not reopen until 1973. The targets of the terror were primarily those of 'bad' class backgrounds, particularly those who were landlords and who had worked in the KMT government before 1949, but the movement was also increasingly characterized by fighting between the various Red Guard factions. Increasingly, in fact, the Red Guard movement offered a vehicle for the expression of class-based resentment (Unger 1982: 100–2). As Unger (2007: 110 says):

> In the heat of the 1966–68 upheaval, under the cover of Maoist rhetoric, socio-economic groups that were disgruntled with their pre-Cultural Revolution situations came into conflict with groups that wished to preserve the status quo.

Broadly speaking, the children at Chinese urban middle schools split into two factions, and this factionalism led to the formation of different Red Guard groups. The first faction comprised the children of cadres and the children of workers and peasants. This faction had the higher class status and had done well since the 1949 Revolution, but the exam-based system of the early 1960s tended to discriminate against it. These children lacked the cultural capital enjoyed by middle-class children, and therefore their exam performance was comparatively poor. This in turn limited their prospects of progression to the best middle schools and ultimately to university. Most of them were therefore strongly in favour of the abandonment of the exam-based system of advancement. The other faction comprised the children of the middle class (clerks, teachers or the former owners of small businesses) and children whose parents had 'bad class' status. Even though these households had not done well in the 1950s, their cultural capital and the examination system ensured that, on average, they did much better at school than working-class, peasant or cadre children. These Red Guards had in effect a strong stake in maintaining the pre-1966 educational system. It was the one advantage that their class retained.

Innocents were inevitably caught up in the process of factional fighting; there are countless examples of the humiliation and torture of cadres, teachers and veteran revolutionaries. The targets of the movement widened as the 1960s wore on. The Ministry of Foreign Affairs, for example, was singled out and diplomats were far from immune. Indeed the process culminated in the burning of the British mission in August 1967, suitably symbolic revenge for the destruction of the Old Summer Palace at the hands of Western troops in the nineteenth century.

The escalating violence and disruption that occurred between 1966 and 1968 had not been Mao's intention. The slogan *tingchan nao geming* ('stop production, make revolution') is often used in Chinese accounts to summarize the policy, but, as we will see, the very purpose of the Cultural Revolution was to use political campaigns as a means towards the end of raising *production*. For example, the Dazhai model of rural development was regarded by Mao as vastly superior to the Chaoyang educational model pioneered in Liaoning, because in the latter political activism was seen as good in itself, whereas at Dazhai it was a means towards the end of raising output (Teiwes and Sun 2007: 341–2). And the burning of the British mission, surely one of the most emblematic acts of these years, was condemned even by Mao as anarchism (Teiwes and Sun 2007: 54).[22]

Yet irrespective of Mao's intentions and endeavours, production undoubtedly suffered in the short run. As Figure 5.3 shows, industrial production fell in absolute terms during 1967 and 1968, and even in 1969 it was not back to its trend. Even the countryside was affected. Although the conventional wisdom has long been that the Cultural Revolution had little impact on rural China, some of the most recent research suggests that the countryside was far from immune to the political campaigns (Walder and Yang 2003). In fact, parts of the rural economy also seem to have been badly affected, with the pattern of rural industrial growth at a provincial level showing marked fluctuations in output from year to year which can only have reflected political factors. In Sichuan, for example, rural industrial performance was especially bad in 1972 and 1975 (Bramall 2007: 248–9).

There was a chance that genuine democracy could have been introduced in China in the autumn of 1967, when the Red Guard movement reached its zenith. But Mao decided instead to use the army to suppress the movement, to restore order and to reopen schools.[23] Classes resumed in October 1967, though it was not until July 1968 that the ground was cut from under the Red Guard movement by the launching of the *xiafang* programme. The reasons for this reversal remain obscure. It is easy to portray it as a loss of nerve on Mao's part or as a response to his perception that he had lost control of a movement that was increasingly threatening to overthrow the Party and perhaps even Mao himself (MacFarquhar and Schoenhals 2006: 247–52). One might alternatively argue that Mao had little

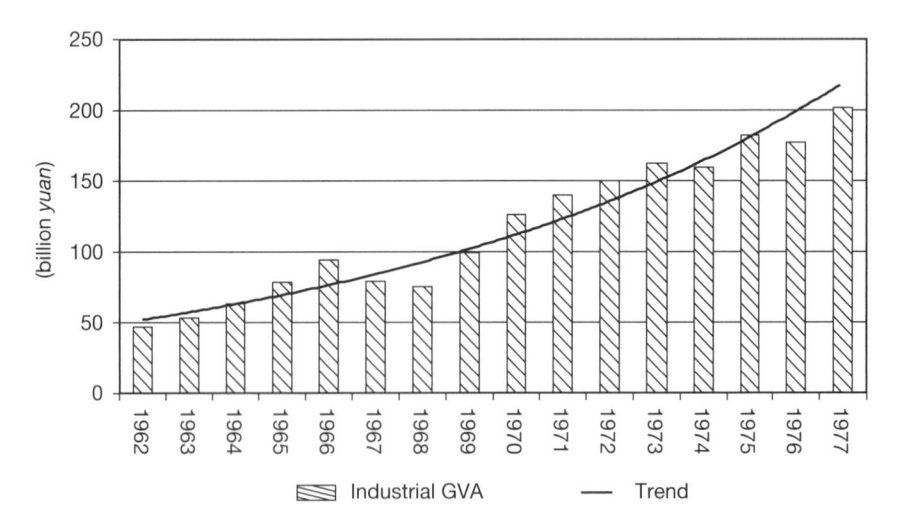

Figure 5.3 Industrial value-added during late Maoism (1987 prices) (Source: Maddison (1998))

choice as the Revolution disintegrated into factionalism. According to Wang Hui (2006: 37): 'The tragedy was a result of depoliticization – polarized factional struggles that eliminated the possibility for autonomous social spheres, transforming political debate into a mere means of power struggle, and class into an essentialized identitarian concept.'

Xiafang: the rustication programme

Whatever the true explanation behind Mao's decision, the vanguard role for the Red Guards was brought to an end in 1968. Chinese society became increasingly militarized during the late 1960s, years which saw a transfer of power to Lin Biao, the Defence Minister and Mao's designated successor. Lin's lack of charisma made him an unlikely cult figure, but he was enormously respected on account of his generalship during the civil war, and his poor health – itself a result of his military service – was understood for what it was. His influence over Mao was considerable, not least because the army was increasingly seen as the only force with China capable of maintaining order and ensuring continued economic development.[24]

The most controversial policy pursued during the late 1960s was that of *shangshan xiaxiang* ('up to the mountains and down to the countryside'), or *xiafang* (rustication) for short. This involved transferring two groups of the urban population to the countryside: middle-school and university students, and industrial cadres and technicians. *Xiafang* dated back to the early 1960s, and at that time it was largely voluntary; according to Chan *et al.* (1980), for example, none of those rusticated from Guangzhou city were coerced into it. In the early 1960s, the aim of *xiafang* was to reduce the size of urban population in the aftermath of the Great Famine, with the twin hopes of thereby increasing the farm workforce (labour shortages were recognized to have contributed to the famine) and reducing the need to extract grain from the countryside in order to feed the urban population. The policy, at least as measured in its own terms, was relatively successful. Ten million were rusticated in 1961 alone (MacFarquhar 1997: 32) and the total urban population declined from 130.7 million in 1960 to 116.5 million in 1963 (SSB 2005a: 6).

There were several motivations for the policy of the late 1960s. Mao (1968) couched the programme in terms of re-education:

> It is absolutely necessary for educated young people to go to the countryside to be re-educated by the poor and lower-middle peasants. Cadres and other city people should be persuaded to send their sons and daughters who have finished junior or senior middle school, college, or university to the countryside. Let us mobilize. Comrades throughout the countryside should welcome them.

Nevertheless, rustication was not seen as an integral part of the Cultural Revolution. Indeed the main periods of rustication pre- and postdate the Cultural Revolution. This suggests that other motives were at work, whatever the ideological cloak given to the programme by Mao himself. Bernstein (1977: 33–83) identifies three distinct aims behind the programme. First, the need to deal with the Red Guard problem and the unsatisfied aspirations of Chinese young people which lay behind the movement. Second, a desire to create space in urban schools and at the same time avoid urban unemployment. The very fact that schools had been closed during the Cultural Revolution meant that there was a backlog of children wanting to enter middle school in 1968. Finding urban jobs for this cohort would not be easy, not least because output and employment opportunities had declined in 1967 and 1968. The only solution was to deem all those who attended SMS schools in 1966 (irrespective of whether they were first-, second- or third-year students) to have graduated, and then to assign them to rural jobs (Pepper 1996: 388). At a stroke, the policy made room in schools and avoided urban youth unemployment by despatching the surplus labour to the countryside.

The third programme aim was to promote rural development. This is clear from the emphasis within the *xiafang* programme on the transfer of skilled cadres and technicians to the countryside to promote Third Front construction (Shen and Tong 185–9). It is no accident that the two regions with the principal concentrations of Chinese industry seem to have contributed most to *xiafang*. Out-migration from Beijing in 1970, for example, was only 70,000. By contrast, net out-migration from Liaoning totalled 248,000 and the Shanghai figures were 275,000 and 312,000 for 1969 and 1970 respectively (RKTJNJ 1988: 233–47; Hu 1987: 77). Of course provincial flows cannot capture the movement in full because much of the rustication was intra-provincial or intra-municipality, whereby those working in county towns or cities were returned to their home villages, or even to state farms within the jurisdiction (the islands in the mouth of the Yangzi river were a common destination for many Shanghai youth). Nevertheless, the exodus from these predominantly urban centres to other provinces certainly captures at least one part of the phenomenon. By the time the programme was brought to an end during 1977–9, some 18 million people, almost all from relatively privileged backgrounds, had experienced *xiafang* (Shen and Tong 1992: 187).[25]

The effectiveness of the *xiafang* programme is open to question. It certainly broadened the horizons of China's urban youth, who would not otherwise have garnered firsthand experience of conditions in the countryside. Nevertheless, the distance of rustication for many Red Guards was often small and the broadening of horizons consequently rather modest. To be sure, Shanghai, Tianjin, Beijing and other big cities sent substantial contingents to western China, and many Chengdu Red Guards ended up in the mountainous highlands of western Sichuan. Other urban youth were assigned to work on state farms in Heilongjiang. Yet many of Shanghai's state farms were no further away than the islands in the mouth of the Yangzi river. And for the rusticated youth of Jimo (Shandong province), it meant no more than a transfer from Jimo's county town to their home village (Han 2000).

However, and even though the transfer was spatially rather limited, it is clear from the copious memoirs of the urban youth involved that most were disaffected by their experience. It is not surprising. The majority of the rusticated were those who had lost out in the fights between Red Guard factions; a much smaller proportion of children from cadre or worker households were rusticated than children from middle- or bad-class families (Unger 1982: 134). Those rusticated often saw themselves as losers, and the very fact that many of them were academically gifted allowed them to give effective voice to their grievances in the 1980s and 1990s. In a very real sense, the literature on the rustication experience is a history written by those who were losers at the time, but who became the victors after Mao's death and the 'reversal of verdicts' that followed the end of the Cultural Revolution.

More generally, as Bernstein (1977: 7) noted: 'Because the transfer program runs contrary to several kinds of preferences, aspirations, and expectations, one would expect that those affected by the programme would regard it as a form of downward mobility.' But the bitterness was intensified by the fact that the *xiafang* programme of the late 1960s (in contrast to the way it operated in the early 1960s) was coercive. Some of those sent down in the late 1960s certainly volunteered, but for the majority participation was compulsory. Yet even when Chinese youth participated voluntarily in the process, many of them returned to urban China in the late 1970s with bitter memories (Gao 2000; Yang 1997). Most Western scholars have echoed this scepticism, pointing to the limited scale of skill transfers (Bernstein 1977) and to its damaging environmental consequences for the fragile ecosystems of border regions such as northern Heilongjiang and Xishuangbanna in southern Yunnan (Shapiro 2001). And Pepper (1996), broadly sympathetic to the goals of the Cultural Revolution, notes the intense level of dissatisfaction voiced by many of those she interviewed. As one of her interviewees admitted, many of those rusticated had an attitude towards the peasantry that was almost racist and therefore it was inevitable that the process would be painful.

This is not the place for a full discussion of the *xiafang* programme. It was conceived at least in part as a means of raising educational standards amongst urban and rural children alike, and accordingly its impact is discussed in the chapter on education below. Nevertheless, the transformative impact of the experience on the Red Guards is clear from even a cursory reading of the literature.[26] Take, for example, the experience of Ma Bo, who spent eight years in Inner Mongolia between 1968 and 1976, and who was imprisoned for part of that time for criticism of the Party leadership. Despite the suffering, he concluded:

> I declare here and now that a generation of young people who left for the mountains and countryside in 1968 to toil on the nation's farms and pasturelands, all the way to the furthest border regions, left an indelible mark on the history of mankind. Red Guards ... were forced to make the agonizing transition from people who bruised their knuckles on the bodies of others to people whose hands grew calloused from manual labour. No longer were they fanatics who yelled 'To rebel is right' while beating their victims and raiding their homes. (Ma 1995: 368)

The moving account offered by Yang (1997), which tells of both the hardship and life-changing nature of the experience of rustication to Heilongjiang, tells a similar tale. So too Anchee Min's (1984) account of life on a state farm in Jiangsu. These accounts may not be representative, but they are certainly emblematic of the experience of many of the Red Guards. For them at least, the *xiafang* movement was not in vain.

Between two deaths: the era of disillusionment

Lin Biao's death in 1971 ushered in the fourth phase of late Maoism. In many respects, this was an era of shattered dreams. The Red Guard movement had energized Chinese youth. Its ruthless suppression therefore destroyed those hopes, and left an ideological vacuum. For a time, the Army stepped into the breach, only for Lin Biao's attempted coup and death to put an end to this hope. After 1971, economic policy remained largely unchanged, except in that the scale of international trade began to expand. But by then the grandiose visions of the late 1960s had largely been abandoned.

The years between 1971 and 1976 were in fact a desperate attempt to inject new momentum into the late Maoist project. The violence wrought by the Red Guards, and the subsequent discrediting of Lin Biao, the man who had been portrayed as responsible for restoring order, undermined much of the political legitimacy of the late Maoist revolution. In political terms, the 1970s revolved around the struggle by the Gang of Four to create the conditions that would allow it to assume and retain power after Mao's death more than anything else. In practice, the violence continued. Unger (2007) characterizes the 'One Hit, Three Antis' campaign of 1970–1 as almost as vicious as the 'Cleansing of Class Ranks' which occurred in 1968. But throughout this campaign, and that which focused on 'Criticizing Lin Biao and Confucius' in 1974, Mao ensured that the Gang was kept weak and that Deng Xiaoping remained protected. There is much that we do not know about the relations between Mao and Deng. However, the very fact that Deng was allowed to survive despite Mao's perception of him as an arch 'capitalist roader' is a testimony both to Mao's pragmatism, and his low opinion of the other personalities competing for the succession. Be that as it may, the very weakness of the Gang made it relatively simple for the army to stage a coup in October 1976, during which the Gang was arrested. One rather suspects that Mao had always intended it that way.

The most significant change in terms of economic policy-making in the early 1970s was the growing reliance on imports of modern producer goods from Japan and from the West. Nixon's 1972 visit led to a gradual thawing of relations and to significant increases in imports. Crucially, a decision was taken in January 1973 to import thirteen sets of synthetic ammonia plants in order to supply increased amounts of chemical fertilizer to the farm sector and hence promote the planting of new dwarf varieties. In fact Zhou Enlai first developed the notion of a ten-year import substitution strategy to run from 1975 to 1985, and even toyed with idea of setting up a special economic zone in 1973 (Reardon 2002: 165 and 175).

The importance of these changes should not be exaggerated; China's economic strategy taken as a whole remained relatively inward-looking. However, the progressive development of trading links with other countries was a sign of what was to come.

The years of Hua Guofeng, 1976–1978

Mao's own death in 1976 inevitably led to a gradual unravelling of the development strategy which had been pursued since 1963.[27] Not that this had been Mao's intention, though it is arguable that his choice of successor made the unravelling inevitable. For the cadre that Mao chose to succeed him was Hua Guofeng, a man of little distinction by most accounts and almost universally derided for advocating that policy should be based upon the 'two whatevers' (*liangge fanshi* – 'adhere to whatever polices were set by Chairman Mao and implement whatever instructions were given by him').[28]

The Foreign Leap Forward

Hua was true to the 'whatever' principle in economic policy: in its fundamentals economic policy-making changed little between 1976 and 1978. The years of Hua Guofeng are therefore properly regarded as a continuation of the late Maoist era. The Dazhai system of collective farming was to continue to be the mainstay of agricultural policy, income inequalities were to be held in check, public ownership of industrial assets was to remain unchallenged and a high rate of investment was to be maintained.

Even the 'Foreign Leap Forward', the phrase which will always be associated with Hua, was little more than a continuation of the process of opening up which had begun in 1971. Nevertheless, Hua gave the strategy more bite and shifted the emphasis to petroleum and machinery imports in the Fifth Five Year Plan (1976–80). In this way, the notion of a 'foreign' or 'outward' leap forward gained wide currency. It was formalized in Hua's Ten Year Plan, which was approved in January 1978, and it centred around 120 industrial projects and a stated aim of 'catching America and surpassing Britain'. The impact of this change in policy can be seen from the data on foreign trade. The share of imports in GDP rose from only 2.2 per cent in 1971 to 5.5 per cent in 1974, and it stayed at between 4 and 5 per cent between 1974 and 1978 (SSB 1999: 3 and 60).

It is moot whether Hua's development strategy would have succeeded if fully implemented. Most Chinese accounts are scathing. And whilst there is no doubt that these accounts were designed to offer a Dengist reading of the politics and economics of the 1970s, the programme imposed a very considerable strain on state finances. Government expenditure on capital construction soared from 30 billion *yuan* in 1977 (which was the average for 1970–7) to 45 billion *yuan* in 1978, and the capital projects initiated help to create a 13.5-billion-*yuan* budget deficit in 1979 – comfortably the highest deficit of any year in the history of the People's Republic (SSB 1999: 8). This seems to have been the essence of Chen

Yun's concern, which replicated the worries he expressed during the 'oppose rash advance' movement of the late 1950s. Many would also argue that the strategy did not address the fundamental systemic weaknesses in the Maoist development strategy, namely its reliance on public ownership.

Nevertheless, although the scale of the (foreign) Leap was large, it was not overly ambitious. Certainly any notion that it would have recreated the famine conditions of the early 1960s seems far-fetched given the revival of agricultural production under way in the late 1970s. Furthermore, the deterioration in state finances owed rather more to the war with Vietnam than to Hua's strategy itself; official defence spending increased by no less than 33 per cent in 1979 (SSB 1999: 8). In retrospect, the criticism directed against the economic strategy seems to have been based more upon a desire to discredit Hua Guofeng than on any reasonable assessment of the underlying economics involved. For all the talk of readjustment during 1978–82, the development strategy adopted during much of the 1980s was little different from that advocated by Hua. Hua after all was only developing the Four Modernizations strategy advocated by both Zhou Enlai and, even more tellingly, by Deng Xiaoping himself during 1974–5.

In practice, the Ten Year Plan never even came close to implementation. This reflected the growing political ascendancy of Deng Xiaoping. Backed by the army and with near-hero status within the Party on account of his work before 1949 and in the 1950s, Deng's position was also enhanced by his being a victim – rather than an architect – of the Cultural Revolution. Accordingly, his eventual coming to power was practically certain once the decision had been taken by the army to arrest the Gang of Four in October 1976. Hua Guofeng, with limited personal stature and negligible military support, was in no position to resist. As Deng, along with Chen Yun, was firmly opposed to the Ten Year Plan, it was effectively scrapped in late 1978.

The political transition

Although Deng had been appointed Vice Premier in July 1977, his position was still weak. His main problem throughout that year was ideological. The Central Committee Circular no. 4 of 1976 (which had been approved by Mao) had explicitly accused Deng of 'not reading books and being ignorant of Marxism-Leninism', of being critical of the Cultural Revolution (which Mao saw as one of his great achievements) and of being utterly untrustworthy (Schoenhals 1991: 249–50). With Hua Guofeng and his followers pushing the 'two whatevers' – that is, promising to uphold whatever actions Mao had taken and whatever instructions he had given – Deng's position was perilous.

However, the ideological climate shifted in Deng's favour and against the 'two whatevers' during 1978. Critical here was the publication of 'Practice is the Sole Criterion for Truth' in the influential newspaper *Guangming Ribao* (11 May 1978); the piece was reprinted in *Renmin Ribao* (People's Daily) the next day. Produced by a number of writers at the Central Party School but masterminded by Hu Yaobang, this article was to become the basis for Deng's repudiation of

Hua's slavish adherence to Maoism. Deng appears not to have known about it, but he came out strongly in favour of 'Practice' in June 1978. With the PLA uniting behind the notion that practice, rather than whatever Mao had said or done, was the sole criterion for truth, Deng's star was in the ascendant. By the autumn of 1978 – even before the famous Third Plenum – his seizure of power was all but complete; during his visit to Japan he was received as *de facto* head of state.

Conclusion

This is not the place for a full evaluation of late Maoism; that task is taken up in Chapter 9, which properly assesses the developmental record of the regime during the 1960s and 1970s. But there is no doubt that much of what happened during the late Maoist era is indefensible, whether it be the widespread violence and persecution, the destruction of priceless cultural relics, the burning of books or the mindless reverence for the writings and speeches of Mao himself. The closure of schools and universities did little to further the cause of economic modernization. The participation of workers in political activities disrupted production. And the attacks on foreign diplomats damaged China's international reputation.

Nevertheless, the late Maoist development strategy lacked neither purpose nor ambition. Mao was not the captive of the spirit of the May Fourth movement that he is sometimes portrayed as, but rather an innovative Marxist thinker. During the 1960s, he rejected the numbing economic determinism that was the hallmark of much Marxist theory and practice, and instead launched a remarkably wide-ranging and coherent programme designed to transform simultaneously the superstructure, and the economic base, of Chinese society. In that the Cultural Revolution was about a redistribution of wealth and status, it struck a chord with the Red Guards. Many of China's young people were disaffected by both the limited opportunities available for study at university and the anti-meritocratic examinations system which effectively ensured that only those who went to a handful of elite schools had any prospects of going to the best universities. The attack on the property acquired by China's new bourgeois elite was equally popular, and again this is not surprising; many of this new urban elite had acquired their status by exploiting the inherited wealth, property and status that they had acquired during the Republican era. The educational system was also an obvious target. China's schools were staffed by teachers who had been educated before 1949 and whose mindsets were, from a Red Guard perspective, both conservative and conventional. Traditional notions of culture propagated by this system were thoroughly elitist, and mass culture invariably sneered at; there was certainly, therefore, a case for the reallocation of state cultural spending.

Furthermore, any attempt at a blanket condemnation of late Maoism must reckon with the evidence suggesting that in many ways its impact was rather limited. Even in so far as cultural destruction took place, we need to be wary about its scale. Much survived intact, and it is at least arguable that far more mindless destruction has been done in the name of economic modernization over the last two decades than by the Red Guards in the 1960s. Members of the CCP elite certainly were targeted, but that too was hardly surprising. As the events of the last thirty years have shown, the rightists within the Party such as Deng Xiaoping and Liu Shaoqi were indeed bent upon a full-scale capitalist restoration. And Liu was a target of particular venom not just because of his status as a 'capitalist roader' but also because he played such a leading role in trying to suppress student unrest in 1966. Not only was he responsible for sending in work teams in the first place to crush the incipient student protest movement, but also his wife played a key role in leading the work team sent to Qinghua University, so much so that she even conscripted her daughter as well.[29] Of course none of this justifies the treatment of Liu, but it does go some way towards explaining Red Guard anger. In short, a case certainly can be made for late Maoism as a programme designed to promote economic modernization by reducing entrenched inequalities and by enthusing the mass of the population, especially young people – many of whom had their illusions dispelled by their travels across China. If it was ultimately a tragedy, the late Maoist era was a tragedy of good intentions.

This programme was recognized for what it was by those who lived through it, and by those who observed it from afar during the 1960s and 1970s. Jack Gray (2006) and William Hinton (1972) may have erred in some of their assessments, but neither was in any doubt that the policies of the 1960s and 1970s amounted to far more than a purge of 'capitalist roaders' within the CCP. But scholarship since 1978 has largely failed to take late Maoism seriously.[30] The book produced by Chang and Halliday (2005) is an especially egregious example, but it is hardly alone. Bo Yibo's account of the events of the period is so partisan that it is barely credible. Shapiro (2001) extends the usual critique of late Maoism to encompass environmental damage. Even MacFarquhar and Schoenhals (2006) provide an account which, though richly informed, offers little by way of analysis and ignores both the underlying development strategy and its achievements; not surprisingly, it is simplistic in its condemnation.

Yet even here there are now signs of change. The volume by Law (2003), for example, offers a much more balanced perspective on the late Maoist era than has long been the norm. And Will Hutton (2007), often criticized for his lack of specialist knowledge on China, shows admirable sense in suggesting that the late Maoist era laid the foundations for the explosive growth of the 1980s and 1990s, and in so doing puts the work of many supposed China experts to shame. Talented Chinese scholars such as Han Dongping (2000, 2001) and Gao Mobo (1999) have drawn the attention of a sceptical readership to the genuine rural accomplishments of the late Maoist era. Many of those who were Red Guards during the Cultural Revolution have come to recognize that *xiafang* was a formative process and that it expanded their horizons. We are still a long way from getting to the truth of late Maoism: much remains to be uncovered. However, at least some of the worst stereotypes are beginning to be exposed for what they are.

Notes

1 Of course criticism was encouraged during the Hundred Flowers movement of 1956, but the difference between it and the SEM was that Hundred Flowers was never conceived as being a means by which rectification of the Party could take place. Moreover, Mao did not regard Chinese intellectuals as suitable agents for bringing about such change, and that partly explains the severity of the anti-rightist movement of 1957.
2 For a good discussion of some of the issues, and the misuse of the term Cultural Revolution, see Law (2003) and Unger (2007).
3 For a useful collection of documents on the Cultural Revolution, see Schoenhals (1996). For the role of Lin Biao – Mao's designated successor – see Teiwes and Sun (1996). The best chronological account is that offered by MacFarquhar and Schoenhals (2006). For the 1970s, see the revealing and detailed account in Teiwes and Sun (2007).
4 For some of the recent literature on the late Maoist era, see Schoenhals (1996), MacFarquhar (1997), MacFarquhar and Schoenhals (2006), Esherick *et al.* (2006) and Teiwes and Sun (2007). Much of this is rather partisan – we lack a good, sympathetic history of late Maoism which takes account of all the materials which have become available over the last decade – but the Chinese literature is far worse, and needs to be treated with great care. A sign of the problem is that figures as important as Lin Biao and Jiang Qing have yet to receive a proper biographical treatment. For her life as a Shanghai actress, we at least have contemporary sources, and they have enabled Vittinghoff (2005) to demonstrate convincingly that Jiang (Lan Ping as she then was) was a brilliant and much-acclaimed Nora in performances of Ibsen's *A Doll's House* in 1935. But we know little of her role in the 1950s and 1960s, and we await a good scholarly study of the role of the Gang of Four (Jiang Qing, Zhang Chunqiao, Yao Wenyuan and Wang Hongwen).
5 One of the best discussions of the evolution of Mao's thought is that offered in Liu (1997). See also the Introduction in Liu (2004).
6 The term 'superstructure' is used here to refer to the sum of the system of law and government, the processes of cultural production (including the educational system and the media) and to ideology. Integral to Marx's work was the idea that the superstructure was a manifestation of the will of the ruling class. On this, the formulation in the *Communist Manifesto* is very clear: 'Your very ideas are but the outgrowth of the conditions of your bourgeois production and bourgeois property, just as your jurisprudence is but the will of your class made into a law for all. ... What else does the history of ideas prove, than that intellectual production changes its character in proportion as material production changed? The ruling ideas of each age have ever been the ideas of its ruling class' (Marx and Engels 1848: 55 and 58–9).
7 The most illuminating critiques of Stalinism are those offered by Louis Althusser (1969; Althusser and Balibar 1968), whose writings were in many ways inspired by Mao's own ideas. For an introduction to Althusserian Marxism and its application to economics, see Kaplan and Sprinker (1993) and Wolff and Resnick (1987). For an analysis of some of the issues which surround the Cultural Revolution and how it relates to Marxist theory, see Healy (1997) and Liu (1997). Mao's influence on Althusser is plain. His essay 'On Contradiction' (1937a) provides the basis for Althusserian thought; indeed there is an unmistakably Maoist ring to Althusser's view that 'The fate of a socialist country (progress or regression) is played out in the ideological class struggle' (Althusser, cited in Liu 1997: 243). Mao's concern was not to put forward a general theory, but to deal with Chinese realities during the 1930s; Althusser's contribution was to provide a more fully developed theory. One of the paradoxes of post-Althusserian theorizing, in both its poststructuralist and postmodernist variants, is that it focuses primary on culture and literature rather than the central economic issue of the transition to socialism which so obsessed Mao.

172 *Chinese Economic Development*

8 However, Mao's ideas have themselves been consistently criticized by other Marxists for what they see as his heretical suggestion that human agency might be more important than material (economic) factors. Even some of those sympathetic to Mao's approach argue that the Cultural Revolution 'lapsed into an instrument of political manipulation and domination, especially in dealing with estranged and dissenting intellectuals' (Liu 2004: 8).

9 Liu (2004: 8) argues that Mao was guilty of this: 'The dialectical reversal of political and ideological revolution vis-à-vis economic development, however, did not give birth to an antideterministic and dynamic conception of history that could serve as a new epistemology for the alternative modernity. Over the years, Mao increasingly subscribed to an ideological and cultural determinism [after 1978] ... Only the "content" of determinism was reversed, as it were, from a cultural ideological determinism to a resolute economic determinism.'

10 As Schoenhals (1996: 4) notes, Lin's talk was seen and approved beforehand by Mao himself. There is no definitive statement by Mao himself on the development strategy of the 1960s and 1970s.

11 According to Hinton (1972: 38), we can think of the treatment of Chinese students from worker or peasant backgrounds as similar to that of the treatment of blacks from the American South, or of those born in the ghetto, in US universities before the civil rights movement.

12 The final possibility was the use the Army to purge the Party and bureaucracy, and that in effect was the approach adopted between 1968 and 1971.

13 There is a degree of *ex post* rationalization here; there is no evidence that Mao conceptualized economic development in quite this way. Nevertheless, the Third Five Year Plan set out the vision clearly enough. To be sure, there were omissions but that was hardly surprising. Part of the reason for these omissions was the need to maintain military secrecy; it would not do for the Third Front programme to be outlined in a Five Year Plan. And partly the omissions reflected Mao's understandable reluctance to state quite so bluntly his desire to purge the upper echelons of the Party of dissident elements. It would therefore be a grave mistake to suppose that late Maoism lacked coherence; on the contrary. The strategy may not have been articulated in the form presented here, but the underlying Maoist vision is unmistakable from the speeches, writings and policies of the period.

14 For a critique of the standard interpretation of Mao offered by (inter alia) Stuart Schram, see Healy (1997).

15 For Chinese population policy, and the attempts that were made to control the growth rate after the late 1960s, see Banister (1987), Scharping (2003), White (2006) and Greenhalgh and Winckler (2005).

16 The launch of the Third Front programme of defence industrialization was even more important in its effects. It is discussed in Chapter 7, below.

17 The campaign exhorted the Chinese people to learn from the diary of Lei Feng, a PLA solider who had worked selflessly for the Revolution and for the cause of socialist modernization. It remains unclear whether Lei Feng ever existed; his diary was certainly an invention of the CCP's propaganda department.

18 The process of 'cleaning up' cadre behaviour began in some parts of China in 1962. The ten points were subsequently revised, so much so that a distinction is usually made between the First Ten Points and the Later Ten Points, which were more detailed and were issued in November 1963. The 'Small Four Clean Ups' set out in the May 1963 were replaced in early 1965 by the 'Big Four Clean Ups', which called for a much more general rectification of cadre behaviour in the fields of politics, economics, organization and ideology. For some of the literature on the SEM, see MacFarquhar (1997: ch. 15), Baum and Teiwes (1968) and Baum (1969).

19 The CCP defined the relationship between the SEM and the Cultural Revolution in the Sixteen Points of 8 August 1966: 'the Great Cultural Revolution enriches and

elevates the Socialist Education Movement and adds momentum to the movement in cleaning up politics, ideology, organization and economics' (cited in Baum 1969: 100). Baum rightly notes that the SEM and the Cultural Revolution were not the same, in that the former was a 'revolution from above' (it was led and directed by the Party and by Party-appointed work teams) whereas the Cultural Revolution was much more of a 'revolution from below' in that it was led by *ad hoc* Red Guard groups. However, because both focused ultimately on promoting economic development by means of superstructural change, they deserve to be treated as part of the same broad strategy.

20 For an account of the Cultural Revolution at Qinghua University, see Hinton (1972) and Andreas (2002). At China's universities, personal interest appears to have been less important in motivating Red Guard membership, because all those at university had already 'made it' to the top of the educational system (Unger 2007: 121–2). However, Unger also notes evidence that those who were about to graduate from university tended to be more loyal to the Party than their juniors, because job assignments were under Party control.

21 For the background of the Red Guards, see Zheng (2006), Chan *et al.* (1980) and Unger (1982). Andreas (2002: 508) argues that conflict at the Qinghua Middle School was initially between the children of old and new elites, but that it increasingly became a struggle between the children of workers and peasants on the one hand, and all elite children (the children of both revolutionary cadres and intellectuals/professionals) on the other. According to him: 'The new political and old educated elites found unprecedented unity in condemning the radical egalitarianism and turbulence of the Cultural Revolution.'

22 And not surprisingly; Britain was one of the few countries trading to any significant extent with China at that time.

23 The contemporary left in China is highly critical of this reversal. For them, the failure of the Cultural Revolution was that it did not go far enough. At the very moment when true democracy was starting to develop, Mao brought the process to a halt.

24 There is, however, little evidence that Lin or the left tried to pursue an independent strategy during the late 1960s. Even the rapprochement with the USA was accepted with little apparent opposition (Xia 2006).

25 For the *xiafang* programme, see Bernstein (1977). Some of the data (much of it published since 1997) on the scale of the programme are summarized in Bramall (2007: 147–50).

26 A useful collection of interviews with former Red Guards is that of Jiang and Ashley (2000).

27 For discussions of the politics of Hua's interregnum, see Sun (1995) and Misra (1998). For an excellent discussion of Hua's 'Foreign Leap Forward', see Reardon (2002: ch. 7). Although Reardon uses some questionable sources and is rather problematic in many of his judgements, this is undoubtedly one of the most interesting discussions of Hua's strategy.

28 Hua's key allies included Wang Dongxing, Chen Xilan, Wu De and Chen Yonggui (the erstwhile leader of the Dazhai production brigade).

29 Hinton's (1972: 62) description of Liu's daughter, the hapless Liu Tao, is evocative: 'Did Liu Tao have talent or leadership ability? Apparently not. She was a spoiled young woman, a debutante type, interested in fashion and personal pleasure, and could not make a coherent speech.'

30 A rare exception is Gao (2008), though he is perhaps a little too uncritical of the notion of a peasant-led modernization programme.

6 The revolution in education

As we have seen, the late Maoist development strategy sought to remake the superstructure of Chinese society. The cornerstone of this programme of superstructural change was to be a radical transformation of China's system of education.[1] The programme was radical in three senses. First, it aimed at a massive expansion of education in the countryside to provide the rural population with the same opportunities as urban citizens and in the process to expand the size of the educated workforce. Second, it sought to achieve a qualitative transformation of the educational system by incorporating work as well as study into the process. Third, the provision of basic education in urban areas was to be expanded so that the children of workers would have an opportunity to attend middle school. None of this was entirely new; similar experiments had occurred in the CCP base area in Yan'an in the 1940s and again during the Great Leap Forward. The distinguishing feature of late Maoism was the scale of the attempted transformation.

Opinion on its impact is varied. According to Hannum (1999: 202): 'the Cultural Revolution, condemned on most counts as an educational disaster, successfully raised educational levels in rural areas and narrowed urban-rural educational differentials.' Moreover, she argues, the success of late Maoism in this regard is etched in sharp contrast by the failures of the post-1978 regime: 'The evidence presented ... points to an extension of educational opportunities across the urban-rural divide through the radical interventions of the Cultural Revolution, and a subsequent contraction of these opportunities in the 1980s' (Hannum 1999: 209). Deng and Treiman (1997) take an equally positive view of late Maoism's effects on inequality and stratification. So too does Suzanne Pepper (1996). Seeberg (2000: 458–9) offers a contrary view: 'rural attainment dropped and it dropped to an unsustainable low level of literacy. Less than functional literacy was provided in urban basic education, and urban educational attainment dropped to the same low level as rural education.'

As we shall see, these and other conclusions stem principally from differing interpretations of the evidence. To begin with, however, I sketch the unfolding of educational policy during the Maoist era.

The Chinese educational system in the early 1960s

The transformation of Chinese education after 1966 was prompted by Mao's view that superstructural change was the crux of the problem of economic development, and that Chinese education had failed between 1949 and the early 1960s.

The system of Chinese education during the early 1950s was based on the American-style approach which had been introduced into China during the early 1920s. Primary education was meant to begin at the age of seven and last for six years. Junior middle school (JMS) was designed to last for three years, senior middle school (SMS) for three years, and university education for four or five years (depending on the subject studied). In practice, the pre-1949 system was very far from comprehensive; the majority of children received little more than a few years of teaching in *sishu*, which were small private schools funded by parents or lineage associations, and typically run by a single teacher. From these, boys (only perhaps 5 per cent of girls attended some form of school) emerged imbued with an understanding of 'Confucian' values such as respect, deference and contempt for the peasantry, and an acquaintance with a modest number of characters, or what might be described as subsistence rather than functional literacy (Pepper 1996: 53).

By the late 1940s, a parallel system of education had developed in CCP base areas, based on the model pioneered in Yan'an, the capital of the Shaanxi–Gansu–Ningxia border region (Seybolt 1971). Initially the Yan'an system followed that of regular schools in other parts of China: those entering secondary school had to be aged between thirteen and nineteen, standard examinations had to be taken and passed and teachers were expected to keep their non-teaching work to an absolute minimum. This system was abandoned in the early 1940s as unsuitable; it was too expensive, full-time study was not very popular with parents and the creation of a small number of regular schools meant that children had to travel long distances to get there. Its replacement, as adumbrated in the directive for elementary schooling of April 1944, altered both the form and the content of education. The standardization which was the hallmark of the regular school system was abandoned, and instead *minban* (literally 'run by the people') schools were promoted. These differed from the regular schools in being run and financed by village communities themselves.

The new Yan'an system was a decentralized and low cost system of education which in many ways was well suited to conditions in a backward base area in which the literacy rate was barely 1 per cent and where a state-funded system of education was hard to finance via taxation. Instead, the villages funded the schools, and had great freedom over whom to select as teachers, the length of schooling and the type of assessment.[2] In some ways, it was simply a development of the *sishu* system. However, *minban* schools appealed to the CCP because they shortened the length of education and reduced the financial burden on the state, which only had to provide a subsidy rather than paying for the full cost of schooling. In this way, it was hoped that the number of those receiving elementary education could be increased. The Yan'an system also changed the content of schooling by reducing its duration and by requiring pupils to combine work with study. Thus secondary schooling was cut back to only three years, and pupils were expected to engage in manual labour for twenty to thirty days per year. The logic was clear. The CCP's aim was to produce the cadres, teachers and skilled workers needed by the base area, rather than preparing children for higher education – which had been the aim of the old system.

The approach adopted after 1949 incorporated two elements. First, all private schools and *sishu* were taken into state control. Second, the CCP sought to marry the regular school system inherited from the KMT with the Yan'an *minban* schools, and to learn from the Soviet Union (rather than the USA) in organizing the new educational system. At the same time, the distinction between junior and senior middle schools was to be abolished, and the length of elementary education cut from six to five years. This vision was set out in the 'Decision on School System Reform' (October 1951), and much of it was implemented. *Minban* schools disappeared and the system was regularized along Soviet lines. Unified examinations and testing, a fixed curriculum and the inspection of teaching were all hallmarks of the new system, as were new *zhongdian* (keypoint) schools, designed to train the best of the age cohort for entry into higher education.[3] This was an avowedly elitist system. Chinese educators were adamant that there must be no sacrifice of quality on the altar of uncontrolled expansion of numbers, a policy which they condemned as 'blind adventurism'. The perspective of the professional educators was that China was simply too poor to fund universal elementary education, still less secondary education; any such steps were widely regarded as premature in the context of the 1950s.

These various pressures meant that an educational system had been put in place across China by 1955 which was far removed from the Yan'an model. It was designed to prepare students for university, rather than for work; the work–study component had virtually disappeared; and the pace of expansion was relatively slow. In fact, primary-school enrolment was virtually stagnant in the period between 1952 and 1956 (Pepper 1996: 198). For all that, the influence of the USSR and the Yan'an tradition ensured that the system of the mid-1950s fell well short of being a Confucian system of providing education for education's sake to a small elite. Enrolments did increase as the 1950s wore on, and one of the features of the era was the development of vocational specialized secondary schools turning out students who had specialized in engineering, agriculture or (the largest single category) learning how to teach.

By 1958, however, this system was regarded as unsatisfactory for a number of reasons. One problem was that elementary school provision was still lacking. By mid 1956, for example, only 52 per cent of the age cohort were entering elementary school and this meant that the overall illiteracy rate (of around 78 per cent) was very slow to decline (Pepper 1996: 212). Another problem was inadequate provision of secondary education in rural areas. In 1958, there were some 37 million children aged between thirteen and sixteen, but the regular school system had only the capacity to educate 7 million of them. The remaining 30 million, mainly rural children, therefore lacked access to secondary education (Pepper 1996: 305).

These weaknesses were identified in the 1956 *National Programme for Agricultural Development, 1956–1967*, which set out the aims of virtually eradicating illiteracy over a seven-year period (defined as knowledge of 1,500 characters), establishing a part-time school in every *xiang*, and achieving compulsory primary education by the end of the twelve-year period (Selden 1979: 362–3). Mao recognized the problem himself in his speech 'On the Correct Handling of Contradictions among the People' in February 1957:

> Currently there still are 40 per cent of the people who have no school to go to. In addition, there is another matter: this can be called the 4 million. This year there are 4 million graduates from higher primary school who cannot advance to middle school, there's no way to advance to middle school, no space, no funds. (MacFarquhar *et al.* 1989: 160)[4]

The Great Leap Forward addressed these issues by means of a complete overhaul of the educational system. In its essentials, the Leap strategy took to heart the dictum of 'walking on two legs'. In the sphere of education, this entailed the development of two separate systems of education. In urban areas, the system set up during the 1950s was to continue. However, all pupils were expected to take part in some sort of productive work (Kwong 1979: 446). Moreover, the curriculum was reduced from twelve to ten years in a renewed attempt to break with the American twelve-year model, an idea first mooted in the October 1951 reform (Unger 1980). Much more radically, and in an attempt to expand educational provision in rural areas, new *minban* primary schools and agricultural middle schools were created by the communes.[5] The schools had much in common with the *minban* schools of the Yan'an era, except that they were more radical in approach: their purpose was to combine work and study in more or less equal proportions. Rural children would thus still be able to contribute to agricultural production, and the costs of education would be both lower and borne by communes rather than by the state. The broad aim of the programme was to universalize primary and secondary education in rural areas, a remarkably ambitious goal for a country so poor. The overhaul seems to have commanded widespread support within the upper echelons of the CCP.[6] For although it was to be castigated during the Cultural Revolution as the pet project of Liu Shaoqi, the 'two systems' approach set out in Liu's speech of 30 May 1958 undoubtedly had Mao's backing (Pepper 1996: 295–301), and the evidence in many ways suggests that Liu's approach in 1958 was more radical than anything Mao had in mind at that time (MacFarquhar 1983: 108–13).

However, the Great Famine inevitably brought these experiments to an end, as it had done so many others. Faced with agricultural disaster, the communes were reluctant to commit the resources needed to maintain middle schools and the experiment was therefore largely abandoned in rural areas. Regular schools fared much better because they were funded centrally. On the eve of the Cultural Revolution, therefore, the system had reverted to the regularized school system of the 1950s, which ensured a high level of urban provision but very little beyond elementary education in most rural areas.

Educational trends, 1953–1965

Despite the vicissitudes discussed in the previous section, the data suggest that the educational policies of the 1950s and early 1960s were successful in the sense that they expanded very significantly the reach of China's educational system.

Figure 6.1 shows the scale of the expansion. In 1953, some 8.2 million new enrolments took place at the primary level. Given that there were nearly 13 million children aged seven at that time according to the 1953 census (RKNJ 1953: 600), the system was inadequate to enrol the age cohort even before any thought was given to enrolling overaged children and adults. From this low base, enrolments grew slowly in the early 1950s and then doubled during the Leap. The famine led to an inevitable contraction, but the 1958 level was regained by 1964. In that year, almost 33 million new enrolments took place, well up on the figure of around 10 million in the early 1950s, as those who had missed out on education during the famine years were enrolled. In many provinces, the growth in enrolments in the early 1960s was based around a big expansion in the number of primary-school teachers; in Anhui, for example, the number of primary teachers was reported to have risen from 80,000 in 1963 to 177,000 in 1965 (SSB 2005a: 495).[7] In large measure this reflected the creation of work–study primary schools, the number of which grew very rapidly during 1964 and 1965 as a result of their promotion by Liu Shaoqi (Unger 1980: 226–7). Across China, there were 1.7 million

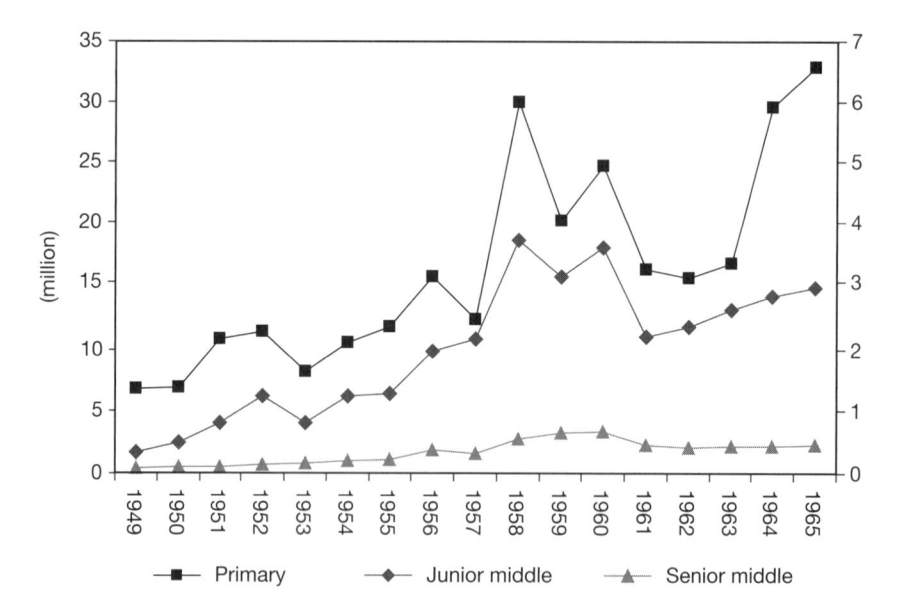

Figure 6.1 School enrolments, 1949–1965 (Source: SSB (2005a: 81–2).)

Note: Primary enrolments are shown on the left-hand axis, and middle school enrolments on the right-hand axis.

teachers working in *minban* primary schools in 1965 out of a total of 3.9 million teachers (ZGJYNJ 1984:1022). The net effect of all this was a definite expansion in educational provision between the early 1950s and the mid-1960s. Given that there were only 20 million children aged seven at that time according to the 1964 population census (RKNJ 1985: 602) and over 30 million being enrolled, it is evident that the system was able to reach out and enrol overaged children and even adults – in sharp contrast to the situation in 1953.

Figure 6.2 shows the long-run trend in enrolments; the gross enrolment rate rose from around 50 per cent in the early 1950s and reached 80 per cent during the peaks of 1958 and 1965.[8] A considerable proportion of those enrolled were overage: the figure was about 30 per cent in 1953 (ZGJYNJ 1984: 1024). This indicates that the primary-school system was doing a fair job in terms of providing basic adult education as well as recruiting from the primary-school cohort. Still, there was far to go. Although enrolment was good in the year of 1964, the net enrolment rate for the whole seven to twelve cohort was still low; only about 50 per cent of this cohort was enrolled in schools at that time.

The success of the educational programmes of the 1950s can also be measured by looking at the data on literacy available from the fertility survey of 300,o00 women carried out in 1982, which, amongst other things, asked women about their education (Lavely *et al.* 1990). These data show a surge in literacy rates for those who were completing their primary education in the 1950s. Assuming that literacy was achieved at the age of eleven, the figures show that around 85 per cent of those born in 1930 – and thus completing their education in the Republican era – were still illiterate in 1982.[9] By contrast, illiteracy amongst the cohort born in 1946 (and hence notionally achieving literacy by 1957) was down to only 40 per cent. However, the famine checked this progress. For those born in

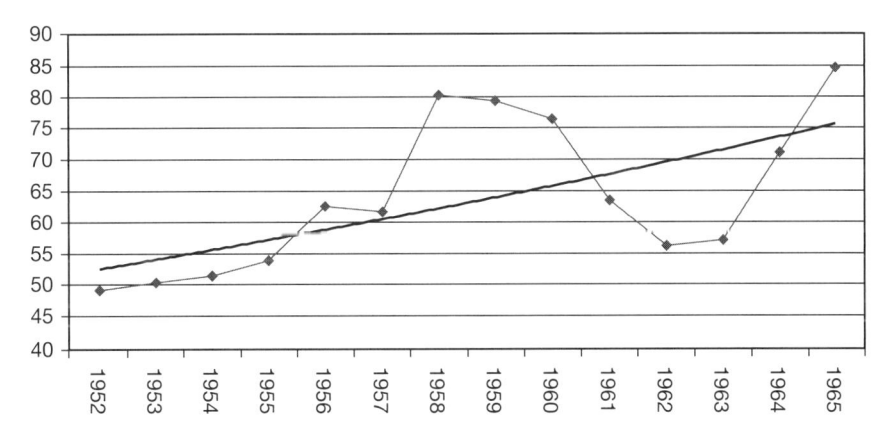

Figure 6.2. Primary school gross enrolment rates (total enrolment as a percentage of the age cohort) (Source: ZGJYNJ (1984: 1024).)

Note: These data are gross rates, i.e. they include the enrolment of overage students. The 1964 census indicates that only around 50 per cent of children aged 7 to 12 were in primary school at the that time.

1952, the 1982 illiteracy rate was up slightly at 43 per cent (Lavely *et al.* 1990: 67 and 71).

Secondary-sector enrolments at the junior level grew equally rapidly during the 1950s, and even more so during the Leap, when there was rapid expansion of the new agricultural middle schools. They first appeared in March 1958 (Unger 1980: 224), and there were over 22,000 of them by 1960, with a total enrolment of 2.3 million.[10] Regular JMS enrolment also virtually doubled in 1958, such that nearly 6 million new students were enrolled in some form of junior secondary education (regular and agricultural schools combined) in that year. Again, however, the Great Famine brought expansion to a halt. The number of agricultural middle schools, for example, fell back from 20,000 in 1958 to only 4,000 by 1963 (ZGJYNJ 1984: 1017), and regular school new enrolments fell back to the 1957 level by 1961–2. Nevertheless, the figure for new enrolments started to rise again in 1962–3. By 1965, total JMS new enrolments reached 3 million, three times the level of 1953. In addition there was a revival of agricultural middle schools, which in turn reflected recovery from the famine and the enthusiasm of Liu Shaoqi (Pepper 1996: 306). By 1965, there were 3 million children enrolled in these schools, well up even on the 1958 figure of 2 million (SSB 2005a: 81).

Senior middle-school enrolments show a broadly similar trend during the 1950s and the Leap. New enrolments increased from around 150,000 in 1953 to 320,000 in 1957. They too surged during the Leap, reaching a high point of 680,000 in the halcyon days of 1958 (SSB 2005a: 81–2). Once again, the decline during 1959–62 was steep. More seriously, there was no real revival in the early 1960s; senior middle-school new enrolments in 1965 were no high than they had been in 1961. Still, the ultimate result of all this was that the three sectors of the Chinese school system grew at the same approximate rate in the long run; there was a tripling of enrolments between 1953 and 1965 across the board. The 'two systems' approach advocated by Liu Shaoqi appears to have been working.

The Maoist critique

Mao was less convinced. One concern focused on the type of education that students were receiving in China's schools and universities. This line of attack was set out retrospectively in the famous 'two assessments' (1971) of the educational policies pursued before the Cultural Revolution:

> [In the seventeen years after 1949,] Chairman Mao's proletarian revolutionary line has not been implemented in the main, as a result of which the bourgeoisie has exercised dictatorship over the proletariat; and the great majority of intellectuals [trained in these seventeen years] still remain basically bourgeois in their world outlook; in other words, they are still bourgeois intellectuals. (Teiwes and Sun 2007: 57)

This apart, the main weaknesses of the Chinese system in the mid-1960s were perceived to be several. First, and despite the expansion of the 1950s, enrolment and graduation rates were still far too low. In order for the growth rate to be increased and sustained, the supply of trained graduates at all points in the educational system needed to be increased. Second, Chinese education remained true to its Confucian heritage. It placed too much emphasis on academic knowledge and too little on work experience (practice). The best statement of Mao's view here is to be found in 'On Practice' (1937b), in which he argued that knowledge depends not only upon ideas (including those acquired through education), but also upon practice (experience).[11] Perhaps more famous was his 1930 statement in 'Oppose Book Worship' (Mao 1930):

> The method of studying the social sciences exclusively from the book is likewise extremely dangerous and may even lead one onto the road of counter-revolution. Clear proof of this is provided by the fact that whole batches of Chinese Communists who confined themselves to books in their study of the social sciences have turned into counter-revolutionaries. ... Of course we should study Marxist books, but this study must be integrated with our country's actual conditions. We need books, but we must overcome book worship, which is divorced from the actual situation.

Third, Mao regarded the educational system as being riddled with inequality. The examination system continued to privilege those of 'bad-class' background because it ensured that children who inherited cultural capital from their parents were able to advance through the academic system even though inequalities in income and wealth had been much reduced.[12] Would-be students were only equal in the sense that examination success offered a route to advancement, irrespective of background. The effect of all this was a profoundly stratified system. Thus, at the elite Qinghua middle school attached to Qinghua University, only 6 per cent of students were of peasant or working-class origin on the eve of the Cultural Revolution (Andreas 2002: 472–3).

In effect, Mao thought of the determinants of educational attainment in terms of the equation

$$E = f(P, Y, C, L)$$

where P refers to personal characteristics (such as health, intelligence, energy and disability), Y is household per capita income, C is household cultural capital (we can think of it as the level of parental education and the extent of their social connections) and L is a locational variable to capture the impact of living in a rural or an urban area. Personal characteristics (with the partial exception of health) were something even Mao could not control, and the worst of China's class-based inequalities had been eliminated via land reform and nationalization in the 1950s, such that differences in household were no longer especially important by the early 1960s in determining educational outcomes. However, the 'great divide' between urban and rural China remained, and one of the explicit aims of late Maoism was to close it by promoting the expansion of rural education. As importantly, the income redistribution of the 1950s had done nothing to address the problem of inequalities in cultural capital. A central aim of the Cultural Revolution in particular, and late Maoism in general, was therefore to break the link between parental status and the attainment of children.

Inadequate provision of school places and the crisis of expectations

There is no doubt that Mao was correct in his first line of criticism: despite rising enrolments, the Chinese system was still turning out very few graduates at all levels. Although elementary education was more or less universal in urban areas, the same was not true of the countryside. Thus in 1965 only 6.7 million students graduated from primary school out of the age cohort of around 15 million thirteen-year-olds. The deficiencies at secondary level were even more obvious, with junior middle schools graduating only 1.7 million students and senior middle schools a paltry 0.4 million students out of age cohorts of 13 and 11 million respectively (RKNJ 1985: 602).

As seriously, the expansion of elementary education was leading to a dangerous escalation of educational expectations which could not be satisfied very easily. The number of graduates at all levels within the system was rising, but the supply of places at the next educational level was not rising in tandem. Part of the problem was the crisis faced by would-be university students. In the mid-1950s, it was relatively easy to gain access to university. In 1956, for example, Chinese universities made 185,000 new enrolments whereas senior middle schools graduated only 154,000 students. By 1965, however, all this had changed because of the growing number of graduates being produced by the senior middle schools. As a result, there was 'a crisis of dwindling opportunities' for these students (Chan *et al.* 1980: 398). The total new enrolment in universities was no higher than it had been in the mid-1950s, but the number of SMS graduates had more than doubled, meaning that only one in two SMS graduates could gain university access (SSB 2005a: 81–2).

The problem was almost as serious lower down the educational ladder. For although the growth rates of student numbers at all levels within the school system were very similar between 1953 and 1965, the change in the absolute numbers was not and this meant a growing number of disappointed students. Figure 6.3 shows the extent of the gap between the number of graduates and enrolments at the next level up. It shows that (for example) over 3.5 million of those graduating from elementary school in 1965 could not go on to JMS because of lack of capacity. At the next level up, fewer than half a million of the 1.7 million JMS graduates of 1965 could enter SMS. In both cases, the situation was far worse than in either 1957 or 1953.

The solution adopted to solve this problem during the Great Leap Forward had been to create agricultural middle schools in order to expand the range of opportunities open to rural children. However, even evaluated on its own terms, this had not worked; the enrolment gaps remained the same during the Leap because the expansion in the secondary sector was matched by the expansion

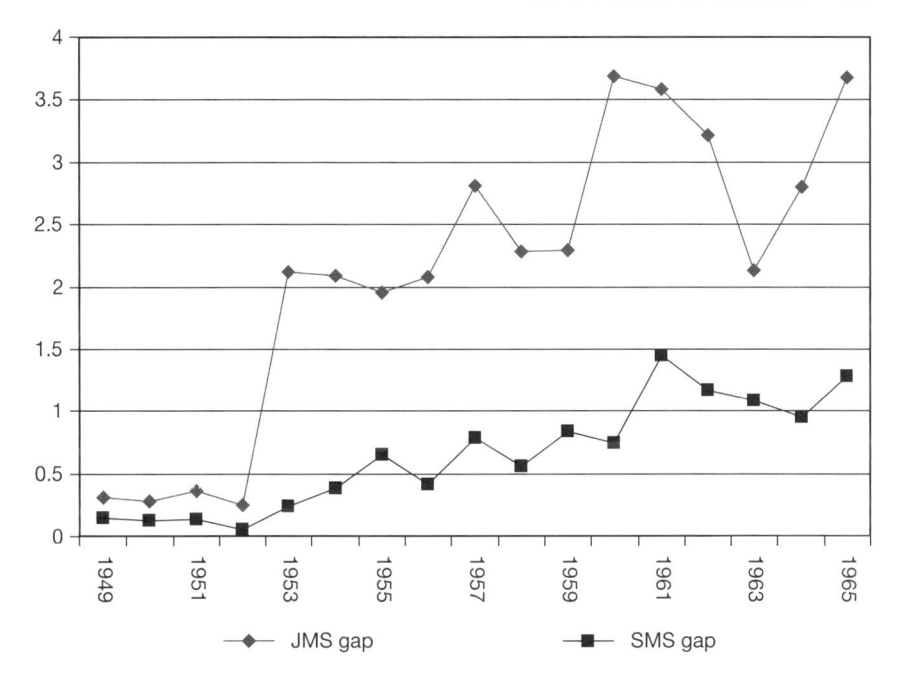

Figure 6.3 The enrolment gap, 1949–1965 (millions) (Source: SSB (2005a: 81–2).)

Note: The JMS gap is the number of those graduating from primary school but not enrolling in junior middle school in any given year. Similarly the SMS gap is the number of JMS graduates minus the number of SMS enrolees in the same year.

of the primary sector. More significantly, the new agricultural middle schools, which were at the heart of Liu Shaoqi's 'two systems' concept, were a failure. Although they answered Mao's desire for children to learn from practice as well as from books, they were not regarded with much favour in the countryside. On the contrary; they were seen as providing a second-class education during which rural children 'earned nothing and learned little' (Pepper 1996: 305–12). The schools were cheap, costing the state only 13 *yuan* per person compared to 187 *yuan* for a regular school place in the case of Jiangsu (Pepper 1996: 305), but the trade-off between the opportunity costs incurred via the loss of labour, even in a work–study school, on the one hand and the gain from a low-quality education on the other was an unfavourable one in the eyes of the rural population. According to one of Pepper's (1996: 309) informants:

> There were two things people did not like because both were inferior and they tried to get rid of them as soon as possible: one was agricultural middle schools; the second was *minban* schools. Peasants did not want to send their children to such schools because the education provided was inadequate. Neither teachers nor peasants liked these schools … despite their convenience

Unger (1980) makes much the same sort of point; the allure of the regular school system and the prospect of university entrance made it almost inevitable that agricultural middle schools would be seen as inferior. The work–study concept even provoked resentment because parents saw their children as working for the school for free instead of working for the household, a consideration strengthened by the temporary revival of family farming during the early 1960s which placed a premium on available household labour. By 1966, the whole approach was being derided as a distortion of the notion of 'walking on two legs'. This helped to seal the fate of Liu Shaoqi, the member of the CCP most closely associated with it. Radical though it had been in 1958, it was no longer seen as such in the mid-1960s. What was needed was an expansion of the work–study concept to urban areas, and that is what the late Maoist strategy delivered.

Educational inequality

At root, the problem China faced in the mid-1960s was one of educational inequality. The Great Leap Forward had led to an expansion in the supply of school places. However, the enrolment gap had widened, leading to a spiral of unfulfilled expectations. Worse, the 'two systems' approach imposed a binary divide between a low-quality rural system and a high-quality urban system. Not only were there not enough places available at middle school level, but access to them was the preserve of the privileged few. To make things worse, the keypoint system was actually strengthened during the Leap and the early 1960s, even though this ran contrary to the logic of reform elsewhere in the system. As Pepper (1996: 347) says, the effect was 'to re-create educational forms and functions modelled directly on those of the imperial bureaucratic past'.

The system in place in the mid-1960s was therefore still a profoundly elitist one. A classic example of such elitism was the State Council decree of 1956 stating that the standard for literacy in rural areas was knowledge of 1,500 characters, whereas 2,000 were required in urban areas. Not that this made literacy harder to achieve in the cities; after all, the lion's share of resources were concentrated there. But the obvious implication – that rural children needed to know fewer characters – captures the spirit of the 1950s very well. Other examples of elitism are not hard to find. Examinations were notionally meritocratic, but in practice they favoured children from privileged families; their family background and inherited cultural capital gave such children a great advantage. Learning was largely divorced from practice, and academic competence in a teacher was judged on the basis of years of schooling. The results were as follows:

> The real beneficiaries of an elite education system are the elite themselves, for the process of giving them privileged training so that they can serve the masses increases the disparity between them and the masses, and puts the elites in a position of authority over them. In short, the new elites become a new ruling class, and like all ruling classes, they are unwilling to give up their power voluntarily. … To avoid this situation, it follows that

educational preference should go to those at the bottom of the social and economic scale – the proletariat and the poor and lower-middle peasants – to raise them to a position of equality with other groups in society. (Seybolt 1971: 666–7)

The data for China during the 1950s and 1960s support this view that access to educational opportunities was very unequal. The official data for the 1950s, for example, show that only 20 per cent of tertiary-school children were from worker-peasant backgrounds in 1952/3, and the ratio was little better in 1957/8, when it stood at 36 per cent (Pepper 1996: 214). An alternative approach to inequality is to look at the numbers of those enrolled in middle schools coming from rural backgrounds (Hannum 1999). The picture here is a remarkable one (Table 6.1); there were more children enrolled in junior middle schools in China's handful of cities than in the whole of the countryside. Even if we classify county towns as rural (and that is probably the correct approach, as they had little in common with Chinese cities), the picture is little better. The cities still accounted for 42 per cent of middle-school students, whereas their share in China's total population was only 13 per cent at the time of the 1964 census (RKTJNJ 1988: 335).[13] To be sure, these data take no account of enrolments in agricultural middle schools, but as these were widely regarded as inferior (as we have seen), the story remains much the same in its essentials. The CCP may have presided over a successful overall expansion of the system, but it is very evident that rural areas were lagging far behind.

The data assembled by Lavely *et al.* (1990) from the 1982 fertility survey show the same pattern. Of those born in 1944 (and who therefore received a few years of secondary education before the famine), only 11 per cent of the women from rural areas interviewed in 1982 reported having some secondary education, compared with 59 per cent of urban women. Deng and Treiman (1997) use the same data to track the relationship between the education of sons still living with their father and the education and occupational status of their father. They conclude that, amongst those born in the late 1940s and thus completing their education before the Cultural Revolution, the sons of cadres and intelligentsia

Table 6.1 Total JMS enrolment by place of residence, 1962–1965

	Total	Cities	Towns	Rural
1962	6.19	2.18	1.72	2.30
1963	6.38	2.49	1.75	2.13
1964	7.29	2.92	1.83	2.54
1965	8.03	3.38	1.95	2.70

Source: ZGJYNJ (1984: 1005).

Note
These data exclude those enrolled in agricultural middle schools; there were 4.4 million of these students in 1965. Regular JMS enrolment data therefore understate the true reach of the secondary educational system.

typically had received 2 to 2.5 more years of education than the sons of peasants by 1982. More generally, their data show that male farmers born in 1950 typically had received only 5.8 years of education when surveyed in 1982, compared with the 8.2 year average for non-farmers (Deng and Treiman 1997: 403). In other words, and despite the massive expansion of education which occurred in the 1950s, educational inequality at middle-school level remained rife in China at the start of the Cultural Revolution.

Inequality was no less apparent at primary-school level despite educational expansion. Table 6.2 hints at the magnitude of the problem. Of the population aged seven to twelve only about 50 per cent were in school at the time of the 1964 population census. However, this single national figure disguises the extent of inequality within the system. In Beijing and in Shanghai cities proper, the enrolment rate was between 80 and 85 per cent, and it was around 70 per cent in the cities of Manchuria. But in rural Shanghai (that is, in the counties under the jurisdiction of Shanghai municipality), the rate of enrolment was only 68 per cent and in Jiangsu province it slipped to 43 per cent. Further west, however, the picture was far worse. The city populations fared quite well; even in Guizhou, about 73 per cent of urban children were enrolled in primary school (RKTJNJ 1988: 388–9). In the countryside, however, early Maoist educational programmes had hardly made a dent in the problem of under-enrolment. Only 35 per cent of Guizhou's rural children were in elementary schools in the early 1960s, and in Gansu and Ningxia the figure fell to 26 per cent, the worst recorded of any province. The provincial data thus range from 83 per cent in Shanghai city to 26 per cent in the Gansu countryside. This was educational inequality on a catastrophic scale.

The overall picture, then, was one of very considerable stratification in the mid-1960s; the meritocratic exam-based system had the effect of privileging those with cultural capital. For all that, some qualification is needed. In particular, the evidence does suggest that the policies of 1963–5 were having considerable

Table 6.2 School enrolment rates for children aged 7–12 in 1964 (per cent of the age cohort)

	Urban	Rural
Provinces with the best urban primary enrolment rates		
Shanghai	83	68
Beijing	81	63
Shaanxi	79	48
Hubei	78	50
Shanxi	76	72
Provinces with the worst rural primary enrolment rates		
Gansu	68	26
Qinghai	59	26
Anhui	57	27
Ningxia	58	30
Yunnan	56	33

Source: RKTJNJ (1988: 388–9).

effects on the extent of inequality within China's educational system. The case of Qinghua University and its attached middle school is instructive (Andreas 2002: 473). The class composition of the middle school exemplifies the Maoist critique; only about 6 and 9 per cent of the children enrolled there were of respectively working-class or peasant origin. Yet at Qinghua University itself – where in many ways one would expect children of elite backgrounds to be even more dominant – worker-peasant students comprised close to 40 per cent of the total. In other words, the process of superstructural change – in this case educational levelling – was already underway even before the beginning of the Cultural Revolution.

Educational policy in the late Maoist era

The solutions adopted to address these perceived failures in the late Maoist era were in effect a reassertion of the Yan'an approach. One aim was thus to expand the scale of rural education, both by means of its active promotion and by sending educated young people and urban teachers down into the countryside to serve as teachers in the newly created rural schools. Urban education was to be made equitable by abolishing university entrance exams and by making entry more dependent upon having a worker-peasant background than on high test scores. And in both sectors, work–study was to be the norm; the distinction between the 'two systems' of regular and *minban* education was to be brought to a swift end.

Mao's (1966) approach was set out in a letter to Lin Biao dated 7 May 1966:

> The students are in a similar position. Their studies are their chief work; they must also learn other things. In other words, they ought to learn industrial, agricultural, and military work in addition to class work. The school years should be shortened, education should be revolutionized, and the domination of our schools by bourgeois intellectuals should by no means be allowed to continue.

These notions were amplified in the CCP circular of 16 May and the 'Decision on the Cultural Revolution' of 8 August 1966 (Schoenhals 1996), which set out the main principles. Most local governments then drew up their own guidelines for educational policy modelled closely on these central directives. In Jimo, the county in Shandong written about by Han Dongping (2000: 99), guidelines were drawn up in April 1968. And in all this, a key aim was to narrow the gap between urban and rural China. According to Mao (1961):

> What shall we do to reduce the rural population? If we do not want them crowding into the cities we will have to have a great deal of industry in the countryside so that the peasants can become workers right where they are. This brings us to a major policy issue: do we want to keep rural living conditions from falling below that in the cities, keep the two roughly the same, or

keep the rural slightly higher than the urban? Every commune has to have its own economic center, its own upper-level schools to train its own intellectuals. There is no other way to solve the problem of excess rural population really and truly.

The expansion of rural education

A key element in the late Maoist strategy was to expand rapidly the number of students attending elementary and middle schools. This translated into the aim of establishing a primary school in every production brigade and a middle school in every commune. The distinction between government (*gongban*) and village-run (*minban*) schools was abolished; they all became *jitiban* (collective) schools. More importantly, the number of middle schools increased dramatically. Much of this was the result of villages pooling resources to build new middle schools (Han 2000: 103). In fact, although the *minban* schools had technically been abolished, it was their construction which actually led the expansion of middle-school education. For although the categories were notionally abolished, many of the statistical publications retain the distinction. To give an example, the *County Records* for Wushan, a poor county in the Yangzi Gorges, show that the number of *minban* schools quadrupled between 1965 and 1976, compared to a 50 per cent increase in the number of *gongban* schools (Wushan xian zhi 1991: 465). In the altogether more prosperous county of Kunshan, located on the outskirts of Shanghai, 1,789 of its 2,385 teachers were employed in *minban* schools (Kunshan xian zhi 1990: 621). This is a clear demonstration of the importance of the *minban* programme in rich and poor areas alike. To be sure, and as Table 6.3 shows, the number of schools did rise in urban areas as well. However, the increase was much more dramatic in county towns than in the cities, and even more so in the countryside, where the number of SMS increased by a factor of about 80 between 1965 and the high-water year of 1977.

Table 6.3 Number of senior and junior middle schools, 1964–1978 (thousands)

	Senior middle schools			Junior middle schools		
	Cities	Towns	Rural	Cities	Towns	Rural
1964	1.35	2.19	0.60	2.79	2.56	9.71
1965	1.32	2.19	0.60	3.08	2.28	8.63
1971	0.86	1.48	11.82	4.88	3.53	72.19
1972	4.00	3.54	20.49	2.55	3.09	59.29
1973	5.14	4.30	19.93	1.93	2.17	63.86
1974	5.85	4.83	20.91	1.57	2.15	65.32
1975	6.17	5.02	27.94	1.81	2.45	80.13
1976	7.01	5.73	47.79	1.94	3.67	126.01
1977	7.61	6.38	50.92	1.88	3.22	131.27
1978	7.11	6.11	36.00	2.70	3.33	107.10

Source: ZGJYNJ (1984: 1005).

However, this expansion in the number of schools did not solve the problem of ensuring an adequate supply of teachers. It was a relatively straightforward task to solve the elementary school problem, because a relatively large number of JMS graduates were available even in rural China. However, staffing junior and especially senior middle schools was much more of a problem because most rural SMS graduates used their success to leave the countryside for ever. Moreover, the antipathy of professional teachers to universal secondary education was profound. According to Pepper (1996: 412):

> [T]eachers had difficulty accepting the basic concept of universal junior middle schooling since it meant that 'no matter what their records in elementary school' everyone was promoted. ... Education was not a right but a privilege to be earned, in accordance with fixed standards, or withheld. Schools that failed to enforce such standards 'were not really schools'.

The solution adopted – much to the consternation of many of those urban citizens affected – was to use the power of central government over job assignments to return urban graduates to the countryside. The motives behind the *xiafang* programme were complex (see Chapter 5). For example, the 1968 'Notification' on job assignments for university graduates stipulated that 'In general, graduates must become ordinary peasants or ordinary workers. A majority must become ordinary peasants' (Schoenhals 1996: 77). This was hardly a policy initiated with the sole aim of promoting rural education, whatever its merits as a scheme devised to widen the horizons of the rusticated youth themselves.

Nevertheless, a significant number of graduates and former Red Guards eventually did become teachers, not least because Chinese villagers recognized that they were fit for little else. Of the eighty-two persons interviewed by Pepper, thirty-three were rusticated youth and of these no fewer than twenty were teachers (Pepper 1996: 391). Others who ended up as teachers were cadres and college teachers sent initially to 'May 7th Cadre schools' for political study. Han (2000: 102–3 and 106) notes that elementary-school vacancies were filled by village graduates. However, the central government played a key role in staffing middle schools by requiring teachers on the government payroll to return to their home village. Thus in Jimo, the number of teachers employed by the Ministry of Education rose from 307 in 1965 to nearly 1,900 in 1977 (Han 2000: 106). This pattern was mirrored in many other parts of China. It was the very fact that the *xiafang* programme filled these key positions – rather than its contribution to the supply of teachers – that was its main contribution to the expansion of rural education.

To be sure, there was no growth at all in the number of elementary schools in rural China during the late Maoist era. In fact, the figure for the late 1970s was around 900,000, well down on the 1.6 million recorded in 1965 (ZGJYNJ 1984: 1022). Not that this signalled any reversal of policy; the number of elementary school pupils continued to rise. Rather, it was simply a reflection of the fact that elementary schooling was available to most Chinese children by 1965.

It was also driven by a recognition that many of the schools which had been established during the rapid expansion of 1964–5 were simply too small to be viable.

Curriculum reform

As important as the expansion of rural education was curriculum reform. The national college entrance exam had mandated the use of national textbooks across China, and these, because they were inevitably geared both towards passing the exam and the needs of urban children, were very unsuitable for rural education (Han 2000: 168). The decision to scrap the exam in the mid-1960s thus had the knock-on effect of allowing local schools much more flexibility over the use of textbooks and indeed to develop teaching materials of their own (Pepper 1996: 405–10). One common effect was the displacement of physics by industrial knowledge, and biology by agricultural science.

The late Maoist era also saw the development of a virtuocracy (as Shirk calls it), whereby educational success depended much more upon having a worker or peasant background than on examination success. In this way, the cultural capital passed on to children by parents who were intellectuals, or who had been prosperous before 1949, was negated. Thus when the universities reopened in 1970–1, a high-school graduate had to have two years of farm or factory experience, and the recommendation of their commune or factory, which in turn tended to be based upon their perceived level of political commitment. As time went by, however, cadre status became increasingly important to gaining university access, because cadres were able to use their connections to exploit the absence of well-defined admissions criteria (Kwong 1983: 94–5).

A second important change was to reduce the length of schooling from twelve to nine years. Practice varied very considerably, and urban schools were more likely to provide five years of middle-school education than schools in the countryside, but the new norm was five years of elementary education followed by four years of middle schooling (Pepper 1996: 403–10). This general approach had been attempted previously, and it is not hard to see its attraction to the Chinese government and to the communes themselves. A saving of three years worth of funding per child was no small matter, and necessarily made it easier to finance higher enrolment rates across the system. The danger, of course, was that it led to a dilution of the quality of education, a matter to which we return later.

Perhaps the most striking policy initiative was the decision to expect all pupils and students across the system to engage in both work and study. The aim was to do away with the binary divide between the *minban* and regular schools which had been a feature of the Leap, and, as we have seen, the notion was based upon Mao's view of the need to combine the acquisition of theory with work-based practice. In some cases, of course, the work experience was of low quality. In the countryside, however, this sort of auxiliary labour made a big contribution to production. As Han (2000) notes, it was almost a matter of course that children would be withdrawn from school in the countryside for a few hours if family needs were pressing, and the whole school system effectively closed during the key planting and harvest periods, when labour was at an absolute premium. More importantly, this labour helped to provide the basis for the expansion of rural industry. Precisely because middle-school students and their teachers had at least some skills, they were able to play an important role as industrial workers and therefore it was quite commonplace for schools to have industrial enterprises attached to them. In Jimo, for example, the Number 1 middle school had a factory, two workshops and two farms attached to it (Han 2000: 114–15). And the rural industries in turn generated a part of the revenue stream needed to finance education. Nevertheless, we should not exaggerate the work component of the new education. Han suggests that work occupied between half a day and one day per week, and Pepper's informants provided the same information (Pepper 1996: 406–7). In other words, perhaps two months per year of traditional teaching time were lost to work. Education remained primarily about book-based knowledge acquisition.

The efficiency of the late Maoist educational system

There is no doubt that late Maoism led to a dramatic transformation of Chinese educational practices. However, the central question is not so much the extent of the transformation, but its impact on efficiency and on equity. Was the total level of educational provision expanded, or was it the case that the increased number of students making their way through the system was offset by a precipitous decline in the quality of education per student? These are the main efficiency questions.[14] As for equity, the avowed Maoist aims were to close the gap between urban and rural China, and to erode the class advantage enjoyed by the children of intellectuals, cadres and those who had prospered before 1949. Were these goals achieved?

Enrolment, graduation and literacy trends

There is no question about the upward trends in enrolments and graduations for elementary-school children. The number of graduates soared from around 5 million in the early 1960s to 25 million in the peak year of 1977. Much of this growth occurred in the rural sector; about 21 million of the graduates were rural in 1977, compared with about 450,000 in 1965. Some of this reflected the increase in the size of the cohort, which rose substantially because of population growth. Nevertheless, the data show a clear increase in the enrolment rate, beginning in 1964–5 and culminating in enrolment rates of well over 90 per cent by the mid-1970s. To all intents and purposes, therefore, primary-school education was close to universal by the time of Mao's death. Although the process of expansion predated the Cultural Revolution, the rise in the enrolment rate (of around 20 percent) which occurred after 1966 was astonishing, and testifies to the effectiveness of the late Maoist strategy.

The increased level of elementary provision was more than mirrored at

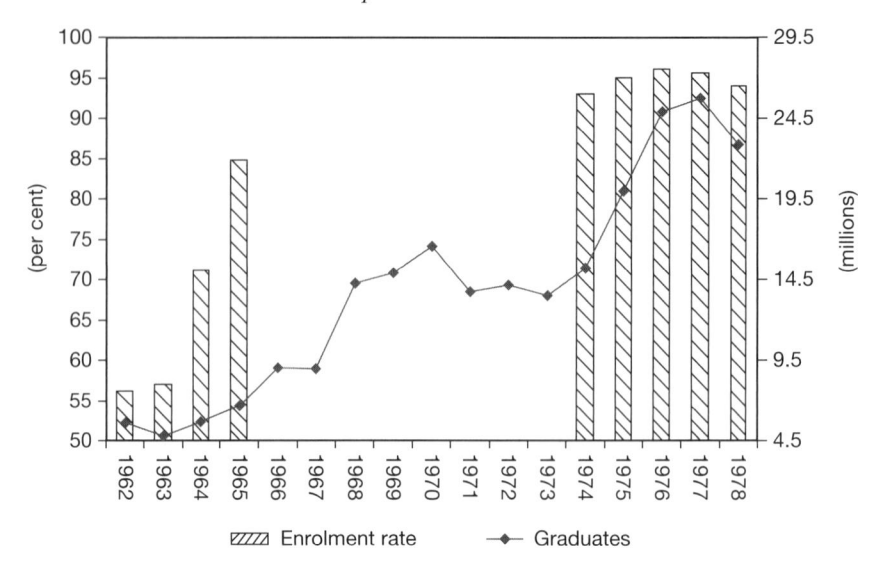

Figure 6.4 Primary enrolment rates and number of graduates, 1962–1978 (Source: ZGJYNJ (1984: 1021 and 1024))

Note: There are no data for enrolment rates during the late 1960s and early 1970s. The data are for the net enrolment rate, i.e. the data include enrolees of primary school age only.

middle-school level. Enrolment rates are not available but we can proxy the trend by looking at the promotion rate, which is the proportion of the graduating cohort in any year enrolling in the next level of the system. The trends here are shown in Figure 6.5. Two features are particularly striking. First, there was a dip in enrolments during 1966–7, when many of China's middle schools were closed. These data suggest that not all schools were closed – in that sense, some of the accounts of the Cultural Revolution are misleading – but it is nevertheless apparent that the Revolution dealt a severe blow to enrolment rates. Second, the data show a pronounced increase in the promotion rate at both JMS and SMS levels. As a result, virtually all Chinese children were able to enter JMS by the end of the 1970s, compared with around half in the mid-1960s. At SMS level, the rise was equally marked; 70 per cent of children were entering senior middle school in the halcyon days of the mid-1970s. It is worth stressing too that many of the gains accrued to urban as well as to rural children. In the Deng–Treiman sample (1997: 403), the sons of farmers born in 1960 (and living in urban areas in 1982) enjoyed on average 8.2 years of education, well up on the 5.8 years received by the cohort born in 1945. For the sons of non-farm men, the rise was from 8.2 years to 10.2 years.

An alternative way to assess Chinese educational progress during the late Maoist era is by looking at the trend in the literacy rate. If more students were making their way through the system and achieving literacy, that would appear to suggest a clear rise in educational efficiency. The most useful data here were

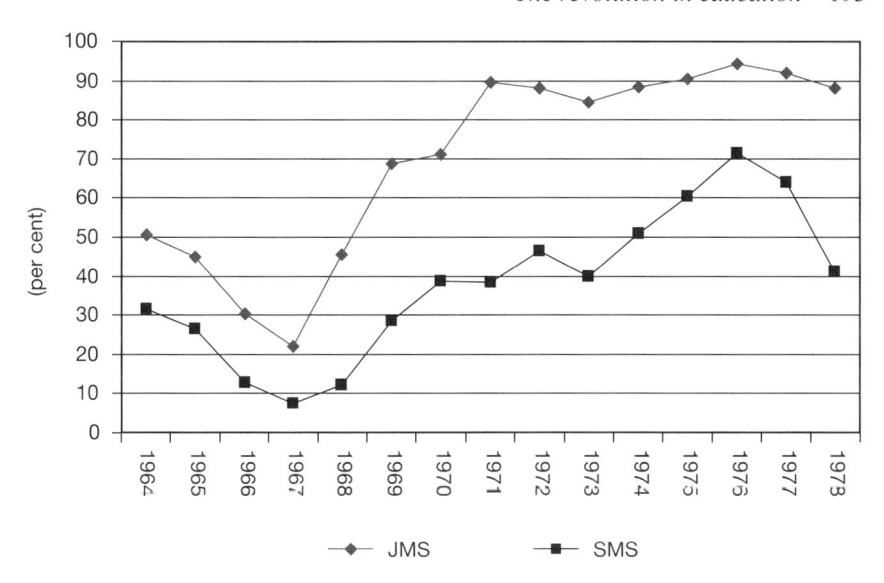

Figure 6.5 Promotion rates to junior and senior middle schools, 1964–1978 (Source: SSB (2005a: 81–2).)

those collected during the 1982 Population Census. Not only were extensive data on literacy rates by age obtained but also, because it was a comprehensive, nationwide census, the data provide an alternative means by which we can assess the impact of late Maoism.

The trend using the 1982 data (shown in Figure 6.6) is striking, especially for girls; see also Lavely *et al.* 1990. Of girls born between 1948 and 1952 – and thus completing their primary education before the Cultural Revolution – the illiteracy rate was well over 40 per cent, compared with only 13 per cent for boys. This demonstrates the extent of the gender inequality built into Chinese culture and the educational system at the time. Thereafter, the male illiteracy rate continued to drop, falling to only 4 per cent amongst those born during 1963–7. But the fall in female illiteracy was far faster, declining from 40 per cent for the 1948–52 birth cohort to only 15 per cent for the 1963–7 cohort, the last to complete its primary education before the end of the Maoist era. This reduction in female illiteracy was a remarkable achievement, and it is thrown into relief by what the data tell us about the cohorts born in 1968, 1969 and 1970. For these children, the illiteracy rate shows stagnation, suggesting that the death of Mao signalled an end to the downward trajectory of illiteracy rates.

To be sure, some qualification to this picture of declining illiteracy is in order. First, the estimates in Figure 6.6 are the rates for survivors. It is likely that illiteracy was greater amongst those who did not live to see the 1982 census, at least if we assume that education is positively correlated with good health. Second, it is evident that the decline in illiteracy predates the 1949 Revolution. Buck's survey recorded that 69 per cent of males and 99 per cent of females were illiterate in

194 *Chinese Economic Development*

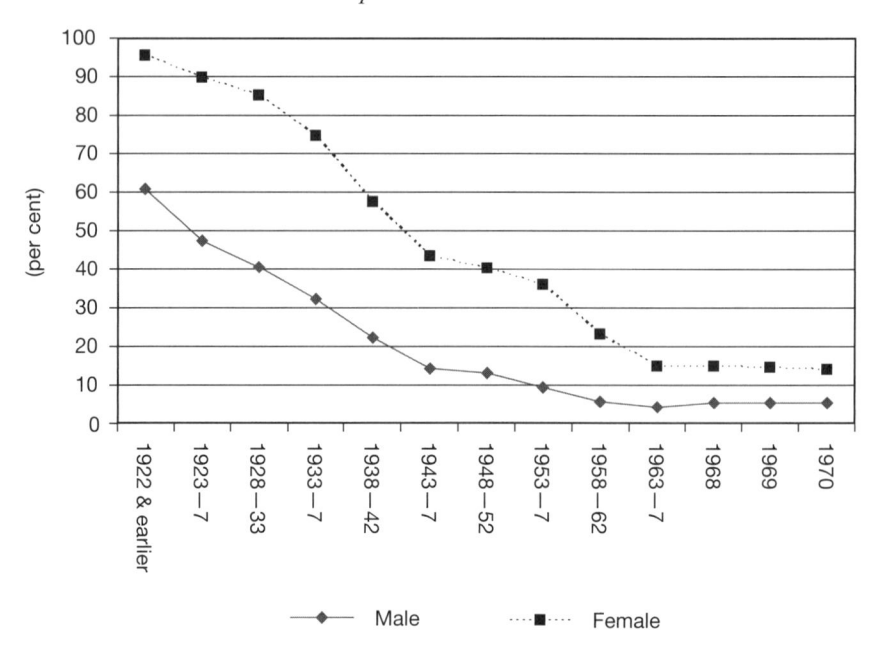

Figure 6.6 Illiteracy rates in 1982 by year of birth (Source RKNJ (1985: 618).)

1929–33 (Buck 1937: 373).[15] However, the situation was changing fast in the 1930s, not least because of the influence of the June 4th movement and the significance that movement accorded to the importance of developing education in the service of modernization. For example, those who were born during 1931–5 were much more likely to be literate than those born in the 1920s, even though their education was disrupted by the Second Sino-Japanese War. This provides testimony to the comparative success of the Republican government in expanding education.

For all that, it is clear that the Maoist regime took the process much further. Significant though the pre-1949 reductions in illiteracy were, it was a much harder task to reduce illiteracy from 28 to 5 per cent than from (say) 80 to 60 per cent because it demanded an expansion of educational provision in very poor parts of rural China. In that sense, the success of late Maoism is especially noteworthy. It was a system built upon the expansion of rural education; this was no elitist system. And the effectiveness of the late Maoist educational programme was enhanced by a number of innovations. The sending-down programme of educated urban youth and other urban professionals certainly helped; Zhou Youguang, the inventor of *pinyin*, was one academic so exiled in the 1960s. Collectivization provided the institutional infrastructure and made possible the extraction of the necessary resources. Probably of equal importance was the introduction of the *pinyin* system of character romanization introduced in February 1958, which made it much easier for children to learn the Chinese language.[16]

The issue of quality

Yet the data on illiteracy and enrolments discussed in the previous section do not settle the question of educational progress. To be sure, the late Maoist educational strategy led to many more Chinese entering and graduating from elementary and middle schools than ever before, and to a big rise in the literacy rate. However, we need to ask whether this increase in numbers was offset by a deterioration in the educational experience. Was expansion bought at the price of declining quality? The CCP leadership in the late 1970s seems to have thought so. Consider the speeches of Deng Xiaoping in 1977 on education. According to Deng, and in contrast to Mao's assessment of the same period, educational policy in the first seventeen years after 1949 (the period before the Cultural Revolution) was successful. According to him (Deng 1995: 80): 'The "two appraisals" in the *Summary of the National Conference on Education* [of 1971] do not accord with reality. How can we dismiss 10 million intellectuals at one stroke?' Furthermore, by arguing that intellectuals were just as much workers as those employed in manual occupations, he signalled an end to the policy of giving preferential treatment to workers and to peasants. He thus 'reversed the verdict' of the 1971 *Summary*. Deng (1995: 55–6) also called for the restoration of the keypoint system: 'It is necessary to bring together, through stiff examinations, the outstanding people in the key secondary schools and the key colleges and universities.' In addition, he was critical of the Maoist policy of requiring middle-school graduates to participate in manual labour before going to university: 'we must make up our minds to restore the direct enrolment of senior middle school graduates though entrance examinations, and to stop the practice of having the masses recommend candidates for admission to colleges and universities' (Deng 1995: 68).

We should not dismiss this as empty rhetoric. As Seeberg rightly points out, we need to think about how data on literacy rates were arrived at and whether they are reliable. In China's case, the approach taken was to look at the level of education completed (Lavely 1990; Ross 2005). The census enumeration form and instructions show this very clearly (RKNJ 1985). If a child had successfully graduated from primary school (and had the certificate to demonstrate it), s/he was deemed to be literate. This was inevitably a less reliable method than testing character recognition, because graduation did not necessarily imply knowledge. In fact, Seeberg argues that we should discount the graduation certificates handed out during the late Maoist era, and concludes that the illiteracy data complied during the 1982 census should not be trusted.

There is some evidence which supports Seeberg's negative conclusion. For example, a study based upon character recognition in 1996 found that the net effect of late Maoism was to reduce the number of characters recognized by the equivalent of one year of education (Treiman 2002). This undoubtedly would have been enough to ensure that some of those who graduated from primary school were illiterate. However, Seeberg's more general argument that late Maoism led to no improvement in literacy rates is extreme. A year's reduction in schooling would certainly reduce literacy rates, but it is hard to see that it would have had a dramatic effect. Literacy was usually gained at the age of eleven, two years before the completion of primary school. Even allowing for a dilution in quality, this still implies that most primary-school graduates would have been literate. Moreover, even if students had not become literate by the time of graduation from primary school, almost all of them had the opportunity to go on to middle school and hence the chance to improve their knowledge of characters. Thus one of Pepper's (1996: 408) most critical informants, whilst claiming that late Maoist primary school graduates had acquired on average only 1,000 characters, recognized that students had acquired 2,000 by the time of middle-school graduation.

In any case, the Treiman results are hardly decisive. There are inevitably question marks over the reliability of a study conducted in 1996 as a means of assessing late Maoist literacy rates. Character recognition may well have diminished in many cases in proportion to the number of years which had elapsed after the end of schooling. In other words, many of the late Maoist cohort may simply have forgotten the characters that they learnt at school. That seems to have been particularly true of manual workers in Treiman's sample. The other problem is that it is very hard in the type of analysis conducted by Treiman to normalize for differences in family background. Observed differences in character recognition may simply reflect differences in cultural capital between the sample schooled in the 1950s and those schooled in the late 1960s and 1970s, rather than any late Maoist effect.

More generally, Seeberg's apocalyptic conclusion about the effect of late Maoism on education is not very convincing, and her conclusions on illiteracy are at variance with those of most other academics (Pepper 1996; Hannum 1999; Peterson 1994a, 1994b; Gao 1999; Han 2000). The central problem is the obvious bias in the way that she interprets the data. Seeberg regards any numbers that are published either before 1965 (the Leap aside) or after 1978 (though not the results of the 1982 Population Census, as we will see) as reliable. However, any data collected during the late Maoist era or the Great Leap Forward are simply dismissed a priori as little more than fabrication. Seeberg is right to recognize the dangers in any unthinking acceptance of Chinese data, but she fails to apply this same principle to her own analysis. A typical statement is that 'Ministry of Education officials in 1983 had admitted to UNESCO that the Cultural Revolution had contributed to an increase in illiteracy' (Seeberg 2000: 319). However, the Ministry of Education officials whom she interviewed, and whom she relies upon in assessing educational quality in the late 1970s and early 1980s (Seeberg 2000: 430–2), were anything but neutral bystanders. Many of them had suffered during the late Maoist era; indeed the headquarters staff of the Ministry had been banished to the poor county of Fengyang in Anhui during 1969–70 (Pepper 1996: 467). They had very strong reasons for being negative about the Cultural Revolution and were anxious to follow the new political line being promoted by the CCP leadership, which was very critical of the educational effects of late Maoism.[17]

There is a more general point here too. Chinese illiteracy data are not ideal in the way in which they are collected. However, an approach based upon school completion rates has long been the norm in most countries, and there too it suffers from the same limitations as the Chinese methodology. In Europe, North America and in China alike, the completion of primary-school education in no sense guarantees literacy. Only very recently has there been a move towards reliance on test scores as a way of judging educational quality. On this basis, the International Adult Literacy Survey has estimated UK rates of functional illiteracy to be around 20 per cent over the last decade, a figure which is far higher than that usually cited in UN statistics.[18] In other words, if we are thinking of China's record in comparative perspective, it is not obvious that the disparity between true illiteracy and illiteracy as measured by primary-school completion rates is any different in China from the disparity in other countries.

The key issue is of course the trend. At any moment in time, Chinese literacy data exaggerate the true level of attainment because they are based on completion rates rather than true tests of reading ability. However, if the extent of exaggeration did not change over time, we are still justified in concluding that the late Maoist development strategy had a positive effect on literacy. Seeberg's argument is that the bias did change; the figures from the 1964 Population Census are relatively reliable whereas those from the 1982 census are not. This is the basis for her claim that late Maoism may even have led to an increase in illiteracy. However, there is absolutely no basis for that conclusion. The methodology which underpinned the estimates of illiteracy was exactly the same in 1964 as it had been in 1982, and the general opinion amongst demographers is that the 1982 census was China's best to date, and certainly far better than most of those conducted in other poor countries (Banister 1987). And the ideological biases in China were probably such as to make the 1982 returns more reliable. The CCP and its Ministry of Education had a very strong incentive to show *high* illiteracy rates in 1982 because they could then be blamed on the late Maoist strategy and its distortion by the Gang of Four. The very fact that illiteracy rates show a clear decline between 1964 and 1982, this political agenda notwithstanding, points powerfully to the conclusion that true illiteracy declined very substantially during the late 1960s and 1970s.

The quality of middle-school and university education

If there was a failure during the late Maoist period, it was not so much in terms of primary education and literacy, but in terms of middle-school and university education. We know that the universities were closed for a long period. We know too that the length of schooling was cut by two or three years on average. And we also know that many schools were staffed by teachers who were poorly trained and badly motivated. It seems reasonable to suppose from this that, although China was successful in reducing illiteracy during the late Maoist era, it was not successful in terms of other aspects of academic education.

This alleged weakness in upper-level education is the essence of Peterson's argument. He acknowledges that literacy rates did improve during the late Maoist era (Peterson 1994a: 120), but that was as far as China's educational success went. Having a knowledge of 1,500 characters, he argues, was enough only to carry out the most basic of tasks. According to him (Peterson 1994a: 117):

The village schools inculcated a basic, poorly funded and limited literacy program. Their economic and social uses terminate at the production team gate.

The products of this sort of education inevitably encountered difficulties in those instances where they gained university entrance. Kwong's (1983: 95–6) interviews in the late 1970s and early 1980s reveal a general view amongst those teaching in institutes of higher education that standards were well below those than prevailed before the Cultural Revolution, and that the average student had no better than a pre-1966 JMS education. Moreover, the peasantry were well aware of the limitations of Maoist rural education, and this proved to be a significant factor in limiting the demand for middle-school education. Pepper (1996) paints a picture of a late 1970s Chinese peasantry who were mortified by the decline in middle-school educational provision that was a feature of the late 1970s and early 1980s (Figure 6.5, above), but the truth, as Peterson points out, was rather more complex. Chinese education had traditionally been seen as an avenue of social mobility, but the rural schooling of the 1970s fell well short of fulfilling that promise.

This question of the quality of middle-school education is difficult to assess. Some of the evidence certainly supports Peterson's negative appraisal. Many of the Chinese educators who were exiled to the countryside were predictably scathing of the impact of late Maoism. One of the teachers interviewed by Pepper (1996: 408) concludes that a JMS graduate knew only 2,000 characters compared with the 3,000 norm prior to the Cultural Revolution. We also saw early that Treiman (2002) had concluded that the impact of late Maoism was to reduce the length of effective education by one year. Other studies too have concluded that late Maoism had harmful effects in the sense that it reduced the number of years of education attained, especially for those urban cohorts most affected by the *xiafang* programme (Giles *et al.* 2007).[19]

Nevertheless, the evidence when taken as a whole is far from easy to interpret. The Giles *et al.* study refers only to urban children and it is hardly surprising that their education was affected by the sending-down programme, because that programme made it far more difficult for them to gain access to a university education. University access depended heavily upon the recommendations of local cadres and sent-down youth were not likely to be favoured. But even if urban youth did lose out, that does not tell us anything about the *overall* effect of late Maoism. We need also to consider whether any loss to urban children was offset by gains to those born in the countryside. As we see in the next section, it probably was. As importantly, a recent study of twins found that the late Maoist strategy had a positive effect on the returns to education (Zhang *et al.* 2007). The advantage of this sort of study is that it normalizes for the effects of family-specific factors on educational attainment, which are otherwise very difficult to measure.[20] Again, however, the results are not decisive, because the sample is small and restricted to urban educational attainment. Nevertheless, the conclusion that those who were educated during the 1980s and 1990s did less well than those educated under late Maoism is a striking one. In explaining the results, the authors hazard the opinion that 'the Cultural Revolution made individuals work harder and become more disciplined and more responsible, which offset the decline in teaching and learning quality' (Zhang *et al.* 2007: 639).

Education and post-1978 Chinese economic growth

We can also think about the quality of Chinese educational programmes during the late Maoist era by looking at the link between macroeconomic performance and education. More precisely, we can consider the link between the educational inheritance of the Dengist regime in the late 1970s and China's subsequent economic performance. There are three logical possibilities. First, that the educational legacies of Maoism hindered economic growth. Second, that there was no real link at all and the pace of growth was independent of the level of education. Third, that the educational legacies of Maoism had powerful positive effect on subsequent growth.[21]

The first of these possibilities can be ruled out. As we shall see in later chapters, the Chinese economy grew at a rate of around 10 per cent per year in the 1980s and 1990s. Whatever else the effects of Maoist education may have been, it certainly did not prevent economic growth from occurring. Of course we can always pose the counterfactual: the Chinese economy would have grown even faster had it inherited a better system of education. But countries simply do not grow more quickly than around 10 per cent per year over a long period of time, and therefore such a counterfactual can safely be discounted.

As to whether Maoist educational legacies were neutral or helpful for growth, some of the macroevidence seems, on the face of it, to suggest that education did not matter very much for growth. To see this, we can use the county-level data on growth rates in China in the 1980s and 1990s and look at the degree to which they are correlated with the county literacy rates of 1982 (Bramall 2007). The evidence shows that literacy rates are statistically significant for economic growth even when we normalize for the initial level of GDP per head, FDI, skills and location. However, the *economic* significance of education is very weak. That is, education has a positive effect on growth but that effect (though statistically significant) is small relative to the effect of other factors. This emerges very clearly when we exclude the counties located in the poorest parts of western China from the econometric analysis. For the vast majority of Chinese counties and cities, increases in literacy seem to have mattered very little: a county or a city with a literacy rate of (say) 70 per cent on average grew no faster than a county or city with a literacy rate of 50 per cent after 1982. These findings for China seem to be very much in line with much of the evidence on other countries (Easterly 2001).

The instances of Jiangsu and Zhejiang provinces further illustrate the point. Both provinces enjoyed remarkably fast economic growth after 1978 by Chinese standards. Yet their average level of education in 1982 was rather low compared with the provinces of Manchuria, where in fact economic growth was slow. Skill levels seem to have been much more important, and here both provinces had done well under Mao, in the sense that rural industry had expanded quickly in the 1970s.

Guangdong, on the face of it, seems to testify to the importance of education. Its educational levels in the early 1980s were high and, as is well known, its economic growth in the post-1978 period was very rapid. However, econometric analysis of differences in county-level growth rates shows that the literacy rate was insignificant (Bramall 2007). In fact, Guangdong's growth seems to have had far more to do with its location, its inherited skills base, and (of course) high levels of inward investment. Finally, Hunan illustrates the reverse of the argument. That province had a very high literacy rate in the early 1980s, yet its growth rate over the next two decades was slow.

However, we should not conclude that Maoist endeavours to expand educational opportunities were pointless. For one thing, this takes no account of the increase in life expectancy that occurred during the Maoist era itself. Given that per capita food consumption increased hardly at all in the late Maoist era, it seems likely that the rise in longevity reflected the combined effect of modest increases in spending on health care and the way in which improved education left the rural population much more aware of the link between sanitation and hygiene on the one hand and disease on the other.

Second, we need to recognize that the impact of educational expansion in the 1960s and 1970s was much more powerful than it was after 1982. This is because there is a threshold effect; once a figure of around 40 per cent literacy is achieved, modern economic growth becomes possible and further increases in literacy have comparatively weak growth effects. This explains the limited impact of levels of literacy on growth rates in the post-1982 era. In the 1960s, however, literacy rates were still below this threshold in many of China's provinces. Consider the evidence in Table 6.4. These data show that there were still twelve provinces where rates of illiteracy were in excess of 60 per cent even in 1964, the year of China's second national population census. This was true even of Jiangsu province. In the rural hinterland of these provinces, the rates were substantially higher. Thus despite the educational expansion of the early Maoist era, many Chinese children lacked access to elementary education. Fifty-seven million children aged between seven and twelve were not in school in 1964, almost exactly half of the age cohort (RKTJNJ 1988: 383 and 388). In Yunnan and Guizhou, the rate was 64 per cent; in Gansu and Ningxia it was over 70 per cent. In other words, the high illiteracy rate in 1964 was not due simply to the very high rates of illiteracy amongst the elderly; there was a clear failure in terms of elementary-school provision as well.

In short, there were many parts of rural China where modern economic growth was impossible in the early 1960s because the literacy rate was not high enough. In these places, Maoist emphasis on extending basic education made eminent sense. Increasing educational levels in Beijing and Shanghai may have done little for growth, but late Maoism was primarily about expanding literacy in provinces like Yunnan and Guizhou; there, the return (in terms of faster growth) was much higher. The great metropolitan centres of China needed little by way of an educational improvement to enable rapid economic growth, but the poor counties of south-west China certainly did – and that is precisely what happened in the late Maoist era.

Table 6.4 Provinces with illiteracy rates of over 60 per cent in 1964

	Population (million)	Semi-literates aged over 12 (million)	Illiterates aged over 12 (million)	Illiteracy (per cent)
Yunnan	20.51	0.64	9.07	73.1
Gansu	12.63	0.34	5.49	71.6
Guizhou	17.14	0.47	7.50	71.0
Anhui	31.24	0.68	13.87	70.4
Ningxia	2.11	0.06	0.85	69.9
Qinghai	2.15	0.07	0.89	67.5
Shandong	55.52	1.91	21.85	66.8
Henan	50.33	1.13	20.33	65.5
Hubei	33.71	1.51	12.04	62.6
Shaanxi	20.77	0.63	7.38	61.0
Jiangxi	21.07	0.98	7.26	60.8
Jiangsu	44.51	1.43	15.94	60.2
Total	689.97	24.78	233.26	58.5

Source: RKTJNJ (1988: 382–3 and 388).

Note
Many official Chinese publications give an illiteracy rate of 33.6 per cent in 1964; see for example ZGTJNJ (2006: 102). That figure is very misleading. For one thing, it excludes semi-literates. For another, and more importantly, it calculates the illiteracy rate as the number of illiterates aged over 12 divided by the total population – when the calculation ought to use the population aged over 12 as the denominator.

Furthermore, the county-level evidence also points to the conclusion that Maoist emphasis on work experience as an essential component of education was of great benefit for growth. Deng Xiaoping (1995: 80–1) admittedly took the opposite view in the late 1970s:[22]

> Why should we enrol students directly? The answer is simple: so as not to break the continuity of study. ... In the past talking with foreign guests I too stressed the advantages of having secondary school students do physical labour for two years after graduation. Facts have shown, however, that after a couple of years of labour, the students have forgotten half of what they learnt at school. This is a waste of time.

But the evidence points towards a different conclusion. Academic education may have suffered, but this loss was more than outweighed by the gains in terms of work experience. The basis for this conclusion is the fact that those counties which had high rates of industrial employment in the early 1980s grew much faster (*ceteris paribus*) than counties which did not (Bramall 2007). I interpret this result as showing that experience mattered. Industrial productivity depends upon learning-by-doing; there is no substitute for industrial experience. Thus those counties across China which successfully developed rural industry in the 1960s and 1970s – and hence gave a larger proportion of their workforce (and school population) experience of industrial employment – grew faster after 1978 than those which did not. The move towards combining work and study during the late Maoist years appears to have generated much greater dividends in terms of growth than increases in the literacy rate in areas where it was already above the threshold needed for modern economic growth.

Summary

The right conclusions from all this evidence seem to be as follows. The effect of late Maoism was in all probability to reduce the quality of any given year's worth of schooling: character acquisition in rural schools was lower for every year spent in the classroom between 1966 and 1978 than pre-1966. Late Maoism also brought about a cut in the number of years spent in school and university by the urban cohorts most affected by the sending-down programme. However, these adverse effects were more than offset by the positive effects of late Maoism. The losses to the upper tail of the urban cohort were more than offset by three factors: the expansion of middle-school opportunities for urban children of working-class origin; the vastly increased number of rural children receiving a primary-school education; and growing opportunities for middle-school education in rural areas. These rural children may have received a somewhat inferior education, but they spent far more years in the classroom than their predecessors and therefore emerged from the experience with at least basic literacy. The rise in the literacy rate between the early 1960s and the late 1970s is therefore no chimera, but a real manifestation of the effectiveness of rural education programmes in ensuring basic education.

Furthermore, even though urban children may have received fewer years of education because of the effects of the late Maoist strategy, the sending-down programme and the broadening of their horizons increased their earning power relative to pre- and post-Cultural Revolution generations. In other words, any loss in terms of academic education was offset by enhanced life skills. Moreover, the macroeconomic data show no sign that higher levels of education would have led to an accelerated growth rate. For a relatively poor economy like China, the educational levels attained by 1978 were in aggregate (though not of course in all regions) perfectly adequate to achieve rapid and sustained economic growth. Education matters for economic growth, but the Chinese evidence points very much towards the conclusion that the attainment of a relatively low educational threshold is all that is educationally necessary to break out of the low-level poverty trap that afflicts many countries across the globe

Educational equity

One of the key educational aims of late Maoism was to reduce inequality of access to schooling. This, as we saw earlier, was acute in the early 1960s. Urban children were privileged relative to rural children, and the educational status of parents was the crucial determinant of educational opportunities for their offspring. On these issues, the evidence is far less equivocal than it is for efficiency: there is

The revolution in education 203

no question that the effect of late Maoism was to reduce inequality across a wide range of educational indicators.

The urban–rural gap

One way of measuring the urban–rural educational gap is to look at differences in progression rates between the two sectors – that is, the percentage of primary graduates enrolling in JMS and the percentage of JMS graduates going on to SMS (Figure 6.7). These progression gaps were very large in 1962; whereas 84 per cent of urban children went on from primary to junior middle school, only 21 per cent of rural children made that progression, making for a progression gap of over 60 per cent. The gap in terms of progression to senior middle school was of the same sort of magnitude: 46 per cent of urban children went from JMS to senior middle school, compared with a paltry 4 per cent of JMS graduates in the rural sector.

By the late 1970s, not much progress had been made in narrowing the SMS gap. To be sure, the progression rate for rural children had increased dramatically; the 4 per cent progression rate of 1962 had become a 64 per cent rate by 1977, the high-water mark. But progression rates had increased equally rapidly in the urban sector, such that there is no real trend decline in the progression gap between the early 1960s and the late 1970s. The data collected by Deng and Treiman (1997: 403) show the same pattern. Boys born in 1950 into a household where the father was a farmer (but which was living in a city in 1982), received seven years of education, but this had gone up to nine years for those born in 1961. Nevertheless, the gap in years of education between non-farm and farm households narrowed

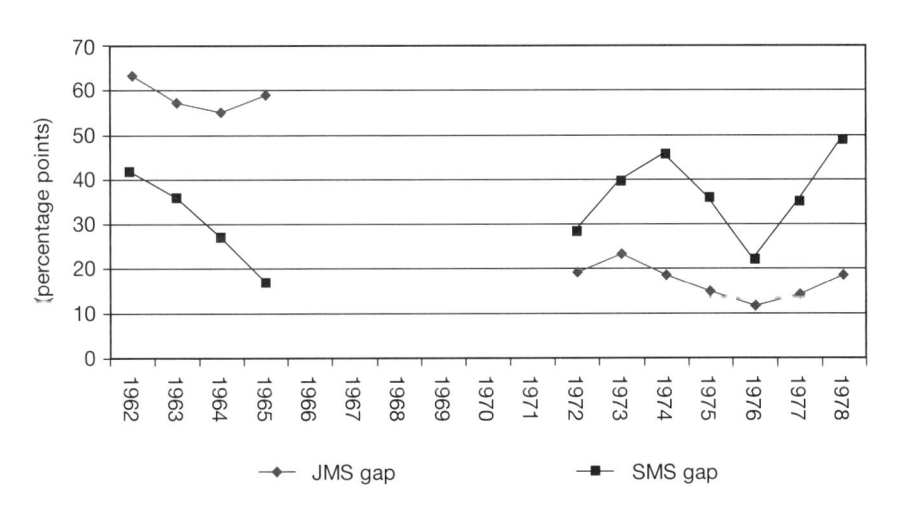

Figure 6.7 The gap between progression rates in urban and rural areas, 1962–1978 (Source: ZGJYNJ (1984: 1006 and 1023).)

Note: The gap is the difference between the urban and rural progression rates, measured in percentage points. The rural figures omit county towns.

only slightly, falling from 2.4 years for those born in 1945 to 2 years for those born in 1960; this was because educational expansion occurred in urban as well as rural areas.

However, the picture was very different in terms of progression to JMS. The progression gap in the early 1960s was around 60 percentage points, but by the late 1970s it had been reduced to little more than 15 per cent. The main reason for this was the strategy of creating a junior middle school in every commune. With little scope for the urban progression rate to increase (it was already quite high in the early 1960s), the rapid growth in JMS numbers in the countryside led inexorably to a narrowing of the differential.

The late Maoist strategy thus made great strides in increasing rural progression. Nevertheless, those strides had not been big enough to eliminate the urban–rural differential. The chances of getting into a senior middle school in the countryside were still much lower than in the cities. Moreover, even though rural senior middle schools had sprung up in great numbers during the late 1960s and 1970s, the quality of education they offered was not particularly high. Above all else, and principally because of the biased internal terms of trade, the communes lacked the funds needed to ensure high-quality middle-school education. Furthermore, the operation of the *hukou* system made it extremely difficult for those born in rural areas to migrate to the cities, and this inevitably limited the extent of mobility (Wu and Treiman 2004b). Without access to the higher-quality education that even during the late Maoist era continued to be available in urban areas, it remained hard for the children of peasants to go to university.

Provincial inequalities

The urban–rural gap was only one dimension of spatial inequality. In fact, it needs to be observed that inequality in education levels between (predominantly rural) provinces remained very significant at the close of the Maoist era. We can see this from differences in county-level literacy rates as measured at the time of the 1982 Population Census. As Figure 6.8 shows, rates were high in Manchuria, in much of Guangdong, in central Hunan and in the areas around Xi'an. But rates were much lower in other parts of China. The south-western provinces, Gansu and Ningxia and much of Anhui all show low literacy rates. As interestingly, the literacy rates in the relatively prosperous provinces of Jiangsu and Zhejiang were not very high by Chinese standards. Maoist policy certainly lowered inter-provincial inequality (as a direct comparison of the variation in illiteracy rates in 1964 and in 1982 reveals. Nevertheless, educational progress remained spatially very uneven.

The influence of parental education and occupation

The egalitarian impact of the late Maoist era was also significant because it *weakened* the relationship between parental education and the educational attainment of their children, and *changed* the relationship between parental occupation and the educational attainment of their children. A high level of parental education

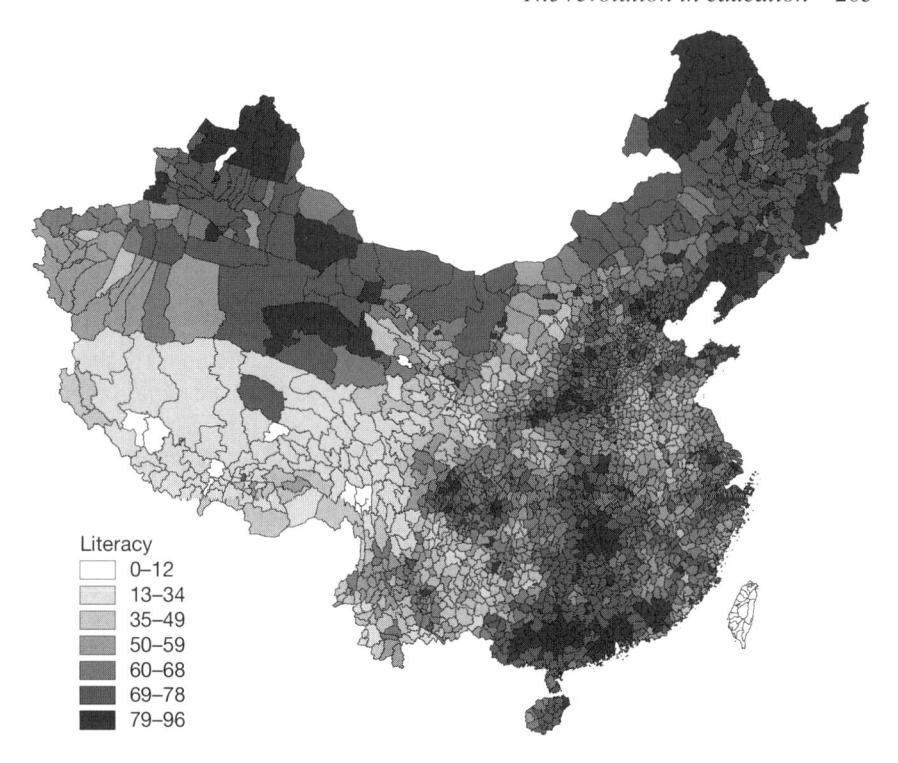

Figure 6.8 Literacy rates by county and city, 1982 (Source: RKTJNJ (1988).)

was no longer a significant advantage for their children in the absence of examination-based progression. Conversely, one of the effects of late Maoism was to elevate the status of workers and peasants, and to lower that of intellectual and urban cadres. Parental occupation still had a key influence on child educational attainment, but the old occupational order was inverted.

In China before 1966 (as is the norm in all OECD countries), there was a strong correlation between the educational level of parents and that of their children. Children brought up in households with large amounts of cultural and social capital (as reflected in parental levels of education) had a much greater chance of progressing to senior middle schools and to universities, because this capital enabled them to do much better in entrance examinations. As Kwong (1983: 106–7) says, the national examination system pre-1966 and post-1977 was egalitarian in only a very narrow sense. In practice, it tended to legitimize the privileged background of children with intellectual or cadre status. And as high-status parents also typically lived in urban areas, it was parental educational status that lay behind much of the urban–rural divide. By the late 1970s, however, this correlation was much weaker. According to Zhou *et al.* (1998: 213):

> In the 1960–65 period, however, the odds of entering college rose systematically with father's education. Having an educated father (one with a senior

high school or college education), rather than an illiterate father, increased the odds of entering college by a factor of 3.6. In sharp contrast, during the Cultural Revolution [defined here as 1966–77], father's education had no significant effect on the odds of college entry; those with educated fathers actually had lower (though not statistically significant) odds of entering college.

The main losers were the sons and daughters of intellectuals, who lost that which they had hitherto regarded as their birthright. This explains much of the bitterness of the Red Guards rusticated to the countryside. Not only had they been deprived of their comfortable urban lifestyle, but also it was hard for them to gain university access because that depended upon a recommendation from their commune, state farm or factory, a recommendation which few of them received. It was not impossible, however, and by opting for worker or peasant status they could do something to change their class label. Paradoxically, in fact, worker status became much sought after in the 1970s. It offered much greater scope for university access, the work involved was less gruelling than in agriculture, and it also afforded some protection against the periodic campaigns directed against households which had enjoyed high status before 1949 or which were headed by intellectuals

The evidence on the dwindling significance of cultural capital is abundantly clear. The work by Deng and Treiman (1997) shows that the advantage enjoyed by boys born into urban cadre and intellectual families diminished over time. For those born in the late 1940s, the sons of cadres and intellectuals typically received 2 to 2.5 more years of education than the sons of farmers. For those born in the mid-1950s, however, the advantage declined to less than one year. In absolute terms, the sons of cadres suffered hardly at all, in contrast to the sons of intellectual fathers (Deng and Treiman 1997: 420).[23] On the basis of the evidence, Deng and Treiman (1997: 424–5) conclude that:

> For nonfarm men from normally advantageous backgrounds, the Cultural Revolution was a disaster. Specifically, the advantage usually associated with coming from an educated professional or managerial family was substantially reduced. The Cultural Revolution succeeded – temporarily – in dismantling a re-emerging stratification system for the benefit of the peasantry.

Admittedly, these results do have their limitations. The Deng–Treiman sample is restricted to urban households, and even then it covers only households in which sons were still living with their fathers. Still, the evidence for rural China also suggests declining stratification. There is in fact some evidence that families of rural cadre families benefited from the policies of late Maoism, because they were able to use their contacts and connections to the benefit of their children (Giles et al. 2007). According to Shirk (1984), late Maoist China was a virtuocracy, rather than an exam-based meritocracy. And in a society where something as intangible as moral virtue ('redness') counted for so much in terms of educational opportunity, the scope for 'opportunism, sycophancy and patronage' (Shirk 1984: 58) was vast. Indeed, the very fact that the children of rural cadres fared well is itself an indication of the demise of the old order. Moreover, even though new inequalities of this sort began to emerge, the gains enjoyed by rural cadres were hardly of a magnitude sufficient to indicate the emergence of a new and privileged elite. As Shirk herself points out, one of the features of the Chinese virtuocracy was that it was unstable. Virtue could easily be lost in a society where much depended upon the correct interpretation of Mao Zedong's thought, as the various Red Guard factions discovered to their cost in the late 1960s. China was therefore very different from most societies, where privilege is easily transmitted from one generation to the next.

Other evidence also points to the conclusion that educational stratification declined. Unger (1984: 132) found that 'bad-class' teachers in rural areas often lost out under late Maoism; their status was undermined by the very fact that they were graduating so many middle-school children (many of 'good-class' origin). More systematic data was collected by Whyte and Parish (1984) on stratification in urban and rural China during the 1970s by means of interviews with émigrés to Hong Kong, which provided information on the émigrés themselves and their neighbours. These sorts of samples were inevitably biased, but the results tally with those based on census data and interviews conducted in the 1990s. For instance, Parish's (1984) work shows very clearly the convergence on nine years of education for the children of all classes during the late Maoist era. The children of peasants and workers increased their average number of years of education over time, whereas the children of intellectuals, the middle class and parents of bad-class background experienced a decline. As interestingly, the number of years of education received by the children of cadre families, which had increased during the 1950s, actually declined during the late Maoist period (Parish 1984: 101 and 103).[24] This suggests that the *guanxi* (connections) enjoyed by cadres in the 1970s

Box 6.1 Summary effects of late Maoism on years of education by class

Class	Effect
children of rural cadres	gainers
children of workers and peasants	gainers
children of urban cadres	losers
children of rural intellectuals	losers
children of urban intellectuals	big losers

Note
These class labels are those which were typically used in late Maoist China. Rural intellectuals here primarily refers to rural teachers.

may not have been as powerful as the Chinese press of the late 1970s and early 1980s suggested that they were (taking their lead from Deng Xiaoping, the media went to great lengths to suggest that late cadres were uniformly corrupt). If rural cadre children were gainers, these gains were offset by the losses suffered by urban cadre children.

There is therefore every reason to conclude that the impact of late Maoism on educational equity was profound. Rustication, Parish argues, may have been misconceived, but if the aim of educational policy is 'to invert the old class order and break the chain of inheritance between privileged fathers and privileged children, then large segments of the Chinese programme may be necessary' (Parish 1984: 119).

For all that, the late Maoist strategy did not break the link between (parental) occupation and (child) educational attainment. The prospects for the children of workers and peasants certainly improved dramatically but nevertheless the extent of mobility within Chinese society was still quite limited. Although some of the urban samples show that the children of peasants living in China's cities typically did very well, this reflects selection bias (Wu and Treiman 2004a). Only untypically adventurous peasants were able to migrate to the cities in the first place, because of the operation of the *hukou* system, and it is therefore not surprising that their offspring did very well in terms of education and occupation. For the bulk of the Chinese peasantry, migration from rural to urban areas was not an option in the late Maoist era. The expansion of rural education expanded their horizons, but, as we have seen, it could not close the urban–rural gap. And if a child's parents had intellectual status or another 'bad-class' label, his or her prospects were dim. Low-status parental occupation was thus transmitted to their children, and in that way the correlation between parental and child status was maintained. It was the *definition* of high and low status that changed during the late Maoist era, not the correlation between parental occupation and the educational attainment of their children. Parental occupation still exercised a decisive influence on the life chances of children, but in ways that the pre-1949 Chinese elites had never imagined. As Parish (1984: 110) concluded:

> Familial influence over the education and the status attainment of children is difficult to erase. After 1966, however, the Chinese came close to doing just that ... after 1966 there was very little an upper-middle class parent could do to help his children succeed in school or find a better job once they were out.

Conclusion

Two educational problems confronted China's planners in the mid-1960s. One was how to create the high-quality educational system needed to enhance the capabilities of the population, thus raising life expectancy and supplying a workforce with the skills needed to accelerate the growth rate. The second was that of educational equity. Income redistribution alone was not enough to guarantee equal access to education for the children of peasants and workers. This was because the cultural capital possessed by higher-status groups translated into exam success for their children. Class privilege as measured by educational access depended upon much more than short-run income and wealth.

In practice, the first problem was never properly solved, because of macroeconomic constraints. The need to finance Third Front construction limited the investible surplus available. The immediate consequence was to force the CCP to make a choice between investment in physical capital and investment in human capital. The conclusion reached by the planners seems to have been that the returns to investment in physical capital were greater than the returns to investment in anything other than basic education. In this, they were almost certainly correct, given China's lack of basic infrastructure (such as railways) and industrial capacity. The result, however, was that China's educational system was poorly funded.

Given the limited resources available, the choice in practice for the planners lay between developing a high-quality system which would be open to a small number of students or a system of mass (but more rudimentary) education for all. Most developing countries have opted for the former strategy: India (with the honourable exception of the state of Kerala) is perhaps the best example. And there is no doubt that the Indian approach has been successful in the sense that some of the graduates from its universities are amongst the best in the world. However, the obverse of the coin was a chronic rate of illiteracy, especially amongst women (Drèze and Sen 2002). Late Maoist China by contrast opted for a system of education for all. China undoubtedly paid a price for this strategy, in the sense that the quality of its graduates (at least measured in academic terms) was comparatively low and their quantity was severely limited. In large measure, this reflected the abandonment of the examination-based system of the early 1960s. In a sense, therefore, the fears voiced by professional educators in the 1950s and early 1960s about the consequences of 'blind adventurism' were realized.

Nevertheless, China was very unusual amongst developing countries in bringing about a rapid and sustained reduction in the illiteracy rate. Accordingly, the overall 'efficiency' of the system – as measured in terms of the average number of years of education per person – undoubtedly increased. Any losses in the university sector were more than offset by gains in terms of basic education. Moreover, the very fact that some evidence suggests that the children of late Maoism did better in terms of earnings in the post-1978 period (after taking into account differences in age, etc.) than their successors is a fascinating one. It suggests that the costs in terms of loss of academic quality may have been offset by the gains in terms of the range of experience acquired by the Red Guard generation. Of course the evidential base for these sorts of claims is rather flimsy. Yet the finding is supported by some of the spatial evidence on growth rates. Jiangsu and Zhejiang provinces entered the 1980s with comparatively low rates of education, yet their average growth rate was faster than that of provinces where educational levels were much higher in the early 1980s. County-level evidence supports this conclusion;

the correlation between literacy rates in 1982 and post-1982 growth is at best weak (Bramall 2007).[25] It therefore appears that an above-average educational inheritance (as measured by literacy) was by no means an essential precondition for rapid economic growth in the post-Mao era. The claim, then, that late Maoist educational policy harmed Chinese growth by lowering the quality of academic education simply does not stand up. In fact, in so far as it allowed students to gain work experience in industry, the policy may well have accelerated the rate of growth.

Late Maoist China did even better in terms of reducing educational inequality. The gap between average levels of attainment in urban and rural areas narrowed. The educational opportunities enjoyed by girls vastly increased. And the traditional link between the level of parental education and the educational opportunities enjoyed by their children was broken. Instead, educational opportunity came to depend much more upon class status and upon virtue ('redness'). As a result, the children of rural cadres, workers and peasants did well, whereas the children of intellectuals, urban cadres and those classes which had been privileged before 1949 fared badly. As a result, the extent of educational inequality narrowed sharply during the 1970s. It was this elimination of traditional class privilege that generated such bitterness amongst the losers during the 1970s, even though they cloaked their antipathy in the lament that late Maoism was producing an educational system of low quality.

It is certainly arguable that China could have done better after 1966. There is considerable evidence that the *xiafang* programme did little to boost rural education, and that the country paid a high price for the alienation of its urban youth. The closure of the schools (between June 1966 and October 1967) and universities (1966 and 1973) did little to promote educational advance. Nor did the persecution of many of China's most talented intellectuals. Furthermore, there must be doubts about the quality of much of the middle-school education, especially in the countryside. The picture painted by Vilma Seeberg is far too apocalyptic and yet at the same time the story told by Han Dongping does not ring entirely true either.

For all that, we need to recognize the extent of China's success in reducing illiteracy and expanding middle-school education. Despite the limitations of the educational system at secondary and tertiary levels, the record of China's system of elementary education was exemplary for a poor country. Moreover, late Maoist policy expanded urban middle-school opportunities as well opportunities in the countryside. It is therefore hard to escape the conclusion that the mass of the Chinese population gained far more than the populations of other developing countries from their government's educational programme during the late Maoist era. Ultimately, however, the virtues of education are largely instrumental. It is a means towards the end of development, rather than an end in itself. The question we therefore need to ask is whether Chinese education helped to promote economic development in the widest sense. This takes us to an accounting of the effects of late Maoism, and this is the subject of Chapter 9. Before that, however, we need to discuss other aspects of the late Maoist development strategy.

Notes

1 The literature on educational developments during the late Maoist era includes Pepper (1996), Han (2000; 2001), Peterson (1994), Seeberg (2000), Lavely et al. (1990), Deng and Treiman (1997), Unger (1982) and Shirk (1982).
2 However, the Party retained control over the textbooks and teaching materials to be used.
3 Keypoint schools then, as now, were essentially college preparatory. They receive far higher levels of state funding than ordinary schools and have first pick of those students who performed best in examinations at elementary or JMS level. Not surprisingly, access to China's 'best' universities depends mainly upon attending the right keypoint schools.
4 The text here is from the 'secret' speaking notes to the speech. The figure given by Mao is different from those subsequently published, which put the total number of primary graduates in 1957 at 5 million and the JMS enrolment at 2.2 million, suggesting a gap of only 2.8 million; see also Figure 6.2, below. Mao may have included in this figure graduates from previous years who had been unable to enrol in junior middle schools.
5 The Chinese data for the Leap are confusing because *minban* primary school data are usually included in the primary totals, whereas agricultural middle school data are usually listed separately (see SSB 2005a: 77–82).
6 For the Leap strategy in education and its contradictions, see Kwong (1979). It is worth emphasizing that the Leap was much less radical than the Cultural Revolution. During the Leap, for example, the regular school system in urban areas was left largely intact and national examinations for university entrance continued to be held (Kwong 1979: 450).
7 This figure needs to be treated with caution. If the 1965 figure is correct, it implies that the poor province of Anhui had more primary teachers per member of the population than affluent Shanghai, which seems highly unlikely.
8 The gross enrolment rate is the total enrolled divided by the number of children of primary-school age. The net enrolment rate refers to those enrolled of primary-school age only, divided by the number of children of primary-school age.
9 Lavely et al. (1990) assume that literacy was normally achieved by the age of eleven. One of Pepper's (1996) interviewees expected a twelve-year-old to have acquired 2,000 characters, and given that the State Council (in 1956) had defined literacy as knowing 1,500 characters, it seems reasonable enough to assume that literacy was achieved at the age of eleven or twelve.
10 Unger gives a figure of 2.9 million (citing an April 1960 edition of *Renmin Ribao*). I use the retrospective figure given in SSB (2005a: 80) and in ZGJYNJ (1984: 1017).
11 Curiously enough, World Bank and Maoist policy were in tandem during the early 1960s, when both emphasized the need to develop vocational and technical education at the secondary level. Manpower planning – meaning the creation of an educational system geared to supplying the needs of the industrial sector – was the order of the day in World Bank circles, and its educational lending focused on the attainment of that goal, rather the development of primary or general education (Psacharopoulos 2006).
12 This notion of cultural capital as a determinant of educational success features prominently in the work of Bourdieu; see, for example, Bourdieu and Passeron (1977).
13 Here I use a definition of the city population which includes those with a rural registration status who were nevertheless living in the cities at the time of the census.
14 One would also, of course, wish to evaluate the success of the Maoist system in terms of educational output per unit of spending, which is the more usual definition of efficiency. The data required to make that evaluation are not available, but we are safe in concluding that the Maoist system was very low cost. In truth, however, a broader definition of educational efficiency is also needed. A system which successfully educated a very small proportion of the population at low cost might be efficient in a narrow economic sense but it would have done little to further the broad cause of 'development'.

15 These are data for those aged seven and over, and therefore overstate true illiteracy because children aged seven to fifteen who are still going through the school system should be excluded. For this reason, the standard UN definition of illiteracy relates to those aged fifteen and over.
16 Whether *pinyin* is an accurate system of romanization is moot, though it should be said that some of the contempt shown towards it by Chinese-language teachers reflects their own elitist prejudices against an innovation which was both Maoist in origin and which facilitated the expansion of mass rural education.
17 In the context of the late 1970s and early 1980s, blanket criticism of the late Maoist era was tricky because that meant criticism of Mao himself, and the limits to that had been carefully set out in the Third Plenum of the CCP in 1978. It was much easier to criticize educational policy, because that was much more closely associated with the Gang of Four (and especially Jiang Qing) than with Mao himself.
18 The UNDP *Human Development Reports* give British illiteracy as less than 1 per cent, and the same is true of the data for other advanced countries. However, even casual empiricism is enough to disprove such overblown claims.
19 Note that this result is only for urban children. Giles *et al.* (2007: 21fn) also note that only Shanghai children from their five-city sample were significantly affected in terms of years of education lost by the sending-down programme.
20 The purpose of this study is to determine the extent to which earnings are related to years of education in each period, and then compare Cultural Revolution and post-Cultural Revolution cohorts ('Cultural Revolution' is used in this study to mean the entire late Maoist period). The number of years of education within each set of twins varied considerably, and there is a clear correlation between earnings and years of education. By looking at each twin, we can separate out the impact of years of education on earnings from the impact of genetic factors, which by definition are controlled. In fact, a study by Li *et al.* (2005) found that the return to an extra year of education post-Cultural Revolution was 8.4 per cent, but that this declined to only 2.7 per cent once genetic factors were filtered out – suggesting that the impact of education on earnings is actually quite small. Once the 'true' return to a year of education for the post-Cultural Revolution cohort is calculated, it can then be compared with the return to the Cultural Revolution cohort.
21 The link between the quantity and quality of schooling and the rate of GDP growth is far from well established in the growth literature. For quantity effects, see Barro and Sala-i-Martin (1995). For a demonstration of the importance of quality (as measured by test scores), see Hanushek and Kimko (2000). However, it is very difficult to establish whether the dominant direction of causality is from schooling to growth, or growth to schooling (Bils and Klenow 2000). Nevertheless, many have taken this evidence to suggest that education does little for growth. For example, Easterly (2001: 73) concluded from his survey of the literature as follows: 'What has been the response of economic growth to the educational explosion? Alas, the answer is: little or none.'
22 Deng was attacked in the mid-1970s for what was perceived as his opposition to work–study and to the *xiafang* programme (Bernstein 1977: 72–6).
23 These results are qualified by the finding that urban cadre families seem to have lost out almost as much as intellectual families in the *specific* sense of access to SMS education for their sons.
24 It is important to stress here that the children of urban cadres remained privileged even during the 1970s (Zhou *et al.* 1998). It was only the *scale* of their advantage which declined.
25 Although, as stressed earlier, those counties where literacy rates were below the threshold needed for modern economic growth almost certainly enjoyed a growth dividend from educational expansion.

7 Collective farming

The collective farm was the centrepiece of the rural development strategy during the late Maoist era.[1] Inspired by the writings of Lenin, the CCP hoped that collectives would allow the mobilization of the rural force on an unprecedented scale. This mobilization would bring about big increases in output and create the conditions for farm mechanization. And mechanization would in turn enable labour to be released for use in China's growing industrial sector. Labour was rural China's main asset. The function of the collective was to put it to good use.

This chapter discusses the extent to which these Maoist dreams were realized. Much of the literature has portrayed the Chinese collective in a very negative light. Nevertheless, even the most severe amongst the critics have recognized the difficulties involved in properly assessing collective performance. One problem is that of how to measure performance. The problem of causality is even more intractable. Was it the collective *per se* that constrained Chinese agriculture? Or was it the way in which collective farming was implemented that was the problem? Alternatively, was collectivized agriculture held back not by its own failings but by a whole range of other factors?

The agricultural context

One of the main challenges faced by the Chinese state during the twentieth century was that of ensuring food security for its population, and the history of Chinese development during this period is in many respects a history of the search for solutions to this overriding problem.[2]

In principle, food security can be achieved by extensive imports. However, this has never been a viable option for China. In the century before 1949, China was a grain importer. For example, rice was imported in significant quantities by Guangdong province from Thailand (Siam), northern Vietnam (Annam) and even Bengal and Burma (Latham and Neal 1983). Lin (1997: 46) suggests that around 13 per cent of Guangdong's consumption was met by imports in the 1930s. Shanghai was also a significant importer. However, the combination of an unstable international political situation, China's underdeveloped transport network – there were no railways in Sichuan, a province comparable in size to France, before the 1949 Revolution – and endemic civil way made reliance on food imports a perilous

214 *Chinese Economic Development*

approach as a *national* strategy. As a result, rice and wheat typically accounted for only about 5 per cent of Chinese imports in the Republican era, which were themselves equivalent less than 5 per cent of GDP (Feuerwerker 1977: 104–5).

The situation was little easier during the Maoist era because of China's poor international relations. During the 1950s, China was a net grain exporter, and indeed the scale of her exports increased despite famine conditions in the late 1950s as the CCP sought to pay off debts to the Soviet Union (Figure 7.1).[3] When the scale of the famine was finally recognized, the position changed abruptly. The 4.2 million tonnes of net grain exports of 1959 became net imports of 4.4 million tonnes in 1961, mainly comprising wheat from Canada. Thereafter, China became a relatively consistent net importer of grain, the scale of these imports being usually a function of the size of the domestic harvest. For example, comparatively poor weather in the late 1970s depressed the size of the harvest and net imports increased. Nevertheless, it is important to emphasize that the scale of China's agricultural trade was small throughout the Maoist period; as a percentage of grain production, imports never amounted to more than the 1961 figure of 3.3 per cent.

China could in principle have imported more; the very fact that it imported large amounts of wheat from Canada in the early 1960s is indicative of the possibilities. From a political point of view, however, this was out of the question as a long-run strategy. It was not so much that Mao was hostile to international trade; far from it, despite what has often been written. The very fact that China opened up very substantially to foreign trade in 1971–2, at the height of late Maoism, is testament to that (see Chapter 11 for a fuller discussion). But reliance on imports to satisfy the demand for basic foodstuffs was fraught with danger.[4] Even if China had relied upon Canada, there was always a danger that the US could bring pressure to bear

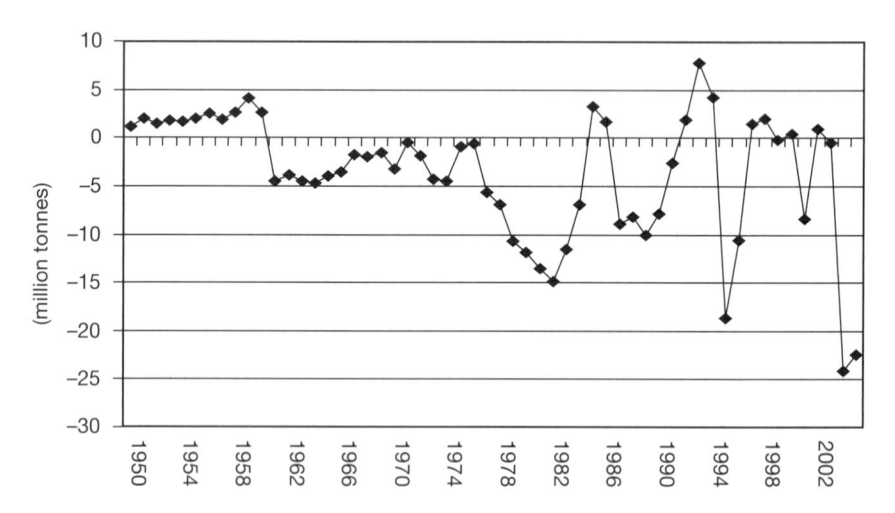

Figure 7.1 Net grain exports (Sources: ZGTJNJ (2006: 744–7); SSB (2005b: 20); MOA (1989: 520–35).)

Note: A minus sign indicates net imports.

on its neighbour or, worse, that the US military might choose to attack supply lines as part of the war against Vietnam. In any case, imports had to be paid for. China could have exported consumer goods to pay for grain imports, but production of consumer goods would have diverted investment away from the key producer goods sector, and slowed the rate of economic growth.

All this meant that China would have to ensure food security by dint of its own efforts. Agricultural production had to be stepped up, and the rate of growth of output needed to be fast enough to meet both the demand of consumers and the needs of producers of alcohol, meat products, silks and cotton textiles. Given the pace of population growth, a daunting challenge therefore confronted China's planners during the whole of the Maoist era.

The CCP solution initially focused on land reform. It was hoped that the elimination of the worst features of the Republican agricultural system – high rents, usurious interests rates, and landless labourers – would lead to a surge in agricultural production. As we saw in Chapter 3, some of these hopes were realized; land reform for example was moderately successful in reducing inequality and in raising agricultural production. Nevertheless, it was never envisaged that family farming would offer a permanent solution to China's agricultural problem. It was a transitional policy, nothing more.

Mao's view was that the collective was far superior to the family farm as an institution of production and rural development.[5] In this, his approach echoed the writings and ideas of Lenin. In essence, Lenin's argument was that the creation of large-scale collective farms was the only means by which mechanization and the expansion of irrigated area could be achieved. Whatever the implications of large-scale farming for yields – and the CCP was hopeful that putting an end to parcellization, the wastage of land in the form of paths and boundaries and

Box 7.1 **Chinese agricultural institutions, 1949–2007**

Period	Agricultural regime
pre-1947	traditional agriculture (family farming and tenancy)
1947–52	*first land reform*
1952–5	family farming
1955–6	*collectivization*
1956–76	collective farming
1977–83	*second land reform (decollectivization)*
1984–2007	family farming

Note
The phases in italics were periods of transition from one regime to another. The periodization used here sidesteps the question of whether periods of transition (such as 1977–83) should be classified as family or collective farming, and this can make a considerable difference to the analysis of performance.

conflict over access to water would increase yields – large farms would more than compensate by increasing labour productivity, and in the process release labour for use in the industrial sector. Furthermore, public ownership of land also held out the possibility of unified and effective provision of welfare, whether income security or health.

And so it was that the collective farm assumed centre stage in Chinese agricultural policy in the years between the creation of collectives during 1955–6 until 1984, by which time they had virtually ceased to exist. The commune functioned badly during the Great Leap Forward, and indeed many within the CCP took the view that the recovery which occurred during the early 1960s was only made possible by the reversion to family farming in many parts of China. But Mao was undaunted. For him, the collective was a key element in the development strategy which unfolded during the late Maoist era. On the one hand, the collective farm would make possible the direct modernization of the economic base via mechanization and the expansion of irrigation. And by mobilizing the agricultural surplus, collectives would create the rural industries which in turn would supply badly need agricultural inputs such as cement, steel and chemical fertilizers. On the other hand, and as importantly, the collective was envisaged to be an important vehicle by means of which the relations of production could be changed. By suppressing private economic activity, reducing income inequalities and by developing the ideology of the peasantry, Mao hoped that the productive enthusiasm of the rural workforce could be developed – and that this in turn would lead to the more rapid development of infrastructure and yields alike.

The Maoist solution to poor agricultural performance broke therefore with both the Marxist tradition, and the solutions being offered by Western economists to developing countries. The Maoist collective was not Leninist, because it placed far more emphasis on the importance of non-material incentives; that was to be especially true of the Dazhai model. At the same time, Chinese collectivization was a solution far removed from the World Bank and Ford Foundation approach (pushed in India, for example), which saw technology in general, and the Green Revolution in particular, as a solution to agricultural underdevelopment. Not that Mao was oblivious to the importance of a technological fix. Rather, Mao believed that high-yielding varieties and mechanization would occur more rapidly, and be more effective, if introduced by collective farms. A purely technological solution was no answer to China's agricultural problems.

Features of the Maoist collective farm

The system of collective farming operated in one form or another between 1955 and 1984. However, it was not until 1963, and after a period of experimentation between 1960 and 1963 (discussed in Chapter 4), that the structure and method of operation of collective farms was set out in a systematic way. The key features of the collective as it operated after 1962 can be set out in the following way.

First, collective farming comprised a three-tier structure, made up of commune, production brigade and production teams (Table 7.1).[6] The communes were

Table 7.1 The size of collective farms, 1959–1981 (persons per unit)

	Communes	Production brigades	Production teams	Household size
1959	21,785	1,070	168	4.35
1963	7,020	872	101	4.23
1970	13,594	1,088	153	4.61
1981	15,060	1,152	136	4.54

Source: ZGTJNJ (1983: 147).

initially very large, comprising around 24,000 people, but they were reduced after the famine to a more manageable 7,000. Thereafter, and largely as a result of population growth, the size of the communes increased such that they were averaging about 15,000 in the early 1980s. However, the key unit of account in the hierarchy was the production team. It was responsible for the organization of production and for the allocation of work points (and work-point earnings) to its members. Such accounting was sometimes carried out at the brigade level (especially in the 1960s). However, the Chinese experience was that this usually did not work because it almost eliminated the link between the value of the work point (which was calculated as an average over the whole brigade) and the amount of work done.[7] It typically comprised 136 people in 1981, or about thirty households. These figures were substantially up on those recorded in 1963, but it is evident that Chinese production teams were relatively small and manageable units throughout the Maoist era.

Second, a key feature of the collective system – as the name implies – was that land, draught animals and big pieces of farm equipment were owned not by individual households but by the collective. Nevertheless, for most of the late Maoist era, households were allowed to operate a private plot of land (in effect, a garden), which they could cultivate in any way they liked but which was often used to grow vegetables and to provide feed for pigs or hens. The size of these private plots varied over time; during the more radical periods, they were eliminated entirely, whereas the average size tended to increase during the late 1970s as moves towards decollectivization gathered momentum and because of population growth; additional land was typically allocated to larger households, and therefore families had an incentive to have more children (Potter and Potter 1990: 112).

The third feature of the collective was the allocation of income on the basis of work points. The value of each work point was determined at the end of the harvest year. Men almost invariably were given a higher work-point rating than women for a day's work (when time-rate systems were operative), and work traditionally regarded as male was allocated more points than female work (when piece-rate systems were in use). Most workers received between seven and ten work points per day. Daily work-point earnings were as high as twelve or fifteen (Hinton 2006: 159) during the peak planting and harvesting periods, but the spread was nevertheless very narrow. In the village studied by Potter and Potter (1990: 120–2), a first-grade male received ten points per day in 1979 compared with the 7.3 points awarded to a fourth-grade woman. In one village the range was from five to ten in 1966, but it had narrowed to nine to ten by the early 1970s in order to avoid conflict between peasants (Unger 2002: 86).

It is worth noting that the system of pay within collective farms varied very substantially over time, and between locations.[8] For much of the late Maoist period, workers on collectives were either allocated a fixed number of work points based upon their sex and their perceived contribution to production (in other words, a time-rate system), or received a given number of work points for completing a specific task (piece rates). It was by no means uncommon for both systems to be in operation in the same village; many points would be awarded on the basis of task completion but some would be allocated on the basis of a worker's labour grade. However, the Dazhai system was also frequently in use during the late 1960s and early 1970s. Under it, work-point earnings were decided on the basis of mass meetings of production team members. This public appraisal system required that workers initially made a self-assessment of their contribution. Other team members would then offer their own appraisal of the worker's contribution and, after discussion, a conclusion would be reached. The Dazhai system also involved a moral or ideological dimension. It assigned some work points on the basis of perceived commitment to the collective, and not just on the basis of work done; in this way, a weaker team member might still receive a high number of work points. The other advantage of the Dazhai system was that appraisal meetings were held infrequently. As the system was practised in Gao village in Jiangxi, for example, work-point recorders took a note of daily attendance to award gross work points. The annual rating of each worker (the number of base points), which was based on skill, strength and attitude, was then applied to this attendance record. As the number of base points was determined annually, this simplified enormously the issue of appraising the intensity of effort (Gao 1999: 61–2).

Theoretical issues: collective versus family farming

Collective farms remain the most controversial of all agricultural institutions. In part, this is because they are coercive. In contrast to cooperatives, membership of collectives is compulsory; this in turn limits labour mobility and hence freedom.[9] It is for good reason, therefore, that collective farming has been seen as similar in its effective to European feudalism. It is further argued that collectivization is futile, because it does nothing to raise yields, the main challenge which faces poor countries. Finally, it is alleged that the supposed main advantage of collectives – that they facilitate mechanization – is not applicable in poor countries, because they lack the industrial capacity necessary to provide tractors in the first place.

However, strong arguments have been put forward for collective farming. For one thing, collectives lead to the creation of large fields and hence save land formerly wasted because it was used for hedgerows, paths and irrigation channels. Second, they facilitate the rapid diffusion of new technology. Third, and most importantly, collectives make possible the mobilization of labour – which in turn makes possible the construction of large-scale irrigation projects and the development of rural industry.

The case against the collective[10]

One of main criticisms directed against collectivization in China is that it was premature. Of course few would deny that labour-saving technical progress offers an adequate solution to the problem of supervision and control: that is why large American and Canadian farms are profitable, and why large farms are much more efficient in (technologically) advanced regions within developing countries than in poor regions. In China's case, the introduction of such technology might well have also succeeded. However, so it is argued, the decision to collectivize in 1955–6 was extremely premature. At that time, mechanization was simply not possible because China's industrial capacity was underdeveloped; its industries could not supply the inputs required. Furthermore, the mechanization challenge which confronted China was greater than in North America because of the essentially aquatic environment within which rice production takes place (Bray 1986). The People's Republic would have done better, it is argued, to have persisted with small-scale family farming until the time was right for full-scale mechanization.

This notion that a transition to socialism can be premature if the forces of production are underdeveloped is of course central to much Marxist theory.[11] Lenin himself had strong views on the subject (Lenin 1919, 1923). His speech to the 8th Congress in 1919 stressed the psychological importance of tractor production for converting the middle peasantry to the idea of collectivization: 'In a communist society the middle peasants will be on our side only when we alleviate and improve their economic conditions. If tomorrow we could supply one hundred thousand first-class tractors, provide them with fuel, provide them with drivers – you know very well that this at present is sheer fantasy – the middle peasant would say, "I am for the communia" (i.e., for communism).' By contrast, the 1923 speech on cooperation stressed the necessity of a lengthy transition period ('a cultural revolution', he called it) during which the peasantry would acquire skills and literacy. Mechanization ought to precede collectivization, and indeed that was the view articulated by Lenin. Thus a poor country needs first to create the necessary conditions for mechanization – by which is meant establishing an adequate machine building capability – before pushing ahead with collectivization. The Soviet Union in 1928 was not in that position and therefore, the transition to collective farming was premature. According to Selden (1988: 60):

> Ignoring Lenin's strictures, beginning in 1929 Soviet collectivization preceded agricultural mechanization, and indeed all technical, administrative, and social preparation for such changes as collectivization. Rather than building on peasant consciousness of the benefits of collective agriculture, it rested on naked state coercion.

And so it was in China during 1955–6. Urban industry had developed quickly, but its focus was on means of production intended for use outside agriculture, and rural industry was in its infancy. Accordingly, mechanization was not a realistic option and therefore collectivization was pointless. It would depress yields. And it would generate few gains in terms of labour release in the absence of mechanization.

Collective farming, it is argued, offered few other advantages. It is widely believed that there is an inverse relationship in farming between farm size and yields. Small farms in general enjoy higher yields than large farms because they use labour much more intensively. Labour productivity may be low, but labour is not scarce in poor countries – whereas land most certainly is. In that small farms maximise yields, they are the ideal mechanism for maximizing agricultural output in poor countries. In essence the argument here is that size creates immense problems for the supervision and control of the labour force.[12] As a result, and in common with managerial farms in developing countries, Chinese collectives used labour much less intensely than small-scale family farms and this depressed both land and total factor productivity (Griffin *et al.* 2002: 286–7). China's experience thus provides, it is said, further support for the well-known inverse relationship between size and land productivity. More general empirical support for the inverse relationship is offered in Berry and Cline (1979), Cornia (1985) and in some of the studies summarized in Ray (1998: ch. 12).

The case for the Maoist collective

In fact, however, the case against collective farming is far less clear-cut than the arguments in the previous section suggest. Moreover, the critics tend to ignore the advantages of collective farming.[13]

For one thing, it is now widely recognized that the alleged inverse relationship between yields and farm size is far more difficult to establish than previous scholarship would have us believe.[14] The empirical evidence is particularly problematic. Too many of the studies have focused on land productivity when our real interest lies in total factor productivity. However, the methodological problems which underpin the calculation of total factor productivity make that sort of approach problematic. As importantly, there are severe normalization problems. Observed variations in yields often reflect differences in land quality, access to irrigation and credit, differences in cropping patterns or differences in input (or product) prices, rather than economies or diseconomies of scale *per se*. These problems are compounded by the fact that comparisons are often between large managerial farms and small family farms, rather than comparisons purely of scale. As a result of these difficulties, studies for a range of countries have arrived at inconclusive results (Dyer, 2004; Khan 2004; Ray 1998: 453–7). And interestingly enough, even Buck (1947: 34) had recognized that prewar Chinese family farms were too small: 'In China at least 80 percent of the farms are too small to be economic units.' Collectivization made possible (as we will see shortly) the exploitation of economies of scale and thus made labour available for use in infrastructural construction and for rural industrialization. But it also allowed much more scope for specialization than was possible on a family farm, and that in turn raised yields (Chinn 1980).

Second, there is much to suggest that the diffusion of new seed varieties and technologies is much faster under collectives than it is under family farming. An agricultural research system of sorts had been created in the early 1950s, but most new varieties introduced in the 1950s were either imports or had been developed before 1949. In fact, the superiority of foreign imports was such that they increasingly dominated cropping patterns (Stone 1988a: 790–1). All this began to change as a result of collectivization. By 1957, a web of nearly 14,000 agricultural technical stations had been created across China, complemented by 1,400 seed stations and 1,900 breeding and demonstration stations. By 1979, the number in each category had risen to 17,600, 2,400 and 2,400 respectively (SSB 1984: 189). This new system for research and development gradually led to the development of new indigenous varieties. Imports were by no means dispensed with; a large amount of dwarf wheat seed was imported from Mexico during 1972–4, International Rice Research Institute varieties developed in the Philippines were introduced in Guangdong, and Pakistan provided a range of advanced seedlings. However, many of these foreign imports proved unsuited to Chinese growing conditions; Mexican wheat is a case in point. It helped China's breeding programmes indirectly, but the lion's share of the credit for the new varieties that spread quickly in the 1970s goes to the Chinese research system. Yuan Longping, a Chinese scientist based in Hunan, is now widely acknowledged to have been the inventor of the world's first true hybrid variety of rice in 1974. More generally, as Stone (1988a: 795–6) says:

> [U]nlike the 1950s, primary credit for Chinese varietal success cannot be awarded to such imports, but rather to the development throughout the country of a strong and broad based complex of agricultural research.

To be sure, mistakes were made in the process. Nolan (1988) makes much of the diffusion of the unsuitable double-wheeled and double-bladed plough in the late Maoist era, and it is equally true that some of the new seed varieties which were pushed by the collectives were ill-suited to Chinese agricultural conditions (Stone 1988a: 792 and 794). Nevertheless, the overall success of the programme is very apparent from the speed at which suitable hybrids and semi-dwarfs were adopted in the 1970s. Moreover, the impact of the new varieties was dramatic. The yield of the latest dwarf varieties of wheat in Sichuan in the late 1970s was around 300 kg per sown *mu*, far above the 70 kg achieved from traditional varieties. Rice hybrids yielded 500 kg compared to the 200 kg yield of the traditional seeds (Bramall 1995: 737).

Of course it may be that a system of family farming and state-funded research and development would have been equally effective. However, China appears to have been far more successful in terms of irrigation and introducing new seed varieties than most other developing countries. Pakistan and India have both shown that HYVs can be introduced on small-scale farms; many Indian farms have done precisely that by using tube wells to make possible the Green Revolution in wheat farming during the 1970s and 1980s. However, we do well to note that both countries benefited enormously from Western aid and technical assistance. In the absence of such US assistance, it is very unlikely that their wheat revolution would have been anything like as successful. Moreover, the chronic inefficiency of farming in other parts of East Asia – notably Japan and Taiwan – demonstrates rather tellingly the limitations of small-scale family farming as a vehicle for modernization. Indeed increasingly frenzied efforts have been made to promote farmland consolidation in both Japan and in Taiwan. In Japan, however, this has proved extremely difficult, because the rising price of land has encouraged many farmers to hold on to their very small holdings. As a result, despite the 1961 Basic Agricultural Law designed to promote consolidation, only 3 per cent of all farms were larger than 3 hectares in size – the minimum required for effective farm operations (Kojima 1988: 733–4). No less than 44 per cent of Japanese farms were smaller than 0.5 hectares in size in the 1980s.

A third argument for collectivization is that it makes mechanization possible. Crucially, it allows for the consolidation of large numbers of small plots – 'noodle strips', as Hinton disparagingly called them – into large fields. Hinton (2006: 141) gives the example of Wugong village, where 1,300 small plots were consolidated into six large fields during the 1950s. Without that consolidation, mechanization would have been out of the question. It is of course true that consolidation in the specific case of Wugong was achieved by cooperatives prior to collectivization, and by implication that it is possible to consolidate farmland by means other than collective farms. However, the larger collectives of the post-1956 era made possible the accomplishment of far bigger and more elaborate consolidation schemes. Potter and Potter (1990) provide one such example for the Great Leap Forward. Such ambitious projects took years to accomplish, but by the 1970s many of them were coming to fruition and mechanization was proceeding apace. Available horsepower rose from 14.9 million in 1965 to 160 million in 1978; over the same period, the area on which mechanized farming took place rose from 16 million hectares to 41 million (MOA 1989: 309–18).

Of course, as the critics rightly note, collectivization by itself is not a sufficient condition for mechanization, but some sort of consolidation process is necessary if mechanization is to proceeded, and collective farming offers a very effective vehicle for mechanization. Moreover, the mechanization of agriculture itself is highly desirable because it saves labour. Labour may not be as scarce as land in poor countries, but labour scarcity remains the principal bottleneck to the expansion of production. By saving labour, mechanization offered to lead to big gains. First, it enabled China's collectives to intensify production by applying more labour per unit of area and to expand the area which was double-cropped, thus relieving the key supply-side bottleneck. The notion therefore that mechanization cannot help to raise yields and output is patently untrue. Second, it enabled agriculture to release labour for use in other sectors, and, especially in the long run, this is perhaps the crucial contribution of mechanization.[15] Labour release was the main contribution to industrialization made by England's agricultural revolution in the late eighteenth and early nineteenth centuries (Crafts 1985), and it is why mechanization is potentially so important for China. The decline in mechanized area that occurred during the early 1980s – it fell from a peak of 42.2 million hectares in 1979 to 36.4 million in 1986 (MOA 1989: 318) – was one of the main failures of decollectivization. In a very real sense, the restoration of 'noodle strips' in the 1980s has delayed Chinese industrialization by preventing the release of labour.

Moreover, the notion that mechanization is impossible in the aquatic environment required by rice farming is grossly exaggerated. To be sure, the mechanization of China's paddy fields was difficult, but we do well to remember that rice was only one of China's grain crops. Even in Sichuan, the key winter crop is wheat, and therefore mechanization has an important role to play during the winter dry season, when wheat is grown. That is still more true for north China, where wheat is the key crop. To argue therefore that mechanization is impossible in Chinese agriculture is therefore at best an exaggeration, and at worst grossly misleading.

However, the main argument for collective farming is that it enables the mobilization of labour for infrastructural programmes, especially water conservancy projects. Given the importance of rice production in Chinese agriculture, that made the case for collectivization in China even stronger than in the USSR.

Labour mobilization in China was possible because a large proportion of the agricultural labour force was idle during the winter months (November to February), especially in north China. An indication of the extent of this underemployment comes from the data collected by Buck (1937) for the early 1930s (Figure 7.2). Twenty-five per cent of all idle time occurred in December and 32 per cent in

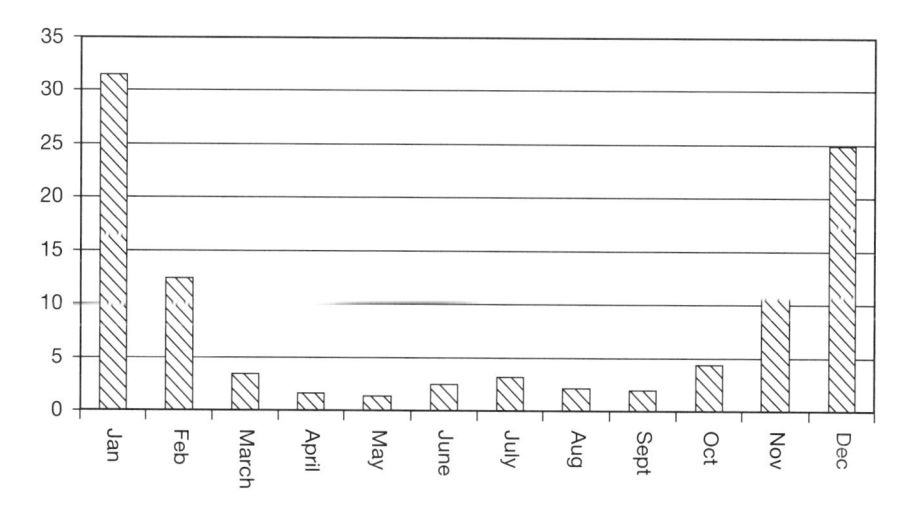

Figure 7.2 Distribution of idle time in agriculture by month in the early 1930s (percentage of annual total) (Source: Buck (1937: 296).)

January, and this pattern was of course weather-related; it was impossible to work productively in the fields of north and even central China during these months. And the totals involved were not negligible. Buck's survey put the total at 1.7 idle months per man per year, and although this may have dropped somewhat in the early 1950s, it is unlikely that the fall was large, simply because alternative employment opportunities were so limited. Buck's conclusion was that one route out of poverty for the rural sector was to use this underemployed labour in developing rural industry, and this was indeed one solution adopted after 1949, as will be seen in the next chapter. However, precisely because so much of the surplus was seasonal, the development of rural industry was not easily accomplished. It was in fact much more straightforward to mobilize the labour force for infrastructural construction during the winter months. The CCP was very much alive to these possibilities, and indeed much of the pressure to create large collectives in the late 1950s was driven by the need to mobilize labour.

The importance of finding a solution to the water problem was compounded by the extent of water shortages on the north China plain and across much of northern China. According to the World Bank (1997d: 88–9), north China was home to 45 per cent of China's population and contributed 45 per cent of cultivated area, but possessed only 14 per cent of national water resources. As a result, per capita water availability was only 750 cubic metres, compared with 3,440 cubic metres in the south in the mid-1990s. The underlying problem is low rainfall. This in turn has enforced high levels of water extraction from rivers, as a result of which many of them (not least the Yellow river) run dry during the winter. It also places a premium on the creation of high-quality water storage facilities, which are essential for irrigation purposes.

The evidence on irrigation points to the conclusion that labour accumulation was remarkably effective in resolving some of these problems (Vermeer 1977). Nickum's (1978: 280–2) estimates suggest that 40–60 million peasants were involved in labour accumulation in the mid-1960s, rising to 120–40 million by 1976–7 as the programme intensified and focused increasingly on supra-brigade and commune water conservancy projects. On average, a peasant engaged in labour accumulation for thirty days per year. Although these data are not entirely reliable, the scale of the programme is attested to in a wide range of local-level studies (Endicott 1988: 74–80; Qin 1995). Once again, Potter and Potter (1990) provide a classic account. Collectivization did not put an end to disputes over access to water, and even village-level cooperation was not enough to resolve all water conservancy issues, because of collective action problems at supra-village level. As one account puts it: 'the commune and brigade authorities refused to organize people from other villages to participate in the project. ... So the project was never carried out and as a result Gao Village is the only village in Yinbaohu commune that did not benefit from the Communist infrastructural frenzy in the PRC's first forty years' (Gao 1999: 23). And there is no doubt that collectivization led to the launching of a number of ill-judged projects that would not otherwise have been attempted (Siu 1989: 232–5).[16] In general, however, collectivization made rational management of water resources far easier, so much so that worries over the implications for water conservancy was one reason for resistance to decollectivization in many places (Endicott 1988: 75 and 134).

The macrodata demonstrate the extent of the expansion of irrigated area in the late Maoist period (Table 7.2). For China as a whole, irrigated area tripled between 1952 and 1978, with much of the increase occurring after 1965. Gains were recorded across all the main agricultural provinces, with spectacular (and probably exaggerated) rises reported in Jiangsu, Shandong and Heilongjiang. This expansion was one of the great achievements of collectivized agriculture, and marked out China from (*inter alia*) India and Vietnam. Crucially, the expansion of irrigated area, combined with the increased labour productivity generated by the creation of large collective farms, allowed for substantial increases in double

Table 7.2. Trends in irrigated area, 1952–1978 (area irrigated in million *mu*)

Province	1952	1957	1965	1978
Beijing	0.37	0.58	3.69	5.13
Tianjin	1.11	2.15	3.30	5.20
Hebei	14.40	23.66	26.29	54.87
Shanxi	3.81	8.72	10.53	16.36
Liaoning	1.51	5.43	4.57	12.78
Jilin	1.75	5.53	3.06	8.99
Heilongjiang	2.04	4.28	5.67	10.02
Shanghai	5.81	5.74	5.52	5.40
Jiangsu	3.33	17.13	29.09	49.08
Zhejiang	16.35	18.10	21.37	22.58
Anhui	15.44	18.74	24.37	35.93
Fujian	9.64	11.54	16.00	12.94
Jiangxi	14.80	19.91	30.01	24.62
Shandong	5.10	11.53	22.68	66.22
Henan	11.82	19.56	17.95	55.83
Hubei	12.47	21.09	33.84	35.33
Hunan	23.07	26.64	32.44	40.31
Guangdong	10.27	16.83	31.90	29.51
Guangxi	8.03	13.09	14.65	22.05
Sichuan	9.97	15.99	23.93	43.02
Guizhou	2.74	4.17	6.14	7.46
Yunnan	1.04	6.64	12.82	13.52
Shaanxi	1.19	7.58	9.42	18.21
Gansu	4.91	6.45	8.00	12.72
Qinghai	0.97	1.72	2.12	2.47
Ningxia	2.23	3.24	3.13	3.64
Total	200.50	296.00	402.50	614.20

Source: Bramall (2000a: 138).

Note
The Heilongjiang figure for 1965 is by linear interpolation. Only incomplete time series data exist for Inner Mongolia, Tibet, Xinjiang and Hainan; they are therefore excluded from this table. Their inclusion would have added 67.31 million *mu* to the total in 1991. For a discussion of the limitations of Chinese irrigation data, see Nickum (1995a).

cropping – which had not been a feasible proposition in the early 1950s because of shortages of both water and labour (Walker 1968). The contrast between China and Vietnam's Mekong delta is especially instructive. In the latter, collective farming was of short duration and only about 10 per cent of farmland was collectivized before the restoration of family farming across Vietnam in 1988 (Ravallion and van de Walle 2001). As a result, most of the delta is still not properly irrigated and is capable of producing only one crop of rice per year. That in turn goes far towards explaining why this is one of the poorest regions of Vietnam despite its very favourable growing conditions.

To summarize, in one sense the strictures against collective farming are correct. China lacked the capacity to carry out mechanization in the late 1950s, and indeed the promotion of rural industry on such a vast scale during the Great Leap Forward was a recognition of this fact. However, the problem with this sort of critique of collective farming is that it fails to recognize the reverse causal relationship between collectivization and mechanization: collectivization may be a necessary condition for mechanization and for the introduction of the full modern technological package. In other words, collectivization in China in the mid-1950s was not premature but instead a necessary precondition for the development of a modern agricultural sector. In other words, once we accept that large-scale farms operating modern technologies are more efficient than small-scale family farming using traditional technologies, and once we recognize the effectiveness of collectives in expanding the irrigated area, it is evident that collectivization has much to recommend it. At the very least, some sort of land reform designed to create *large* farms is imperative. Whether it takes the form of expropriation by the landlord class acting in concert with a coercive state (as in nineteenth-century America or seventeenth-century England) or state-led collectivization (as China or the former Soviet Union) is moot. But the notion that voluntary land consolidation schemes will solve the problem is utopian.

The performance of collective farms

The short- and medium-term test of the effectiveness of collective farming in China is whether it led to the rapid growth of agricultural output, and whether it boosted productivity. The longer-run question is whether the expansion of irrigated area and the development of rural infrastructure led to gains even after decollectivization. In other words, did the Maoist collective pave the way for the agricultural 'miracle' of the 1980s? We consider short-and medium-term trends in output and productivity in this chapter; the longer-run question is considered in Chapter 11.

Output growth

In terms of raising food production and meeting the basic food requirements of its population, the policies pursued in China since 1949 have been very successful. Over the period 1952–2006, value-added in China's primary sector rose annually

Collective farming 227

by 3.7 per cent in real terms, a higher figure than the average for low- and middle-income countries during 1965–80 (2.8 per cent), 1980–90 (3.4 per cent) and 1990–2003 (2.4 per cent) (World Bank 1990a: 181; World Bank 2005: 200). China's rate of growth was also faster than the world average of 2.3 per cent for the period 1961–2000 (Federico 2005: 20). Furthermore, and crucially in terms of food security, the production of food crops rose rapidly as well. The key food crop was of course grain, and in China grain output grew by 2.5 per cent per year between 1952 and 2006, very much in line with population. There is thus every reason, and especially so given the nature of the land constraint, to conclude that the output performance of Chinese agriculture was extremely good during the second half of the twentieth century.

The most interesting question is of course the relative performance of Chinese agriculture under family and collective farming. However, this type of comparison is not straightforward. For one thing, it is not clear whether we should focus on the overall growth of output, or the growth of grain production (the key food crop). In addition, the value-added data for the Maoist period are problematic; there is a good case for using gross output data.[17] The other issue concerns the relevant time periods we should use to compare family and collective farming. As far as the collective era is concerned, the years used by Hinton (2006) are 1954 to 1983. However, this too is rather problematic. Family farming was still the dominant system in 1954, and the collective was no longer home to the majority of households after 1981. It is therefore more plausible to use 1955 (the last year of family farming) and 1981 (the last year of collective dominance) to demarcate the impact of collectivization. That said, there is something to be said for looking at the period 1963–81. The logic here is that 1955–64 was a period of transition. The communes set up in 1958 were experimental and much modified after the disaster of the Leap. Furthermore, family farming re-emerged in the early 1960s in many parts of China, and collective farming was not really restored until 1963. As for the era of family farming, a case can be made for using 1983–2006 (Hinton's approach) or for 1981–2006 (if 1981 is agreed to be the last year of collective farming).

For all these reasons, it is important that we use a range of indicators and look at different temporal definitions, before drawing any conclusions. Some of the possible definitions of the collective era are presented in Table 7.3.

The comparison in growth rates achieved under the two systems is in fact significantly affected by these procedures. If we contrast 1963–81 with 1981–2006 – the comparison which places collective farming in the best light – it is evident that family farming outperformed collectives on the criterion of gross output value by a margin of around 2 per cent per annum, a very substantial differential. However, the differential is much less dramatic if we use value-added data, falling to about 1 percentage point. This is because the use of intermediate goods in the production process (fertilizer, electricity, etc.) spiralled after 1978, thus reducing value-added ratios across the agricultural sector. And if we restrict the comparison exclusively to grain production, then the superiority of family farming disappears. Indeed the growth of grain output between 1963 and 1981 was more than three times *faster*

Table 7.3 Chinese agriculture under collective and family farming (percentage annual growth rates)

	Gross output value (1980 prices)		Volume (tonnes)	Value-added (comparable prices)
	Farming	Agriculture	Grain	Agriculture
Collective farming				
1954–83	2.9	3.3	2.9	2.7
1955–81	2.8	3.2	2.8	2.6
1963–81	3.3	3.6	3.5	2.9
Family farming				
1981–2006	4.5	5.6	1.3	4.2
1984–2006	4.3	5.5	1.0	3.9

Sources: MOA (1989); SSB (2000a); SSB (2005b); ZGTJNJ (2007).

Note
The Chinese definition of agriculture includes forestry, livestock and fisheries as well as farming. Household sidelines are excluded from the data before 1981 because the series includes village industry; the post-1980 data include sidelines in farming. Some of these definitional issues are discussed in ZGTJNJ (2006: 500).

than the rate achieved after 1984 (3.5 per cent compared with 1 per cent). This is shown very clearly in Figure 7.3; the indices of agricultural output and grain production move very much hand-in-hand until the early 1980s, and then the two series diverge. Given that the primary aim of the Maoist regime was to satisfy the basic needs of the population, there is undoubtedly a case for focusing on grain production. Conversely, the aim of the post-1978 regimes has been to foster the growth of a more diversified agricultural sector, and therefore it is not unreasonable to look at the overall rate of agricultural growth after the early 1980s in judging the extent of success.

Note, however, that the analysis in the previous paragraph takes official data at face value. In fact, there is considerable evidence that collectives underreported output to evade procurement quotas (Oi 1989; Shue 1988). And Hinton (1990) argues that much of the apparent increase was generated by reducing stocks. As far as the evidence is concerned, there is little doubt that a large part of the increase in the early 1980s reflected a process of reintermediation.[18] The pre-1981 private sector was either not included in the commune accounts, or its output was understated. The effect of decollectivization was to bring all types of economic activity within the ambit of the statistical authorities, who relied upon survey data (instead of the commune crop reporting system).[19] As a result, output surged because of a change in the reporting system, and no attempt has been made to readjust the data to allow for this. And its impact was by no means small:[20]

> One major difference in the current system is that the income from the private plots, private pig raising and other household sideline activities is included in the public accounts for the first time. As a result, the figures after 1982 are

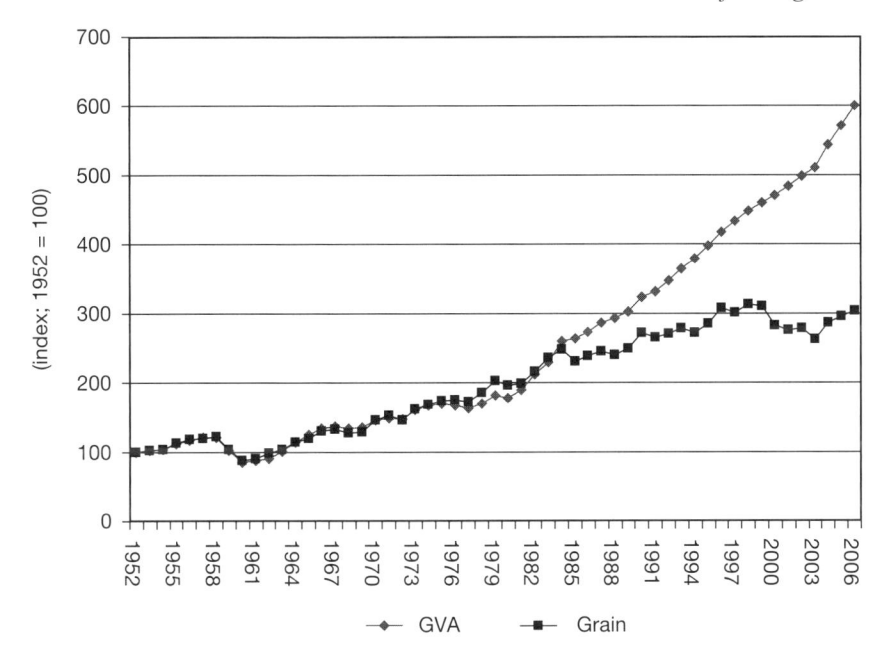

Figure 7.3 Growth of agricultural output, 1952–2006 (Sources: SSB (2005a: 12 and 45); ZGTJNJ (2007: 59 and 478).)

Note: Agricultural GVA is at comparable prices.

greatly inflated compared to those of previous years. To make them equivalent the accountants at Magaoqiao suggested that the post-1982 figures should be scaled down by 40 percent. (Endicott 1988: 142)

Taken together, the evidence discussed in this section suggests that comparisons are sensitive to the time periods used, the output measure employed and the assumptions made about underreporting of output by collectives. It is therefore far from unreasonable to conclude that the rate of agricultural growth under collective farming was not so very different from that achieved after 1982. True, there is little basis for the claim that collective farming was superior to the family farm. But these data go a long way towards refuting some of the more outlandish criticism which has been directed against the Maoist collective.

Productivity

The other way to evaluate the performance of late Maoist agriculture is in terms of its productivity record. To do that, it makes sense to compare the record of collective farms with the small-scale family farms which succeeded them after 1983. Three measures of productivity are considered in what follows. Land is the factor of production which is most scarce in China; the trend in land productivity is therefore of central importance. However, one of the main aims of development is to raise per capita output, and that in turn implies that the aim of policy should be to maximize labour productivity in farming. The principal disadvantage of both these measures is that they are partial; they consider only one input. The most general measure of productivity is total factor productivity, though this suffers from a number of methodological limitations.

(a) Land productivity

Consider first land productivity. The best measure of this is the grain yield, and the trend is summarized in Table 7.4.

Despite limited use of other inputs (such as chemical fertilizers) until the mid-1970s, collectivization mobilized labour on a scale never previously seen in China or in other countries. This enabled grain yields to approximately double between 1955 and 1981, a remarkable achievement, and clear evidence that collective farming hardly failed in China. In fact the growth rate of grain yields was substantially faster during 1955–81 than it was between either 1952–5 or 1981–2006. The growth rate even accelerated between 1965 and 1981 as the infrastructural projects undertaken in the late Maoist era started to be completed. These are significant findings. For although it can be argued that a comparison of grain *output* growth across these periods is misleading (because far less area was sown to grain under family farming), the same is not true of the yield data. These data provide a measure of land productivity, and they demonstrate rather clearly that collective farming was far more effective in raising yields than family farming. When due note is taken of the other constraints on agriculture in the Maoist era (see below), we may fairly conclude that the record of Chinese collective farming was very far from being poor.

When placed in international perspective, China's ability to increase rice yields was impressive in both Maoist and post-Mao eras. As Figure 7.4 shows, Chinese yields gradually converged on those of Japan and the US (which became the world leader by the end of the millennium). Even though India started from a lower base (which was compounded by 1965 being a bad year), China's rate of yield growth was faster during the period 1965–81. Thereafter, Chinese growth slowed down. Nevertheless, by 2004, China's rice yields were high by international standards. The USA remained ahead of other countries, with average yields of around 7.5

Table 7.4 The growth of land productivity, 1952–2005 (growth of grain yields per annum)

Period	System	Growth of yields
1952–55	family farming	2.1
1955–81	collective farming	3.2
(1965–81)		(3.4)
1981–2006	family farming	1.6

Sources: SSB (2000a: 40); ZGTJNJ (2007: 474 and 478).

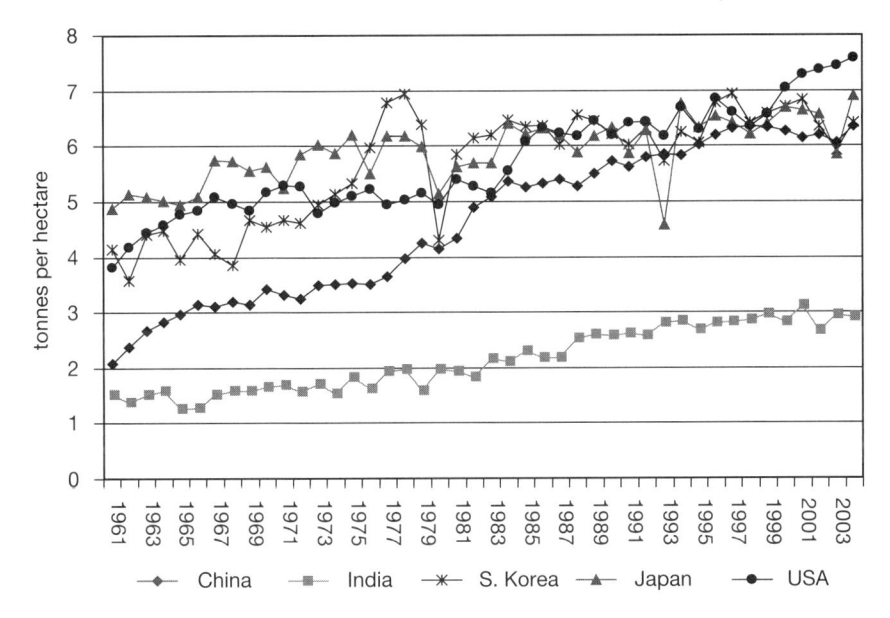

Figure 7.4 Rice yields in Asia and the USA, 1961–2004 (Source: IRRI (2007).)

tonnes per hectare. Nevertheless, China's average yield was on a par with South Korea, and approaching the levels attained in Japan. In China's most advanced provinces, rice yields were above the US and Japanese average; the rice yield in Jiangsu, one of China's leading producers, was no less than 8 tonnes per hectare by 2000.

As for wheat yields, China did even better. In 1965, the average wheat yield in the People's Republic was 1.02 tonnes per hectare, considerably below that in the USA (1.79 tonnes). By 1981, however, China (2.11 tonnes per hectare) was fast approaching the level attained in the USA (2.32 tonnes), and by 2005, China was far ahead. By then its average wheat yield was no less than 4.28 tonnes, whereas that of the US was only 2.82 tonnes (FAO 2007). China is also achieving wheat yields which are well above those recorded for other major wheat producers such as Canada (surpassed by China in 1981) and Argentina (surpassed in 1975). This remarkable record reflects the development and rapid introduction of new high-yielding varieties, which has been occurring at regular intervals since the early 1970s. The process began in the late Maoist era, allowing Chinese yields to go past those of Argentina and Canada, and the growth continued thereafter; the US was overtaken in 1983/4.

In short, the Chinese record on land productivity is impressive. The People's Republic closed inexorably the yield gap for wheat and rice during the 1960s and 1970s, and the process of yield growth has continued since then, so much so that it is fair to say that China uses its available land far more productively than any other large-scale agricultural producer on the planet.[21] On other productivity indicators, however, China lags behind. To these we now turn.

(b) Labour productivity

Many have argued that, for economic development to be successful, the key contribution that agriculture must make is to release labour. This of course was the key element in the celebrated Lewis model. A central precondition for successful development, he argued, was an agricultural revolution based around an increase in labour productivity in farming. Such a process would create surplus labour – which could then be released for use in the modern industrial sector. In many ways this is precisely what happened in England during its Industrial Revolution. Small-scale family farming pushed up yields in England between 1520 and 1739, a process which Allen calls the 'Yeomen's Revolution'. However, in so far as there was an agricultural 'revolution' during the second half of the eighteenth century, it was one presided over by landlords (the Landlords' Revolution). They drove a process in which average farm size increased, and English yeomen (small-scale landowners) became tenant farmers. Women and children were the main losers:

> [T]he facts support the Marxist view. The employment per acre of men, women and boys all declined with size. The decreases were greatest for women and boys. Eighteenth-century farm amalgamation rendered most rural women and children redundant in agriculture. ... The main contribution of the landlords' agricultural revolution was a further shedding of labour in the eighteenth century. (Allen 1992: 18–19)

This process was brutal, but it did lead to rising labour productivity and the creation of a labour surplus – which was then available for use in the great manufacturing centres of east Lancashire and west Yorkshire (Moore 1967; Crafts 1985; Allen 1992, 1999).[22]

What of China? On this question, it is usually argued that the record of collective farming was extremely poor, and the data bear this out. The agricultural labour force increased very substantially between the mid-1950s and the late 1970s. Combined with slow output growth, the outcome was that output per agricultural worker shows hardly any increase in the late Maoist era (Figure 7.5). The annual growth rate of GVA per worker was only 0.8 per cent per year between 1955 and 1981, whereas it grew at a rate of nearly 5 per cent per year after 1981. Moreover, the number of hours worked per labour day probably stayed around the same. Workers may have put in less effort, but the number of hours spent per worker on collective tasks remained much the same.

Local studies support this pessimistic appraisal of labour productivity in Chinese agriculture in the late Maoist period. According to Huang (1990: 249): 'the phenomenon of "loitering labor" [was] such that by the late 1970s, the same farm tasks ... were taking one and a half times as long to accomplish as they required under family management.' And even Hinton, one of the leading defenders of Chinese collective farming, quotes a collective worker as follows:

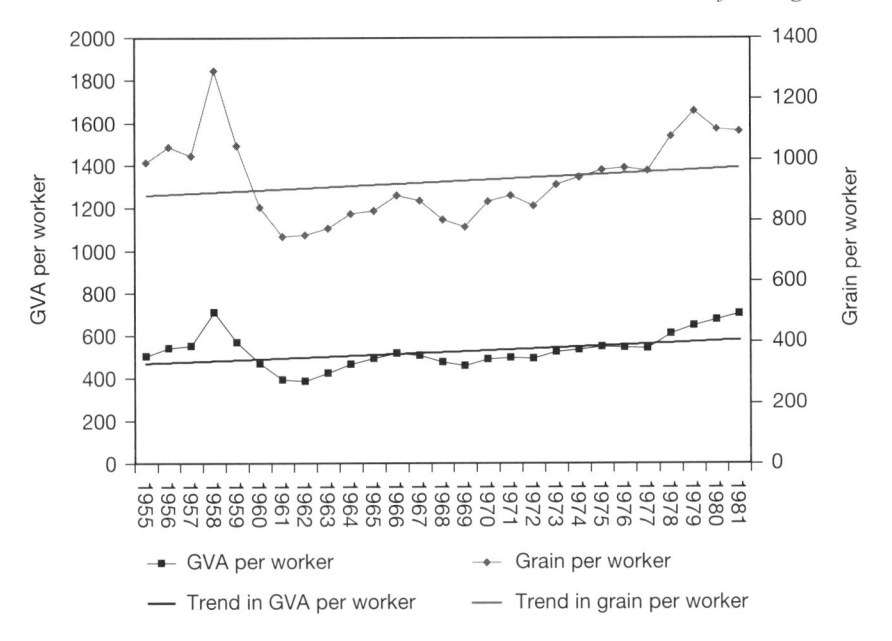

Figure 7.5 Trends in labour productivity under collective farming, 1955–1981 (Sources: MOA (1989: 106–9); SSB (2005b: 116–17).)

Note: GVA in agriculture is in yuan at 1980 prices. Grain is measured in terms of kg per worker.

> In our cooperative [collective] days we used to work all day, every day, year-in and year-out, but we got almost nothing done – work a little, take a break, work a little more, take another break. We felt harassed and we produced very little. What we were doing looked like work but in fact we were stalling around. Now we make every minute count. (Hinton 1990: 53)

Of course, if one accepts this view that shirking was commonplace, it does mean that China had already gone some way towards creating a labour surplus by the late 1970s, because, by then, much of its agricultural labour force was underemployed for a considerable part of the day – and yet agriculture was producing enough output to meet the (basic) needs of the Chinese population and its industry.[23] Some of this underemployment was of course illusory in that a part of the time not spent on collective farms was spent on private sideline production; as we have previously noted, the inclusion of the private sector in the agricultural data would raise both total output and by implication all measures of productivity. But some of the underemployment took the form of leisure, as the quotation from Hinton makes clear. The effect of decollectivization and the improvement in the intersectoral terms of trade was to eliminate much of this underemployment; labour inputs (in terms of hours worked) surged in the late 1970s and early 1980s. Following the second land reform, every minute was made to count on the family farm.

Paradoxically, therefore, the return to family farming in the early 1980s harmed industrialization. It boosted labour productivity in farming. However, by encouraging greater effort per hour worked on the family farm, it made the release of labour *more* difficult because it locked labour into agricultural production more closely. And, by any sensible definition, this was not a good use of labour, because the marginal productivity of labour in agriculture was much lower than in both rural and urban industry. The elimination of underemployment did boost agriculture production; the marginal productivity of labour in farming was not zero. But it would have made much more sense for China to move this low productivity labour out of farming and into the industrial sector.

And this of course is precisely what happened. The process of labour release began in the Maoist era. As Huang (1990) argues, the historical process of involution – the increasing application of labour to an essentially fixed supply of land – was coming to an end by the late 1970s. In part this was simply because of slowing population growth; it was no longer possible to increase intensification at the pace achieved in the 1960s. But more fundamentally, there was widespread recognition that rural industrialization offered the only viable route out of poverty, and this resulted in the creation of new rural industries by the state (at the county level) and by individual communes and brigades. By the early 1970s, this process of rural industrialization was in full swing (Bramall 2007). It was particularly rapid in the more advanced parts of rural China – notably Jiangsu and Zhejiang provinces – where the scope for agricultural intensification was very limited by the end of the 1970s. In Songjiang, the county studied by Huang (1990: 242), rice yields peaked in 1979. In the 1980s, as is well known, rural industry took off across China and in the process caused both an ascent from rural poverty and the release of farm labour.

The data on the size of the agricultural labour force bear these trends out. Between 1965 and 1981, the size of the agricultural labour force increased by about 60 million to almost 300 million workers. However, its share in the total had fallen from 82 per cent to only 68 per cent; clear evidence then of some release of labour. The absolute size of the agricultural labour force peaked in 1991 at 381 million, but by then accounted for only 60 per cent of the work force, and by 2004 this has fallen to only 47 per cent (SSB 2005a: 7). The main reason for the release of labour was the growth of the rural industrial sector, which offered significantly higher wages. The true size of the sector is hard to measure, because we should include county industries in the total and data on these are not readily available. But TVE employment alone soared from 28 to 139 million between 1978 and 2004, and a further 30 million workers were employed in county enterprises and organizations (not just industries) of one form or another in 2004 (Bramall 2007: 58 and 78). The very fact that industry was able to grow so rapidly is a tribute to the capacity of Chinese agriculture to raise output and at the same time release labour.[24]

Nevertheless, and even though output per worker rose in the 1980s and 1990s, low labour productivity remains a fundamental feature of Chinese agriculture. Measured in terms of value-added per worker, Chinese labour productivity in the late 1990s was only a tenth of that of Australia, and even less than that relative to the USA (OECD 2001: 75). In short, for all its success in terms of land productivity, China has failed to resolve the problem of low labour productivity, and this failure has limited its ability to release labour for use in other sectors of the economy. We will come back to this issue in Chapter 10.

(c) Total factor productivity

The productivity indicators discussed so far are partial measures, and that is their principal limitation. If, for example, relatively low Chinese labour productivity merely reflects greater use of capital per worker in other countries then we cannot conclude that Chinese agriculture is inefficient. We need a broader measure of efficiency.

One measure commonly used is of course total factor productivity (TFP). The data here show a clear contrast between the performance of the agricultural sector under collective and family farming. Maoist collective farms experienced a trend decline in total factor productivity of more than 1 per cent per year between 1955 and 1981 (Wen 1993: 27 and 33). Thereafter, the transformation was abrupt. Between 1981 and 1989, TFP grew by 6 per cent a year and over the long period 1981–96 by nearly 4 per cent per year (OECD 2001: 73–5).

However, these estimates are suspect in a variety of ways. Wen's (1993) approach is problematic because he used sown area (which rose) rather than cultivated area (which fell) as his measure of land inputs. This procedure in effect treats a process which many would regard as technical progress (increasing the multiple cropping index) as simply an increase in land inputs. Such concerns have persuaded other scholars to use arable land instead to measure land inputs (Fan and Zhang 2006). Additionally, the weights assigned to inputs are very arbitrary, necessarily so given that price data bear little relation to marginal costs. For example, the weight assigned to labour inputs varied between 0.12 and 0.50 in the studies summarized by Wen (1993: 27).[25] The recent study by Fan and Zhang (2006: 143) gives a weight of 0.42 to labour, which is not very different from Wen's 0.35 – but assigns a weight of only 0.20 to land, compared to Wen's 0.36. The relative weights given to land and labour are certainly important. given that the trend in labour inputs was strongly upwards (at least in terms of the headcount) whereas that for cultivated area was downwards. It is also true that the record of the post-Mao system is less good if we exclude the years of decollectivization and look just at the growth rate between 1985 and 1996; using Wen's methodology, TFP growth falls from 3.8 per cent per year for 1981–96 to only 2.2 per cent for 1985–96.

In fact, it is quite possible to turn the conventional wisdom on its head. The Fan and Zhang study, undoubtedly the best available, shows the way in which the results are sensitive to the underlying assumptions. By using Divisia weights (i.e. weights that change annually to reflect changing input shares) and by correcting for overreporting of fish and livestock production, they reduce the TFP disparity between collective and family farming considerably. Their series has TFP growth at 0.3 per cent between 1955 and 1981, but at only 2.7 per cent between 1981 and 1997 (Fan and Zhang 2006: 146–7).[26] As they say, even though post-1978 growth was 'respectable', they are in no doubt that 'the official statistics overestimate both aggregate output and input, resulting in biased estimates of total factor productivity growth. Furthermore, the official data overstate the impact of the rural reforms on both production and productivity growth' (Fan and Zhang 2006: 149). If we then assume that the output of private plots was not properly included in the pre-1981 output data, as discussed earlier, we end up with near convergence of TFP growth rates between the two periods. That conclusion would be strengthened by excluding the period 1981-5, when much of the apparent TFP rise was due to an increase in labour hours, rather than an increase in true efficiency. And in the process, the alleged superiority of family farming is wiped out.[27]

Income inequality within Chinese collectives

If the primary aim of collectivization was to raise agricultural output, its secondary purpose was to reduce inequality, or at least prevent polarization. More precisely, and as we have seen in Chapter 3, the concern within the Party in the early summer of 1955 was that the reduction in inequality brought about by land reform was only temporary. By that time, inequalities were increasing and the long-run prospect was that of polarization.

Now whether this diagnosis of China's situation in 1955 was accurate is moot; many Western academics have interpreted the evidence from the 1954 survey in a much less negative way (Nolan 1988; Selden 1988). But there is no doubt that an income gap between rich peasants and poor peasants persisted in the mid-1950s (Table 3.7). The gap in part reflected differences in labour power and productivity. However, differences in the ownership of means of production – land, draught animals, tools and carts – were more important. According to Shue (1980: 282–3):

> [T]he much greater income of rich peasant households was not primarily attributable to superior cultivation techniques and a high rate of productivity but merely to their greater ownership of means of production, especially land and labor.

None of this is surprising; after all, the land reform settlement was very much a 'wager on the strong' in that it was designed to preserve the rich peasant economy in order to motivate agricultural producers. But the price that was paid for this pro-growth policy was persistent inequality. To be sure, intra-village income inequalities were held in check by a variety of means (Shue 1980). Private trade was discouraged. Cheap loans were provided to the new producer cooperatives in the hope that this would encourage rich peasants to join them. Agricultural taxation was progressive. The creation of rural credit cooperatives offered a means by which poor peasants could gain access to cheap loans. And the creation of supply and marketing cooperatives helped realize economies of scale, and helped to guarantee poor and middle peasants a fair price for their products. Nevertheless, agricultural policy in the mid-1950s was in no sense designed to reduce inequality to a level below that achieved in the immediate aftermath of land reform. Moreover, there was considerable resistance to cooperatives within the countryside. Rich peasants feared that they would lose out by pooling their land and equipment with other peasants. Moreover, cooperative members were very reluctant to grant membership to households with little labour power (Hinton 1983: 140).[28]

The decision to enforce collectivization in 1955–6 indicates that the Party was no longer content either to preserve the rich peasant economy, or to accept the exclusion of some of the poorest rural households from the cooperatives. It was time to move on. And the structure of collective farming as it operated in the 1960s and 1970s was very much geared towards achieving a much more egalitarian distribution of income within China's villages than had been achieved in the early 1950s.[29] This redistributive intent is evident from the mechanisms embedded in collective farms. The range of work points awarded for a day" work was narrow. The pooling of land, draught animals and tools was designed to make incomes much more dependent upon labour power. The suppression of private trade and commerce eliminated opportunities for profits outside farm production. And the determination of communes to ensure that private plots did not account for more than about 5 per cent of arable area restricted the scope for income generation from sideline activities.

In addition, collective farms worked at reducing two other sources of inequality. First, the expansion of rural education and the development of health care both had the effect of raising the productivity of the poorest members of the rural community. These policies therefore had the effect of increasing the number of work points that could be earned by peasants who previously would have been unable to work or who had few skills. As labour power was the key potential asset of each peasant in the collective, this was of great importance. Education, not surprisingly, was especially significant. To give one illustration: a 1983 survey for forty-three counties in Sichuan found the average incomes of illiterates was 198 *yuan* whereas those with a senior middle school education earned 282 *yuan* (Sichuan nongcun yanjiuzu 1986: 720). The literacy drive in Maoist China therefore contributed very significantly to an erosion of income differentials.

Second communes set up a social security system to ensure that even households which lacked labour power did not starve.[30] Part of this was the provision of a basic grain ration to all individuals, irrespective of the amount of work done. This grain was not a gift but a loan; households which became indebted were expected ultimately to repay their debts. But the grain ration had the effect of ensuring that short-term distress – illness or injury leading to a temporary decline in the ability to work – did not have dire consequences. For households which were chronically short of labour, outright subsidies were provided. These were the 'five guarantees' (of food, clothing, housing, medical care and burial) which were set out as one of the aims of collectivization as early as the National Programme for Agricultural Development of January 1956. Such payments recognized that some households lacked able-bodied members and could not survive without subsidies.[31]

The net effect of these redistributive mechanisms on income inequality is difficult to judge. We would ideally compare intra-local inequality in the countryside in 1955 with intra-local inequality in the villages in 1978. However, the data are lacking. Published rural Gini coefficients for the early 1950s (Roll 1980) and the late 1970s (Adelman and Sunding 1987; SSB 2000b) suggest that there was little change over time; the rural Gini remained at slightly over 0.2.[32] However, these Ginis are based on very unreliable survey data, especially that for 1978; illiterate households were undersampled and non-farm rural households were ignored (Bramall and Jones 1993: 46; Bramall 2001). In any case, these Ginis incorporate spatial factors – the Gini is a function of both intra-local (within-village) inequality and spatial (between-village) inequality. The very fact that the Gini shows little change over the late Maoist period probably indicates that reductions in intra-local inequality were offset by increases in spatial inequality (the latter is discussed further in Chapter 9).

We can throw some light on the particular issue of intra-collective inequality by looking at the available village studies for the late 1970s.[33] However, these too have their limitations (Vermeer 1982). Many of the estimates are based upon the distributed collective income, a measure which ignores income from private plots, which typically accounted for at least 20 per cent of total household income. As there is no reason to suppose that private income was distributed in the same way as collective income, any analysis of distributed collective income is likely to be misleading. A second limitation is that that the villages surveyed were unrepresentative. It is therefore very hard to generalize on the basis of a handful of such studies. The other main problem is that the income distribution was changing very quickly in the Chinese countryside in the late 1970s as decollectivization gathered momentum and, much more importantly, restrictions on both private commerce and on the size of private plots were lifted. It therefore matters a great deal whether one uses data for (say) 1977 or for 1980.

Nevertheless, logic tells us that the distribution of income within China's villages at the time of Mao's death could only have been very equal by world standards because polarizing forces were weak. All this started to change in the late 1970s, but not before 1977. The private sector was virtually non-existent; land, draught animals and tools were under public ownership; and even the significance of differences in labour power between households had been much reduced. The two main factors making for continuing inequality were rural industrialization and differences in land quality across production teams. The development of rural industry in the 1970s was important because industrial jobs paid far more than jobs in farming and were few in number. Accordingly, those peasants who were able to work in industry enjoyed a substantial income premium and this pushed up inequality. Furthermore, although distribution within teams was otherwise equal, there is no doubt that there was inequality between teams and brigades in the same commune because of differences in land quality. A production team based on the plains had a great advantage compared to one located in the hills. Nevertheless, neither rural industrialization nor differences in land quality can have had a dramatic effect in the 1970s. Rural industrialization was still comparatively limited in most parts of China, and differences in land quality within a commune were typically comparatively small. Thus, in the sample assembled by Griffin (1984: 44), the Gini for within-brigade inequality was only around 0.05 in the early 1980s. Spatial inequality mattered, but the contrast between coastal counties and those located on the Himalayan plateau was far more important than within-county inequalities.

Bearing these qualifications in mind, the fact remains that the village studies which are available largely confirm the assessment of comparatively modest inequalities between rural households within communes. A useful compilation of studies is that by Griffin (1984: 41), which suggests that the average within-team Gini coefficient was less than 0.20. These studies are hardly conclusive; most of them are for the early 1980s (which exaggerates inequality in the mid-1970s, when rural industrial development was much less advanced) and they are misleading (as previously noted) because they cover only distributed collective income and hence exclude the growing private sector.[34] It also needs to be emphasized that collectivization did nothing to reduce spatial inequality, which remained a critical influence on the overall rural income distribution in the 1970s. Nevertheless, there is nothing in the evidence to suggest high levels of income inequality at the village level; on the contrary. Despite the limitations of the data, we may therefore reasonably conclude that the rural distribution of income within China's villages was certainly no more unequal than it had been in 1955, and was probably more equal. In terms of avoiding rural polarization, collectivization was therefore a considerable success.

Causality: why did Chinese collectives fail to live up to expectations?

The discussion in the previous section suggests that the collective farms of the late Maoist era performed much less badly than has often been alleged. The productivity record in particular was far better than commonly thought. Nevertheless, it is fair to conclude that their performance did not live up to the expectations voiced during the late 1950s and early 1960s. For many scholars, this was not surprising, because of what they saw as the inherent weakness of collective incentive systems. In fact, however, the issue is much more complex. Collective farming *per se* may have held back the growth of agricultural production, but a range of other factors was at work as well – so much so that it is by no means unreasonable to conclude that, but for these other constraints, Chinese collectives might well have been successful.

We therefore need to discuss the full range of factors which affected agricultural performance. These of course include the way in which the collective itself operated. But we need also to consider the constraints (domestic and international) within which the Maoist agricultural sector had to operate. And finally we need to discuss the impact of late Maoist policy, and especially the extent to which agriculture was constrained by the emphasis placed on grain production and the way in which the internal terms were biased against agriculture.

Collective incentive systems

The usual critique of Chinese collective farms focuses on their size (Nolan 1988; Griffin et al. 2002). Economies of scale are extensive in industry but agriculture, so it is said, is different. The creation of large units of production in rural China was therefore a mistake.[35] However, as we have seen, the international evidence is ambiguous. Much the same is true of the studies of Chinese agriculture before 1949 (Buck 1937; Huang 1985; Brandt 1989).

The absence of a clear inverse relationship in many of the empirical studies reflects the fact that there are two possible solutions to the problem of supervision and control, either of which is sufficient to reverse the inverse relationship.[36] One solution is institutional innovation – that is, the creation of a system of incentives which adequately motivates the workforce such that the need for supervision is much reduced. The second solution is to introduce labour-saving technical progress; the replacement of labour by capital reduces the need for supervision. If a case is to be made against Chinese collectives, it must therefore be that they failed to establish an adequate incentive system and that they failed to introduce labour-saving technologies – rather than that they were simply too large. In other words, it is not size *per se* that is the problem. Large agricultural units can be made to work either via the design of an appropriate incentive system, or by simply economizing on labour.

To see this, we can think of the collective incentive system in terms of the following equation:

$$y_i = w_i \cdot (X - R)/W$$

where:

- y_i = the annual income of the ith worker;
- w_i = number of work points earned by the ith worker over the year;
- X = net annual output of the collective;
- R = taxes + deductions for collective welfare provision
- W = total number of work points awarded by the collective to all workers during the year (such that $W = \sum w_i$).

Under this system, the income of the ith worker depended upon the number of work points earned by that worker (w_i) multiplied by the value of each work point, which is given by $(X - R)/W$.

In principle, this type of system embodies strong incentives. This is because, in contrast to wage employment, a peasant receives both a wage (work points) and a dividend (a share in the output of the organization). Peasants on collective farms are in fact over-incentivized to allocate time to collective work (Sen 1966). However, the problem for the Chinese collective was to ensure that a high time allocation translated into an equally high effort allocation because of potential free-rider problems. Unless the workforce was properly motivated, it would have a strong incentive to acquire as many work points as possible (a high time allocation) but to put in little effort. A low effort allocation would reduce total output, and therefore the value of the work point would fall. However, this effect would be more than offset by the increased number of work points earned.[37] And the size of the unit of account matters here. On a very large unit, the marginal effect of a slacking worker on the value of each work point is necessarily much less than on a small unit. For this reason, team-level accounting tended to provide stronger productivity incentives than brigade-level accounting. Note too that the shirking peasant received a side-benefit for slacking. By devoting little effort to collective work, s/he had more energy to work on the household's private plot during the evening. Thus the optimal strategy for a peasant was to maximize the number of work points earned, but to put little effort into the work. In Liu Minquan's (1991a, 1991b, 1994) phrase, the system encouraged a high time allocation but a low effort allocation.[38]

The challenge therefore for the Maoist collective was to devise a system whereby this type of shirking could be prevented.[39] In principle, close supervision and control offered the answer: a worker who shirked would have his or her working point earnings reduced. This was the approach adopted in Chinese production teams. The completion of tasks would be monitored by work-point recorders whose jobs was to be out in the fields observing work and ensuring that the full quota of work points was awarded for a particular task only if it were completed to a satisfactory standard. In judging that, a whole range of factors came into play, such as the weather, the hardness of the soil, the degree to which a task had been completed only by over-working a farm animal, etc. The work-point recorder would then hand over the records of his day's activity to the production team accountant, who would enter the data into the team accounting books.

This supervisory system is used in most factories, and on managerial (capitalist) farms. However, it requires a high input of labour to ensure that supervision is adequate. Furthermore, it is much harder to supervise farm work than assembly-line manufacture. A large period of time necessarily elapses in agricultural production from planting to the final harvest, and if the crop is small it is much harder to identify the underlying reasons unless every stage of the work has been supervised. By comparison, the assembly of a car takes much less time; the quality of each component part is easily assessed; and if the final assembled product fails to perform adequately, it is a straightforward matter to take it apart and identify the underlying source of failure. By contrast, it is hard to disassemble a potato. Agriculture is not unique in terms of problems of supervision and control of the labour force; coal mining poses similar problems. But there is no doubt that supervision and control is much harder than in manufacturing. This largely explains why large managerial farms are comparatively rare in countries where labour is the main input, though it is arguable that this is more down to the nature of ownership (managerial capitalism) than it is to the pure effects of size.[40]

There are other potential solutions to the problem of worker incentives. One is to rely more upon ideological and political motivation. The ideal is one in which peasants would be self-motivated by the notion of 'building socialism' (or in the local context raising the prosperity of the entire village), and there is a little doubt from many of the accounts that some villagers were extremely idealistic in the late Maoist era. However, the scope for free-riding in this sort of system is immense, and it also needs to be observed that many of China's peasants had become disillusioned by the mid-1960s. This reflected the debacle of the Great Leap Forward, the intensity and regularity of political campaigns in the countryside, and limitations on labour mobility. It is for example certainly arguable that (voluntary) cooperation would have been a better solution than (coercive) collectivization if the aim was to motivate the workforce.

The third solution was that used to good effect in the Dazhai production brigade. As noted above, this relied upon mass meetings as a way of ensuring quality control. A peasant who slacked might be subject to merciless criticism at such public meetings, and this threat acted as a powerful disincentive to shirking, because of the potential loss of face involved. There is considerable evidence that this sort of peer pressure was very effective in Dazhai, just as it has been in other contexts.[41] In practice, however, the system worked less well than had been hoped. The main problem was that many team members were reluctant to voice criticism of their fellow villagers in public, mainly because of the implications of such public criticism for social relations – and hence for the harmony of village life, which was itself important to maintain given the need for household cooperation on infrastructural projects. And the very fact that the Dazhai system encouraged the awarding of work points for attitude as well as for work done introduced a highly subjective component into the appraisal: how precisely was socialist morality to be judged and evaluated? Partly for these reasons, the Dazhai system fell out of favour in many villages in the 1970s (Unger 2002: ch. 4). For example, Long Bow, the village studied by Hinton, found it difficult to implement the Dazhai incentive system (Hinton 1983: 695–6).

Nevertheless, whilst we must recognize the problems encountered in devising an adequate incentive system, the weaknesses in the system of incentives incorporated into Chinese collectives are typically overstated by the critics of the Maoist system. For example, there is some evidence that the abandonment of the Dazhai system had more to do with the fall of Lin Biao in 1971 than its intrinsic problems. One account of its use in Sichuan between 1967 and 1971 suggests that it was preferred to the piece-rate system because personal work-point ratings needed to be set only once a month or so (Endicott 1988: 124–7). In Gao village in Jiangxi, the key appraisal meeting was annual (Gao 1999: 62).[42] Under a piece-rate system, there was a need for either on-field monitoring or daily meetings:

> [D]ifferences of opinion over entitlement to work points could lead team members into hours of argument in long meetings. One peasant summed up the attitude toward such meetings by saying: 'Doing a little extra work won't kill me, but this damn staying up all night will'. (Endicott 1988: 125)

In any case, for many of China's peasants the loss of notional negative freedoms was more than compensated for by a range of positive freedoms: access to education and health care, the existence of a social security system and the elimination of the exploitative class relations which typified the Republican countryside. In fact, Chinese collective farms continued to operate effectively in most parts of the countryside until their abolition in the early 1980s. This was not a system on the brink of collapse, a conclusion attested to by the fact that so many collectives were resistant to being broken up in the early 1980s. As Hinton (1990, 2006) plausibly argues, leadership was very important; where it was good, collective farms found few difficulties in devising and operating an effective system of incentives.

I conclude from all this that the incentive failures said to have afflicted late Maoist collective farming have been greatly exaggerated. Problems there certainly were but, in so far as collective performance was poor, we need to look elsewhere for a complete explanation.

Constraints: the closed arable frontier

The best place to look is to the macroeconomic constraints on agriculture. For the fact of the matter is that Chinese agricultural conditions were simply not very conducive to a rapid and sustained increase in production, whatever the incentive system.

The main problem was that China had more or less reached its arable frontier by 1949 (Figure 7.6).[43] As a result, the land constraint on Chinese agriculture was much more binding than in much of Africa or in Latin America. In Brazil, for example, cultivated area grew by no less than 175 per cent between 1950 and 1985 (Baer 1995: 310). In China, there was still some scope for expansion in the south-west and especially in Heilongjiang; cultivated area in the Manchurian province rose from 6.5 to 9.2 million hectares between 1952 and 1996 (SSB 1990: 290; HJTJNJ 1996: 220). Increases were also recorded in other parts of the north and west, such as Ningxia and Inner Mongolia (Ho 2003). This helped to push up the national figure during the 1950s from about 98 to 112 million hectares. Such a level of usage was unsustainable; by the middle of the 1990s, total arable area was virtually the same as it had been at the time of the Revolution, and the trend has been steadily downwards since the early 1960s. Yet to maintain cultivated area at above its 1949 level was no mean achievement; the demands of urbanization placed considerable pressure on arable land, especially around urban centres.

But simply maintaining arable area was not good enough to ensure food security, because of population growth. The trajectory of this growth is well known thanks to China's relatively reliable population censuses and the work of Banister (1987: 353). The population in 1949 was about 560 million if we back-project from the data for 1953, the year of China's first proper population census. Growth then averaged around 2.2 per cent per year between 1949 and 1957, well above the probable Republican rate of around 0.5 per cent per year. Although China's population actually declined between 1958 and 1962 because of the effects of the Great Famine, growth resumed in 1962 and averaged well over 2.5 per cent in the late 1960s. After 1968 (when the rate of growth hit 3.1 per cent), the pace of growth

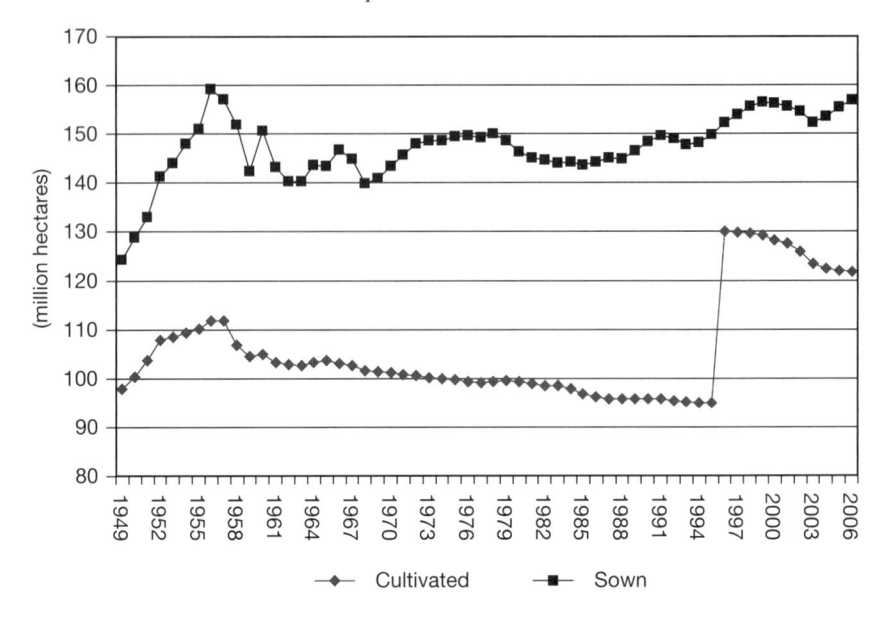

Figure 7.6 Cultivated and sown area, 1949–2006 (Sources: SSN (2000a: 21 and 34); ZGTJNJ (2007: 474); MOA (2004: 135): SEPA (2004, 2005, 2006a).)

Note: The First Agricultural Census of 31 October 1996 led to an upward revision in cultivated area from 95 to 130 million hectares; hence the spike in the series. However, the output data were not revised, suggesting that much of this 'new' land was of very marginal quality and that its production had already been incorporated into yield estimates.

gradually declined, reaching 1 per cent in 1984 and 0.5 per cent by 2006. The net result of all this was that China's population approximately doubled between 1949 and 1989 – with the effect that arable area per capita halved during the second half of the twentieth century.

It is partly true to suggest that a growing population was of China's own making. Mao was fiercely anti-Malthusian, and Ma Yinchu, the noted demographer, was purged in the late 1950s for his allegedly Malthusian warnings about the dangers of population growth. Nevertheless, it is too easy simply to blame Mao. At the most basic level, China's ability to manufacture contraceptives was very limited. And the planners were very well aware of the population problem, and tried to raise both the age of marriage and female enrolment rates in schools in a bid to reduce the birth rate. More fundamentally, a big increase in China's population was inevitable during the 1960s and 1970s because of the age structure of the population and the falling death rate, which declined as a result of big improvements in sanitation and mass inoculation campaigns. Chinese agriculture was in a sense a victim of the country's success in improving levels of human development.

In order to meet spiralling domestic demand, all this meant that it was imperative to increase either yields or the sown area. In fact, as Figure 7.6 shows, China was quite successful in raising sown area.

Although the peak of the late 1950s proved unsustainable, sown area by the mid-1990s was still around 20 per cent higher than it had been in 1949, and much of the increase was achieved in the Maoist era.[44] This reflected increases in the multiple cropping index, itself made possible by the expansion of irrigated area and growing use of chemical fertilizer. Total sown area has trended upwards since the early 1970s, but it is evident that the rate of increase has been very slow; it remains to be seen whether China can maintain it at above 150 million hectares, the level around which it has hovered since the early 1970s. Much of the difficulty here is simply the climate. The growing season is typically not long enough to support three crops in the big producing provinces along the Yangzi, notably Sichuan and Jiangsu. Attempts to do precisely this foundered during the Maoist era, when it was found that one rice crop was yielding more than two crops simply because the growing season was too short. As a result, and although growing availability of plastics eased the problem to some degree, these experiments were largely abandoned in the late 1970s (Donnithorne 1984; Leeming 1985).

The problem then for collective farming was that it had to increase production at a rate at least equal to the rate of growth of the population against a backcloth of limited scope for increases in area. That meant that output targets had to be met by increasing yields. In other words, the collective farms of the late Maoist era faced a colossal challenge, something which is often forgotten when international comparisons are made. The very fact that agricultural output did rise as fast as population during the late Maoist era is in many ways a tribute to the effectiveness of collective farming.

Policy constraints

The challenge faced by the Maoist collective were compounded by the broader constraints imposed on agriculture by Chinese macroeconomic policy. There were two main priorities. First, the expansion of industrial production. Second, the need to supply the grain needs of the population. The first meant that the internal terms of trade were biased against agriculture, thus discouraging production. The second forced overemphasis on grain production on marginal land at the expense of higher value-added products, which depressed the growth of value-added.

(a) The terms of trade and the supply of modern inputs

Much of the literature focuses on the causal role played by incentive systems in determining the pace and pattern of agricultural growth. However, the interaction between the state and the rural sector via the operation of taxation and the manipulation of the intersectoral terms of trade also played a key role, and in the main it served to depress the rate of agricultural growth in the Maoist era.

At first glance this notion that the pattern of intersectoral resource flows hampered agricultural growth appears unfounded. A good deal of the literature has argued that even though agriculture was a net contributor to industrialization in the 1950s (Ishikawa 1967), this was not the case for the bulk of the Maoist period (Ishikawa

1988; Nakagane 1989; Karshenas 1995). The basis for the argument is that the rate of land taxation was declining over time. State investment in agriculture was rising, and the intersectoral terms of trade moved in agriculture's favour during the Maoist period. Hinton puts the point with characteristic clarity: 'grain prices in China were almost never lower and were quite often higher than in America. The state was not expropriating grain from the peasants, but was paying going world rates or better. I often wished that I could sell my 800-ton corn harvest in China' (Hinton 2006: 122).

And the data seem to bear this out. The agricultural tax was a lump sum. As a result, the revenue raised barely changed during the Maoist era. In 1981 it raised 2.8 billion *yuan*, a large figure but one which was virtually unchanged from the 2.7 billion raised in 1952, when the level of agricultural production was much lower. In fact, as a share of state revenue, the agricultural tax fell from 15 per cent in 1952 to only 2.6 per cent in 1981 (MOA 1989: 362–3). As for price trends, the trend improvement in the internal terms of trade is very clear in Figure 7.7. Whereas the prices of industrial goods selling in rural areas were virtually constant during the Maoist era, agricultural procurement prices rose steadily.

However, this analysis of the intersectoral terms of trade is misleading because it takes no account of changes in productivity.[45] Industrial productivity was increasing

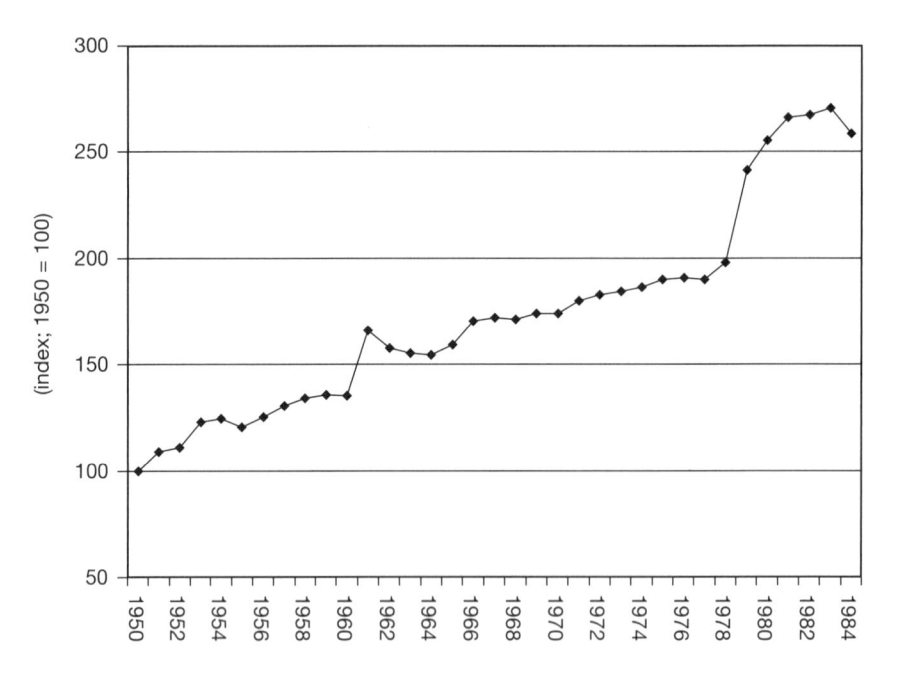

Figure 7.7 The internal terms of trade, 1950–1984 (Sources: Han and Feng (1992: 525); SSB (2005a: 32–3); SSB (2005b: 203).)

Note: The internal terms of trade is the index of agricultural product prices (procurement prices before 2001) divided by the index of agricultural producer good prices (industrial goods selling in rural areas before 1978).

much more quickly than agricultural productivity during the Maoist period. In a market economy, this would have translated into very substantial declines in the prices of industrial inputs (chemical fertilizer, plastics and machinery) sold in rural areas. In fact, industrial prices did decline, but by nothing like the amount implied by the rise in productivity. As a result, the prices of industrial producer goods were far out of line with their marginal cost of production. The double factorial terms of trade – the terms of trade adjusted for sectoral productivity – moved against agriculture. In effect, the value of goods produced by an industrial worker was being exchanged for a progressively larger volume of agricultural goods. This is the phenomenon usually called 'unequal exchange' in the Chinese literature, a literature which suggests that unequal exchange may even have increased during the Maoist era. Estimates of its absolute extent range from between 20 to 50 per cent in the 1970s (Chen and Buckwell 1991: 106; Li 1985: 233; Yan et al. 1990: 67).

Unequal exchange occurred because the Maoist development strategy was predicated upon the extraction of resources from agriculture to finance industrial development. The key extractive mechanism was the intersectoral terms of trade, which allowed the industrial sector to generate very large supernormal profits; not only was the sale of producer goods to the farm sector highly profitable but, more importantly, low food prices meant that industrial enterprises could pay low wages – thus generating high profits across the entire industrial sector.[46] The primary objective of this policy was to generate the funds and the real resources needed to invest in new industries, especially the Third Front projects located in western China. And the aim of industrialization was to secure China against the perceived foreign threat posed by the USA and the Soviet Union.

The significance of biasing the terms of trade against agriculture is very clear from the data on farm profitability; the plain facts of the matter are that many types of farm production were simply unprofitable by the late 1970s. In 1977, for example, rice cultivation yield a profit of only 6 *yuan* per *mu*, whereas the cultivation of both wheat and vegetable oil meant a loss of 11.4 *yuan* per *mu* (Bramall 2000a: 314).[47] It was not the system of collective incentives that discouraged production, but the impossibility of turning a profit given the prevailing price structure.

In addition, Maoist agriculture was handicapped by the limited volume of investment which went into the production of the modern inputs needed by agriculture. Even if the relative price structure had been more favourable, Chinese farmers would not have been able to get hold of chemical fertilizer during the Maoist era because it was simply not available in sufficient quantities. Only in the 1970s did this begin to change (Figure 7.8). Given that chemical fertilizer was a crucial part of the modern technological package – HYVs, water and chemical fertilizer – its limited availability constrained China's ability to introduce the Green Revolution technology needed to bring about big increases in yields. Irrespective of the management system in operation, China could not have transformed its agricultural production until the Green Revolution technology became available in the late 1970s, whatever its system of farming.

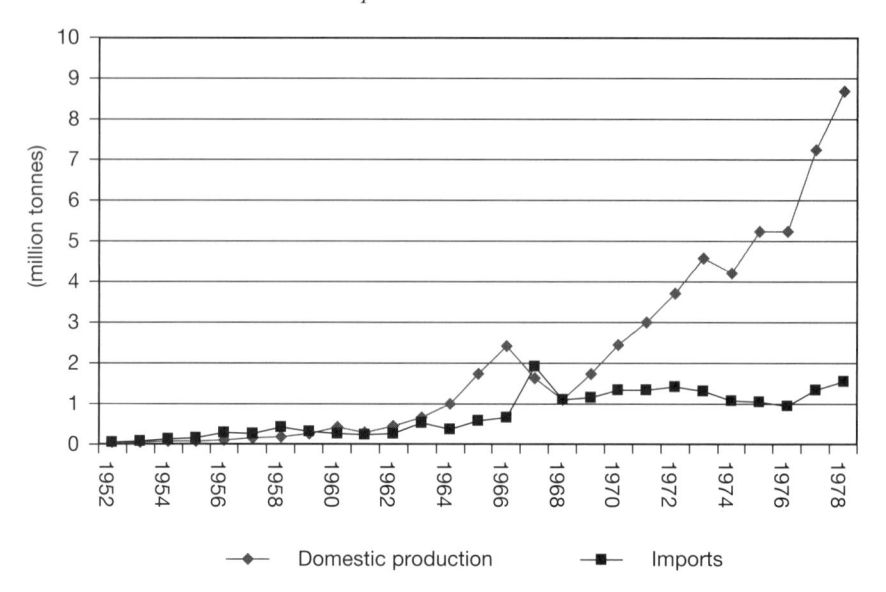

Figure 7.8 Production and imports of chemical fertilizer (Source: MOA (1989: 324–5).)

(b) Grain first

The other constraint on Maoist agriculture was the overemphasis placed on grain production. The logic of such a strategy is that, by altering the composition of sown area, more of the total was given over to food crops and less to cash crops and orchards.

However, single-minded emphasis on grain production is a strategy fraught with peril. For one thing, an emphasis on low value-added crops inevitably constrains the growth of overall agricultural gross value-added. Second, a grain monoculture runs the risk that grain will displace other crops on land to which grain production is patently unsuited, especially hillsides, leading to erosion, leaching of the soil and desertification. And this is precisely what happened during the Maoist era, suggest some (Smil 1984; Shapiro 2001; Eyferth 2003); according to these writers, the slogan *yiliang weigang* (take grain as the key link) was interpreted all too literally to mean that grain production had absolute priority. Some of the evidence supports this view. There is no doubt that much of the expansion that occurred during the Leap was ill-conceived, and the very fact that area fell back sharply from its 1958 peak demonstrates that point (Figure 7.2). And there is certainly some evidence of ill-advised schemes; Shapiro (2001), for example, discusses the filling-in of parts of Dianchi lake in Yunnan for grain use. In short, there is little doubt that 'grain first' did constrain agricultural production.

However, late Maoist agricultural policy was very different from the straw man that is set up in so much of the literature. The attempts by the Dazhai production brigade to increase grain production by terracing hillsides have often been mocked, but the evidence suggests that it was very successful (Qin 1995; Hinton

1983, 1990). In fact, much of the evidence points to the conclusion that the full Maoist slogan in relation to grain production – which was 'take grain as the key link and promote overall development and diversification' (*yiliang weigang quanmian fazhan duozhong jingying*) – was understand very well; grain production was important, but only as part of a comprehensive strategy for agricultural development (Hinton 2006). As a consequence, animal husbandry – not grain production – was even placed centre stage in many pastoral regions (Ho 2003). Chinese provinces were certainly encouraged to be more self-reliant in grain production. This much is clear from the scaling down of procurement quotas and inter-provincial grain transfers. The province worst affected by the famine was Sichuan, and there is no doubt that the province's role as a key supplier of grain to other provinces and to the USSR during the 1950s and the Leap had contributed to famine conditions (Bramall 1993). In recognition of this, Sichuan was no longer required to be a net supplier of grain after 1960; only Heilongjiang, where there was still scope for the expansion of arable area, played this role after the Leap debacle (Walker 1984). Nevertheless, to argue that a policy of regional self-sufficiency was pushed to the extreme is simply not supported by the evidence. The grain trade between provinces may have dwindled, but intra-provincial trade if anything expanded as groups of counties were designated as grain bases.

Perhaps the clearest indication of the sense of Maoist policy is provided by the data on the composition of grain sown area. In 1952, grain accounted for 88 per cent of sown area. This declined steadily to reach 81.5 per cent in 1959, the height of the Leap. It then increased somewhat as famine conditions made it imperative to cultivate grain; the grain share rose to a peak of 86.7 in 1962. Thereafter, however, the decline resumed. By 1968, the share was only 83 per cent, and by 1976 it was down to 80.6 per cent – precisely the reverse of what we expect to see if the monoculture claims were correct (SSB 2000a: 64). In other words, the evidence points decisively to the conclusion that Chinese agriculture became progressively *more* diversified as the late Maoist era evolved.[48] Chinese agriculture was much more characterized by mono-culture in the 1950s than at the time of Mao's death.[49]

Nevertheless, and despite this trend, the central conclusion remains. Extreme overemphasis may have declined over time, but the focus of the late Maoist strategy on grain production constrained the growth of agricultural output.

Assessment

In sum, the problems of Chinese agriculture in the 1960s and 1970s were as much structural as they were incentive-based. The scope for expanding arable area was limited by the end of the 1950s. The only way forward for China was a strategy of agricultural intensification based around raising yields.[50] That in turn required the application of what is usually called 'Green Revolution' technology: chemical fertilizer, high-yielding and chemical-fertilizer-responsive seed varieties and irrigation. But Green Revolution technology could not be introduced overnight. The fertilizer needed to be produced – and that meant industrial development, which in turn squeezed agriculture in the short run because it required the extraction of surplus. Similarly, the irrigation systems needed to be built. As India's experience demonstrates, Green Revolution technology in the case of wheat was more easily implemented because it was less demanding of irrigation development. But India's record in respect of rice production has been much less impressive; here, the Maoist system had the advantage because the communes were able to mobilize the vast quantities of labour required to construct gigantic irrigation systems. Nevertheless, the expansion of irrigated area – as with industrial production – could not be achieved in the short term despite the mass mobilization of Chinese labour (Nickum 1978, 1990). Even then, a vast research effort was needed to produce the hybrid HYVs which would thrive in Chinese conditions. China embarked upon such a research programme in the early 1960s, but it was not until the mid-1970s that the new varieties started to become widely available. It is highly unlikely, therefore, that the early implementation of decollectivization would have made very much difference to China's agricultural prospects.

Evaluating the impact of decollectivization

The previous section has shown that there were three sets of potential constraints on late Maoist agricultural performance: collective farms, limited scope for increases in sown area and policy factors, notably the biased internal terms of trade and the emphasis on grain production. The key analytical question is therefore to identify the specific role played by collective farming. The logical test of collective farming is to assess what happened as a result of the decollectivization which occurred between 1977 and 1983. To what extent can the surge in output which occurred be attributed to decollectivization?

The fable of decollectivization

There is no doubt that a process of decollectivization occurred in China in the late 1970s and early 1980s, nor that it coincided with a marked increase in output.[51] As Table 7.5 shows, decollectivization did not take place especially quickly; the figure of 50 per cent family farming was achieved only in the summer of 1982. Nevertheless, despite this slow pace, family farming had been fully restored by late 1983. It is therefore inevitable that the plaudits have been awarded to the restoration of family farming for China's agricultural miracle.

However, there are several problems with the decollectivization hypothesis. The first relates to timing. There is no doubt that output growth rose in the late 1970s and early 1980s. Between 1976 and 1980, for example, agricultural value-added increased by 4.6 per cent per year, and this climbed to 10.1 per cent per annum between 1980 and 1984; both figures were well in excess of the 2.5 per cent growth rate which was the average between 1965 and 1976 (Bramall 2000b: 122). But there is a problem with causality here because, as Table 7.5 shows, much of Chinese agriculture remained collectivized in the late 1970s. Given that so few teams had abandoned production teams before 1980 – only 5 per cent had introduced *baogan* (family farming) by December 1980 (Chung 2000: 64) – it is hard

Table 7.5. The decollectivization of Chinese agriculture (percentage of production teams using each system)

	Baochan daohu	Baogan daohu	Baochan daozu
January 1980	4.1	0.02	24.9
December 1980	18.5	5.00	23.6
October 1981	26.6	38.00	10.8
June 1982	19.7	67.00	2.1
December 1982	8.7	70.00	neg
December 1983	neg	94.00	neg

Source: Bramall (2000a: 328).

Note
Baochan daozu (contracting production to the workgroup) was the least 'radical' of these reform models; workgroups were no more than small production teams. *Baochan daohu* (contracting production to the household) was more radical, but the allocation of income was still controlled by the collective; only the organization of production was contracted to the household. *Baogan daohu* (contracting everything to the household), or *dabaogan* as it was sometimes called, amounted to a *de facto* return to private farming; households under this system were responsible for production and were allowed to keep any profit they made after paying a tax to the village. In a strict sense, the *baogan* system was not private farming, because property rights were insecure; land remains the property of the state, and local government retains a good deal of power over how land is used. Nevertheless, the system is far closer to private farming than any of the systems in operation in the late Maoist era. Note that rows do not add to 100; the residual is of course the percentage of teams still under full collective management.

to argue that family farming played a key role in the acceleration of growth; the numbers simply don't add up. Indeed, even if we add the *baochan daohu* figure to the *baogan* total (to produce a household figure of 24 per cent in December 1980), the numbers still look implausible; it is hard to believe that this 24 per cent of teams alone could have produced a growth blip of the order of magnitude observed.[52] In fact, we can go further. If we make a direct comparison between counties which decollectivized early and those which decollectivized late in Sichuan province (China's biggest agricultural producer), the data show that counties which retained collective farming until mid-1982 experienced a growth rate of output and grain production which was at least as high as (and perhaps even higher than) counties where decollectivization occurred early (Bramall 1995: 749–51). The most logical conclusion is that reforms to the system of collective farming, in conjunction with other policy changes, were decisive – not family farming itself.

Moreover, just as a whole range of factors affected agricultural performance in the late Maoist period, so a whole series of changes occurred between 1977 and 1983 that make it hard to trace out the precise effects of decollectivization. For one thing, as we saw in the previous section, the supply of chemical fertilizer increased sharply. Without the increase in production – output rose by about 50 per cent between 1978 and 1982 (SSB 1990: 18) – it is highly unlikely that farm output would have increased so rapidly. Second, new seed varieties were becoming available in large quantities. According to Stone (1988a: 795):

> HYV extension progress for all major cereal crops during the final two Maoist decades was exceedingly rapid, culminating in 1978 with hybrids covering

60 per cent of corn area, 13 per cent of rice area and around 40 percent of sorghum area. Semi-dwarf rice (including hybrids) covered no less than 80 percent of rice, and semi-dwarf wheat covered 40 percent.

The introduction of HYVs was made possible by the completion of many of the large-scale irrigation projects begun in the 1960s. As we saw earlier, irrigated area expanded steadily in the 1960s and 1970s across the whole of China, a remarkable achievement given that many of the projects were large scale and therefore required a high degree of cross-village cooperation.

As importantly, macroeconomic policy became much more pro-agriculture. Zhao Ziyang took the lead in Sichuan in reducing procurement quotas, increasing the scope for private plots and putting an end to some of the less well-advised attempts to introduce double rice cropping in areas where it was simply not possible (Donnithorne 1984; Bramall 1993). All this gave communes more freedom over cropping patterns and (in conjunction with the emergence of private markets) the option of selling output at a higher price to the private sector instead of to the state. The net effect was to increase the profitability of farm production. More importantly, procurement prices for commodities sold to the state were increased. The Chinese state recognized the problem in 1979, when it increased procurement prices by 22 per cent on average and grain prices by no less than 31 per cent (Sicular 1989; Han and Feng 1992). As a result, a tonne of grain sold for 361 *yuan* in 1980 compared with 263 *yuan* in 1978 (MOA 1989: 463). This price rise, combined with unchanged industrial input prices, led to a big improvement in the internal terms of trade. At a stroke, this greatly increased farm incomes and provided a strong incentive to raise production.

However, the impact of this shift in the terms of trade towards agriculture is controversial (Stone 1988a, 1988b; Bramall 1993). In theoretical terms, the impact is uncertain because the income and substitution effects of a relative price rise operate in different directions. On the one hand, peasants were able to achieve a given income by producing and selling less (the income effect). On the other hand, the price rise encouraged them to reallocate labour time towards the more profitable activity of farming (the substitution effect). Its impact on agricultural production is therefore hotly debated; see the discussion in Bramall (2000a: 313–23). There is no question that it raised profitability across a range of farm crops. For example, profits per *mu* of rice rose from 6 *yuan* in 1978 to 25 *yuan* in 1979, and from 0.5 *yuan* to 13 *yuan* for corn. Much more controversial, however, is the degree to which these price rises stimulated productivity and thus contributed to the surge in agricultural production in the early 1980s. The subject is particularly controversial, because if we attribute the bulk of the output increase to a price response we are by implication suggesting that decollectivization was less important as a source of growth. For what it is worth, most scholars have taken the view that price rises had a relatively small effect (Lin 1992; Putterman 1993; Hua *et al.* 1993). Others, myself included, are less convinced. In part this is because the impact of the 1979 price rise is masked by the poor weather of 1980 and 1981. It is also because it is hard to see how the surge in HYV and chemical fertilizer use in the late 1970s and early 1980s could have been financed without the surge in the profitability of collective farming. Price rises may not have had a spectacular effect on productivity, but they did pay for the surge in input use by collective and family farms.[53] As Stone (1988b: 147–8) says:

> Of course it is virtually impossible to sort out the effects of the price changes alone in the presence of such sweeping reforms. It is quite possible that they would not have been so effective without the other important changes in rural incentive structure allowing farmers to keep most of their increased output or to sell it profitably in the free markets. But it is also clear that without the price changes, the additional application of fertilizers indispensable to such a massive increase in yields might not have been possible.

The econometrics of decollectivization

There is no doubt, then, that a range of factors came together in the late 1970s and early 1980s which were all favourable for agricultural production. Decollectivization was one factor. However, it was not the only factor at work. The poor weather of 1978–81 gave way to the excellent weather of 1982–4; many of the irrigation projects begun in the mid-1960s were brought to completion; new HYVs became available in very large quantities as the research programmes of the 1960s bore fruit (Stone 1988a; Bramall 1995); chemical fertilizer availability soared; and the intersectoral terms of trade shifted powerfully in agriculture's favour. Table 7.6 summarizes these trends.

The econometric studies, which attempt to tease out the respective contributions of these various factors, point to a contribution of between 27 and 71 per cent from decollectivization. Of these studies (summarized in Bramall 2000a: 333–4), the best is probably that of Lin (1992), which ascribes 47 per cent of the growth between 1978 and 1984 to decollectivization. However, none of this is very convincing. These studies are all dependent upon the use of neoclassical production functions, a methodology which has been roundly condemned by a range of writers going back to Kaldor and Robinson in the 1950s. The impact of the lagged effect of the irrigation projects completed in the late Maoist period has been ignored. And no proper attempt has been made to deal with the impact of weather by, for example, smoothing the time series data. This is of very great importance, because a comparison of 1978 with 1984 is a comparison between a very bad year for weather and one of the best years of the century, which tends to inflate very substantially the growth rate. It is no accident that growth falls off after 1984; 1985, in fact, was a year of very poor weather. As 1980 and 1981 were also years of poor weather, whereas 1982 and 1983 were years of good weather, it is evident that the comparison is firmly loaded in favour of the decollectivization hypothesis. It is in fact little more than a trough-to-peak comparison.

In short, the econometrics of decollectivization is inconclusive. There is no doubt that decollectivization was a favourable factor, and this suggests that the incentive problems which have been much remarked upon stifled the growth of agricultural production. Nevertheless, it is not clear that decollectivization was

Table 7.6 Output and conditions of agricultural production, 1974–1984

	Agricultural GVA	Chemical fertilizer use	Procurement prices	Hybrid rice area	Weather index	Family farming
	(1952=100)	(kg per mu)	(1950=100)	(m ha)		(per cent of teams)
1974	167	11	205	neg	−23	0
1975	170	12	209	neg	−13	0
1976	167	13	210	0.14	2	0
1977	163	14	209	2.30	29	0
1978	170	19	217	4.20	54	0
1979	181	24	266	4.74	12	4
1980	178	27	284	4.95	47	24
1981	190	28	301	5.12	27	64
1982	212	31	308	5.61	8	79
1983	230	34	321	6.75	10	94
1984	60	35	334	8.84	3	96

Sources: MOA (1989: 341 and 436); IRRI (2007); Kueh (1995: 299); SSB (2005a: 12).

Note
Kueh's index measures the percentage deviation from the 1952–84 average; a positive number indicates poor weather. The family farm figure here is the total of *baochan daohu* and *baogan daohu*; see Table 7.5. The 1981 figure is for October, whereas the others are year-end figures.

the critical factor. Many other factors were clearly important as well. As Hussain (1989: 238) rightly says:

> [A] large credit for the rates of growth since 1978 must go to technical change, interpreted broadly to include increased application of inputs made possible by the introduction of HYVs in the past. The shift over to family farming has indeed led to a more efficient utilization of technical possibilities, but it was the introduction of HYVs and the massive investment in irrigation that created those possibilities in the first place.

The case against collective farming is therefore very far from compelling. Moreover, if we give the credit to the expansion of irrigated area and the development of the agricultural research system, the calculus in favour of the collective is even stronger. Indian economists and social scientists are often laughed at for advocating collective farming in India, but the evidence from China is far more ambivalent than the conventional wisdom allows.

Conclusion

Late Maoist agriculture did not fail. It was a more than creditable record to raise farm output at the same rate as population. Nevertheless, its performance did not live up to the hopes of the Party and the claims of its most ardent admirers.

Part of the reason for this failure was the nature of the collective farm. It proved extremely difficult to devise an incentive system which would properly motivate the rural workforce, and as a result labour productivity grew slowly, if it grew at all. Shirking was a fact of life on the average Chinese collective farm in the late Maoist era. And in any assessment of collective farming, we cannot ignore the suppression of the freedom to travel and migrate, one of the most basic of all human rights, that collective farming necessarily involved.

For all that, the literature on collective farms continues to exaggerate the defects of the collective and to downplay its merits. And merits there were aplenty. The Chinese peasantry in the late Maoist era achieved an unprecedented expansion of the irrigation system, and in so doing laid the foundations for both mechanization and the effective introduction of high-yielding hybrid and semi-dwarf varieties. As a result, late Maoist agriculture was able to meet the needs of the economy even though labour productivity was low. Moreover, the return to family farming hindered Chinese development, in that, by discouraging shirking, it increased the volume of labour inputs in farming at a time when the needs of the economy would have been better served by releasing this surplus labour for industrialization. To be sure, some agricultural labour was released in the 1980s and 1990s, but larger farms would have accelerated the process of industrialization.

In any case, the slow growth of output and labour productivity on China's collectives had far more to do with macroeconomic policy failure than with any intrinsic weakness in collective organization *per se*. Chinese macroeconomic policy throughout the late Maoist era was heavily influenced by international constraints. China's isolation, and the growing threat to its borders posed by the USA and the Soviet Union, forced upon Mao a programme of defence industrialization. For Mao, the Party and the Chinese people, there could be no going back to the 1930s, and China's treatment at the hands of the Japanese. China had stood up in 1949, and it would not kneel again.

From these nationalist imperatives, the rest followed. Defence industrialization had to be financed, and the only source for the resources required was the agricultural sector. In consequence, the internal terms of trade were shifted against agriculture in order to hold down the price of wage goods and industrial inputs, thus boosting the profits of the industrial sector and its capacity to reinvest. In the process, the production of chemical fertilizer and other key farm inputs was neglected, and, even if they had been available, the terms of trade were such that the farm sector would have been unable to afford them. Chinese agriculture was thus thrown back on its own resources. However, the very fact that farming was not profitable in the 1970s resulted inevitably in low wages and low levels of labour motivation. Big increases in farm output brought no tangible reward, and by the time of Mao's death it was simply no longer possible to motivate a workforce denuded of all but the most basic material commodities. Only by dint of a supreme effort, and aided by the growing availability of HYVs produced by China's own agricultural research system, could even these basic needs be met.

For all that, the China of 1978 stood on the edge of an agricultural revolution, and the collective farms deserve the lion's share of the credit. By the late 1970s, the strategic threat was much diminished, and it proved possible to increase relative agricultural prices and to raise the supply of industrial inputs. The result was a surge in agricultural production the like of which has rarely been seen, and much of this surge was accomplished under collective – not family – farming between 1977 and 1982. Even after its abolition, the influence of the collective continued to be felt. For without the irrigation projects brought to a successful completion during the 1970s, the continuing growth of production that occurred during the 1980s and 1990s would simply not have been possible.

Notes

1. Most collectives were established during 1955–6. However, the form and organization of collectives were not regularized until the early 1960s. It therefore makes sense to associate collective farming with the late Maoist era.
2. For discussions of general agricultural policy issues in China, see Brown (1995), Findlay and Watson (1999), Huang *et al.* (1999), Carter and Rozelle (2001), OECD (2001) and Dong *et al.* (2006). For useful summaries and analyses of the Maoist era, see Walker (1984), Perkins and Yusuf (1984), Nolan (1988) and Ash (2006). For pre-1949 agriculture, see Perkins (1969).
3. The Chinese definition of grain includes soybeans and potatoes. Four kilograms of potatoes were assumed equal to 1 kg of other grain types before 1964; thereafter, the conversion ratio used has been 5 to 1. Chinese grain production data are almost always given in terms of unhusked grain (*yuanliang*), but data on grain commerce and procurements are usually in terms of trade or husked grain (*maoyiliang*).
4. One of Mao's clearest statements on comparative advantage and the dangers inherent in reliance on trade is to be found in his 'Reading Notes on the Soviet Text *Political Economy*': 'Above all, agriculture must be done well as far as possible. Reliance on other countries or provinces for food is most dangerous' (Mao 1962, section 60).
5. The terminology used in the Chinese context is confusing. However, the word 'collective' or the phrase 'collective farming' is typically used to refer to advanced or high-stage agricultural producer cooperatives between 1956 and 1958, to communes between 1958 and 1963 and to encompass the entire three-tier system of communes (more precisely, people's communes), production brigades and production teams set up after 1963. For a description of the structure and operation of collectives, see Donnithorne (1967: chs. 2 and 3).
6. In many cases (though not all), a production brigade was a natural village and teams were hamlets or village districts.
7. That is, the value of each work point was determined by dividing the total value of production team output by the total number of work points awarded to team members. Income therefore depended upon the number of work points earned (which was directly under a worker's control) and the value of each work point (which depended upon the efforts of the entire unit of account).
8. Fine overviews of many of the issues are provided in Tsou *et al.* (1979), Potter and Potter (1990: chs. 5–7), and Unger (2002: ch. 4). For Dazhai, see Tsou *et al.* (1979) and Qin (1995). The case for collective farming is well put in Hinton (1983, 1990, 2006) and Liu (1991a, 1991b, 1994).
9. We do well, however, to remember that the 'freedom' enjoyed by workers under capitalism is a very special sort of freedom. They have the freedom to choose which capitalist to work for, but not the freedom to choose whether to work or not. Moreover, workers under capitalism are still coerced into producing surplus value. The freedom of workers in a capitalist system is notional rather than real because they lack capital, and it is very far from clear that giving them the right to migrate expands their freedom very much. Accordingly, the frequently heard charge against collective farming that it constrained migration is hardly a compelling sort of critique.

10 For the literature putting the case against the Maoist collective, see Selden (1988), Nolan (1988) Hua *et al.* (1993), Friedman *et al.* (1991) and Putterman (1990, 1993).
11 For Marxist thinking on the collective, see Bottomore (1991). Marx's own writings are more ambivalent than Lenin's. In his famous 'Letter to Vera Zasulich' (1881), it is evident that Marx believed that the traditional Russia commune (obshchina) could in principle develop into a collective farm; in other words, the introduction of capitalism into the Chinese countryside was by no means an historical necessity: 'in Russia, thanks to a unique combination of circumstances, the rural commune, still established on a nationwide scale, may gradually detach itself from its primitive features and develop directly as an element of collective production on a nationwide scale. ... Theoretically speaking, then, the Russian "rural commune" can preserve itself by developing its basis, the common ownership of land, and by eliminating the principle of private property which it also implies; it can become a *direct point of departure* [original emphasis] for the economic system towards which modern society tends; it can turn over a new leaf without beginning by committing suicide; it can gain possession of the fruits with which capitalist production has enriched mankind, without passing through the capitalist regime, a regime which, considered solely from the point of view of its possible duration hardly counts in the life of society' (Marx 1881).
12 Griffin *et al.* (2002) put forward a variation on this suggesting that large farms use less labour because of their monopsony power in the labour market. The existence of such power entices them to use less labour in order to hold down wages and boost profitability.
13 For studies sympathetic towards Chinese collective farming, see Bramall (1995, 2000a, 2004), Hinton (1983, 1990, 2006), Liu (1991a, 1994) and Qin (1995).
14 For useful discussions of the problems with the inverse relationship, see the special issue of the *Journal of Agrarian Change* (January and April 2004) and Federico (2005: ch. 7).
15 It should be noted here that labour productivity grew very slowly under collective farming (Tang 1984; Wen 1993); the annual rate of growth of GVA per agricultural worker (1980 prices) averaged about 0.7 per cent per annum between 1955 and 1981. compared with a rate of nearly 5 per cent between 1981 and 2005. This differential reflects the lagged impact of the introduction of new seed varieties and the completion of irrigation projects in the 1970s, and the rapid growth of other inputs post-1978 (which boosted the growth rate of a partial measure like labour productivity without necessarily producing big increases in total factor productivity).
16 Some questions have been raised about the quality of these irrigation schemes, especially those built during the Great Leap Forward, and there is some evidence of dams collapsing during the 1970s. One example widely quoted is the collapse of the Banqiao and Shimantan dams in Henan in 1975, which may have killed as many as 230,000 people (Yi 1998). However, these particular dams were constructed in the 1950s, and their collapse was due more to a decision to allow the size of the reservoirs they controlled to increase to a point far beyond the design capacity than to any intrinsic flaw. The very fact the most of the irrigation systems established in the late Maoist era have not been dismantled since 1978 is perhaps the clearest indicator of their continuing effectiveness.
17 It does not seem to matter, however, whether we use 1952, 1957, 1970 or 1980 relative prices to value agriculture; the growth rate is little different. In other words, the percentage adjustment in grain prices at various points in the Maoist era was very similar in magnitude to the adjustment in animal product, forestry and other prices. The choice of prices does affect overall GDP growth because earlier relative price sets give a higher weight to industry which was the faster growing sector, but none of this is relevant in an appraisal of agricultural performance.
18 A good discussion is provided in Endicott (1988: 142–3).
19 Collective sidelines were included in the pre-1981 accounts but not private sidelines.

258 *Chinese Economic Development*

20 In some parts of China it was by no means uncommon for private plots to account for 10 per cent of arable area (Gao 1999: 54 and 63–4). Gao's account suggests that the effect of private production was to double household income in the 1970s.
21 In terms of value-added, China's land productivity was (US) $2181 per hectare in 1998 (at 1989–91 prices), well ahead of the USA ($853) and India ($727). Japan did better ($3086), but it is a small-scale producer by comparison; Japanese arable area in the late 1990s was 4.5 million hectares, far below the figures for France (18 million), Canada (46 million), India (162 million) and the USA (177 million). Although these international comparisons of land productivity in value terms are inevitably affected by the exchange rate used, there is no doubt that Chinese land productivity was relatively high, not just in terms of grain yields but across a wide range of crops (OECD 2001: 74).
22 Yields and output in agriculture did grow significantly in the period between 1800 and 1850 according to Allen's analysis, but it was the release of labour that was the revolutionary feature of English agriculture.
23 However, it should not be inferred that there was literally surplus labour in agriculture in the late 1970s, at least if by 'surplus' we mean a body of labour that could readily be moved out of agriculture and into industry without loss of agricultural production. Much of China's labour surplus at the end of the Maoist era was only notional. In part, the problem was structural: the entire labour force was needed during the peak harvest period. More importantly, the incentive system (by which I mean the *combination* of the collective system of work-point payments and the intersectoral terms of trade) was such that the removal of 'surplus' workers from agriculture would not have resulted in those workers left behind increasing their productivity; their effort allocation would probably have remained the same. Only after the incentive system was changed in the late 1970s and early 1980s by decollectivization and agricultural price rises does it make sense to talk of surplus labour (Bramall 2000: 167–8). In the late 1970s, labour could be redeployed to rural industry, but only provided that it was still available for agriculture during the key harvest months.
24 Chinese agriculture may actually have been far more successful in terms of labour productivity than these data suggest. Rawski and Mead (1998) argue that the official data overestimated the farm labour force by as much as 100 million in the early 1990s, implying that a very substantial release of labour has already occurred. Nevertheless, this does not overturn the general point that Chinese labour productivity remains low by world standards.
25 For a useful compilation of TFP studies on Chinese agriculture, see Kalirajan and Wu (1999: 29–51), Putterman and Chiacu (1994) and Maddison (1998). Carter (1999) offers both an excellent survey and a judicious critique of the literature which attributes the bulk of growth to decollectivization. He rightly recognizes the key role played by technical progress, and the way in which an inadequate treatment of weather has led to biased results.
26 Rozelle and Huang (2006: 50) suggest that China's TFP growth rate was around 2 per cent per annum between the mid-1980s and the mid-1990s. This is very close to Fan and Zhang (2006: 146–7) figure of 2.2 per cent growth between 1985 and 1996.
27 Some studies point towards an underestimation of TFP growth after 1978. Rawski and Mead's (1998) downwards revisions to the labour force data would imply much faster TFP growth.
28 For a discussion of agricultural issues and problems relating to the distribution of income in the mid-1950s, see the general accounts offered by Luo (1985), Selden (1988), Shue (1980) and Schran (1969), as well as the more detailed local studies by Endicott (1988), Crook and Crook (1966), Hinton (1983) and Friedman *et al.* (1991).
29 For excellent discussions of the operation of the late Maoist collective, see Chan *et al.* (1984), Endicott (1988), Potter and Potter (1990) and Gao (1999).

30 Labour power is crucial in an agrarian economy, but it was less important in driving inequality on collective than on private farms. In Sichuan's still collectivized economy in 1978, for example, labour-rich households enjoyed a per capita income which was 33 per cent higher than in labour-poor households. By 1984, however, the differential had gone up to 47 per cent as collective mechanisms for redistribution fell into abeyance (Nongcun xiaozu 1986: 3).

31 Five-guarantee households typically accounted for a very small proportion of the households in any production team. In most cases, outright poverty was temporary and could be dealt with by loans. The 1956 National Programme set out the objective in the following terms: 'Agricultural producers' cooperatives should make suitable arrangements in production and livelihood for those members who are short of labor power, widows, widowers, orphans and childless people who have no one to depend upon for their livelihood, and disabled veterans, in order that they be guaranteed food, clothing, fuel, education (for their children and young people), and burial, and enable them to have something to depend on in birth, growing up, death, and burial' (cited in Tsou *et al.* 179: 160).

32 An excellent study of changing patterns of intra-village inequality between the 1930s and the 1970s is that of Blecher (1976). See also Griffin and Saith (1982: 184).

33 For some of these studies, see Whyte (1975), Blecher (1976), Tsou *et al.* (1979), Vermeer (1982), Griffin and Saith (1982) and Griffin (1984).

34 Griffin (1984: 51–9) has long argued that private sector income is equalizing; this neopopulist/Chayanovian view is restated in Griffin *et al.* (2002). There is some evidence to support this in Griffin's own studies but also in the national data. The 1980 survey of peasant income shows that effect of including sideline income was to reduce the ratio of per capita income between top (earning over 500 *yuan*) and bottom (earning less than 60 *yuan*) from 14.5 to 1 to a little under 10 to 1 (SSB 2000b: 27–8). However, this probably reflects spatial factors. Sidelines were liberalized much earlier in poor provinces and in poor countries than in richer parts of China and hence made more of a contribution to total income in poor areas. Thus 1980 is an unrepresentative year because the pace of reform was much faster in poor areas than rich ones. More generally, it is unlikely that sideline income was so redistributive *within* villages because the very factors that reduced income from collective sources for poor households – low skills and low labour productivity – would also have restricted income from sidelines. For critiques of Griffin, see Vermeer (1982) and Bramall (2004).

35 Note that this criticism relates to the direct effects of size on productivity. It is widely acknowledged that there are economies of scale in agricultural marketing and agro-processing.

36 Khan (2004: 89–91) provides a lucid summary of these key issues.

37 This is especially clear at the margin. A peasant might work a whole day and earn (say) seven work points but actually do no work at all. S/he would be much better off, but there would be no increase in total output.

38 On a family farm, the problem does not arise to the same extent because there is a much more direct link between the work done by household members and the output (income) of the household. The household is in effect a very small collective.

39 This is of course a standard principal–agent problem. The challenge for the principal, faced with limited information, is to devise an incentive and monitoring system which ensures a high level of productivity.

40 For useful discussions of these issues in Chinese agriculture before and after 1949, see Chinn (1980), Nolan (1988: ch. 2), Huang (1985), Liu (1991a, 1991b, 1994) and Kung (1994).

41 The high rate of debt repayment achieved by the Grameen Bank in Bangladesh reflects the fact that lending is to groups of women. As the entire group risks denial of loans

260 *Chinese Economic Development*

if one member defaults, peer pressure acts as an extremely powerful deterrent against default.
42 Gao Mobo (1999: 62) concluded of its operation: 'One can imagine how important the annual evaluation of base points was for the villagers. My experience was that the system worked quite well and did more or less reflect the true contribution each member made to the team, gender inequality aside.' Elsewhere, however, it worked less well; in the account offered in Siu (1989: 229–32), 'Women cried and men fought' even when the appraisal was made much more frequently than once per year.
43 A measure of China's problem is that its arable area in 1998 was 124 million hectares, less than in both India (162 million) and the USA (177 million) – which has less than a quarter of China's population (OECD 2001: 74).
44 As the figure shows, much of the rise occurred in the early Maoist era. However, without the mobilization of labour and expansion of irrigated area that took place after 1963, it is doubtful whether it would have been sustained at over 140 million hectares.
45 The best discussion of the issues is that offered by Sheng (1993). It is worth noting that estimation of the pattern of intersectoral resource is fraught with difficulties, both conceptual (how should sectors be defined? What prices should be used to value output?) and empirical (should transfers be measured using real or financial flows? To what extent do the available data fully capture resource flows?).
46 The average pretax rate of profit in the state sector was no less than 35 per cent in 1978 (GYWSN 2000: 53–4).
47 And if the 6 *yuan* figure for rice sounds impressive, we do well to remember that it rose to 25 *yuan* following the 1979 increase in farm prices. See Bramall (2000: 313–23) for a full discussion.
48 A study by Lin and Wen (1995) tends to confirm this conclusion by arguing that the promotion of regional self-sufficiency in grain production, a policy which certainly was pursued during the Maoist era, had only a small (negative) effect on agricultural productivity.
49 Chinese data on forested area are not very reliable for the early 1950s, but it is by no means impossible that there was an increase during the Maoist era. Ross (1988: 34–5) suggests that forested area may have increased from around 94 million hectares in 1949 to 122 million hectares by the mid-1970s.
50 Perhaps the best summary of China's development of the Green Revolution package is that offered by Stone (1988a,b).
51 The process of decollectivization is discussed in more detail in Chapter 10.
52 This 24 per cent figure is from Su (1982: 6). Chung's (2000: 64) figure is much lower at only 14 per cent.
53 Cuts in procurement quotas in the late 1970s also left collectives with a much greater share of the surplus, which was thus available either for self-consumption or for sale on the re-emerging private markets (Bramall 1995); see also Carter (1999).

8 The Third Front and rural industrialization

Rural industrialization was the third key element in the late Maoist development strategy alongside the expansion of rural education and collective farming. The underlying conception here is summarized in the slogan 'walking on two legs'. The People's Republic inherited a significant industrial base, but most of these industries were located in the urban centres of Manchuria or the great urban centre of Shanghai. The aim of the rural industrialization strategy was to redress the spatial balance, and in so doing serve the needs of defence (by creating a less vulnerable industrial base) and of agriculture by expanding the production of agricultural inputs such as tractors and chemical fertilizer. By exploiting local resources which might otherwise be neglected, and by holding down transport costs, it was hoped that rural industry would serve to complement the urban industrial sector.

One component of the rural industrialization strategy was the development of Third Front industries, in western China and in the mountainous hinterland of China's eastern provinces. Often thought of as an urban industrialization programme, this was nothing of the kind. To be sure, some Third Front investment was directed towards existing urban centres, but the bulk went into creating new industrial centres on green-field sites such as Panzhihua in Sichuan and Liupanshui in Guizhou. In essentials, therefore, the Third Front was a programme of defence industrialization in rural areas. Running alongside it during the 1960s and 1970s was a more general programme of rural industrialization in which small-scale enterprises were created and managed by China's counties and by its collectives. Commune- and brigade-level industry is more famous, but the county-run industries were more significant in terms of their overall level of production and employment.

Most scholars agree that China expanded its industrial capacity before 1978.[1] However, they claim, the Maoist industrialization programme was overly ambitious, and led to the creation of an industrial sector that was chronically inefficient and excessively geared towards satisfying the needs of other industries, rather than those of consumers.[2] The legacies are felt even now, so much so that contemporary China is an example of an economy which is overindustrialized. China's bloated industrial sector is woefully inefficient, absorbing vast quantities of capital and skilled labour to little effect. As a result, the service sector is not large enough to meet either the demands of the population or to provide the jobs necessary for China's growing workforce in an age in which manufacturing production is increasingly capital-intensive. What was needed during the 1960s – and is needed still – was the privatization of state-owned industrial assets, and the creation of fully functioning market institutions and property rights

I shall argue that this type of interpretation is misconceived. By adopting a very narrow definition of efficiency (one that focuses on short-run productivity), it ignores the central point that China moved far during the late Maoist period towards creating an efficient industrial sector – in the (macroeconomic) sense of an industrial sector capable of serving the needs of China's development. Those needs were military security and the expansion of per capita GDP if at all possible, not some arbitrary productivity target. Moreover, we should recognize late Maoist industrialization for what it was: a programme of learning-by-doing. The industrial strategy was not pretty and it involved a great deal of short-run resource misallocation. In the process, however, the Chinese workforce acquired a range of skills, skills which provided the foundation for the industrial expansion of the 1980s and beyond.

The late Maoist industrialization strategy

We saw in Chapter 3 that defence considerations played a key role in influencing the industrialization strategy adopted during the First Five Year Plan; the most obvious indicator was the expansion of heavy industrial production in the 1950s. These considerations continued to influence industrial policy throughout the late Maoist era. Just as the First Five Year Plan had emphasized the development of industry in the Chinese interior, so too did late Maoism. The only real differences were that the focus of defence industrialization moved from central to western China, and that the scale of the response was much greater, which was perhaps inevitable given that China was isolated in the 1960s (whereas in the 1950s it at least enjoyed the support of the Soviet Union). Thus the centrepiece of late Maoist industrialization was the programme of Third Front construction in the western provinces and in the mountainous interior of the coastal and central provinces.

Yet late Maoist industrialization was different in character from that of the early Maoist period in one key respect: the greater focus it accorded to rural industrialization. In part this is illustrated by the spatial pattern of Third Front investment; much of it went into developing green-field sites, rather than merely expanding industry in existing urban conurbations. More generally, however, rural industry was also seen as more than just a solution to the problem of defence. It was also regarded also as a solution to the problem of underdevelopment in the Chinese countryside. For if the living standards of the peasantry were to be increased, more would be needed than just collective farming. Rural industrialization would be needed as well.[3]

Rural industrialization

Mao's conception of industrialization in the mid-1950s deviated little from the Soviet orthodoxy. He had come to the conclusion by the summer of 1955 that the acceleration of development in the countryside required collectivization.

However, there is little in his speeches and writings to suggest that he saw rural industry as a key part of that process. Modern industrial inputs would be needed for rural modernization. However, these could be best supplied from industries located in urban centres.

In some ways, in fact, Mao's approach became more conventional in 1956. 'On the Ten Great Relationships' – the key speech of that year – signalled a shift away from industrialization in the interior and placed renewed emphasis on the modernization of industry in China's existing urban centres along the coast, namely Shanghai and Manchuria (as discussed in Chapter 4). Liu Shaoqi had made precisely the same argument at the Eighth Party Congress in September 1956 (Liu 1956):

> We must make full use of the favourable conditions existing in the coastal provinces, develop the industries there in a suitable way and use them to support the development of industries in the interior, and so accelerate the industrialization of the country. Liaoning, Shanghai, Tientsin and other industrial areas have made an outstanding contribution in this respect in the period of the First Five-Year Plan. In the second five-year period, in addition to making maximum use of the industrial bases in Northeast and East China, we must also appropriately bring the facilities of Hopei, Shantung and South China into full play in developing industry.

Mao's major speech of 1957, 'On the Correct Handling of Contradictions among the People', did little more than reiterate that point. To be sure, Mao argued, it was necessary to develop small and medium-sized enterprises but the industry inherited from the Republican era needed to be exploited to the full – and that in effect meant giving emphasis to urban industry (Mao 1957). By the end of 1957, however, Mao's views appear to have changed. Instead of placing such emphasis on urban industrial development, the Great Leap Forward would be led by rural industry. This was the strategy of 'walking on two legs'; rural industrialization would take place at the same time as urban industrialization, instead of in sequence. The Leap was thus about balanced development in the sense that it emphasized both rural and urban industrialization. Oddly enough, however, the clearest statement of the need for rural industry was given by Liu Shaoqi in May 1958 (Selden 1979: 394):

> In the period of the first five-year plan, we paid attention first of all to the development of industries run by the central government, to giant enterprises; this was absolutely necessary. But not enough attention was paid to the development of local industries and small and medium-size industries; this was a shortcoming. In the past two years or more, the Central Committee has repeatedly pointed out that this shortcoming must be rectified. ... This will inevitably result in: (1) quickening the pace of the nation's industrialization; (2) quickening the pace of mechanization of agriculture; and (3) quickening the speed at which differences between city and countryside are reduced.[4]

The logic behind this approach is easily set out. Rural industrialization would make use of labour which would otherwise be under- or unemployed. The very seasonality of agricultural work meant that it was not possible to transfer agricultural labour from the rural to the urban sector. The labour had to be available in the countryside to collect the harvest. But rural industry offered a way of squaring the circle; it could be shut down during the key harvest months, and the workforce employed to collect the harvest. Rural industry was also advantageous because it offered a means by which transport costs could be reduced. Given too that long-distance trade was vulnerable to attack, the development of rural industry also made military sense. Moreover, the development of rural industry offered a means by which the enthusiasm of the peasantry could be mobilized. For Mao, the failure to make the most of peasant talent was one of Stalin's greatest failures and he did not want China to repeat it.

The first concrete manifestation of the shifting Maoist vision was the launch of the Great Leap Forward in 1958. The CCP's Chengdu plenum in March 1958 gave a green light to the development of rural industry, and in particular to a remarkably ambitious programme to develop iron and steel production. Even the revised data on industrial production published at the end of the 1980s show steel production increasing from 4.5 million tonnes in 1956 to 18.7 million tonnes in 1960 (SSB 1990a: 18). The targets were even more ambitious; that for 1960 was an astounding 50 million tonnes, rising to 80–100 million tonnes by 1962 (Chan 2001: 76).

In retrospect, the industrialization attempted during the Leap was too ambitious and too narrow in its focus. It was too ambitious because the rural workforce lacked the skills necessary for iron and steel production, and because the targets set were implausibly high. As a result, the targets were not met, and the quality of much of the iron and steel produced was extremely low. It was too narrow in its scope because an exclusive focus on iron and steel made little sense; the need for other inputs – chemical fertilizer and cement in particular – was equally desperate. Worse, the industrialization programme played a key role in causing the devastating famine of the early 1960s by diverting labour away from farming and into industry. The programme did yield benefits in terms of learning-by-doing, and in some parts of northern China – where coal supplies were ample and where there was a tradition of iron- and steel-making – the Leap was even relatively successful in promoting industrial development (Wagner 1995). On the whole, however, the programme was a failure, in the short term at least. China would have done better to have focused on the expansion of traditional industries such as furniture, paper-making and food processing.

Nevertheless, the collapse of the Leap proved to be only a temporary setback. Mao's determination to promote rural industrialization remained intact, and once the famine was over, the process of industrialization began anew. The continuities in industrial policy between the Leap and the late 1960s are clear. The industrial development strategy continued to emphasize the importance of state ownership: there was no move towards privatization in the late Maoist era. Furthermore, the expansion of large urban-based industrial companies – such as the Anshan steel plant and the Daqing oilfield – continued and absorbed a large fraction of China's skilled labour. More importantly, the attention given to rural industry during the Leap continued: there was no going back to the urban-focused strategy of the 1950s. To be sure, production was far more diversified than the iron and steel focus of the Leap, and there was a clear recognition of the dangers inherent in promoting rural industry at the expense of agriculture: in both senses, lessons from the Leap had been learned. But rural industrialization remained a key component of the late Maoist strategy.

The Third Front

The main discontinuity in industrial policy between the late Maoist era and the Great Leap Forward was in terms of the emphasis placed on defence industrialization in the former. In the late 1950s, the threat to China was seen to be less serious and therefore defence considerations were less important. As Mao (1956) said in the 'Ten Great Relationships':

> Not so long ago, there was still fighting in Korea and the international situation was quite tense; this could not but affect our attitude towards coastal industry. Now, it seems unlikely that there will be a new war of aggression against China or another world war in the near future and there will probably be a period of peace for a decade or more. It would therefore be wrong if we still fail to make full use of the plant capacity and technical forces of coastal industry.

By 1964, however, Mao's optimism had evaporated. As a result of China's break with the Soviet Union and the growing American military presence in Vietnam, China was strategically isolated and the threat of war was very real. To compound the problem, Chinese industry was located predominantly in the coastal or frontline (*qianxian*) provinces and in Manchuria. It was therefore highly vulnerable to attack by US aircraft based in South Korea, Taiwan and Japan, and to a Soviet attack into Manchuria. The very fact that the Leap had seen rapid industrial development in the coastal provinces only made the situation worse. For Mao, China needed to meet the threat by developing a large and secure industrial base, as his speech to the Politburo on 6 June 1964 concerning the Third Five Year Plan (1966–70) made clear:[5]

> As long as imperialism prevails, there is always the threat of war. We must therefore establish a strategic rear. This by no means excludes the coastal areas. These must also be well organised, so that they can play a part in aiding the construction of new bases. ... We have two fists and one bottom. Agriculture and national defence are our two fists. But if we want to make our fists strong, the bottom must sit securely. The bottom is our basic industry. (Mao 1964: 132)

The concrete result of these concerns was the Third Front programme of defence industrialization which began in 1964 and continued until the end of the 1970s.

The significance of the Front is evident in part from the defence budget. Defence spending as a percentage of central government spending declined from over 40 per cent in the early 1950s to less than 10 per cent in 1960. By 1964, however, it was back to around 20 per cent, and in the late 1960s it exceeded 25 per cent. Even by the time of Mao's death, and in the wake of improved relations with the USA, the defence share was still around 15 per cent.[6]

In purely economic terms, the Front was far more important than the Cultural Revolution, not least because of the investment resources poured into it by central government.[7] Much Third Front investment went into what was called the large Third Front (*da sanxian*) region in western China, and the provinces of Sichuan, Gansu, Guizhou and Yunnan in particular. There were clear echoes here of the Nationalist strategy adopted during the Second World War, when Sichuan was developed as an industrial base after the loss of Shanghai and Manchuria to the Japanese. However, the spatial scope of the programme continued to expand over time. During 1969–76, the Third Front extended into the mountainous western prefectures of Hunan and Hubei provinces. Even before then, all provinces were enjoined to develop their own Third Front programmes; Shaoguan thus became Guangdong's little Third Front region, and Shanghai set up Third Front projects in Anhui province.

The Third Front exerted an overwhelming influence on the Chinese economy in the late 1960s and during the early 1970s. This was mainly because of the Front's sheer scale. This cannot be easily quantified because of the difficulties involved in distinguishing precisely between Front and non-Front investment, and because of the exclusion of some categories of defence spending. However, there is no doubt that the development of many of the western provinces – but especially Sichuan and Gansu in the mid-1960s and Hubei and Hunan in the early 1970s – was massively affected; in all of these provinces, investment surged at the height of the Front.

The Front led to a further reconfiguration of China's industrial geography. The pre-1949 period had seen the establishment of modern industry in eastern China, predominantly in the port cities of Shanghai and Tianjin, and in Manchuria; this was the First Front. The First Five Year Plan, as noted above, focused much more on the development of industry in Second Front areas, that is in central China. The Third Front was the culmination of this historical process in that it shifted the focus to the western provinces, and to Sichuan and Gansu in particular.

In that the Front expanded industrial production in some of China's cities it was a strategy of urban development. But the Front was pre-eminently a programme of rural industrialization (Bramall 2007: 12–19). Perhaps the best illustration of this was the construction of new cities in the Chinese countryside, such as the steel centre at Jiuquan (Gansu), the coal centre at Liupanshui in Guizhou, Shiyan in Hubei (the site for the Second Automobile plant, which focused on lorry production) and most famously the steel city of Panzhihua built astride the Jinsha river in south-western Sichuan. And as part of the programme, new railways were constructed across the countryside of western China, notably the line linking Chengdu and Kunming via Panzhihua.

The impact of the Front is reflected to some extent in the provincial growth rates. The median industrial growth rate (at current prices) between 1964 and 1978 for China's provinces was 9.3 per cent. However, in the two provinces singled out for Third Front investment – Sichuan and Gansu – the growth rates were 16.5 and 12.5 per cent respectively (SSB 2005a). But the province is too large an aggregate of analysis to allow us to identify properly the impact of the Third Front; even in Sichuan and Gansu, many counties were largely untouched by the programme. It is therefore more useful to look at specific Third Front centres and to contrast their growth rate with other industrial centres (Table 8.1).

It is evident from the data in Table 8.1 that some areas outside the Third Front did well. Wuxi, where industrial output increased more than fourfold between 1965 and 1978, is a good example. Even in Shanghai, where rapid growth was difficult to achieve because the base level of industrial output was so high, nearly tripled its industrial output. But the growth rate in a typical Third Front centre was much faster. In Shaoguan, the centre of Guangdong's little Third Front programme, output rose nearly sixfold. In Liupanshui (Guizhou), an eightfold increase was recorded. Tianshui in Gansu achieved a thirteenfold rise.

Yet the growth of cities such as Tianshui was dwarfed in significance by the growth of the new steel-producing city of Panzhihua, which emerged from the

Table 8.1 Growth of industrial output in Third Front centres, 1965–1978

	GVIO per capita in 1965 (current yuan)	GVIO index in 1978 (comparable prices; 1965 = 100)
Front centres		
Panzhihua	26	11,477
Liupanshui	17	781
Xiangfan	35	890
Tianshui	21	1,346
Shaoguan	96	559
Chongqing	220	240
Baoji	148	503
Deyang	61	571
Other cities		
Shanghai	2,110	287
Shenyang	1,098	235
Guangzhou	698	291
Nantong	137	402
Wuxi	355	465
National	193	367

Source: Bramall (2007: 17).

Note
Data refer to the entire jurisdiction, i.e. city proper plus counties under the jurisdiction of the city. The GVIO figures probably exclude brigade industry and below in most cases, but the sources are unclear on this. Note that the GVIO data for the municipalities in which brigade industry grew most quickly – Nantong and Wuxi – do include all types of industrial production. In the other jurisdictions, brigade-level industry was far less important that SOEs and COEs owned at the county level and above, and therefore the comparison between Third Front and other regions is a fair one.

mountain fastness of south-western Sichuan.[8] This area was little more than a green-field site in the early 1960s, at the confluence of the Jinsha and Yalong rivers in Sichuan. There, the two counties of Yanbian and Huili together had a population of around 270,000 in 1952, and agriculture made up around 84 per cent of GDP; even in 1962 agriculture still accounted 64 per cent of the total. However, the site was rich in minerals, which included coal, iron ore, vanadium (60 per cent of national total) and titanium (93 per cent of national total). And Mao was obsessed by the idea of developing it, as his talk on the Third Five Year Plan in June 1964 reveals:

> Unless the Panzhihua steel plant is fully developed, I cannot go to sleep at night. If there is no Panzhihua steel plant, I will have to ride on a donkey to get to meetings. If we do not have enough money, use the royalty payments on my writings. (cited in Li X. Q. 2006: 178)

The decision to exploit these reserves by developing the iron and steel complex of Panzhihua and to create the city of Dukou in 1965 put an end to the dominance of agriculture in the area for once and for all. After 1965, the share of industry soared, and with it GDP. By 1978, real GDP was 4.6 times greater than it had been in 1965 and Panzhihua's population had more than doubled; by 2000, real GDP was nineteen times larger than it had been in 1965. However, the rapidity of industrialization is more evident from the share of industry in GDP, which rose from its 1962 figure of 6 per cent to no less than 76 per cent (Figure 8.1).[9] This was industrialization on an unprecedented scale, and in one of the poorest parts of China.

Yet Panzhihua encapsulates all that was good and bad about the Third Front. On the one hand, it demonstrates the effectiveness of the programme in raising industrial production. As Shapiro (2001: 157–8) says:

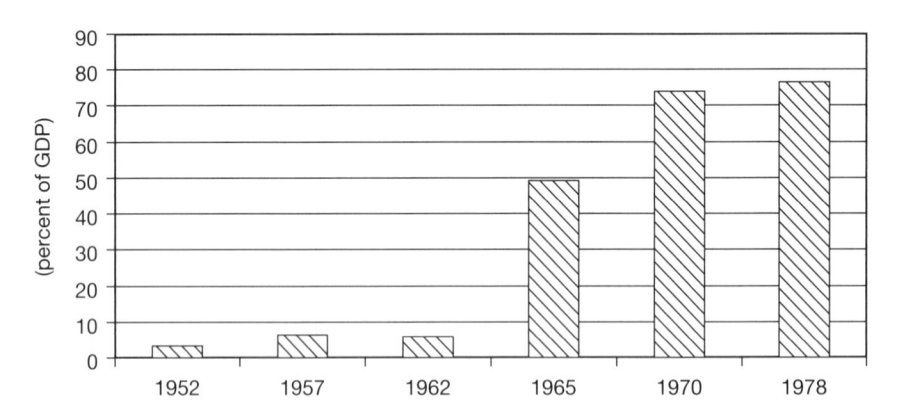

Figure 8.1 The share of the secondary sector in GDP at Panzhihua, 1952–1978 (Source: Panzhihua tongjiju (2001: 58).)

Note: The share is calculated at current prices. By way of comparison, the national share of the secondary sector in GDP in 1978 was 48 per cent.

[S]ome may see Panzhihua as one of the few Third Front success stories in that it did indeed give China access to a wealth of mineral resources, while the Chengdu–Kunming railroad associated with the project opened up a great section of the country.

However, the development of industry at Panzhihua was an environmental disaster (Shapiro 2001). Moreover, the Panzhihua complex was not very efficient, even by the close of the 1970s (Bramall 2007: 44). The value of output per worker there was little different from that of other Chinese steel plants in the early 1980s. However, Pangang (Panzhihua steel) was far less efficient than either the new plant steel plant constructed at Baoshan on the outskirts of Shanghai in the 1980s, or world leaders such as POSCO and Nippon Steel, even in the 1990s (Nolan 2001: 641). Panzhihua undoubtedly is an example of learning-by-doing, but there is no question that the learning process was a slow one. The programme of late Maoist industrialization certainly did leave in its wake a range of legacies, but the Third Front – precisely because of its defence orientation – was one of its least effective elements. Too much of the industry created was simply located in the wrong places to further the cause of industrialization in the 1980s and 1990s.

The development of county, commune and brigade industries

Equally important in the rural industrialization strategy of the 1960s and 1970s was the development of small-scale industries owned by Chinese counties, communes and brigades. This expansion programme had of course been at the heart of the Great Leap Forward but rural industrialization had practically come to a halt in the early 1960s. This standstill was an inevitable consequence of the Great Famine, which was widely recognized to have been caused by the diversion of labour from farming to iron and steel production. The CCP leadership had no desire to see a repetition of those horrors, and so insisted that the rural labour force focused on farm production. This policy was made effective by imposing severe restrictions on counties, communes and production brigades, most notably by limiting access to the rural bank loans needed to start up new companies.

However, and the debacle of the Leap notwithstanding, Mao had not given up on the desirability of rural industrialization. His own evolving views on the desirability of rural industrial developments were set out in his letter of 7 May 1966 to Lin Biao:

> The communes do their main agricultural work (including forestry, fishing, animal husbandry and subsidiary trades), but they must also learn military affairs, politics and culture. When circumstances allow, they should collectively set up small-scale factories and take part in criticizing the capitalist class. (Mao 1966).

This steer from above, and extent of the recovery of the agricultural sector from the nadir of 1959–61, helped to restart rural industrialization. As importantly, it was increasingly apparent to local cadres that rural industry offered a way out of the involutionary *cul-de-sac*, because productivity in the industrial sector was much higher than in farming.[10] Once, therefore, the famine was over, rural cadres were keen to redeploy labour from low-productivity agriculture to higher-productivity industry. In addition, there was growing recognition that rural industrial growth was essential for the modernization of the farm sector; urban industry was simply incapable of supplying the chemical fertilizers and other inputs required (Riskin 1971, 1978 and 1987; Bramall 2007). The whole process was given further momentum by the financial decentralization of the early 1970s, which gave local government in the Chinese countryside the resources needed to finance industrialization.

The first step in the rural industrialization process was the expansion of county-owned SOEs after 1968. In the early 1970s, the focus shifted to commune and brigade industries, especially after the North China Agricultural Conference of 1970 and the National Conference on Rural Mechanization of September 1971. Five particular areas were selected ('the five small industries'): cement, chemical fertilizer, iron and steel, machinery and power. Although this did little to raise living standards in the short run, it helped to provide the inputs necessary for the expansion of irrigation networks, the construction of basic infrastructure (roads and housing) and to begin farm mechanization.

As Figure 8.2 shows, the strategy bore fruit. Up until 1965, rural industry had languished as efforts in the countryside focused on the revival of farm production. In 1963, for example, 82.4 per cent of the total workforce were engaged in agriculture, some 1.2 percentage points higher than it had been in 1957; this shows that the process of rural industrialization stalled during in the early 1960s.[11] Thereafter, however, rural industrial growth was rapid. It averaged 24 per cent per year in the commune sector and 11 per cent for brigade industry. This overall growth rate (15 per cent per year) was significantly higher than the overall rate of industrial growth of 11 per cent. Even though the commune and brigade sector began its growth from a very low base, there is clear evidence here of the Maoist commitment to rural industrial development. As a result of this various efforts, an extensive rural industrial sector had been created across the Chinese countryside. By 1978, perhaps 40 million workers were employed in rural industrial enterprises, about half the total industrial workforce.[12]

An evaluation of late Maoist industrialization

It is hard to assess properly the utility of China's late Maoist industrialization strategy because it was never called upon to meet the defence imperatives which had led to its creation. But if we confine our assessment to the economics of the strategy, four questions needed to be answered. Was late Maoist rural industry efficient in terms of productivity? Was it efficient in the wider macroeconomic sense of being able to satisfy China's demand for manufactures? Did it provide an adequate foundation for continued growth after 1978? And did rural industrial expansion in the 1960s and 1970s lead to a narrowing of spatial inequality?

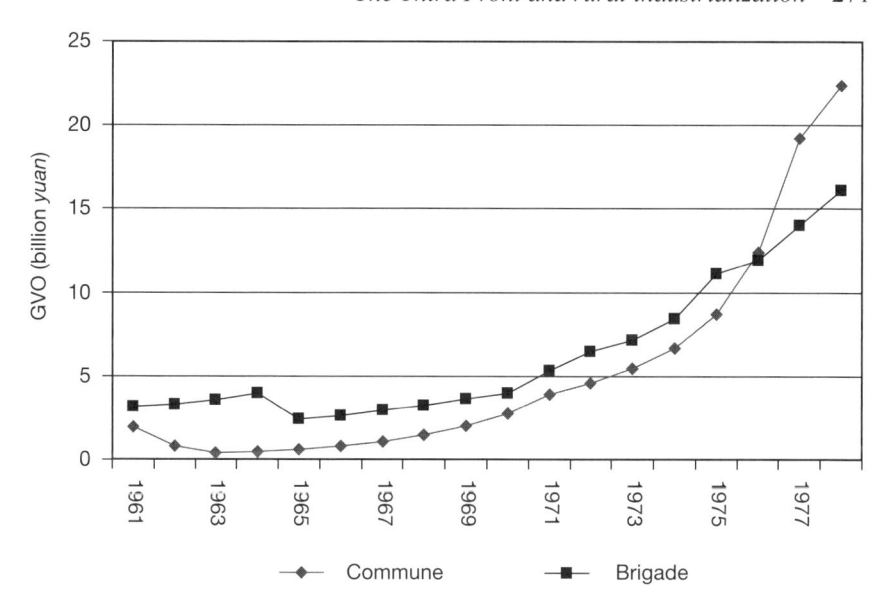

Figure 8.2 Growth of commune and brigade industrial output, 1962–1978 (Source: He (2004: 24, 28, 31 and 38).)

Note: These figures exclude all types of sub-brigade industry, including private and individual enterprises. However, very few of these enterprises existed before 1978 and therefore the distortion is small. Data are at 1980 constant prices.

The productivity record

As measured by the usual metric of productivity, there is no doubt that the Third Front sector was woefully inefficient (Naughton 1988; Bramall 2007). It could hardly be otherwise given the location and small scale of many of these enterprises. Front planners had wanted enterprises to be small in scale and dispersed across the Chinese countryside precisely because they were worried about the vulnerability of industry to aerial attack. Indeed the key slogan for the programme was *fensan yinbi kaoshan* (dispersed, concealed and near mountains) Economic considerations were of secondary importance.

The productivity record of commune and brigade industry is more controversial, but there is little real doubt that this subsector of rural industry was also inefficient (Wong 1991; Whiting 2001; Bramall 2007: 37–47). Here, the debate is more about whether than inefficiency was due to state ownership (Whiting 2001), the absence of fiscal decentralization, which would have forced communes to ensure that their industries were efficient (Oi 1999), or whether it was because these industries were infants and still had far to progress along the learning curve. I have argued elsewhere (Bramall 2007) that we do better to see these nascent industries as infants, which grew up during the 1980s and 1990s. This argument is taken up below.

Underindustrialization

From the perspective of the leadership, however, China's underindustrialization at the close of the 1970s was even more of a problem than low industrial productivity. The CCP had undoubted strategic ambitions. The first was to ensure military security. Ultimately, however, the CCP wanted China to assume its rightful place in the sun and achieve great power status, thus reversing the humiliations of the century after 1839. To achieve these ambitions, China needed above all else a large industrial sector. Yet despite heroic efforts during the late Maoist era, China remained industrially underdeveloped at the close of the 1970s. To be sure, the share of industry in GDP was much higher by 1978 than it had been in 1952 (Table 8.2). Indeed by international standards, the 1978 figure seems to have been extremely high. The World Bank data for 1980 (World Bank 1998: 212–13) show that the industry share in China was 49 per cent (here industry includes construction). This was well above the average for low-income countries (32 per cent), and higher than for many middle-income countries (which averaged 45 per cent). Some oil- and mineral-rich countries had higher shares, but that is not surprising. Russia and some of the other Soviet Republics had higher shares too, but it is far from self-evident that China's shortfall in this regard constituted failure; arguably these states were overindustrialized

However, these official output data overstate the extent of Chinese industrialization under Mao. For one thing, the output data are misleading because they are distorted by the Chinese relative price structure: 1978 Chinese prices were those set by the state. Industrial prices were far too high and agricultural prices were far too low in relation to both presocialist Chinese market prices (i.e. those of the early 1950s) and to international prices in 1978. The effect of this price distortion is to overstate the value of industrial production and understate that of agriculture. Maddison's (1998: 68 and 157) estimate of Chinese GDP uses 1987 prices – on the grounds that these were far closer to market prices than those of 1978 – and these show a substantially different picture. The industrial share (including construction) increased substantially during the Maoist era, but the 1978 figure was still only 38 per cent of GDP (up from only 12 per cent in 1952). Compared with the international averages cited in the previous paragraph, that implies that China at the close of the Maoist era was only a little more industrialized than the average low-income

Table 8.2 The share of industry in employment and GDP, 1952 and 1978

	Share in GDP		Share in employment	
	1952	*1978*	*1952*	*1978*
Primary	50	28	84	71
Secondary	21	48	7	17
Of which: Industry	18	44	n/a	n/a
Tertiary	29	24	9	12

Source: SSB (2005a: 7).

country and less industrialized than the average middle-income country, where the industry share was 45 per cent.

This analysis suggests that late Maoist China was underindustrialized, and this is reinforced by an examination of employment shares. If we look at employment shares, the secondary sector employed only 17 per cent of the Chinese workforce in 1978, far below the peak of 48 per cent recorded in Britain (the classic workshop economy) in 1955 (Rowthorn and Wells 1987: 208). This reflected in part the capital-intensive nature of Chinese industrial production; mineral extraction and lumber, both relatively capital-intensive sectors, were of great importance, and heavy industry played a much greater role than light industries such as textiles and garments. However, China's low level of industrial employment also signified the continuing underdevelopment of its industrial sector. The corollary to the low industry share in employment was the continuing dominance of Chinese agriculture, which still employed 71 per cent of the workforce at the time of the Third Plenum. Remarkably enough, this was only thirteen percentage points less than in 1952 – powerful testimony to the limited extent of industrialization during the Maoist era. To put this in some sort of perspective, only 29 per cent of the male British workforce was employed in agriculture as early as 1840 (Crafts 1985: 57). In other words, China's industrial sector was not efficient in 1978. On the one hand, absolute productivity levels were well below world levels. More importantly, however, the industrial sector was simply too small to support China's economic and political ambitions, and in that sense its industrial sector was inefficient in a broader macroeconomic way.[13] That is, by increasing the size of the industrial sector, China could have increased its per capita GDP very substantially. It is in this respect that the failure of late Maoist industrialization was most apparent.

Furthermore, China's pace of industrialization under Mao was actually quite slow compared to that of Britain in the early stages of development. It took Britain forty years (1800 to 1840) to increase the share of male employment in industry from 30 to 47 per cent (Crafts 1985: 62–3); the ten-percentage-point increase achieved in China between 1952 and 1978 represented a comparable pace of increase. However, Britain was already a relatively industrialized nation on the eve of its Industrial Revolution, whereas China was not. In other words, given China's low base, one might have expected a faster pace of industrialization. That conclusion is reinforced by the fact that the growth rates of GDP (and industrial output) have accelerated over time amongst countries setting out on the path to development. Britain, for example, could not do better than increase its GDP by around 2.5 per cent in the first half of the nineteenth century, whereas countries starting their industrialization after 1960 have, when successful, achieved growth rates of closer to 10 per cent per year. In principle, therefore, China ought to have industrialized more quickly than it did.[14]

This 'failure' was clearly recognized by the leadership in 1978. Of course it was unrealistic to expect China to follow in Britain's footsteps; the prevailing industrial technologies of the late twentieth century were much more capital-intensive than those of 1840. Nevertheless, there is little doubt that China was underindustrialized in 1978. Whereas 17 per cent of China's labour force was employed in the secondary sector in 1978, 40 per cent of Japanese men (28 per cent of women) and 32 per cent of South Korean men (24 per cent of women) were employed in industry in 1980 (World Bank 2001a: 52–3). Another symptom of this underindustrialization was the high urban unemployment rate at the end of the 1970s. The official figure was 5.4 per cent in 1979 (SSB 2005a: 7), and this national figure masked considerably higher rates in some provinces. In Sichuan, for example, the 1978 unemployment rate was almost 11 per cent (SCTJNJ 2006: 96). This was partly due to the return of those sent down to the countryside during the late Maoist era, but it also owed much to the failure of the economy to create an adequate number of jobs in the manufacturing sector.

In short, the China of 1978 remained an underindustrialized economy despite the Maoist programme of economic development. Chinese planners were rightly as anxious to expand the scale of industrial production – in both urban and rural areas – as they were to increase its efficiency. A bigger industrial sector offered a far more cost-effective solution to the short-run development problem than any ill-conceived attempt to raise productivity within the industrial sector itself.

The legacies of late Maoist industrialization

The really interesting question, however, is whether the rural industrialization of the late Maoist era laid the foundations for the rapid industrial growth of the 1980s and 1990s. In other words, and even if it is reasonable to conclude that late Maoist industrialization was a short-run failure, is it sensible to view the programme as successful in the long run in expanding the industrial capacity of the Chinese economy?

This notion that the legacies of late Maoist rural industrialization were both large and favourable is by no means fanciful given the extent of development which had taken place by the end of the 1970s. China may have been underindustrialized still, but we should not underestimate the scale of the Maoist programmes. It is, to be sure, hard to argue that the physical capital legacies of the Maoist era were especially important. Too much of the machinery was ill-suited to the market conditions of the 1980s. More importantly, much of the rural industrial capital was tied up in defence projects in dubious locations and with little future. The conversion of defence equipment to civilian use was not impossible, and the Dengist regime had some success by going down this road. But most Third Front industrial capital was beyond salvage.

However, the idea that Maoist rural industrialization led to the creation of human capital, and hence provided the basis for future growth, is much more compelling. My own explanation of post-1978 rural industrial growth is that we should see Maoism as a process of learning which created the skills base without which industry could not have flourished in the post-Mao era (Bramall 2007). Only by virtue of their employment in often inefficient rural industry before 1978 were workers (and managers) able to acquire the skills, experience and competencies needed to ensure efficient industrial production. The *xiafang* programme also helped. The very fact that those parts of China where rural industry was already well established by 1978 industrialized most quickly demonstrates the importance of prior learning-by-doing. Geography certainly played a role in the process; the more successful counties in this regard were invariably located near large urban conurbations, and benefited from their proximity in terms of both skills and product demand. But the impact of the Maoist legacy is undeniable.

The other explanations for post-1978 rural industrialization are far less persuasive.[15] One such view is that much of the rural industrialization in the 1980s and 1990s was path-dependent (Whiting 2001). That is, rural industrialization in places like Sunan was so extensive by the late 1970s that it developed a momentum of its own. However, this path-dependent industrialization could not provide a basis for sustainable growth in the long run because so many of the rural industries of the late Maoist era were inefficient; rural industrialization in Sunan was a road to ruin. In fact, rural industrialization after 1978 was only successful because the private and foreign sectors increasingly assumed centre stage, and displaced the failed Sunan approach (not least in Sunan itself in the 1990s, where local government officials belatedly realized the error of their way). Foreign and private entrepreneurs introduced new skills and technologies, and in the process transformed the Chinese rural landscape. The classic illustration of the sheer dynamism of the process is that of Wenzhou municipality in Zhejiang province, which is alleged to have grown rapidly because it wholeheartedly embraced small-scale household industry at the end of the 1970s (Nolan and Dong 1990). The Wenzhou model was increasingly adopted across China, displacing the more statist Sunan model after 1996, when it became clear that many of the *xiangzhen* enterprises were chronically inefficient. Similarly, rural industry flourished in south-eastern China because foreign influence was most strongly felt there.

However, Whiting's account has much of the air of a fable about it. For one thing, the numbers just do not add up if we are to use the expansion of the private and foreign sectors as an explanation for rural industrialization before 1996. There is no doubt that private industry existed, nor that some industries which were ostensibly owned by local government were simply private enterprises in disguise. But there is nothing to suggest that these industries made up more than a fraction of the output total; even in the mid-1990s, the value-added share was only about 40 per cent.[16] The data have been revised in recent years to show that the private sector was more important than previously thought. Nevertheless, the conclusion remains clear. As emphasized in the work of revisionists such as Jean Oi (1999), the majority of enterprises were owned by China's towns and villages, not by the private sector. Second, the privatizations of the late 1990s were driven not by concerns about efficiency but by a desire on the part of local cadres to raise money very rapidly and enrich themselves in the process. It was, in other words, a classic privatization process. A revenue-raising scheme was disguised an efficiency-driven policy initiative. Finally, the lessons from Wenzhou are much less clear than its advocates allege. For one thing, its growth record was not especially impressive given the low base from which started. As importantly, Wenzhou's growth was not a triumph for private enterprise but a product of special conditions: capital inflows from abroad (especially Taiwan) and heavy government investment. And the key role played by child labour in the Wenzhou miracle is a cause for condemnation, not celebration. None of this is to deny the growing importance of the private sector across China after the privatizations of the late 1990s. By 2003, the non-public subsector of rural industry provided close to 80 per cent of employment and around 65 per cent of value-added. But the essential point remains: the contribution of the private sector to pre-1996 growth was small, and much of the increase after 1996 was down to privatization rather than organic growth.

The contribution of the foreign sector to the rural industrialization process before the mid-1990s is also spectral. Foreign capital assuredly helped to fuel the rural industrialization of Wenzhou, and played a significant role in parts of Fujian (notably Jinjiang) and in Guangdong. However, the reach of the foreign sector was limited (see Chapter 11). Total FDI was very small before the early 1990s, and even thereafter it was concentrated in the coastal provinces. Further, it is only in the case of Guangdong that we can really talk about growth being export-led; even in provinces such as Zhejiang and Jiangsu, domestic factors were critical in the late 1990s. Any notion, then, that the foreign sector played a decisive role in driving rural industrial growth must rest on spillover effects. There is no denying that there have been some; there has, for example, been extensive migration from the interior to the Pearl river delta, and both return migration and remittances have helped to promote growth in the interior. Again, however, the numbers are not compelling. There is no empirical evidence to suggest that FDI spillover effects have been anything other than relatively weak (Bramall 2007: ch. 4). The evidence for China on this point is thus very similar to that for other countries.[17]

An alternative and more plausible explanation of rural industrialization after 1978 focuses on the fiscal decentralization of the early 1980s. This is said to have given local government both the means and the incentive to create new industrial enterprises (Oi 1992, 1999). By allowing local governments to retain a substantial proportion of enterprise profits, local cadres were given very strong incentives to create successful enterprises. The profits they made enabled them to pay large increases in cadre salaries and improve conditions of employment. As cadre promotion was closely tied to their performance in promoting economic development, this too functioned as a strong incentive mechanism. Furthermore, decollectivization removed an important source of revenue and forced local officials to look to rural industry to finance public sector expansion and development. In short, the hard budget constraints associated with fiscal decentralization galvanized local officials into action.

There is much which is plausible in this explanation. One of the great strengths of this sort of literature is that it recognizes the role of incentive structures in influencing public policy-making. Successful economic development is about agency and incentives as well as capability. Moreover, the fiscal decentralization hypothesis helps to explain the geography of rural industrialization; those areas where physical and economic geography were favourable were able to take advantage of the decentralization. Those regions hampered by geography suffered from the process. Thus Jiangsu and Guangdong were two of the chief beneficiaries from this process of 'playing to the provinces' (Shirk 1993), whereas rural industrial development occurred very slowly in the poorer western provinces.

This revisionist hypothesis is to my mind far more plausible than the one offered by Whiting *et al.* because it rightly recognizes the central role played by local government in the rural industrialization process. Nevertheless, it is still some way short of being a compelling explanation. The principal limitation of the decentralization hypothesis is that it overemphasizes agency and downplays capability. The Chinese fiscal system was already comparatively decentralized by the early 1970s, yet rural industry did not take off. And it makes little sense to explain the failure of the Great Leap Forward in terms of any lack of agency. It was the capability to fashion an effective programme of rural industrialization which was lacking. By the mid-1970s, the industrial capability of the Chinese countryside had greatly expanded, and it is no accident that the process of rural industrialization began to accelerate.

Still, it is hard to explain rural industrialization purely in terms of learning, because there is no real evidence that industrial *take-off* was actually underway in the late Maoist era. To be sure, the acceleration in the growth rate was marked. In the 1960s, the growth rate of commune and brigade output was a rather modest 6 per cent, but thereafter it accelerated, averaging over 23 per cent per year in real terms between 1971 and 1978. With county-run industries increasing their output at a similar rate, it is evident that the Chinese countryside was in the process of transformation – well before the supposed 1978 climacteric. However, we do well to note that the growth of the 1970s began from a very low base and it is therefore not surprising that it was so rapid. In fact, rural industrial growth was even faster after 1978 in most parts of China than it was during the previous decade, and it is this more than anything else which suggests that we should date take-off from the 1980s. Table 8.3 brings together the data for a selection of provinces. It shows that commune- and brigade-level industrial output grew faster after 1978 in the province of Zhejiang even though it already had a well-established industrial base. Even more telling is the case of Jiangsu. By 1978, this was the most industrially developed part of rural China. Nevertheless, output still rose by over 30 per cent per year between 1978 and 1989.

In short, there are good reasons for concluding that the post-1978 reform package – institutional reform and fiscal decentralization – did play some sort of role in the accelerating pace of output growth. It is not easy to see how the growth rate would have otherwise accelerated in the way that it did. Nevertheless, without the skills base inherited from the Maoist era, the pace of growth would have been altogether slower. It is the absence of such legacies in most parts of the developing world – such as Vietnam's Mekong delta, well served in most respects but for the lack of any rural industrial heritage – that explains why they have been unable to follow in the footsteps of China. In other words, the expansion of capability and the provision of adequate incentives together explain the explosive rural industrialization of the 1980s and 1990s. The late Maoist legacies mattered, even if they were only part of a bigger process.

278 *Chinese Economic Development*

Table 8.3 Growth of commune and brigade industrial output by province, 1962–1989 (per cent per annum; 1980 prices)

	1962–1971	1971–1978	1978–1989
Fujian	4.7	12.1	22.1
Guangdong	5.1	24.1	29.1
Hebei	18.2	27.8	14.1
Henan	21.4	28.7	13.4
Hubei	4.7	16.6	21.9
Hunan	11.5	13.9	15.1
Jiangsu	17.5	30.6	30.5
Jiangxi	22.1	11.0	18.0
Ningxia	5.5	16.4	13.4
Shanxi	9.5	17.4	16.4
Sichuan	17.0	18.7	21.2
Zhejiang	13.7	21.1	33.7
Sample median	12.6	18.1	19.6

Sources: SSB (1990a); SCZL (1990: 23); GDFZ (1990: 10–15).

Notes
a Growth rates are based on gross output value data. These data typically exclude all types of sub-brigade industry, including private and individual enterprises; systematic national data for pre-1984 do not seem to exist for these categories (see for example MOA 1989: 294–5). As a result, the growth rates for post-1978 understate true growth rates, although those for the earlier periods are generally reliable, because so little sub-brigade industry existed in the late Maoist period. The general argument that output growth was fast pre-1978 is therefore not affected by these omissions.
b The Jiangsu series terminates in 1988 instead of 1989. There are no systematic data on brigade industrial production in the province for pre-1965, seemingly because the brigade sector was extremely underdeveloped before the mid-1960s (Mo 1987: 98–9); the growth rate given here for 1962–71 is actually for 1965–71.
c The Fujian and Guangdong (excluding Hainan) data are for brigade and below industries only.
d Jiangxi's high growth rate for the 1960s does appear to be correct, at least in the sense that the data given in SSB (1990a) are the same as those in the provincial statistical yearbook.

Industrialization and spatial inequality, 1963–1978

Any assessment of the effectiveness of the rural industrialization programme should also consider whether it served to hold spatial inequalities in check. As has been noted in previous chapters, the erosion of spatial inequality was not high on the agenda in the late 1950s; Mao's speech on the 'Ten Great Relationships' had given renewed emphasis to developing the coastal region. Only after 1963 was great emphasis placed on reducing spatial disparities, and on closing the gap between China's cities and its countryside. For the next decade and more, the CCP hoped that the strategy of 'walking on two legs' would bring about this result by accelerating the rate of industrial growth in relatively underindustrialized regions and in the countryside in particular.

The data suggest that China was relatively successful in this regard (Figure 8.3). It is true that the overall coefficient of variation for per capita industrial output at the provincial level increased marginally between 1964 and 1978, and indeed the trend was upwards over that period. However, this was very much driven by the

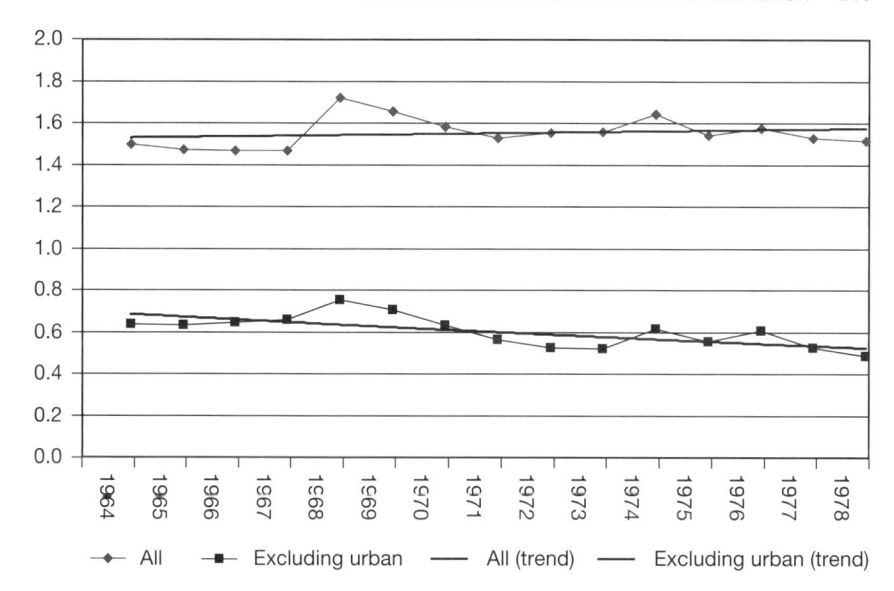

Figure 8.3 Coefficients of variation for per capita industrial output (current prices) (Source: SSB (2005a).)

inclusion of the large industrial centres and the cities – Shanghai, Beijing, Tianjin and Liaoning. If we exclude these four and look at the dispersion of industrial output between provinces – that is, predominantly rural areas – then it is clear that spatial inequality declined rather significantly. In fact, the coefficient of variation in 1978 was only 0.49, well down on the figure of 0.64 in 1964. This suggests that it was the urban–rural gap that drove the overall pattern of spatial inequality. As a strategy designed to narrow the gap in industrial development between the rural coastal provinces and the provinces of the rural interior, the late Maoist strategy was rather successful.

As a strategy designed to eliminate the urban–rural gap and the 'great divide' between city and countryside, late Maoism failed. For all Mao's ambitions, and despite both the *xiafang* and Third Front programmes, the gap increased. Why? The answer to this question seems to lie in the commitment of the regime to rapid industrialization. In order to achieve that growth, it was necessary to raise investment in the industrial sector. This in turn required the maximization of industrial profits, and the best way to achieve that was to keep costs down. Some of China's industries were reliant upon agricultural products as inputs; cotton is a good example. Nevertheless, the main cost item was that of labour, and the easiest way to hold down labour costs was by ensuring that food was cheap for the urban workforce. The upshot of these considerations was a deliberate policy of biasing the internal terms of trade – the price of agricultural relative to industrial goods – against the agricultural sector.[18] This imposed a powerful constraint on the agricultural sector, as we saw in Chapter 7. And precisely because the bulk of Chinese industry was to be found in urban centres – Liaoning and Shanghai – industrial bias meant urban bias. The policy of rural industrialization, which gathered momentum as the 1960s wore on, imposed a check on this process; Jiangsu, a predominantly rural province, was able to mitigate the most harmful effects of urban bias by developing rural industry. Nevertheless, the check imposed on the urban–rural differential was slight. In general, urban areas were privileged by the Maoist industrialization strategy.

The role of urban bias in driving industrial growth is also evident from accumulation rates. We would expect to find higher rates of investment in urban jurisdictions because larger industrial profits had to finance investment. By contrast, we would expect a predominantly agricultural province such as Sichuan to have had a lower investment rate because of its large and relatively unprofitable agricultural sector. And the evidence shows precisely that (Figure 8.4). The average accumulation rate in the fastest-growing five provinces was 34.6 per cent between 1964 and 1978. In the slowest growing five, it was only 27 per cent.[19] The story is even more clear if we look at the extremes of the distribution. The main reason that Gansu grew much more rapidly than Jiangxi was that the latter achieved an investment rate of only 22.6 per cent, whereas the Gansu figure was 39.1 per cent (SSB 1990a).[20] In other words, urban bias plus a large industrial sector translated into a high rate of accumulation and, in so far as this process led to further increases in industrial production and profits, the process was self-reinforcing

This investment-based explanation of growth and spatial disparities is very much in accord with both traditional growth theory and the worldwide empirical evidence. The distinctive feature of rapid growth achieved by the USSR between 1928 and 1960, and East Asia throughout the postwar era, was the high rate of

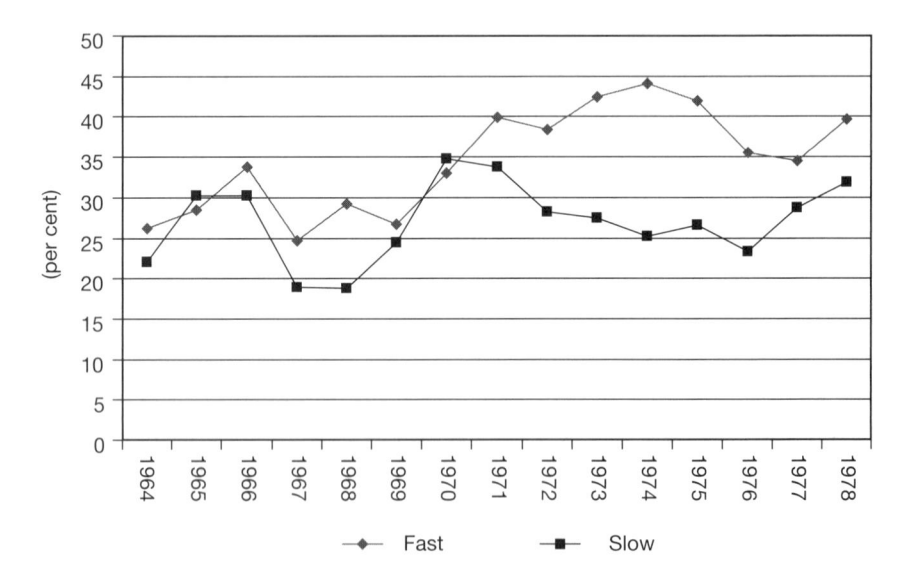

Figure 8.4 Share of accumulation in national income in fast and slow-growing provinces (current prices) (Source: SSB (1990a).)

investment. Nevertheless, although a major part of the Chinese story, it is not the only part. A comparison between Liaoning and Guizhou makes this clear. The two provinces had similar investment rates, yet Liaoning grew far faster – despite starting from a much higher base. This suggests that the *efficiency* of investment was much higher in Liaoning, and that undoubtedly was the case. The problem for the south-western provinces such as Guizhou, Yunnan and Sichuan was not so much government malfeasance or incompetence in investment allocation, but rather the nature of the task. All these provinces lacked the most basic industrial infrastructure. Not only was their 1964 industrial base very small, but also they lacked the railway infrastructure needed for the development of an industrial economy. The new industrial city of Panzhihua was built quite literally on a greenfield site. Educational and skill levels were also very low. As a result, the lion's share of investment carried out by central government in these provinces had to be directed towards establishing the preconditions for industrialization. By contrast, an industrial foundation had been firmly established in Liaoning under Japanese colonial rule, and therefore the payoff to investment in terms of increases in industrial production was direct and relatively immediate. Shanghai had vast reserves of skilled labour and its growth was subject to the sort of increasing returns discussed by Alfred Marshall and the new economic geographers (Krugman 1991). Shanghai's initial development in the early nineteenth century may have owed much to accident, but its subsequent development provides a classic demonstration of the impact of the interaction of increasing returns and relatively low transport costs. And the Third Front programme was so effective in Gansu precisely because a relatively large industrial sector had already been established before 1964, partly of course in order to develop China's nuclear capability. In short, investment rates and history interacted to determine spatial outcomes. Maoist redistributional policy in the form of the Third Front investment was not enough to overturn the positive historical legacies enjoyed by Shanghai and Liaoning.

The spatial pattern of industrialization at the end of the Maoist era shows the lingering influence of history and the continuing impact of physical geography on industrial development. A significant level of industrialization had been attained across China, not least in and around the provincial capitals. However, there were three main concentrations of Chinese industry at the time of the 1982 census (Figure 8.5).

The biggest concentration was in Manchuria, the development of which had begun in the Republican era, when it was a Japanese colony. It also owed much to the region's extensive mineral resources. The concentration around Shanghai, and extending both north into Jiangsu and south into Zhejiang, is equally marked. Shanghai was the centre of this and of its development long predated the 1949 divide. And of course rural industry was well established in the Zhejiang–Jiangsu region in the 1930s, thus providing a firm industrial foundation on which to build. The third concentration (though that is not really the right word) of industry was in resource-rich areas in the interior, but especially in parts of Inner Mongolia, Xinjiang and western Sichuan. Here late Maoism and the Third Front had certainly left its mark; development in these areas had been negligible before the

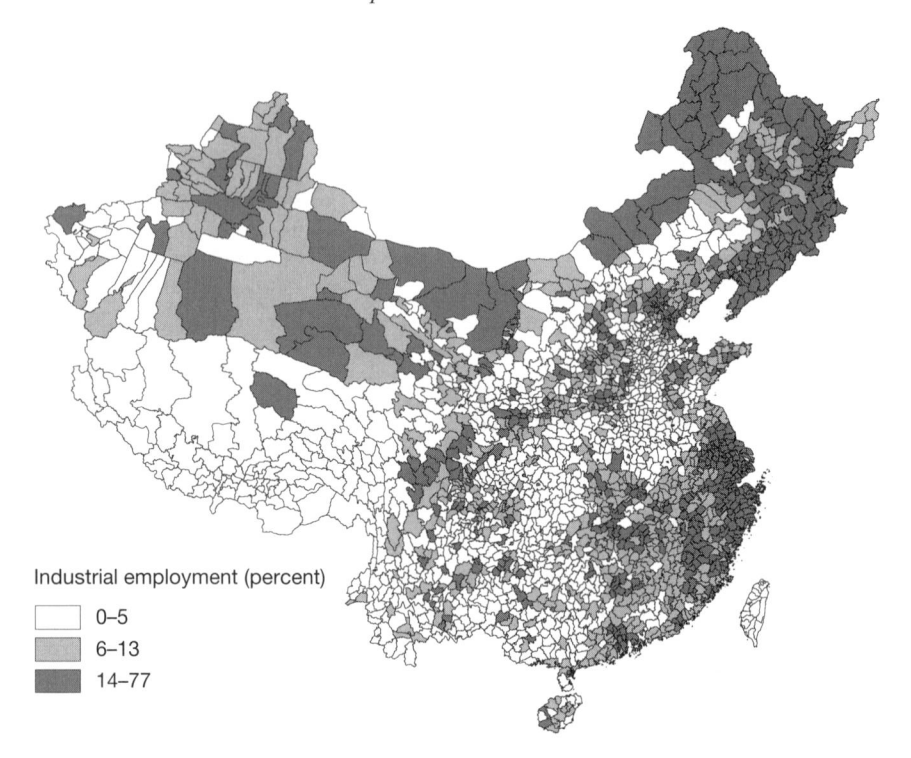

Figure 8.5 Industrial employment in 1982 by county and city (percentage of the total county and city workforce) (Source: RKTJNJ (1988).)

Note: Mean industrial employment across China's 2,000-plus counties and cities was 14 per cent of the workforce in 1982.

1950s. Again, however, industrialization was based around resource extraction and lumbering, rather than around manufacturing.[21]

In other words, state policy can help to hold in check the centrifugal forces created by geography and history; and to some extent that is precisely what happened in the late Maoist era as a result of *xiafang* and Third Front investment. But to suppose that the late Maoist strategy did, or could have, created a geography of industrialization which was independent of China's history and physical geography is wishful thinking: rural industrialization proceeded most rapidly where physical geography was favourable and where access to large urban markets was easy. The persistence of spatial inequality was very hard to counteract.

Conclusion

In narrowly economic terms, rural industrialization contributed little in the short term to Chinese development. This is especially true of its Third Front component.

Much of the industry was geared directly towards military production, such as the weapons base at Chongqing. Front enterprises were widely dispersed (and were even located in caves), thus preventing the effective exploitation of economies of scale. Skilled labour was lacking and had to be transferred into Front regions from the eastern provinces. And production was hampered by the high transport costs associated with production in peripheral regions far from the main concentrations of population. In other words, this was a high-cost programme of industrialization which plainly failed to build upon China's existing industrial base. Moreover, the rural industries established by Chinese counties, communes and brigades were hardly in the vanguard of a technological revolution. Productivity was low, and workers in these industries faced a steep learning curve. It could hardly be otherwise for a workforce that had been brought up to be a generation of farmers.

However, all this is rather beside the point. The rationale for Front construction was strategic rather than economic, and rural industrialization was about learning and the development of skills rather than the achievement of productive efficiency and profitability in the short run. And the long-run effects of rural industrialization on the development potential of western China in particular, and rural China in general, were very considerable. By creating an industrial base, a rudimentary infrastructure and, perhaps most importantly of all, the development of industrial skills via learning-by-doing, the foundations for broader industrialization in western China were created. Many Front, commune and brigade enterprises turned out to be unprofitable even after restructuring in the early 1980s, and have since been closed. However, the pace of rural industrialization in the 1980s and 1990s would not have been anything like as fast but for Maoist rural industrial development. There is a clear spatial correlation between the pace of rural industrialization after 1978 and the level of industrial development achieved by the end of the 1970s, and to this latter the Third Front contributed enormously.

To be sure, we must not exaggerate the significance of the Maoist contribution to Chinese industrial development. The pattern of Chinese industrialization in the late 1970s bore the indelible imprint of its past. And measured in terms of the conventional metric of profit and productivity, Chinese rural industry was inefficient. The agricultural sector continued to hold sway in terms of rural output and employment. And there is little to suggest that rural industrialization had taken off in the late Maoist era; growth rates actually accelerated after 1978 even though the base level of output was much higher than it had been in the early 1970s. In no small measure, this was because of agency and incentive problems; it was only after further fiscal decentralization in the early 1980s that rural industrialization really exploded into life. Nevertheless, Mao in his twilight years presided over a remarkable expansion of rural industrial capability – especially skills – which laid the foundation for the extraordinary growth of the 1980s and 1990s and hence provided the basis for rural China's ascent out of poverty. In that sense at least, some of the high hopes voiced by the planners in the early 1960s have been met.

Notes

1. For a critical perspective on Maoist rural industrialization, see Wong (1991), Naughton (1988) and Whiting (2001). For a more positive view, see Putterman (1997) and Bramall (2007).
2. The classic statement of this view is Sachs and Woo (1994).
3. I define rural industry here using the approach adopted in Bramall (2007); any type of industry, irrespective of its ownership, which operated within a jurisdiction designated as a county is classified as rural. This is wider than the usual commune and brigade definition which proliferates in the literature, but which in my view quite wrongly ignores county-run SOEs. Chinese counties did of course have urban settlements (towns) within their borders, but these had little in common with China's cities. By any Western standard, Chinese counties were rural jurisdictions.
4. 'Local industry' here refers to both commune industry but also, and more importantly, to industries owned by county governments. Liu uses it here also to include SOEs owned by provincial and city governments. Many of these local industries (though not all) were clearly rural.
5. A fuller version of Mao's June 1964 speech, as recollected by Bo Yibo, is given in Reardon (2002: 139–40).
6. See Figure 12.2 in Chapter 12, below, for more detail on these trends.
7. For further discussion of the Front, see Naughton (1988), Wei (2000), Bachman (2001), Shapiro (2001), Chen (2003) and Bramall (2007). For a sympathetic account of the programme by one worker transferred from Beijing to Guizhou to work on the Front, see Sang (2006: 59–72).
8. The city of Dukou was created on the site of Panzhihua in 1965 out of the counties of Huili, Yanbian (Sichuan) and out of parts of Yongren and Huaping (Yunnan). Miyi county was placed under its jurisdiction in 1978. The city was renamed Panzhihua (the name of the key industrial enterprise) in January 1987.
9. Panzhihua is interesting in other ways as well. It was reputedly one of the few places in China where baseball was played in the late Maoist era.
10. By involution is meant the application of ever-increasing amounts of labour to a fixed amount of land, a process which over time drives down the average and marginal product of labour. For a useful discussion of involution in China, see Huang (1990).
11. The agricultural share in the total did not return to its 1957 figure until 1968 (SSB 2005a: 7).
12. The results from the 1982 Population Census for the occupational composition of the population produce a figure of about 43 million rural industrial workers, some 10 per cent of the rural workforce. The total was certainly somewhat lower in the late 1970s, but not by very much.
13. A full discussion of this broader macroeconomic definition of efficiency is to be found in Chapter 12.
14. China's problem was that it needed to be self-sufficient in food production because of the external constraints that it faced, and therefore it does not really make sense to take about industrial failure. By contrast, Britain after 1815 did not need to be self-sufficient; its victory in the Napoleonic Wars gave it unquestioned naval supremacy in the Atlantic – and elsewhere for that matter – for the next century. That made it less necessary to rely on domestic production, and in fact Britain was importing over 20 per cent of its food requirements by the early 1820s (Crafts 1985: 126). For China, by contrast, the knock-on effect of military weakness was that the bulk of its labour force was needed for agricultural production.
15. This analysis, and subsequent paragraphs in this section, are based on Bramall (2007).
16. The share of the private sector in total TVE employment was much higher than its share in value-added, but that simply reinforces the point about the small contribution of the private sector, because it demonstrates the very low level of labour productivity.

17 In part this is because FDI and competition from imports has been a destructive as well as a creative force. For a recent survey of the international evidence, see Crespo and Fontoura (2007).
18 The coal industry also suffered from low product prices. Low energy prices were part of this deliberate strategy designed to boost the rate of growth of manufacturing industry, especially metallurgy and machine-building.
19 The five fastest-growing provinces were Beijing, Liaoning, Shanghai, Tianjin and Gansu; the five slowest-growing provinces were Sichuan (including Chongqing), Jiangxi, Guizhou, Xinjiang and Nei Menggu.
20 These rates are accumulation shares in net domestic material product. I have not used expenditure-based measures of GDP because these are distorted by the high relative price of exports in the case of the major cities. Shanghai's net export share in GDP in the mid-1970s, for example, is far too high.
21 Note too the small concentration in the Pearl river delta. This gives the lie to the notion that FDI and trade created an industrial sector in Guangdong. On the contrary; one was established there already.

9 Late Maoism
An assessment

We have seen in the previous chapters that the late Maoist development strategy pursued between 1963 and 1978 was nothing if not ambitious. Its most radical element was the programme of superstructural change which will for ever bear the name of the Cultural Revolution. But late Maoism was about much more than that. It was in its essentials a strategy of rural development. Collective farming was seen as the answer to the problem of low productivity in farming. Rural industrialization would transform the countryside, facilitate the modernization of agriculture and provide the basis for China's military security. And the expansion of rural education would not only underpin both programmes, but would also help to bring about an increase in life expectancy and a reduction in morbidity. To what extent did late Maoism succeed?

The history of the victors

Assessments of the late Maoist era have tended to be negative. One line of criticism has been to focus on motive. The notion of a late Maoist development strategy is not taken seriously; instead, Mao is portrayed as some sort of power-crazed dictator, bent upon revenge and the elimination of his opponents. The account offered by Mao's doctor has contributed much to this type of assessment (Li Z. S. 1996). But Western writing has also tended to view Mao as little more than a monster. According to Becker (1996: 253–4), for example, late Maoism singled out for persecution the very people who had 'saved' China by bringing the Great Leap famine to an end. A variant on this theme goes further, to argue that late Maoism was a holocaust, and that there is thus a clear parallel between Nazi Germany and late Maoist China (Chang 1991; Chang and Halliday 2005). An alternative, and less apocalyptic, interpretation portrays late Maoism as no more than a distorted application of the values Mao acquired during the May 4th movement of 1919 and the early 1920s. It was distorted because of its xenophobia, because of Mao's reverence for European romanticism and youth (which led to the vanguard role for the Red Guards in the movement) and because of the way in which Mao used violence as a tool to attack Confucian values. A variation on this theme is the suggestion that late Maoism amounted to no more than a sinified version of Stalinism in its intent (Nolan 1988). For example, it has been suggested that the policy of 'walking on two legs' – narrowing the gap between urban and rural China – was window dressing for a continuing process of urban bias.[1] The avowed aim of late Maoism may have been to eliminate the 'three great divides' (*san da chabie*) between urban and rural, between physical and mental labour and between peasant and worker. However, policy in practice was based around the extraction of surplus from the rural sector and its reinvestment in the expansion of Chinese industry. It therefore resulted in an expansion of the gap between the towns and the Chinese countryside.

The other line of criticism of late Maoism has focused on its effects. Much Chinese scholarship is the work of the very cadres and intellectuals who suffered most during the 1960s and 1970s, and it is therefore not surprising that suffering has coloured their assessments.[2] The history that they write is therefore an ideological project; it is a history of the victors, or as some might say the history of the survivors. In this project, these scholars have been aided and abetted by the post-1978 regime, which has sought to magnify its own achievements by repudiating much of what went before. Not that this is a straightforward ideological project; in fact, the official 1981 CCP verdict was less damning than some had wanted, because of pressure from the army (Sun 1995: 126–30). To be sure, the verdict was critical enough:

> Comrade Mao Zedong's prestige reached a peak and he began to get arrogant ... He gradually divorced himself from practice and from the masses, acted more and more arbitrarily and subjectively, and increasingly put himself above the Central Committee of the Party [p. 608] ... The history of the Cultural Revolution has proved that Comrade Mao Zedong's principal theses for initiating this revolution conformed neither to Marxism-Leninism nor to Chinese reality. They represent an entirely erroneous appraisal of the prevailing class relations and political situation in the Party and state [p. 599].
> (Central Committee 1981)

However, criticism of Mao was muted, because many of those who presided over the growth of the 1980s were deeply implicated in the events of the 1960s and 1970s. One of the reasons that Deng was able to command so much respect after 1978 was that he had suffered more than most, but even his reputation was sullied by his support for the Great Leap Forward, and the very fact that he survived at all.

More generally, any attempt to repudiate late Maoism risked undermining the Party itself. If Mao's actions during the 1960s and 1970s became a legitimate subject for criticism, so too did his actions in the 1950s and even before the Revolution. If Mao was wrong during the 1960s, then perhaps he was wrong before 1949 as well. The history of the 1960s and 1970s therefore remains treacherous ideological terrain for the CCP even now. It is therefore much easier to argue that the 'correct' Maoist vision had been 'distorted' by the Gang of Four, and especially by Jiang Qing.[3]

Some Chinese scholars and most Western intellectuals have had few such qualms in evaluating the effects of late Maoism. Whatever its intention, its effects were disastrous. Wu Jinglian (2005: 408) argues that: 'The Great Cultural Revolution caused a mammoth catastrophe and drove the Chinese national economy to the verge of collapse.' The detailed study offered by MacFarquhar and Schoenhals (2006: 373) concludes that: 'the Cultural Revolution had failed miserably to benefit those for whom it was supposedly launched.'[4] According to Seeberg (1990: 468): 'Not only China, but the world will continue to suffer from the ecological and population problems caused by Maoist policies for a long time to come. It is wrong to separate out individual pieces of policy from the gruesome big picture. It recalls the immorality of the claims that Hitler made the trains run on time in Europe.'[5] And according to Chang and Halliday (2005: 569), the death toll of the Cultural Revolution was around 3 million.

There is a basis in fact for some of these claims. The notion that late Maoism was little more than a purge of his opponents within the Party is supported by abundant evidence showing the persecution of CCP officials in the late 1960s and early 1970s, some to death. The list includes Liu Shaoqi (1969), Peng Dehuai (1974), He Long (1969), Tao Zhu (1969) and Chen Yi (1972). And there is no doubting the violence of campaigns such as the 'Cleansing of Class Ranks' (1968) or the 'One Hit, Three Antis' movement of 1970–1. Furthermore, recent research has uncovered evidence of the mass killings of 'class enemies' in provinces such as Guangxi and Guangdong (Su 2006; Unger 2007: 113fn). There is even evidence of officially endorsed executions and cannibalism of the victims in parts of Guangxi province (Zheng 1996).[6]

However, it is important to recognize that criticism of the late Maoist development strategy is by no means uniform. Drèze and Sen (2002), for example, compare the record of Maoist China very favourably with that of India. More generally, of course, the writings of the 1970s, and not least those of Althusser, the great French philosopher, were often adulatory. Maoism inspired in these writers a belief that the Chinese road represented an alternative, and much more attractive, path to modernity than either capitalism or Stalinism. Furthermore, a considerable number of recent Chinese accounts have also been much more positive about the effects of late Maoism on rural living standards and education, many of them written by those who lived in rural China during that period (Wu 1993; Ma 1995; Yang 1997; Han 2000, 2001; Gao 1999; Li 2003). Many of China's New Left intellectuals have also sought to rehabilitate the late Maoist development strategy, though the efforts of (*inter alios*) Liu Kang and Cui Zhiyuan have been hampered by the violence associated with the Cultural Revolution. That inevitably colours interpretations of the period (Kipnis 2003).[7]

Moreover, much of what has been written about the Cultural Revolution is at best distortion and at worst a blindness that is almost wilful. For example, Wu Jinglian's view that late Maoism was an economic 'catastrophe' is simply wrong. To be sure, the economy was on the verge of collapse in 1967–8 when Red Guards ran riot, but (as we shall see) the rise in per capita GDP and life expectancy which occurred in the late Maoist era suggests a very different interpretation for the period as a whole. Suffering there was aplenty, but the living standard of the average Chinese increased very significantly. As for the notion that late Maoism was no more than a purge of the Party, the fact remains that Deng Xiaoping and Chen Yun – both very obvious targets for all sorts of reasons – survived. The contrast between late Maoism and (say) Stalin's purge of the Red Army in the late 1930s is illuminating. In the latter, the Soviet Union's best generals perished, suggesting that Stalin really was motivated by personal animus. By contrast, China's most talented planners survived, irrespective of their role in the Leap and its aftermath.

Moreover, late Maoism was certainly was not a 'holocaust'. The death toll was not low, but it does not compare to the scale of European mortality. More importantly, there was no genocidal intent in China; neither the Cultural Revolution nor late Maoism was intended to be a deliberate programme of extermination. To my mind the implicit comparison with Nazi Germany is fanciful. In China's case, Mao shed few tears over the death of 'counter-revolutionaries', but there is no evidence of any genocidal intent. Even MacFarquhar and Schoenhals (2006: 184) recognize that 'Mao seems never to have ordered the liquidation of a senior colleague during the Cultural Revolution. Unlike Stalin, he did not feel the need for the safeguard of a final solution.' Although there is a danger in accepting Mao's speeches as a true indication of his intent, certain passages from 'Ten Great Relationships' summarize his approach to counter-revolutionaries very accurately:

> [K]illing these counter-revolutionaries won't (1) raise production, (2) raise the country's scientific level, (3) help do away with the four pests, (4) strengthen national defence, or (5) help recover Taiwan ... Counter-revolutionaries are trash, they are vermin, but once in your hands, you can make them perform some kind of service for the people. (Mao 1956: 14)

These are chilling words, but they also reflect Mao's own rather instrumental approach to dealing with enemies of the regime: far better to employ then for some productive purpose than to eliminate them. All this is very different from the intentions of Hitler in the final years of the Second World War, when military defeat and the destruction of German cities were regarded as secondary in importance to the extermination of European Jews. Preserving Jewish lives and maximizing their output would have been a far better strategy if military victory had been the overriding aim.

We need, then, to get away from thinking about late Maoism as a holocaust or as a personal vendetta. Instead, we need to take late Maoism seriously as a programme of economic development, and assess it in those terms. To what extent did it succeed in increasing per capita GDP and raising life expectancy? Was the Chinese economy performing up to its potential in the late Maoist era?

Late Maoist data

Although it is easy enough to disprove some of the more fanciful claims about the impact of late Maoism, any proper assessment of the era as a programme of economic development is hampered by the quality of the data. Many of the figures which are now available were published retrospectively; publication of data was effectively suspended between the mid-1960s and 1980, the year that the Chinese Statistical Publishing House was established (Yue 1990: 238–40). The first *Chinese Statistical Yearbook* (with data up to 1981) appeared in 1982, and by 1983–4 national time series data on most key economic magnitudes had been published going back to 1949. This process of retrospective publication was gradually extended to include provincial and sectoral data, but most notably the publication of *County Records* for every one of China's 2,000-plus counties and cities.

Taken as a whole, the data published during the last twenty-five years on the late Maoist era are far more reliable than those that were published in the late 1950s, the 1960s and the 1970s. In particular, the data published during the course of the Great Leap Forward were pure fiction. Nevertheless, we need to treat all the data with care. Many of the SSB's personnel were sent down into the countryside during the Cultural Revolution; by 1969, the SSB employed only 15 staff compared with 675 at its peak in 1957 (Matsuda 1990: 333). As result, it must be fair to assume that the process of data *collection* was limited at best. Moreover, the fact that the retrospective data published on the Great Leap in the 1980s were very round – 1958 grain output was given as exactly 200 million tonnes and as 170 million tonnes in 1959 in the authoritative MOA (1989) compilation of the late 1980s – points to the particular dangers associated with using the data for the period 1958–62.[8] We also need to recognize that the system of statistical collection and reporting at the enterprise level effectively collapsed during the Cultural Revolution, and therefore many of the data for 1966–8 are suspect. Furthermore, because the statistical system followed the Soviet model in focusing on material product, the data on service production which are needed for the reliable calculation of GDP were simply not collected in any systematic fashion. Finally, it needs to be said that there has long been a tendency within China's statistical reporting system to confuse current and constant prices. Data that purport to be at constant prices are often current price data, and even now that continues to be an issue.

For all that, China's statistical data even for the Cultural Revolution are at least on a par with those available for most developing countries. The population census data collected in 1953, 1964, 1982, 1990 and 2000 tend to underestimate infant mortality rates but are nevertheless far more complete than for many other countries. The macroeconomic data, save for the period 1958–61 and 1966–8, are also fairly reliable. Moreover, there is very little evidence of outright fabrication; for example, the economic data are internally consistent. They could of course be consistent lies but if so, it suggests an incredibly efficient and well-organized system of statistical fabrication, which was probably beyond the capability of the Chinese state. Moreover, some data which are known to be reliable can be used as a check on the plausibility of other data. For example, the figures on international trade are usually reliable because two countries are involved and therefore one set of data can be used to check the other.

The main problem lies not so much with the numbers themselves but in interpreting them. One problem, albeit something which China has in common with other countries, is a tendency to redefine sectoral boundaries over time; commune and brigade industry, for example, was included within the definition of agriculture during the Maoist era. This makes the calculation of consistent time series data across the 1978 divide quite difficult; the same is true for international comparisons. But the real problem is that many Chinese economic concepts used during the Maoist period are unusual (stemming in the main from the use of the Soviet material product system between 1949 and 1992 rather than the UN's System of National Accounts (SNA)), and they need to be interpreted with great care, something which is lacking in many Western and most Chinese publications.[9]

Yet perhaps the key point to bear in mind in thinking about the quality of economic statistics in Maoist China is that even quite substantial adjustments to the official Chinese data would not lead to any *qualitative* difference in the way we evaluate its development record. Of course it matters whether 20 or 40 million people died in the famine of the late 1950s and early 1960s, but acceptance of the lower figure does not alter the way we look at Maoism; only compelling evidence demonstrating that there was no such famine would do that. Similarly, there is no plausible manipulation of the GDP data which would show either that China's growth record under Mao was dismal, or that it was on a par with the rates achieved in South Korea, Taiwan or Japan. In short, the limitations of the Chinese data have little substantive significance. They are unreliable enough to preclude sophisticated econometric analysis, but solid enough for us to tease out China's economic trajectory during the Maoist era with a fair degree of certainty.

And the main story told by the Maoist data in respect of long-run developmental trends is that China did far better in terms of human development than it did in terms of opulence. Considerable growth of per capitab output and consumption did occur between the early 1950s and the time of Mao's death, but the record of the People's Republic on raising life expectancy was much better. The remainder of this chapter discusses these trends in more detail.

Late Maoist GDP growth

Three different sets of estimates of the growth rate of GDP per head in the late Maoist era are summarized in Table 9.1. It is immediately evident that growth rates are sensitive to the set of relative prices used to value GDP. Measured at 1952 prices, GDP grows much more quickly than if measured at 1990 prices. For the whole 1963–78 period, in fact, the per capita growth rate is almost doubled if we use 1952 instead of 1990 prices. The inconsistency arises because 1952 relative prices give a much higher weight to industry than do 1990 prices; by 1990, agricultural prices had risen substantially (the Chinese state has manipulated agricultural prices since 1978 in order to stimulate production), whereas industrial prices had fallen (because of rapid productivity growth). As industry was the faster-growing sector between 1952 and 1978, 1952 prices produce a higher GDP growth rate.

Table 9.1 Estimates of GDP growth, 1963–1978 (per cent per annum at constant prices)

	Period	Constant price set	Growth of GDP	GDP per capita growth
Maddison	1963–78	1990 prices	5.1	2.6
Official	1963–78	1952 prices	7.5	5.0
	1963–78	1970 prices	6.4	4.0

Sources: Maddison (2006b); SSB (1999: 1 and 4).

In measuring Chinese growth, Angus Maddison contends that 1990 prices are preferable, partly because the data by then are more plentiful (which makes it easier to estimate value-added), and partly because prices were much more market-determined, and therefore provide a better guide to relative scarcity.[10] However, his use of 1990 prices to value GDP is problematic because it implicitly uses the preferences of the population in 1990 as the basis for the prices ascribed to goods. This is problematic because it does not make much sense to use the post-Mao population's preferences, as expressed in terms of demand, to evaluate the Maoist regime. The relative prices set for 1970 are not much better because these are not market prices but rather the prices assigned by the planners; therefore they do not reflect the preferences of the population. One can argue that planning prices are in some sense 'better' than market prices if we assume that consumer preferences are irrational, that markets are distorted and that planning prices were more rational. But that is to make a very strong argument. My own view is that it is much more logical to use 1952 prices, because these reflect the preferences (desires) of the population at the start of the Maoist era. The question we are trying to answer in assessing Chinese 'development' is the extent to which the state met the demands of the population; it is therefore logical to use 1952 prices, because these reflect the market-expressed priorities of the population at the start of the Maoist era.[11] These preferences assign high prices to producer goods (which were in short supply) and relatively lower prices to basic consumer goods (like grain), which were available in adequate amounts for survival.

It is of course easy to see that the prices we use produce none-too-subtle differences in the performance of the late Maoist regime. Any critic of the regime would use 1990 prices, and any apologist would incline towards the use of 1952 prices. In fact, and as noted above, it does not really matter very much because neither 1952 nor 1990 prices convey a *qualitatively* different picture of China's GDP record under Mao. A per capita growth rate of 2.6 per cent per annum or 5 per cent per annum amounts to a respectable rather than spectacular performance for a relatively poor country. There was nothing especially remarkable about China's GDP record whichever price set is employed; as Table 9.6 shows, Chinese GDP growth was significantly slower than in Japan, Taiwan and South Korea during their 'miracles'. Equally, however, it is fair to conclude that estimates of this sort demonstrate rather conclusively that any claim that late Maoism was a 'catastrophe' is flatly contradicted by the evidence.

The consumption record

As regards food consumption, we need to recognize that there are a number of data problems. There are two ways of estimating food consumption. One way is to start with estimates of production, and calculate from these the amount available for food consumption after allowing deductions for waste, animal feed, milling, seed and industrial use, and after additions as a result of net imports. This is the food balance approach used by the FAO and by a number of scholars (Piazza 1986). Alternatively, one may use the results obtained from surveys of peasant consumption carried out by China's State Statistical Bureau. However, surveys of this ilk are problematic (Bramall 2001). The main weakness of the surveys carried out in the late 1970s and early 1980s was that they were very small, and that they tended to exclude many of the rural poor (mainly because they were illiterate and innumerate, and therefore were not able to keep the records required by the surveyors). One manifestation of the limitations of the survey data is the fact that they put rural calorie consumption at only 1,834 kcals per person per day in 1978 (SSB 2006c: 34), a wildly implausible number. For one thing, this is well below subsistence, which was probably around 2,200 kcals given that Chinese rural population was so heavily engaged in manual labour. For another, it is hard to square a food consumption level of 1,834 kcals with what we know about life expectancy. As data on life expectancy were collected during the course of the highly reliable 1982 population census, there is every reason to be suspicious of the 1,834 kcal figure. It is also worth noting that the provenance of the figure of 1,834 kcals is uncertain. The official data published in the early 1980s, which are supposedly based upon the same survey as the data published in 2006, show per capita consumption of 2,224 kcals in 1978 (ZGTJNJ 1983: 509). Quite why a figure of 2,224 kcals has become a figure of 1,834 kcals is unclear.

For these reasons, the estimates of food consumption based upon production appear to offer a much firmer basis for assessing the achievements of the late Maoist regime.[12] These food balance estimates show that the late Maoist record on food consumption largely parallels its GDP record (Figure 9.1). Average per capita daily consumption certainly increased over time, climbing from around 1,800 kcals per day in 1963 to around 2,400 kcals by 1978.[13] Of course consumption in 1963 was still depressed in the aftermath of the famine, and it is worth noting that the 1950s peak was 2,300 kcals (in 1956). In other words, a comparison between 1956 and 1978 suggests only a modest improvement in per capita consumption over time. An even more pessimistic interpretation would be to argue that, if we compare consumption levels in the late 1970s with those of the 1930s, food consumption may even have fallen. That was my reading of the evidence for Sichuan, then the largest province in China (Bramall 1989). I may have been too pessimistic given what we now know of output underreporting in the late 1970s. But whatever the reality, there is little to suggest any big improvement in average food availability during the late Maoist period.[14]

For all that, there is no question that there was an improvement in nutrition for many in the *poorest* parts of China in the 1960s and 1970s. We can see this from

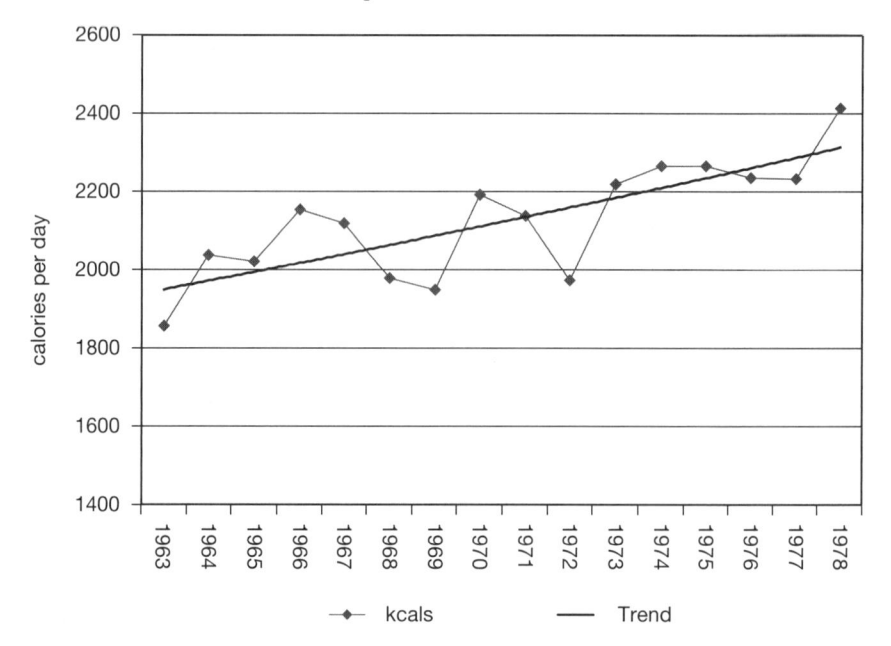

Figure 9.1 Food consumption in China, 1963–1978 (kcals per capita per day) (Source: Piazza (1986).)

Note: FAO estimates using a methodology very similar to Piazza's put calories intake at 1,972 kcals in 1965 and 2,247 kcals in 1978 (FAO 2006). This latter seems to fit very well with what we know of life expectancy in the early 1980s; it is hard to believe that daily food consumption can have been less than that.

the change in the average height of seventeen-year-olds between 1958 and 1979. In Chengdu city, the average seventeen-year-old boy was 4 cm taller than in 1958; the average seventeen-year-old girl was 3 cm taller (Liu 1988: 262). In Anhui province, seventeen-year-old boys in the rural parts of Hefei were 8 cm taller than they had been in 1958 and girls almost 3 cm taller (Zheng and Gao 1987: 348). This evidence seems to suggest that, even if *total* calorific availability increased comparatively little, the distribution was much more equal, benefiting urban and rural poor alike.

Human development

Late Maoism was about much more than increasing levels of per capita consumption. One of its priorities was to raise levels of human development by the expansion of health care and education, especially in rural areas.

The record on human development in the 1960s and 1970s is far from uniformly positive because of the loss of life incurred during the violence of the late 1960s and 1970s. It used to be thought that the effects of the Cultural Revolution and the campaigns of the 1970s were felt almost exclusively in the cities. However,

Table 9.2 Life expectancy (official data; years at birth)

	Male	Female
1929–31	25	24
1973–5	63	66
1981	66	69

Sources: RKTJNJ (2005: 253); ZGRKNJ (1985: 883, 886, 1065–6); Barclay *et al*. (1976: 618–20).

Note
The basic data for 1929–31 were collected by Buck's team (1937: 391). Without adjustment, they suggest life expectancy of about 35 years at birth. However, Buck's team recognized that this figure was too high because of underreporting of infant deaths: 'deaths of infants were probably the least completely recorded of all … The results of other studies support the internal evidence that the rate of 156 was too low' (Buck 1937: 389). The data were subsequently adjusted for underreporting of infant deaths by Barclay *et al*. (1976) and these adjusted data are those given in the table. The 1973–5 data were collected as part of a nationwide mortality survey; for a discussion of their reliability, see Banister (1987: 91–5) and Chen *et al*. (1990). Underreporting of infant mortality was a problem, and for that reason Banister has readjusted the life-expectancy estimates downwards; she puts true male life expectancy during 1973–5 at 61 years and female life expectancy at 63 years (Banister 1987: 389). A recent further readjustment to allow for greater underreporting reduces male life expectancy to 59 years, and female life expectancy to 61 years (Banister and Hill 2004: 71). However, these are quantitative rather than qualitative adjustments; the trend after the early 1950s is unambiguous. The data for 1981 were collected during the 1982 Population Census and are on the whole reliable, though they probably underreport the number of infant deaths.

recent work suggests that the violence extended to many parts of the countryside. Based upon an analysis of the records published on over 1,500 of China's counties, Walder and Yang (2003) estimate that there may have been between 750,000 and 1.5 million excess deaths in the late Maoist era. This estimate has the air of speculation about it, based as it is upon a very large adjustment for what they believe is underreporting. For all that, this figure for the number of deaths is by no means implausible

Nevertheless, the deaths that undoubtedly occurred during the political campaigns of these years should not draw our attention away from the remarkable trend improvement in longevity which occurred during the late Maoist era. The data on life expectancy tell much of this story.[15] In the early 1930s, the average life expectancy at birth in rural China was extremely low. At little better than twenty-five years, it was well below the figures of forty-three years reported for Japan in 1921–5 (Mosk 1996: 8) and fifty-three years for England and Wales during 1901–5 (Woods 1992: 29). All this changed after 1949. By the mid-1970s, life expectancy at birth had soared to the dizzying heights of sixty-three to sixty-six years, and by 1981 female life expectancy was close to seventy years.

The rise in life expectancy was in part a statistical artefact; the fall in fertility which commenced in the late 1960s as a result of the 'two-child policy' necessarily reduced the number of infant deaths, because fewer children were being born.[16] Yet the very fact that the decline in mortality commenced in the 1950s – well before fertility started to decline – suggests other forces were at work. Of these, two were crucial. For one thing, and as a result of asset redistribution in the countryside and the creation of communes in 1958, per capita food consumption by the poor rose significantly, even though *average* food consumption rose only slightly. This undoubtedly went some way towards increasing life expectancy. More important, however, were improvements in public health. Large-scale vaccination programmes and improvements in sanitation (such as the anti-schistosomiasis campaigns) had a major effect in reducing death from infectious disease, especially in rural areas (Banister 1987). In this regard China's strategy was far more effective than India's (Drèze and Sen 2002); in fact, barely a country in the world has matched the pace of mortality reduction achieved by the People's Republic in the postwar era. It is a classic demonstration of how a poor country can reduce mortality even in the absence of large increases in GDP per head.

Less certain is the role played by the expansion in rural education in reducing mortality, but only because it is hard to trace out the precise nature of the link between education and health. Certainly there is some cross-sectional evidence which suggests that educational improvement led to increases in life expectancy. Table 9.3 shows data on provinces with above- and below-average levels of life expectancy in 1982. As is evident, the top six provinces in terms of life expectancy all enjoyed above-average literacy rates. Conversely, four of the worst six provinces in terms of longevity also did badly in terms of literacy.

To be sure, the relationship between life expectancy and literacy is anything but tight. Xinjiang provides a good example. It had the lowest longevity of any

Table 9.3 Provincial deviations in life expectancy and literacy from the national average in 1982

	Life expectancy (years)	Literacy (percentage points)
Provinces with high life expectancy		
Shanghai	+5	+9
Beijing	+4	+11
Hebei	+3	+1
Liaoning	+3	+10
Guangdong	+3	+7
Tianjin	+3	+9
Provinces with low life expectancy		
Shaanxi	−3	−1
Sichuan	−4	0
Guizhou	−6	−7
Qinghai	−6	−6
Yunnan	−7	−8
Xinjiang	−7	+3

Sources: State Council (1991: 30); Banister (1992: 6).

Note
Deviations are measured as life expectancy of the province (in years) minus the national average, and the literacy rate of the province (as a percentage) minus the national average. A plus sign indicates above-average life expectancy or literacy. Life expectancy data refer to life expectancy at birth. The literacy rate refers to the population aged 15 and over.

Chinese province even though its literacy rate was above the average. There are other notable exceptions too. Jilin, Heilongjiang and Hunan all enjoyed literacy rates which were well above average, but did not fare very well in terms of life expectancy; longevity in Hunan, for example, was two years below the average. However, none of this is especially surprising or affects the general conclusion. Mortality rates were inevitably higher in counties located on the Himalayan plateau; infant mortality rates in many of these counties was very high, even though both per capita incomes and literacy were above average. This testifies to the impact of water shortages and altitude. We can therefore probably conclude on balance that improvements in education contributed to the rise in average life expectancy.

The key factor behind the rise in life expectancy was a sustained reduction in infant mortality, which had been the main factor behind the very high mortality rates of the 1930s. In the early 1930s, the infant mortality rate in rural China stood at about 300 per 1,000 live births (Barclay *et al* 1976: 617–18), almost three times higher than in Britain. By 1963, the national figure had fallen to around 73 per 1,000 and the decline continued during the late Maoist era. Figure 9.2 shows the trend using the official data and adjusted figures estimated by Banister (1987). By 1978, the rate was down to around 40 per 1,000, about half the figure recorded in 1963 Local data show the same trend. In Shifang county in Sichuan, for example, the rate declined from about 100 per 1,000 in 1965 to about 50 per 1,000 by 1978 (Lavely 1984: 369). Even allowing for a degree of underreporting in the official data, the late Maoist achievement was a remarkable one. In fact, as Figure 9.2 shows, Banister's estimates converge with the official data for 1978, and, because

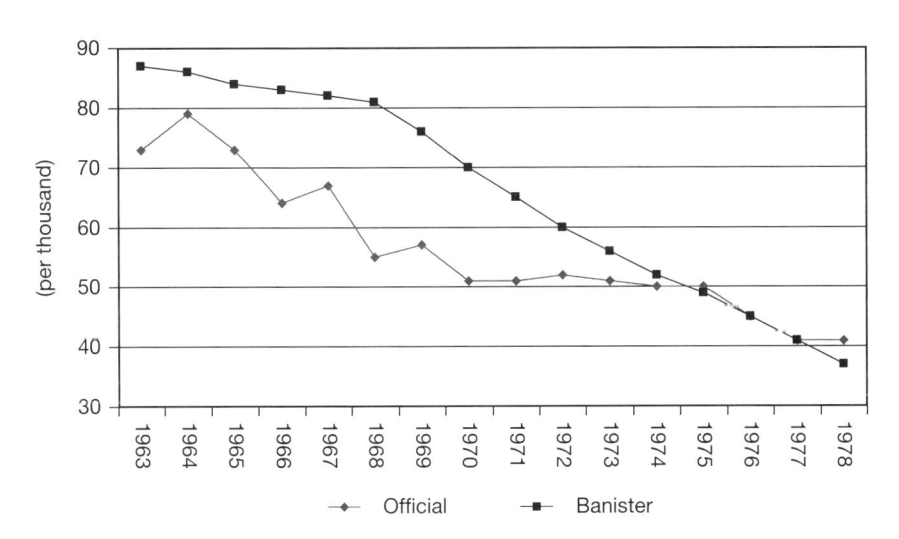

Figure 9.2 Chinese infant mortality rates, 1963–1978 (Sources: RKNJ (1991: 537); Banister (1987: 352).)

Note: These are official data.

she has a higher estimate for the early 1960s, her figures show a faster rate of decline than do the official figures.

To get some indication of just how impressive this late Maoist record was, the average for developing countries in 2005 was still as high as 57 per 1,000, and for the least developed countries amongst them, the figure was 97 per 1,000. Even outside sub-Saharan Africa the rates in 2005 were often still higher than in China at the close of the Maoist era. India, for example, recorded an infant mortality rate of 56 per 1,000 in 2005, and the figures for Pakistan and Bangladesh were 79 and 54 per 1,000 (UNDP 2007: 262–4).

Distributional issues

The impact of late Maoism on inequality and poverty is much more difficult to assess than its effect upon human development. Part of the difficulty is that we lack good data on the personal distribution of income. The other problem is that the trends are by no means easy to interpret; there is little consistency in the inequality and poverty trends.

Inequalities in per capita income

In principle, the best way to assess inequality is by using data on the distribution of personal income collected using household surveys. We can think of the overall Gini coefficient as a function of the rural Gini, the urban Gini and the intersectoral gap.[17] If we had data on all three, we would be able to estimate the overall Gini coefficient.

However, there are acute problems in using the personal income data to estimate trends in Chinese inequality. First, we know very little about the extent of inequality in the early 1960s. It was noted in Chapter 3 that Roll (1980) estimated the Chinese rural Gini coefficient as being 0.22 in 1951–2, and that there was probably comparatively little change in the rural distribution between 1952 and 1963. However, we know very little about the urban distribution, and even less about the gap between urban and rural areas. Part of the problem here is inadequate data; Adelman and Sunding (1987: 156 and 163) estimate the overall 1952 Gini coefficient as being 0.26 but, as they readily acknowledge, this figure is obtained by simply assuming that urban inequality in 1952 was the same as in 1978. Even if we accept that intra-city inequality changed little over time (which is probably a fair assumption), we cannot discount the possibility of rises in the income gap between cities. There are also serious definitional problems involved in determining the appropriate scope of the 'urban' and 'rural' sectors.

Second, the data we have for 1978 are also rather fragile. Official SSB estimates put the Gini coefficients for per capita income at 0.21 for the rural sector and 0.16 for urban China. However, the samples from which these estimates are derived were small and unrepresentative (Bramall 2001). The urban figure in particular seems very low, although the absence of an informal sector in Chinese cities in the late 1970s means that it is not entirely implausible, and in fact other evidence does support it; for example, the data collected by Whyte and Parish (1984: 44) from a small sample of interviews produced a Gini coefficient of only 0.25. As this was for household rather than per capita income, and because rich households tend to be larger (which depresses their per capita income advantage), the SSB figure is low but not perhaps extraordinarily wide of the mark.

However, the real problem in evaluating Chinese income inequality is that the overall Gini coefficient is very sensitive to estimates of the hard-to-measure gap between the urban and rural sectors. The SSB data show that average per capita living expenditure by urban households was about 2.7 times greater than living expenditure by rural households (SSB 1999: 22). However, this takes no account of the subsidies paid to the urban population in respect of housing, education, transport, etc. (Lardy 1984). In fact, Adelman and Sunding (1987: 163) show that the overall Gini varies between about 0.32 (if urban subsidies are ignored) and 0.44 (if urban subsidies are included). But given that urban subsidies are not easily estimated (much depends on how one measures the implicit value of urban housing), the plausible range of estimates is probably much greater.

Our primary interest is in the trend between the late 1950s and 1978. Given the data problems, it is hard to be absolutely certain about what happened in the late Maoist era. However, the usual conclusion in the literature is that inequality within the urban and rural sectors narrowed under the combined influences of collectivization, the Dazhai system of narrow work-point differentials, relatively limited wage gaps in the urban sector and the ruthless suppression of private industry and commerce across the People's Republic. Furthermore, the income gap between workers living in different provinces and municipalities (urban spatial inequality) also seems to have declined; the coefficient of variation for the eighteen provinces and municipalities on which we have data declined from 0.16 in 1957 to 0.11 in 1980 (SSB 1999: 138). Moreover, the data we have on personal income inequality between provinces and municipalities for peasants shows at worst a modest increase; for the twenty-one provinces and municipalities on which we have data in 1957 and 1978, the coefficient of variation shows a rise from 0.24 to 0.27 (SSB 1999: 137–8).

However, the gap between urban and rural areas in terms of per capita income widened appreciably. This was not because of big increases in cash incomes in the urban sector. It is true that participation rates rose in China's cities as women joined the workforce in increasing numbers, offsetting stagnant urban wages. However, cash incomes in the rural sector also rose appreciably (some 63 per cent) between 1957 and 1978 (SSB 1999: 22). Thus the notional urban–rural gap actually declined from 3.1 to 1 in 1957 to only 2.7 in 1978. For all that, the real urban–rural gap increased because of the payment of subsidies to urban workers which were not matched by similar payments to the peasants. According to Lardy (1984), these subsidies were vastly higher than in the mid-1950s; by 1978, they amounted to no less than 80 per cent of the urban wage. It is therefore entirely possible that this rising urban–rural gap offset – or even exceeded – the impact of those factors making for a reduction in the overall degree of inequality. China at the end of the Maoist era was certainly not capitalist, but the operation of geographical factors may well have ensured that inequality was not especially low by international standards. Adelman and Sunding's estimate of a Gini of over 0.44 in 1978 is therefore certainly plausible.

Inequalities in per capita output

In view of the doubts about the quality of the income data which were discussed in the previous section, it is sensible also to look at what the data on per capita output (particularly GDP) tell us about inequality. This is because GDP data for China are much more comprehensive in coverage, and therefore tend to be more reliable than those on income. However, to calculate an overall Gini coefficient for GDP per head, we need data on three magnitudes: the gap between provinces and municipalities (which is *de facto* the urban–rural gap);[18] the gap between counties and cities within provinces; and the gap in terms of output per capita between households in counties and cities. As data on inter-household per capita output within cities and counties are not available (indeed it does not make sense to talk about household output outside agriculture and the small business sector), we cannot calculate an overall Gini coefficient for per capita output.

However, we can use per capita GDP data to assess the spatial component of inequality. This is especially important in the Chinese case because, as we have seen, the most controversial issues are the trend in the urban–rural gap, and the extent to which inequalities between provinces diminished over time. Few doubt that intra-local inequality declined (or at least remained very low), but the real issue is whether late Maoism was successful in reducing spatial inequality, and especially the gap between the cities and the countryside.[19]

Figure 9.3 shows the trends.[20] It shows two series, one for inequality for all provincial-level units and the other for Chinese provinces only. The contrast between the two series is stark. If we look just at the inequality between provinces (i.e. exclude Beijing, Tianjin, Shanghai and Liaoning from the calculation),[21] the coefficient of variation for per capita GDP declined from 0.36 to 0.26 between 1963 and 1978. To be sure, the absolute degree of spatial inequality amongst the provinces was still quite considerable in 1978; per capita GDP ranged from 558 *yuan* in Heilongjiang to 174 *yuan* in Guizhou. Nevertheless, it was the poorer provinces which tended to grow faster in the late Maoist era. Jiangsu provides a very good example. Its level of GDP per head in 1964 was actually lower than those recorded in the mineral-rich northern provinces such as Heilongjiang, Shanxi, Xinjiang and Inner Mongolia, and therefore its above-average growth rate served to reduce the overall degree of spatial inequality. Even the differential between coast and interior was far from clear-cut – interior provinces such as Gansu, Ningxia, Henan and Shaanxi all grew faster than the average. In other words, intra-rural inequality declined, a finding which testifies to the effectiveness of the strategy of 'walking on two legs'. Rural industrialization in general, and the Third Front programme in particular, succeeded in reducing this dimension of spatial inequality.

By contrast, the coefficient of variation for all jurisdictions shows a clear increase. Once the predominantly urban centres of Beijing, Shanghai, Tianjin

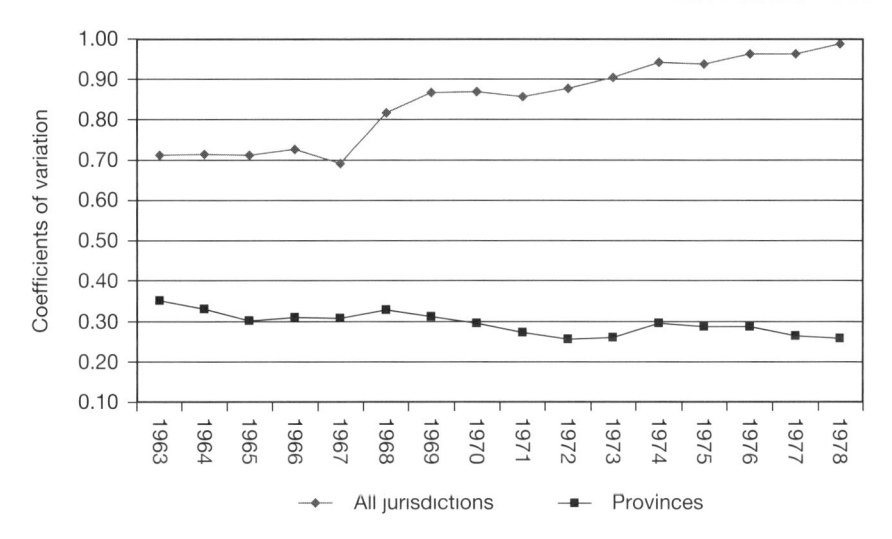

Figure 9.3 The dispersion of per capita GDP by province and municipality (Source: SSB (1999).)

Note: The coefficient of variation (CV) is the standard deviation of provincial GDP per capita divided by mean per capita GDP. 'All jurisdictions' covers every one of China's provincial-level municipalities except Tibet (Hainan and Chongqing are included in Guangdong and Sichuan respectively). The CV labelled 'Provinces' excludes Beijing, Tianjin, Shanghai and Liaoning, the key urban centres. GDP per capita data are at current prices.

and Liaoning are included in the sample, the coefficient of variation climbs from 0.71 to 0.99. Of the five fastest-growing jurisdictions, only Gansu was essentially rural. Moreover, the growth differential between these fast-growing urban areas and the rest was by no means small. Beijing and Shanghai were growing at well over double the rate of advance being achieved in the south-western provinces of Sichuan, Chongqing, Yunnan and Guizhou. It is scant wonder that the coefficient of variation shows such a pronounced rise. It indicates that the per capita GDP differential (the urban–rural gap) between cities and countryside increased during the late Maoist era. Figure 9.4 shows this divergence very clearly.

Why did the urban–rural gap (and hence the overall coefficient of variation) rise in this way given the apparent late Maoist commitment to reducing the 'great divide' between China's cities and its countryside? One superficially plausible answer would be that the cities benefited from slower population growth (see Table 9.4).[22] Shanghai's population actually declined somewhat, whilst the populations of poor provinces like Anhui, Sichuan and Guizhou grew at a rate of over 3 per cent per year, very fast rates when sustained over a decade and a half. However, this neoMalthusian hypothesis is not very compelling. For one thing, the rapid population growth which occurred in Guangxi and Gansu did not prevent these provinces from increasing their per capita GDP quickly. In other words, rapid population growth was not destiny; even if it was harmful, those adverse effects were easily swamped by GDP growth. Second, and more importantly, it is not

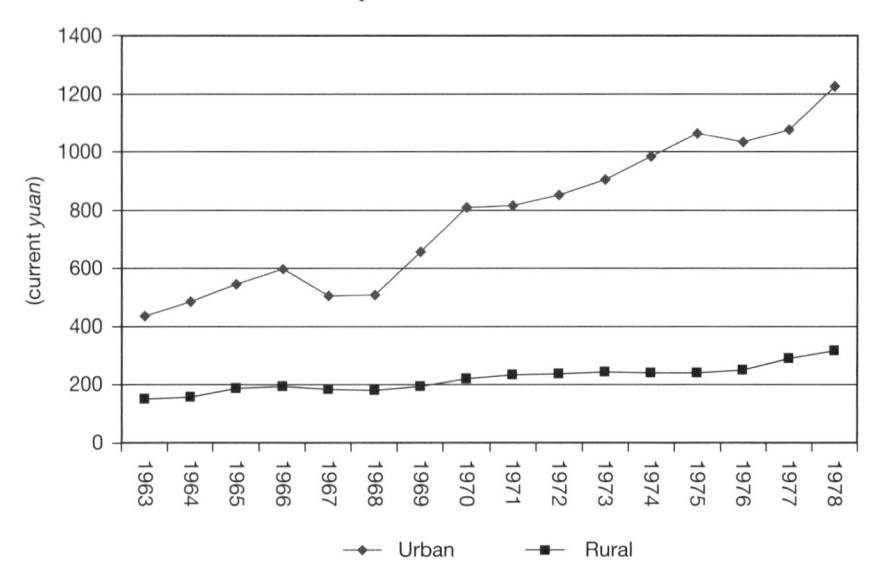

Figure 9.4 The urban–rural gap in terms of per capita GDP, 1963–1978 (Source: SSB (1999).)

Note: Urban GDP per head is the median for Beijing, Shanghai, Tianjin and Liaoning (a predominantly urban province). The rural figure is the median for all other provincial-level jurisdictions except Tibet (Hainan and Chongqing are included in Guandong and Sichuan respectively). These data are in current prices, but there was comparatively little regional divergence in prices in the late Maoist period. The absolute gap was of course affected by price factors, but the absence of regional divergence means that the trend shown here is fairly reliable.

obvious that Shanghai gained from its slow population growth. That city experienced a massive drain of its young people and many of its skilled workers as a result of the *xiafang* and Third Front programmes. Moreover, a larger supply of unskilled labour would probably have helped to depress labour costs, and hence boosted industrial profits. The proposition is hard to demonstrate conclusively, but one cannot help but conclude that Shanghai's growth would have been even faster if its population had grown quickly.

A much more plausible explanation for rising spatial inequality centres on differences in initial levels of industrial development, which had the effect of setting up a process of cumulative causation. The data in Table 9.4 show the significance of industrial growth; there is a fairly close correlation between rates of GDP per capita growth, and rates of industrial growth. However, it is only a 'fairly close' correlation because the impact of industrialization also depended upon the size of the industrial sector in each province.

To see this, note that Sichuan and Tibet both enjoyed rapid rates of industrialization, but slow overall growth rates. By contrast, GDP growth in Shanghai and Tianjin was rapid even though industrial growth was below the national median. This apparent contradiction is explained by the respective sizes of the industrial sector in these provinces in the early 1960s. In Anhui, industry accounted for

Table 9.4 Trends in GDP per capita by province and municipality, 1964–1978 (ranked by growth of GDP per head)

Province	GDP per capita (current yuan)		GDP per capita	Growth rates, 1964–1978 (per cent per annum)	
				Population	Industrial output
	1964	1978	1964–78	1964–78	1964–78
Beijing	464	1,248	7.9	0.8	10.3
Shanghai	927	2,485	6.8	–0.1	7.3
Gansu	153	346	6.3	2.8	12.5
Tianjin	486	1,142	6.0	1.0	7.6
Liaoning	319	675	5.8	1.5	9.0
Guangxi	115	223	5.5	2.6	12.0
Shandong	128	315	5.5	1.8	10.5
Hebei	142	362	5.3	1.7	12.3
Jiangsu	199	427	5.2	1.8	12.1
Ningxia	190	365	5.2	3.7	15.7
Henan	101	231	4.8	2.4	9.9
Shaanxi	140	292	4.7	2.2	10.6
Hunan	152	285	3.8	2.3	9.1
Anhui	141	242	3.7	3.0	9.2
Guangdong	217	367	3.7	2.2	8.7
Zhejiang	180	330	3.7	1.9	8.6
Qinghai	256	425	3.6	3.7	14.8
Fujian	153	271	3.3	2.7	9.8
Hubei	180	330	3.3	2.2	7.2
Shanxi	211	363	3.1	2.2	7.4
Tibet	210	372	3.1	2.1	20.4
Jilin	241	382	2.9	2.2	7.1
Hainan	204	311	2.8	3.0	8.7
Yunnan	140	223	2.8	2.9	9.2
Heilongjiang	332	558	2.7	3.2	7.8
Sichuan	129	261	2.5	2.7	16.5
Chongqing	164	255	2.3	2.5	5.8
Jiangxi	164	273	2.3	2.9	8.6
Guizhou	113	174	1.0	3.2	9.5
Nei Menggu	260	318	1.0	2.8	5.9
Xinjiang	290	317	–0.2	3.6	7.5
Median	180	330	3.7	2.4	9.2
Coefficient of variation	0.696	0.973			

Source: SSB (2005a).

22 per cent of GDP in 1964, and the share was only 18 per cent in Sichuan in 1965 (SSB 2005a). By contrast, industry accounted for 70 per cent of GDP in Shanghai and for 54 per cent in Liaoning. In other words, it was the *combination* of industrial growth and the initial size of the industrial sector that mattered in determining GDP growth rates. Shanghai's industrial growth rate may have been

lower than Sichuan's but its vastly larger industrial sector meant that its industrial growth rate was much more significant for GDP than the number alone suggests. By contrast, Sichuan was held back by the fact that it had a large but slow-growing agricultural sector; with 59 per cent of GDP attributable to agriculture in 1965, only very rapid agricultural growth would have increased Sichuan's GDP growth rate by a significant amount in the short and medium term. By contrast, the success of Gansu in terms of GDP growth had much to do with the fact that industry already accounted for 36 per cent of GDP in 1964, approximately double that in Sichuan. The Third Front programme was more successful in Gansu than elsewhere precisely because it already had a large industrial sector by 1964. In short, the Maoist strategy of rural industrialization was successful in its own terms – rates of industrial growth were faster in underindustrialized provinces, thus reducing inequalities in industrial production – but it did little to reduce inequalities in GDP per head because the industrial sector was so small in China's poorest provinces. The problem for the poor provinces was that agriculture was growing much less quickly than industry, and agriculture was the largest sector.[23] Even if agriculture had grown a little faster, spatial inequality would still have increased. An agricultural miracle was what was called for.

In other words, much of the increase in spatial inequality which took place across China between 1964 and 1978 was unavoidable given the commitment of the CCP to industrialization. The well-developed metropolitan centres enjoyed first-mover advantage: they already boosted large and well-established industrial sectors at the inception of the late Maoist era. They were therefore in poll position to take advantage of the post-1963 industrial development programme. As Figure 9.4 shows, that is exactly what happened. The Third Front, vast programme of investment in the interior though it was, could not close the urban–rural gap because of the very underdevelopment of so much of western China. In any case, the primary purpose of the Front was to promote national security, rather than to promote economic development; a more civilian-orientated development programme would inevitably have been more successful in raising the growth rate of industrial output.

However, the real constraint on the capacity of the rural provinces of both eastern and western China to close the gap between themselves and the great metropolitan centres was that they were still predominantly agricultural in 1964. It was to take more than a decade and a half of painstaking, state-led, rural industrial development and skill expansion before even Zhejiang and Jiangsu had a large enough industrial base to be able to increase GDP more quickly than Shanghai and Liaoning. Moreover, the late Maoist rural strategy actually made it harder for poor rural provinces to close the per capita GDP gap because it prioritized industrial growth. Rural industrialization would inevitably be more successful in those areas where some sort of industrial base had already been established because the learning curve was so steep. Moreover, in so far as rural industrialization was financed by resource extraction from agriculture, it meant that the income gap between mainly agricultural and mainly industrial regions would increase. Indeed the very fact that the same instrument used to finance rural industrialization – the biasing of the internal sectoral terms of trade against agriculture – benefited the industries of Manchuria and Shanghai ensured that the gap between urban and rural regions tended to widen, rather than diminish. A much more pro-agriculture development strategy would have been needed to reduce spatial inequalities in GDP per head, but that would necessarily have implied a much slower pace of industrialization. And this was one of the inherent contradictions in the late Maoist development strategy. It was simply not possible to reconcile the needs of defence industrialization and rapid agricultural growth. Collective farms helped to square the circle by making full use of the labour force, the only rural resource which could be spared, but ultimately it was not enough.

In sum, only if we focus on income inequality within communes and factories, or inequality between rural Chinese provinces, can we really claim that the Maoist system was egalitarian in its effects. The system has often been portrayed as one of socialism *par excellence* but the widening urban–rural gap seems to make a mockery of any such claim. The gap between city and countryside in late Maoist China was probably as wide as in most other developing countries at the close of the 1970s. Whatever the intentions of late Maoism, the outcome was a process of urban bias driven by the needs of defence-orientated industrialization.

Status inequality

Late Maoism was as much about reducing status inequality as anything else. As we have seen, one of the motivating factors behind Red Guard membership was a deep sense of grievance directed towards middle-class and professional households by workers and peasants on the one hand, and by the children of cadres on the other. Although land reform and the abolition of private enterprise had reduced inequalities in income and in wealth by very substantial amounts, the children of China's old elites were overrepresented in the universities and best schools. The problem was not one of discrimination at the point of entry; anybody with sufficiently high grades could be virtually certain of access to the best schools and universities, provided they did not come from a 'bad-class' (counter-revolutionary, rightist, landlord, etc.) background. But worker, peasant and cadre households lacked cultural capital; that made it almost impossible for them to compete on a level playing field in the exam-based educational system. Income and wealth redistribution was not enough to erode these advantages. Accordingly, one of the themes running through the late Maoist development strategy was an attempt to level the playing field by getting rid of examinations, making educational (and hence occupational) advancement dependent upon 'virtue' ('redness') and by introducing a mandatory work component into education.

As we saw in Chapter 6, there is considerable evidence that late Maoism succeeded. According to the work of Parish (1984) and Parish and Whyte (1984), income and educational gaps narrowed substantially during the Cultural Revolution: 'after 1967 there was very little that a well-educated father could do to help his children succeed in school or find a better job once they were out. Education was no guarantee of occupational success. Government policy to break the reproduction of status groups was indeed effective, and it had the side effect of reducing males advantages in education, occupation and income as well' (Parish and Whyte 1984: 51). For the first time in Chinese history, the children of intellectuals aspired to become workers.

There are, however, important qualifications to all this. As Parish and Whyte note, the 1960s and 1970s saw the emergence of new classes. The late Maoist strategy did not so much eliminate inequality as bring about the replacement of one elite group (the old professional and intellectual elite) with another (cadres and the military). To be sure, not all cadres did well. As the Cultural Revolution deepened, so the target shifted away from the middle classes and the intellectuals, and more towards the urban cadres and Party members who had done well for themselves in the 1950s and early 1960s, Moreover, the fall of Lin Biao weakened the awe in which the army had previously been held. Nevertheless, being the child of a soldier helped social mobility. Moreover, many rural cadres seem to have enjoyed a big improvement in their relative status. Chen Yonggui, who moved from being the leader of the Dazhai production brigade to Politburo membership, provides the paradigmatic example of the peasant made good.

Second, the obstacles to upward mobility for the Chinese peasantry remained enormous because of the operation of the *hukou* system, which made it difficult for them to migrate from the countryside to the cities. The Parish and Whyte samples show the children of peasants who had made it to urban areas doing well, but as Wu and Treiman (2004a) point out, this is a very biased sample. To have made it to a Chinese city in the first place was a clear indication that the peasant in question was possessed of extraordinary talent or contacts. That the children of such peasants do well is not surprising. For most peasants, however, a 'great wall' separated the countryside from the cities. For example, the probability of gaining CCP membership was perhaps twenty times higher for a person of urban origin (Wu and Treiman 2004b: 373). Moreover, though the proportion of rural children going to SMS increased significantly during the late Maoist era, the proportion increased just as fast in urban areas, so that the progression gap remained largely unchanged. Furthermore, urban children still enjoyed on average around two years more education than rural children in the late 1970s; this gap hardly narrowed at all in the late Maoist era (Deng and Treiman 1997). In other words, late Maoism reduced educational poverty; the average level of educational attainment increased significantly in rural areas. But it did comparatively little to reduce one of the key dimensions of educational inequality: the gap between urban and rural China remained largely unchanged.

These results broadly conform with those on income. The late Maoist development strategy appears to have been highly successful in reducing intra-local inequality in both income and status, whether *within* cities or *within* the countryside. However, it did little to narrow the urban-rural gap, and perhaps even widened it.

Inequalities in human development

Inequalities in terms of *human* development were also still substantial at the end of the Maoist era. According to the detailed 1973–5 mortality survey, the average life expectancy of a woman born in Shanghai was nearly seventy-five years. This was substantially greater than the fifty-nine years that was the lot of a woman born in Guizhou at the same time (RKNJ 1985: 1066). Educational inequalities between provinces were also considerable. There were 59,649 secondary-school teachers in Shanghai in 1978, or 177 people per teacher. In the whole of Guizhou, however, there were only 56,681 teachers, meaning 456 people for every teacher (SSB 2005a).

A more systematic picture of the extent of such spatial inequalities in human development emerges from the county-level data on human development at the time of the 1982 census (Figure 9.5). Ideally, we would use data on life expectancy to illustrate these disparities because this is the best single measure of human development (as discussed in Chapter 1), but these data are not available at the county level. However, we can use infant mortality data as a proxy.[24] They show that the median county-level infant mortality rate (IMR) was 25 per 1,000 in 1982. However, regional variation was very considerable. In three areas, the

Infant mortality rates in 1982 (per 1,000 live births)

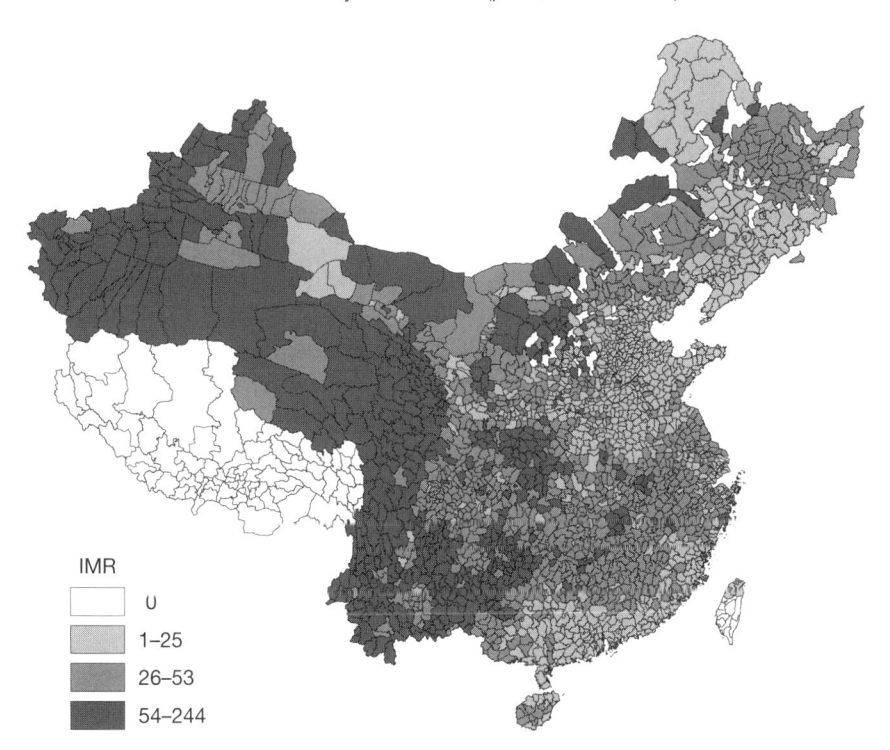

IMR
- 0
- 1–25
- 26–53
- 54–244

Figure 9.5 Regional variations in infant mortality at the time of the 1982 census (Source: RKTJNJ (1988).)

Note: 0 here indicates no data.

IMR was very low. Most striking is the low IMR across the North China plain; even in a poor province like Henan, the IMR was below the all-China median almost everywhere. But also very apparent are the low IMRs along the coasts of Guangdong and Fujian provinces, and in southern Manchuria. Apparent too are concentrations of low infant mortality around Shanghai, in north-western Heilongjiang province and along the Longhai railway running from Zhengzhou through to Lanzhou in Gansu. The other enclaves were invariably cities. A curiosity in all this is that infant mortality rates were by no means low in Zhejiang and Jiangsu provinces, even though the two were more industrialized than most Chinese provinces.

In much of western China, however, county IMRs averaged between 54 and 108 per 1,000 (or between double and quadruple the median). IMRs were also high in southern Shaanxi, along the Shaanxi–Nei Menggu border, and in some parts of Hubei and Hunan. More striking, however, are the very high rates recorded in southern Qinghai and western Sichuan and in the far west of Xinjiang. In these areas, IMRs of well over 150 per 1,000 – over six times the national median – were the norm, and in eight counties the rate exceeded 200 per 1,000. By contrast, the IMR rate was below 10 per 1,000 in no fewer than thirty-eight of China's jurisdictions. Physical geography was a key constraint in western China. The Qinghai–Sichuan concentration undoubtedly owed much to altitude; all these counties are on the Himalayan plateau. In Xinjiang, the high IMR along the border with Kazakhstan again reflected the adverse desert conditions. In short, spatial variation in the IMR was pervasive at the end of the Maoist era.

Moreover, there was only a modest decline in the urban–rural mortality gap in the late Maoist period. Figure 9.6 shows the gap in terms of infant mortality. In 1963, rural infant mortality was approximately double that in urban areas (89 compared with 45 per 1,000). By 1978, that had declined to a ratio of about 1.8 to 1. To be sure, rural infant mortality fell sharply in the 1960s and 1970s; it was only 49 per 1,000 in 1978, clear evidence of the effectiveness of the late Maoist health care system. However, the urban infant mortality rate declined almost as fast; by 1978 it was down to only 27 per 1,000. As a result, the urban–rural gap declined only modestly. This nevertheless stands in sharp contrast to the widening of the per capita GDP differential between urban and rural China over the same period. In terms of human development at least, the urban–rural gap did narrow, albeit slowly, in the late Maoist era.

Poverty

The late Maoist development strategy certainly was instrumental in greatly reducing urban poverty. Estimates vary depending upon the poverty line used. A World Bank study put urban poverty at 4.4 per cent of the urban population in 1978, falling to 1.9 per cent in 1981 as returnees from the *xiafang* programme found jobs (World Bank 1992: ix and 146). Official data give a poverty rate in 1981 of 0.8 per cent using the old urban poverty line, and 6 per cent using a new line reflecting the level of income deemed necessary for subsistence in the early twenty-first century

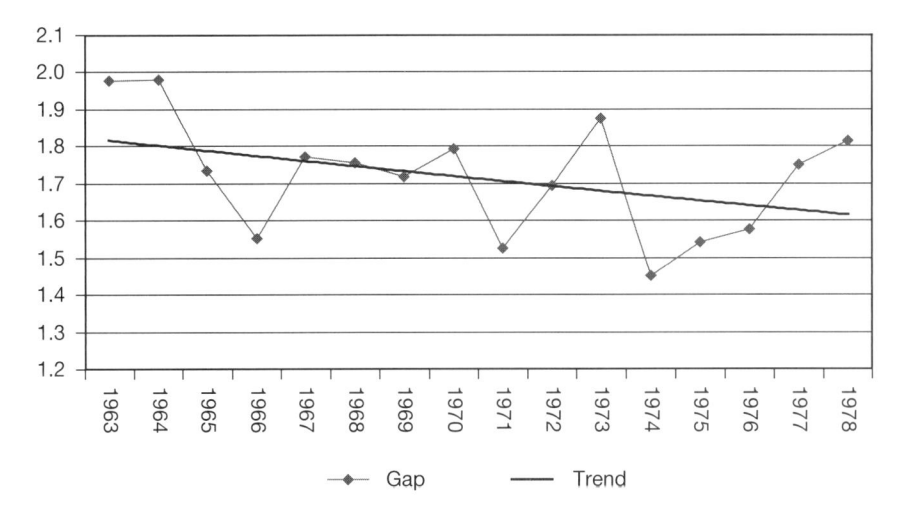

Figure 9.6 The urban–rural infant mortality gap, 1963–1978 (Source: RKNJ (1991: 537).)

Note: The gap here is the rate of infant mortality in the countryside divided by the rate in the cities.

(Ravallion and Chen 2007: 40).[25] However, despite these differences, it is clear that China was unusual amongst developing countries in having all but eliminated urban poverty. This achievement reflected the rapid growth of the urban sector (which reduced the dependency ratio), low levels of unemployment, the payment of large subsidies (as previously noted) and the absence of an informal urban sector, where most poverty tends to be found in other poor countries.

The record on rural poverty – at least as measured in terms of income – was much worse. Again estimates vary. The commonly quoted figures for 1978 are the World Bank's (1992: 146) 260 million and the SSB figure of 250 million, or 31 per cent of the rural population (SSB 2003: 74).[26] However, using the World Bank's more recent $US1 per day as the poverty line the total goes up to 470 million (60 per cent). More recently devised poverty lines using 1990 prices suggest that no less than 41 per cent of the rural population was living in absolute poverty in 1980, a figure which rises to a colossal 76 per cent using a poverty line based on 2002 prices (Ravallion and Chen 2007: 39). Moreover, although much of this rural poverty was to be seen in western China, there were large concentrations of poor people in the central and coastal provinces as well.

Table 9.5 demonstrates the widespread nature of Chinese rural poverty by summarizing the number of counties in each province which were poor in each of the years 1977, 1978 and 1979. It also provides an indication of persistent poverty by giving the number of counties, and the percentage of the population, which were poor in all three years. It is clear that persistent poverty was concentrated in two areas – Guizhou province in the south-west and in the arid Gansu–Ningxia region in the north-west. But the data for 1977 in particular show that rural poverty was actually widespread. Even in provinces which are coastal and

Table 9.5 Poor counties in China, 1977–1979

	Poor counties in each year (number)			Counties which were poor in all three of the years 1977–1979	
				(number)	(population in poor counties as percentage of total rural population)
	1977	1978	1979	1977–9	1977–9
Shandong	63	46	26	24	20
Guizhou	52	58	53	43	61
Hebei	51	17	13	11	7
Henan	49	45	31	26	27
Yunnan	45	28	32	23	20
Sichuan	39	7	3	2	2
Gansu	35	27	32	26	41
Shaanxi	30	24	13	11	8
Fujian	23	22	12	11	23
Shanxi	22	24	10	8	16
Anhui	20	15	11	10	22
Jiangsu	18	6	2	2	4
Zhejiang	15	5	3	3	4
Xinjiang	13	9	9	8	16
Guangxi	8	8	6	5	5
Guangdong	7	11	7	3	4
Ningxia	6	4	5	3	32
Liaoning	5	2	0	0	0
Heilongjiang	3	0	1	0	0
Nei Menggu	3	17	11	1	0
Jiangxi	2	5	1	1	5
Hunan	2	0	0	0	0
Hubei	2	1	0	0	0
Qinghai	2	0	2	0	0
Total	515	381	283	221	

Source: MOA (1981).

Notes
a The final column is the population living in poor counties as a percentage of the total rural population resident in each province.
b The poverty line used here is a per capita distributed income of 50 *yuan*. This measure excludes income from private plots used for crops, vegetables and pasture and, because some of the poor counties may well have done well on this score, these data needed to be treated with a little caution. The category 'always poor' denotes a county in which per capita distributed income fell below the 50 *yuan* mark in all three years.
c This measure of poverty is based merely on county averages. Poor households living in a county where average income was above the 50 *yuan* mark are thus excluded from this poverty count, which helps to explain why the total number of poor identified here (88 million) is well below the 250 million figure for total rural poverty in 1978. Note that the population of Chinese counties (there were over 2,000 of them at the end of the 1970s) typically varied in the range 0.5–1 million. In predominantly ethnic minority counties, the figure was almost always much lower.
d These data were undoubtedly compiled in order to show that the policies adopted during 1977–9 were working. Not only is the total number of poor counties shown to be falling, but also the reduction is seen to be greatest in Sichuan – the very province in which the process of reform (under Zhao Ziyang) was most advanced.

we now think of as affluent, poverty was commonplace; obvious examples are Fujian, Zhejiang and Jiangsu.[27] The most remarkable example, however, is that of Shandong, where there were no fewer than sixty-three poor counties in 1977, over 60 per cent of the provincial total. This spatial distribution of rural poverty shows rather clearly that Chinese poverty at the close of the 1970s was only partly a result of adverse geography. Much of the poverty in Gansu, Guizhou and Ningxia then (as now) reflected geographical factors, but the same cannot be said of poverty in the coastal provinces like Shandong.[28] Rather, it is a clear indicator of the slow pace of growth of per capita production across rural areas during the Maoist era and illustrative of a more general policy failure.

The other way to see the extent of poverty is in terms of GDP per head, the most general measure of per capita income. We do not have the data to calculate per capita GDP by county at the end of the Maoist period, but it is possible to estimate the figures for 1982 (Bramall 2007). The main concentrations of poverty – defined as a per capita GDP of less than two-thirds of the mean of 453 yuan – were in three areas. First, in the south-western provinces of Guizhou and Yunnan, and the western half of Sichuan (which became Chongqing in 1997). The second concentration was in the north-western provinces of Ningxia and Gansu. Third, a considerable number of poor counties were to be found in the central provinces of Shaanxi and, particularly, Henan. This spatial distribution largely corresponds to that of the poor counties identified in Table 9.5.

For all that, a good deal of caution is in order before leaping to conclusions about poverty at the end of the Maoist era. This is because the data that we have on rural life expectancy for China in the late 1970s are not consistent with estimates of very high levels of income poverty. Given that the census-based life expectancy data are much more reliable than those for poverty, Yao's (2000: 461) claim that the official estimate of 270 million rural poor in 1978 'is most likely a gross understatement of the real poverty situation, one which was provided by the government to cover up the failure of Mao's economic policy' is not very convincing. It is simply not possible to square a life expectancy at birth of sixty-five years in 1978 (Banister 1987: 352) with Yao's (2000: 464) notion that 596 million rural Chinese were living below subsistence in 1978. Moreover, the very fact that the IMR was below 50 per 1,000 in so many of China's counties by the end of the 1970s is telling (Figure 9.5). After all, as noted earlier, the *average* IMR for developing countries even in 2005 was no less than 57 per 1,000. By this criterion, China's late Maoist record in reducing the extent of rural human poverty was quite extraordinary, and it needs to be recognized as such.

The late Maoist environmental record

China under Mao has also been accused of having a poor record on the environment. One argument is that socialism inevitably causes more environmental damage than other types of economic systems because of the absence of secure property rights (Smil 1984, 2004). Firms therefore have no incentive to economize on their use of inputs; they are therefore as environmentally inefficient as they are economically inefficient. In addition, public goods (such as forests) are overused or depleted because they are not properly protected by the state. By implication, conferring private property rights would help to resolve the problem. Second, Maoism is said to have been damaging because it led to rapid population growth and hence to growing pressure on scarce resources; this is the force of the argument advanced by Qu and Li (1994). A third argument focuses on the structure of production and suggests that overemphasis on heavy industry was especially harmful (as it was in the Soviet Union). It led, for example, to very heavy consumption of low-grade coal, which causes acid rain and high levels of pollution in coal-producing centres, notably across Shanxi province. Fourth, a number of specific Maoist polices were disastrous. The *xiafang* programme led to mass migration to environmentally-sensitive regions such as Yunnan and Hainan island (where native woodland was cut down and replaced by rubber plantations) and northern Heilongjiang, and hence to enormous damage (Shapiro 2001; Hansen 1999). According to a source cited in Shapiro (2001: 173–4):

> [T]hen the educated youth arrived, from Beijing, Shanghai, Kunming and Sichuan, many tens of thousands of them. All these people had to eat. They couldn't take over the Dai lowlands, so they asked the Aini and Lahu to teach them to slash and burn to open up space in the mountains. They didn't know when to cut. In this way the advanced educated youths became the backward slash-and-burners.

In addition, late Maoist China's overemphasis on grain production is said to have been even more damaging because it led to widespread deforestation and encroachment upon freshwater lakes like Dianchi in Yunnan (Shapiro 2001: 95–138).

There is certainly force to many of these arguments. Overgrazing and desertification on the fringes of the Gobi desert were partly driven by population growth and excessive growth in animal numbers. By the 1970s, the carrying capacity of areas such as the Ordos plateau in Inner Mongolia was exceeded; by 1980, for example, there were some 80 million sheep equivalents grazing in Ejin Horo county compared to capacity of around 26 million (Jiang 1999: 69). There is evidence that forested area declined during the Great Leap Forward (when wood was needed for iron and steel smelting). There is also more systematic evidence of wholesale deforestation, especially in the south-west; according to Heberer (2007: 9): 'almost the entire forest stock was cut down between 1950 and the early 1990s' in Liangshan prefecture in south-western Sichuan. And there is no denying the environmental impact of heavy industry in many parts of China.

However, we need some perspective on all this. First, it needs to be emphasized that late Maoism was an environmentally benign developmental strategy model in a number of respects. We should, for example, take note of the reliance placed on the bicycle as a form of urban public transport. In that regard, Maoist China was far ahead of the rest of the world. Moreover, some of the criticisms directed against late Maoism by (*inter alios*) Shapiro are exaggerations. As noted in Chapter 7, the 'grain first' campaign actually emphasized all-round development as much as it did the production of grain itself, and therefore caused far less degradation than usually claimed (Ho 2003). In addition, the argument that it was simply an absence of private property rights that was the source of the problem is significantly undermined by the fact that massive deforestation occurred during the process of agricultural reform in the late 1970s and early 1980s. The expansion of private plots from 5 to at least 15 per cent of cultivated area applied to forestry as well as farming, and together with the re-emergence of a private timber market at the same time led to widespread deforestation on a scale that was little different from that which occurred during the Great Leap Forward (Ross 1988: 69–73).

Second, the data we have on environmental trends during the Maoist era are virtually non-existent and certainly not reliable. The data usually cited by the Chinese government suggest total afforested area of around 83 million hectares in the 1940s, rising to around 122 million hectares by the mid-1970s.[29] Moreover, it seems that the widely quoted comparison between 1976 and the 1940s is not based upon comparable area (Ross 1988: 35–7). It has in fact been suggested that there was a decline from 15 per cent of area in 1943 to only 12 per cent in 1966 (Zhang 2000: 54). But given the unreliable nature of the forest survey of 1943 – after all, the Kuomintang government controlled only a part of the Chinese mainland at that time – we simply do not know what happened over time. Third, some of the damage reflected climatic events rather than the agency of man (Jiang 1999: 29–30). The retreat of the elephants across China over the last few millennia was driven partly by climatic change, which led to episodes of colder weather which lasted for several centuries (Elvin 2004: 6 and 9).

Fourth, the notion that the CCP inherited a pristine environment only to destroy it is far from true. As the work of a number of environmental historians has shown, much of the deforestation and desertification occurred many centuries ago (Elvin and Liu 1997; Elvin 2004). As Elvin (2004: 9) says, elephants roamed the area around Beijing 4,000 years ago before they were pushed by back the encroachment of man, which destroyed the trees which are the natural habitat of the elephant. Qu and Li (1994: 13–26) identify three main periods of environmental damage that were mainly the result of population growth. The first period was from 221 BC to 57 and the second from 755 to 1403. Thereafter, the pace of degradation accelerated:

> Cultivated areas and cities of the Han and Tang dynasties in the North and Northwest were literally submerged by sands during the Ming and Qing reigns. Both the Dunhuang grotto and the Silk Road are surrounded by a seemingly endless sea of sand. (Qu and Li 1994: 25)

Furthermore, we cannot have the argument both ways when it comes to the impact of economic growth. If it is accepted that Maoism led to comparatively slow economic growth and that late Maoist China was poor by world standards (and both propositions are true), then it must follow that the environmental damage done was also relatively slight. This is because there is unquestionably a link between per capita GDP and environmental damage. In saying this, I do not claim that the well-known environmental Kuznets curve is some sort of well-established empirical regularity. It is not; and in so far as environmental indicators have improved in many OECD countries over the last two decades, that improvement surely reflects the impact of institutional change rather than growth *per se* (Deacon and Norman 2004). Nevertheless, the idea that an increase in per capita output usually leads to environmental damage – especially in a poor country – is hard to deny given that environmental goods are inputs into the productive process just like other types of inputs. In Maoist China's case, poverty and the absence of a bourgeois middle class meant bicycles rather than cars. Accordingly, the very fact that per capita GDP in China was still so low by 1976 surely means that the level of environmental damage was comparatively slight. In fact, as we will see, the extent of environmental degradation under Maoism has been dwarfed by what has happened since 1978. Late Maoism was hardly an environmental model for other countries to follow, but it is hard to argue that China's record in this regard was worse than that of other developing countries at a comparable level of GDP per head. The basis for an environmental critique of Maoism certainly existed, but much of the literature exaggerates China's failings.

Conclusion

It is clear from the discussion in the previous sections that many of the hopes of the late Maoist development strategy were not realized. Per capita output and consumption levels certainly increased, but not by very much. Despite attempts to reduce the 'three great divides', the income gap between urban and rural China widened during the 1960s and 1970s. Official data suggest that some 250 million rural Chinese continued to live below the (income) poverty line in the late 1970s. And economic growth brought with it considerable environmental damage.

Yet achievements there were aplenty. In terms of human development in particular, China did remarkably well; the long-run reductions in mortality and in illiteracy which were achieved were the envy of much of the developing world. Moreover, the urban–rural gap as measured in terms of mortality certainly declined, albeit rather slowly, because the decline in (for example) urban infant mortality was almost as rapid as the decline in rural areas. Income and status inequalities within the workforce were remarkably small as a result of the virtual extinction of the private sector, powerful curbs on wage differentials, collective farming and the educational revolution of the 1960s and 1970s.

At first glance, therefore, the overall Maoist record does not appear especially distinguished, with successes often matched by failures. Even Mao himself recognized the failures of the Cultural Revolution in looking back on it from the vantage point of 1975:[30]

> Regarding the Cultural Revolution ... it is a 70/30 distinction, 70 percent achievement, 30 percent mistakes ... The Cultural Revolution committed two mistakes, 1. knocking down everything, 2. widespread civil war. In knocking down everything a part was correct, for example concerning the Liu and

Lin cliques. A part was mistaken, for example [knocking down] many old comrades. ... widespread civil war, grabbing guns, shooting off most of them, fighting a bit, is also physical training. But beating people to death, not giving first aid to the wounded, this is not good. (Teiwes and Sun 2007: 3)

However, we need to be more systematic in our appraisal and use the criteria set out in Chapter 1, above. What can we conclude?

The pre-1949 historical comparisons are largely in late Maoist China's favour; indeed it is hard to think of a criterion on which the Republican or late Qing regimes did better. However, the comparison with early Maoism is less clear cut. The tendency in Chinese policy-making circles in the early 1980s was to look back on the early 1950s as a sort of Leninist 'golden age' during which the socialist system worked well. It is not hard to see why this rose-coloured view is proffered. The early 1950s, after all, was an era of relatively fast and balanced growth, declining inequality and a period unsullied by famine. Moreover, the early Maoist was largely free of the intra-Party violence that marred the lives of many cadres during the 1960s and 1970s. In reality of course, and as previously discussed, it is not entirely clear that this sort of adulatory assessment of early Maoism is appropriate. Most obviously (at least according to Maddison's data), the growth rate was no better in the early Maoist period than between 1963 and 1978. Indeed the Party itself in 1955–6 concluded that the strategy needed to be changed. And it far from difficult to argue that much of the seeming rise in output that occurred between 1949 and 1955 was no more than a recovery from the depredations of war and civil war, and that the growth which did occur was simply not sustainable given the weakness of the agricultural sector. At root, however, the early Maoist failure was not so much that short-run performance did not live up to potential, but that the development strategy did very little to expand the long-run potential of the Chinese economy.

If we evaluate the late Maoist developmental record by comparing it against that of other countries, the calculus is less favourable than if we make historical comparisons. In terms of growth rates in particular, late Maoist China did much less well than the smaller East Asian NICs (Table 9.6). Per capita output grew at barely a third of the rate achieved by these countries during their economic miracles, and this shortfall in performance has often been used to argue that Maoist

Table 9.6 Per capita GDP growth during the East Asian miracles (per cent per annum; constant prices)

	Period	*Growth rate*
Japan	1950–73	8.2
South Korea	1961–97	7.4
Taiwan	1961–97	6.3
China (1990 prices)	1963–78	2.6
China (1952 prices)	1963–78	5.0

Source: Maddison (2001: 304; 1998: 157).

China performed far less well than it ought. Even if we use official data and value GDP at 1952 prices (the approach which is most favourable to late Maoism), China still did less well in the 1960s and 1970s than its Asian rivals. Given also that, it is conventionally argued, inequality was much more muted in South Korea, Taiwan and Japan than in most other parts of the world, the case for late Maoism is not very strong.

To my mind, however, this sort of international comparison is flawed in its detail and suspect in its methodology. For one thing, the record on inequality of the East Asian NICs is masked by both statistical fabrication – many of the Taiwanese data simply ignore the top and bottom ends of the income distribution and focus instead on inequality amongst wage earners – and by the fact that all three are much smaller countries. This latter means that it was almost inevitable that spatial inequality would be much greater in China than in the other three. Second, the comparison between China and America's East Asian satellite states is really rather bogus. Such a comparison ignores the international relations of the era, which favoured China far less than the other three (as will be discussed shortly when we think about economic potential). It also typically assumes that a China–East Asian comparison is valid because all four were in some sense Confucian and hence of common culture – as nonsensical a basis for comparison as one could think of. Even Morishima, who has gone further down the cultural path than most, distinguishes between Chinese and Japanese Confucianism.

The more sensible comparison is between China and India – large, poor, blank and essentially unaligned in the post-1960 era. And here the comparison is far more in China's favour. Despite the famine, late Maoist China's human development record was far better than that of India, and its GDP growth rate was faster. Between 1963 and 1978, per capita GDP grew at only 1.3 per cent per annum in India, only a little more than half the Chinese rate when measured at 1990 prices (Maddison 2006b). More strikingly, China caught up. In 1950, per capita GDP in China was only 70 per cent of that of India. In 1978, Chinese per capita GDP exceeded that of India for the first time (Maddison 2003: 304). Although these sorts of bilateral comparison are fraught with difficulties, it is hard to fault the underlying story. India at independence was in a much better position to grow quickly:

> [India in the 1950s] ... was an excellent horse to put your bets on. Her leadership was world class: Mahatma Gandhi and Jawaharlal Nehru were names to conjure with. ... The civil service, the mandarin system left behind by the British, was renowned for high competence and incorruptibility. As you looked across the Third World, it was indeed hard to find a country that offered more if you were judging development potential. (Bhagwati 1993: 8)

Yet China was able to catch up. And India's record on income inequality and poverty was certainly no better and probably worse: there is rather strong evidence that absolute rural poverty rose into the mid-1970s. Further, although most reported Indian Gini coefficients are fairly low, this has much to do with the use of data on per capita expenditure, which tends to be more equally distributed than income. Moreover, the Deininger and Squire (1988) data seems to suggest that Indian inequality is U-shaped, first falling and then rising (Fields 2001).

The third means by which we can evaluate the late Maoist record is by comparing actual performance against potential, the approach which (as discussed in Chapter 1) is the one I prefer in assessing short- and medium-term development records. This criterion raises all sorts of interesting questions since we can reasonably argue that the potential of the late Maoist economy was rather limited, both because of the failures of the 1950s and, more importantly, because of the international environment. I have noted elsewhere (Bramall 1993) that the late Maoist strategy was heavily constrained by China's international isolation. Growing US involvement in Vietnam forced the abandonment of Zhou Enlai's 'four modernizations' strategy in the early 1960s in favour of the defence-orientated Third Front, and deteriorating Sino-Soviet relations led to a fresh burst of Third Front investment in the early 1970s. The effect was to divert scarce resources away from consumption and civilian investment, and instead direct it towards the defence sector. In such circumstances, it was hardly surprising that China's growth rate was much slower than in Japan, Taiwan and South Korea, all of which were little more than US colonies. Had, for example, Taiwan been forced to rely upon its own resources for defence, its economic record would have been dismal.

Of course it is easy to claim with hindsight, as Naughton (1987) has done, that China's response – and hence the diversion of resources from civilian to military use – was disproportionate to the threat. It was far from so straightforward at the time in the climate of the Cold War; and documentation released in Britain and in the USA in recent years has demonstrated that the two governments had seriously contemplated massive bombing campaigns and even nuclear strikes against the People's Republic. The very fact that China moved so quickly after 1971 to scale back the Third Front, and increase its foreign trade, suggests a regime well aware of the limitations of the strategy of autarkic defence-orientated industrialization which it had been forced to pursue after 1964. The late Maoist regime was remarkably pragmatic in its approach to policy-making.

That having been said, there was a powerful ideological component to Chinese economic policy-making during the entire Maoist era. In practical terms, this meant that China's isolation was in part self-inflicted. Certainly China saw itself as threatened in 1958, but it hard indeed to argue that the Great Leap Forward was an appropriate policy response. By any real standard, the Leap was a policy-making disaster and little can be said in mitigation of the regime's ill-starred approach. Perhaps the best we can say is that it was indeed a tragedy born of good intentions. Furthermore, China continued to pay a price in the 1960s and 1970s for Mao's ill-starred intervention in the Korean War; without that legacy of distrust, it is certainly arguable that Sino-US relations would have improved much earlier. More significantly, the breakdown in relations with the Soviet Union was surely avoidable. It is not difficult to see why Mao baulked at Khrushchev's 'revisionism' but the maintenance of cordial relations ought to have been possible – and that in turn (not least because of improved relations between the USA and the USSR) might have rendered the Third Front unnecessary. Accordingly, the argument certainly can be made that China's economic potential was rather greater in the late Maoist era than has sometimes been suggested – and accordingly that the development record was less good than it might have been even in terms of human development. For if China had spent less on defence, there can surely be little doubt that life expectancy and levels of educational attainment would have been considerably higher by the late 1970s than they were.

Accordingly, if a case is to be made for late Maoism, the strongest argument is not so much that at its short-run performance lived up to potential, but that Mao bequeathed to his successors a range of positive economic legacies. The late Maoist developmental record may have been indifferent but – in contrast to early Maoism – the era greatly expanded the long-run potential of the economy. As we shall see, it was to be the Dengist regime which was to reap the benefits, and to claim the credit for itself. For example, China in 1976 was on the verge of an agricultural revolution. New HYVs were becoming available in large quantities, and production of chemical fertilizer was increasingly sharply on the back of rural industrialization and the importation of chemical fertilizer plants from abroad. As importantly, the massive irrigation projects launched in the late 1950s, and completed during the 1960s and 1970s at vast cost in terms of labour inputs, laid the foundation for the agricultural miracle of the late 1970s and early 1980s. Even many of the Leap projects paid off. Potter and Potter (1990: 78) provide a good example of the experience of Zengbu village (Dongguan county, Guangdong) in carrying out a new water-control project:

> Everyone from Zengbu worked on the project, and every adult was given a quota for moving rocks and mud ... The work was almost unbearably arduous and, quite literally, backbreaking. The peasants, who worked for three appalling winters moving mountains of rocks and dirt to build the levees, paid a high price in exhaustion and lasting physical injuries, primarily back injuries from carrying. People speak of that time almost in awe of what they were able to accomplish ... The results were worth the effort and the sacrifice ... By 1962, the land was drained, irrigated and completely encircled with protective embankments. Zengbu was no longer poor, marshy, and marginal, but fruitful land well-suited to rice agriculture and secure from flooding. Rice production rose dramatically.

China's transport infrastructure was also vastly improved. Its pre-1949 railway network was largely confined to eastern China, and the historic contribution of late Maoism was to extend the network to, and across, the provinces of the north- and south-west. Without this inheritance, the growth of the 1980s and 1990s would swiftly have faltered and died. Yet most important of all were the human capital legacies. The expansion of secondary education across rural China after 1963 ensured a population which was far better able to exploit the employment opportunities that were increasingly on offer in the 1980s. Still more importantly, the late Maoist era set in motion a vast process of learning-by-doing in the countryside (Bramall 2007). The first steps taken during the Leap in developing rural industry were abortive, but even that episode taught the population much about the skills and techniques required of industrial workers. Learning then accelerated during the 1960s and 1970s as Third Front investment in China's rural fastness created new opportunities for the peasant population, and as the establishment of local small-scale industries by counties, communes and brigades created a diverse and dynamic industrial sector. Many of these industries were inefficient if we measure their performance in terms of profits or productivity, but the rural workforce acquired in the process of learning-by-doing an array of skills and competencies which were to make possible the meteoric rural industrialization of the 1980s and 1990s. It was this process of prior learning in the countryside that has given post-1978 Chinese industrialization much greater depth and vitality than industrialization in countries such as Vietnam and India, which have attempted to follow in China's footsteps without having the preconditions to make it possible.

Mao's egalitarian inclinations were thwarted by the arithmetic which the sheer size of the agricultural sector in China's poorest provinces imposed. Only an exceptionally rapid and sustained agricultural growth rate would have reduced spatial inequality, and that was impossible given that China's arable frontier had already been reached. The Third Front and rural industrialization were not enough. Industrialization simply served to benefit those cities and provinces which were already relatively industrialized by the early 1960s. It was arithmetic that ensured that Sichuan's 17 per cent industrial growth rate did not lead to a narrowing of the GDP gap between it and Shanghai, even though industrial production grew in the latter at only around 7 per cent. There were some things that not even Mao could change. As Marx (1852: 32) put it: 'Men make their own history, but they do not make it just as they please in circumstances they choose for themselves; rather, they make it in present circumstances, given and inherited.'

Notes

1 I discuss some of these issues in Bramall (2006).
2 Typical examples of the 'Mao ruined my life' genre include Cheng (1986) and Chang (1991).
3 Though this is not an easy line to sustain, because it is entirely possible that Jiang was as much a victim as Liu Shaoqi in the way that she was manipulated by Mao, and subordinated her own life to his. We cannot know for sure until the archives are opened up – indeed we may never know – but there is no question that the definitive account of the politics of the late Maoist era has still be written. Given that there is not a shred of evidence that Jiang had any power base of her own, and that she was little more than a tool of Mao, a critique of her role in the 1960s and 1970s takes us back to a criticism of Mao himself.
4 The references by Wu, MacFarquhar and Schoenhals to the Cultural Revolution are to the entire 1966–76 period.
5 Seeberg's claims would carry more weight if they had been tempered by a little more respect for the evidence. For example, it was Mussolini who was credited with getting the trains to run on time, not Hitler as she claims (Seeberg 2000: 468); German trains have always run on time. For a scathing review of Seeberg's book, see Bakken (2002). Even the indictment of the Gang of Four in November 1980 accused them only of persecuting 727,420 people and killing 34,274 – chilling enough figures but hardly sufficient to justify the use of the term 'holocaust'.

6 The reliability of this source is, however, open to doubt. Zheng, a former Red Guard and now a Chinese dissident, is of course far from neutral.
7 For the New Left and some of their ideas, see Liu (2004) and Zhang (2006).
8 The grain figures for the Leap have been further revised in recent publications, especially for 1961; see SSB (2000a: 37).
9 For example, several of the submissions made by Western scholars to journals for which I have refereed have mistakenly interpreted the Chinese concept of gross output value as a measure of value-added. Most Chinese economists are even more cavalier in their treatment of the data; the recent 'textbook' produced by Wu Jinglian (2005) is a classic example.
10 Maddison (1998: 157) used 1987 prices; his more recent comparative estimates of international growth rates use 1990 prices. However, the argument (and his estimate of late Maoist growth) is little affected whether one uses 1987 or 1990 prices.
11 1952 prices across China were market-determined, though they were increasingly subject to state control as the decade wore on.
12 In fairness, there are also questions about the reliability of the production data which have been used to calculate food balance sheets. In particular, there is a widely held view amongst Western scholars that the data for the late 1970s are too low because of underreporting (itself a strategy devised by communes and households to avoid high procurement quotas). According to Oi (1989) and Shue (1988), the underreporting was of the order of at least 10 per cent. I suspect, however, that any adjustment for this would not alter the interpretation offered in this chapter. That is because underreporting was almost certainly as much of a problem in the early 1960s, in the aftermath of the famine. Precisely because high procurement quotas contributed to the famine (urban areas suffered comparatively little because rural procurement was so high), communes typically underreported output by significant amounts in the period after 1962. In other words, the production data may be too low in absolute terms, but the trend in output (and hence consumption) between 1963 and 1978 shown by the official data is reliable.
13 Poor weather depressed output in 1976–8 in many parts of China according to Kueh's (1995: 299) index. The comparison of 1963 with 1978 is therefore probably a little unfair to the late Maoist era.
14 For a discussion of trends in grain availability under Mao, see Ash (2006). As Ash notes, adequate levels of per capita grain consumption were maintained only by suppressing the growth of other types of agricultural production.
15 For a useful discussion of Chinese mortality in the late Maoist era in comparative and historical perspective, see Reddy (2007).
16 China made little attempt to control population growth before the late 1960s, and indeed the chief proponent of population control (Ma Yinchu) was imprisoned for his advocacy of what his opponents called a Malthusian policy. However, that changed in the late 1960s when the policy of *wan xi shao* (late marriage; longer intervals between births; fewer children) was introduced. This brought about a big reduction in fertility, well before the start of the much better known one-child policy in the late 1970s. For good discussions of Chinese population policy, see Banister (1987) and Scharping (2003).
17 Here the rural and urban Ginis themselves can each be thought of as determined by the combination of within city (county) inequality and between city (county) inequality – that is, as determined by a combination of intra-local and spatial factors.
18 Of course all of China's provinces have urban concentrations, but it makes more sense in analytical terms to think of them as essentially rural jurisdictions. Conversely, China's big municipalities have counties within their jurisdiction and hence a significant rural population; it is nevertheless helpful to think of them as urban entities. The gap between the provinces and the municipalities is therefore a useful (albeit imperfect) proxy for the urban–rural gap.

19 Trends in net domestic material product – which approximates GDP – are discussed in Lyons (1991), Tsui (1991) and Wei (2000: ch. 2). These writers tend, however, to understate the significance of the declining gap between the provinces.
20 Comparatively little work on spatial inequalities within provinces has been done, mainly because time series data are hard to obtain. Wei and Kim's (2002) work on Jiangsu is a rare exception, and this shows little change in inequality between counties over time. My own research on Sichuan (Bramall 1993) suggests that rural spatial inequality was lower by the end of the Maoist era than it had been in the late 1930s and early 1940s, but I am the first to admit that one needs to make a lot of assumptions in making these sorts of comparisons across the 1949 divide. More generally, we have no data on intra-county and city output. This rules out the production approach to measuring overall inequality; we can track spatial inequality but we have no data on intra-local inequality
21 Liaoning has long been heavily industrialized and urbanized; it was therefore very different in character from other Chinese provinces even in the late Maoist period, and it therefore makes sense to treat it as a *de facto* urban jurisdiction.
22 It matters little whether we use 1963 or 1964 as the starting-point for analysis. I use 1964 in Table 9.4 because that year marks the inception of the Third Front programme.
23 The growth rate of GDP is a weighted average of the growth rates of industry, agriculture and services, where the weights are sectoral shares. In arithmetic terms, a large weight (the sectoral share) is given to the slow-growing sector (agriculture) in poor provinces, whereas a small weight is assigned to the fast-growing sector (industry) in richer provinces and in the cities. Thus slower industrial growth in Shanghai relative to Sichuan led an increase in the per capita GDP gap between the two because faster industrial growth in Sichuan was not enough to offset the impact on GDP of its slower agricultural growth because that was the sector that had a very large weight.
24 IMR data provide a much better insight into mortality patterns than (say) crude death rates because they are not influenced by the age structure of the population.
25 It is quite usual for absolute poverty lines to be revised upwards as countries become more affluent; the range of commodities needed to avoid poverty is deemed to be greater. These revisions to the notion of subsistence do show that even absolute poverty lines have a relative component to them. Of course it is not entirely clear that it is appropriate to use a current poverty line to judge the extent of historical (i.e. 1978) poverty. But one can equally argue that the 1978 poverty line is just as inappropriate for the analysis of poverty in (say) 2008. This is the standard pricing problem encountered when assessing trends over time; should the criterion for assessment be initial or end year conditions? In fact, China's poverty line increased from 100 *yuan* in 1978 to 300 *yuan* in 1990 and to 637 *yuan* in 2003 (SSB 2004: 47).
26 This implied a poverty line of about \$US0.66 per day; the SSB assumed that the Chinese population could get by on much less than suggested by the World Bank. For a discussion, see World Bank (1996).
27 For an illuminating discussion of poverty in Fujian, see Lyons (1994). For a perspective on poverty in rural Shandong under Mao, see the autobiographical account of Li (2003).
28 In fairness, many of the poor counties in coastal provinces were located in the provincial interiors. For example, most of Shandong's poor counties were to be found in its western prefectures such as Heze.
29 The figure for the 1940s is a Guominadang estimate made in 1943. The figure for the mid-1970s is from China's first proper survey of forests (Wang 1993; Zhang 2000).
30 For a collection of essays assessing the social and economic impact of the Cultural Revolution, see Joseph *et al.* (1991) and Law (2003).

Part 4
Market socialism, 1978–1996

10 The era of market socialism, 1978–1996

The death of Mao in 1976, and Deng's seizure of power in 1978, ushered in what has justly been described as a new era in Chinese development. The 'Gang of Four', Chen Boda (Mao's secretary) and five officers accused of plotting to assassinate Mao in 1971 were tried and imprisoned after a Stalinist show trial in November 1980 which was little more than a demonstration of the justice of the victors. The Party was purged of those, like Hua Guofeng and Chen Yonggui, who had been committed to the late Maoist development model. And late Maoist economic structures were progressively abandoned. Instead, China moved unequivocally in the direction of creating a market-orientated economy based on private ownership and presided over by an authoritarian state.

Nevertheless, there was nothing abrupt about this process of transition. On the contrary, its hallmark was gradualism.[1] This gradual process of change distinguished China from (say) Russia and the nations of the former Soviet Union, where moves towards democracy and privatization were abrupt. As a result, whereas the epithet 'capitalist' can justly be applied to these countries by the middle of the 1990s, the Chinese economy of the mid-1990s was still in all essentials a market socialist system. In other words, China began its transition much *earlier* than Russia, but it was well *behind* in terms of privatization and marketization by the time of Deng's death in 1997.

This chapter charts the unfolding of Chinese policy after 1978. However, because the progressive opening-up of the Chinese economy, and its extraordinarily rapid industrial development, have garnered so much attention, I have given them chapters in their own right (Chapters 11 and 12). In this chapter, I focus on the debates about which path China should take, the evolution of macroeconomic policy and the agricultural revolution.[2] Implicit in the time frame of 1978–96 adopted here is the assumption that Deng's death in early 1997 marks the beginning of a new era, during which the policy of gradual transition was abandoned in favour of a breakneck rush to embrace capitalism

Alternative modernities

The Third Plenum of the Eleventh Central Committee of the Chinese Communist Party in December 1978, to give the full and tedious title of the meeting, confirmed

Deng's accession.³ The Plenum also ushered in a new phase in China's political and economic development. However, the Plenum itself did little more than lay the groundwork. The Party had to face up to the complex task of how to assess the history of the previous twenty years in such a way that the Cultural Revolution (and much of the late Maoist development strategy) could be repudiated without undermining the hegemony of the CCP. A communiqué on some of these issues was released at the end of the Plenum, but the definitive pronouncement did not appear until June 1981.⁴ Note too that the Plenum did not announce a radical new economic policy; there was no real agreement amongst the leadership on the way forward at that time.

In some respects, in fact, there was continuity across the 1978 divide: Deng Xiaoping showed no inclination to promote Western-style democracy in the 1980s and no disinclination to persecute dissident Party members. The members of the Gang of Four were duly tried for their supposed 'crimes', Hua Guofeng was retired, Hu Yaobang was summarily dispensed with during 1987 for failing to combat 'bourgeois liberalism' and Zhao Ziyang was placed under permanent house arrest for his part in 'encouraging' the Tian'anmen protesters in 1989.⁵ Some writers have made much of the supposed change in style in the treatment of Party opponents, but in fact the fate of the Gang was little different from that of Liu Shaoqi or Peng Dehuai during the Cultural Revolution. Moreover, the hand of retribution extended down to lower levels within Chinese society. Many of those seen to have profited 'unfairly' during the late 1960s and 1970s were purged and imprisoned during 1983 and 1984 (Unger 2007: 116). The justice of the 1980s was in truth little different from that of the 1970s; in both cases, it was the justice of the victors. Moreover, the Party remained only too willing to encourage mass protest by students whenever it served their purposes; the racist demonstrations directed against African students studying in China during 1985–6 are but one example. If the late Maoist era was marred by violence, the 1980s were little different.

Nevertheless, policy changed in many respects after 1978. For one thing, the post-1978 era was one in which economics, rather than politics, was in command. Deng's approach was thus much closer to the orthodox Marxian notion that the development of the forces of production should take priority, and that superstructural (political) change was subordinate to that goal. In concrete terms, this meant the repudiation of class struggle.⁶ However, and in a clear break with Marx, the working assumption was adopted that China was in the primary stage of socialism: 'socialism' because the bulk of industry was in public ownership and exploitation had been ended, 'primary stage' because the development of the productive forces was essential and therefore a range of material incentives (inequality) was functionally necessary to raise productivity.⁷ Whereas Marx had argued that capitalism had to precede socialism, the CCP took the view in the 1980s that a primary stage of socialism could serve as a substitute for capitalism. Zhao Ziyang (1987) summarized the approach thus:

> China is now in the primary stage of socialism. There are two aspects to this thesis. First, Chinese society is already a socialist society. We must persevere

in socialism and never deviate from it. Second, China's socialist society is still in its primary stage. We must proceed from this reality and not jump over this stage [p. 641] ... precisely because our socialism has emerged from the womb of a semi-colonial, semi-feudal society, with the productive forces lagging far behind those of the developed capitalist countries, we are destined to go through a very long primary stage. During this stage we shall accomplish industrialization and the commercialization, socialization and modernization of production, which many other countries have achieved under capitalist conditions [p. 642] ... The principal contradiction we face during the current stage is the contradiction between the growing material and cultural needs of the people and backward production. Class struggle will continue to exist within certain limits for a long time to come, but it is no longer the principal contradiction [p. 644].

On all this, there was wide agreement within the CCP during the 1980s. The economics of late Maoism needed to be abandoned and replaced by some sort of strategy of *gaige kaifang* (reform and opening up). For all their disagreements, Deng Xiaoping, Chen Yun, Li Peng, Zhao Ziyang, Hu Yaobang, Zhu Rongji and Jiang Zemin shared a common desire to repudiate many of the key tenets of Maoism. And yet, if the leading members of the Party were clear on what they were against, there was little agreement on what they were for. In particular, there was great uncertainty as to the scope of *gaige kaifang*, and considerable disagreement over the pace of the transition process. It is in this sense that Chinese economic policy-making after 1978 has been characterized as *mo shitou guohe* ('crossing the river by feeling for the stones').[8] In principle, three choices were open to China. It could revert back to the economic system of the earliest Maoist era (socialism). It could make a rapid transition to a market-orientated economic system (capitalism). Or it could put in place a system which combined elements of markets and planning (market socialism).

Back to the future? A return to the early Maoist model

The logic behind the first of these strategies would be to reform the system of central planning in an attempt to make it function more effectively. This was in essence the 'Old Left' view advanced by Chen Yun at the end of the 1970s, and it amounted to a return to the structures of the 1950s. More concretely, it would involve the restoration of family farming in agriculture, the removal of many of the restrictions on private industry and commerce and – perhaps most importantly for Chen – a reallocation of state investment away from defence, metallurgy and machine building, and towards light industry, and agriculture. This was the policy of 'Readjustment' which was pushed between 1978 and 1982. The focus was on structural rather than systemic change; private ownership would be countenanced, but the dominance of the state sector was to be preserved. In some ways, the model here was the New Economic Policy pursued in the USSR between 1921 and 1928.[9] Markets would be allowed to function, but this NEP model was not some form of market socialism, because price-setting would remain in state hands.

The NEP model continued to have its adherents throughout the 1980s. Readjustment (which, as we will see, was in many respects an attempt to restore the pre-1955 system) was abandoned after 1982, and in retrospect 1978–82 was the swansong for the Old Left; even the Tian'anmen massacre and the economic debates of that period did not lead to any significant policy reversal. Nevertheless, the Leninist NEP model continued to attract Old Left intellectuals such as He Xin well into the 1990s. For example, He Xin and others famously characterized the attempts by the World Bank to impose neoclassical economics on China as 'cultural imperialism' on the part of the US establishment and as economic suicide for China. When allied to He Xin's fierce nationalism, this doctrine made for a powerful cocktail and attracted many adherents. The survival of some of these ideas was further strengthened by the emergence of a New Left, as represented by (*inter alios*) Wang Shaoguang and Cui Zhiyuan, during the 1990s. Both offered coherent and searching critiques of the market socialist model. Wang, for example, has argued powerfully against decentralization; only fiscal centralization (and hence central government transfers from east to west) offers a viable solution to the problem of regional inequality. And Cui's support of workplace democracy in the mid-1990s – his model was based on Mao's famous Angang Constitution – offered an appealing solution (not, however, to the Old Left) to the problem of SOE inefficiency. In a sense, Cui takes the democratizing logic of the Cultural Revolution one stage further. Thus the left was never entirely marginalized during the 1982–96 period and as inequality increased, so the appeal of its underlying message grew.[10]

The capitalist alternative: Anglo-Saxon, Rheinish and neoauthoritarian capitalism

The second theoretical possibility in the early 1980s was to make a complete transition to some form of capitalism. One variant on this theme, and the most radical solution, was of course to adopt the Anglo-Saxon model, in which state ownership was all but non-existent. The Japanese, French and West German 'Rheinish' model of indicative planning, plus state ownership of some key industries, was also attractive. But the adoption of either form of capitalism would require a massive programme of privatization, and it was obvious that such a step might lead to very big rises in unemployment and hence threaten regime stability. Unlike many of the Western economists who have advised post-socialist regimes, the Chinese leadership was entirely realistic about the social consequences of privatization and hesitant about proceeding down that path. There was also a recognition that the underpinning of property rights by parliamentary democracy, a free media and an independent judiciary – all hallmarks of the Western democracies – would be impossible to combine with a one-party system. Accordingly, the models of authoritarian capitalism (or neoauthoritarianism as it was usually called in the debates of the late 1980s and early 1990s) adopted in Singapore, Taiwan and South Korea appealed much more, especially to Zhao Ziyang.[11] The Russian failure to prosper under an essentially democratic regime in the early 1990s served only to strengthen the position of the neoauthoritarians. Its central tenet was set out by Wu Jiaxiang: 'neo-authoritarianism is an express train toward democracy by building markets' (Wu 1989: 36). The long-run objective was democracy, but neoauthoritarianism was seen as the means to that end in the short run. This model thus combined a market economy – that is, essentially private ownership and market-based price-setting – with continued CCP rule. It would not be possible to combine authoritarian rule with a *fully* market-orientated economy because the property right uncertainty for private agents resulting from authoritarianism would lead to sub-optimal levels of investment. Private entrepreneurs would not invest if they risked profit and property confiscation, as they would in an authoritarian state. Accordingly, some state-led investment would be a necessity under this sort of system – as it is in Singapore. Nevertheless, compromise or not, such a system of authoritarian capitalism would be a world removed from the Maoist economic system which Deng inherited.

Chinese market socialism

The final alternative was to move much further down the path of market socialism than envisaged by Chen Yun or as practised in the early Maoist era. Chen's NEP model was built around the principles of extensive state ownership and price-setting by the state. However, one could in principle combine extensive state ownership with *market*-based price determination; this is the type of model which features prominently in John Roemer's (1994, 1996) conception of market socialism. Such a decentralized approach to price-setting would, at a stroke, remove the informational problems which had bedevilled central planners in the USSR, Eastern Europe and indeed China itself and thereby improve allocative efficiency. However, by retaining a large measure of public ownership, the equity objectives that are integral to socialism could nevertheless be realized. In effect, Roemer's vision of market socialism does away with inequalities which derive from share ownership and from profits. Inequalities are allowed to exist, but only in so far as they reflect differences in productivity in the labour market.[12] Although few of China's planners consciously conceptualized the issues in this way, it was – as we shall see – precisely the model with which the People's Republic ended up in the mid-1990s.

The evolution of policy

In practice, the CCP chose to adopt the early Maoist model in the aftermath of the 1978 Third Plenum. Late Maoism was repudiated, and so to Chairman Hua's 'foreign leap forward'. However, there was no attempt at privatization in either urban or in (most of) rural China. Nevertheless, the set-up of new non-state firms was allowed, prices were altered by the state to more closely reflect notional market conditions and the more relaxed international environment meant that the defence industrialization of the late Maoist era could be brought to a conclusion. By 1982, however, there was a general perception that the more market-orientated of China's experiments had been most successful, and therefore that a more radical strategy was possible, and indeed desirable.

Between 1982 and 1989, therefore, policy-making became much more radical. Ownership reform was very much on the agenda as a wholesale process of agricultural decollectivization was pushed through across the Chinese countryside. Many price controls were lifted, as market forces were given an increasingly free rein. The process signalled the abandonment of the Leninist model, and a recognition that nothing less than some form of market socialism – characterized by liberalization and by the retreat of the state to occupy only the commanding heights of industry and infrastructure – would serve to generate rapid growth. However, price reform combined with macroeconomic expansion ignited an inflationary bubble which led directly to the democracy movement, and ultimately to the Tian'anmen massacre and the fall of Zhao Ziyang in 1989.

Box 10.1 **Chinese economic policy, 1978–1996**

Phase	Title	Policy
1978–82	Readjustment	Industrial liberalization
		Readjustment of fiscal priorities
		Changes in the state-set relative price structure
		SEZs established
1982–9	The beginnings of market socialism	Decollectivization
		Further industrial liberalization
		Beginnings of market-based price determination
1989–91	Rectification: the Tian'anmen massacre and macro contraction	Suppression of student and worker dissent
		Cuts in government spending
		Transition to market socialism halted
		Pause in the policy of opening-up
1991–6	Completion of the market socialist project	Price liberalization completed
		Acceleration in the pace of opening-up
		Introduction of stock markets
		Fiscal and monetary expansion

The drift towards market socialism began anew in the early 1990s. Price reform was completed between 1991 and 1996; the Tian'anmen repression and more contractionary macropolicy made that easier to accomplish by holding down demand and by cowing the workforce into accepting rises in the prices of key wage goods. In many ways, this was a classic neoauthoritarian programme. At the same time, many of the restrictions on foreign trade and inward investment were removed in the wake of Deng's 'southern tour' in 1992, which extolled the virtues of the special economic zones. However, macroeconomic policy again became overly expansionary, leading to a new inflationary bubble in the mid-1990s. For all that, a genuinely market socialist economy had been created by the time of Deng's death in 1997. Large swathes of the industrial sector remained in state hands, but virtually all prices had been liberalized and the open door policy had been implemented so fully that membership of the WTO became a realistic policy option.

This rather chequered path demonstrates one of the key truths about this era: there was no blueprint for reform, and no country which China could easily copy. The experiences of the East Asian newly industrializing countries were instructive, but the legacies of Maoism made China's situation unique. A new Chinese model of development had to be developed from scratch. It is therefore worth looking in more detail at the way in which policy unfolded after 1978.

Readjustment, 1978–1982

Economic policy-making between 1978 and 1982 was dominated by the theme of 'Readjustment'. More precisely, Party policy was encapsulated in the slogan 'readjusting, restructuring, consolidating and improving the national economy' approved by the Central Committee in April 1979.[13] The central idea was that the growth rate could be accelerated by reallocating state investment from less efficient sectors (defence, metallurgy and machine-building to name but three) to more efficient sectors (in particular those which produced inputs for agriculture and consumer durables). The corollary was that ownership change was unnecessary. Structural change rather than systemic reform was all that was needed to accelerate the growth rate. Nevertheless, even though Readjustment was not an especially radical policy initiative, its adoption heralded the end of Hua Guofeng's 'foreign leap forward'.[14]

Several areas were identified for Readjustment: the ratio of agricultural to industrial production, the ratio of light to heavy industrial production, the structure of heavy industry itself (meaning increased production of inputs destined for agriculture and light industry) and the structure of agriculture (meaning less attention to grain production). Self-evidently, this was an agenda for balanced growth which was directed primarily towards the task of raising living standards by increased production of (non-grain) agricultural commodities and industrial consumer goods (Liang 1982).

The other key component of the Readjustment strategy was a change in the relative price structure. Policy here was designed to align state-set prices more closely with social marginal costs in an attempt to provide incentives to producers. This was a particular concern in respect of agriculture, where state procurement prices were so low by the late 1970s that it was impossible for communes to make any sort of profit on the production of a wide range of agricultural commodities; these included wheat, corn, vegetable oil and cotton, all of which were unprofitable to produce at some point or other during 1975–8 (Han and Feng 1992). This pro-industry bias in the internal terms of trade meant that there was little incentive for peasants to increase production, and it is therefore fair to conclude that one reason for slow agricultural growth under Mao was this distorted price structure.[15] China's planners sought to address this issue early in the Readjustment period. Accordingly, procurement prices were increased on average by 22.1 per cent in 1979, the margin between the quota and above-quota price was increased and the state paid still higher 'negotiated' prices on still higher sales (Sicular 1988, 1989). This shift in the terms of trade towards agriculture continued thereafter. If the index of the terms of trade is set at 100 in 1978, it had risen to 150 by 1985 and to 189 by 1996 (Bramall 2000a: 315). However, more general attempts to estimate an 'optimal' relative price structure which could simply be imposed by the planners on the economy were far less successful. The central problem of how to calculate prices in a non-market economy without reference to demand remained (Naughton 1995: 129–30). Indeed it is revealing that very little attempt was made to adjust the price of energy even though Chinese energy prices were well below world levels. The coal price rose by about 6 per cent in 1980, and it increased by more than the average for industrial products during 1980–2 (ZGTJNJ 2000: 305). Nevertheless, this change was far smaller than the adjustment required, and the price of energy was actually allowed to fall in 1980 and 1982 even though there was massive excess demand across the economy.

The period 1978–82 also saw considerable change in the structure of ownership, even though there was no attempt at privatization. By October 1981, nearly 40 per cent of production teams had abandoned the collective and restored family farming. Controls on the operation of private industry were tacitly lifted in some parts of the Chinese countryside in the late 1970s. Wenzhou municipality in Zhejiang province was the pacesetter here; by 1982, about 12 per cent of total gross industrial output value was being contributed by the private sector (WZTJNJ 2001: 203).[16] Some attempts were also made to reinvigorate state-owned enterprises. For one thing, the freeze on urban wages in force between 1963 and 1977 was lifted.[17] In addition, SOEs were allowed to retain a large proportion of their profits, and were granted much more autonomy in respect of the wage scales and the payment of bonuses; launched in Chongqing in 1978, these reforms were extended across most of the state sector during 1979 and 1980 (Wu 2005: 145). Furthermore, SOEs were allowed to sell some of their products at market-determined prices once they had met the requirements of the plan, an issue discussed further below. Still, it is worth emphasizing that no attempt was made to promote privatization during the Readjustment period. It was simply not on the agenda in the early 1980s.[18] The aim of industrial policy during this period was liberalization, not privatization

The other important initiative in the Readjustment period was the establishment of four Special Economic Zones (SEZs) in Shenzhen, Shantou, Zhuhai (all in late 1979) and in Xiamen (October 1980). The aim was to attract foreign direct investment, and hence promote both exports (from newly established joint venture companies) and technology transfer. In order to do that, a relatively relaxed regulatory regime was established and tax holidays were granted. Two important but often neglected points about the SEZs need to be made.[19] First, the decision to establish the SEZs in south-east China – rather than in the key industrial centres of Shanghai and Liaoning – was only partly motivated by the proximity of Hong Kong. As importantly, it was a deliberate attempt to avoid 'capitalist contagion'. Guangdong and Fujian, the two provinces which hosted the SEZs, were comparatively under-industrialized and therefore little damage would be done if the SEZ programme spiralled out of control. Interestingly enough, Deng Xiaoping seems later to have concluded that it had been wrong not to have given SEZ status to Shanghai:

> In retrospect, one of my biggest mistakes was leaving out Shanghai when we launched the four special economic zones. If Shanghai had been included, the situation with regard to reform and opening in the Yangzi delta, the entire Yangzi river valley and, indeed, the whole country would be quite different. (Deng 1992: 363–4)

Second, the construction of the SEZs was financed to a very considerable extent by central government. For example, as well as direct financial subsidies, some 25,000 PLA engineers and workers were sent to Shenzhen (Kleinberg 1990: 58). Foreign investors certainly contributed, but the SEZ programme would simply not have happened without central government investment in infrastructure.

The macroeconomic aggregates show the impact of these various Readjustment policies (Figure 10.1). In fact, Chinese Readjustment was almost a classic example of a World Bank structural adjustment programme in that it cut government spending and shifted resources away to a more 'efficient' sector of the economy. Government spending as a proportion of GDP was cut sharply, falling from 31.5 per cent in 1979 (when it was partially inflated by the war against Vietnam) to just over 22 per cent in 1982. At the same time, the balance of industrial production shifted sharply away from heavy industry and towards light industry. As a result, the share of light industry in industrial output rose from 43 per cent in 1978 to 51.5 per cent in 1981. In some of the provinces, the change was even greater. In Beijing, Liaoning, Sichuan, Jiangsu, Shaanxi and Shandong, the light industry share rose by 10 percentage points or more between 1978 and 1981 (SSB 1990).

Particular sectors singled out for investment cuts were defence (especially Third Front projects), rural education and the production of agricultural machinery. For example, the abandonment of the campaign to 'learn from Dazhai', at the heart of which had been the promotion of agricultural mechanization, led to a sharp fall in the production of agricultural machinery; its share in total industrial production more than halved between 1977 and 1981. Textiles were the main beneficiary; production as a percentage of gross industrial output value rose from 12.4 to 16.7 per cent during 1977–81 (SSB 1985: 34–5). The Readjustment programme made

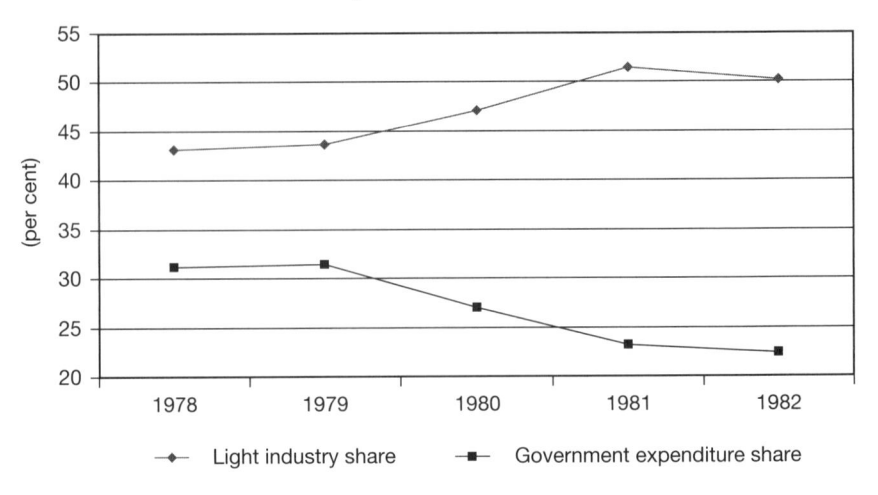

Figure 10.1 The impact of Readjustment (Sources: SSB (1990: 10); SSB (1999: 6 and 8).)

Note: The government (budgetary) expenditure share is as a percentage of GDP at current prices. The light industry share is the share of light industrial production in the gross value of all types of industrial production (GVIO) at current prices.

itself felt particularly strongly in the rural CBE sector. The number employed in agricultural enterprises fell from 6 million in 1978 to 3.4 million in 1982, a period during which total employment in the sector rose from 28 to 31 million (MOA 1989: 292). However, the CBE industrial sector experienced extensive restructuring. The production of building materials and electrical equipment was sharply reduced, as was that of nitrogenous and phosphate fertilizers. By contrast, the production of textiles in CBEs greatly increased (XZNJ 1989: 44, 56, 59; MOA 1989: 298–9). In the process, labour productivity increased significantly; it more than doubled in agricultural enterprises and rose by over 50 per cent in industrial CBEs.

The most visible short-run consequence of the Readjustment programme was a reduction in the growth rate of GDP. As Figure 10.2 shows, the rate of growth dipped from nearly 12 per cent in 1978 to a mere 5.2 per cent in 1981. This was well below the post-1978 trend and in fact, as we shall see, only in 1988 and 1989 was the annual growth rate below this for the entire 1978–2005 period. The readjustment may have been necessary, but the loss of output (relative to potential) that occurred during 1979–81 was very considerable for a comparatively poor country.

The long-run impact of the Readjustment programme is much more difficult to gauge. In part, this is because of the rash of systemic changes which occurred after the middle of 1982. It is therefore very hard to judge whether post-1982 trends reflected the medium-term impact of Readjustment or the accelerating rate of systemic change. Nevertheless, the impact on industrial structure was relatively long-lived. To be sure, the light-industry share fell back from over 51 per cent in 1981 to 47 per cent in 1985, but it was back up to 49 per cent by 1988. In any case, even the 1985 nadir of 47 per cent was still well up on the 43 per cent of 1978.

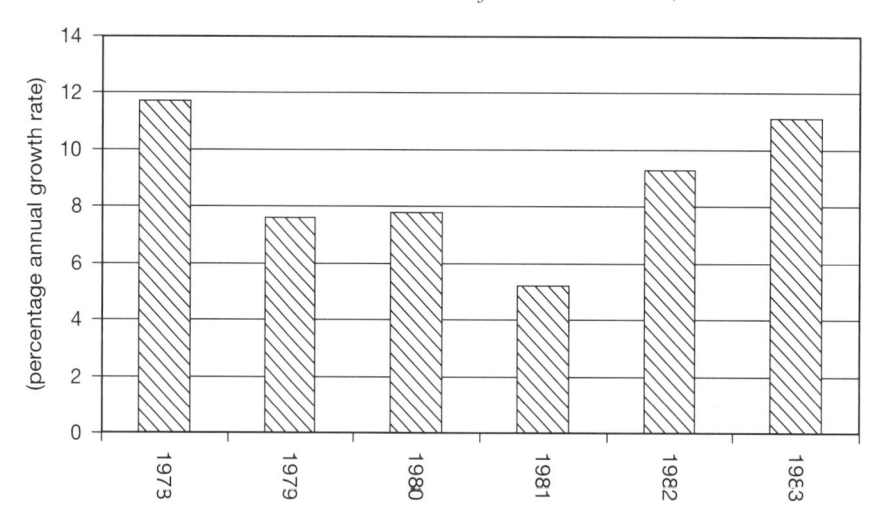

Figure 10.2 Annual growth rate of GNI during Readjustment (percentage change; comparable prices) (Source: ZGTJNJ (2005: 53).)

It therefore seems fair to conclude that the balance of Chinese industrial production was permanently altered, and there is little doubt that the increased supply of consumer goods did much to raise material living standards and to build a coalition of support behind Deng's reform programme.

For all that, the consensus amongst most Chinese and Western economists is that the Readjustment programme did not go far enough to reinvigorate the economy. Even those sympathetic to the notion that extensive state intervention is a *sine qua non* for rapid growth have noted that the policies of 1978–82 left China with an economy which was still very recognizably Leninist: price-setting remained in state hands and only very limited privatization had been carried out. Much more change was needed if China was to create a genuinely market socialist economy. Those of a neoclassical persuasion within the Chinese policy-making bureaucracy itself were even more critical: for them, capitalism was the only way to guarantee rapid growth, and accordingly the reforms of 1978–82 were derisory in scope and impact. The Readjustment programme (similarly structural adjustment programmes) may have been essential to restore macroeconomic stability, but it did not go far enough in addressing the issue of continuing state ownership. Only privatization could resolve the fundamental problem of inefficiency caused by soft budget constraints.[20] The scene was thus set for a more neoliberal approach to economic policy-making after 1982.

Decollectivization, price reform and the road to Tian'anmen, 1982–1991

As has been seen, economic policy-making between 1978 and 1982 focused on Readjustment rather than on systemic reform. After 1982, however, the advocates of Readjustment were increasingly marginalized, and the reformers assumed centre stage. The guiding principle for them was that it was entirely possible to combine a market economy with socialism. A number of Deng's speeches and statements during 1985 set out this agenda, which was to guide policy-making throughout the remainder of the 1980s and during the early 1990s (Deng 1985: 152):

> It is clear now that the right approach is to open to the outside world, combine a planned economy with a market economy and introduce structural reforms. Does this run counter to the principles of socialism? No, because in the course of reform we shall make sure of two things: one is that the public sector of the economy is always predominant; the other is that in developing the economy we seek common prosperity, always trying to avoid polarization. The policies of using foreign funds and allowing the private sector to expand will not weaken the predominant position of the public sector, which is a basic feature of the economy as a whole. On the contrary, those policies are intended in the last analysis to develop the productive forces more vigorously and to strengthen the public sector. So long as the public sector plays a predominant role in China's economy, polarization can be avoided.

Nevertheless, and it is a point that has often been made, the process of Chinese transition was gradual, and stands in sharp contrast to events in Russia (Nolan 1995). Not only did China travel a much smaller distance down the path towards a market economy in the 1980s and early 1990s (especially in that privatization was largely avoided), but also, in so far as China did liberalize, the pace of change was slow. In a very real sense, therefore, it makes sense to describe Chinese reform as gradualist, a process of 'crossing the river by feeling for the stones' (*mo shitou guohe*) or 'growing out of the plan' (Naughton 1995).

The result of this progressive reorientation of policy was a dramatic acceleration in the pace of change after 1982, at least compared to what had happened between 1978 and 1982. The two most dramatic changes were agricultural reform and the removal of price controls. Other changes did occur. Decision-making and fiscal powers were decentralized; China increasingly opened itself up to foreign trade; controls on private industry were progressively relaxed; and attempts were made to improve the performance of urban industry. However, the significance of some of these changes can easily be exaggerated. As will be shown in Chapter 11, China remained only partially integrated into the world economy before 1992; little FDI was attracted during the 1980s and tariffs remained high. The changes in the urban industry sector fell far short of anything that could be styled privatization; Chapter 12 discusses these issues in more detail. Most would-be Chinese entrepreneurs were very reluctant to establish large industrial enterprises; they worried about being labelled as capitalist roaders. The private industrial sector therefore remained small. And the impact of fiscal decentralization has been exaggerated in much of the literature. As will be discussed in Chapter 12, it was less important in driving the growth of rural industry than has sometimes been claimed. The really significant changes in the 1980s were in agriculture and in price-setting. Let us consider these in turn.

The agricultural revolution

The Third Plenum of 1978 was chiefly important in an economic sense because it gave approval to a number of experiments. For all the continuities between the early 1970s and the era of Hua Guofeng, Hua's time in office was one of significant experimentation in economic policy-making. For example, the Plenum gave approval to small-scale attempts to invigorate state-owned industry by providing managers with greater decision-making power; Sichuan was in the vanguard.

However, experimentation was most dramatic in the sphere of agriculture, where the introduction of family farming and private markets in poor regions were more or less condoned by local officials.[21] This process of agricultural experimentation was especially marked in Anhui under the leadership of Wan Li, and in Sichuan province (presided over by Zhao Ziyang). The reforms there were judged to be a great success by 1978; the famous slogan *yao chifan Zhao Ziyang; yao chimi zhao Wan Li* ('if you want to eat grain, call Ziyang; if you want to eat rice, call Wan Li') was already in wide circulation.

The initial reforms in agriculture, especially in Anhui and Sichuan, focused not on changing ownership or even the management of collectives but rather on reducing the tax and procurement burden, and giving teams much more discretion over cropping patterns. For example, many aspects of Maoist agricultural policy were reversed under the slogans of *fangkuan zhengce* ('relax government controls') and *tiyang shengxi* ('recuperate and multiply'), which were popularized across Sichuan as early as the spring of 1977. Private commerce, for example, was encouraged. Triple cropping of grain was largely abandoned; it had proved impossible to achieve in many areas because of labour shortages and because the growing season was too short. Instead, communes were given much more freedom over the range of crops cultivated.[22] And the policy of *tiyang shengxi* led to big reductions in taxation and procurement quotas in poor areas. In conjunction with better weather (1976 was a particularly bad year) and the introduction of the full Green Revolution package, the effect was to bring about a surge in agricultural production in 1977 and 1978.

Indeed, although the restoration of private farming occurred in some poor parts of China during 1976–1982, there was no *general* programme of decollectivization in the late 1970s and indeed the process of decollectivization was very slow.[23] Accordingly, although some (for example Sachs and Woo 1994) have characterized Chinese agricultural reform as an example of shock therapy or big bang, it actually makes more sense to characterize the process of change as gradual (Box 10.2).

The initial management reforms divided production teams into smaller units or groups. This was the system of *baochan daozu*, and in its essentials was little different from collective farming.[24] The logic behind *baochan daozu* was that the problems of supervision and control of the labour force which afflicted Chinese collectives could be obviated by creating smaller units of production. Production groups, being smaller than teams, would ensure that the value of each work point

Box 10.2 Agricultural institutions, 1976–1984

Chinese name	Translation	Peak year
baochan daozu	contracting production to work groups	1980 (25 per cent)
baochan daohu	contracting production to households	1981 (26 per cent)
baogan daohu (or dabaogan)	contracting everything to households	1983 and after (94 per cent in December 1983)

Source: Chung (2000: 64–5).

Note
The peak year data refer to the year in which the highest percentage share of teams using that system was recorded.

would be much more closely related to labour productivity, and hence discourage shirking (Liu 1994). The system of *baochan daohu* was much more of a hybrid because it restored most management decisions to households even though decisions concerning income distribution remained in the hands of the collective. Only the system of *baogan daohu* was family farming proper, because, as the name suggests, this involved contracted all decision-making, and transferring assets, to households.[25] This system has also often been called the household responsibility system because it delegates the responsibility for farm management to households.

Anhui is the province usually credited with pioneering reform, and there is no doubt that decollectivization did occur early in some of it as counties; the case of Fengyang, where decollectivization began in 1977, is the best-known example, However, Anhui as a whole moved rather slowly to embrace family farming. In fact, Guizhou was the only province where more than 50 per cent of production teams had adopted family farming by the end of 1980. Nationally, the 50 per cent figure was reached only in December 1981, and even this figure included households practising *baochan daohu* (which was not family farming at all). Sixty-seven perc ent of teams had introduced the *baogan* system prior to June 1982, and given that the bulk of the harvest is sown and collected during the summer and early autumn, we are justified in seeing 1982 as the first year in which a preponderance of the harvest was produced on family farms. Only by December 1983 was the process of decollectivization complete; by then, 94 per cent of teams had restored family farming (Chung 2000: 64–5). The following year, the final step in the process was taken when it was announced that communes, production teams and the production would be abolished, their administrative functions being taken over by the newly restored *xiang* (township) and *cun* (village). The agricultural system has remained largely unchanged ever since.

Given this relatively slow pace of change, there is an argument for seeing the entire period between December 1976 and December 1983 as a transition period between collective and family farming. Alternatively we can use December 1981 as the point at which the dominance of family farming was restored.[26] Yet however we date it, evidently the second land reform was a gradual process, certainly much more so than the introduction of collective farming during 1955–6. Family farming – the system of *baogan daohu* – had been adopted by less than 40 per cent of production teams even as late as the autumn and winter of 1981. In other words, the Chinese countryside was still dominated by collective farming at the end of 1981.

It remains a matter for debate whether this process of Chinese decollectivization was spontaneous or pushed from above.[27] My own interpretation is that much of the initial decollectivization, especially in mountainous and poor areas, was driven by popular demand and encouraged by local leaders. Given that material living standards and yields had risen only very slowly in these areas in the late Maoist era, it was almost inevitable that a return to family farming would be looked upon favourably; almost anything was deemed worth trying. In more prosperous parts of China – the counties on the Chengdu plain (Endicott 1988: 134), Sunan, Yantai in Shandong and virtually the whole of Manchuria – decollectivization was widely resisted. In Heilongjiang, for example, only 9 per cent of teams had adopted *baogan* even as late as May 1982, by which time the national figure was around 70 per cent (Bramall 2000a: 328–9). In part this resistance reflected the hostility of provincial leaders, but it was grounded in a recognition that a return to small-scale farming would hamper mechanization and the maintenance (still more the expansion) of irrigation systems. As a result of the 1979 price change, the introduction of new seeds and greater availability of chemical fertilizer, the agricultural sector was booming in many parts of China during the early 1980s and it is therefore far from obvious that collective farming was an obstacle to agrarian progress. Thus, as Hinton (1990) argued so eloquently, decollectivization imposed real costs on the Chinese countryside, and its universal imposition across China was arguably as unwise as the earlier decision in 1955–6 to impose collectives.

(a) Agricultural performance after 1978

There is no doubt that the *package* of agricultural reforms was very successful in the sense that output surged in the late 1970s and early 1980s.[28] Table 10.1 brings together data on the growth of overall agricultural output and grain production. It shows that there was a period of very rapid transitional growth between 1981 and 1984, reflecting a combination of weather (1980 and 1981 were years of flooding whereas 1984 was a very good year), a reduction in underreporting of output and a range of policy changes, both institutional and structural.

But the sort of miraculous growth achieved between 1981 and 1984 was not sustainable; the trend rate of growth between 1984 and 2006 fell back to about 3.9 per cent per year.[29] Of course this was considerably faster than the trend growth rate between 1963 and 1981 of about 2.9 per cent per year; as Figure 10.3 shows,

Table 10.1 Agricultural growth rates, 1963–2006 (per cent per annum)

	Growth of agricultural GVA	Growth of farm sector output	Growth of grain production
1963–81	2.9	3.3	3.5
1981–84	10.6	9.5	6.8
1984–2006	3.9	4.3	1.0

Sources: SSB (1999: 4 and 31); ZGTJNJ (2006: 59, 462 and 466); SSB (2000a: 37 and 462); ZGTJNJ (2007: 465 and 478).

Note
GVA is at 1980 prices. Farm sector output refers to the gross value of farm output (not value-added), measured at 1980.

the growth rate was clearly faster (the trend line is steeper) after 1984 than it had been between 1963 and 1981. Nevertheless, the difference in growth rates between the two periods is by no means as dramatic as often suggested.

Why did growth accelerate in the 1980s? In essence, the explanation lies in the package of agricultural reforms introduced in the late 1970s and early 1980s. The combination of decollectivization, new seed varieties, the completion of irrigation

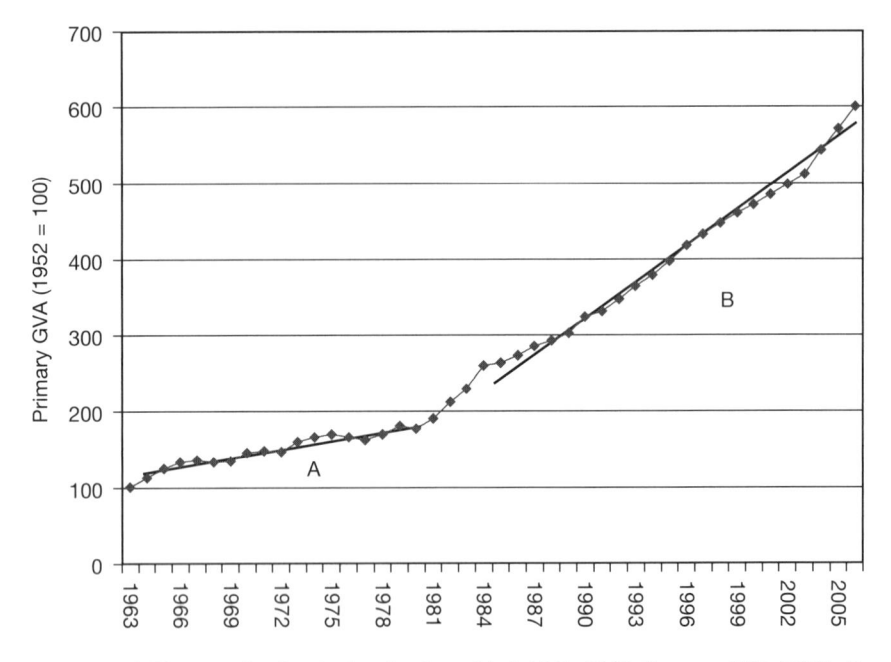

Figure 10.3 The growth of agricultural value-added, 1963–2006 (Sources: SSB (1999: 4); ZGTJNJ (2007: 59).)

Note: The solid lines A and B indicate approximate trends during the periods 1963–81 and 1984–2006 respectively. They are provided for illustrative purposes only. Agricultural GVA is at comparable prices and calculated by aggregation of subsectors.

projects, greater supplies of chemical fertilizer and more favourable relative prices proved highly effective (Chapter 7). One part of this package particularly deserves emphasis because it is often neglected, namely the changing composition of agricultural output. A change in macroeconomic priorities, in conjunction with the decentralization of decision-making to farm households, led to far less emphasis on grain production, and indeed less emphasis on farming in general. As Table 10.1 shows, the rate of growth of grain production was much slower after 1984 than it had been during the Maoist era. This provides a clue as to what has going on. In effect, China has been shifting its rural labour force and its inputs away from grain farming and towards more profitable subsectors such as animal husbandry and fisheries. In 1978, farming accounted for 80 per cent of GVAO, and animal husbandry and fisheries for 15 and 2 per cent respectively. By 2006, farming was down to 51 per cent whereas husbandry stood at 32 per cent and fisheries at 10 per cent (ZGTJNJ 2007: 465). Thus the rapid growth of agricultural GVA reflects not so much the dynamism of the individual agricultural subsectors, but rather the increasingly greater weight of animal husbandry, fisheries and non-grain crops in total output. None of this is to criticize the post-1984 agrarian strategy, but we do need to recognize that agricultural growth has been driven as much by a change in policy objectives as it has by the reform package per se.

(b) Continuing agricultural problems

Chinese agriculture has grown quite quickly during the 1980s and 1990s, as we have seen. However, its efficiency remains low and it is beset by a range of problems. Even relatively optimistic scholars such as Rozelle and Huang (2006) have drawn our attention to some of China's failures (and its productivity implications) even whilst emphasizing the more positive aspects of China's record on technical progress in the farm sector.

For one thing, Chinese agriculture has become very reliant on massive inputs of chemical fertilizer. Total usage in 1975 was 5.5 million tonnes but this had risen to 17.4 million by 1984, 40.8 million in 1998 and to 47.7 million tonnes by 2005 (SSB 2005b: 44; SSB 2006: 469). As a result, China's per hectare usage was second only to Japan by the mid-1990s (Maddison 1998: 113). The People's Republic is nearing the point where further growth will lead to declining yields, and the environmental consequences (especially in terms of pollution of water) are already apparent (Smil 2004: 118–19). Widespread use of plastics is also causing considerable problems, not least for the use of agricultural machinery, and declining use of organic fertilizers is likely to produce declining soil fertility in the near future (Veeck and Wang 2000: 66 and 76)

A second problem is the deterioration of China's irrigation system, which had a seriously adverse effect on total factor productivity in the rice sector and offset the positive effects of the introduction of new varieties. The Green Revolution technologies introduced across the world in the late twentieth century comprised a package of technology: irrigation improvement (such as tube wells, drip irrigation systems and large-scale water control projects), high yielding (and increasingly

GM) varieties and increased use of chemical fertilizer. Without increased water availability to complement the other elements in the package, the rise in yields is typically small. Irrigation is therefore crucial, and in this regard the decollectivization of the early 1980s caused a range of problems. In particular, it fragmented control of the irrigation system and made it difficult to mobilize labour for irrigation maintenance and construction, which produced a growing number of disputes between households over access to water, especially in the north of China. Many scholars have drawn attention to the problem (Vermeer 1997; Nickum 1990b; Watson 1989; Nickum 1995: 67–70; Hinton 2006: 194), and whilst Vermeer is right to caution against the conclusion that the water conservancy system has collapsed, there is no doubt that it has deteriorated significantly in quality as structures (including tube wells) have been neglected or abandoned. In addition, although the introduction of water fees in the 1980s may well have encouraged a more efficient use of water – a point celebrated by some authors (Johnson *et al.* 1998) – the reduction in consumption has delayed the introduction of high-yielding new varieties which are water-using.

The third key problem is that of small farm size, compounded by the fragmentation of holdings (Hinton 2006: 193). This problem dates back to the decollectivization settlement of the early 1980s, which sought to equalize the quantity and quality of land allocated to households by dividing village land up into small plots. The net result was that a typical household received plots of land which were scattered across the village. The data for 1986 show that 51 per cent of farms were less than 0.3 hectares in size, and this figure had gone up to 54 per cent in 1990. And the comprehensive Agricultural Census of 1997 found that no less than 79 per cent of holdings were of less than 1 hectare in size; the comparable Japanese figure was 71 per cent in 1986. In fairness, however, it remains a matter for debate whether average farm size is too small. For example, some studies have found little evidence of economies of scale (Wan and Cheng 2001), though these types of studies do not properly allow for the gains from the mobilization of labour for infrastructural projects.

The case against parcellization is much more generally accepted. The data show that a typical farm was divided into nearly ten non-contiguous parcels in 1984–5. This had fallen to around six plots by 1990, about the same degree of fragmentation as reported in Buck's prewar survey (Bramall 2004: 125–6). A number of recent studies confirm that parcellization hampers technical efficiency (Nguyen *et al.* 1996; Tan *et al.* 2006); one estimate suggest that an end to fragmentation might increase grain output by as much as 70 million tonnes (Wan and Chen 2001: 192). Other trends associated with parcellization are also a cause for concern. Small-scale tractor use increased more than tenfold between 1978 and 2005, and the usage of agricultural machinery has increased approximately sixfold since 1978. However, small tractors were used as much for transport purposes as for agricultural work; China's agricultural parcels were too tiny even for small tractor use in many cases. More significantly, the number of large and medium-sized tractors increased very slowly after 1983 and peaked in 1987 at 881,000. Thereafter it declined, to reach a low of 671,000 in 1996. The total has increased since; the figure for 2005 was

1.4 million (SSB 2005b: 36; SSB 2006: 467). Nevertheless, the slow overall pace of growth serves to underline the way in which decollectivization recreated small-scale farming and thereby slowed down the release of labour. Decollectivization has served to recreate the prewar agricultural landscape, with all its embedded inefficiencies.

The conundrum which confronts the Chinese authorities is the same as that with which the governments of Taiwan and Japan have wrestled since the end of the Second World War. The solution lies in land consolidation schemes. But the difficulty is in devising policies and institutional structures which will promote such consolidation. Even in Japan, and despite much postwar effort, the percentage of farms of less than 1 hectare in size fell from 73 per cent in 1955 to only 71 per cent in 1986 (Kojima 1988: 733–34). In Taiwan, considerable energy has been put into carrying out what has been styled a second land reform based around land consolidation, but the process has been very slow (Liu *et al.* 1998).

The final constraint that China confronts is that large-scale agricultural imports are not really an option, and therefore the need to ensure food security by means of domestic production remains. It is true that the political constraints on China's foreign trade have eased immeasurably since the late 1970s. Furthermore, reductions in transport costs (especially within China as a result of Maoist investment in railways) and the development of international grain markets make large-scale grain imports an altogether more plausible proposition. Nevertheless, China's policymakers continue to shy away from reliance on large-scale imports of food, principally because that would entail dependence on the USA. That is not surprising given that the two countries are fast becoming global competitors. In principle, however, China could significantly increase its dependence on imports and at the same time ensure diversity of supply by reliance on Canada, Brazil and south-east Asia as well as the USA. In fact, the problem is more economic. Precisely because China is not a small country, it is not a price-taker in world markets. Accordingly, even a comparatively slight rise in imports would exert significant upward pressure on world food prices, thus adversely affecting China's terms of trade. That in turn would require China to export every increasing quantities of industrial goods, at falling prices and against a background of all the protectionist concerns that this type of policy would ignite in industrialized countries. Moreover, China's entry into the World Trade Organization has restricted its freedom for manoeuvre because it limits the extent to which barriers to imports, whether tariffs or subsidies, can be utilized.[30] It therefore seems likely that China will become a growing net importer of grain over the decades ahead.[31] The rise in net imports during 2004–5 therefore seems to offer a portent of what is to come.

(c) A property rights solution?

It is relatively easy to enumerate the problems faced by Chinese agriculture. It is much harder to identify the solutions. In essence, however, we can think of two different approaches to the agricultural problem. One sees the solution in more secure property rights and improved market functioning. The other regards the state as part of the solution rather than the essence of the problem.

The market-led approach sees agricultural inefficiency in China as rooted in insecure property rights and malfunctioning markets. This insecurity discourages investment and technical progress.[32] In particular, it discourages land sales and the creation of larger farms operating non-fragmented plots of land. Larger farms would make it easy to resolve irrigation problems (by reducing the collective action problems which inevitably stem from having a myriad of small family farms), as well as allowing the exploitation of those economies of scale which do exist in farming. The creation of proper land and rental markets, as well as the development of rural labour markets, is therefore crucial to agrarian progress. From this perspective it also follows that the development of capital markets is necessary so that farmers can borrow the funds required for land purchase, and for agricultural investment.

From this market-led perspective, Chinese decollectivization did not go far enough, because it did no more than transfer land management rights, rather than ownership, to households. And fifteen-year land management contracts introduced after decollectivization did little to encourage investment. Even though many were replaced by thirty-year year contracts in the late 1990s, many villages continued to award comparatively short-term (five- to ten-year) contracts (Krusekopf 2002). At the same time, the Chinese state did little to encourage the development of rental and finance markets, both necessary concomitants for land consolidation to occur.

These problems persisted into the 1990s (OECD 1997; Nyberg and Rozelle 1999). However, a number of academics have argued that the functioning of Chinese rural markets has improved significantly in recent years. Commodity markets are well integrated, land markets have developed quickly since the 1990s and many of those left behind by the process of out-migration have benefited from the increased scope for renting arable land (Carter and Rozelle 2001; Brandt *et al.* 2002; Rozelle and Huang 2006). From this perspective, China is moving in the right direction but a good deal more needs to be done if the productivity of agriculture is to be increased significantly.

Part of the solution to the problem of insecure property rights lies in reduced government intervention. It is argued that the problem is not merely that local government across China is guilty of sins of omission but that it has committed sins of commission. That is, farm land continues to be owned by village-level government, and this level of government has periodically redistributed land from household to household ensuring that even land management rights were insecure (Judd 1992; Zhu and Jiang 1993). In part the aim has been to hold inequality in check by ensuring that even the poorest households continue to have access to land. But, perhaps more importantly, China's villages have tried to allocate land in such a way as to concentrate it in the hands of the most efficient farmers. The most common system of land management is the *liangtianzhi* (two-field system). This involves households being allocated two types of land in addition to private plots First, households received *kouliangtian* (grain ration land) as part of the decollectivization settlement. This land was usually allocated on a per capita basis, the aim being to ensure that each household managed enough land to meet its subsistence requirements. Second, and in addition, households could usually sign a contract with the village to manage additional land (responsibility land or *zerentian*) in return for agreeing to meet a part of the procurement quota imposed by central government. In 1990, *zerentian* land accounted for 360 million *mu* in those parts of China using the *liangtian* system; *kouliangtian* accounted for a further 180 million *mu*. In addition, Chinese villages retained a reserve of land. Some of this was used to provide feed for pigs. And some was rented out (*chengbaotian*) in return for a fee and the households agreeing to take on an additional part of the village's procurement quota. Crucially, the allocation of land was not set in stone at the time of decollectivization. As households have died out or migrated, *kouliang* land reverts to the land reserve controlled by the village government. Conversely, the village allocates more *kouliang* land to households which are growing in size. Additionally, it is village government which makes decisions about how much land would be contracted out and whether households wishing to contract land represent a good or bad risk. To be sure, a secondary land market exists whereby households which have contracted land in turn lease out that land to other households. Nevertheless, it is local government which continues to exercise control. As a result, the market for land in rural China is far removed from that found in most other countries, whether developed or underdeveloped. Usufruct rights are to some extent permanent and heritable, but the system is altogether less market-driven than is the norm in both developed and developing countries.[33]

(d) Beyond property rights: the role for the state

The market-driven perspective on China's agricultural challenges outlined in the previous section is problematic. Some scholars are sceptical as to whether insecure property rights are holding back agricultural investment (Kung 1995). More fundamentally, secure property rights would not circumvent collective action problems and coordination failures: market failure is inevitable, and there is thus a *prima facie* case for state intervention. The development, maintenance and expansion of irrigation networks provides a classic example of a collective action problem which is not easily resolved by reliance on market-led interaction amongst small family farms. It is for precisely this reason that the expansion of irrigation in India was less rapid than in China in the late Maoist era. It is also telling that the introduction of a land law in Vietnam in the early 1990s explicitly designed to promote land sales has largely failed to increase farm size (Ravallion and van de Walle 2001). Landlessness has increased (mainly because well-to-do farmers have sold their land, rather than because of distress sales), but small-scale farming and fragmentation remains a severe problem, especially in the relatively fertile rural region around Hanoi.

The market-driven perspective is also problematic because, as noted above, the redistribution of farmland by the state between households has played a key role in holding income inequality in check. Any move towards a fully market-based system would run the risk of producing big differences in income from farming, and thus exacerbating the high pre-existing level of inequality in the countryside (which stems from differences in the amount of income derived by each household from the non-farm sector). In short, China's pressing need is for *more state intervention* in the rural sector rather than for less. That need not presage a return to collective farming but it does suggest the need for a very different state-led approach if the problem of agricultural inefficiency is to be resolved.

The logical conclusion to draw from this critique of the market-led approach is that the solution to China's continuing agricultural problems lies in increased state intervention designed both to hold down inequality and to promote farmland consolidation schemes. The logic here is clear: market-led solutions may push the process of consolidation along in the right direction, but are unlikely to be carried out as quickly or as effectively as they can be by a proactive state. The same is true of essentially cooperative solutions aided by state funding, as in Taiwan's second land reform of the late 1970s and early 1980s. These schemes did help to increase farm size and yields (Liu *et al.* 1998) but in general have been only a partial success, seemingly because of the reluctance of governments to fully commit to consolidation schemes (Bain 1993). The Chinese government has also been rather reluctant to proceed too rapidly down this route, even though the evidence points strongly to the benefits from the Comprehensive Agricultural Development programme which was introduced in the late 1980 (Wu *et al.* 2005).

Implementing a state-led solution to China's agricultural problems will not be easy. In particular, a renewed attempt by the state to boost agricultural output by increasing farm prices seems unlikely to succeed. Trends in relative prices between the late 1970s and the late 1980s were largely favourable to agriculture; as Figure 10.4 shows, the internal terms of trade were on an upward trajectory throughout the 1980s. This helped to maintain the growth of the early 1980s. After 1988, however, agriculture did much less well. In that year, the terms of trade reached their highest level in the post-1949 era, and thereafter prices shifted against agriculture. The trend between 1994 and 2000 was particularly unfavourable, the index declining from 303 to 213. In no small measure, this was because of big rises in agricultural production, which depressed product prices in the market-orientated environment of the late 1990s. But in a sense, it was almost inevitable that relative farm prices would fall as China became more integrated into the world economy. Grain prices were typically well above world prices at the end of the 1970s, and even in 2000 that remained true for many commodities when differences in quality are taken into account.[34] The Chinese wheat price, for example, only appears to be lower than the world price because Chinese wheat is of much lower quality than the high-grade wheat which is imported; contrast the results in Huang *et al.* (2004: 89) and Carter (2001: 80). It is therefore likely that the long-run effect of WTO accession will be to depress the price of maize, cotton, sugar and soybeans, though meat, rice and horticultural prices will probably rise (Huang *et al.* 2004: 89 and 94).

There has been some revival in the terms of trade since the nadir of 2000, but it is clear that China's agricultural sector has been operating in a much more hostile

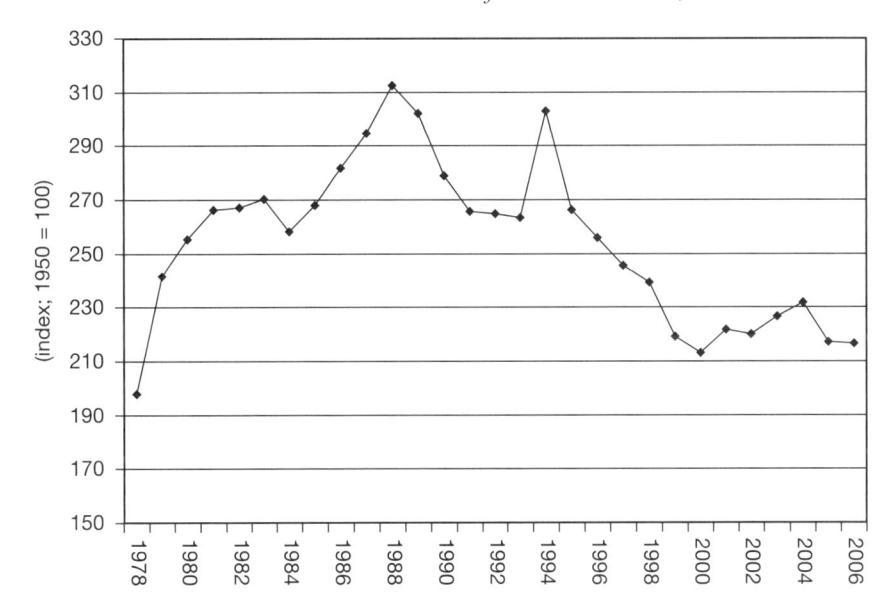

Figure 10.4 The internal terms of trade, 1978–2006 (Sources: SSB (2005a: 32–3); SSB (2005b: 203); ZGTJNJ (2007: 325 and 327).)

Note: The internal terms of trade is the index of agricultural product prices (procurement prices before 2001) divided by the index of agricultural producer good prices (industrial goods selling in rural areas before 1978).

macroeconomic environment during the last two decades than in the halcyon days of the late 1970s. These adverse price trends have impacted severely upon farm incomes, as will be discussed below. Worse, there is no easy solution to this problem. A policy of direct price-based subsidies to farmers seems to offer an obvious way forward; this was the course followed by the EU in the postwar era. However, this type of policy is largely ruled out by the terms of WTO accession. In any case, it would be extremely expensive given the size of China's farm sector, and arguably of doubtful utility because the subsidies would probably be 'captured' disproportionately by richer farmers. Pricing policy may have been effective in accelerating growth in the late 1970s, but the scope for such a policy no longer really exists. The agricultural problem will have to be solved by other means.

Fiscal policy offers one such means, not least because the state's treatment of agriculture has not been especially generous since 1978 (Huang *et al.* 2006). Measured purely in terms of financial flows (and thus ignoring any resource extraction via the terms of trade), agriculture was a net contributor to the rest of the economy. These flows were partially via the fiscal system. The contribution of agriculture to total state revenue rose during the post-1978 period, mainly because higher taxes on fruit and vegetable production offset declining income from grain. Mandatory procurement quotas also imposed an implicit grain tax on the farm sector.[35]

Furthermore, state investment in agriculture hardly changed between 1978 and 1997; a significant decline in irrigation investment is especially apparent. Nevertheless, total state investment in agriculture exceeded taxation and in that sense the priorities of the Chinese state were clear. The primary channel for financial outflows was in fact the banking system, and in this way a very substantial proportion of agricultural savings financed investment in the industrial sector. Nor is it evident that things have changed dramatically in response to the perceived crisis of the late 1990s. For example, the share of state spending on agriculture rose substantially in 1998 but, taken as a whole, there was no real trend between the late 1980s and 2004; the figure remained at around 8 per cent (SSB 2005b: 77).

The other possible solution is to reduce the price of agricultural inputs. The Chinese industrial sector has of course become much more market-orientated since 1978 as SOEs have faced growing competitive pressure from imports, from TVEs and from the private sector. Nevertheless, the rapid pace of productivity growth has not translated into substantial price falls for agricultural means of production such as plastics, chemical fertilizers and machinery. This suggests that Chinese manufacturing continues to enjoy a considerable degree of protection and monopoly power – as it has done since 1949. In other words, the problem of unequal exchange remains. Further liberalization in this area may be the best way forward for a China serious about promoting the development of agriculture.

Price reform

The second main focus of policy between 1982 and 1989 was price reform. There were two obvious differences between China and Western economies in the late 1970s. For one thing, asset ownership was vested in the Chinese state, and little changed in this regard until the late 1990s. Second, Chinese prices (including wages and interest rates) were set by the state instead of by market forces. The relative price structure was altered during the Readjustment period, as we have seen, but the fundamental approach remained: prices were set by the state rather than by market forces. All this changed during the mid- and late 1980s (Chan 1989; Yabuki 1995).

There were several arguments in favour of a move towards price-setting by market forces. The main problem for economic planners in the 1970s was the impossibility of determining whether a sector was efficient. This was because profit rates were far more closely related to the prices which enterprises were allowed to charge than to underlying economic performance. For example, mining and large swathes of agriculture were unprofitable because the prices set by the state for their products were far too low.36 By contrast, enterprises which manufactured consumer goods were immensely profitable by virtue of the high prices which could be obtained. There were thus vast differences in profit rates in 1984 which largely reflected the distorted price structure. The rate of pretax profit in light industry was 56 per cent and 76 per cent for chemicals, whereas that for the coal industry was only 3 per cent (Zhang 1988: 90–1).

One solution to this problem was for the state to alter the price structure; there was no need to introduce a market-based system of price determination simply to deal with this problem. Indeed Oscar Lange famously argued in the mid-1930s that it was quite possible for a socialist state to set prices. The central planning bureau only needed to start with prerevolutionary prices and then adjust them to reflect the evidence of shortage and oversupply; it need not compute the price for every good at every moment in time. By the late 1970s, however, it was clearly recognized that the whole business of state price-setting was a much more complex process.[37] For one thing, a vast range of commodities (each of different qualities and specifications) existed. Even if the state responded to shortages and surpluses only in the manner prescribed by Lange, the costs involved in setting prices for all these commodities were very high and therefore the inevitable tendency was for prices to be changed only very slowly – which meant that prices were out of line with those that the planners felt desirable. In addition, it made for an exceptionally difficult planning process. Precisely because so many goods were inputs into other types of production, the planners needed to consider very carefully the impact of any given price change. For example, increases in agricultural prices necessarily cut urban wages and reduced profitability in the food-processing sector. That was not necessarily a bad outcome, but there were clearly both economic and social consequences which needed to be considered. A big increase in coal prices also had profound ramifications for the rest of the economy. The obvious alternative approach was to leave price determination to market forces, though that too was not without its costs. That was because a shift to a market-based system of price determination would inevitably reintroduce a high degree of uncertainty into economic life as a result of speculation and fluctuations in both demand and supply.

Yet, and irrespective of whether the solution adopted was price adjustment by the state or reliance on market forces, the main problem posed by price reform was that it would produce general inflation. Relative price adjustment would invariably take the form of a price increases rather than falls; a cut in the average price level would require a cut in money wages, the hardest of all things to achieve given worker resistance. These price increases would feed into inflation directly, and any attempt to cushion the blow by providing price subsidies would have fiscal implications – and as likely as not fuel demand-pull inflation. Of course inflation could in principle be controlled readily enough by complementing relative price adjustment with contractionary fiscal and monetary policy, but that would tend to depress the growth rate.

In the mid-1980s, the CCP took the view that inflation was a price worth paying for the allocative gains that would follow from adjusting the relative price structure, and for the maintenance of rapid growth. Influential here was the view of Li Yining, who was a close adviser to Hu Yaobang (the Party secretary) and Hu Qili. Li saw little cause for concern in inflationary pressures. He perceived the increase in the money supply, which was the consequence of pressure on the state budget, as largely benign in that it was growth-promoting; much better, he argued, for demand to exceed supply than the converse (Li 1990). Li doubted that the Chinese population had a high degree of 'social tolerance' for inflation but was even more sceptical of the utility of combining price reform with macroeconomic contraction.

The centrepiece of the price reform strategy of the mid-1980s was the dual-track pricing system. There were two elements to this. First, enterprises were allowed to sell a significant (and rising) proportion of their output outside the plan. Second, the price at which extra-plan sales could take place was allowed to diverge from planning prices. Between 1982 and 1984, the permitted range within which above-plan sales could take place was plus or minus 20 per cent of the centrally-determined price. However, it was increasingly recognized that this type of restriction was unworkable. In October 1984, therefore, this restriction was removed; the 'Decision of the Central Committee of the CCP on Reform of the Economic Structure' effectively allowed above-plan sales at *market* prices. This policy certainly had the effect of providing an incentive to firms to increase production. However, it also created abundant opportunities for corruption; by buying commodities at central planning prices and selling at market prices, speculative profits could be made; thus was born the phenomenon of *guandao* (profiteering) and spiralling income inequality. Moreover, the scope for making speculative profits was very large indeed because of the divergence between market and plan prices. In December 1988, for example, the average market price of steel was, yuan compared to a plan price of 592 *yuan*. As for trucks, the price for a *Dongfang 12o* selling in Shenyang was 63,800 *yuan* compared with a plan price of 25,800 *yuan* (Yabuki 1995: 130).

The dual-track pricing system was only one part of the price reform process. In addition to introducing the dual-track approach, the number of commodity prices subject to any form of state control was reduced. The prices of 160 commodities were fully liberalized in September 1982, and another 350 in the autumn of 1983 (Chan 1989: 312). More agricultural and light industrial products were liberalized in January 1985. Most radically of all, the prices of non-staple consumer goods – including vegetables, fish and meat – were significantly increased in 1985 (Shirk 1993: 301). In the main, however, these price rises were offset by subsidies to the urban population, and the net effect was a combination of rapid growth but spiralling inflation. The steady post-1979 increase in farm procurement prices had not been accompanied by any corresponding increase in the consumer prices charged to urban residents. In effect, therefore, the state was paying a growing price subsidy to the urban sector, and the scale of these subsidies was running at around 30 billion *yuan*, or 13 per cent of government spending by 1988 (SSB 1999: 8). Although the subsidy burden in percentage terms had not increased since 1981, the need to finance a growing absolute volume of spending inevitably put great pressure on public finances and contributed to inflationary pressure within the Chinese economy. Indeed it was only with some difficulty that the inflationary bubble of 1985–6 was brought under control, albeit at the cost of abandoning the big change in industrial producer prices which had been initially planned for 1986 (Shirk 1993: 296–309).

The apparent insouciance of Hu Yaobang over the effects of rising prices (like Li Yining, he saw moderate inflation as a price worth paying for rapid growth), as well as his perceived failure to act more decisively against the student disturbances of 1986, left him politically isolated even though the inflation rate in 1985 was still running at less than 10 per cent (Figure 10.5). Hu was replaced as Party secretary in early 1987 by Zhao Ziyang, who had successfully portrayed himself as a relative conservative in abandoning the mooted 1986 price reforms (Shirk 1993: ch. 13). Under Zhao, and acting on the advice of Wu Jinglian, China sought to combine continuing relative price reform with a more contractionary macroeconomic stance after 1986. In this, Zhao was backed by Deng Xiaoping (1988: 257–8): 'We cannot speed up the reform without rationalizing prices … we have no choice but to carry out price reform, and we must do so despite all risks and difficulties.'

Zhao's strategy focused on lifting controls on four non-staple commodities, namely meat, eggs, vegetable and sugar, without any attempt to cushion the blow by paying subsidies. Moreover, it was announced that these changes were but the beginning of a more extensive process of price reform, and indeed much of this was accomplished; by the end of 1988, only 25 per cent of commodities were subject to full-scale state control, leaving around 25 per cent subject to floating prices (i.e. prices were allowed to vary within a specified band) and the remaining 50 per cent being market-determined (World Bank 1990: 59). In retrospect, it was a mistake to announce such radical price reform in advance. Its effect, combined with actual price rises, fuelled panic buying and this served only to intensify inflationary pressure. In February 1988, retail prices were 11 per cent higher than they had been in January 1987. By August, the inflation rate was running at 23 per cent

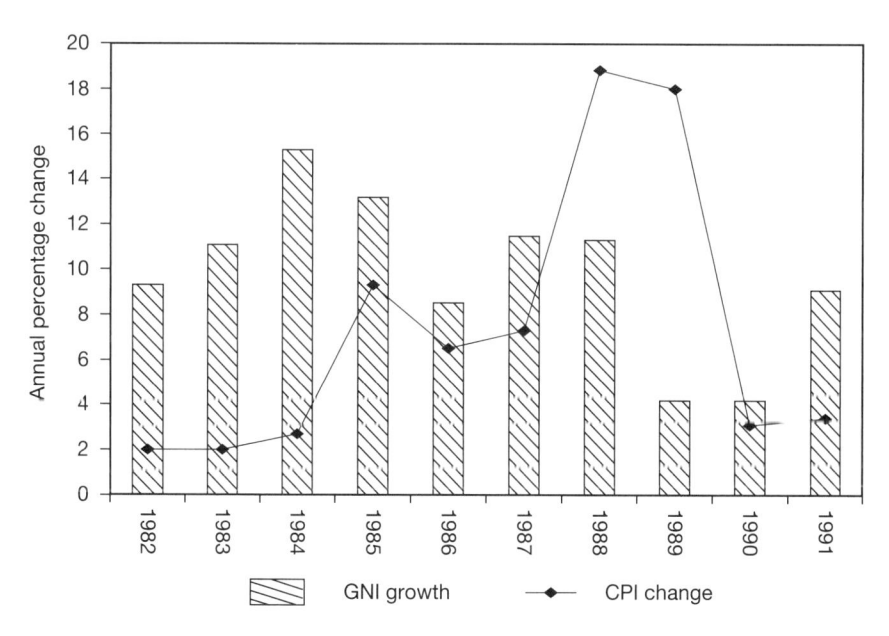

Figure 10.5 Growth of gross national income and the consumer price index, 1982–1991
 (Sources: ZGTJNJ (2005: 5): SSB (1999: 21).)

Note: The growth of GNI is at constant prices. The CPI is the official consumer price index.

and in February 1989 it peaked at 27.9 per cent. For some goods, the inflation rate was much higher; the inflation rate for vegetables peaked at 48 per cent (August 1988) and that for meat, poultry and eggs at 44 per cent in October 1988 (World Bank 1990: 165).

With the CCP bent upon pushing through these relative price changes, the only way to deal with the inflationary spiral was a process of fiscal and monetary contraction.[38] This was the approach adopted during 1988–9, and it triggered a collapse in output growth. As Figure 10.5 demonstrates, macroeconomic contraction was ultimately successful in that sense that the inflation rate was brought down; from a peak of nearly 19 per cent in 1988, the rate fell back to a mere 3 per cent by 1990. However, the cost in terms of growth was very considerable. Deng Xiaoping (1988: 258) had hoped as late as May that 'the growth rate for 1988 may still exceed 10 percent' and in that respect he was right; actual growth exceeded 11 per cent. But growth slowed markedly thereafter, with GNI registering increases of only a little over 4 per cent in both 1989 and 1990.

The contraction of 1988–90 was costly in terms of bankruptcy and rising unemployment in the small-scale private sector. More importantly, the price rises of 1988 and 1989 fuelled the democracy movement by encouraging urban workers to join with students, culminating in the great demonstrations and massacre at Tian'anmen Square in June 1989.[39] This was the classic demonstration of Deng's new authoritarianism: an increasingly market-orientated economy underpinned by an authoritarian and ruthless state. Hu Yaobang had been purged in 1987 for his support for bourgeois liberalism, and Zhao Ziyang paid the same price in 1989. For those who died in Tian'anmen Square and the subsequent witch hunt, the penalty was much greater. In addition, the need to deal with the political turmoil necessarily brought the process of economic liberalization to a halt. The process of reform was not to resume until 1991.

The last hurrah: Deng's southern tour and beyond, 1991–1996

The transition to market socialism was relaunched in 1991. The background to this was the collapse of the Soviet Union (and the failure of the attempted coup there in August 1991), and the triumph of the coalition forces in the First Gulf War, which provided a startling demonstration of US military capability. These events made it clear that the CCP faced a stark choice if it was to remain in power. It could reverse the transition process, attack corruption and inequality and recentralize the planning process – thus preserving the sort of Leninist state which Gorbachev had dismantled in the USSR during the late 1980s but running the risk of halting the growth process in its tracks. Alternatively, the CCP could attempt to rally popular support by abandoning the contractionary macroeconomic policies of 1988–90 (thus increasing the pace of economic growth) and using some of the fruits of growth to promote defence modernization and hence a nationalistic agenda.[40]

Deng's choice was to accelerate the pace of economic growth and to relaunch the marketization process. He signalled this course during his trip to Shanghai

(February 1991), and his *nanxun* (southern tour) to Shanghai and to Shenzhen in February 1992. Many parts of his 1992 speeches reveal Deng's intent very clearly, namely to push ahead with reform, to secure socialism by means of authoritarianism and state ownership of the key industries and to increase the growth rate:

> We should be bolder than before in conducting reform and opening to the outside and have the courage to experiment. We must not act like women with bound feet ... So long as we keep level-headed, there is no cause for alarm. We have our advantages: we have the large and medium-sized state-owned enterprises and the rural enterprises. More important, political power is in our hands ... Right tendencies can destroy socialism, but so can Left ones. China should maintain vigilance against the Right but primarily against the Left. The Right still exists, as can be seen from disturbances. But the Left is there too ... Our three-year effort to improve the economic environment and rectify the economic order was a success. But in assessing that effort, we can say it was an achievement only in the sense that we stabilized the economy. Should not the accelerated development of the preceding five years be considered an achievement too? (Deng 1992: 360, 361, 363 and 365)

Two of the main themes of the 1990s were the rapid opening-up of the economy to foreign trade and investment, and renewed attempts to enhance the efficiency of the industrial sector. I discuss both in later chapters. Yet more important than anything in rekindling the growth process was monetary and fiscal expansion, and Deng (1992: 364–5) seems to have regarded it as perfectly normal to have periods of rapid growth (such as 1984–99) broken up by short periods of rectification and stabilization. The government accounts show the renewed expansion very clearly (Figure 10.6). State capital construction, which had stagnated in the late 1980s, helped to pull the economy out of the doldrums in 1990, and accelerated the pace of growth during 1994–5. Government consumption expenditure helped to moderate the downturn in 1989 and provided a massive stimulus in 1991 and 1992, when it grew by 20 per cent in each year. At the same time, and in order to prevent the central government deficit spiralling out of control, a process of fiscal recentralization was initiated by Zhu Rongji, the new Premier, starting in 1994. Its central aim was to reverse the trend whereby central government budget revenue had fallen from about 35 per cent of GDP to only 15 per cent between 1979 and 1993.[41]

The net result of all this was accelerating growth. In each of the years 1992–4, the growth rate of real GNI comfortably exceeded 12 per cent, well up on the 4 per cent recorded in 1989 and 1990 (ZGTJNJ 2005: 53). That the inflation rate also spiralled – the consumer price index rose by 15 per cent in 1993 and 24 per cent in 1994 (ZGTJNJ 2005: 301) – suggests that these sorts of growth rates were unsustainable, and Zhu Rongji moved quickly to take the growth rate down to around 9 per cent by the late 1990s. For all that, the achievement of such rapid growth points to the underlying vitality of the Chinese economy right up to the time of Deng's death in early 1997.

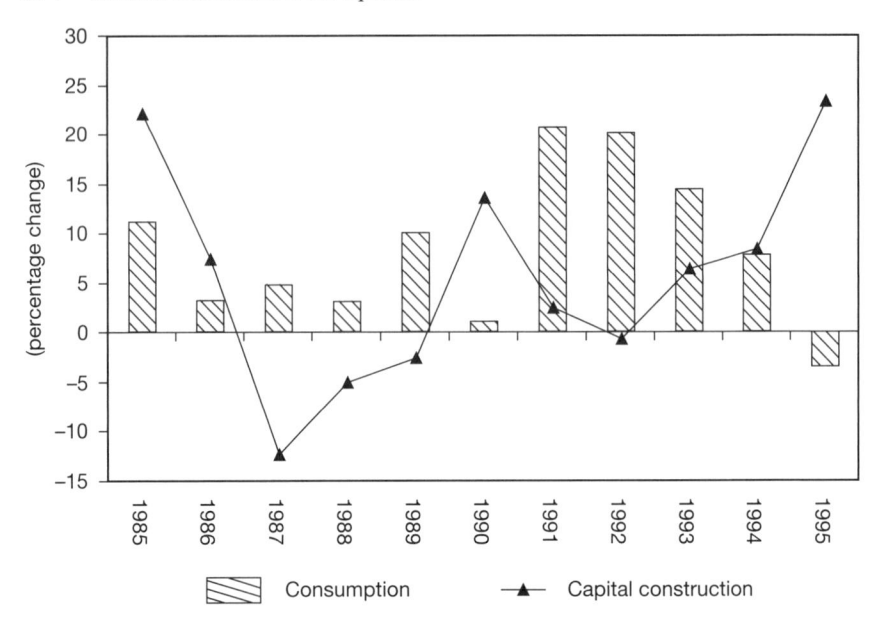

Figure 10.6 Growth of government consumption and capital construction expenditure
(Sources: World Bank (1997a: 124); SSB (1999: 11).)

Note: 'Consumption' is the annual growth of real general government consumption expenditure (GDP basis), measured at 1990 prices. The growth of capital construction expenditure by government is measured at current prices.

It deserves to be emphasized that the rebound of the economy, as well as the rapid growth which had been achieved between 1982 and 1988, was achieved under a system of market socialism. The 'market' features of the system were market-based price determination and the liberalization of entry by private firms. By 1995, for example, 78 per cent of the value of producer good sales, 89 per cent of retail sales and 79 per cent of farm commodity sales were at market prices (OECD 2005: 29). By that time, too, the intensity of competition was high across the whole economy as the result of entry by private and foreign-owned firms. And the People's Republic was deeply embedded in the world trading system. In all these respects, it makes sense to describe the Chinese system using the word market. But in many key respects, this was still a socialist economy. As we have seen, the industrial sector continued to be dominated by state-owned enterprises operating in both rural and urban areas. Tariff barriers, though lower than they had been in the 1980s, were still high; in that sense, China's international economic integration was only partial. Controls on the migration of labour between urban and rural China were easing, but they were still powerful in the mid-1990s. Stock markets had been created in Shanghai and Shenzhen, but these were weak and sickly things. And the extent of income inequality, though much higher than it had been in the early 1980s, was not extreme by international standards. By the end of 1996, the transition to capitalism had not been completed, and there is every reason to suggest that this was by design, and not by accident.

Conclusion

The Chinese economy of 1996 that Deng surveyed from his deathbed was recognizably different from that he inherited in 1978. Collective farming had been swept away and replaced by a system of small-scale family farming. China had opened up further to the world economy, and was increasingly a magnet for foreign direct investment as well as a supplier of cheap but low-quality manufactured exports. Rural industry had enjoyed more than a decade and half of extraordinary growth. Virtually all prices were determined by the market instead of being set by the state.

Yet the China of 1996 was still far removed from being a market economy. Property rights were vague and insecure, posing a threat to investment in agriculture and industry alike. The average rate of tariff protection on imports continued to be high, and levels of inward investment were still very low. Guangdong province was relatively open, but the rest of China bore the characteristics of a closed economy. Perhaps most importantly, the bulk of the industrial sector remained firmly in the hands of the state. In fact, the role of the state had actually expanded in the Chinese countryside: the most numerous industrial enterprises were those owned by townships and villages, not those owned by the nascent private sector. And in the cities, large state-owned enterprises continued to hold sway. To be sure, the official data show a slightly different picture (Jefferson and Singh 1999: 27). By 1996, those enterprises formally designated SOEs produced only 29 per cent of gross industrial output. But when one adds to this the output of collective enterprises – urban collectives, county-owned collectives, township enterprises and village enterprises – the true share of the state sector rises to around 70 per cent.[42] Given that SOEs and urban collectives were larger and boasted higher productivity than household industries, their share in value-added was even higher. Some of the collective enterprises may have been private enterprises in disguise; many private sector capitalists feared a policy reversal which might leave them vulnerable. But even allowing for this, we still have the conclusion that the state sector was producing well over 50 per cent of industrial output in 1996. This is far above the share controlled by the state in advanced capitalist economies.

We are therefore entitled to regard the Chinese economy of 1996 as still recognizably different from that to be found in other countries. The drift to capitalism in China had gone far, but this was still a market socialist economy at the time of Deng's death. The very fact that it was a hybrid – that it combined elements of state and market in a way that was different from both the China of 1978 and the America of 2007 – helps to explain why it was able to generate such rapid growth in the two decades after Mao's death. That, however, takes us ahead of our story and to an assessment of China's performance as a market socialist economy. Before moving on to that, we need to document the extraordinary changes which occurred in the industrial sector, and in China's relations with the world economy, between 1978 and 1996.

Notes

1. For some of the literature and debates about the extent to which the Chinese model was characterized by gradualism, see Sachs and Woo (1994), Nolan (1995), Naughton (1996) and Bramall (2000).
2. I take the story on agriculture all the way through to 2006. There has been no real change in agricultural policy or performance since 1996 and therefore it makes little sense to impose such an artificial dividing line.
3. A useful, though necessarily partial, biography of Deng is that of Yang (1998). For a summary of Deng's reacquisition of power during 1977–8, see Huang (2000: ch. 7). The 1978 'truth criterion' debate is discussed in Schoenhals (1991). It is sometimes suggested that policy after Mao's death was dictated by the 'Eight Immortals' (Deng Xiaoping, Chen Yun, Peng Zhen, Yang Shangkun, Bo Yibo, Li Xiannian, Wang Zhen and Song Renqiong), a phrase traditionally used to refer to eight Daoist deities, but now used by some Chinese scholars in a more contemporary context. All eight certainly played a role in the Chinese Revolution but, Deng and Chen aside, this was a group of mediocrities. This was undoubtedly one of the reasons Mao was content to dispense with their services during the Cultural Revolution; indeed, Li Xiannian's disastrous handling of the economy in the early 1970s forced Mao to recall Deng Xiaoping (MacFarquhar and Schoenhals 2006: 377–9). As for the contribution of the others, Song Renqiong's very status as one of the eight is uncertain (some accounts list Wan Li), Yang Shangkun was purged in the early 1990s for attempting to usurp power, and seven of them (Deng was the exception) were part of the Readjustment faction which vehemently opposed marketization in the early 1980s (see below). The part played by Zhao Ziyang, Zhu Rongji and even Li Peng in formulating and executing the development strategy of the 1980s and 1990s was far greater than that of the 'Immortals' (again Deng is the exception). In short, the contribution of the 'Immortals' to Chinese economic development was as negligible as that of the Daoist sages on whom they were modelled. It is for this reason that the phrase is used much more by Western journalists than by Chinese scholars.
4. This was the document 'On Questions of Party History', which has been reprinted in translation in a number of sources, e.g. Liu and Wu (1986).
5. Hua 'volunteered' his resignation as Premier in September 1980, and was forced to resign as Chairman of the Central Committee and of the Central Military Commission in June 1981.
6. As noted in the previous chapter, the notion of self-reliance was progressively abandoned after 1972. Although post-1978 policies are often called *gaige kaifang* (reform and opening up), the process of *kaifang* had been initiated by Mao and continued by Hua Guofeng.
7. According to Zhao (1987: 644), the 'primary stage of socialism' would last for about a hundred years (starting from the 1950s, when socialism was established). The term itself first seems to have been used by Su Shaozhi. The phrase 'primary stage of socialism' does not feature in Marx's writings.
8. There is now an extensive literature on the post-1978 policy package. For a variety of perspectives, see Naughton (1995), Nolan (1995), Bramall (2000), Lin *et al.* (2003), Wu (2005) and Hart-Landsberg and Burkett (2005). For a good diagnosis of many of the problems faced by China in 1980, see Xue (1981). For the policy debates of the 1980s, see Sun (1995), Hsu (1991) and Shirk (1993). Most of the best Chinese literature focuses on the problems which have emerged in the late 1990s as a result of this transition strategy, and will be discussed in the next chapter.
9. For an introduction to NEP in the Soviet Union, see Davies *et al.* (1994). See also Chapter 3, above.
10. The problem for the Old Left was its inability to articulate a plausible economic alternative to traditional state ownership in the industrial sector. As Cui Zhiyuan has argued,

some form of worker management constitutes a plausible alternative in one sense (cooperative management certainly can work), but that was not really acceptable to the Old Left, because it amounted to conceding state control to the working class. It did not help that He Xin's intellectual background was in literary studies, though paradoxically it allowed him to understand rather better than most economists the manner in which the master discourse cloaks its true agenda beneath the mantle of freedom and choice. For the views of such critically engaged intellectuals, see Fewsmith (2001) and Zhang (2006).
11 Key advocates of neoauthoritarianism in the circles around Zhao Ziyang were Wu Jiaxiang, Zhang Bingjiu and Xiao Gongqin.
12 It is simply not true that Chinese inequalities by the 1990s reflected no more than differences in productivity. However, the Dengist conception of *an lao fenpei* (distribution according to work done) was unambiguous enough in principle.
13 For discussions of the economics and politics of readjustment, see Xu (1982) and Fewsmith (1994).
14 In political terms, we can think of 1978–82 as a period of struggle between the 'readjustment' (*tiaozheng*) and the 'reformist' (*gaige*) factions within the CCP over the degree to which systemic (ownership) change to the economic system was needed. The readjustment faction was led by Chen Yun and the grouping included Li Xiannian, Peng Zhen, Wang Zhen, Bo Yibo, Deng Liqun, Hu Qiaomu and Yao Yilin. Its economic analysis was supported by the bulk of economists based at the State Planning Commission and the People's University in Beijing. Zhao Ziyang, Hu Yaobang, Wan Li and Hu Qili were much more closely associated with the notion that reform was needed, and economic advice was provided to them by (*inter alios*) Xue Muqiao, Dong Fureng, Yu Guangyuan, Sun Shangqing, Liu Guoguang and Chen Yizi. This group increasingly advocated a neoclassical policy solution: only privatization and a hardening of budget constraints offered a proper and lasting solution to the problem of industrial inefficiency.
15 The extensive literature on intersectoral resource flows and pricing issues includes Ishikawa (1967), Nakagane (1989), Karshenas (1995), Sheng (1993) and Knight and Song (1999). The constraint imposed on pre-1978 Chinese agriculture by the relative price structure is discussed in Chapter 7, above.
16 For an introduction to the development of Wenzhou, see Nolan and Dong (1990).
17 Urban incomes did increase during this period, but only because of growing participation rates amongst women.
18 One of the best accounts of initial industrial reform in China is that given in Chai (1998). See also Naughton (1995: ch. 3) and Otsuka *et al.* (1998: ch. 2).
19 One of the very few useful accounts of the SEZ programme is that of Kleinberg (1990).
20 From a theoretical viewpoint, there is a recognition that a readjustment programme almost inevitably leads in the long run to the collapse of planning. Kornai (1992) is the classic source here. Leninist systems have a coherence about them, but attempts to make incremental changes will lead to their collapse because of the emergence of all manner of contradictions between the market and non-market sectors. China's dual-track pricing system, for example, was a recipe for corruption and could lead only to pressure for further, more dramatic, changes.
21 Agriculture is divided into four subsectors in China: farming, animal husbandry, forestry and fisheries. Household sideline activities (such as handicraft production), though a separate category during the 1980s, are now included within farming.
22 Triple cropping of grain – two rice crops and one wheat crop – was widely promoted in the late 1960s and early 1970s. The literature on these agricultural reforms includes Shambaugh (1982), Donnithorne (1984), Wang (1988), Bramall (1995) and Chung (2000).
23 For a discussion of the reform process, see Ash (1988), Du (1996) and Bramall (2000). For discussions of decollectivization, see Chung (2000), Kelliher (1992), Zhou (1996) and Unger (2002).

24 This sort of system was by no means uncommon in the late Maoist period. Magaoqiao production brigade in Sichuan, for example, used it in the early 1960s, and reintroduced it again after 1971 (Endicott 1988: 127 and 129). In that sense, the continuities between the Maoist era and that of Deng are much stronger than is usually recognized.
25 It needs to be emphasized, however, that full ownership rights – especially the right to sell assets – were not transferred to households, something which has arguably caused problems in the late 1980s and during the 1990s (as will be discussed below).
26 There is no sense, however, in seeing 1978 as the turning-point, at least as far as output trends are concerned.
27 For some of the literature, see Watson (1984), Zhou (1996), Kelliher (1992) and Chung (2000). For all the brio of Zhou's account, I find it very hard to take seriously her notion that it was 'a spontaneous, unorganized, leaderless, non-ideological, apolitical movement' (Zhou 1996: 15).
28 I stress 'package' here because, as we saw in Chapter 7, there is much debate about the role played by decollectivization in the process of accelerating output growth.
29 Inspection of the data suggests that there was a clear break in the series in the early 1980s, with comparatively steady growth on either side. The trend growth rate was undoubtedly higher after 1984, indicating an apparent step-change in agricultural performance.
30 For international trade issues and the effects of WTO entry on Chinese agriculture, see Garnaut *et al.* (1996), Garnaut (1999), OECD (2001), OECD (2002b), Diao *et al.* (2003), and Bhattasali *et al.* (2004).
31 The picture, however, is complex. Rice and wheat were not subject to much protection in 2001, whereas maize and cotton both benefited from export subsidies; imports of these last two are likely to increase. However, the Chinese government retains a good deal of discretionary power to limit imports, especially via the way the way in which VAT is levied on imports but not on many agricultural commodities traded on the domestic market (Bhattasali *et al.* 2004: 5–7 and 81–98). Given that the level of protection on Chinese imports has declined steadily since 1978, WTO entry should be conceived of as being another step in the liberalization process, rather than a climacteric.
32 This approach is typical of much contemporary development theorizing, as exemplified by Ray (1998). The development 'problem' is reduced to one of incomplete or missing markets, an approach which grapples adequately with neither the problem of pervasive uncertainty (which ensures that markets will always fail to generate efficient outcomes) nor that of the ways in which class relations bias market outcomes against both efficiency and equity. The very possibility that the only way to deal with market failure is to eliminate the market in question is rarely considered. Ultimately, of course, the problem is to identify the second-best solution: is it a badly functioning market or ill-conceived state intervention? There is no theoretical high ground to be seized here; that which works in practice is inevitably very context-specific, depending as it does on state capacity and the quality of governance.
33 The property law passed by the NPC in March 2007 is unlikely to change the situation very much, because its focus was essentially on urban property rights. It does help somewhat by allowing leases on farmland to be renewed when they expire. However, the power to appropriate land enjoyed by local government remains, and the law does not allow the mortgaging of land, which is a necessary step if a land market is to develop properly.
34 The crux of the problem for Chinese farmers in the late 1970s was that input prices were too high (as reflected in the high rates of profit being made in the industrial sector), not that product prices were too low.
35 The rate of extraction from the rural sector (as opposed to the agricultural sector) was much higher because of taxation levied on township and village enterprises.

36 According to Wright (2006: 165): 'up to the mid-1990s, the state's economic priorities expressed through the fixing of prices were the most important negative influence on coal mining profits.'
37 This formed the basis for the critique of price-setting (and hence the very concept of socialism as an operational economic system) by von Mises and Hayek. For a discussion of the Lange model and criticism thereof see Gregory and Stuart (1974: ch 9), and Nove and Nuti (1972).
38 The process of rectification also led to the reimposition of controls on some prices. By 1990, the prices for seventeen agricultural products were still set by the state and a further eleven were subject to state guidelines. The prices of twenty-four primary products or processed agricultural products (e.g. wheat flour) were similarly controlled. As for industry, the prices of some 742 products were subject to state control (Yabuki 1995: 128).
39 The massacre was applauded by a number of Western academics, who dismissed the suggestion that the number of deaths ran into the thousands as exaggeration, and argued that it was functionally necessary to uphold the authority of China's neoauthoritarian state.
40 For the politics of the revival of the reformist agenda, see Fewsmith (2001: ch. 2).
41 The Chinese fiscal system and the 1994 reforms are usefully discussed in Brean (1998).
42 China's collective enterprises were *de facto* state enterprises. Many of them were actually more closely controlled by the state than the SOEs themselves.

11 Foreign trade and inward investment since 1971

One of the most remarked-upon features of Chinese economic development since 1978 has been the pace at which the People's Republic has opened up to foreign trade. Western shops are awash with cheap Chinese goods. Foreign direct investment has flooded in. And Western brands are a commonplace sight across the Chinese mainland.

No wonder China's opening-up is so commented upon. The country's share of world exports of manufactures rose from 0.8 per cent in 1980 to 8.3 per cent by 2004 (Winters and Yusuf 2007: 36). The share of exports in Chinese GDP appears to have increased even more rapidly; as Figure 11.1 shows, it rose from about 5 per cent in the late 1970s to 37 per cent by 2006, a remarkably high figure for a comparatively large economy like China.[1] On the other side of the balance of payments, China is a big importer of fuels and raw materials from Australia, Africa and Latin America. It imports vast quantities of components and assembles them into finished manufactures for export.[2]

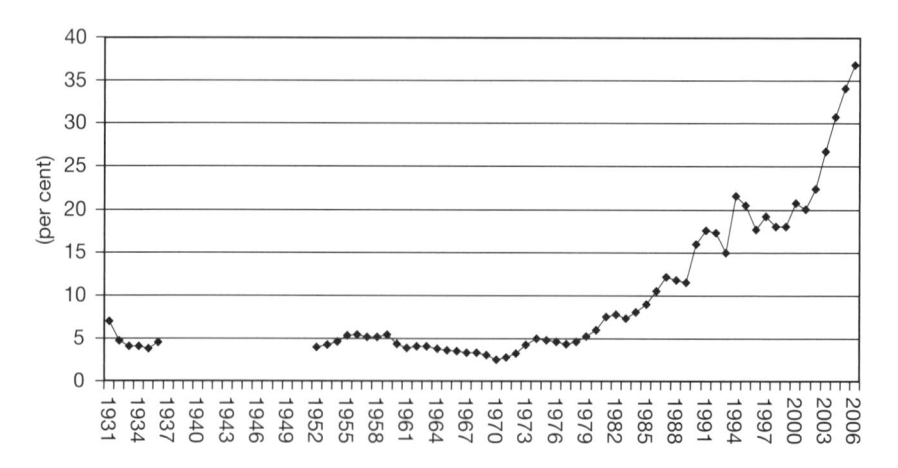

Figure 11.1 The share of exports in Chinese GDP, 1931–2006 (GDP measured at national prices) (Sources: ZGTJNJ (2007: 57 and 724); SSB (2005a: 9 and 68); Yeh (1979: 98).)

Note: Data for 1931–6 are at 1933 prices. Subsequent data are at current prices.

Three conclusions have usually been drawn from these data on China's growing integration into the world economy. First, it is widely believed that foreign trade and FDI have been the motors of Chinese economic growth over the last thirty years (Bergsten et al. 2006; Winters and Yusuf 2007; Hutton 2007; Glyn 2006). Second, China's development is viewed as having had a dramatic impact on the demand for global commodities, leading to rising world prices for many raw materials. Third, Chinese exports have been held to blame for a large part of the decline of low-skill jobs in manufacturing in the USA and the European Union.

However, much of this analysis is controversial. Admittedly a full discussion of the impact of the rise of China is well beyond the scope of this book, but many of the arguments about China's global influence are overstated.[3] It is certainly true that competition from Chinese manufactures in world markets has impacted heavily upon other low-wage countries such as Mexico, Turkey and Vietnam. It is also true that North–South trade has caused jobs losses amongst the unskilled (Wood 1994; Sachs and Shatz 1994). However, the role played by Chinese imports in the deindustrialization of the USA and Europe is small. There is certainly an apparent correlation between growing Chinese imports and rising unemployment, and much political debate in the USA focuses on the 'threat' to American jobs posed by Chinese imports. But most imports originated in other developed countries in the 1980s and 1990s. Indeed, the worsening trade balance between China and the USA has been offset by its improving balance with Hong Kong, Taiwan and Japan – which itself reflects the shifting of production in these Asian economies to China (Bergsten et al. 2006: 90). Most jobs in the OECD economies are in the non-tradable sector and therefore insulated from competition from Chinese manufactured exports (Glyn 2006: 99). Moreover, China's growth has sucked in imports from the West, thus leading to job creation. And, more fundamentally, there is a good deal of evidence to suggest that the loss of unskilled jobs has much more to do with labour-saving technical progress than it has with imports (Lawrence and Slaughter 1993). Trade with the South between 1992 and 2002 perhaps accounts for 25 per cent of job losses in manufacturing in the EU and around 50 per cent in the USA, but, as manufacturing accounts for only a quarter of total employment in these countries, the overall impact of trade with all low-income countries is comparatively small (Glyn 2006: 111). Calls for protection are therefore wide of the mark in many cases.

The role played by the foreign sector in driving Chinese economic growth is equally debatable; as we will see, there are many questions that remain unresolved. In fact, however, it is by no means fanciful to argue that the character of Chinese growth has changed very little between the late nineteenth century and the beginning of the twenty-first. This is because the Chinese economy remains dualistic in several respects. Trade and inward investment had a crucial impact on a small coastal enclave in the 1930s and again during the 1980s and 1990s. However, the Chinese interior was and is only weakly integrated into the world economy, and its growth was driven by domestic demand for most of the period. Only since 2000 can it be plausibly contended that exports and FDI were the engines of growth, and even for this period the linkages between the export and domestic sector are fragile. This chapter begins, however, with another neglected aspect of China's trade policy: late Maoist China did not pursue an autarkic trade policy and indeed the open door began in the early 1970s.

Antecedents: foreign trade before 1971

The inevitable consequence of the international isolation which followed the Sino-Soviet split in 1960 was limited trade. By 1970, the nadir of China's foreign trade, the share of exports was down to around 2.5 per cent of GDP, considerably less than half the share recorded in 1956 of 5.4 per cent (Figure 11.1).

However, Chinese policy during the 1960s was not built around a strategy of self-reliance. Table 11.1 shows that even Sino-Soviet trade remained substantial in the early 1960s, the split between the two powers notwithstanding. Even in 1965, imports from the USSR still accounted for 9 per cent of all Chinese imports. The case of Sichuan provides a good illustration of the degree of continuing trade. The value of that province's exports to the USSR was 40.8 million *yuan* in 1958 and 88.8 million in 1959. In 1965, however, Sichuan was exporting 61.1 million *yuan* to the Soviet Union and a figure of 28.7 million *yuan* was recorded in 1966; only then did it fall sharply, averaging only about 4 million *yuan* per annum for the remainder of the 1960s and during the early 1970s.

In fact, the value of Chinese exports in 1966 was actually higher than it had been in 1956 and 1957. In the main this was because of an expansion of trade with Western Europe and Japan.[4] Imports from the latter increased from $US42 million in 1962 t0 $US583 million by 1970, and imports from Britain rose from $US32 million to $US386 million over the same period (ZGTJNJ 1981: 355 and 364).[5] As Table 11.1 shows, 1964 was the turning point in the reorientation of Chinese trade away from the Soviet Union; in that year the shares of Japan and Western Europe exceeded the Soviet share in Chinese imports for the first time since before 1949. By 1971, Japan and Western Europe together accounted for

Table 11.1 Chinese imports by country of origin, 1963–1971 ($US million)

	Total	USSR	Japan	W. Europe
1963	1,270	194	64	133
1964	1,550	134	161	161
1965	2,020	186	262	263
1966	2,250	165	334	444
1967	2,020	56	304	515
1968	1,950	59	335	505
1969	1,830	27	382	513
1970	2,330	24	583	702
1971	2,210	68	594	436

Source: ZGTJNJ 1981 (1982: 355–67).

Note
Western Europe here comprises the UK, France and West Germany.

around 50 per cent of Chinese imports, and their absolute value was no less than five times greater than it had been in 1963. The 1960s, in other words, was a period in which China diversified its sources of imports away from both the USA and the Soviet Union.[6]

Chemical fertilizer provides an interesting illustration of the approach of the People's Republic to foreign trade. China's capacity to produce chemical fertilizer was very limited in the early 1950s; production in 1952 (in terms of nutrient or effective weight) was around 40,000 tonnes. The long-term solution was to increase domestic production, but imports provided a solution in the short and medium term. It is therefore not surprising that imports rose from 45,000 tonnes in 1952 to 261,000 tonnes by 1962. Much more surprising, at least if one starts from the assumption that China was a closed economy in the 1960s led by a leader firmly opposed to foreign trade, is that this figure rose steadily over the following decade, reaching 1.1 million tonnes in 1968 and 1.3 million tonnes in 1970, about one third of total supply (MOA 1989: 324–5). Imports were thus making an important contribution to Chinese agricultural modernization.

This example, as well as the more general evidence, suggests that China was anything but a closed economy even in the late 1960s. The geographical pattern of its trade certainly altered, and trade as a percentage of GDP declined. But the Chinese economy was never closed, and its strategy never autarkic. In fact, measured in $US, the value of exports in 1970 was around 50 per cent higher than it had been in the mid-1950s (SSB 2005a: 68). In short, the People's Republic continued to trade on the world market, and to fulfil its international obligations. The picture we have is of a country keen to engage with the world economy where possible, but limited in its opportunities by China's relative isolation.

Opening the door: trade policy in the 1970s

Any notion that Mao was implacably hostile to international trade is not supported by the evidence for the 1970s.[7] As Teiwes and Sun (2007: 51) put it: 'it was the Chairman who opened up the policy of borrowing from the West that would expand dramatically in the post-Mao era.' The key step here was Nixon's decision to reverse the US policy of containment by ending the ban on non-strategic US exports to China in spring 1971 (Foot 1995: 75). Nixon's desire to broker some sort of settlement in Vietnam with the help of China helped to pave the way for his February 1972 visit to China and to improved Sino-US relation.[8]

Following the resumption of trade between China and the USA in 1971, trade flows increased steadily. However, improved relations with the USA were in themselves of little significance in the short run; Sino-US trade remained limited during the 1970s, with the US supplying less than 7 per cent of Chinese imports even in 1978. However, the events of 1971–2 were still of great significance because they led to the normalization of relations between Japan and China (Yokoi 1990), and hence to a massive increase in trade between the two countries. It was this expansion of Sino-Japanese trade which was especially important for China in the

1970s.[9] Japan, in an echo of its policies of the prewar era, wanted access to Chinese natural resources, including oil. China needed more advanced technology. And so the stage was set for a process of mutually beneficial trade. Between 1971 and 1975 (the Fourth Five Year Plan), China imported no less than $US3.1 billion in plant and technology from Japan, and followed this with a further $US9.4 billion between 1976 and 1980. Fifty-nine per cent of all contracts were signed with Japanese firms in the early 1970s (Yokoi 1990: 697–8). More generally, Western Europe and Japan together accounted for over 40 per cent of Chinese imports in every year between 1971 and 1978. If Chinese modernization was driven after 1971 by external forces, those forces resided in Europe and Japan.

The principal aim during the 1970s was to use improved relations with Japan and the West to deepen the process of import substitution by importing advanced equipment. It was 1973 that proved to be the key year. It was decided to import four chemical fibre plants, steel rolling equipment for the Wuhan steel plant (from Japan), a benzene works and three petrochemical plants (Liu and Wu 1986: 384). This expansion was made possible by the development of the Daqing oilfield (where production began in 1960), and by the big rise in the world oil price in 1973. It therefore made great sense for China to increase its oil exports, and that is exactly what happened. In 1970, exports of crude oil amounted to only 190,000 tonnes. By 1974, this was up to 5 million tonnes, and the figure reached 11.3 million in 1978 (ZGTJNJ 1983: 433). Once again, it illustrates the central feature of Chinese trade policy: the CCP was more than willing to trade on the world market when the opportunities presented themselves.

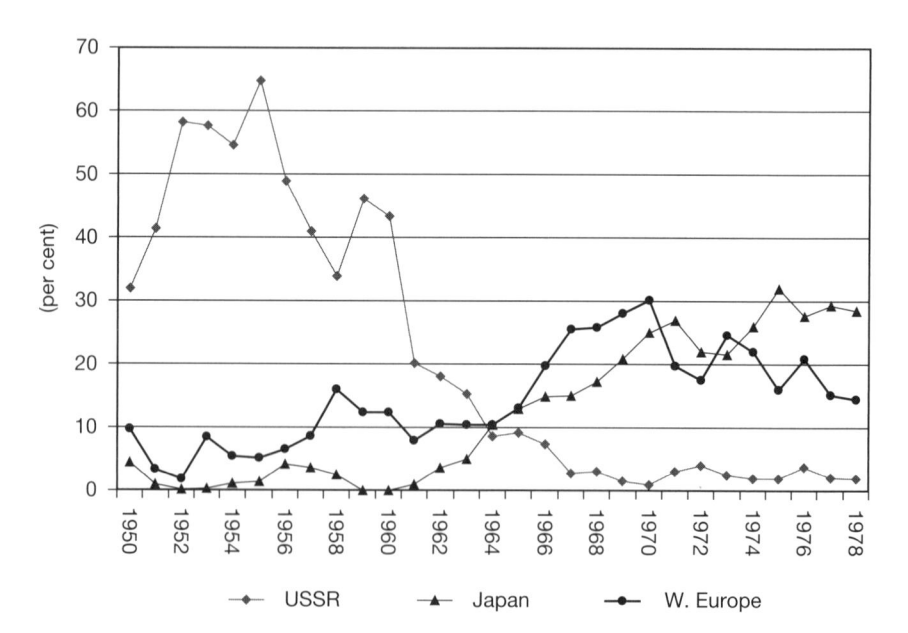

Figure 11.2 The changing composition of Chinese imports, 1950–1978 (percentage of total imports by source) (Source: ZGTJNJ (1982: 355–67).)

Perhaps most importantly of all, thirteen sets of chemical fertilizer equipment from the USA, Europe and Japan were ordered, with a view to vastly expanding China's capacity to produce chemical fertilizer. The effects of this decision – in conjunction with expansion of production in small-scale plants in the countryside – are apparent. In 1970, imports amounted to nearly 36 per cent of total supply. By 1978 this was down to only 15 per cent, as the total volume of imports stagnated at around 1.3 million tonnes, whereas domestic production soared from around 2 million to over 12 million tonnes (MOA 1989: 325). In other words, imports were crucial when domestic production was inadequate, but once import substitution had taken place, the value of imports dropped.

Nevertheless, the development of China's foreign trade in the 1970s was not smooth. This may have stemmed from the continuing opposition of the Gang of Four to greater integration into the world economy, though the Chinese evidence is not to be trusted on this point. More importantly, China's trade was in deficit because of her inability to generate enough export revenue to pay for essential imports. For although the oil price rise of 1973 helped in one way, it harmed China's prospects in the sense that it plunged the OECD economies into recession. The value of imports surged from $US2.9 million in 1972 to $US7.6 billion in 1974, but because export growth was slow, the balance of trade deteriorated. In fact, the trade surplus of $US660 in 1973 became a deficit of $US670 million in 1974 (SSB 2005a: 68), and the turnaround in some ways confirmed the view that foreign entanglements created difficulties rather than opportunities.

Mao's death led to an acceleration in the pace of integration. The most visible change was the 1977 launch of the 'great leap outward', or 'foreign leap forward' by Hua Guofeng. The foreign leap placed particular emphasis on imports of raw materials. Imports of rolled steel in particular soared, rising from 2.4 million tonnes in 1972 to 4.9 million in 1976 and to a peak of 8.6 million tonnes in 1978 (ZGTJNJ 1983: 435). In order to finance this programme, China was forced to intensify the programme of oil exports which had been launched in the early 1970s. As a result, exports of both crude oil and refined petroleum soared in the mid- and late 1970s (Figure 11.3). The opportunity costs incurred in terms of the constraint imposed on road transport was of course considerable. Total oil production in 1978 was about 104 million tonnes, and crude oil exports alone accounted for around 15 per cent of production.

Yet for all the drama of the foreign leap forward, the strategy was no more than a continuation of the policy that China had been adopting since the early 1960s. To be sure, the scale of foreign trade increased significantly over the course of the 1970s; the dollar value of exports rose from 2.6 billion in 1971 to 9.8 billion in 1978; in that sense we are justified in regarding 1971 as a climacteric. Nevertheless, Chinese policy in the 1960s and 1970s was consistent in the sense that the CCP leadership throughout showed a readiness to engage with the world economy that was conditioned far more by realism than it was by a raft of ideological presumptions. No less a figure than Deng Xiaoping (1978a) made clear the Chinese approach:

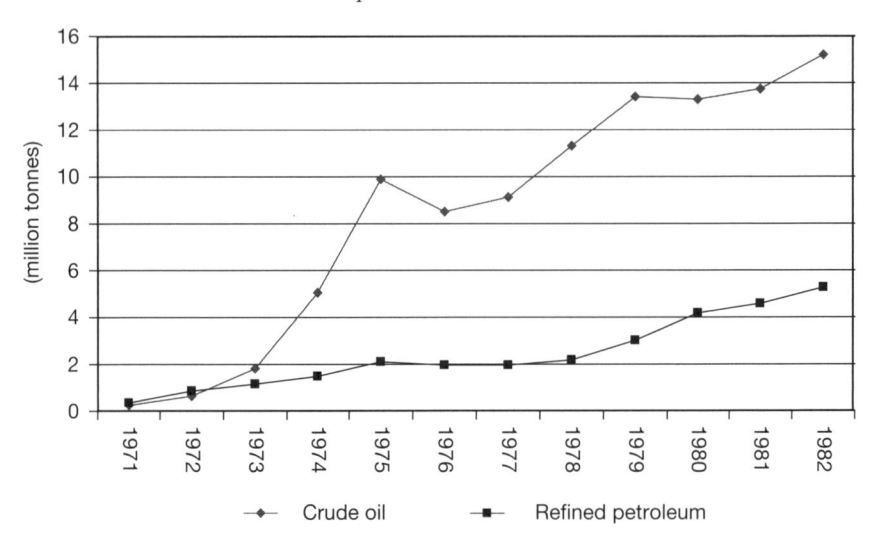

Figure 11.3 Exports of crude oil and refined petroleum, 1971–1982 (Source: ZGTJNJ (1983: 433–4).)

> [W]hile Comrade Mao was still living we thought about expanding economic and technical exchanges with other countries. We wanted to develop economic and trade relations with certain capitalist countries and even to absorb foreign capital and undertake joint ventures. But the necessary conditions were not present, because at the time an embargo was being imposed on China.

The leitmotif throughout the late Maoist era was import substitution, and the expansion of trading possibilities after 1971 served only to deepen the process, rather than to initiate it. Moreover, as we have seen, fluctuations in China's trade during the 1970s had far more to do with balance of payments problems than ideology. No matter how much the leadership wished to modernize by means of technology transfer, it was simply not possible given China's inability to generate more rapid export growth.

The door opens wider, 1978–1996

Chinese trade expanded more quickly after 1978. The phrase 'the policy of opening to the outside world' was used by Deng Xiaoping (1978b) in October of that year, but China was pursuing a more liberal policy towards foreign trade even before the celebrated Third Plenum of 1978. For example, the value of imports grew by no less than 51 per cent in 1978 alone (ZGTJNJ 1981). Thereafter, the process accelerated, and a key factor was undoubtedly the restoration of diplomatic relations between China and the USA on 1 January 1979, which in turned paved the way for an expansion of trade via the granting of Most Favoured Nation status to China by the US Congress in 1980.

1978 was a year of qualitative as well as quantitative significance. That is because it marked China's renewed willingness to accept foreign direct investment. The first step was the announcement by Li Xiannian in the immediate aftermath of the Third Plenum in December 1978. More significant, however, was the July 1979 decision to establish special economic zones in Bao'an county (the Shenzhen SEZ) and in Zhuhai, followed by an announcement in May 1980 of further zones in Shantou and Xiamen; the first three were in Guangdong, the last in Fujian province. These SEZs were archetypal free trade zones characterized by low rates of taxation and slimmed-down bureaucratic procedures, and aimed at encouraging technology transfer. The choice of Guangdong and Fujian as the home for the SEZs was driven in part by the hope that it would make it easier to tap the capital of overseas Chinese living in Hong Kong and Taiwan. But it also demonstrates the wariness of the CCP.[10] The relative absence of Chinese industry in these two provinces meant that any competitive threat would be far less than if the zones had been established in Shenyang or Shanghai, even if Deng later admitted (as we saw in the previous chapter) that Shanghai's exclusion was a mistake.

Although the initial SEZ programme was seen as less effective than had been hoped in several respects – too much of the FDI had gone into property, and much of the production in the zones was little more than processing and assembly work – it was decided to persist with it.[11] In large measure, this decision was driven by a desire to 'level the playing field'.[12] The CCP had come under pressure from other provinces and cities to confer upon them the same advantages granted to much of Guangdong and Fujian, and this was a hard argument to resist. There was of course a recognition that the promotion of the open door would almost certainly lead to a widening of the gap between the Chinese coast and the interior; however, it was hoped that a process of trickle-down would close this gap in the long run. Perhaps more important than anything else in driving the implementation of further policies designed to attract FDI was a recognition that the China of the 1980s was far behind the West in almost every respect. If China was ever to recapture its former glories – the nationalist agenda was never far from the fore – the Celestial Empire would have to achieve a much faster rate of growth. And that in turn meant exploiting the opportunities for catch-up by attracting FDI and thus emulating the path taken by the East Asian NICs in the 1960s and 1970s. Inward FDI would also help to promote export expansion, a strategy strongly advocated by Wang Jian on the grounds that it would allow China to take advantage of its comparative advantage in labour-intensive production and would generate the foreign exchange needed for defence and industrial modernization.

As a result, the opening up of the late 1970s continued in the 1980s. May 1984 saw the opening up of fourteen coastal cities to FDI in a step which was effectively an increase in the number of SEZs; most of the fourteen were former Treaty Ports.[13] The Zhujiang and Yangzi deltas, the Xiamen–Zhangzhou–Quanzhou triangle (in southern Fujian) and the Liaodong and Jiaodong peninsulas were similarly opened up in 1985. Hainan island was granted provincial and SEZ status in 1988. Perhaps most importantly of all, work began on the creation of a new industrial zone in Pudong in Shanghai in 1990 (it was mooted in 1986, but only approved four years later) with a view to modernizing what remained the centre of Chinese industrial production.[14] The television series *River Elegy* (broadcast in 1988), with its bold assertion that China needed to look out to sea (and by implication to the West) rather than inland if it were to modernize, captured the spirit of Zhao Ziyang's approach – and, predictably perhaps, attracted a torrent of criticism from the left and from nationalists (Fewsmith 2001: 96–7).

After 1992, China's engagement with the world economy increased further (Wu 2005: 297–8). The catalyst here was Deng's southern tour of 1992, taking in Shanghai as well as the special economic zones. One feature of this new liberalization programme was the strategy of the 'four alongs', which amounted to opening up various regions of China to foreign direct investment – along the coast, along the northern border provinces of Xinjiang, Heilongjiang and Nei Menggu, along the railway (the Longhai line and its westward extension, which linked Urumqi with Xi'an, Zhengzhou and ultimately the coast) and along the Yangzi river. Thus the opening up of the Pudong development zone in Shanghai was followed in 1993 by the decision to open up the Yangzi cities of Wuhu, Jiujiang, Wuhan, Yueyang and Chongqing, and to press ahead with construction of the controversial Three Gorges dam on the river between these last two cities. In addition to the 'four alongs', it was also decided in 1993 to open up eleven provincial capitals, and to make Harbin, Changchun, Hohot and Shijiazhuang open cities, which in practice meant granting these cities the same range of privileges and freedoms granted to the fourteen open coastal cities in 1984. The underlying logic here was of course to level the playing field: that is, to extend the preferential treatment previously enjoyed by only the coastal region to much of the interior in the hope that the trickle-down effects of FDI (in terms of employment and technology transfer) would be accelerated. The whole process went a stage further in March 2007, when a law was passed which harmonized the rate of corporation tax on domestic and foreign enterprises.

This promotion of FDI was complemented by a progressive reduction in tariff rates on imports. The logic here was to reduce the extent of protection enjoyed by Chinese industries in the hope that growing competition would force them to raise productivity by innovation and by cost-cutting. As a result, the unweighted average tariff rate fell from 43 per cent in 1992 to 18 per cent by 1998, and the weighted tariff rate fell from 41 to 16 per cent over the same period (Prasad 2004: 10). Nevertheless, the CCP sought to expand exports at the same time that it was allowing an expansion of imports. Crucial here was exchange rate policy; the *renminbi* was allowed to fall from 1.7 *yuan* per dollar in 1978, to 5.5 *yuan* in 1992 and to 8.3 *yuan* by 2004. This helped to increase the competitiveness of China's exports. It also, however, helped to cause the East Asian financial crisis of 1997. The crucial step here was devaluation of 1994, which cut the dollar value of the *renminbi* from 5.76 in 1993 to 8.62 to the US dollar in 1994. This move undermined the competitiveness of a number of South and East Asian countries, and hence their ability to repay foreign loans. But from a Chinese perspective, it served its purpose: Chinese exports soared.

WTO entry and exchange rate issues, 1996–2007

Chinese trade policy before 1996 can be characterized as one of strategic (i.e. limited) integration with the world economy. The broad aims were to expand exports and to use the revenue to import key producer goods, whilst maintaining relatively high tariffs on imported consumer goods. After Deng's death, however, policy shifted dramatically towards the creation of a free-trade economy. More precisely, policy-making during the late 1990s was dominated by discussions about WTO accession, and after entry by debates centred around China's exchange rate.

As far as the politics of WTO accession are concerned, it appears that Jiang Zemin had been in favour of entry as early as 1993–4.[15] Indeed his enthusiasm was not even tempered by the Asian financial crisis of 1997–8, even though that event provided an excellent illustration of the dangers inherent in international economic integration.[16] However, membership was opposed by Li Peng, and it was only after March 1998 – when Li was replaced as Premier by Zhu Rongji – that the impasse was broken. From that point on, Zhu and Jiang worked together to bring about accession.[17] Initially, they met with failure. Talks between China and the US broke down in April 1999, and the US did great damage to Zhu's political standing in China by releasing a list of the concessions he had offered on China's behalf. These concessions, combined with the US bombing of the Chinese embassy in Belgrade, created much resentment amongst Chinese nationalists; Zhu was accused of being a traitor and of selling out China's national interests to court favour with the USA. Nevertheless, Jiang stood by Zhu, and, despite opposition from Li Peng – the only dissident during the Standing Committee vote (Fewsmith 2001: 224) – China and the US reached agreement on WTO accession in November 1999. Full agreement with WTO members was not reached until a year later, but the agreement with the US was the key step.

The economic rationale for membership was that it would serve to undermine domestic interest groups; without tariff and non-tariff barriers, Chinese enterprises in both manufacturing and service sectors would be exposed to proper competition.[18] This, it was argued, would speed up the rate of innovation and productivity growth, and it of course resonated with the *zhuada fangxiao* policy (see Chapter 12) of reducing subsidies, accelerating restructuring and exposing SOEs to intensified competition from the domestic private sector. Not surprisingly, it was opposed by members of the Old and New Left (such as Cui Zhiyuan), who wished to retain trade barriers on classic infant industry grounds: only by means of protection would enterprises (especially in the high-tech sector) be able to grow large enough to exploit economies of scale, and be given the time needed for learning-by-doing. The critics were also concerned that the removal of capital controls would make China vulnerable to the sort of capital flight that had caused so much damage to the economies of Indonesia, Thailand and South Korea in 1997–8.[19] Nevertheless, the very fact that little concrete information was released by the Chinese government on the precise terms and conditions of entry prior to accession meant that many of the potential critics were not even aware of what China was signing up to.

Ultimately, the free-trade inclinations of Zhu and Jiang Zemin, in conjunction with the absence of powerful domestic opposition, prevailed. As Figure 11.4 shows, China's engagement increased rapidly in the late 1990s. Between 1996 and 2004, the share of exports in Chinese GDP almost doubled, and the volume of FDI increased by about 50 per cent. Indeed China was receiving more FDI than any other country by 2003 (World Bank 2005: 342–3). These trends were driven both by WTO accession itself, and by preparatory steps even before accession in December 2001. Tariff cuts in fact started in earnest in 1993, when the unweighted rate fell below 40 per cent for the first time (Lardy 2002: 34–5). By 1998, as we have seen, the rate was down to 18 per cent and by 2002 it had fallen to only 12 per cent. As for the weighted rate, its trajectory shows a decline from 41 per cent in 1992 to 16 per cent in 1998, and to only 6 per cent in 2002 (Prasad 2004: 10).[20] Such aggregates mask the dramatic falls for some products; for example, the tariff rate on cars fell from 123 per cent in 1995 to 29 per cent in 2001, and that on tobacco declined from 137 to 43 per cent over the same period (Ianchovichina and Martin 2004: 216). These are startling figures, and demonstrate a marked contrast between the relatively inward-looking China of the 1980s and the infinitely more outward-orientated country that entered the new millennium. In its trade regime at least, China was avowedly capitalist by the time of WTO accession.

Nevertheless, accession to the WTO played little role in driving the inexorable rise in exports seen in Figure 11.4. Much more important here was China's competitive

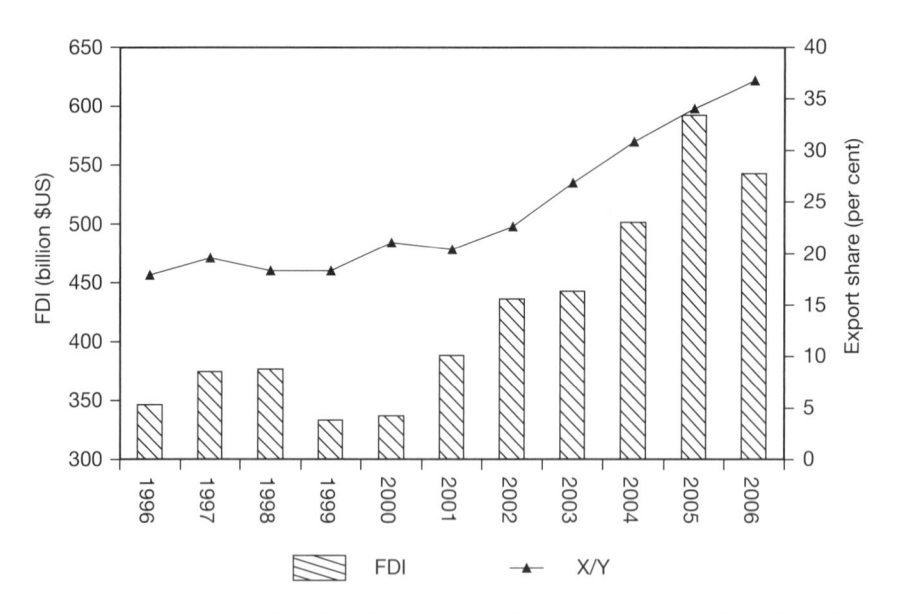

Figure 11.4 Trends in foreign direct investment and the share of exports in GDP, 1996–2006 (Source: ZGTJNJ (2007: 57 and 742).)

Note: X/Y is current price exports as a percentage of GNI (national prices). FDI is realized foreign direct investment.

nominal exchange rate relative to the USA. In 1981, one dollar exchanged for approximately 1.7 *yuan* (ZGTJNJ 1981: 393). By 1990, the *renminbi* had depreciated such that it was trading at 4.8 *yuan* per $US and by 1994 it had fallen to 8.6 *yuan*. And from 1995 to July 2005, the dollar–renminbi rate was pegged by the Chinese government at approximately 8.3 *yuan* per $US (ZGTJNJ 2005: 627). In conjunction with low relative labour costs (admittedly offset by low levels of productivity for many types of goods), it ensured that Chinese exports were highly competitive in US markets and therefore that China enjoyed sustained export growth during the late 1990s and after the turn of the century.

Not perhaps surprisingly, China has been increasingly criticized for this policy in the US. At one level, this criticism was driven by the implications of Chinese competitiveness for the US balance of payments. Amongst many economists, the policy was seen as irrational, because this type of exchange rate regime caused the *renminbi* to be undervalued.[21] For although depreciation was perceived as an appropriate market-driven response in the 1980s, when China was attracting little FDI and running current account deficits in most years, the same was not true after 1993. In fact, for the 1993–2006 period, China not only enjoyed a large (and rising) current account surplus but also attracted large FDI inflows. Market pressures were thus tending to produce *renminbi* appreciation and therefore the dollar peg led to *renminbi* undervaluation. Accordingly, the CCP came under increasing pressure to allow the *renminbi* to appreciate, and finally (in July 2005) it moved a little in that direction.

For all that, it is far from clear that Chinese policy between 1993 and 2006 was either flawed or deliberately mercantilist. For one thing, although the *renminbi* was pegged against the dollar, the overall trade-weighted exchange rate appreciated by over 20 per cent between 1994 and 2004 precisely because the dollar appreciated during this period against other currencies (Goldstein and Lardy 2005: 19). In other words, it is misleading to focus on the dollar–*renminbi* rate when the US takes only about 20 per cent of Chinese exports. When we look at the trade-weighted rate instead of merely the dollar rate, it is hard to argue that the Chinese government has pursued a systematic policy of overall exchange rate undervaluation. The *renminbi* may be undervalued relative to the dollar but that is not quite the same thing. The second issue centres around the meaning of the equilibrium exchange rate. At one level, it can be argued that the equilibrium should be the purchasing power parity rate, and this is the general premise which underpins the Western literature. An alternative approach is simply to argue that the rate which equalizes the underlying balance of payments is the appropriate objective of policy; see for example Goldstein (2006). However, it is not very difficult merely to achieve balance of payments equilibrium. The hard thing is to achieve balance at socially acceptable levels of employment, output and inflation. From this perspective, it is wholly reasonable to argue that China was right to maintain a competitive exchange rate, because that served to promote rapid output and employment growth – which were the key goals of macroeconomic policy.[22] Indeed there are real dangers that uncontrolled appreciation will have extremely damaging effects on China's export industries and on those parts of the agricultural sector which are export-orientated. Appropriate domestic policy – reflation and redistribution in favour of the regions and sectors adversely affected – can mitigate these dangers (Blanchard and Giavazzi 2006), but this type of sophisticated macroeconomic management is not easily accomplished and is well beyond the capacity of a Chinese state beset by rent-seeking coalitions.[23]

The effects of opening up

Deng Xiaoping (1984: 3–4) had few doubts about the importance of opening up for the Chinese economy:

> China's past backwardness was due to its closed door policy. After the founding of the People's Republic, we were blockaded by some, and so the country remained partially closed ... the experience of the past 30 years or more proves that a closed door policy hinders construction and inhibits development

His view has been echoed in the writings of many other economists, as we saw at the beginning of the chapter. For many it is almost an act of faith that China's open-door policy has been the engine of growth – that is, growth has been driven by exports, by technology transfers and by FDI. One result is that governments across the world have concluded that, in order to accelerate economic growth in their own countries, they need to copy China. Vietnam provides one example; in government circles there, it is the conventional wisdom that FDI has been crucial for growth in China, and that Vietnam must go the same way if she is to catch up.

Yet the reality of China's experience is more complex. Trade and FDI have certainly been the handmaidens of growth, but it is a very big stretch from there to the conclusion that the open door was the engine of growth. The crux of the matter is whether trade was merely an adjunct to the growth process, or whether it was a prime mover. The issue is that of causation. Trade growth and FDI growth have coincided with rapid economic growth in the 1980s and 1990s but is that relationship causal? And, even if there is causality, has the open door exerted a significant – or a trivial – impact on growth?

A useful way of starting to address the issues is to distinguish between the experience of China in the 1980s and her experience after the process of opening up was given renewed vigour by Deng's southern tour in early 1992 and China's decision to join the WTO. We begin with the period up to 1992.

The impact of the open door in the 1980s

As far as the 1980s are concerned, there is almost universal agreement on two points. First, the Chinese economy was far more open by 1988–9 than it had been in 1978.[24] Second, the impact of greater trade on the pace of economic growth was positive. Trade did involve some costs, but it is hard indeed to argue that the costs outweighed the benefits. The question of causality is altogether more difficult to answer. However, one way to proceed is to look at the spatial pattern of growth, and to use the cross-sectional evidence to establish the extent of causation between trade/FDI and growth.

This spatial approach is useful because there were considerable differences in both the pace of growth and the degree of openness across provinces. To see this, we can look at the experience of four provinces: Guangdong (the province most affected by opening up), Jiangsu (a coastal province but one which traded comparatively little in the 1980s) and Sichuan and Guizhou (interior provinces and amongst the poorest in China). It makes sense to look at their experience up to and including 1988, because thereafter the pattern of trade and FDI was distorted by the recession of 1989–90 and the political repercussions of the Tian'anmen massacre (Table 11.2).

Nevertheless, there is much in the data presented in Table 11.2 to suggest the positive impact of trade. The most obvious feature is the correlation between expanding trade shares and accelerating GDP growth in the 1980s. All four provinces experienced very large increases in their trade share, and simultaneously achieved a considerable acceleration in their growth rate. In all four cases, the increase in the trade share is dramatic. A casual inference is therefore suggested: increased openness led to a more rapid rate of economic growth. This is reinforced by the correlation between trade shares in 1988 and growth rates during the 1980s. Guangdong province had by far the largest trade share, and also enjoyed the fastest rate of growth. Guizhou, with the slowest rate of growth, had a lowest trade share amongst the four.

Nevertheless, the open-door hypothesis is far from confirmed by these data. One problem centres on the data for 1978. Guangdong in 1978 was the most open of the provinces in this sample, and by some distance, yet its growth rate in the late Maoist era was much *slower* than the rates achieved in Jiangsu and Sichuan.[25] This suggests that the Hong Kong connection did Guangdong little good in the

Table 11.2. Trade shares and growth rates in selected provinces, 1978–1988

	Guizhou	Sichuan	Jiangsu	Guangdong
Trade shares				
1978	0.6	0.3	2.9	14.7
1984	1.4	1.4	1.0	11.4
1988	2.7	4.6	10.4	39.8
GDP growth				
1965–78	4.9	5.6	6.7	5.3
1978–88	7.8	9.7	12.5	13.3

Sources: SSB (2005a); SSB (1990a).

Note
The trade share is the sum of exports and imports in GDP, measured in $US at official exchange rates in each year. GDP growth rates are percentages per annum based upon comparable price indices. Chinese time series data on foreign trade are often inconsistent because they mix Customs and Ministry of Foreign Trade series; the data presented above are consistent Ministry of Foreign Trade figures. Sichuan includes Chongqing; Guangdong excludes Hainan.

1970s. In part this was because the central government was appropriating most of the foreign exchange earnings generated by Guangdong exports. But it was also because much of Guangdong's exports were rice and vegetables destined for Hong Kong. In fact, Guangdong became China's leading rice exporter, increasing its export volume from 80 to over 200,000 tonnes per year by 1975 (Vogel 1989: 339). The central government played a key role in this by designating some prefectures – Foshan was the first – as export production bases and providing them with cheap steel and chemical fertilizer. However, agricultural exports are rarely a route to prosperity, especially exports of low value-added products; linkages effects are too weak and agricultural prices are too volatile. And so it was for Guangdong.

Second, and assuming for the moment that trade shares based upon official exchange rates accurately measure the degree of openness (and, as we will see shortly, this is very debatable), the main problem is that the trade shares of two of the four provinces were still very small in 1988. Even Jiangsu's trade share of 10 per cent indicates an economy essentially closed, rather than open. A comparison with the larger European economies is useful here because, in terms of population and geographical size, they are comparable to a Chinese province like Jiangsu. In 2003, Italy recorded a trade share of 50 percent, France 51 per cent, the UK 53 per cent and Germany 68 per cent (World Bank 2005: 230–2). In the same year, the South Korean trade share was 74 per cent and even Japan – despite being a much larger economy and therefore needing to trade less – recorded a figure of 22 per cent. Given this disparity in trade shares between the European economies and most Chinese provinces in 1988, it is very hard to argue, even though the trade shares of China's provinces grew quickly, that foreign trade played anything other than a minor role in the growth process during the 1980s. Can we really argue that a trade share of only 2.7 per cent of GDP was instrumental in causing Guizhou's growth rate to rise from 4.9 per cent during 1965–78 to 7.8 per cent between 1978 and 1988? Surely not. And this conclusion is reinforced by the fact that the rise in the trade share was due more to exports than imports. This is of significance because the usual argument for exports is that they solve demand-side deficiencies. But Guizhou did not suffer from any real demand-side problem in the 1980s; the domestic market was growing quickly, and export demand was almost trivial by comparison. In 1987, for example, domestic consumption rose by 1,585 million *yuan* – whereas exports increased by only 107 million *yuan* (SSB 2005a: 884 and 900). To see Guizhou's growth as export-led therefore makes little sense. To see it as import-led on the basis of the diffusion of technology is equally unconvincing, given that imports were barely a third of the value of exports and that there was inevitably a lag between imports and diffusion to the domestic sector. A far more plausible explanation would focus on the growth of agriculture between 1978 and 1984, and the surge in production in the TVE sector (only a part of which was exported by provinces such as Jiangsu, Sichuan and Guizhou).

These disparate provincial experiences demonstrate that the Chinese economy of the 1980s was dualistic. A part of the coastal region – the SEZs and the delta of the Pearl river – was closely integrated into the world economy.

Foreign trade and inward investment since 1971 375

However, the rest of China was only weakly linked to the outside world. As Naughton (1997: 312) says:

> Despite the immense flood of foreign investment into Guangdong and Fujian, the GDP growth rates of these provinces have been only slightly above the national average. ... while China has experienced rapid growth in both exports and GDP, the provincial evidence is not clear on the causal relationship between the two. Foreign trade and investment have been highly geographically concentrated, but the acceleration of economic growth has been very broadly based.

Moreover, an argument in favour of the open door based around the impact of foreign direct investment is even less plausible than one based on trade, because the scale of FDI was tiny in the 1980s. Jiangsu received only $US103 million in 1988, and the figure for Guizhou was a paltry $US14 million. To be sure, Guangdong received $US919 million in FDI in 1988 but even this was derisory relative to provincial GDP (3 per cent). In the early 1980s, the sums involved were far smaller. Given that much inward investment went into hotels and property, and that joint ventures aimed primarily at using China as a low-wage base from which to export, there is little basis for arguing for rapid technological diffusion either. It is therefore hard to disagree with Vogel's (1989: 374) conclusion that 'Guangdong's explosive export growth owed surprisingly little to foreign capital.'

In fact, the limited integration of the Chinese economy was a deliberate result of policy. As we have already noted, Shanghai was not awarded SEZ status in the late 1970s precisely because the CCP was reluctant to open up the Chinese economy to competition from imports in order to provide a measure of protection for its domestic industries. The Party's aim was not free trade but strategic integration – that is, to import technology and key raw materials, but to limit imports of manufactured goods. To that end, tariff and non-tariff barriers remained high throughout the 1980s and 1990s. The unweighted tariff rate did decline in the 1980s, but only by a small amount; the data show an unweighted rate of 56 per cent in 1982, and this had declined marginally to a still-very-high rate of 43 per cent in 1992 (Prasad 2004: 10). In such circumstances, it is no wonder that it is hard to find clear evidence to support the open-door hypothesis in analyzing the 1980s.

The open door after 1992

Any notion that trade and FDI were the engines of Chinese growth is much more compelling for the period after 1992. In large measure, this is because the volume of trade and inward investment was far greater relative to the size of the economy than it had been in the 1980s.

The macro data tell much of the story. As Figure 11.1 shows, the share of exports in GNI (valued using Chinese prices) soared. By 1989, the export share was up over 11 per cent of GNI, more than double its 1978 share. By 1996 it reached

19 per cent and it stood at no less than 37 per cent in 2006. The share of imports tracked that of exports fairly closely, and the net result was a China far more open to foreign trade than it had been in the Maoist era. By contrast, the increase in FDI was much more gradual. By 1989 it was some ten times greater than it had been in 1979, but because it started from a low base, the total volume attracted in the late 1980s was still very small. By the late 1990s, however, all that had changed; the volume of FDI being attracted into China was huge. To be sure, the official data undoubtedly overstate the true inflow. In fact, a substantial proportion of FDI was from Chinese firms who were channelling their investment via Hong Kong back into the mainland in order to take advantage of tax breaks. Nevertheless, there is no question that much of the inflow was a real addition to domestic investment.

The genuine FDI that China did receive was of great importance. Its contribution was not so much in terms of increasing the supply of savings; China was awash with saving in the 1980s and 1990s. Rather, FDI was crucial because it was a conduit for technology transfer and because it played a pivotal role in the rise of exports. Foreign-invested enterprises contributed 17 per cent of Chinese exports in 1991, but by 2005 the figure was up to 58 per cent (Chan *et al.* 1999: 25; ZGTJNJ 2006: 751–2). Foreign companies, in other words, were at the heart of China's export growth. Indeed some centres of Chinese industry were quite literally created by FDI. Shenzhen is the most famous example, but Dongguan is an equally good example. In the latter, GDP grew by more than 20 per cent per annum between 1980 and 2005, as what had been a green-field site was transformed by FDI and in-migration. Dongguan had been an exporter of rice in the 1970s (Vogel 1989: 339); by the 1990s, its export trade was dominated by manufactures.[26]

Another development during the 1990s was the that the geography of Chinese export production shifted substantially (Figure 11.5). Guangdong remained the single most important province, and its exports increased fourfold between 1991 and 2005. However, the centre of China's export boom had shifted towards the Yangzi delta because of the removal of controls on Shanghai's development and the growing maturity of Jiangsu's rural industry. By 2005, the combined value of exports from Jiangsu and Shanghai had almost matched the Guangdong figure, driven by a tenfold increase over the previous decade. As a result, Jiangsu's exports as a percentage of those of Guangdong rose from 13 to 52 per cent; the equivalent figures for Shanghai were 21 per cent in 1991 and 32 per cent in 2005. In short, China's integration into the world economy was far more broadly based by 2005 than it had been in the early 1990s, and that inevitably meant that the spatial impact of the open door were proportionately greater.

It is also worth emphasizing the extent to which the commodity composition of Chinese exports has changed over the last twenty years. Guangdong provides the clearest illustration. It is not so much that the province increasingly focused on manufactures rather than primary commodities; even as early as 1987, manufactures contributed 85 per cent of Guangdong's export earnings. This figure had risen to 97 per cent by 2002, but the most remarkable change was the shift away

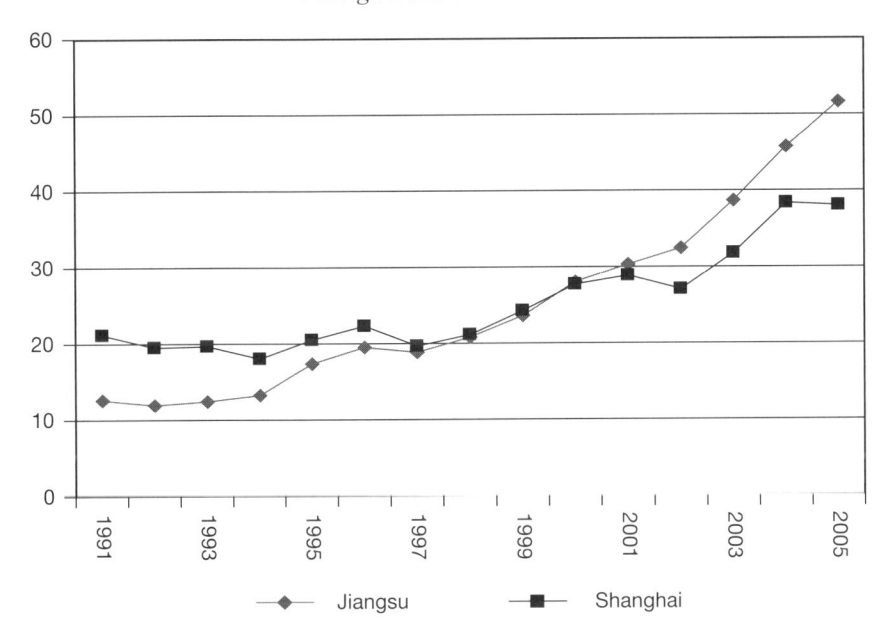

Figure 11.5 Ratio of the value of exports from Jiangsu and Shanghai to those of Guangdong, 1991–2005 (per cent) (Sources: ZGTJNJ (2006: 749); SSB (2005a: 390, 424 and 730).)

from traditional manufactures (processed food, garments and textiles) towards electronics and machinery. By 2002, mechanical and electrical products contributed no less than 61 per cent of the province's exports and in absolute terms amounted to more than four times the value of textiles and apparel (GDTJNJ 2003: 410 and 416–17). Jiangsu was little different. In 2005, the value of machinery and transport equipment exports was 57 per cent of provincial exports (JSTJNJ 2006: 342–3). China thus moved a long way up the value chain during the course of the 1990s.

The notion that spillover effects were more significant after 1992 is also more plausible. The strongest argument for this is the evidence on labour migration. Much migration was driven by a range of macroeconomic factors, but primarily by the combination of growing demand for labour in the industrial sector (in both urban industries and in burgeoning TVEs) and the yawning real wage gap between agriculture and industry. However, a considerable volume of migration was driven by the open-door policy. The SEZs in particular, and the south-eastern coastal region in general, began to experience considerable labour shortages by the mid-1980s. This excess demand for labour was met initially by drawing labour from the hinterland of provinces such as Guangdong but increasingly by labour attracted from much further afield. A feature of the 1990s was thus the migration of large numbers of young people – often women – from the province of Sichuan to Guangdong, and from Anhui to Shanghai. An unusually complete data series for Tianjin provides a more systematic insight. It shows that the difference between the actual and the registered population was only 30,000 in 1987, but by 1995 that had gone up to 470,000; in 2004 it was 911,000 (SSB 2005a: 130).

The data collected during the 2000 population census reveals the scale of the migration across China.[27] According to that census, there were 42 million long-distance temporary migrants in 2000.[28] The spatial breakdown is still more revealing, showing that a large proportion of the temporary population in the big cities comprised long-distance migrants. Some 95 per cent of Beijing's floating population was made up of long-distance migrants, whilst the equivalent figures were 93 per cent for Tianjin and 72 per cent for Shanghai. None of this is especially surprising; the large prosperous metropolitan centres were inevitably more attractive than poorer coastal provinces for large numbers of long-distance migrants. More interesting, however, is the fact that China's provinces were also magnets for migrants. Zhejiang proved to be an especially attractive province; no less than 68 per cent (3.7 million) of its floating population were long-distance migrants. The figure for Xinjiang, a province booming on the basis of its mineral resources, was also attractive. It attracted some 1.4 million long-distance migrants, or about 74 per cent of its entire floating population.

In all these cases, whether cities or provinces, it was rapid economic growth that fuelled growing demand for labour and hence migration. The case of Guangdong, however, was rather different in that it was the open door that triggered in-migration. That is the only way to explain the sheer scale of the migration into the province. According to the 2000 census, it had a floating population of 25.3 million, of whom no less than 15 million (72 per cent) were long-distance migrants (Liang and Ma 2004: 476; ZGTJNJ 2002: 102–3). These inflows continued into the next decade. As a result of the 1 per cent population survey of 2005, Guangdong's population was adjusted upwards from 83 million in 2004 to 91.9 million in 2005 at a time when its natural growth was only 0.7 per cent per year (ZGTJNJ 2004: 94; ZGTJNJ 2005: 100).

The main sources of Guangdong's migrants were the provinces of Hunan and Sichuan; the latter experienced a net outflow of around 4.4 million migrants aged five and over between 1995 and 2000, and Hunan exported 2.9 million (Fan 2005: 308). The bulk of these migrants into Guangdong were woman (66 per cent) aged between sixteen and twenty-five (Ng *et al.* 1998: 179). Within Guangdong, migration centred on the Pearl river delta.[29] Shenzhen, the first of the special economic zones, was an obvious destination, but other cities also experienced a massive influx. Dongguan is perhaps the best example. According to the data collected by Yeung (2001: 242–3), its migrant population rose from 16,000 in 1986 to 1.4 million in 1997, or around 50 per cent of the municipality's total population. Ng *et al.* (1998: 178) record the total rising from 58,000 in 1982 to 872,000 in 1995. According to different figures also quoted by Ng *et al.* (1998: 178) for the mid-1990s, only 179,000 out of Dongguan's labour force of 1.6 million were local – 849,000 workers had migrated in from other parts of Guangdong and a further 586,000 from outside Guangdong entirely. Dongguan was not alone. Of Guangzhou's total workforce of 3 million in the mid-1990s, only about 2.1 million were locals and the corresponding figures for the city of Zhongshan were 159,000 locals out of a total of 821,000.

Given the extent to which Guangdong attracted migrant workers compared to other parts of China, there is no doubt that the open door played a key role in driving the migration process. This in turn raises the possibility of powerful spillover effects via labour migration. Two main channels have been suggested. The first centres on the remittances paid by migrants to their home villages. Widely varying figures appear in the literature (Murphy 2006). Khan and Riskin (2005: 363) put the figure at only around 3 per cent of peasant income. Other sources suggest that Sichuan alone received 202 billion *yuan* in 2000 (Murphy 2006: 7) – an utterly implausible number (and probably a misprint) because it would imply that Sichuan's approximately 5 million migrants were each remitting 40,000 *yuan* per year even though average urban incomes were less than 10,000 *yuan* per year. A more plausible estimate can be derived from Murphy's (2006: 8) own contention that the average migrant remits around 3,000 *yuan* a year. In Sichuan's case, that would imply total remittances of around 15 billion *yuan* per annum, or 220 *yuan* per capita for the rural population – which would amount to around 12 per cent of income. An alternative approach is to treat the category 'outside wage income' as reported in the rural household surveys as income from migrants. This arguably overstates remittances, because the definition of an 'outside worker' here is a worker employed outside the *xiang* of official residence (SSB 2003b: 330). In other words, the remittances made by very short-distance migrants are included in this category, and it is clearly debatable whether such workers should be classified as migrants at all. Be that as it may, the data on outside income for 2005 give a figure of 459 *yuan* across China, amounting to about 14 per cent of per capita net rural income (SSB 2006c: 278–80). More interestingly, many of China's poorer provinces did better than this. The Sichuan figure was 601 *yuan* (21 per cent of rural income) and 635 *yuan* (24 per cent) was the figure recorded for Anhui.[30] Of course not all these flows can be attributed to the open door; much remittance income was generated by employment in TVEs within the same county or provinces, and many of these TVEs were largely unaffected by capital inflows or were at best weakly integrated into the world economy. For all that, it is plausible enough to argue that the open door did generate a flow of remittances to the Chinese interior which was anything but insignificant.

The second type of migrant-induced spillovers were technological; that is, spillovers caused by migrants returning to their home villages with a new set of skills which provided the basis for the development of new products and new production processes in their home villages. These skills were often used by return migrants not merely in farming but instead to set up new businesses. The migration process in effect created new rural entrepreneurs (Murphy 2002; Zhao 2002; Gaetano and Jacka 2004). In other words, the externalities generated by inward investment may have been so powerful that the volume of FDI alone gives no indication as to its true impact.

Finally, in considering the open-door hypothesis, it is worth noting the extent to which Chinese economic growth has come to rely upon imports of key producer goods and inputs. Although China has a large landmass, its mineral and land resources per capita are relatively limited, and this, combined with rapid economic growth, has forced it to become a significant importer of raw materials. In fact, Chinese foreign policy has become increasingly dominated by concerns over access to mineral resources. The support provided to the Burmese government in 2007 was driven by these sorts of considerations, and China's courting of African governments stems from the same considerations. For example, China is the biggest foreign investor in (and supplier of arms to) Zimbabwe in order to secure access to gold, tobacco and the platinum seen as crucial for its car industry. Chinese growth is also fuelled by uranium from Niger, manganese from South Africa and copper, nickel and iron ore from across the continent.

Oil is the best example of China's growing dependence on imports. In 1980, with oil imports amounting to less than 1 per cent of domestic consumption, China was a big net exporter to the tune of around 17 million tonnes (ZGTJNJ 1994: 196).[31] Little changed in the early 1980s; the import share was still below 1 per cent in 1985. Thereafter, however, imports steadily grew as domestic production failed to keep pace with economic growth. By 1990, China was importing around 7 per cent of its oil (ZGTJNJ 2007: 263), and 1993 was its last year of oil self-sufficiency. By 2000, the share of imports was 43 per cent and by 2006 it had reached 56 per cent of domestic consumption (ZGTJNJ 2007: 263). As significantly, China increasingly sought to reduce its dependence on oil from the Middle East. Imports from Russia and Venezuela are both significant, but it is to Africa that China has turned. By 2005, 17 per cent of Chinese oil came from Angola (second only to the 22 per cent provided by Saudi Arabia), and in 2006 Angola became the largest supplier of Chinese oil needs. Angola is not alone. Nigeria and Equatorial Guinea have been important suppliers and so too Sudan; the latter provided around 7 per cent of China's imports by the middle of the decade. Without access to these resources, Chinese economic growth would fade and die.

Taken together, all this evidence suggests that there is no doubt that growing international trade has helped the process of Chinese economic growth since Mao's death, and especially during the 1990s. FDI flows have increase substantially since the early 1990s. Technological spillovers have occurred. Much internal migration within China has been driven by the jobs created in the foreign sector, and the remittances flows associated with it have helped to alleviate poverty in the western provinces. And without the importation of a range of key inputs, Chinese growth would have foundered.

The limitations of the open-door hypothesis

Yet whilst there is no doubting the contribution of trade and FDI to growth, four problems remain with the open-door hypothesis as a plausible explanation of growth. First, conventional measures of GDP lead to a gross overstatement of the trade share and hence exaggerate the open door's quantitative importance. Second, the evidence on technological diffusion is weak. Given that the impact of the open door was so spatially limited, this is of great significance, because the only way we can argue that trade and FDI were the engines of growth in the interior is if the spillover effects from coastal development were large. Third, China's ability to generate indigenous technical progress greatly increased during the Maoist era. As a result, the intercession of 'the foreigner' was far less necessary for productivity growth than had once been the case. Finally, it is not even clear that the effect of the open door has been positive; certainly the calculus of costs and benefits is less clear-cut than is usually suggested.

The problem of measurement

One of the biggest problems with the hypothesis that the open door was instrumental in China's post-1992 growth is that estimates of the trade share in GNI are very much lower when GNI is measured at purchasing power parity instead of the official exchange rate. More precisely, the official exchange rate understates true GNI, and to a very substantial degree. The World Bank's estimate of Chinese GNI per person at purchasing power parity (PPP) for 2005 was $4,091, vastly greater than GNI measured at national prices, which was a mere $1,721 (World Bank 2007b: 22). As exports are measured at world prices, the effect of the purchasing power parity calculation is to reduce the export share of China (and indeed most poor countries) very substantially. This in turn leads to a very different perception of the extent to which China is an open economy. Table 11.3 provides an illustration of the impact of revaluing GDP using purchasing power parity.

When measured using national prices, the China of 2005 appears to be an open economy. At 38 per cent, its export share was much greater than those of the US, Japan and India. But when GDP is measured using PPP, China's export share falls back from 38 per cent to only 16 per cent. The same readjustment is evident for all poor countries, whereas for rich countries it depends on whether they are relatively high-price countries (like Japan or the countries of Scandinavia). This

Table 11.3 International evidence on export shares, 2005 (exports of goods and services as a percentage of GDP)

	When GDP measured at purchasing power parity (per cent)	*When GDP measured at national prices (per cent)*
Brazil	9	17
China	16	38
India	4	21
Japan	18	13
South Korea	33	43
UK	31	26
USA	10	10

Sources: World Bank (2007a: 218–20 and 246–8; 2007b: 22–4).

Note
The figures are based on the preliminary results of the 2005 round of the International Comparison Project.

382 *Chinese Economic Development*

evidence suggests that China, even after joining the WTO, was still a relatively closed economy, in contrast to countries like South Korea or the UK.

Of course there can be no denying that a considerable part of Chinese manufacturing is exposed to international competition, whether in the Chinese or the world market; nobody would pretend that contemporary China is a closed economy. Furthermore, estimates of purchasing power parity are subject to a large number of uncertainties.[32] China did take part in the International Comparison Project for the first time in 2005, and therefore we may fairly conclude that the latest estimates we have are better than the old ones. In fact, the latest World Bank estimates increase the Chinese export share at PPP from 8 to about 16 per cent of GDP; compare the estimates in World Bank (2007a: 14) and World Bank (2007b: 22). The result of these revisions makes China a considerably more open economy than, say, the USA.

For all that, there is little to suggest that China is an open economy. For one thing, the latest ICP estimates almost certainly exaggerate Chinese price levels and therefore underestimate true PPP GDP; if true, that would imply that China's export share is considerably less than 16 per cent.[33] Moreover, the notion that the Chinese economy was still relatively closed is entirely plausible. For one thing, and as Table 11.3 shows, large economies like the USA, Japan and India in general do not trade very much; this is because they have large domestic markets (and therefore can exploit economies of scale without exporting much) and a substantial resource base. The precise opposite is true of city-states like Singapore. China thus appears to have been simply a normal large country in terms of the volume of its trade in the years immediately after joining the WTO. Second, the common perception in the West of a China exporting large quantities of manufactures does not imply a large export share. Precisely because the Chinese economy is so large, even modest levels of exports have a major effect on China's trading partners, and that is what has happened in the 1990s and beyond. However, China's large service and agricultural sectors remain largely unaffected by trade flows, and this is reflected in the small share of both exports and imports in GNI. Finally, note that even *The Economist* (3 January 2008), usually only too keen to argue that growth across the world is export-led, seems to accept that China's growth has been driven primarily by domestic factors:

> Contrary to popular wisdom, China's rapid growth is not hugely dependent on exports. ... If exports are measured correctly, they account for a surprisingly modest share of China's economic growth. ... China's economy is driven not by exports but by investment, which accounts for over 40% of GDP.

Limited technological spillovers

The second problem with the open-door explanation of Chinese growth is that spillover effects remained weak even after 1992. There is no denying the extent of migration in the 1990s. Nor is there any question that return migrants carried with them back to their home villages a range of useful skills. However, the impact of this return migration on rural industrialization was limited. China's township and village industries began to grow quickly in the 1970s, well before the open-door policy was of any significance. The key agent of rural industrialization was local government. In this process, local government was aided and abetted by the development of links between China's hinterland and its most advanced industrial centres – technology transfers from, for example, Shanghai and Wuxi to the Jiangsu countryside, or from Chengdu and Chongqing to the Sichuan countryside, were considerable. But the agents of change here were skilled technicians with many years of experience in rural industry, and even then a long process of learning by doing was needed before a high productivity industrial workforce could be established. To suppose that a handful of young women with a range of experience limited to the shop floor of low-technology factories based in Dongguan and Shenzhen had a galvanizing effect on the Chinese countryside in the 1990s is preposterous. In those areas where rural industrialization was relatively straightforward – regions close to big cities and well favoured by economic geography and with a substantial stock of skilled labour – the process of rural industrial growth was already well underway by 1992, and return migrants were irrelevant. In other parts of the Chinese hinterland, it would take far more than a few return migrants to break out of the poverty trap.[34]

As for other types of technological spillovers, the evidence suggests that these were quite weak.[35] One reason for this was the geography of the open-door policy. The very fact that it focused on the SEZs, a handful of coastal cities, and was not extended even to provincial capitals until the mid-1990s necessarily limited the spillover effects. The dynamism of the Yangzi delta broadened the extent of spatial interaction but the engagement of China's interior provinces with the world economy remained very limited in the years after WTO accession. Take Hunan province. In 2005, its population of 63 million accounted for about 5 per cent of the national total. Its exports, however, accounted for only 0.5 per cent of the all-China total despite being adjacent to Guangdong province. Guizhou, poorest of all Chinese provinces, contributed 3 per cent of the population total but only 0.1 per cent of Chinese exports (ZGTJNJ 2006: 100 and 749). Even the mountainous hinterland of Guangdong was little affected by spillovers from its special economic zones. Indeed many economists see the absence of trade and FDI in its interior as a prime reason for spatial inequality. The open-door policy would have been far more effective if, from the start, it had focused on the traditional centre of Chinese industry – Manchuria – and had attempted to promote industrialization in the Chinese interior. However, and as we have seen, the CCP was so afraid in the late 1970s that opening up would lead to deindustrialization that it adopted a highly conservative policy, confining the SEZ to parts of China was there was little indigenous industry with which foreign firms and joint ventures could compete.

A second limiting factor in technological spillovers was that foreign firms located in China did very little either to sell goods to the Chinese market or to promote technology transfers. To be sure, foreign firms contributed enormously to total exports; their share in Chinese exports rose from 5 per cent in 1988 (Chan *et al.* 1999: 25) to over 50 per cent by the time of WTO entry. But these companies generated few backward linkage effects; they imported large quantities of intermediate inputs and fashioned them into finished products, adding little by way of value in the process. The data tell much of the story. Dongguan exported $US35 billion in 2004, but its imports (mainly intermediate inputs) amounted to no less than $30 billion in the same year (Gill and Kharas 2007: 11). In 2005, foreign-invested firms exported goods to the value of $US94 billion from Jiangsu, far above the $2.9 million exported in 1995. However, these same firms imported goods to the value of $US91 billion (JSTJNJ 2006: 340). As Bergsten *et al.* (2006: 105) say:

> More than half of all of China's exports and almost 90 per cent of its exports of electronic and information technology products are produced by foreign-owned factories located in enclave-like settings where interaction with domestic firms appears somewhat limited

Laptop computers offer a good example. Most are produced by Taiwanese-owned factories in China but the chips are from Intel, the software from Microsoft and the LCD screens and chips from South Korea and Taiwan. Only a third of gross value-added is Chinese (Bergsten *et al.* 2006: 106). The primary aim of these firms, predictably enough, is to locate in China merely in order to cut costs – that is, to use China as a low-cost base from which to export goods to the rest of the world. In this respect they were very successful. But to suppose that improving the balance sheets of Western multinationals did much for China is delusional.

Another reason for the limited reach of the open door was that inward investment from the USA was limited. This is of considerable significance because the US was, and remains, the world technology leader in most sectors of manufacturing. The very fact that few of the world's leading companies were located in China necessarily limited the transfer of best-practice technology. In one sense, of course, this made sense from a Chinese point of view; cutting-edge technology could not easily be absorbed by Chinese companies in the 1980s and early 1990s. But the absence of US firms in the late 1990s and after 2000 necessarily made it difficult for China to close the productivity gap between itself and the world leader.

The limited effect of the open door on the Chinese economy is confirmed by a range of more formal econometric studies. The results of these are especially interesting, because most of the economists who have carried them out have done so in the hope of documenting the existence of powerful spillovers from the foreign to the domestic sector. However, the studies show that spillover effects were as weak in China as in other countries.[36] As a result, the open-door policy has had the effect of widening spatial disparities across China. This is not surprising. As the work of Borensztein *et al.* (1998: 134) has shown, countries can only make effective use of FDI if they have the requisite absorptive capacity:

The most robust finding of this paper is that the effect of FDI on economic growth is dependent on the level of human capital available in the host economy. There is a strong positive interaction between FDI and the level of educational attainment (our proxy for human capital).

These findings are replicated in my own work on China (Bramall 2007).[37] Those parts of the People's Republic which have experienced rapid rural industrialization since 1978 have been regions with geographical advantages and a well-developed human capital base. FDI helps the process, but only in combination with other favourable conditions. And precisely because human capital is sparse in so many parts of China, so the reach of the open door has been limited.

The technological inheritance

There is no doubt that China has been comparatively successful in developing an indigenous innovative capacity which is much greater than might be expected of a country with its level of per capita GDP (Rodrik 2006b). The development of a modern semiconductor industry is one example of China's success in this regard, and it is undeniable that FDI and technology transfer have facilitated the process. Nevertheless, we do well to recognize that the impact of the open door in this regard has been less significant than it might have been precisely because of the extent to which China's indigenous technological capability expanded during the Maoist era. The intercession of the foreigner was far more necessary before 1949 than it was in the 1980s and 1990s, because by that time China had long since broken out of any low-level equilibrium trap.

There are many examples of indigenous technical progress in the Maoist era.[38] Perhaps the best example was China's successful development of high-yielding varieties (Stone 1988a,b). Precisely because HYVs need to be tailored to the specific growth conditions which obtain in the country, the scope for direct technology transfer is limited. As a result, the strains of high-yielding dwarf wheat developed by Norman Borlaug and used to good effect in Mexico, India and Pakistan were not suited to Chinese growing conditions. Instead, China developed its own varieties of wheat and other crops (such as cotton and maize) during the 1960s. These became available in large quantities in the mid-1970s, revolutionizing yields and making possible the surge in production in the late 1970s and early 1980s. In that the rural development of the 1980s was very much based upon increased agricultural production, it was a rural revolution made in China.

More generally, and as documented in previous chapters, the development of rural industry, the Third Front programme of defence industrialization, the sending-down programmes of the late 1960s and the expansion of education all played important roles in developing human capital and hence underpinning productivity growth in the 1980s and 1990s. The China of the late 1970s was thus far better able to generate rapid industrialization than it had been in the late 1940s. The clearest indication of this is the extraordinarily rapid growth of rural industry, a development which owed remarkably little to exports or to foreign technology. Jiangsu's exports may have grown very quickly in the late 1990s and in the first decade of the new millennium, but they did so by exploiting the rural industrial base which had been created in Suzhou, Wuxi and Kunshan during the Maoist era, and which expanded in the 1980s. Technological modernization in these areas has certainly been facilitated by new technology from (*inter alia*) Singapore (which has developed close links with Suzhou) and Japan, but much of the technological know-how required for the relatively simple types of production carried out in Chinese rural industries was already available in China in the 1980s. In no small measure, this reflected the Maoist inheritance and the types of goods being produced. The key rural industries which flourished in the 1980s and 1990s were those producing garments, beer, cement, bricks and paper, not those producing consumer durables for Western markets. Thus the open door may have helped Chinese industrialization, but it was very far from being a necessary condition. Had the open-door policy operated in the 1950s, the impact would have been altogether greater.

The costs of the open door

The final difficulty with the open-door hypothesis is that it is not self-evident that its effects on China's growth and development have been positive. The impact of opening-up can be assessed under four headings: average living standards, absolute poverty, inequality and political economy effects.[39] As far as the first is concerned, the impact of the open door is not in doubt. The most powerful argument for free trade is that it raises consumer living standards by depressing prices and increasing the variety of goods available. There is little doubt that this is precisely what happened in China after 1978, with the result that a large proportion of China's population benefited from the process.

The other effects are more uncertain. There is a large international literature suggesting that globalization reduces absolute poverty by job creation, and that there is a close relationship between the rate of economic growth and the rate of absolute poverty reduction (Dollar and Kraay 2002). Dollar and Kraay (2004: F47) go further to argue that there is a close relationship between growing openness to trade and FDI, and absolute poverty reduction:

> [C]hanges in trade volumes have a strong positive relationship to changes in growth rates. Furthermore, there is no systematic relationship between changes in trade volumes and changes in household income inequality. The increase in growth rates that accompanies expanded trade therefore on average translates into proportionate increases in income of the poor. Thus, absolute poverty in the globalising developing economies has fallen sharply in the past 20 years.

However, and *pace* Dollar and Kraay, the debate is not resolved so easily. The problem is that, as Bardhan (2006) and Ravallion (2006) have emphasized, there is no simple relationship between trade and absolute poverty reduction. Trade can reduce poverty by virtue of increased employment (derived from the export of both labour-intensive manufactures and farm products), cheaper input prices and increased competition (and thus enhanced productivity). However, growing competition from imports may cause deindustrialization and undermine farm incomes in so far as food imports undercut domestic production. In China's case, it is not difficult to observe these sorts of effects, whether positive or negative. Most obviously, FDI generated a large number of jobs in south-east China and indeed was responsible for the *creation* of new industrial centres such as Dongguan and Shenzhen. In the process, a significant number of poor farmers were able to escape from poverty by becoming industrial workers. There is no doubt that this new proletariat was an exploited one, but real per capita incomes assuredly rose on the back of such exploitation. On the other side of the coin, cheap wheat imports have reduced the incomes of some farmers, and competition from imports has undermined China's traditional industries, leading to spiralling urban unemployment. However, these negative effects are themselves hard to assess. Guangdong had little industry to speak of at the end of the Maoist era and therefore the extent of deindustrialization in the region most affected by liberalization cannot have been very great. And China's farmers in the interior were protected against the impact of imports by high transport costs and growing barriers to inter-provincial trade (Poncet 2003). There are two further complications. For one thing, much of the observed urban unemployment in China reflects domestic restructuring of both SOEs and TVEs, rather than trade factors. For another, it is hard to determine the degree to which Chinese export growth reflects Chinese liberalization, and the extent to which it reflects the growth of the world economy.

These various factors are hard to disentangle in order to arrive at some overall estimate of the impact of liberalization on poverty. However, the use of large general equilibrium models is widely believed to help to resolve these measurement difficulties. Such computable general equilibrium models suggest that liberalization between 1995 and 2001 (the run-up to WTO accession) had positive effects, and that WTO membership itself will continue the process (Bhattasali *et al.* 2004). Ianchovichina and Martin (2004: 221) put China's welfare gain at $31 billion between 1995 and 2001, and an additional $10 billion between 2001 and 2007. Similar models predict that the Doha round of trade liberalization will have further positive effects – in China's case, the short-run effect will be a reduction in poverty of 4.6 million, mainly via increased Chinese agricultural exports. Full world trade liberalization is predicted to reduce Chinese absolute poverty by 8.3 million (Hertel and Winters 2006: 27).

Such optimistic results need, however, to be qualified. One problem of course is that they are derived from equilibrium models and therefore take scant account of market failure; in other words, markets are assumed to clear and therefore implied equilibrium prices can be used to evaluate welfare effects. As it is fair to assume that markets never clear, the results of computable general equilibrium models need to be taken with a pinch of salt. Yet the most striking feature of the models is that they predict such small effects on welfare as a result of trade reform. A telling commentary here on the size of the welfare effects is that the studies have widened the impact of WTO accession to the period 1995–2001 on the grounds that the changes that occurred during these years were made in preparation for accession. Some sort of an argument can be made along these lines, but given that talks between China and the US on WTO entry broke down as late as April 1999, it is a bit of a stretch to use 1995 as the baseline for such studies. But putting this to one side, the numbers involved are still very small. In fact, a study by Chen and Ravallion (2004) on welfare effects of liberalization under the auspices of the World Bank reaches a similarly damning conclusion; mean income rose by 1.5 per cent, but this occurred entirely in the period prior to WTO accession.

Worse, the Chen–Ravallion study suggests that poverty actually increased as a result of accession; this is because the average income of the rural population fell by 18 *yuan* between 2001 and 2007 as a result of falling farm prices for rice, wheat, vegetables and fruit (Chen and Ravallion 2004: 267). Even a World Bank study estimated that the wages of unskilled farm workers fell by 0.7 per cent between 2001 and 2007, implying a rise in rural poverty as a result of WTO entry (Ianchovichina and Martin 2004: 221). None of this is at all implausible. The main gains from WTO accession will be garment and consumer good manufacturers located in already affluent parts of China such as the Pearl river and Yangzi deltas. Poverty in these regions is limited and therefore the poverty-reducing effect of WTO entry there is small. Conversely, the regions which are the main losers – farmers in western and central China and workers in the Manchurian rustbelt – are the regions where the poverty problem is most acute. Manchuria of course used to be a rich region, but state-led restructuring of the industrial sector under the auspices of *zhuada fangxiao* has put an end to much of that by creating urban unemployment. The impact of WTO entry is therefore to reinforce the problem.

Now the adverse effects of WTO entry should not be exaggerated. The farmers of the interior are protected by high transport costs and by the reluctance of central government to sanction large-scale food imports. Moreover, the unemployment problem in Manchuria is primarily a consequence of state-led industrial restructuring, as will be seen in the next chapter. But it is very hard to make the case for growing integration into the world economy on the grounds that it will reduce poverty. Moreover, even the more optimistic assessments of the effects of liberalization between 1995 and 2001, as well as expectations for the Doha round and full trade liberalization, need to be placed in context. Even if poverty falls by 8 million, it is hard to see this as anything but modest in the context of the events of the previous twenty-five years. To be sure, the absolute poverty headcount was quite low by 2001. However, we do well here to remember that Chinese rural poverty fell by an extraordinary 200 million in the 1980s – at a time when trade was negligible and the volume of FDI almost laughably small. As Ravallion (2006: 1381) concludes:

> [I]t is hard to even make the case from the available data that trade has helped the poor. ... More plausible candidates for explaining China's success against poverty can be found in the role played by the agrarian reforms starting in the late 1970s, subsequent agricultural growth (which had an unusually large impact on poverty given a relatively equitable allocation of land achieved in

the wake of the early reforms to de-collectivize agriculture), reduced taxation of farmers, and macro-economic stability.

As for the effects on inequality, it is evident that most of the studies suggest that the gains for the rural sector were typically rather small, whereas those for the urban sector were considerably larger – thus implying that trade liberalization widened the urban–rural income gap. For example, Chen and Ravallion (2004: 268) have urban incomes rising by 29 *yuan*, whereas rural incomes fell by 18 *yuan* between 2001 and 2007. But even here there was a marked regional component. As will be discussed further in Chapter 15, the main losers were those parts of western China where farming was the key source of income, and the cities of the north-east, where livelihoods were based around employment in heavy industry. The main region to gain was of course the south-east, and especially Guangdong province.

The political economy issues effects of the open door, and especially WTO entry, are more complex. In essence, however, the main consequence of opening up has been a loss of policy autonomy. In practice this means that the Chinese government is now extremely circumscribed in terms of the degree to which it can pursue industrial policy designed to support and develop infant industries. Given that world historical evidence points unequivocally to the conclusion that protection and subsidies are a *sine qua non* for catch-up (Chang 2002), China's abandonment of these developmental tools is a crucial mistake. It will mean that China will never be more than a middle-income country.

Conclusion

The engine of Chinese growth since 1978 has been the domestic economy. Powered by the twin motors of domestic capital accumulation (physical and human) and productivity increases, output growth has surged ahead at a rate of close to 10 per cent per year. If there has been an economic miracle, it has been a miracle made in China.

The basis for the claim that the contribution of the foreign sector has been small is easily set out. In part, the contribution of the foreign sector has been meagre because China is a large country with a low per capita resource base. That means that its domestic market is large enough to allow the exploitation of economies of scale in most industries. It also means that China lacks the resource base enjoyed by natural-resource-rich countries like Saudi Arabia or Botswana. In consequence, export-led growth based around primary commodities has been neither possible not desirable. And the numbers bear this out; the share of Chinese exports as percentage of Chinese GDP (measured at purchasing power parity) has been small in the post-1978 period by international standards.

The notion that Chinese growth has been import-led is a little more persuasive. Many of China's imports have either been capital goods or raw materials; this is because the tariff structure during the 1980s and 1990s discriminated firmly against imported consumer goods. Imported raw materials have helped fuel China's long boom in a very literal sense; imported oil has become critically important to Chinese growth. And imports have been a useful conduit for technology transfer, alongside foreign direct investment. Furthermore, both trade and FDI have been more important than the raw numbers suggest because of technological spillovers and because of induced labour migration.

Nevertheless, we need to retain some perspective on all this. Before the middle of the 1990s, the numbers point very clearly to the conclusion that the contribution of raw material and imported technology was comparatively limited. The extent of raw material imports was small: China was a net oil exporter until 1993. The reach of the open-door policy was very limited, largely confined as it was to the southern coastal provinces. Internal labour migration, though increasing, provided a highly imperfect transmission mechanism for new technology to the Chinese interior. Furthermore, the real engines of growth in the twenty years after Mao's death were agriculture and rural industry. The growth of the former owed much to the reform package of the late 1970s and 1980s, not least the surge in domestic chemical fertilizer production and the diffusion of the new high-yielding crop varieties which had been developed during the late Maoist era. The growth of the latter reflected both policy change and the foundation provided by the technological and skill legacies of the Maoist era. These developments in the rural sector provide a far more coherent explanation of the pace of growth in western provinces like Gansu, Guizhou and Sichuan – where GDP growth was in the order of 5 to 7 per cent per year in the 1980s and 1990s – than foreign trade and inward investment.

After 1992, the world economy undoubtedly played a greater role in Chinese growth; the data on the share of imports and the growing levels of FDI admit of no other conclusion. However, the shares of FDI and imports are still comparatively small relative to GDP, and almost all the econometric evidence suggests that spillover effects have continued to be rather weak. The fact is that most of the manufacturing carried out in the foreign sector in China is little more than assembly work. Moreover, favourable spread effects have been at least partly offset by powerful backwash effects on neighbouring regions – including Hunan, Guangxi and even the hinterland of Guangdong itself – as a result of the rapid industrialization of the Pearl river delta. All these regions have suffered from an exodus of skilled labour, which has undermined their capacity to generate industrial growth. And deindustrialization in parts of Manchuria is undoubtedly at least in part a consequence of growing international integration. Finally, we need to recognize that even the most outward-looking parts of southern China have based much of their prosperity on their geography (large concentrations of population and low transport costs) and on their industrial inheritance from the Maoist era. True, some green-field sites have been utterly transformed by inward investment; Shenzhen and Dongguan offer perhaps the best examples. But the industrialization of the Yangzi delta region owes as much to its Maoist inheritance, its favourable geography and the removal of controls on the growth of the great metropolitan centre of Shanghai as it does to inward investment.

Foreign trade and inward investment since 1971   391

In short, for all the attention lavished on China's open-door policy and its WTO accession, internal factors were the mainspring of economic growth in most parts of the People's Republic in the thirty years after Mao's death. Foreign trade and capital flows have facilitated the process, but they have been handmaidens, rather than engines of growth.

Notes

1 In 2005, the average export shares (goods and services) were 25 per cent for low-income countries and 36 per cent for middle-income countries (World Bank 2007a: 220).
2 As with most countries, the long-run trajectory of imports tracks that of exports very closely. If we are measuring the extent of trade, it therefore matters little whether we look at the value of imports or of exports.
3 For general discussions of the economic dimensions of globalization, see Glyn (2006), Stiglitz (2002) and Bhagwati (2004).
4 Trade between Japan and China practically ceased in 1959 and 1960, but this reflected not so much Chinese emphasis on self-reliance as the aftermath of the Nagasaki flag incident of 1958 (the Chinese flag was pulled down in a shop in Nagasaki and no action was taken over this 'crime' by the Japanese government because the CCP was not recognized as the legitimate government of China). However, trade resumed in the early 1960s, and its growth was abetted by the lack of support offered by Japan to the US over Vietnam.
5 Only after 1966 – the height of the Cultural Revolution – was there a decline in the absolute *renminbi* value (SSB 2005a: 68).
6 Trade with Indo-China also rose in the 1960s. Sichuan's trade with Vietnam expanded as the Third Front gathered momentum and China's involvement in Indo-China increased. Provincial exports rose from about 1 million *yuan* in 1963 to 14.6 million *yuan* at their peak in 1972 (ZSSWY 1984: 591–2).
7 Shirk's (2007: 14) view that 'Chairman Mao reached out [in 1971] to the United States to end China's two-decade-long self-imposed isolation' is far too simplistic an interpretation of Sino-American relations in the 1950s and 1960s. It was, after all, the US which had imposed and maintained the trade embargo.
8 Lin's death in September 1971 may also have helped, but recently released documents suggest little evidence of any opposition within China to Mao's wish to improve relations with the USA (Xia 2006).
9 For some of the literature on trade between Japan and China, see Ishikawa (1987) and Yokoi (1990).
10 One of the very few good accounts of the opening-up process is Kleinberg (1990). Foot (1995) covers the politics of improved Sino-US relations.
11 It is worth noting that Shenzhen explicitly moved its focus away from infrastructural development and towards export promotion in 1985. Nevertheless, foreign-invested companies of all types were supplying only about 10 per cent of all Chinese exports by 1990 (Chan *et al.* 1999. 25).
12 For a discussion of these debates and an outline of the process of opening up, see Hsu (1991: ch. 4), Lardy (1992), Shirk (1993) and World Bank (1994, 1997).
13 The fourteen were Tianjin, Shanghai, Dalian, Qinhuangdao, Yantai, Qingdao, Lianyungang, Nantong, Ningbo, Wenzhou, Fuzhou, Guangzhou, Zhanjiang and Beihai.
14 For a useful discussion of the SEZs in the context of the decision to develop Pudong, see Chan (1991).
15 The discussion in this paragraph is based on Fewsmith (2001: 206–24). It is important to note that the CCP had long been in favour of GATT and then WTO membership because of the symbolism involved. However, it was only in the late 1990s that the

392 *Chinese Economic Development*

      CCP leadership showed itself ready to remove China's remaining tariff and non-tariff barriers.
16 Indeed the crisis led to rethinking even by advocates of globalization in the IMF, the World Bank and Western economics departments. By the end of the millennium, it was still normal for economists to advocate free trade, but many were much more equivocal as to the desirability of unrestricted capital flows; see for example Bhagwati (2004: ch. 13).
17 However, there is some evidence that Zhu was opposed to WTO membership in the early 1990s (Lardy 2002: 20).
18 For the literature on changes to China's tariff regime and the implications of WTO entry, see Lardy 2002, Bhattasali *et al.* (2004), OECD (2002) and the special issues of *China Quarterly* (September 2001) and *China Economic Review*, 11 (4) (2000).
19 Many Chinese liberals, such as He Qinglian and Qian Yingyi, seem to have supported accession on the paradoxical grounds that further integration into the world economy would weaken the Chinese state by exposing the economy to financial and balance of payments crises, thus demonstrating the state's impotence and leading to its collapse. A variant on the theme is the notion that WTO membership would necessarily force China to adopt international rules of law, and that this would pave the way for a more general process of reform which would culminate in the Chinese state itself being subject to the law. Thus any short-term economic costs would be offset by longer-run political gains (Zhang 2006).
20 An alternative series shows the weighted tariff rate fell from 32 per cent in 1992 to 6 per cent in 2004 (World Bank 2005: 338).
21 A typical estimate puts the extent of *under*valuation at over 20 per cent in 2003, whereas in the late 1970s it was *over*valued by at least 50 per cent. For some of the literature, see Chang and Shao (2004), Goldstein and Lardy (2005), Goldstein (2006) and Goldstein and Lardy (2006).
22 Of course a weak exchange rate does not serve as a check on inflation and that is one reason why China's exchange rate policy has attracted the opprobrium of the inflation-obsessed World Bank and the IMF. But given that China's pre-eminent price problem after 1996 was deflation rather than inflation, it is hard to argue that using the exchange rate as a nominal anchor in the fight against inflation was an appropriate approach to policy. More generally, the disastrous experiences of countries which have fixed their exchange rate at an inappropriately high level in a desperate (and ill-conceived) bid to ensure credibility in the fight against inflation – the UK's entry into ERM in the early 1990s offers a classic example – surely demonstrates that the central danger for a poor country lies in over- rather than undervaluation.
23 The ending of the *renminbi*–dollar peg does at least mean that the Chinese government can now use the interest rate as a tool of domestic policy rather than having to use the instrument to control the exchange rate. In that sense, its freedom of action has been enlarged.
24 I focus here on the period up to 1988 because the recession of 1989–91 distorts the growth record. However, whether one looks at 1988 or 1992 as the end-point matters little because the economy was no more open in 1992 than it was in 1988.
25 Guangdong's trade share fluctuated between a low of 11 per cent in 1965 and 18 per cent in 1974, so the 1978 share is representative enough of the period.
26 A concise discussion of the rise of Dongguan is given in Gill and Kharas (2007: 10–12). For a more detailed treatment, see Yeung (2001).
27 The national pattern of migration is discussed in more detail in Chapter 9.
28 'Temporary' (or floating) in the sense that their official place of residence (or *hukou*) was outside the place in which they were residing in 2000. 'Long–distance' here refers to migrants who had crossed a provincial boundary.
29 Note that the data are very inconsistent across sources, reflecting both the scale of illegal flows and also differences in definition. It is rarely clear whether a figure for

migrants includes both temporary and permanent migrants, whether the figure is a stock or a flow (i.e. the total number living in the city on any given day or the inflow over the course of the year in question), whether the migrants are long- or short-distance or whether the figure includes intra-county (or intra-municipality) as well as inter-county migrants.
30 The Guangdong figure was a colossal 1,550 *yuan*, which shows just how many of its poorer villagers were working in the factories of the Pearl river delta.
31 Consumption here includes oil which is stockpiled.
32 A useful discussion of some of the older PPP estimates is to be found in OECD (2005: 70–1).
33 The World Bank (2007b: 68) study estimated Chinese GDP by extrapolation using prices drawn from eleven cities. Although the price surveys covered the (rural) counties under the jurisdiction of the city governments as well as the urban areas, the cities chosen were hardly representative. The list (Beijing, Shanghai, Ningbo, Qingdao, Guangzhou, Xiamen, Dalian, Harbin, Wuhan, Chongqing and Xi'an) is very much biased towards the coastal region. Only Wuhan Chongqing and Xian are interior cities, and even then all three are very much tourist and trading centres. The deep interior – provinces such as Xinjiang, Gansu, Guizhou and Yunnan – is not represented at all even though this is the poorest part of China, relatively unintegrated into the world economy and characterized by prices which are lower than the national average. It looks very much as if the cities were deliberately chosen by China's SSB in order to minimize Chinese GDP so that the People's Republic can still claim to be a very poor country.
34 Furthermore, the open door had paradoxical effects in that it lead to the growth of local protectionism as local governments tried to prevent a drain of skilled resources and raw materials to the coastal provinces. At the same time that China became more integrated into the world economy, so its domestic economy became less integrated (Poncet 2003).
35 Moreover, in so far as technology transfers were occurring, it is not clear that trade and FDI were key instruments in the process. Paul Romer has argued that the prime requirement for growth in LDCs is that they close the 'ideas gap' between themselves and more advanced countries, but that in itself need not require a large volume of trade. It is the type of trade, as well as openness to new ideas and technologies, that is much more important than its volume.
36 Global studies, including those of Blomstrom and Kokko (1998), Görg and Greenaway (2004) and Borensztein *et al.* (1998), find little evidence of strong spillover effects from FDI. For the Chinese evidence, see Li *et al.* (2001), Brun *et al.* (2002), Hu and Jefferson (2002), Fu (2004), Liu (2002), Cheung and Lin (2004), Zhang and Felmingham (2002) and Thompson (2003).
37 See also Gao (2005).
38 They include the development of a nuclear capability and artemisinin, which has proved to be a highly effective treatment of malaria and which was developed entirely independently of the West in the early 1970s. Of course innovation in China was partly based upon inventions imported from elsewhere; Chinese nuclear weapons would not have been developed without initial Soviet help. However, we should not get too precious about this: after all, the development of American nuclear technology was facilitated by the work of British and German scientists.
39 These broad distributional issues are discussed in more detail in Chapter 15. The focus here is on the trade-related aspects of the income distribution.

12 Industrial development since 1978

As discussed in Chapter 8, the late Maoist industrial sector was weak in two respects. First, it was too small to supply the producer goods needed to make China a superpower and the consumer goods needed to slake the demand of its population. Second, Chinese industry was inefficient. Industrial policy in the post-1978 era has been an unending search for a solution to these twin problems.

The weakness of Chinese industry at the close of the 1970s is not surprising. Chinese industrialization in the Maoist era was driven by defence considerations to the exclusion of other factors. The development of the Third Front industries in caves and in inaccessible parts of western China can only be understood in these terms. China's improved relations with the USA by the end of the 1970s put an end to all that. Instead, the Party faced the genuine difficulty of trying to formulate an industrial policy that would be suitable for peacetime.

This chapter discusses the theoretical issues involved in formulating such a strategy and the arguments for a state-led industrial policy which focuses on the provision of subsidies to a small number of targeted industries. It then moves to discuss the way in which industrial policy was carried out in practice. The most important issue, however, and the issue which is central to this chapter, is whether post-1978 industrial policy was successful. On this point, the literature is largely negative. Chinese industrial performance may have been better than it was in the late Maoist era but the scholarly consensus is that China moved far too slowly after 1978 in privatizing state-owned industry. In fact, China compounded some of the problems of the late Maoist era by allowing the expansion of state-owned industries in rural areas. That private industry was nevertheless allowed to develop in tandem with this state sector expansion meant that the planners were protected from the full consequences of their actions: the private sector was dynamic enough to provide the subsidies required to keep the ailing state sector afloat. Nevertheless, there was a real opportunity cost here. By diverting resources into propping up inefficient industries, China has hampered the expansion and development of its educational system, its health care, its transport infrastructure and the relief of poverty in western China. It is the poor quality of education and health care that is the true cost of industrial failure.[1]

I shall take issue with this assessment, and argue that Chinese industrial development has actually been very successful since 1949. When the concept is properly defined – to mean a sector capable of serving the wider needs of the Chinese economy rather than merely in terms of profitability or productivity – we may fairly concluded that the 'efficiency' of China's industrial sector has improved dramatically since the Revolution.[2] To be sure, Chinese industry has a considerable distance to go before it is able to compete outside those markets where price competitiveness is the critical factor. And in the long run high productivity (though not competitiveness *per se*) is essential for high living standards, and hence for the very goal of development itself. The very fact, therefore, that productivity growth in China's industrial sector has been fitful is a cause for concern. However, an obsession with competitiveness and productivity is likely to be disastrous if it leads – as it has done since 1996 – to the closing down of large numbers of enterprises. Productivity does need to be increased in the long run, but an ideologically driven industrial closure programme will hinder its attainment by bringing to a halt the process of learning-by-doing and by creating social unrest. Indeed successful catch-up almost certainly requires that China leaves the WTO, and embarks upon a renewed process of limited (strategic) integration into the international economy – and in so doing abandons its recent, wholesale and unseemly conversion to the nostrums of the Washington consensus.

Theoretical issues

Few would deny the proposition that industrial development is a *sine qua non* for prosperity for most countries; few indeed are the instances of countries which have prospered on the basis of financial services, tourism or agriculture. Furthermore, as has long been recognized, manufacturing in particular is an engine of growth because of the extensive scope therein for technical progress and the exploitation of dynamic economies of scale (Kaldor 1966). There is some evidence that manufacturing is becoming less important as a source of job creation; services are increasingly playing that role in some countries, such as India (Dasgupta and Singh 2006). Nevertheless, manufacturing remains critical as a source of exports and of technical progress, functions not easily performed by the service sector.

Nevertheless there is much controversy over industrial development strategies, in respect of the objective of policy, and about ways and means of achieving that objective. Nobody doubts the importance of industrial growth. Much less clear is the need for competitiveness in world markets. Although many policymakers focus on the need for countries to achieve competitiveness, it is by no means obvious that this is a sensible policy goal, especially in the short run. Second, there is much debate about ways and means. Is growth best achieved by leaving things to market forces (with state spending on education and infrastructure as an essential adjunct) or by means of state-led industrial policy designed to select the industries of the future and to subsidize them during their infancy? 'Leaving well alone' is of course the implication of the well-known Solow growth model.

Precisely because technical progress is exogenous – and therefore cannot be explained – it is not amenable to increase by government action. It is tempting for a government to introduce policies designed to raise productivity, but in truth it would do better to leave well alone.

Competitiveness and productivity growth

One of the central assumptions in much of the literature on Chinese industry is that the creation of an 'efficient' industrial sector is imperative. By 'efficient' is meant a sector which has internationally recognized brands and which is able to compete in world markets without having recourse to low wages. In neither respect is contemporary China doing especially well (Hutton 2007). To be sure, low-wage economies can always compete in world markets, but there is a clear contradiction in terms between the notion of a low-wage economy and an economy which is developed. If China wishes to be developed, it has to increase its real wages and by implication a development strategy based on cheap exports is not sustainable. Similarly, a strategy based around a continuous depreciation of the currency (designed to offset wage increases) is unlikely to succeed. It will only serve to ignite an inflationary spiral as workers seek to offset the effects of rising import prices by demanding higher money wages.

The goal of competitiveness is itself a red herring (Krugman 1994; 1996; Lall 2001; Lall and Albaladejo 2004). It is always possible to compete on the basis of cheap labour or a low exchange rate, and therefore increasing competitiveness does not matter very much. In the *long run*, it is productivity – not competitiveness – which is the principal determinant of living standards. Krugman (1994) makes the point very clearly:

> Productivity isn't everything, but in the long run it is almost everything. A country's ability to improve its standard of living over time depends almost entirely on its ability to raise its output per worker [p. 13]. Compared with the problem of slow productivity growth, all our other long-term economic concerns – foreign competition, the industrial base, lagging technology, deteriorating infrastructure, and so on – are minor issues. Or more accurately, they matter only to the extent they may have an impact on our productivity growth [p. 18].

To see this most clearly, consider a closed economy. In such circumstances, competitiveness does not matter, because there is no international trade. But without increases in productivity, the population cannot raise per capita real income in the long run because productivity is a *sine qua non* for increasing the availability of goods. The long-run challenge for China, as for other developing countries, is therefore that of creating a high-productivity industrial sector.

In the *short run*, however, it is not clear that productivity – output per employed worker – matters very much for a developing country. This is not obvious in most neoclassical models, because they simply assume that the economy is at a full employment equilibrium (or at the natural rate), and therefore that there is no unemployment problem. In this sort of world, the economy is always operating at its potential and any unemployment is voluntary; in effect, the problem of unemployment is assumed away. In practice, however, the 'problem' of underdevelopment is as much about a failure to mobilize the labour force as it is about low productivity. That is, the typical underdeveloped country is characterized by endemic under- or unemployment. In such circumstances, per capita income can be increased by mobilizing 'surplus' labour to create a bigger industrial sector even if there is no rise in industrial productivity. The most obvious way to do this, and indeed the classical route to development, is to transfer surplus labour from agriculture to the industrial sector. Industrial productivity may not increase in the process, but industrial production rises and economy-wide productivity increases (because the share of the low productivity agricultural sector becomes lower). In fact, the second-best outcome could even be one in which industrial productivity falls provided that total employment and industrial output rises. This is the basis for the definition of industrial efficiency put forward by Ajit Singh, one which rightly recognizes that we need to think about efficiency in macroeconomic terms:

> [A]n 'efficient' manufacturing sector must be able to provide (currently and potentially) sufficient net exports to meet the country's overall import requirements at socially acceptable level of output, employment and exchange rate. It is in this important sense that, in spite of the growth in productivity, there is evidence that the UK manufacturing sector is becoming increasingly inefficient. (Singh 1977: 136)

Once, of course, the economy achieves full employment the calculus becomes altogether different, and the need to raise industrial productivity comes sharply to the fore. But in acknowledging the long-run truth in the argument advanced by Krugman, we need to recognize that the short-term policy issues are rather different. In fact, we can go further. As has long been recognized (Arrow 1962), one of the characteristics of industrial production is learning-by-doing. It follows from this that the creation of an industrial sector which is inefficient in the short run (in terms of productivity) may nevertheless lead to long-run increases in productivity via the process of learning. Indeed it is arguable that this is precisely what has happened in China, not least in its rural industrial sector (Bramall 2007). In other words, the extent of learning is a function of the level of production. The expansion of industrial production, even though that production is inefficient in the short run, is crucial for long-run success.

The role for industrial policy

The role for state-led industrial policy – by which I mean selective assistance to a comparatively small number of enterprises – in growth promotion is equally controversial. One view is that industrialization is best promoted if the state confines itself to the provision of a range of public services, infrastructure and the development of human capital – and avoids anything that resembles (as it is pejoratively called) 'picking winners'. This rejection of industrial policy is of course the approach summarized by the term 'Washington consensus', first used by John Williamson to describe the policy orientation of the Washington-based institutions during the 1980s and 1990s. This analysis does not deny that a capitalist economy will be handicapped by a range of market failures. Rather, the argument for limited state intervention is made on the grounds of second-best. Public goods are best provided by government, but state failure will be extensive if any attempt is made to pick winners. It is not a straightforward task to select the industries of the future, and governments would do well not to try. Living standards may depend upon productivity, but governments can do little to increase it (Krugman 1993a, 1993b).

Over the last decade, the Washington consensus has increasingly emphasized the importance of institutional development (the rules of the economic game) rather than simply arguing for privatization, competition policy and the liberalization of prices. The underlying idea here is that economies are characterized by uncertainty and transaction costs. Secure property rights are a *sine qua non* for investment, and one of the primary failures in transition economies has been adequate attention to creating a proper legal system within which private enterprise can flourish. Institution building is therefore as essential for a successful market economy as competition and market forces.

This market-led approach to industrialization has been rejected by a number of economists inspired by the work of List and Chalmers Johnson. The heterodox approach encapsulates several ideas. In one respect, they share common ground with orthodox economists in believing that the growth rate can be increased in poor countries in the short run by raising the rate of investment. If a government mobilizes savings, it can raise per capita income by raising the capital–labour ratio.[3] Stalin's Soviet Union provides the classic example, and in the postwar era Singapore has adopted a similar mobilizational strategy, achieving an investment share in GDP in excess of 40 per cent. Of course few orthodox economists would recommend the adoption of the Stalinist strategy; on the contrary. But in principle, the creation of secure property rights and financial deepening underwritten by the state would also raise the savings rate.

So much, then, is common ground. Where heterodox writers differ from their opponents is in arguing that increases in investment will generate externalities and hence long-run growth. This view goes back to the work of Kaldor, and (in one form or another) is an integral component of new growth theory.[4] Accordingly, the Krugman–Young notion that East Asian growth is unsustainable because it is based upon capital accumulation is therefore simply wrong from a heterodox perspective. And there is evidence to support the heterodoxy. As a range of studies have shown, even if we use the (methodologically dubious) total factor productivity approach to calculating technical progress, it is by no means obvious that the East Asian economies have been unable to innovate. For example, a study by Bosworth and Collins (2003) put the contribution of total factor productivity growth at fully 35 per cent in South Korea, Singapore and Taiwan.[5]

The second key heterodox idea is that the state should reallocate investment from low-priority to high-priority sectors, rather than leaving investment decisions to market forces. In other words, dynamic rather than static comparative advantage should be decisive in guiding the pattern of investment. Industries that are unprofitable in the short run may prove to be the industries of the future, and therefore should be targeted. In practice, this has meant that governments have shifted investment from light to heavy industry at a much earlier stage in the development process than was the norm in Britain and the USA during the nineteenth century. The classic British strategy ('textiles first') is thus displaced by one focusing on steel, chemicals and machine-building. Germany provides a nineteenth-century example; Japan, Taiwan and South Korea (post-1960) provide more contemporary illustrations.

To be more precise, there are two justifications for selective industrial policy. The first is military. If a country faces an overwhelming external military threat, markets will inevitably fail because the calculus of security is necessarily different from that of profit maximization. Of course private-sector companies can make very large monopoly rents (supernormal profits) during periods of war, but investment is certain to be sub-optimal given uncertainty. Such military considerations were the key motivating force behind the Soviet First Five Year Plan (1928–32); the German threat required breakneck industrialization during the 1930s if the Soviet Union was to survive. In a sense, of course, this is an *ex post* justification; Soviet survival was based around its well-developed industrial base. Nevertheless, it is very clear that defence considerations were an important factor in the design of the five year plan, even if the nature of the German threat was far less transparent in the late 1920s than it was to become. It is arguable that it was the more general Allied intervention in the Russian civil war (1917–21) that prompted Soviet defence industrialization, rather than any specific German threat.

The other justification for selective industrial policy is that put forward by Chalmers Johnson (1985) in the context of Japan, and subsequently developed by a range of writers, especially in the context of East Asia (Amsden 1989; Wade 1990). The underlying idea here is that catch-up requires state intervention because of the first-mover advantage enjoyed by developed countries. The infant industries of a late-starting country simply cannot compete in most world markets because of their initial inability to exploit economies of scale, and because productivity will only approach world levels after a long process of learning. In Amsden's famous phrase, late starters 'industrialize by learning'. In a world of perfect information and perfect capital markets, this would not of itself provide a justification for state intervention. With perfect information, the banking sector would be prepared to lend to infant industries, confident in the knowledge that its loans would be repaid out of future profits. In a world of imperfect information, however, there is no such guarantee – not least because some infants are bound to fail. The financial system will be risk averse, and therefore late starters will lack the finance necessary to invest and to become competitive in the long run. Furthermore, stock markets tend to be both an unreliable source of industrial finance and remarkably inefficient at promoting the development of efficient companies. The evidence on stock markets points overwhelmingly to the conclusion that merger and takeover activity does not lead to improvements in long-run productivity growth; efficient companies are often taken over and stripped of their productive assets, and the growth of inefficient companies continues unchecked. As Keynes recognized many years ago, stock markets bear all the hallmarks of a casino – limited information, price manipulation and unscrupulous regulation.

> Speculators may do no harm as bubbles on a steady stream of enterprise. But the position is serious when enterprise becomes the bubble on a whirlpool of speculation. When the capital development of a country becomes a by-product of the activities of a casino, the job is likely to be ill-done. ... It is usually agreed the casinos should, in the public interest, be inaccessible and expensive. And perhaps the same is true of stock markets. (Keynes 1936: 159)

China's market offers a classic demonstration of these failures (Zhang 2006).[6] Such capital market failure provides a compelling case for state-led direction of finance.

Even in relatively developed economies, there is a case for state-led industrial policy. Capital markets are little more efficient (in the sense of identifying companies likely to be profitable in the long run) in developed economies than in poor countries; a failure to lend to small companies in Britain has been the staple of financial reports in Britain going back to the 1931 Macmillan Committee. In addition, mature economies are likely to suffer from sclerosis as formerly dynamic industries find themselves at a competitive disadvantage; contemporary Germany provides a good example. Market forces will ultimately serve to reallocate some factors of production, both labour and capital, from inefficient to more efficient sectors. However, this process is likely to be remarkably slow, not least because workers displaced in declining industries will inevitably resist. In such circumstances, the state can accelerate the process of industrial restructuring by means of targeted spending on education and training, and by providing some form of welfare guarantee (perhaps simply in the form of a commitment to full employment) to displaced workers. Accordingly, the need for industrial policy does not disappear simply because an economy becomes more mature. From this perspective, the way to deal with high levels of contemporary European unemployment is by means of *more* state intervention, not less. Attempts to make the European labour market more like that of America will lead to a further hollowing out of manufacturing and (at best) do nothing more than create a large number of low-paid jobs. For all the alleged vitality of the American model, the fact remains that the inflation-adjusted median weekly wage of American men without a high-school education has fallen from $517 in 1979 to $402 in 2004 (Blank 2006: 670) – a staggering indictment of American capitalism.[7] Successful industrialization requires not just jobs but well-paid jobs.

The basis, then, for the heterodoxy is that market failure is pervasive in capitalist economies. There is thus a *prima facie* case for state intervention. However, there is more to the issue than that; the substitution of state failure for market failure represents no viable way forward. Accordingly, a central element in heterodox thinking is that states need to be of the Weberian kind – that is, 'strong', forward-thinking and capable of good governance – if industrial policy is to be successful. In part this is because of the need to limit rent-seeking behaviour by the private sector, but it is also because the industrial policy model is based around the notion of selective intervention – that is, the state needs to select certain industries for support (whether via tariffs or subsidies), and be prepared to withdraw support if the industries in question fail to meet targets for productivity and export growth. The state also needs to restrict entry by firms to key sectors in order to ensure that economies of scale can be properly exploited. In other words, excessive competition is likely to be damaging. South Korea's failure to prevent this in the early 1990s led to the creation of industrial overcapacity, and ultimately to the unravelling of its hitherto successful industrial policy.

The heterodox vision does not necessarily imply that dictatorship is necessary, though many of those who have advocated selective industrial policy have pointed to its association with dictatorship across East Asia. Singapore is the exemplar of this type of approach, and of its limitations.[8] As residents of Hong Kong are apt to say, Singapore resembles nothing if not a big, clean prison. However, one clear implication of the heterodox analysis is that weak states would do better to avoid selective industrial policy. For many of the countries of sub-Saharan Africa and South Asia, the second-best strategy is a market-orientated development strategy – not an industrial policy along South Korean or Japanese lines. The government of Vietnam, for example, appears to have recognized that it is incapable of the sort of selective intervention required, and has increasingly moved away from industrial policy over the last decade. The clearest sign is the decision to merge the Ministry of Planning and Investment with the Ministry of Finance. Nevertheless, theory suggests that the right conclusion is that industrial policy can succeed in the right set of circumstances. Accordingly, to suggest to governments that they should avoid industrial policy is very much a counsel of despair.

Industrial inefficiency at the close of the Maoist era

There was no thought of abandoning some form of industrial policy at the close of the 1970s. Nevertheless, it was widely recognized within the CCP that China's industrial sector was inefficient, especially in the (Singhian) sense that it was far too small. In conjunction with continued urban industrial growth, the rural industrialization programme of the Maoist era had gone some way towards addressing this problem. Nevertheless, as discussed in Chapter 8, rural industrialization had not proceeded far enough; the industrial sector was still far too small to meet China's developmental needs.[9]

To be sure, the industrial sector was profitable; profit rates averaged 25 per cent in SOEs and 27 per cent in COEs in 1980.[10] However, it was well understood that this owed much more to the high prices charged by the state for many consumer goods than to enterprise efficiency. For example, the rate of profit in enterprises using farm inputs was no less than 55 per cent in 1980, reflecting the way in which the internal terms of trade had been systematically biased against the farm sector in the late Maoist period (Jefferson and Singh 1999: 75 and 77). Most of the variation in Table 12.1 can be explained in the same way. The coal industry was no more inefficient than the rest of Chinese industry; its low profitability reflected the constraint imposed by the low state-set product price (Wright 2006).

In addition, profit rates in the SOE and collective sectors were inflated by the absence of competition. Although international trade had increased considerably during the 1970s, Chinese industries faced little competition from imports and were in any case shielded by high tariff barriers. Foreign direct investment was non-existent; there was therefore no competition from foreign-owned companies based in China. As the indigenous private sector had been suppressed in the 1960s and 1970s, there was no threat from that quarter either. No wonder, then, that so much Chinese industry was profitable.

The productivity data provide a better indication of efficiency, and they show an upward trend in labour productivity during the late Maoist era across the industrial sector. As Figure 12.1 shows, overall output per worker rose from around 6,500 *yuan* per worker in 1965 to over 8,000 *yuan* per worker by 1978.

Nevertheless, the late Maoist record on labour productivity growth in manufacturing was not especially impressive in international perspective. Wu's (2001: 184) estimates indicate that gross value-added per employed worker relative to the USA increased by only 1.5 per cent per year in the 1960s and 1970s. As a result, the level of manufacturing productivity was a mere 4.5 per cent of that of the USA, only marginally up on the 3 per cent recorded in 1952. Worse, Wu found no evidence that the gap closed at all between the mid-1960s and 1978; in fact, his estimates suggest that the gap widened. If industrial productivity is measured in terms of total factor productivity – a better measure in some ways than labour productivity because the latter takes no account of increased capital per worker – China's record was equally bad. Although estimates vary, one calculation has TFP

Table 12.1 Profit rates in the state industrial sector at the end of the Maoist era

Sector	All-China profit rates for state-owned industry, 1978	Jiangsu profit rates for state-owned industry, 1982
Metallurgy	11	22
Coal	3	−4
Power generation	18	38
Oil	55	137
Chemicals	22	37
Building materials	12	33
Timber	11	48
Machinery	12	34
Textiles	44	100
Food processing	53	88
Paper	18	50

Source: Zhang (1988: 174, 248–51).

Note
The all-China profit rates are tax and profit as a percentage of the gross capital stock. The basis of the Jiangsu data is not specified. 'State' here covers only SOEs.

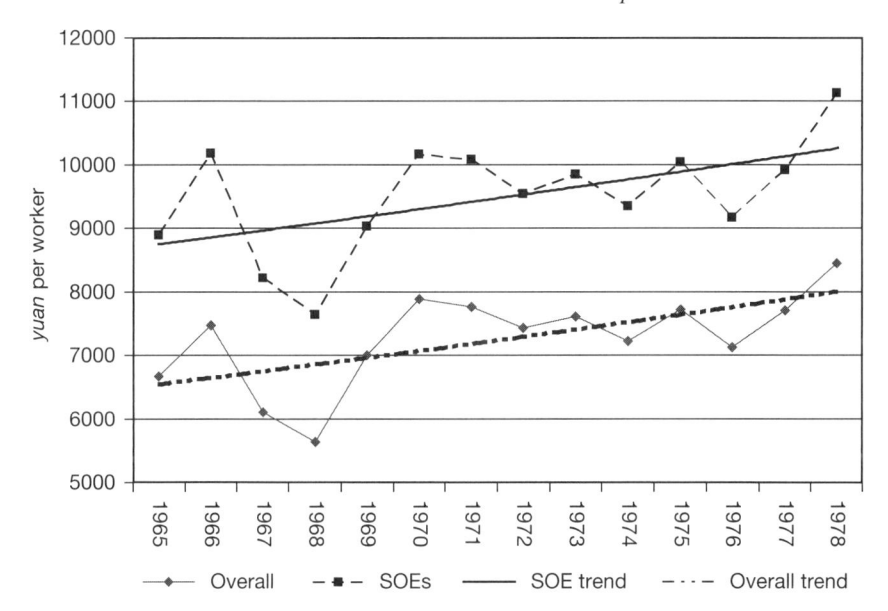

Figure 12.1 Trends in labour productivity in Chinese industry, 1965–1978 (Source: SSB (1990b: 68).)

Note: Data are based on GVIO at 1980 constant prices for *xiang*-level industry and above.

rising by only 0.9 per cent between 1965 and 1978 (Chen *et al.* 1988a,b). Given that TFP is regarded by most neoclassicals and Chinese reformers as the best measure of efficiency, this provided a damning commentary on the efficiency of the Maoist industrial sector.[11]

This retrospective academic analysis was shared by many of those engaged in the operation and direction of Chinese industry at the time of Mao's death. By the end of the 1970s, there was a consensus amongst Chinese industrial economists and leading members of the CCP that great swathes of China's industrial sector were inefficient.[12] There was also a high degree of agreement as to the causes of that inefficiency.

For one thing, too much of Chinese industry was located in the western provinces as a result of the Third Front programme, and the economic geography there ensured low profitability and productivity. The importance of the Front before 1978 also meant that too much of Chinese industrial production was military in its orientation, rather than civilian. It was suited to the needs of a war economy, but not to one in which the external threat had markedly diminished – as it had in China after the late 1970s. A second problem was that of 'too many mothers-in-law'. By this, Chinese economists mean that the work of factory directors was too much subject to interference by the enterprise's Party secretary, by local government and by the various ministries. There was a widespread view that granting SOE factory directors more autonomy would lead to improved performance.

Chinese industry also suffered from three weaknesses commonly encountered in state socialist countries. First, the structure of industrial production was too much geared towards machine building and metallurgy. As a result, the supply of many key inputs – such as chemicals and inputs for the agricultural sector – was deficient. Further, Chinese industry was far too geared towards meeting the needs of industry itself rather than supplying consumer goods. Thus low Chinese living standards were in no small measure a consequence of the low level of consumer good production. Second, techniques of production were too capital-intensive. Given that China had abundant supplies of labour in the late 1970s, efficiency considerations dictated greater use of labour and less use of capital in the production process. Third, the scale of production in many enterprises was too small to allow the effective exploitation of economies of scale. One reason for this was the emphasis on vertical integration, itself in no small measure a consequence of defence considerations and a resulting desire for enterprises to be as self-sufficient as possible.

There was also some recognition that state ownership was a significant part of the problem. However, to suggest privatization as a policy option in the late 1970s or early 1980s was political dynamite, because it challenged both the Maoist vision and the very *raison d'être* of the Party itself. There was thus more or less a consensus that all other options should be tried first before any serious consideration of privatization could be entertained.

Industrial policy, 1978–1996

The solution adopted to resolve the problem of Chinese industrial weakness was twofold. First, a continued expansion of industry production in rural areas was promoted. The Third Front programme was brought to an end; its *raison d'etre* had disappeared with China's improved relations with the USA. But there was no attempt to rein in the growth of the commune and brigade industry. On the contrary; its growth was actively promoted by local government. The second policy solution focused on the problem of industrial inefficiency. Privatization was out of the question in the late 1970s and early 1980s, and never seriously entertained as a policy option. However, it was hoped that a range of policies designed to remove restrictions on production by private and foreign firms would both increase total industrial production and – by dint of competitive pressure – improve the efficiency of the state sector. Liberalization, rather than ownership change, was seen as a major part of the solution to China's industrial problems.

The growth of township and village enterprises

Just as the planners of the 1960s recognized that one solution to the problem of industrial underdevelopment was to promote the growth of rural industry, so did the planners of the post-Mao era. In this sphere China has been more successful than any country on the planet (Bramall 2007). The private sector played a role in this process, and the scale of production in county-run enterprises (county SOEs and COEs) was far from negligible throughout the period. However, the engines of growth were the enterprises owned by township and village enterprises.[13] Only after the privatizations of the late 1990s did this change. The high tide of rural industrialization was therefore very much a state-driven process, not one predicated on privatization or the creation of a system of private property.

China's commune and brigade enterprises (CBEs) were very numerous at the close of the Maoist era. In the eyes of the planners, however, they were also inefficient. The first task in the late 1970s, therefore, was to restructure the sector in such a way as to make it more efficient and thus create the foundation for a new phase of industrial expansion. This process of restructuring was undertaken as part of the more general readjustment of the Chinese economy which took place in the early 1980s. The emphasis was mainly on the closure of agricultural CBEs and the transfer of their assets to households as part of the process of decollectivization. As Table 12.2 shows, one result was that the number of workers employed in agricultural TVEs fell from 6.08 million in 1978 to 3.44 million in 1982 (MOA 1989: 292).

By contrast, employment in the industrial subsector rose, though less quickly than output. The net result was a marked rise in labour productivity, which more than doubled in agricultural enterprises and rose by a still impressive 57 per cent in industrial CBEs. But the industrial sector also experienced re-structuring. The share of building materials in CBE industrial output declined from 30 per cent in 1978 to less than 21 per cent in 1980, and that of electrical machinery fell from 33.5 per cent to 26 per cent (XZNJ 1989: 44, 56, 59). The transformation was rather less marked in those provinces where CBEs were well established. In Jiangsu, for example, the share of electrical machinery declined by only 4 percentage points (from 32 to 28 per cent). But even there, the structure of industrial output altered: one sign of this was the rise in the share of the textile sector from 11 per cent in 1979 to 19 per cent in 1981 (Mo 1987: 192).

Once the process of restructuring had been completed, rural industrial growth commenced once more, and with great vigour. In the TVE subsector (the most

Table 12.2 The readjustment of the commune and brigade enterprises, 1978–1983

	Employment (millions)		Gross output value (billion yuan)		Labour productivity (yuan per worker)	
	Agriculture	Industry	Agriculture	Industry	Agriculture	Industry
1978	6.08	17.34	3.62	38.53	595	2,222
1979	5.33	18.14	3.85	42.35	722	2,335
1980	4.56	19.42	3.94	50.94	864	2,623
1981	3.80	19.81	3.90	57.93	1,026	2,924
1982	3.44	20.73	4.01	64.60	1,166	3,116
1983	3.09	21.68	4.37	75.71	1,414	3,492

Source: MOA (1989: 292–5).

Note
These data exclude sub-village enterprises. Gross output value is measured at current prices.

dynamic component of rural industry), output grew by about 19 per cent per year between 1978 and 2004. That of industrial TVEs was even faster at around 23 per cent (Bramall 2007: 56). Even more impressive (because of its implications for rural living standards) was the growth of TVE employment (Table 12.3). By 2004, employment in TVE industries stood at around 81 million, over four times higher than in 1978. Employment in county-run SOEs and COEs increased much less quickly, but over 100 million Chinese were employed in some form of rural industry by the middle of the 1990s and the number continues to rise.[14]

Table 12.3 Employment in the TVE sector since 1978 (million workers)

	TVE employment				All rural employment	TVE share
	Agriculture	Industry	Other	Total		(%)
1978	6.08	17.34	4.85	28.27	306.38	9.2
1979	5.33	18.14	5.62	29.09	310.25	9.4
1980	4.56	19.42	6.02	30.00	318.36	9.4
1981	3.80	19.81	6.09	29.70	326.72	9.1
1982	3.44	20.73	6.96	31.13	338.67	9.2
1983	3.09	21.68	7.58	32.35	346.90	9.3
1984	2.84	36.56	12.68	52.08	359.68	14.5
1985	2.52	41.37	25.90	69.79	370.65	18.8
1986	2.41	47.62	29.34	79.37	379.90	20.9
1987	2.44	52.67	32.94	88.05	390.00	22.6
1988	2.50	57.03	35.92	95.45	400.67	23.8
1989	2.39	56.24	35.04	93.67	409.39	22.9
1990	2.36	55.72	34.57	92.65	477.08	19.4
1991	2.43	58.15	35.56	96.14	480.26	20.0
1992	2.62	63.36	40.27	106.25	482.91	22.0
1993	2.85	72.60	48.00	123.45	485.46	25.4
1994	2.60	69.62	47.95	120.17	488.02	24.6
1995	3.14	75.65	49.83	128.62	490.25	26.2
1996	3.36	78.60	53.12	135.08	490.28	27.6
1997	2.77	76.35	51.38	130.50	490.39	26.6
1998	2.74	73.34	49.28	125.37	490.21	25.6
1999	2.47	73.95	50.62	127.04	489.82	25.9
2000	2.22	74.67	51.31	128.20	489.34	26.2
2001	2.00	76.15	52.71	130.86	490.85	26.7
2002	2.05	76.68	54.15	132.88	489.60	27.1
2003	2.90	78.56	54.27	135.73	487.93	27.8
2004	2.85	81.61	54.20	138.66	487.24	28.5
2005	n.a	n.a	n.a	142.72	484.94	29.4
2006	n.a	n.a	n.a	146.80	480.90	30.5

Sources: He (2004: 217); XZNJ (2003: 7, 473); ZGTJNJ (2007: 129); LDTJ (2005: 495).

Note
Pre-1984 data are for township and village enterprises only and thus exclude the private and self-employed subsectors. The main components of 'other' in 2002 were construction (14.6 million workers) and commerce (16.9 million), up from 2.36 and 1.44 million respectively in 1978.

Of all China's post-1978 achievements, this was perhaps the most remarkable: such a process of rural industrialization is without parallel anywhere in the world. Apparently it even took the Chinese leadership by surprise. According to Deng Xiaoping (1987: 236):

> In the rural reform our greatest success – and it is one we had by no means anticipated – has been the emergence of a large number of enterprises run by villages and townships ... this result was not anything that I or any of the other comrades had foreseen; it just came out of the blue.

The restructuring of state and collective industry15

The growth of TVEs in the post-Mao era helped to resolve one of the weaknesses in the Chinese economy identified at the end of the 1970s, namely the problem of underindustrialization. However, it was well understood that much more than industrial expansion was required. China's planners and leaders were united in believing that the People's Republic also needed to improve the efficiency of its industrial sector. The central question which confronted the CCP in respect of industrial productivity was that of how to fashion an reform strategy which was effective – and yet fell short of outright privatization.

The CCP's answer was to proceed on three fronts. The first of these, which featured heavily during the Readjustment period, was structural change. In practice this meant shifting state investment away from defence, machine-building and metallurgy, and towards consumer goods and towards the agricultural subsector of heavy industry (especially chemical fertilizer production)

The second strategy focused on price reform (discussed in Chapter 10) and liberalization. It was hoped that the dual-track pricing system would stimulate production in that output beyond the state plan could be sold on free markets. It was also recognized that price reform would raise profits in those industrial sectors which had previously been penalized by low product prices, and hoped that this would spur cadres in those sectors to increase production. Furthermore, by ensuring that prices were set at values which were close approximations to marginal costs, it made SOE performance much more transparent; no longer could a sector hide behind the excuse that its product prices were set at too low a level to allow profits to be made. Most CCP hopes were placed upon liberalization. In concrete terms, liberalization meant the removal of barriers to entry by private or foreign companies, and the hope was that this would intensify the degree of competition. Protected by the soft budget constraints which went hand-in-hand with state ownership, SOEs would not collapse. But competition would lead to a haemorrhaging of staff, and real wage and salary growth would be much lower than in more efficient private and foreign companies. These developments would in turn encourage SOE managers and workers to raise productivity and profitability, enabling wage and salary growth to keep up. Structural change

Box 12.1 Strategies designed to improve SOE performance, 1978–1996

Policy	Rationale
Structural adjustment	Shift state investment towards more dynamic sectors (consumer goods; light industry)
Price reform (see Chapter 11)	Make SOE performance more transparent and provide incentives to increase production
Liberalization	Intensify the competition faced by SOEs and encourage innovation and improved productivity
Governance reforms	Provide more discretion to factory directors over enterprise decisions. Put 'experts' (engineers) rather than 'reds' (Party secretaries) in command of decision-making

aimed also to raise productivity, but the objective was to do so by means of investment reallocation between sectors.

Nevertheless, there was a recognition that more than structural adjustment and liberalization was needed to turn industrial performance around. Improvements in industrial governance were also recognized to be essential, and this was the third industrial reform strategy adopted. Here the CCP focused on providing factory directors with much greater control over wage setting, hiring decisions and production decisions, as well as far more discretion over the disposal of industrial profits. However, ownership change in the SOE sector was not on the agenda. As a result, Chinese industrial policy between 1978 and 1996 was characterized by a range of hesitant steps, all of which had one thing in the common: they fell well short of privatization. In fact, China did not pursue any privatization programme worthy of note before 1996, in sharp contrast to most countries which have abandoned Communism.[16] Indeed China has actively *expanded* the role of the state in the rural sector by encouraging local governments to establish new township and village enterprises. Chinese industrial reform in respect of ownership patterns has therefore been characterized by gradualism and not by shock therapy. That is, the non-state sector has been allowed to expand, but its expansion has not come at the expense of the state sector. We can thus think of China's industrial liberalization strategy as dual track – it has preserved state industry, but allowed a non-state sector to develop in parallel.

This brief sketch of post-1978 industrial policy makes it plain that the CCP did not aim to create a capitalist economy, at least during the 1980s and 1990s. The central aim was instead to maintain state control of the bulk of the industrial sector, and at the same time invigorate performance by a range of other policy measures. We can now move on to discuss these various policy initiatives in more detail.

(a) Structural adjustment

The first policy that was implemented in a bid to improve industrial efficiency was a programme of structural reform. A central part of this strategy was to alter China's industrial product structure in order to give greater weight to light industry and to the civilian sector. In principle, this was easy enough to achieve. Precisely because the government controlled the pattern of investment in those industries which it owned, product structure could be changed simply by changing the pattern of investment. In practice, the question was whether the Chinese state was willing and able to overcome the vested interests of the heavy industry lobby. The various ministries responsible for defence and heavy industry had prospered under Mao, and any attempt to dismantle their empires was bound to be greeted with disfavour. Did the Dengist state successfully overcome this resistance?

There is considerable debate in the literature on this question. According, for example, to Lardy (1989: 284):

> The interindustry allocation of investment also changed, but only for a brief period. ... The traditional emphasis on heavy industry or producer goods was modified, at least in the short run, with its share of industrial investment falling from about 90 per cent during 1966–75 to about 80 per cent in 1981–82. But heavy industry's share began to rise after 1981, exceeding 82 per cent in 1982 and 88 per cent by 1984.

The World Bank (1990: 157) offered a similar conclusion on the extent of structural change during the 1980s. But some others have argued that structural change was extensive (Field 1992; Lo 1997; Bramall 2000a).

In fact, the evidence available suggests that the planners were able to rein in the heavy industry lobby. For one thing, light industry grew faster than heavy

Table 12.4 Growth rates of light and heavy industry (per cent per year; net output value; current prices)

	Light industry	Heavy industry
1952–78	8.7	11.9
1978–89	15.4	12.9
1989–99	15.1	16.6

Source: ZGTJNJ (1990: 419; 2000: 414); SSB (1990b: 64).

Note
Data for 1952–89 for all industries. The 1989–99 data are for independent-accounting industries at the township level and above. As many of the below-township industries excluded for 1989–99 were labour-intensive rural enterprises, these data tend to understate the growth of the light industrial sector after 1989.

410 *Chinese Economic Development*

industry in the 1980s so that the biases of the Maoist period were much reduced. Since 1989, the two sectors have grown at similar rates (Table 12.4). Second, the transition era has seen the development of 'new' industries (electronics, chemicals, pharmaceuticals). By contrast, traditional heavy industries, e.g. mining, logging, metal fabricating, have grown much more slowly. By 1999, relatively 'traditional' industries like textiles and food processing were still important, but so too were more 'modern' industries such as chemicals, electronics and transport equipment (ZGTJNJ 2000: 414).[17]

As for military spending and defence industrialization, there is no doubt that the emphasis has changed significantly. A key element has been a series of defence conversion projects (Folta 1992; Brömmelhörster and Frankenstein 1997); many of the Third Front industries now produce civilian outputs as varied as motor cycles, chemicals, cars, TVs and bronzes. And the air-raid shelters under the big cities have been converted into shopping malls. But many Third Front enterprises have simply been closed down. Perhaps the most tangible sign of the revised priorities of the planners is the fall in military spending (Figure 12.2). As a share of central government spending, defence peaked during the Korean War, and then again in the late 1960s at the height of the Third Front programme (and when war with the USSR seemed like a real possibility), at around 25 per cent. Thereafter, however, it fell back. By the late 1970s it was running at around 15 per cent, and by the mid-1980s defence spending was below 10 per cent.

In fairness, there are many uncertainties about levels of defence spending; a considerable proportion of defence-related activity is not reported in China's

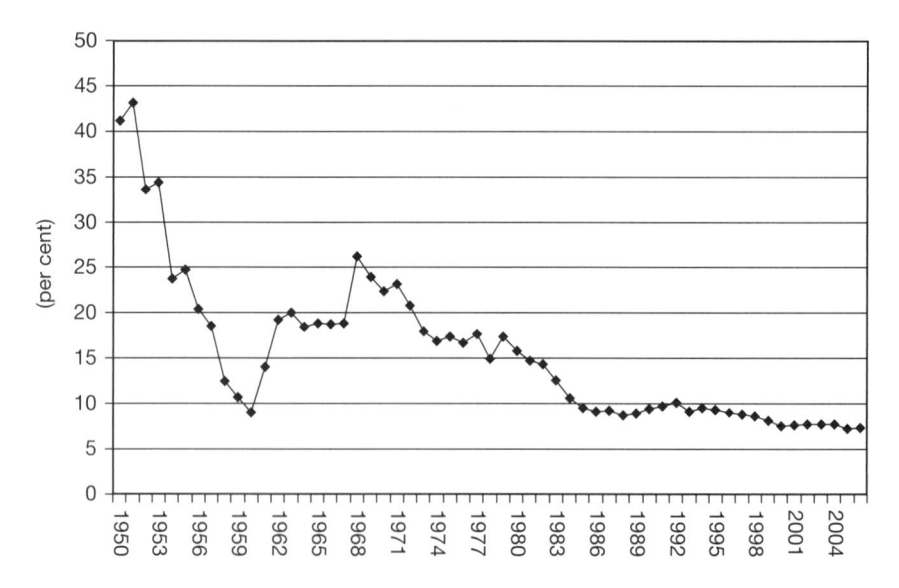

Figure 12.2 Trends in defence spending (defence as a percentage of government spending) (Sources: SSB (2005a: 18 and 22); ZGTJNJ (2007: 279 and 281).)

Note: These are official Chinese data.

national accounts. The data omit many items of spending: true spending was probably double official estimates in 2001, and comparable with UK and France (Shambaugh 2002: 222). For all that, scholars agree that a sharp decline in spending occurred in the early 1980s, and this allowed the Chinese state to divert resources towards the civilian sector. Indeed, an example of the weakness of the military is the ease with which defence cuts were imposed in 1980 and 1981; the decision to make cuts was of course helped by the army's dismal performance in the war with Vietnam in early 1979. Army numbers were further reduced in 1984/5, and a number of senior officers were retired at the same time without precipitating a military coup.

(b) Liberalization

The period between 1978 and 1996 also saw a thoroughgoing process of liberalization, during the course of which most of the controls on the establishment of private and foreign companies were removed.

Three main policies were adopted. First, the controls on the creation of private-sector companies imposed under Mao were lifted. Private firms had been banned under Mao and individual enterprises were heavily restricted in terms of their ability to borrow from the banking sector; only about 300,000 individual firms existed in 1978, most of them simply household businesses (Chai 1998: 175). These controls were lifted officially in 1984, though in parts of China private industry developed quickly in the late 1970s as local governments turned a blind eye to central government policy; Wenzhou was the pace-setter here. The aim was to allow the re-emergence of the sort of private industrial sector to be found in more 'capitalist' economies, although private entrepreneurs were not allowed to join the Party until the late 1990s. Second, controls on foreign companies investing in China were also gradually removed with the objective of encouraging inward investment. This has led to growth of joint ventures in particular (firms jointly owned by Chinese and foreign partner), but also to the appearance of wholly-owned foreign companies since the early 1990s. A third liberalization policy has been the removal of controls on the growth of collectively owned rural enterprises.[18] The main type of restriction in place in the early 1980s was that the banking sector was limited in how much money could be lent to TVEs. That restriction was lifted in 1983/4 (Chai 1998: 169).

These policies of industrial liberalization have worked in the sense that the share of the non-state sector in industrial output increased considerably between 1980 and 1996 (Table 12.5). It shows a considerable decline in the size of the broadly defined state sector, i.e. SOEs and COEs combined.[19] Conversely, it shows sharp increases in the contribution of the private and foreign sectors. But the most significant feature of Table 12.5 is that it demonstrates the continuing importance of the state sector in the 1990s. Even in 1996, and twenty years after Mao's death, SOEs, shareholding enterprises and COEs together still contributed about 70 per cent of Chinese industrial output, far more than either the private/household or the foreign sectors. In other words, it would be very misleading to suppose that

Table 12.5 The structure of Chinese industrial output, 1980–1996 (shares in gross output value by ownership type)

	1980	1989	1996
Urban SOEs and COEs	89.0	72.2	40.2
Rural COEs	10.5	19.6	27.7
Private and household	neg	4.8	15.5
Foreign	0.0	3.4	13.3
Shareholding enterprises	0.0	0.0	3.3

Sources: SSB (1990b: 7); ZGTJNJ (1997: 411 and 416).

Note
Many of the share-holding enterprises were in effect state-owned. The rural COE category refers to township and village enterprises; it excludes county-owned COEs, which were included in the urban collective category here. Household – officially called *geti* (individual) – enterprises are smaller than private enterprises; we can think of them as small family businesses.

China's industrial ownership pattern was similar to that of a capitalist economy in the mid-1990s. China has liberalized its industrial sector, but the state continued to play a dominant role in industrial production.

(c) Governance

The third element in China's reform of industrial SOEs and COEs focused upon attempts to improve the governance of these enterprises. In essence, the strategy amounted to the transfer of decision-making power (including the use of profits) to factory directors. The principal–agent problem would be resolved by aligning the incentives of principals and agents. The central government wished to create profitable enterprises, and the best way to do that was to give its agents (the directors of SOEs and COEs) an incentive to make profits. That meant both allowing a substantial degree of profit retention and, as importantly, giving directors discretion over the use of such profits. In a sense, this was an attempt to apply the household responsibility system – the pseudonym for agricultural decollectivization – to industry. It would grant directors greater responsibility and power without going down the avenue of privatization.

And there was no reason in principle why the governance of SOEs could not be made to work. The principal–agent problem is exactly the same as that which confronts shareholders in controlling managers in capitalist companies. Indeed there are many examples of state-owned industrial companies which have performed effectively in both the developed and underdeveloped world. Even in the case of Britain – often regarded as the classic example of an economy where state ownership failed – the evidence was far more equivocal about the performance of nationalized industries than advocates of Thatcherism allowed.[20] Moreover, in some ways it is easier for an authoritarian regime to solve the principal–agent problem, because the sanctions that the regime can employ against 'dissident' directors are much greater. The threat of a spell in a labour camp is likely to concentrate the mind in a way that shareholder sanctions cannot.[21]

Industrial policy reform therefore focused on transferring greater decision-making power to factory directors – which was tantamount to weakening the power of both Party secretaries within enterprises and the power of central government ministries. This type of enterprise reform began in 1978 and it widened in scope as the 1980s progressed. The reforms of 1983–4 introduced profit-sharing contracts (soon converted into a system of taxes on profits) agreed between the SOEs and the state finance department. By fixing the amount or percentage of profit to be delivered to the state, it was hoped that this would given enterprises an incentive to profit maximize. Furthermore, it was hoped that the introduction of the Factory Director Responsibility System in May 1984 would improve performance further by placing enterprise management in the hands of 'experts' (factory directors) rather than 'reds' (Party secretaries) (Naughton 1995: 204–20; Chevrier 1990). The system was further developed during 1986–7, and the autonomy enjoyed by factor directors was expanded (Wu 2005: 146–8). This sort of system was strongly advocated by many economists (notably Li Yining), who believed it offered a real way forward, especially when combined with the growing competitive challenge posed by TVEs and imports.

Others were more sceptical. Those of a neoclassical bent regarded this system of contracting as bound to fail because the contract was not properly enforceable in the Chinese context. The state would always be able to vary it, and that necessarily created uncertainty and insecurity over the extent to which the enterprise would be able to retain its profits. Even if a notionally arm's-length relationship was created between the principal (the state) and the agent (the factor directors), the state would not be able to resist the temptation to meddle in enterprise operations. In any case, because there was no real possibility of bankruptcy, there was no proper incentive to be efficient; only by introducing hard budget constraints could this problem be resolved.[22]

Privatization therefore had its advocates in China.[23] In fact, the standard neoclassical case for privatization was increasingly appreciated by the mid-1980s. Dong Fureng, who had interpreted the growth of small-scale private industry in Wenzhou as a sign of what could be accomplished with privatization, was one advocate. Hua Sheng put forward a similar view in the mid-1980s. Nevertheless, there was little general enthusiasm for this approach during the 1980s mainly because of a view that the dominance of public ownership was a *sine qua non* for socialism. Despite a number of creative attempts to redefine 'dominance' in terms of influence rather than merely the size of the state sector, privatization was not really on the agenda. A bankruptcy law was promulgated in December 1986, and some in the West heralded this as the first step towards privatization. In practice, however, the law was almost never applied in the remainder of the 1980s and or during the early 1990s.

Yet even those who were less ardent in their advocacy of privatization had little confidence that the new system could work. Wu Jinglian, for example, argued powerfully that the granting of a great deal of autonomy to enterprises under the provisions of the 1988 Enterprise Law (and in the process granting directors *de facto* ownership rights) ran the risk that the directors would use their power to sell off, lease out or simply neglect state assets (Wu 2005: 151–3). As importantly, Wu argued that SOEs would never be invigorated unless they were forced to operate within a proper market environment in which profitability was determined primarily by enterprise efficiency, rather than by the relative price structure. Wu also stressed the adverse effects of continued price subsidies on the public finances and the way in which the dual-track pricing system had encouraged rent-seeking behaviour (Wu 2005: 68–74 and 139–54). By 1988, Wu was advocating full price liberalization within the next three years in order to avoid crisis (Hsu 1991: 159).

The events associated with the Tian'anmen massacre put a break on the governance reform programme, but it began anew after 1991, when the agenda continued the themes of the late 1980s. It is true that some privatization of small-scale TVEs occurred in the early 1990s. But there was no attempt at mass privatization, and the public sector continued to dominate. Even the more recently released Chinese figures on ownership structure, which have revised upwards the shares of the private and household sectors, confirm this phenomenon.[24] By 1996, about 55 per cent of TVE employment was provided in private and household industries. However, the share in value-added was only about 40 per cent, suggesting that the TVE sector continued to be dominated by enterprises owned and managed by local government (Bramall 2007: ch. 3). It is true that many provinces appear to have privatized 50 per cent or more of their small SOEs by the end of 1996 (Imai 2003; Garnaut and Song 2003; Garnaut *et al.* 2005; Cao *et al.* 1999). Nevertheless, the contribution of these SOEs to total industrial output was by definition small, and therefore the dominance of the remaining (large) SOEs and TVEs owned by local government remained effectively unchallenged; the remaining SOEs alone contributed about 29 per cent of GVIO in 1996 (Jefferson and Singh 1999: 27) and, because of their greater efficiency, a large share of industrial value-added.

Yet although the pace of privatization remained slow, the early 1990s saw a continuation of the attempts that had been made in the late 1980s to enliven SOEs. Price liberalization was all but completed by the mid-1990s, and, in conjunction with the fall in the tariff rate and continuing growth of private and foreign sectors, it ensured that the extent of competition in industrial markets intensified. A further move down the road to the creation of a market economy was the creation of stock markets in Shenzhen (1991) and Shanghai (1990). The first steps here were tentative, but the intent was in one sense clear. Those companies which were deemed to be efficient would find it easier to raise capital, whereas those that were seen as chronically inefficient would lose out (and, as the market developed, even face the threat of merger and takeover). The stock market would thus act as a disciplinary device to encourage improved enterprise efficiency, just as it is supposed to do in Western economies. In practice, however, China's stock markets failed to flourish. The culture of insider dealing and the provision of fraudulent information to would-be investors made their activities resemble those of a casino. Furthermore, the primary aim of the Chinese state was to use the stock market to raise money to finance

Industrial development since 1978 415

government spending. By creating shareholding companies out of SOEs and then selling off a minority stake on the stock markets, very large sums of money were raised (Zhang 2006). In this sort of calculus, efficiency considerations were secondary.

(d) Industrial efficiency, 1978–1996

The effectiveness of the various policies outlined in the previous section in best judged by the extent to which they succeeded in raising profitability and productivity. The trend in profitability in China's SOE sector is shown in Figure 12.3. There is a clear decline in the rate down to the mid-1990s, indicating an apparent deterioration in performance.

However, as noted earlier, profitability is not a very good measure of performance. For example, the high profit rates in the late 1970s reflected monopoly power (as a result of the absence of competition from private and foreign companies) rather than efficiency, and much of the decline in profitability reflected the subsequent increase in the degree of competition which resulted from liberalization (Naughton 1995).

Productivity data are much more useful. Here, however, the trend during the 1980s and early 1990s was by no means certain. A large number of studies have

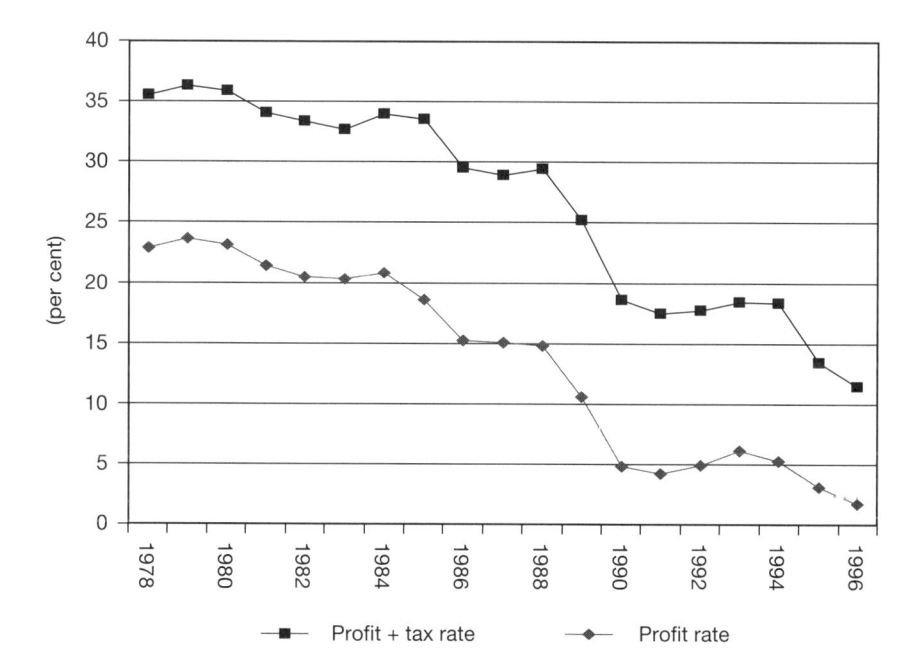

Figure 12.3 Rates of profit in the SOE sector, 1978–1996 (Sources: GYWSN (2000: 53–4); ZGTJNJ (2006: 527–8); ZGTJNJ (2007: 519–20).)

Note: The denominator is the net fixed capital stock.

Table 12.6 Total factor productivity growth in independent-accounting industrial enterprises, 1980–1996 (per cent per annum; adjusted for inflation)

	SOEs	COEs	ODEs	FIEs
1980–4	2.1	3.1	n/a	n/a
1984–8	3.8	5.2	n/a	n/a
1988–92	2.1	3.1	2.1	1.1
1992–6	−1.1	4.3	3.1	0.7
1980–96	1.7	3.9	n/a	n/a

Source: Jefferson *et al.* (2000: 12).

Note
SOEs = state-owned enterprises; COEs = collectively owned firms; ODEs = other domestic enterprises; FIEs = foreign-invested firms. The companies covered here are at the township (*xiang*) level and above; small enterprises are therefore excluded.

been conducted using rather different methodologies, and they have produced very different results (Bramall 2000a: ch. 10; Jefferson and Singh 1999). There is some evidence that the rate of growth of total factor productivity (TFP) picked up in the SOE sector in the early 1980s, and indeed the rate achieved between 1984 and 1988 was impressive by most standards (Table 12.6).

However, by no means all academics agreed with this conclusion (Steinfeld 1998; Woo 1998). The estimates made by Woo (1998: 42), for example, show that SOE TFP rose by only 0.5 per cent per annum between 1984 and 1991, considerably down on the figure for the early 1980s. In any case, the optimism of writers like Jefferson and Rawski was tempered by the evidence that the growth of TFP in the SOE sector tailed off after 1988, and did not revive, even during the boom years of 1992–6. Their results also show that the SOE sector was being outperformed by other industrial sectors in the mid-1990s. For example, the estimates of Jefferson *et al.* (2003: 100) for large enterprises during 1995–9 showed that SOE TFP was rising at only 1.9 per cent per year, well below the figures of 4.5 per cent in COEs, 5.4 per cent in foreign companies and 28.8 per cent in the private sector. Thus the consensus by the late 1990s amongst academics was increasingly pessimistic.[25] Even those like Jefferson *et al.* (2000) and Nolan (2002) – who had argued that industrial reform had been comparatively successful in the 1980s and early 1990s – were driven to conclude that the rate of improvement had at best slowed down. Furthermore, in so far as Chinese SOEs had moved forward, the industries of the OECD countries had moved forward even more quickly, such that the prospects for catch-up were increasingly remote. According to Nolan (2001: 20–1):

> If China had not opened itself to the international economy through trade and foreign investment after the 1970s, the progress in its large enterprises would not have been anything like as great as has been achieved. However, the pace of change in global big business has massively outpaced that of China's large enterprises. ... Given the differential rate of change in business structures and

technological capability, it is hard to imagine that even a much greater length of time under current industrial policies could enable China to produce firms that could challenge the global giants.

The data on value-added per worker in manufacturing tell much the same story. Between 1978 and 1998, Chinese value-added per worker in manufacturing more than doubled in real terms, and in the process rose more quickly than in any of Japan, the USA and Russia. A process of catch-up was under way, especially in respect of Russia; the ratio of Chinese to Russian labour productivity narrowed from 16 to 54 per cent, as a result of poor Russian and improved Chinese performance. Nevertheless, the pace of catch-up was extremely slow. Even by 1994, Chinese value-added per worker was still only about 10 per cent of the levels achieved in Japan and the USA. With US manufacturing productivity rising sharply in the mid-1990s, the medium-term prospects for rapid catch-up did not appear promising.[26]

There is no doubt that the CCP was increasingly aware of the comparatively poor productivity record of the SOE sector, and what this seemed to imply about the effectiveness of the industrial reforms undertaken after 1978. Whether this pessimism was justified is moot. As is widely recognized, the total factor productivity

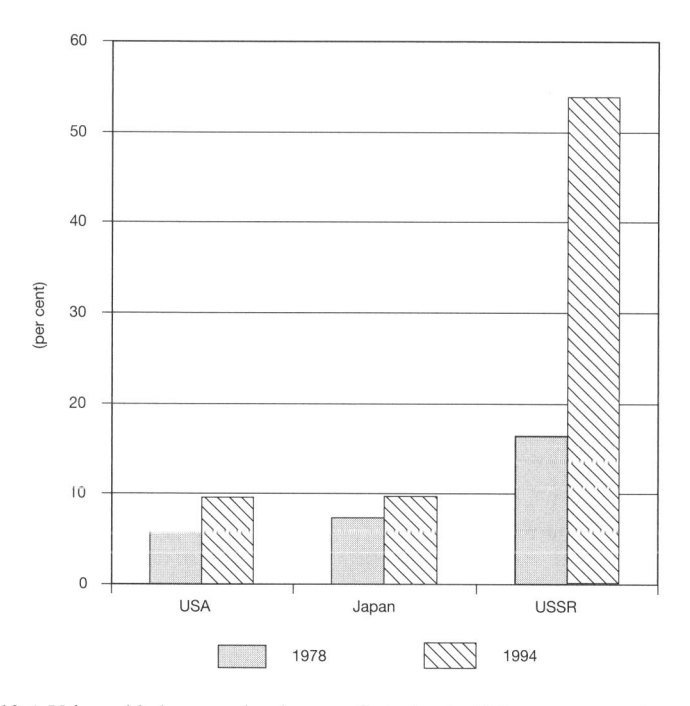

Figure 12.4 Value-added per worker in manufacturing in China as a percentage of value-added in other countries, 1978–1994 (Source: Maddison (1998: 81).)

Note: The underlying value-added data are in $US and are at 1985 prices.

methodology employed in so many of these studies is very dubious because of the grave difficulties involved in measuring the capital stock. Furthermore, the performance of the larger SOEs was far better than that of smaller SOEs, implying that ownership *per se* was not really the problem.[27] In addition, as Holz (2002) points out, the higher tax rate faced by SOEs, and the fact that a larger proportion of SOE assets are in the form of housing, distorts their true performance record. Nevertheless, by the time of Deng's death there was a generally held view that a different range of policies needed to be adopted.

The growth of industrial production, 1978–1996

However, the record on profits and productivity tells only part of the story. Even though these measures of efficiency tell a doleful story, a broader definition of efficiency – the extent to which the industrial sector contributed to development and hence to raising per capita GDP – tells a different tale. In particular, we need to acknowledge the contribution to Chinese development made by the sheer expansion of total output and employment in the industrial sector. Table 12.7 demonstrates this point. Between 1978 and 1996, real industrial GVA grew by over 12 per cent per year. This was a rapid rate of growth in two senses. First, it was faster than the rate achieved during the late Maoist era (1965–78) even though the base level of industrial output by 1978 was much higher than it had been in 1965. Second, it was an impressive performance by international standards; the average growth rate for low-income countries was only 2.8 per cent between 1990 and 1999, and the 4.3 per cent average for middle-income countries was little better (World Bank 2001a: 196). China also outperformed large developing countries. India managed only 6.7 per cent growth, and the rates in Brazil, Nigeria and Indonesia were well below that at 2.7, 1.7 and 6.5 per cent respectively.[28]

The data on sectoral shares in GDP support this more positive assessment of industrial performance. By 1995, the industry share (including construction) in GDP had risen 47 per cent, well up on the figure of 38 per cent recorded in 1978 (Maddison 1998: 69).[29] By comparison, the 1999 average was 30 per cent for low-income countries and 36 per cent for middle-income countries (World Bank 2001a: 200). On the basis of these figures at least, China had effectively accomplished its industrial transition by the mid-1990s.

Table 12.7 Growth of industrial output and employment, 1965–1996 (per cent per annum)

	Industrial gross value-added		Secondary employment
	SSB (comparable prices)	Maddison (1987 prices)	
1965–78	10.3	9.0	8.4
1978–96	12.1	8.5	5.1

Sources: Maddison (1998: 157); ZGTJNJ (2006: 60, 126 and 130); LDTJ (2005: 9); LDTJ (1997: 10).

The People's Republic did nearly as well in terms of employment growth. There are no reliable data on employment in industry for China before 1978, but the secondary sector data offer a fair proxy (most of the employment growth appears to have been in industry rather than in construction). These figures show employment rising by around 5 per cent per year between 1978 and 1996, rather more slowly it is true than between 1965 and 1978 (8.4 per cent), but hardly surprisingly given the high 1978 base and the increasing capital intensity of industrial production across much of the world. In fact, despite growing capital intensity, total employment in manufacturing rose from 53 to 98 million between 1978 and 1996 (LDTJ 1997: 10).

In short, China moved far after 1978 towards the creation of an industrial sector which was efficient in the sense used by Singh (1977). The expansion of the late Maoist era continued and indeed accelerated; in the process, large numbers of new jobs were created. China was assuredly underindustrialized in 1978, but it was much less so by 1996. The productivity record may have been poor, but by increasing industrial output and employment, China ensured a dramatic increase in per capita GDP as much of the surplus labour was mopped up. China's success in this regard stands in sharp contrast to the deindustrialization experienced in the former Soviet Union, and the faltering pace of industrialization across much of the developing world. Too much emphasis on the productivity record is apt to draw our attention away from China's broader record of industrial achievement.

Industrial development after 1996

Chinese industrial development between 1978 and 1996 was very successful in the sense that output and employment grew markedly. Nevertheless, the mid-1990s marked a dramatic change in policy as China embarked upon a programme of breakneck privatization.

There are two ways of explaining this change of direction. One is to argue that many of those who advocated privatization were not animated by a desire to improve performance but by a desire to enrich themselves by asset-stripping. This was especially true of Party members but also of SOE managers, who were the main beneficiaries of the many management buy-outs which occurred. One of the leading critics of the process (he was even prosecuted for libelling the companies involved) was Lang (Larry) Xianping. However, the Party would have none of this: the property law passed by the National People's Congress in March 2007 effectively legitimated this process by allowing urban citizens to pass on their assets (housing, factories, machinery and land) to their children.

By contrast, most scholars have argued that the change of strategy in the mid-1990s was based upon a growing perception, based upon the evidence, that the reforms undertaken up until that time had failed. As Figure 12.3 (above) shows, the profit rate in the SOE shows a steady decline; whether measured as profits plus tax as a percentage of fixed assets or simply as (post-tax) profits, the downward trend is unmistakable. Even allowing for questions over the reliability of the data on the value of the capital stock, there is little doubt about the trend, and this was as apparent to the CCP as it was to scholars in China and in the West.

However, the decline in profitability did not in itself signify policy failure. There were three possible explanations: continued state ownership, growing competition and macroeconomic fluctuation.[30] Of these, the last offers little explanation for the whole period because it amounts to no more than a theory of the trajectory of profits over the cycle, not the secular trend. The fact that the profit rate did not recover during the boom of the mid-1990s suggested that slow growth of demand was not the only factor at work. By contrast, the competition-based argument is much more plausible (Naughton 1995). The monopoly rents of the late 1970s, as manifested in the profit rates of the time, were bound to decline after the advent of competition; from this perspective, the fall in profitability was not a cause for concern.

For all that, most scholars have concluded that the decline in profits was indicative of poor performance, and that this poor performance stemmed from continued state ownership. In taking this stance, there is no doubt that the trends in total factor productivity – the growth of which seems to have deteriorated in the state sector in the early 1990s (Table 12.6, above) – and the failure of China's industrial sector to catch up with other countries were very influential. Nevertheless, there was also a sense that an industry-wide solution was not sufficient. This is because there was a recognition that losses were concentrated in a relatively small number of industries (such as coal mining and textiles); see the discussion in Jefferson and Singh (1999: 144) and Cheng and Lo (2002). It was also realized that large and medium-sized (LME) state-owned enterprises were performing better than small SOEs, both because of the higher quality of their management and the greater scope they enjoyed for the exploitation of economies of scale.

Industrial policy: zhuada fangxiao

The policy solution adopted was a mixture of privatization, closure and restructuring, the latter with the hope that the transformed LME sector would be able to improve its performance. The 5th Plenum of the 14th Party Congress in 1995 saw the beginnings of what was to become a two-pronged strategy which aimed at the transformation (*gaizhi*) of China's industrial sector, and which was encapsulated in the slogan *zhuada fangxiao*.

On the one hand (*fangxiao*), the Chinese state sought to privatize, merge or close most of China's small SOEs (many of which were owned by local government and were to be found within China's counties) and TVEs. This sort of privatization was already well underway in places such as Shunde (Guangdong), Zhucheng (Shandong) and Yibin (Sichuan) before 1996. The decisions of 1995–7 simply extended the process to the whole of China. The underlying rationale here was not so much that ownership was at fault, but rather that most of these enterprises were too small to exploit economies of scale and therefore had no realistic hope of becoming profitable.[31]

The second element (*zhuada*) in the strategy focused on the larger enterprises. In part, *zhuada* aimed at creating large, dynamic and (hopefully) globally competitive firms by merger and by channelling state financial support in their direction. A group of 120 enterprise groups were selected to be 'national champions'. Of the 120, the first 57 were identified by the State Council in 1991, and a further 63 were added in 1997 (Nolan 2001: 87–91).[32] The Chinese government envisaged that these would become the equivalent of the Japanese *keiretsu* and the South Korean *chaebols*. They were drawn from across the ranks of the industrial sector, ranging from companies in energy supplies and electronics to pharmaceuticals and aerospace. The main characteristic of the companies was that they were amongst the largest operating in each sector; together, the national champions controlled over a third of SOE assets by 2003. These national champions are directly under the control of the State Council and now make up the bulk of the 161 enterprises that are still owned by central government.

Perhaps more significantly, the strategy of *zhuada* also aimed to create a larger number of enterprise groups (*jituangongsi or qiye jituan*), of which there were 2,692 in existence by 2003. Some of these were state-owned, but by no means all; many converted to shareholding and limited liability companies of one form or another in the late 1990s. A number of these enterprise groups were owned by central government. One example is Shougang, which in 1996 was a large enterprise group with twenty-seven wholly-owned subsidiaries, including trading, banking and electronics companies; four of these subsidiaries were listed in Hong Kong. The extent of diversification and restructuring had gone so far that only 50,000 of Shougang's 220,000 workers were employed in its 'core' business of steel production by the late 1990s. The core steel operation made profits of 966 million *yuan*, although group net profits were lower (324 million *yuan*) because of losses in its construction, mining and machinery divisions.

However, provincial governments also played a key role by identifying what might be called provincial champions, and channelling support in their direction. In Sichuan, there were eighty-eight enterprise groups in 2005, of which only a handful were national champions and therefore directed by the State Council rather than by the provincial government (SCTJNJ 2006: 571). As Guest and Sutherland (2006) say, the very fact that provincial governments were so actively engaged demonstrates that Chinese industrial policy continues to be on a grand scale, perhaps more so than in other East Asian economies.

Once the aims of the *zhuada fangxiao* or *gaizhi* process were understood, SOE restructuring began in earnest. By means of merger, and by converting enterprises into shareholding enterprises and then privatizing them, the SOE sector was pruned dramatically. The process involved two stages (Garnaut *et al.* 2005). The first stage was one of enterprise valuation, during which enterprises were converted into shareholding corporations. The second stage involved asset transfers, typically to employees (which in practice has meant the transfer of assets to managers given that few other employees had either the ability or the inclination to run the new companies). Typically, the non-productive assets owned by SOEs – hotels, hospitals, canteens and schools – were handed over to local government. An integral part of the whole process was the implementation of a policy of layoffs (*xiagang*) of surplus workers. This began in 1996, and it applied across the newly privatized companies and enterprises remaining in state hands. Between 1998 and 2002, the state sector laid off some 27 million workers (LDTJ 2003: 134) and although the number of layoffs has fallen since, these data indicate a vast process of restructuring. Pressure from the state had much to do with this: Zhu Rongji (the Prime Minister) expected all SOEs to be in profit within three years (Jefferson *et al.* 2003: 89). In addition, the CCP sought to reinvigorate Chinese industry by instructing the PLA to divest itself of its business empire in 1998 in the hope that these enterprises would be more efficient if run by civilians, rather than by the military

The scale of the restructuring of the state sector is apparent from the data. The number of state-owned industrial enterprises fell from nearly 65,000 in 1998 to only 31,750 by 2004. There were in fact only 161 centrally owned SOEs across China by the end of 2006, down from 196 in 2003, and the aim is to reduce this to fewer than 100 by 2010. Revealingly, total employment in industrial SOEs fell from 37 to 20 million, which represented a fall in the SOE share from 61 to only 34 per cent (ZGTJNJ 2005: 494 and 499–500).[33] The share of the SOE industrial sector in industrial value-added declined less abruptly. In 2004, it still accounted for 42 per cent of the total produced by large industrial enterprises, though when the production of small enterprises is included, this falls to 37 per cent (ZGTJNJ 2005: 51 and 488). Slightly different data compiled by the OECD (2005: 81) show

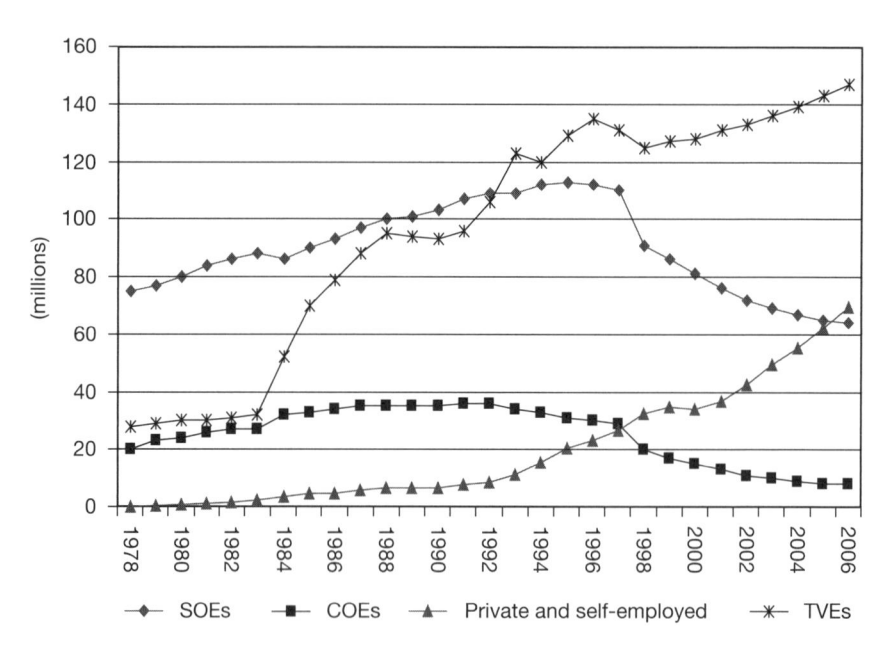

Figure 12.5 Industrial employment by sector (Sources: ZGTJNJ (1990: 114 and 400); ZGTJNJ (1994: 84–5); ZGTJNJ (2007: 128–9).)

Note: The data here are for all types of non-agricultural enterprises and organizations, not just industrial. The TVE figure includes rural private enterprises. The private and self-employed category is for urban areas only. Foreign-owned companies (including Hong Kong-, Taiwan- and Macao-owned companies) based in urban areas employed about 14 million workers in total in 2005.

the share of the state sector in non-farm business value-added falling from 41 per cent in 1998 to 37 per cent in 2001 and 34 per cent in 2003.

The restructuring of the TVE sector is equally apparent. In 1995, employment in township- and village-owned TVEs amounted to 61 million, but this had been cut to only 29 million by 2003. Over the same period, the private sector increased its level of employment from 9 to 46 million (Bramall 2007: 78). Even in Jiangsu, the heartland of TVEs owned by local government, the local state share in employment was down to 25 per cent in 2001, 14 per cent in 2002 and by 2004 it was a mere 6 per cent (JSTJNJ 2002: 170; 2003: 206; 2005: 186). And the situation was little different in neighbouring Zhejiang, where local state-owned enterprises had also flourished in the 1980s; by 2004, the private sector provided 88 per cent of TVE employment (ZJTJNJ 2005: 296). To all intents and purposes, TVEs owned by local government had been wiped out during the course of a decade.

How should all these changes be interpreted? It is tempting to conclude from the fact that the state sector remains so large that the change has been quantitative rather than qualitative. China has completed its transition to state capitalism perhaps, but the state continues to be a key actor in the developmental process. Indeed, an ideological justification for this sort of approach could still be constructed. The formula adopted by Jiang Zemin and his successors was to argue either that the significance of the state sector was not measured by its size, or that the nature of ownership was irrelevant as long as income inequality remained within acceptable bounds. A quotation gives a flavour of the approach (Jiang 1997):

> On the premise that we keep public ownership in the dominant position, that the state controls the life-blood of the national economy and that the state-owned sector has stronger control capability and is more competitive, even if the state-owned sector accounts for a smaller proportion of the economy, this will not affect the socialist nature of our country

This sanguine interpretation of the continuing importance of the state is supported by the continuing emphasis placed on the development of both enterprise groups and the subset of 100 national champions. It is of course true that not all these enterprises are owned by the state, but ownership *per se* is not necessarily decisive. The experience of Japan, South Korea and Taiwan in the postwar era teaches us that state control can be exercised without formal ownership via the allocation of finance.

Nevertheless, whilst recognizing the continuing importance of the state sector, the reduction in its role since the mid-1990s has been dramatic. To see this, consider the data on employment in corporations as recorded by the first National Economic Census on 31 December 2004. These corporations represent the formal sector (the data exclude the self-employed, whether those living in urban areas or the vast number of farm households). Corporations employed nearly 215 million workers at the end of 2004 (out of a total of some 770 million workers and the self-employed). Of the 96.4 million employed in industrial corporations, only 12.8 million were employed in the state sector, and a further 7.33 million in collective enterprises (which function in ways very similar to state enterprises). In other words, the broadest definition of the state gives it a share of only 21 per cent in formal sector industrial employment, on a par with the foreign sector and well behind the private sector's 35 per cent.

Furthermore, it needs to be said that the justification offered by Jiang appears to be little more than a ideological fig-leaf to cover the nakedness of the process of asset transfer that has occurred. More than anything else, it begs the question of who controls the state; it is hard in fact to see the Chinese state as anything other than in the thrall of the capitalist class which emerged as the 1990s wore on.[34] To be sure, China has essentially copied the approach taken by Japan and South Korea to industry policy in the 1960s and 1970s – but the East Asian model is one of capitalist, rather than socialist, development, and therefore to say that China is simply following the East Asian model does not in itself suggest that China's approach should be applauded.[35] And to argue, as Jiang does, that Chinese inequality is still within acceptable bounds is nonsensical. Not only was measured inequality high (as we will see in the next chapter), but also the pattern of income differentials owed little to productivity and almost everything to the ability of economic actors to capture rents by virtue of their position and status. The asset stripping undertaken by the managers of SOEs during the process of insider privatization in the late 1990s is the obvious example. As a result, a capitalist class has emerged. According to Lin (2006: 255), there were four distinct types of capitalists and quasi-capitalists by the end of the 1990s. First, the petit bourgeoisie, or small business people running *getihu* (individual enterprises). Second, a group of genuinely private entrepreneurs, often running relatively large companies (*minying*). Third, public-sector managers (*guoying or dajiti*) to whom the management of public companies has been contracted out and who therefore have much in common with private-sector entrepreneurs. Finally, and by some way the most affluent, are the *guanying* (or *guansheng*). These are the former officials and managers of SOEs who have become private owners of SOE assets following the insider privatizations of the late 1990s. In short, capitalism is alive and well in China.

The Chinese model of state capitalism may yet prove a highly effective way of generating rapid economic growth. But this is a separate question (some preliminary evidence is discussed in the next section). The point that we must not lose sight of here is that Chinese socialism has been abandoned. Whatever words we may use to describe the Chinese path to development, it is not socialist, because the model is no longer based around either equality or public ownership.

Industrial performance after 1996

The remaining issue concerning Chinese industry since 1996 is whether the policy of *zhuada fangxiao* led to a significant improvement in industrial efficiency. Part of the answer is that it is too early to tell, not least because definitional changes in the late 1990s make it difficult to assess changes in performance. Nevertheless, some preliminary conclusions are in order.

(a) Profitability

First, there is clear evidence of a recovery in the rate of profit (Figure 12.6). The pretax rate for example, climbed from its nadir of around 11 per cent in 1996 to 28 per cent by 2006, and the trend in the post-tax rate is similar. However, several words of caution are in order. For one thing, some of the improvement seems to have reflected the transfer of debts from the balance sheets of SOEs to those of the banking sector. For another, part of the recovery was cyclical; the pace of growth picked up considerably after the mid-1990s. Additionally, some of the improvement reflected a transfer of welfare provision from enterprises to the Chinese state, e.g. health care and education; the underlying cost of providing the services did not change. Finally, and most importantly, much of the recovery reflected the steep rise in world oil and raw material prices. As more disaggregated analysis reveals, a very large proportion of total industrial profits (29 per cent) were made in the oil sector – suggesting that the improvement in industrial profitability was by no means general.[36] We are thus probably best advised to conclude that industrial performance has improved, but not by very much.

(b) Industrial output trends

A second conclusion to be drawn from the post-1996 data is that the overall pace of industrial growth continued to be quite rapid. It dipped between the mid-1990s and 2001, mainly as a result of the policy of macroeconomic contraction introduced by Zhu Rongji, which was designed to puncture the inflationary bubble of the middle of the decade. Thereafter, however, the pace has accelerated, and in 2006 industrial value-added rose by 12.5 per cent. This rate was not as fast as in

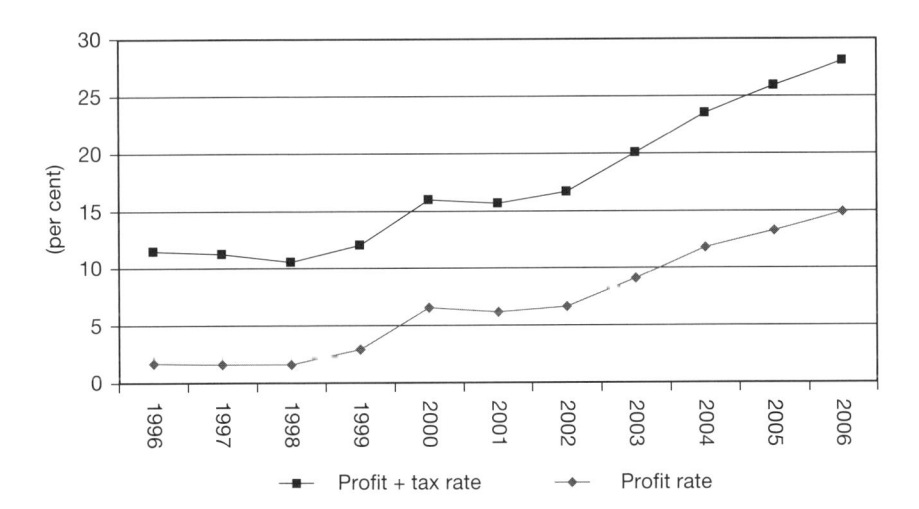

Figure 12.6 The rate of profit in the SOE sector since 1996 (Sources: GYWSN (2000: 53–4); ZGTJNJ (2006: 527–8); ZGTJNJ (2007: 519–20).

Note: The denominator is the net fixed capital stock.

the early 1990s, when the official rate of increase exceeded 20 per cent, but by most standards it was still impressive, especially because China has now sustained industrial growth rates over more than 10 per cent for some three decades.

(c) The growth of industrial unemployment

Nevertheless, it is arguable that the growth rate of the industrial sector has not been as fast as it should have been. Indeed perhaps the most alarming feature of the decade is the trend in manufacturing employment. There were some 25 million layoffs across the urban sector according to the official data between 1998 and 2002 (Giles *et al.* 2006: 587). Manufacturing bore the brunt: employment declined from 98 million in 1995 to 80 million in 2001 (ZGTJNJ 2006: 130). Admittedly these figures are problematic in several respects. Part of the reason for the decline was statistical; laid-off workers were no longer included in the manufacturing total after 1997, and this explains some of the decline. Other problems include the treatment of workers in TVEs (which are not included in these totals), and the limited coverage of migrant workers. Nevertheless, Banister's (2005) revisions to the data, which attempt to take into account these problems, show a similar trend: total manufacturing employment peaked in 1996 at 130 million before declining to around 109 million in 2002. These figures broadly tally with the data on secondary-sector employment, which declined from 166 million workers in 1998 to 158 million in 2002 (ZGTJNJ 2006: 126).

Some of the decline in employment which occurred between 1996 and 2002 seems to have been arrested in recent years. Although comprehensive data on manufacturing employment have not been published for the years after 2002 even in the most recent editions of the *Chinese Statistical Yearbook*, the trend

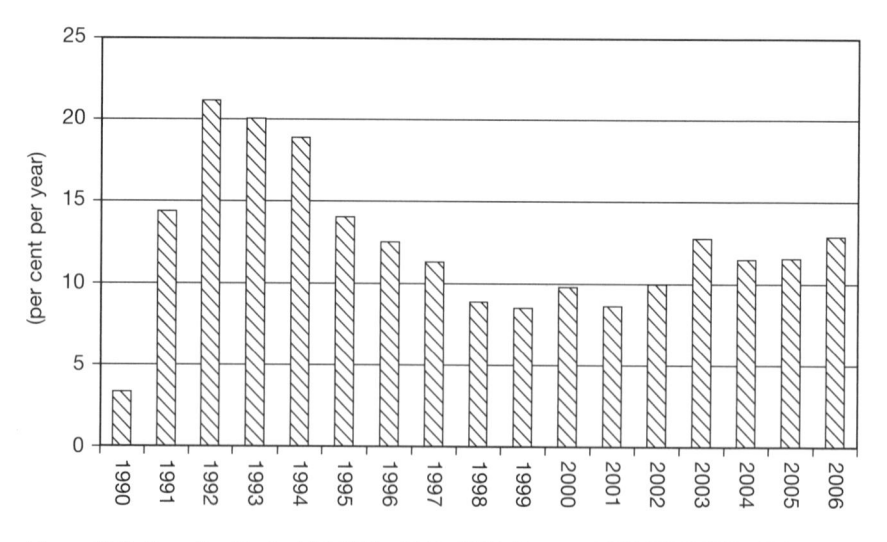

Figure 12.7 Growth of industrial GVA, 1996–2006 (Source: ZGTJNJ (2007: 60).)

is evidently upward. Even in urban units (i.e. excluding the self-employed and those employed in the private sector), the least dynamic sector of the Chinese industrial economy, manufacturing employment rose from 29.8 million in 2003 to 32 million in 2005 (ZGTJNJ 2006: 131).

Nevertheless, and despite the post-2002 revival, it is evident that Chinese industrialization in the decade since 1996 has created remarkably few jobs. Table 12.8 tells much of the story. Between 1978 and 1995, the share of industry in total employment rose from 17 to 23 per cent of the total. However, there was almost no change between 1995 and 2006; almost all the increase that did occur was in 2006 alone. In so far as employment growth was being generated, it was mainly in the service sector.

In suggesting that China's record on industrial job creation has been poor since 1996, it needs to be recognized that it is not necessarily a sign of failure. India, for example, has generated comparatively few jobs in its industrial sector despite rapid industrial growth in recent years (Dasgupta and Singh 2006). Furthermore, given the global trend towards increasing capital intensity in industrial production, it is by no means self-evident that we would expect China to come even close to replicating the British industrial share of 48 per cent recorded in 1955. The per capita income turning-point when it comes to the share of manufacturing employment is estimated to have fallen from $10,000 to only $3,000 (Dasgupta and Singh 2006: 6). China's per capita GDP was well above that when measured at purchasing power parity; by 2005 it stood at over $4,000 (World Bank 2007b). Accordingly, it is not self-evident that we should regard Chinese deindustrialization as premature. There is a case for saying that China is now an industrially mature economy, and therefore we would expect to see the industrial share in employment on the wane.

The real test of the performance of Chinese industry is the extent to which it is capable of ensuring full employment, either directly or indirectly via its exports and linkage effects with the service sector. And here the evidence points towards failure. Chinese unemployment data are admittedly hard to interpret because they only cover the formal urban sector. The official data suggest levels of unemployment rising from around 4 million in 1993 to over 8 million in 2006 (LDTJ 2005: 157; ZGTJNJ 2007: 127). However, these figures exclude laid-off workers. To obtain the level of unemployment in the formal sector in any given year, we therefore need to add the total number of laid-off workers. At the end of 1997, there were a total of 11.5 million laid off workers, which, combined with 5.77 million officially unemployed, gives

Table 12.8 Sectoral shares in total employment (percentages)

	1952	1978	1995	2005
Agriculture	84	71	52	43
Industry	7	17	23	25
Tertiary	9	12	25	32

Sources: ZGTJNJ (2007: 127); SSB (2005: 7).

Note
Industry includes construction, mining and utilities.

428 *Chinese Economic Development*

a total of around 17.3 million unemployed. However, even these data are incomplete, because they exclude unemployment in the private sector and unemployment amongst migrants.[37] There is no doubt that some of those unemployed in the formal sector found work in the private sector, but this positive effect was probably offset by increased unemployment amongst migrant workers. UNDP estimates (2000: 58) suggest that this affected over half a million migrants in the late 1990s.

Figure 12.8 shows the trend in unemployment over time once these adjustments are made. The total rose from around 7 million in 1993 to a peak of nearly 18 million in 1997, a very high level of unemployment by modern Chinese standards. Even these data disguise the extent to which unemployment rose in those parts of the country which were most affected by the restructuring of the textile and mining industries in the late 1990s. For example, total employment in mining and quarrying fell from 9.3 million in 1995 to 5.6 million in 2002 (ZGTJNJ 2006: 130). This led to sharp rises in unemployment in mining areas. In Datong, the centre of Shanxi's coal-mining industry, the rate was 15 per cent according to the 2000 Population Census. In Fushun (Liaoning province), the rate was a staggering 33 per cent. In Fuxin, also in Liaoning, the 2000 unemployment rate was 27 per cent, and it was 28 per cent in both Beipiao and Gaizhou (Cai 2005: 312). For Liaoning as a whole, the official 2002 rate was 6.8 per cent, substantially above the national average (SSB 2005a: 267). Textile centres were also hit badly. The unemployment rate in Tianjin city, for example, was almost 16 per cent in 2000. In

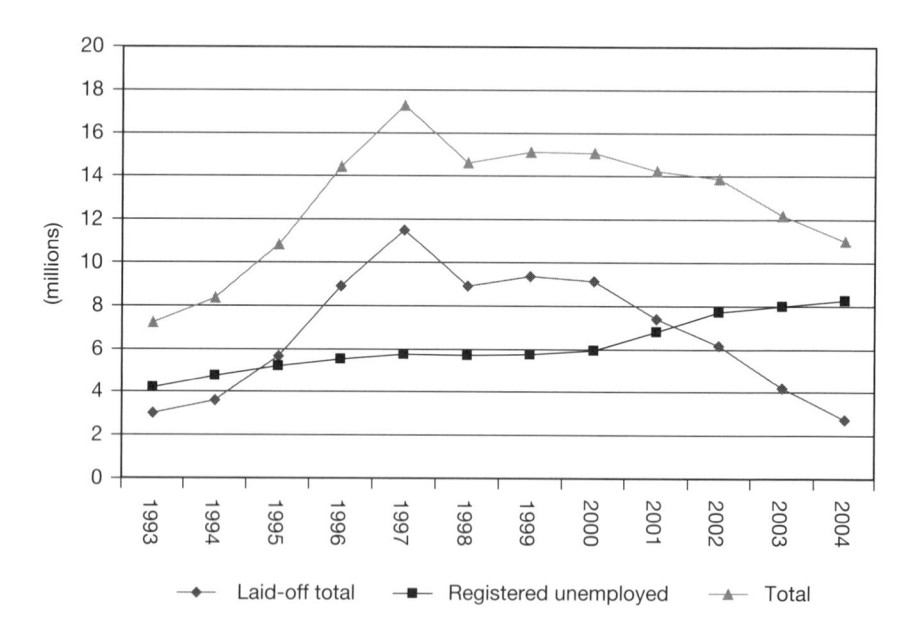

Figure 12.8 Urban unemployment after 1993 (Sources: MOLSS (various years); LDTJ (2005: 163; 2003: 135; 2002: Table 2.6; 1997: 213); UNDP (2005: 58).)

Note: The data are year-end totals and cover SOEs, COEs and other 'units' but not the private sector.

Shanghai too, unemployment was above the national average. Of course some of those made unemployed were absorbed into the informal sector, but nevertheless the shedding of labour was very substantial in the late 1990s.

It is likely that the unemployment trend has been downwards since 2002, not least because of the accelerating pace of industrial growth. However, given that even the official unemployment figure for 2006 was 4.2 per cent (SSB 2007), it is evident that China continues to have a very considerable unemployment problem. It is therefore by no means difficult to conclude that, contrary to some of the views expressed in the literature, China needs a much larger industrial sector, and that the failure to expand it further after 1996 represents a wasted opportunity. In a sense, the clearest evidence of failure is that the Chinese government has accepted that unemployment will rise; the Eleventh Five Year Plan assumes that the unemployment rate will rise between 2006 and 2010.

(d) Productivity since 1996

It remains to be seen whether the changes of the late 1990s and the Tenth Five Year Plan have led to any significant change in productivity growth. Nevertheless, the evidence on TFP growth – in so far as it can be taken as an indicator of trends in efficiency – suggests that the record has been quite impressive and that, in this respect at least, the programme of *zhuada fangxiao* has been successful.

Estimates by Islam and Dai (2007) suggest TFP growth of around 5 per cent in 2002. Bosworth and Collins (2007: 26) estimate the increase for the whole of the period 1993–2004 at no less than 6.2 per cent across the industrial sector, well above the rate for 1978–93 (3.1 per cent) and far above India's rate of growth during 1993–2004 (1.1 per cent). Not surprisingly they conclude that 'we find no support for some of the recent arguments that China is experiencing a significant deceleration of growth in TFP due to wasteful and excessive expansions of capital investment' (Bosworth and Collins 2007: 22). Another recent TFP study by Ozyurt (2007) shows industrial TFP accelerating after the mid-1990s. Jefferson and Su (2006), though they emphasize the wastefulness of much Chinese investment, are also optimistic. According to them, privatization led to the adoption of more labour-intensive technologies during the period 1995–2001.[38]

Whether much store should be set on any of this is moot. For one thing, TFP estimates are so unreliable that one would be foolish in the extreme to draw any conclusions from such studies. For example, Ozyurt's (2007: 15) paper is very interesting because it shows that China's TFP growth was at least as fast in the late 1960s as it is at the moment, a conclusion which I find a little implausible given the impact of the Cultural Revolution. If true, it implies that China would do at least as well to return to the late Maoist strategy if it wishes to maximize TFP growth. For another thing, the work of Guest and Sutherland (2006) on national champions is not very positive about their record. To be sure, these enterprise groups have not performed badly. However, there is little evidence that they have performed better than other large industrial enterprises, and much of their growth has been as a result of merger rather than organic.

One cannot therefore help but conclude that China has thrown out the baby with the bathwater. The *zhuada fangxiao* has not led to any clear-cut efficiency gains, Furthermore, the surrender of policy autonomy which has resulted from WTO membership means that it will become increasingly difficult for China to manufacture a globally competitive industrial sector. This problem has been compounded by insider privatization, which has served to transfer state assets to the private sector, and in the process encouraged the emergence of powerful rent-seeking coalitions. Faced with such private-sector resistance, the state will find it hard to engage in the sort of selective industrial policy which is required. In one sense, none of this matters enormously. It is not, for example, very clear why China should want to create globally competitive companies. As Krugman has rightly argued, competitiveness *per se* matters very little, especially for a large economy, Productivity does, and the creation of globally competitive companies will help that cause (though much less so than in a small open economy like Taiwan). However, in the short and medium term China's interests will be far better served by maximizing GDP per person (by ensuring full employment) rather than by trying to maximize output per industrial worker. And the maximization of GDP per person requires a large, rather than a small, manufacturing sector. It is manufacturing which is the engine of growth, both because of its capacity for generating dynamic economies of scale and because of its linkage effects. The deindustrialization of the last decade, and the unemployment to which it has contributed, is making the challenge of development harder, rather than easier. It may well be that China will be left with a high productivity industrial sector, but one which is too small to ensure full employment.

Conclusion

There is very little international or historical evidence to suggest that industrial catch-up is possible on the basis of the adoption of free trade and a market-driven economic system. The USA succeeded in catching up with and surpassing the UK during the late nineteenth century on the basis of its abundant natural resources and its adoption of an industrial policy based around tariffs and subsidies. Germany followed a similar path. So, more relevantly for China, did Japan, Singapore and South Korea in the second half of the twentieth century.

This type of industrial policy was not really an option for China during the Maoist era because of military considerations. Defence industrialization was the only viable strategy in the face of the external threat posed by the USA and the Soviet Union, and that necessarily led to the creation of an industrial sector which in many respects was inefficient. Since 1978, however, the threat to the territorial integrity of the People's Republic has much diminished, and accordingly the scope for the adoption of industrial policy has increased.

Yet China has failed to make the most of this opportunity. Its industrial strategy in the 1980s and early 1990s was very much along the right lines, focused as it was on the expansion of the state sector in the countryside, the restructuring of defence industries and the reinvigoration of its urban industrial sector. In many respects, this was the industrial policy model at its best. Since 1996, however, this strategy has been abandoned in favour of the adoption of the Washington Consensus at the very time that consensus has been increasingly challenged even by mainstream opinion (Rodrik 2006a). As part of this acceptance of the dictates of global capitalism, China has incorporated targets for the expansion of its service sector into the Eleventh Five Year Plan but not for industry, and has even accepted that unemployment will be higher in 2010 than it was in 2006. To be sure, there is some evidence that productivity growth has accelerated and the profit rate has recovered. But even if true, the fact remains that the programme of *zhuada fangxiao* has reduced the size of China's industrial sector to the point where it is no longer capable of ensuring full employment. In this sense, the Chinese industrial sector has become increasingly inefficient since the death of Deng Xiaoping.

It is therefore all the more surprising that there is a remarkable degree of hubris about Chinese policy-making at the moment. It is as if the leaders of the CCP believe that China is already a developed economy and therefore that a decline in the size of the industrial sector is desirable. But China will not catch up on the basis of such premature deindustrialization. It is the road to ruin. And this policy is all the more foolish because China – in contrast to almost every country in the world – has no need to conform to the dictates of globalization. It has the size to allow it to exploit economies of scale, a respectable enough natural resource base and it has the military capability to resist American pressure. For China, there really is an alternative to free trade.

Notes

1 For statements of this type of analysis, see Steinfeld (1998), Chang (2001) and Studwell (2002).
2 This is a macroeconomic approach to efficiency of the sort put forward by Singh (1977). It is discussed further below.
3 A proposition easily demonstrated by using a Solow-type model. An increased savings rate alters the equilibrium, and during the process of transition to this new equilibrium the growth rate rises.
4 Admittedly there is much disagreement on the causal processes at work. Should technical progress be viewed as an externality or in more neoSchumpeterian fashion as the product of an oligopolistic industrial structure? And there is little agreement as to whether it is investment in plant and equipment, human capital or in some more nebulous notion of ideas that is the key factor in ensuring that growth becomes a self-sustaining process.
5 A useful summary of the issues and the estimates of TFP is to be found in Akhand and Gupta (2005). As they say: 'The war of numbers has resulted in a wide range of TFP growth estimates which are very sensitive to the specific assumptions of each study, the methodology and data used, and the time period covered in each study. Often, these studies lead to contradictory results. It appears that by reworking the data *one can arrive at almost any plausible conclusion*' (Akhand and Gupta 2005: 54).
6 For a more recent survey of the literature on stock failures, see Singh and Zammit (2006).
7 High-school and BA graduation rates have remained stagnant even though one might have expected the growing education-related wage premium to have provided strong incentives to the low paid to improve their education. This suggests that financial constraints and low employment expectations serve to create a poverty trap which can only be broken by dint of concerted state action.

8 The most recent literature refutes the traditional view offered by (*inter alios*) Lipset and Huntington that development must precede democracy (Halperin *et al.* 2005: ch. 2). In fact, the empirical evidence suggests that democracy has a clear advantage over dictatorship in respect of growth and human development when China and the more successful East Asian economies are excluded from the sample. When they are included, the evidence is less conclusive, but it broadly supports the notion of an advantage for dictatorship (partly because there is no data available on dictatorships which we know are performing poorly, e.g. North Korea).
9 For some of the literature on the state of Chinese industry at the end of the Maoist era, see Jefferson and Singh (1999), Naughton (1995) and Xu (1982).
10 It is hard to measure the efficiency of rural industry directly because the data simply do not exist; the general consensus is that it was low, as will be discussed at the end of this section. Here I focus on the overall efficiency of the Chinese industrial sector. That, after all, was the main macroeconomic consideration. Note, however, that the profit rates in Table 12.1 should be seen as no more than a rough guide. The estimates of the capital stock are little more than guesswork. This is partly because the value of the Chinese capital stock was distorted by the same pricing problems which made it hard for the coal industry to make a profit. In addition, it is not clear how housing, defence and other non-productive assets owned by SOEs should be treated. See Chen *et al.* (1988a) for some of these problems.
11 Even more pessimistic results for iron and steel – a key Maoist industry – were arrived at by Jefferson (1990). Other estimates of industrial TFP growth include that by Heytens and Zebregs (cited in Yusuf and Nabeshima 2006: 37), which has it declining by 0.5 per cent per annum between 1971 and 1978. However, these estimates are very sensitive to the measurement of the capital stock. If we assume that Chinese capital was of very low quality – which is one implication of the usual critique of defence-based industrialization – that implies a much lower shadow price (valuation) for capital and in turn much higher rates of TFP growth. For if output expanded despite little increase in the true value of capital, it implies that Chinese industry must have become much more efficient during the late Maoist era. Those who criticize Maoist industrial performance cannot have it both ways; if investment in the Third Front was largely unproductive, then the rise in industrial output that occurred must have been achieved by substantial increases in the efficiency of civilian industry; that was the only way in which industrial output could have been increased.
12 A good summary of many of the problems as perceived in China at the time is provided in Xu (1982).
13 Commune and brigade enterprises were renamed township and village enterprises in 1984. The category was also widened to include private enterprises operating in rural areas.
14 It is hard to be precise about these magnitudes because of definitional problems centring around the treatment of migrant workers and county towns (many of which have been created since 1978). The *xiangzhen* definition of 'industry'used by the Ministry of Agriculture and which appears in the *Labour Force Yearbook* (LDTJ 2005: 495) gives industrial employment of 82 million in 2004. The definition of 'rural industrial employment' used in the *Chinese Statistical Yearbook*, which defines 'rural' using the jurisdictions in existence at the time of the 1964 census (*sic*!), gives a figure of only 60 million (ZGTJNJ 2006: 464). The only certainty in all this is that there has been a large increase in industrial employment in the Chinese countryside since 1978; the *Chinese Statistical Yearbook* definition gives a sixfold increase between 1980 and 2004, compared to the fourfold rise shown in the *Labour Force Yearbook*.
15 Chinese terminology is confusing. One key point to recognize is that state industries were to be found in both urban and rural China (many SOEs were owned by country governments); it is therefore wrong to identify SOEs with the urban sector. The term

'collective' is also used in Chinese accounts and in official sources to include village- and township-owned industries, as well as COEs owned by country governments and at higher levels in the administrative hierarchy. In this section, I exclude TVEs from the definition of collective enterprises because the issues confronting TVEs were very different from those confronting COEs in the urban sector and owned by county governments. In fact, it is best to think of these urban collectives as little different to SOEs; for an illuminating discussion of the issues at the county level, see Blecher and Shue (1996).
16 Privatization has been pursued much more actively since 1996, as we will see below. Many county-level SOEs have been sold off or closed down; many TVEs have met a similar fate. Nevertheless, the output of the state industrial sector remains of massive importance to the Chinese economy.
17 One sign of China's success was the growing sale of refrigerators to the US market; by 2002, the Chinese company Hai'er controlled a major share of this market.
18 These firms had been allowed in the late Maoist era, but the Party at that time was concerned primarily to maximise agricultural production (especially the production of grain). Rural industry was seen as a type of economic activity which diverted scarce labour away from farm production, and was therefore heavily controlled.
19 This is a little controversial. Some scholars (such as Wing Thye Woo and Kate Zhou) believe that many COEs – especially those operating in rural areas – during the 1980s were actually private enterprises. This situation occurred, they argue, because entrepreneurs were afraid to have themselves labelled as 'capitalists' and therefore hid behind the title 'collective'. By the late 1990s, this was much less of a worry. Indeed, Jiang Zemin called for the admittance of private entrepreneurs into the Communist Party itself in July 2001.
20 A useful recent study is Florio (2004).
21 On the other side of the coin, socialist regimes are constrained in terms of the remuneration package they can put in place by socialist norms *vis-à-vis* equity. For an excellent discussion, see Stiglitz (1994).
22 A full discussion of the effectiveness of the industrial reforms of the 1980s and early 1990s is to be found in the next section of this chapter. But it is worth noting here that the average SOE profit rate fell substantially during the 1980s; the Jefferson *et al.* (1999: 75) data show the pretax rate falling from 25 per cent in 1980 to 12 per cent in 1990. It is the interpretation of this decline – did it reflect growing inefficiency or was it a natural consequence of intensified competition as suggested by Naughton (1995)? – that is controversial.
23 Useful discussions of these debates are to be found in Hsu (1991: chs. 3 and 5), Shirk (1993: chs. 12 and 13) and Sun (1995).
24 The original data published in the 1990s were misleading because (as previously noted) some private enterprises had disguised themselves as collective (i.e. state) enterprises for political purposes, and therefore their true contribution was understated.
25 For an especially pessimistic appraisal of the steel sector, see Steinfeld (1998).
26 These comments need to be qualified in one important sense. As we have seen, China experienced far more dramatic structural change than these other countries in the 1980s and 1990s. This reflected the growth of rural and private firms. As most of these new companies were infants (and small), their productivity levels tended to be considerably lower than the SOE average, thus dragging down the Chinese average.
27 For a fine discussion of the issues involved in assessing Chinese industrial performance, see Wright (2006).
28 The Maddison estimates result in industrial growth which is slightly slower between 1978 and 1995 (8.5 per cent) than it was between 1965 and 1978. Nevertheless, China's performance even according to these revised estimates was much better than the developing country norm.

29 Official data on the industry share at current prices give exactly the same figure for 1995 (ZGTJNJ 2006: 58)
30 For the scholarly debates on these issues, see Naughton (1995), Cheng and Lo (2002), Jefferson and Singh (1999), Yusuf *et al.* (2006) and Lo (1999).
31 For a discussion of the privatization and restructuring of small enterprises, see Oi and Walder (1999), Garnaut and Song (2003), Imai (2003), Garnaut *et al.* (2005), Cao *et al.* (1999), Mako and Zhang (2003), Li and Rozelle (2000; 2004), Yusuf *et al.* (2006) and Wu (2005: 192–8).
32 Guest and Sutherland (2006) give 55 and 63 respectively for the 1991 and 1997 figures. These seem to be the number still in existence from the two cohorts in 2003, by which time the total had fallen from 120 to 113 as a result of mergers.
33 The industrial sector was redefined in 1998, and for that year (and subsequently) the employment and enterprise data refer only to large and medium-sized enterprises (those with annual sales of over 5 million *yuan*). It is therefore not possible to give a consistent series on employment in industrial SOEs going back to the 1980s. An alternative approach is to look at trends in employment in *all* types of SOEs, which does produces a consistent time series, though at the expense of covering all manner of government organizations as well as enterprises. This series shows total SOE employment falling from 112 million in 1996 to only 67 million in 2004. The fall in urban COE employment (it is clear that the data refer to urban collectives only; compare the data in ZGTJNJ 2005: 119 and 120) is even more abrupt: the total declines from 31 million to only 9 million over the same period (ZGTJNJ 2005: 120).
34 Hutton (2007) portrays Chinese entrepreneurs as constrained by the predatory state, but it makes far more sense to think of the newly emergent capitalist class as controlling the state, rather than vice versa. Hu Jintao and Wen Jiabao have little by way of a power base that makes them independent of capitalist interests – in contrast to Mao and Deng, who held power in the final instance on the basis of their popular appeal (itself based upon their role in the founding of the People's Republic) and the support of the Army.
35 East Asian Gini coefficients may suggest otherwise but, as discussed earlier, these official data convey a thoroughly misleading picture by estimating inequality from the distribution of wage income alone.
36 Here profit is the sum of total profits, taxes and charges and VAT (ZGTJNJ 2007: 515). Tobacco contributed 13 per cent of total profits, ferrous metal smelting 8 per cent and power generation a further 18 per cent in 2006. In other words, large swathes of the SOE sector made very little profit. Coal mining, for example, employed 20 per cent of the workforce but contributed only 5 per cent of total profits. This performance was much better than in the early 1990s, and the trend across the industrial sector was upward. Nevertheless, these sectoral data show rather starkly that we should not conclude from the recovery of the average profit rate than the efficiency of the SOE sector had been transformed. Moreover, sectoral profit rates still reflect in part the manipulation of relative prices by the state; partial price deregulation in the early 1990s did much to revive profits in the coal sector (Wright 2006: 170).
37 For some of the literature on unemployment, see Ghose (2005) and Giles *et al.* (2005).
38 By contrast, an OECD (2005: 73) study shows economy-wide TFP growth falling from over 4 per cent per annum in 1993 to less than 3 per cent in 2003. However, the use of a Cobb–Douglas production function and the associated assumption of no economies of scale make this methodology very suspect.

13 China's developmental record in the era of Deng Xiaoping

There continues to be intense debate over the reasons for China's rapid economic growth between 1978 and 1996. Many development economists see China's success in Manichean terms. Good (capitalism) supplants evil (socialism), and economic growth offers the perfect happy ending. According to Collier (2007: 66):

> In the 1960s Mao Zedong hurled China into ruin, to an adoring chorus from the Western media. But in response to failure the Chinese political elite swung policy 180 degrees and generated the biggest economic success in history (Mao made his own invaluable contribution by dropping dead).

For Collier, 'heroes' are needed to effect fundamental changes in economic policy, and China found its hero in Deng Xiaoping.

China specialists offer much more nuanced perspectives. To be sure, scholars like Nolan (1995) and Naughton (1995) attribute China's success to policy change. For them, however, it was the adoption of an *incremental* reform strategy, rather than a breakneck charge towards capitalism, that was crucial in China's success. There was no 180-degree policy change; instead, the late Maoist development model was dismantled slowly. The gradual opening up of the economy to foreign trade, and the decision not to privatize state-owned industries until the mid-1990s, avoided wholesale deindustrialization. At the same time, the growth of the TVE and private sectors provided a home for displaced SOE workers (thus allowing the state sector to shed some of its surplus labour and raise its productivity) and an important source of tax revenue. Even decollectivization was imposed across the whole of China only when it was seen to have worked in those areas where it had been tried in the late 1970s. For Nolan and Naughton, the contrast between the Chinese experience and that of the Soviet Union and African countries is stark. Whereas China moved from Maoism to market socialism, the USSR, Eastern Europe and many sub-Saharan African countries all followed the IMF policy prescriptions advocated by Collier and others and moved towards free trade, privatization and a minimalist state. As a result, the economies of Eastern Europe and sub-Saharan African collapsed, whereas China forged ahead at a rate of close to 10 per cent per annum. Thus liberalization and decentralization helped to restructure the Chinese economy in a way that privatization could not. The limits to market socialism may have been reached by the mid-1990s, in the sense that more radical policy initiatives were needed to complete the transformation of the state sector; according to Nolan (2002), the gap between China's enterprises and multinational companies (MNCs) was widening, not narrowing, in the mid-1990s. But for eighteen years the Dengist strategy of gradual reform had worked well.

Other scholars, such as Sachs (2005) and Sachs and Woo (1994), offer an interpretation which is much closer to that offered by Collier and by the IMF. They argue that the gradualist strategy adopted by the CCP did little to promote Chinese growth. In fact, the slow pace of reform in many sectors hampered the pace of advance. Where Chinese policymakers moved least rapidly – the reform of SOEs – economic performance was poor. Where China moved rapidly – the open door and agricultural decollectivization – it reaped the benefits. At root, however, China's success owed far more to its favourable initial conditions than to its economic strategy. China, in contrast to the Soviet Union, enjoyed all the advantages attendant upon entering the transition era with a low level of GDP and hence enormous scope for catch up; it enjoyed 'the advantages of backwardness'. The People's Republic was particularly lucky, argue Sachs and Woo, that the process of Maoist industrialization had proceeded so slowly. The few regions where the Maoist development strategy had left its mark – Manchuria, southern Jiangsu and some Third Front centres – were severely handicapped after 1978. This was because surplus agricultural labour had been absorbed by the inefficient state-dominated sector in the Maoist era, which made the emergence of TVEs and private industry all but impossible to engineer. Economic growth after 1978 was slow in all these regions because the costs of demolishing this failed Maoist industrial legacy were so high; growth was therefore path-dependent. But elsewhere, notably in the provinces of Guangdong and Fujian, an abundance of surplus labour existed, and it was therefore a simple matter to mobilize the labour to serve in the new industries being established by Chinese entrepreneurs, whether based in China or in Hong Kong, Taiwan, Macao or Singapore. Moreover, China was also much luckier than much of sub-Saharan Africa and central Asia. It lacks natural resources (and therefore has avoided Dutch disease) and ethnic tensions, and has a long coastline, all of which are supposedly causally related to economic success (Collier 2007). These preconditions made it easier to develop the sort of labour-intensive manufacturing that is the key to economic growth.

My own writings reject any notion of the path dependency hypothesis: China's economic history was not a constraint on its economic development. On the contrary; the legacies of China's Maoist past played a critical role in promoting the growth of the 1980s and 1990s (Bramall 1993, 2000a, 2007). These legacies included well-developed irrigation and railway networks, a pool of educated workers and, crucially, the rapid expansion of industrial skills brought about by the rural industrialization programmes of the 1960s and 1970s. Late Maoist rural industries may have been inefficient in the short run, but they provided the vehicle for a remarkable process of learning-by-doing. By the late 1970s, rural industrialization was already underway in many parts of China, and it is no accident that the provinces which enjoyed the most rapid growth after 1978 – Jiangsu,

Zhejiang and Guangdong – had the best-developed rural industrial foundation.[1] Furthermore, the introduction of new high-yielding crop varieties in combination with growing production of chemical fertilizer and the maturation of the massive irrigation systems begun in the 1960s had created the conditions for a surge in agricultural production well before decollectivization. China's market socialist development strategy moved the process forward by allowing a private sector to emerge; for example, the suppression of private economic activity under Mao made little economic sense. But without the massive investment of the Maoist era in infrastructure and human capital, the market socialist strategy would have faltered in China – just as it did in Vietnam.

The question of how well China performed under Deng Xiaoping is much less controversial than the question of how strategy, path dependency or Maoist legacies impact upon post-1978 growth and development. Indeed the CCP itself has been anything but backward in proclaiming its economic achievements under Deng's regime. Chinese scholars have echoed this positive assessment. The incremental reform strategy did lead to new problems, but it is axiomatic that it played a critical role in the acceleration of growth (Wu 2005: 57). Western scholars have tended to follow this lead. To be sure, a number of weaknesses in Chinese performance have been widely canvassed, not least the continuing inefficiency of state-owned industrial enterprises and the contradictions caused by the gradual transition to capitalism.[2] But few doubt that performance was impressive. Nolan (1995), for example, paints a flattering picture of Chinese performance when compared with Russia. Chow (2002: 63) also attributes some of China's success to its refusal to privatize its state-owned enterprises.

Still, even on this point in assessing China's post-1978 record there have been dissenting voices. The suppression of the Tian'anmen democracy movement in 1989 was roundly condemned, and the flow of FDI temporarily declined. Amongst scholars, Sen (1989) pointed to the failure of the Dengist regime to reduce mortality rates. Most Marxists, whether Chinese or otherwise, have capitulated to the embrace of the neoliberal agenda since 1978 and especially since the fall of the Soviet Union. But those who adhere to Marxian principles castigate the growth in exploitation and corruption, as well as the abandonment of the Maoist commitment to narrowing the gap between rich and poor. Even the World Bank belatedly rediscovered Chinese inequality in the mid-1990s, albeit only to argue that the solution to the problem was to complete the transition to the market by removing residual barriers to labour migration and privatizing the remaining state-owned enterprises. Where, then, does the truth lies amidst these conflicting accounts?

Material living standards

Considerable doubts surround China's GDP growth rate after 1978. China has made a gradual transition from the MPS to the SNA system of national income accounting, but the very fact that the MPS system was the norm in the 1980s inevitably causes conversion problems in going from NDMP to GDP. A second problem is that the statistical collection system used by the State Statistical Bureau was not properly re-established and staffed until the mid-1980s. Third, there is widespread evidence of overreporting of output levels by local-level agencies and by state-owned enterprises; in some years, every province has reported a rate of GDP growth which has exceeded the national average. And finally confusion over the meaning of constant prices has made it difficult for the SSB to obtain reliable data on output value from factory directors.[3]

In recognition of these problems, and in an attempt to arrive at estimates of true GDP, a full economic census was carried out in December 2004. As a result, GDP estimates for the entire 1993–2004 period have been adjusted upwards by the SSB, mainly because of a revaluation of the production of the service sector.[4] Manufacturing output has also been increased. However, these revisions have themselves been viewed as suspect. Most Western scholars were of the view pre-2004 that Chinese GDP estimates were too high. This was driven by two assumptions. First, that there was widespread overreporting of industrial production in the 1990s by lower-level administrative units anxious to achieve plan targets. Second, it was widely believed that China was badly hit by the 1997 Asian crisis. Yet the impact of the 2004 Economic Census was to *increase* Chinese GDP for every year after 1993, and the new GDP series constructed by back-projecting the 2004 results still showed no sign that the Asian crisis had any impact. This continuing scepticism on the part of Western scholars has been reinforced by the fact that even Xu Xianchun, Director General of SSB national accounts, has acknowledged that Maddison has made a major contribution to providing good estimates of Chinese GDP, and has even suggested that Maddison's estimates should be regarded as a lower bound and the official SSB figures as an upper bound (Maddison 2006a: 123). In view of these doubts about Chinese data, two sets of competing estimates of GDP growth are given in Table 13.1.

Yet the conclusion about China's growth record is qualitatively the same whether we use the SSB or the Maddison data, and in that sense the debate about the Chinese data is rather academic. For the most striking feature of the data in Table 13.1 is that China's growth rate between 1978 and 1996 was at a historical

Table 13.1 Chinese GDP growth after 1978 in historical perspective

	Period	Prices	GDP growth rate (per cent per annum)	Per capita GDP growth (per cent per annum)
Maddison	1952–5	1990	4.5	2.1
	1963–78	1990	5.1	2.6
	1978–95	1990	7.8	6.3
SSB	1952–5	1952	8.6	6.2
	1963–78	1970	6.4	4.0
	1978–96	1970	10.4	8.9

Sources: Maddison (1998: 157); Maddison (2006b); SSB (1999: 3–4); ZGTJNJ (2005: 53).

Note
The Maddison estimates are a part of his wider International Comparison Project.

high, far superior to the rate achieved before 1949 and significantly above the rates achieved in both early and late Maoist periods. And with population growth slowing after 1978, the differential between the Maoist and Dengist eras in terms of per capita output was even greater. Furthermore, even Maddison's more conservative estimate of GDP growth of over 7 per cent (and growing at no less than 6.3 per cent in per capita terms), suggests an economy performing spectacularly well by international standards, at least in terms of the GDP metric. These estimates will no doubt be refined further, but it is very hard to believe that any form of statistical manipulation will convincingly overturn this conclusion.

Perhaps the clearest way of seeing China's achievement is to compare its record on GDP per capita with those of the economies of Eastern Europe and the former Soviet Union (EEFSU) during the first thirteen years of transition.

Figure 13.1 shows just how well China performed. The time frame is a short one (1978 to 1991 for China, 1990 to 2003 for the others) and in some ways therefore underplays the true achievement of the People's Republic because China's growth accelerated after 1991. In other words, lengthening the transition period would make China's comparative record appear still better (unless of course EEFSU growth rates were to accelerate dramatically over the next decade). But even if we confine the comparison to a thirteen-year period, it is particularly striking just how well China has done. In the EEFSU countries, median GDP per head initially declined and even by 2003 it had not recovered to its pretransition

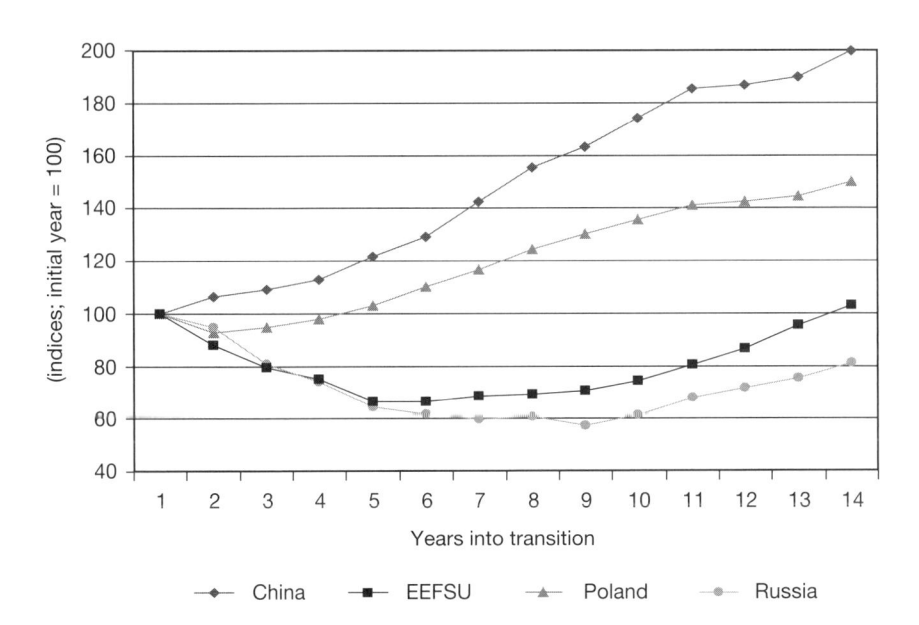

Figure 13.1 Indices of per capita GDP in transition economies (initial year = 100; original data at 1990 prices) (Source: Maddison (2006b).)

Note: The figure for EEFSU is the median for the twenty-two countries. For EEFSU, Russia and Poland year one is 1990. For China, year one is 1978.

level. By contrast, China forged ahead. As a result, Chinese GDP per head by 1991 was approximately double its 1978 level, whereas Russian per capita GDP was still well below its 1990 level even in 2003. Poland, the best performing of the EEFSU economies, was also well behind China after thirteen years – even though it has been admitted to the EU and has enjoyed massive flows of inward investment from Germany.

It is of course fair to say that China started from a much lower base than the EEFSU countries. One would not have expected the much more prosperous economies of EEFSU to have grown as quickly as China. However, some of the Asian republics of the former Soviet Union started from a point not dissimilar to China's and yet their growth rates have not been impressive. Moreover, although most of the EEFSU countries did not enjoy the advantages of backwardness, this hardly excuses the abrupt initial fall in output experienced outside China. Rather, it points to the conclusion that it was the EEFSU strategy that was flawed.

China's post-1978 record was also good in that its population enjoyed a marked improvement in consumption levels during the Dengist era. Per capita food consumption provides the best example. Official estimates of calorie consumption based upon household surveys show consumption rising from around 1,800 kcals per day in 1978 to about 2,500 kcals by 1984, at which level it remained during the late 1980s and early 1990s. At the same time, consumption of grain shifted away from potatoes and other coarse grains towards wheat and rice. Fat consumption rose more dramatically, reflecting increased intake of meat and dairy products. It doubled between 1978 and 1990, and although it declined somewhat in the early 1990s, intake stabilized at about twice the 1978 figure by the mid-1990s (SSB 2000b: 10; 2006c: 34).

It is true that these household surveys of income, expenditure and consumption are not very reliable. For example, the surveys show rural calorie consumption rising from 1,834 kcals in 1978 to 2,325 kcals in 1980 (SSB 2006c: 34). However, an increase in consumption by as much as 500 kcals over a two-year period seems far too large to be very plausible.[5] Furthermore, it is hard to believe that the 1978 figure of 1,834 kcals per capita would have been enough to support a population predominantly engaged in heavy agricultural work. Moreover, it is worth noting that the estimates of consumption in SSB (2006) are at variance with earlier official data – even though they are all supposedly based on the same rural household surveys. The early SSB estimates show that consumption levels were already running at 2,224 kcals in 1978, from where they rose to 2,806 kcals by 1983 in the rural sector. In the urban sector, consumption rose from 2,715 kcals to 3,183 kcals over the same period (ZGTJNJ 1983: 509; ZGTJNJ 1984: 480). These older estimates are probably more plausible than the recently published figures, especially for 1978. However, they are rather on the high side for 1983, and therefore they too deserve to be treated with caution.

Given the dubious nature of these survey data, we do better to rely on the production-based food-balance approach. These data show that grain production increased by only 5 per cent over the period 1978 to 1980 (SSB 2005a: 45). Piazza's (1986: 77) estimates of consumption based on these production figures therefore show only a modest rise in food consumption, up from 2,413 kcals in 1978 to 2,473 kcals by 1980. Of course the production data could be wrong; reintermediation of underreported output probably did occur between 1978 and 1980 as the procurement burden was lessened. Nevertheless, the Piazza estimates seem far more plausible for 1978 than the latest SSB consumption figures, and recent FAO data lean much more towards the Piazza view than the SSB consumption surveys. These FAO figures show that average calorie consumption averaged 2,247 kcals per person per day across the whole economy in 1978. By 1984, at the height of the agricultural miracle, the figure had gone up to 2,624 kcals, and it rose further, to reach 2,709 kcals in 1990 and 2,980 kcals in 1996 (FAO 2006a).

Still, whether one uses production estimates or consumption survey data, the trend is unmistakable. There is surely no question that rural food consumption increased significantly during the post-Mao era, and especially during the late 1970s and early 1980s. By the mid-1990s, indeed, food was so readily available that obesity was beginning to emerge as a problem, especially in the cities. In most respects, then, the situation in the mid-1990s was a far cry from the famine conditions which had prevailed in the early 1960s. The phrase 'China, land of famine' had seemingly been banished to the pages of history.

Fluctuation

This mention of famine, and its absence after 1978, leads on naturally to the more general question of output fluctuation. As discussed in Chapters 4 and 9, the Maoist era was one of considerable economic instability. Output collapse in the early 1960s and industrial production plummeted during the early years of the Cultural Revolution (1966–8). Even in the 1970s, output fluctuated because of the impact of poor weather, and because of political campaigns.

By contrast, the economy was remarkably stable between 1978 and 1996. To be sure, fluctuation was by no means absent (Figure 13.2). The marked slowdown in output growth in 1989–90 led to rising unemployment and poverty. Furthermore, the rapid growth of the early 1980s, and again during the early 1990s when the real growth rate hit a peak of 14 per cent, ignited inflationary pressures; the 1980s episode was amplified by price reform, which led to sharp increases in the prices of key commodities. As a result, the inflation rate soared in 1988–9, and again in 1993–5, to more than 20 per cent – a high figure by most international standards. To be sure, these inflationary episodes were a world apart from the hyperinflation experienced in parts of Latin America in the 1960s and 1970s – and indeed in China itself during the late 1940s. Nevertheless, inflation in the Dengist era was severe enough to lead to substantial shifts in the distribution of income, and there is little doubt that it contributed to the Democracy Movement of 1989 by radicalizing a large section of the urban workforce.

For all that, the years of Dengist rule were an era of great stability when contrasted with the convulsions of the Great Famine and the Cultural Revolution, or when set against either the catastrophic events of 1937–45 or the warlordism of the 1920s and early 1930s. During 1989–90, for example, all that happened

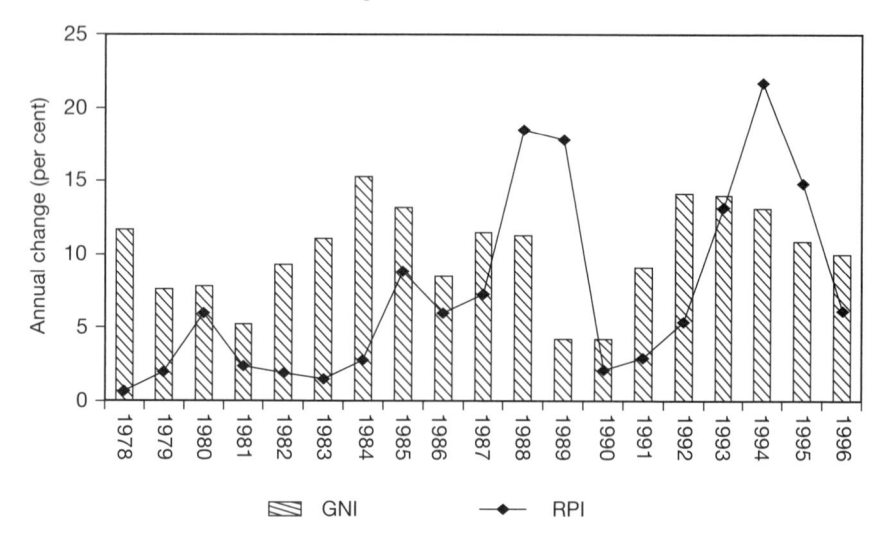

Figure 13.2 Fluctuations in GNI and the retail price index, 1978–1996 (Sources: ZGTJNJ (2005: 53 and 301); SSB (1999: 21).)

Note: The growth of GNI is measured at comparable prices. RPI denotes the retail price index.

was that the growth rate slowed down. There was no collapse in output such as was experienced in (say) the West during the Great Depression of the 1930s, or across the former Soviet Union in the early 1990s. China's record was hardly ideal, but one would be hard to put to argue that it did not mark a substantial improvement.

Human development

China's post-1978 record on human development – whether in respect of education or in terms of health – was much less good than its record on growth.

Education

In the sphere of education, almost the first step taken by Deng's regime in the late 1970s was to allow those who experienced *xiafang* to return home. The second was to cut spending on rural education, thus reversing one of the key achievements of the Cultural Revolution and effectively restoring the elitist educational model of the 1950s (Pepper 1996).

The upshot was that rural enrolment rates plummeted at middle-school level: the proportion of primary graduates entering junior middle school fell from 91 per cent in 1975 to 66 per cent in 1982 (Figure 13.3). Furthermore the proportion of junior middle school graduates entering senior middle school fell from 60 per cent to 32 per cent between 1975 and 1982 (SSB 1999: 100). By any standard, this was a wretched record. It is true that 1982 marked the nadir. Thereafter, enrolment

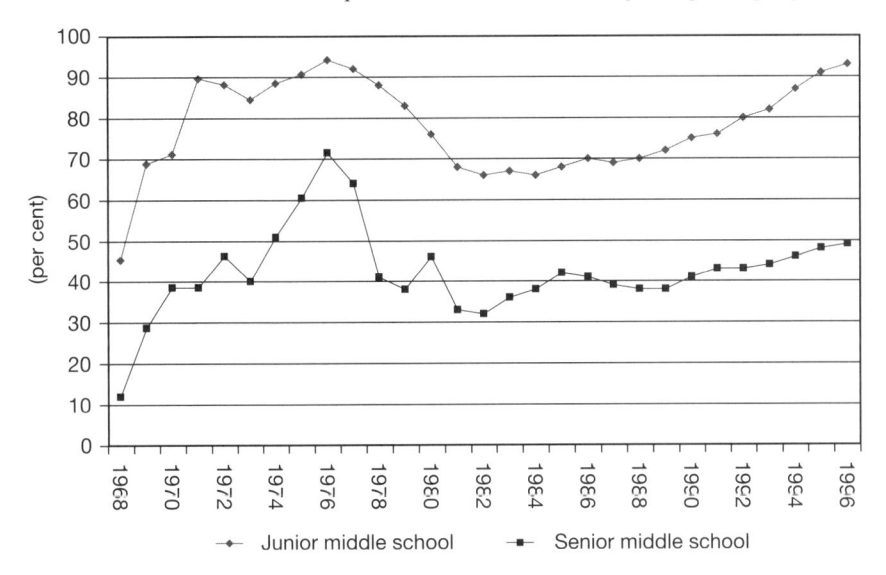

Figure 13.3 Junior and middle school enrolment rates, 1968–1996 (Sources: ZGJYNJ (1984: 1001 and 1021); SSB (2005a: 84).)

rates started to rise again, but they did not reattain their 1975–6 levels until the mid-1990s.

To be sure, Chinese illiteracy rates steadily dropped during the 1980s and 1990s. In 1982, the rate of illiteracy and semi-literacy was 23 per cent. It had fallen to 16 per cent by 1990 and was down to 7 per cent by the time of the 2000 census (RKTJNJ 2005: 252).[6] However, we do well to remember that most of China's illiterates in 1982 were aged sixty or over. It follows that mortality alone had the effect of reducing the overall illiteracy rate – and that signally lessens any credit the Dengist regime can take for the measured fall in illiteracy. Furthermore, the level of public spending on education remained below the international norm. In 1996, for example, public spending on education in China stood at only 2.5 per cent of GDP, significantly less than the international average of 3.7 per cent and despite the fact that the official target was to achieve a rate of 4 per cent of GDP by 2000 (UNDP 2005: 50–1).[7] Even India, which has had a poor record on promoting mass education post-Independence, was spending nearly 4 per cent of its GDP on education in the early 1990s (UNDP 2007: 294–7).

Mortality

China's record on mortality reduction after 1978 was better than its record on education. Admittedly the crude death rate trended slightly upwards after 1978, rising from about 6.3 per 1,000 to 6.6 per 1,000 in 1996 (RKTJNJ 2005: 251; SSB 1999: 1). However, this trend is misleading because the crude death rate takes no account of changes in the age structure of the population. As deaths are highly concentrated amongst infants and those aged sixty-five and over in all populations (including China's), it follows that a fall in the proportion of the population aged between one and sixty-five will tend to increase the crude death rate even if age-specific death rates are unchanged. In China's case, the proportion aged sixty-five and over rose from 5 per cent in 1982 to 7 per cent in 2000 – thus increasing the crude death rate (RKTJNJ 2005: 252). By contrast, there were 13.8 million infants (1.1 per cent) in 2000 compared with 20.8 million (2.1 per cent) in 1982 (RKTJNJ 2003: 71; RKNJ 1985: 604). This fall in the number and proportion of infants would, *ceteris paribus*, have depressed the crude death rate. With these two age-compositional effects working in opposite directions, we have no means of saying a priori whether the crude death rate under- or overstates true mortality. The way to circumvent these problems caused by the changing age structure is to estimate life expectancy, which takes account of both age structure and age-specific death rates. The official data here show a much more benign picture. By the time of the 2000 Population Census, male life expectancy at birth had reached 69.6 years, up from 66.4 years in 1981. Female life expectancy had increased even more, rising from 69.3 years in 1981 to 73.3 in 2000 (RKNJ 1985: 883 and 887; RKTJNJ 2005: 253).

It is of course true that these official data on life expectancy are not reliable. The central problem here is the extent to which underreporting of female deaths has occurred over the post-1978 period (Banister and Hill 2004). There is no doubting the phenomenon. The introduction of the one child per family policy in 1979, combined with Chinese cultural and old-age-security-based preferences for boys has manifested itself in both sex-selective abortion and in the systematic neglect and even murder of infant girls. According to Banister (1992: 28–31), age-specific mortality rates for female infants were 90 per 1,000 for 1990 compared with only 57 in 1981 (Banister 1992: 28–31).

However, we cannot be absolutely sure about the scale of what has happened. In fact, there seems little doubt that the very low numbers of infant girls recorded is in part simply a problem of the underreporting of the birth of girls; these girls have not been killed, but have been placed in orphanages or fostered out to ethnic-minority families to whom the one-child policy does not apply.[8] The extent of this underreporting of births remains uncertain, but a good deal of evidence suggests that it may well have been as high as 30 per cent during the 1990s in many parts of the countryside (Scharping 2003: 204). All this shows up in the decennial population censuses; there were 116 million children aged nought to four in 1990 and yet in 2000 there were 125 million children aged ten to fourteen (RKTJNJ 1998: 214; RKTJNJ 2005: 71). This discrepancy probably occurs because, as children of school age enrol at school, their existence can no longer be denied, whereas there is no need for full-scale reporting at birth – and in fact, given the pressure on local government to control birth quotas, every reason for households and local government to collude in denying the occurrence of above-quota births. But whatever the reasons, this evidence on the reappearance of 'missing girls' does suggest that some of the strongest criticisms of China's record on female infant mortality may be misplaced.

Most Western demographers have therefore concluded that, although China's record has been sullied by excessive female mortality, true life expectancy increased between the mid-1970s and 2000 (Table 13.2). Thus Banister concludes that true male life expectancy rose from fifty-nine years in 1973–5 to seventy years in 2000, and female life expectancy climbed from sixty-one years to seventy years over the same period – despite the rise in female infant mortality (Banister 1998; Banister and Zhang 2005: 23 and 29). This rise in life expectancy occurred because of a reduction in mortality rates amongst children:

> China achieved relatively high life expectancy for a poor developing country by the beginning of the economic reforms in 1978, but in comparison to mortality levels at other ages, the death rates for young children past infancy were still high. … the major success story of the economic reform period in China has been a dramatic reduction in the mortality rates of children in the ages one through four. Almost as impressive has been decline in mortality rates of children ages five through nine. (Banister and Zhang 2005: 29 and 33).

The provincial data back this up. In every one of China's provinces, the infant mortality rate in 1995 was lower than it had been in 1981, and some of the provinces recorded very big reductions (Woo and Bao 2003). The highest achievers were the provinces of the south-west, Qinghai, and Xinjiang – the very provinces where infant mortality rates were highest in the early 1980s. This is a very clear indication that the gains from the 'reforms' of the Dengist era were not confined to the coastal provinces

Nevertheless, the achievements of the market socialist era – though real – are much less impressive when placed in their proper historical and international perspective. For one thing, although every province recorded a reduction in infant mortality between 1981 and 1995, the rate increased in four of them (Jilin, Anhui, Jiangxi and Henan) between 1981 and 1990. This demonstrates that much of the decline in infant mortality during the Dengist era occurred in the early 1990s. Life expectancy offers a broader measure of human development, and here too the record is not that impressive. For example, the rate of improvement in life

Table 13.2 Chinese life expectancy, 1973–2000 (years at birth)

	Male	Female
1973–5	59	61
1981	65	67
1990	66	67
2000	70	73

Sources: Banister (1992: 28–31); Banister and Zhang (2005: 23).

Note
These data are the official figures adjusted by Banister and Zhang for underreporting of infant and child deaths. The underlying 1973–5 data are from the Cancer Survey of that period; other data were collected during the 1982, 1990 and 2000 Population Censuses.

expectancy in the 1980s was less fast than in the late Maoist era. That in itself is not surprising; the starting-point was much higher in 1980 and therefore the scope for improvement was arguably less. Yet the rate of improvement was actually higher in the 1990s than in either the 1970s or the 1980s, suggesting that the effect of a high base was rather small and therefore that the poor performance during the 1980s constituted a real policy failure (Sen 1989).

However, the better comparison is international, because then we can normalize for any distortions caused by differing base levels of life expectancy. This comparison shows that the rate of improvement in China was much less than the average in other countries which entered the 1980s with a similar level of life expectancy. Furthermore, it took most poor countries fewer years to achieve the increase in longevity that China achieved in the nineteen years between 1981 and 2000. During this nineteen-year period, male life expectancy in China increased by 3.2 years. But for what China needed nineteen years to achieve, Cuba required only five years; it reached China's 1981 level of life expectancy in 1967, and attained China's 2000 figure by 1972. Tunisia, Ecuador, Syria and Colombia all took less than ten years to match China's increase in life expectancy once they had achieved China's starting level of 66.4 years. The story for women is similar. Syria needed only seven years to accomplish that which took China nineteen (Reddy 2007: 56).

There are two probable explanations for China's rather poor record. One is a decline in the quantity and quality of food consumption amongst the Chinese poor caused by the increases in food prices which occurred in the late 1980s and during the 1990s. More important was the collapse of the system of rural health care. This was itself a result of the collapse of the communes, which put an end to the provision of basic health care. Instead, user fees were introduced, and these acted as a strong disincentive to the take-up of health care (Reddy 2007: 63–4). By the late 1990s, 87 per cent of the rural population and 44 per cent of the urban population had no form of health insurance or access to free health care (Banister and Hill 2004: 67).

Whatever the reason, the slow rate of improvement in longevity offers a powerful indictment of the Dengist regime. This indictment is especially powerful because the slow rate of longevity improvement took place against a background of sharply rising GDP, which in principle ought to have made possible vastly improved levels of health care. We can probably go far as to describe the 1980s as a lost decade. With infant mortality rising in some provinces, and life expectancy essentially stagnant between the censuses of 1981 and 1990, there is little doubt that China's record on human development was poor during the Dengist era.

Absolute poverty

Viewed through the telescope of the CCP, China did exceptionally well after 1978 in reducing absolute poverty in rural areas.[9] Nevertheless, most of China's poverty achievements appear to have been concentrated in the period before 1984. Thereafter, progress has been much more fitful.

Rapid rural poverty reduction, 1978–1984

In one sense, the Dengist regime started from a favourable position: urban poverty was very low by the end of the Maoist era. However – at least according to the official data – rural poverty was much more extensive; the official SSB data put total rural poverty at 250 million in 1978 (Table 13.3). The transformation thereafter was remarkable. By the mid-1990s, the number of those living in absolute poverty in the countryside had fallen to only about 60 million. In taking some 200 million people out of poverty within less than two decades, China's record was without international parallel.

The main reason for the decline in poverty in the late 1970s and early 1980s was the surge in agricultural production. Even though the distribution of income became more unequal, the pace of growth was such that a clear process of trickle-down occurred.[10] The main factor at work here was that China's poorest regions depended heavily upon farm income, and therefore the agricultural 'miracle' had a powerfully positive effect upon the rural poor.

Intermittent progress in rural poverty reduction, 1984–1991

Progress in rural poverty reduction was much less good in the late 1980s. To be sure, the official data show a clear downward trend: the rural poverty rate falls from 15 to about 10 per cent (Table 13.3). However, a number of Western

Table 13.3 Official estimates of rural poverty

	Poverty line (yuan)	Poverty rate (per cent)	Number living in absolute poverty (millions)
1978	100	30.7	250
1979	n/a	n/a	n/a
1980	130	26.8	220
1981	142	18.5	152
1982	164	17.5	145
1983	179	16.2	135
1984	200	15.1	128
1985	206	14.8	125
1986	213	15.5	131
1987	227	14.3	122
1988	236	11.1	96
1989	259	11.6	102
1990	300	9.4	85
1991	304	10.4	94
1992	317	8.8	80
1993	350	8.2	75
1994	400	7.7	70
1995	530	7.1	65
1996	580	6.3	58

Source: SSB (2004: 47).

estimates suggest progress that was at best fitful (Figure 13.4). The World Bank's (1992) series has total rural poverty as unchanged between 1984 and the early 1990s at around 100 million, and Yao's (2000) series shows a big increase in poverty between 1984 and 1989, a result driven by rising prices and slower agricultural growth.

Paradoxically, this rather poor record occurred despite both accelerating rural industrialization and the development of an explicit poverty-reduction strategy by the Chinese state. After 1984, the growth of the rural non-farm sector, and in particular the growth of rural industry, provided a large number of well-paid jobs. The number employed in the burgeoning *xiangzhen* industrial sector alone rose from 17 million in 1978 to 79 million in 1996. By 'leaving the land but not the countryside' (*litu bu li xiang*) large numbers of China's peasant population were in principle able to raise themselves out of poverty because industrial wages were in general so much higher than in farming. By contrast, in those regions where rural industry developed slowly, per capita incomes were generally low. Here the contrast between (rich) Zhejiang and (poor) Yunnan provinces is instructive. The data for 1999 (the position was little different in 1996) reveal that per income from farming in Yunnan was actually higher (1,056 compared to 1,018 *yuan*). However, total per capita income in Zhejiang was 4,793 *yuan* compared with only 2,210

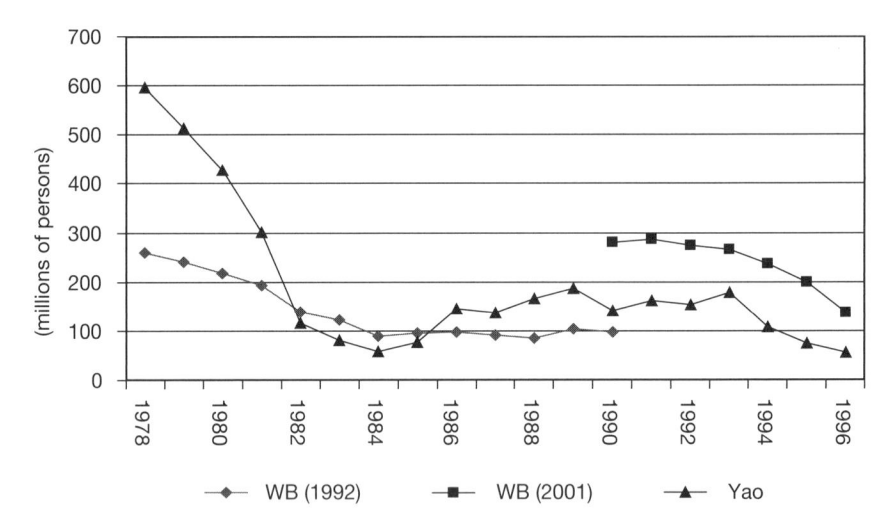

Figure 13.4 Poverty in rural China, 1978–1996 (Sources: World Bank (1992, 2001b); Yao (2000).)

Note: WB (1992) indicates the estimates which were published in World Bank (1992: 4); similarly WB (2001) refers to the data in World Bank (2001b: xv). The estimates published in 2001 use the Bank's 'international' poverty line, which is much higher than the line used by the bank in its 1992 publication and therefore increases the total number in poverty very significantly. One justification for this is that Chinese conceptions of absolute poverty had themselves changes by the early 1990s, and therefore the use of the lower poverty line was no longer appropriate A second justification is that international notions of subsistence are typically more generous than the Chinese norm, and therefore produce more absolute poverty.

yuan in Yunnan, reflecting big differences in wage income (1,738 to 215 *yuan*) and income from running household industry (357 *yuan* to only 36 *yuan*).

In promoting rural industry in this way, local government was doing no more than echoing the views of many Chinese rural specialists. Few were better known than Fei Xiaotong who, writing of Kaixian'gong village in Sunan in 1981, commented as follows:

> As early as 1936 I noted the importance of village industries as a means of raising the standard of living in rural areas where there is enormous population pressure on very limited land. ... It is my opinion that village industries will remain a key to the solution of China's rural economic problems. ... In a highly populated country such as China, once the basic problem of subsistence is solved, a major solution to the problem of rural poverty must be to spread a great variety of smaller-scale industries throughout the vast rural areas rather than to concentrate a small number of large industries in the big cities. (Fei 1983: 203 and 209)

Why then did rural industrialization not lead to big reductions in poverty? The reason appears to be that the main beneficiaries of rural industrialization were those whose incomes were already above the poverty line. In part, this was because the poor typically possessed few skills and a low education, and therefore found it difficult to gain access to industrial jobs even in regions where rural industry was booming. But there was also a regional dimension to all this. Those parts of China where most poverty was to be found in 1984 were typically regions where physical geography militated against rural industrialization.[11] Here agricultural growth – and in particular the development of animal husbandry and forestry – was necessary for poverty reduction, and yet performance across the whole agricultural sector was much less good after 1984 than it had been in the previous six to eight years. Even in the mid-1990s, the prosperity of the farm sector was a crucial determinant of the extent of poverty in those areas where the development of industry was almost impossible because of high transport costs. According to the UN Development Programme (UNDP/ILO 2000: 2): 'A major reason for the exclusion of the poor from the benefits of growth lies in the stagnation of agricultural output and fluctuating terms of trade for agricultural products.'

Moreover, those parts of China where agricultural growth continued to be rapid in the late 1980s were areas where the extent of poverty was already fairly limited. For example, per capita rural incomes rose dramatically in Jilin and Heilongjiang provinces because of agricultural prosperity; the opening up of the arable frontier combined with low population density made grain farming a highly lucrative occupation in these Manchurian provinces. But precisely because the rural population there was already quite well off, agricultural growth only served to reinforce prosperity.

Government policy also appears to have contributed little to poverty reduction in the late 1980s. In fact, the rapid poverty reduction that occurred before 1984 was achieved during a period in which the state had no antipoverty strategy at all.

This only changed after 28 September 1984, when the Central Committee and State Council issued a circular ('Circular on Assistance to Poor Areas to Transform their Conditions as Soon as Possible') identifying a number of dimensions of the problem (Propaganda Office 1988: 182 and 285). This was followed in 1986 by the establishment of the Leading Group for the Economic Development of Poor Areas (*Pinkun diqu jingji kaifa lingdao xiaozu*) by the State Council. Fourteen poor regions were initially identified by the CCP and the State Council in its 'Document no. 19' in 1984, and the Leading Group increased this to eighteen areas in 1986 (Propaganda Office 1988: 175–6). A more complete survey was published by the Leading Group in 1989, which set out the extent of poverty in 1986. It identified 663 poor counties, of which 363 received support from provincial and prefectural governments – leaving 300 counties to be funded by central government (NCGY 1989: 639–43).[12]

Why then did state policy fail? The key to understanding this seems to be that the Chinese state wrongly viewed poverty as almost entirely geographical in origin. The central government's approach to poverty reduction was predicated on the assumption that income inequality *within* counties was limited as a result of the egalitarian policies pursued in China under Mao. In other words, there was little poverty to be found in counties where the average level of per capita income was well above the poverty line. By contrast, there were many poor counties, because the obstacles posed by physical and economic geography were extremely hard to overcome. Accordingly, absolute poverty in China was held to be caused by adverse geography, and therefore central government policy aimed to resolve the problem by providing subsidies to these disadvantaged areas, located primarily in western China. The World Bank has tended to concur in this geographical approach. It is especially evident in the way the Bank's poverty relief programmes had a strong regional flavour during the 1980s and early 1990s. For example, some of its earliest projects – Gansu Provincial Development and Northern Irrigation – complemented the central government's focus on the Sanxi region (Ningxia–Gansu). Two more recent projects have centred on poverty relief in the Sichuan–Shaanxi–Ningxia border region (the Qinba Mountains Project) and in ethnic minority areas in Guizhou, Yunnan and Guangxi (South West China Poverty Reduction Project). The Leading Group on Poverty Reduction took the same view. Government relief funds (both central and provincial) have been allocated primarily to counties identified as poor and the National 8–7 Poverty Reduction Plan of 1994 focuses explicitly on institution building, investment in human capital, promotion of labour migration and infrastructural development in these poor counties.

This sort of geographical approach to poverty reduction received much criticism from Western scholars in the 1990s. The existence of extensive absolute poverty was, for example, addressed at some length in Riskin (1993a, 1993b) and the data demonstrate rather clearly that there is no simple link between geography and rural incomes. Of the 924 counties identified in 1990 as being located in mountainous areas, 65 had an average per capita rural income in excess of 800 *yuan*, far above the 275 *yuan* poverty line used by the World Bank for that year (NCGY

1992: 338; World Bank 1992: 32). The average income in these 65 counties was 890 *yuan*. This replicates one of my findings, that many of ethnic minority counties of western Sichuan were actually rather prosperous by provincial standards in the early 1980s (Bramall 1993). This was because of the development of forestry (a strategy which was admittedly increasingly unsustainable in the long run) and because of relatively high late Maoist prices for livestock products.

Of course it cannot be denied that there was some link between the incidence of poverty and physical geography. Of the 797 counties located on the plains of China, only in 19 was average per capita income below 300 *yuan* (presumably such counties were mainly found in the deserts of the north-west). By contrast, incomes in 198 of the 924 mountainous counties fell below the 300 *yuan* mark (NCGY 1992: 338 and 362). Nevertheless, there is no doubt that the Chinese government has been slow to take on board the non-geographical origins of rural poverty. Indeed China's western development programme of the late 1990s continued to take an essentially geographical approach to poverty alleviation. Khan and Riskin (2001) have argued that the Chinese government was simply mistaken in its view that the overwhelming bulk of the rural poor were to be found in a relatively small number of state-designated poor counties. Rather, persistent rural poverty (and the re-emergence of poverty in urban areas) was a product of the transition strategy itself (UNDP/ILO 2000: 1).

Rural poverty trends, 1991–1996

There is nevertheless some evidence that the process of rural poverty reduction started once again after 1991. This is very evident from both the series developed by Yao and that developed by the World Bank (Figure 13.4). For this period, the Bank has used a revised 'international' poverty line which vastly increased the total number of those in poverty. However, the post-1991 trend is unmistakable; by 1996 the headcount was down to 138 million, barely half the 1990 total.

The main reason is said to be the resurgence of rapid economic growth after 1991, which led to a process of trickle-down. More precisely, the spread of rural industrialization into poor regions, the improved performance of agriculture, and growing opportunities for labour migration all served to increase rural incomes. A geographical core of poverty remained, but the trend was firmly downwards. Nyberg and Rozelle (1999: 95–6) reiterated this World Bank view; considerable poverty remained in China in the mid-1990s, but the trend was unmistakable. Yao's (2000) estimates show the same trend. Using the actual poverty in three provinces (Liaoning, Jiangsu and Sichuan) in 1988 and the apparent relationship between poverty on the one hand and inequality and per capita mean income on the other, he calculates a national trend which has absolute rural poverty falling from 178 million in 1993 to 57 million in 1996.[13]

Other Western scholars have tended to be rather less sanguine about the effects of the resumption of growth in 1991, arguing that poverty changed very little in the early and mid-1990s. The basis for this reassessment is the use of revised estimates of income. Whereas the World Bank and the SSB has made use of the

SSB's income and expenditure surveys, Khan and Riskin (2001) and Riskin and Li (2001) have revised these data in a number of important ways in an attempt to overcome the well-known biases in the SSB surveys (Bramall 2001). It seems that the effect of using provincial price indices and including the value of imputed rent (poor households do badly on this) was to raise significantly the extent of poverty in the mid 1990s (Riskin and Li 2001: 334–7). Even using the official poverty line, the Riskin–Li estimate for 1995 was 11.4 per cent, well above the SSB estimate of 7.1 per cent (Table 13.3). The stagnation in the pace of poverty reduction has been caused by China's growing integration into the world economy, and by the mistaken view of the Chinese government that the overwhelming bulk of the rural poor are to be found in a relatively small number of state-designated poor counties. Particular factors singled out as contributing to this failure include the sharp rise in income inequality, regressive taxation and continued restrictions on migration to urban areas (UNDP/ILO 2000: 10–13). China, therefore, it is argued, needs to rethink its entire economic development strategy, and not merely the policies directly specifically towards poverty reduction.

In sum, the record on rural poverty reduction in the market socialist era is mixed. To be sure, a simple comparison between 1978 and 1996 seems to show a very big reduction in absolute poverty. However, there are reasons for supposing that the 1978 data exaggerate the extent of poverty at the end of the Maoist era, and therefore overstate the extent of the decline. As discussed in Chapter 9, it is hard to see how the (reliable) data showing high life expectancy in the late 1970s can be reconciled with the suggestion that there were between 250 and 600 million rural Chinese living below the absolute poverty line in 1978. Second, even if the decline between 1978 and 1996 is correct, it is evident that most of reduction occurred before 1984. In other words, state anti-poverty policies and rural industrialization utterly failed to make a dent in rural poverty. Third, there was still a very large number of poor people living in the Chinese countryside in the mid-1990s. For all its achievements, the regime still had far to go in eliminating rural poverty by the time of Deng's death.

Urban poverty

The evidence on poverty trends in the urban sector is difficult to interpret. Both World Bank (1992) estimates and the more recent work of Ravallion and Chen (Figure 13.5), which uses a rather high poverty line, show the proportion of the urban population in poverty falling from around 6 per cent in 1978 to around 0.6 per cent of the urban population in the mid-1990s.

However, there are two important qualifications. The first is that urban poverty rates soared during the inflationary period between 1985 and 1989, reaching no less than 7 per cent in 1989. This is a very different picture from that portrayed by the World Bank's (1992) data). The apparent increase in urban poverty owed much to price reform, which increased the prices of key urban commodities – such as meat and eggs – by very large amounts. Acceptance of these urban poverty

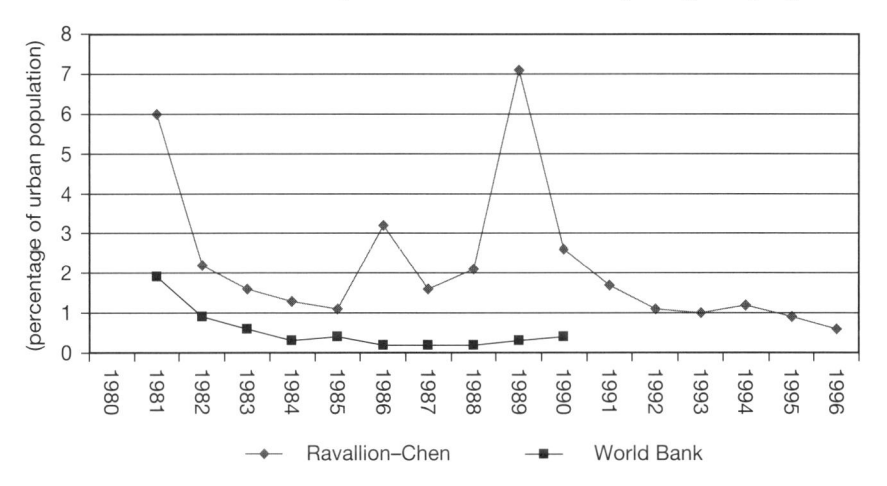

Figure 13.5 Estimated rates of urban poverty (Sources: World Bank (1992: 146–7); Ravallion and Chen (2004: 40).)

Note: Data are for absolute poverty amongst that part of the population officially classified as urban. This includes the population of county towns, as well as the cities.

estimates provides a strong socio-economic explanation for the power of the Democracy Movement in urban China in 1988–9.

A second qualification is posed by the fact that the work of Khan and Riskin (2000) and Riskin *et al.* (2001) suggests that some measures show a rise in urban poverty between 1988 and 1995. Their estimate of deep poverty (which uses a poverty line of 80 per cent of their broad poverty threshold) shows an increase from 2.7 per cent in 1988 to no less than 4.1 per cent in 1995. The incidence of broad poverty shows no change, remaining at around 8 per cent (Riskin *et al.* 2001: 129). As the survey excludes migrants (who receive low incomes whilst in work and find it relatively more difficult to find employment), this may even understate the true level of urban poverty. For them, 'The conclusion is inescapable: Economic reform in China has not succeeded in reducing urban poverty, and by most measures urban poverty has increased' (Riskin *et al.* 2001: 128). More than anything else, this appears to have reflected the very slow growth of urban employment, itself the result of industrial technologies becoming more capital-intensive over time. Urban unemployment, caused by the restructuring of state-owned industries, was also starting to be a considerable contributing factor to urban poverty by the mid-1990s. Official unemployment was running at about 6 million (3 per cent of the labour force) in 1996 but the true total may have been around 16 million (Khan and Riskin 2000: 110–112).[14]

Ultimately, these competing estimates of urban poverty are driven by how poverty is measured (and in particular the prices used to set the poverty line), and therefore it is difficult to reach unambiguous conclusions about the trend in urban poverty during the years of Deng's rule. The only thing that is certain is that China's record on urban poverty reduction was not especially good.

Inequality

The worst aspect of economic performance in the Dengist era was the record on income inequality. China did extraordinarily well in terms of absolute poverty reduction, but the extent and pace of the rise in inequality – whether in terms of income, consumption or educational access – was almost unparalleled anywhere in the world.[15]

Trends in income inequality

Official estimates of income inequality in urban and rural China are summarized in Table 13.4. They suggest that the rural Gini increased by about 50 per cent between 1978 and 1996, and that the urban Gini coefficient almost doubled. The overall Gini coefficient was of course higher than the average of the two sectoral Ginis because of the persistent urban–rural income gap. Measured using the official data, however, this gap did decline. Real per capita net rural income rose 4.2-fold between 1978 and 1996, whereas per capita real urban incomes rose by a factor of only slightly over 3 (ZGTJNJ 2005: 335). However, the nominal gap was largely unchanged at about 2.5 to 1.[16] As a result, with intra-urban and intra-rural inequality rising but an essentially invariant sectoral gap, the overall Gini coefficient climbed, reaching about 0.4 by 1996.

The Chinese government has not shown itself to be overly concerned by this rise in income inequality, arguing that a Gini coefficient of 0.4 was not especially

Table 13.4. SSB estimates of Chinese income inequality

	Rural Gini	Urban Gini	Overall Gini
1978	0.21	0.16	n/a
1979	0.23	n/a	n/a
1980	0.24	0.16	0.28
1981	0.24	0.16	n/a
1982	0.23	0.15	n/a
1983	0.25	0.15	n/a
1984	0.26	0.16	n/a
1985	0.26	0.19	n/a
1986	0.29	0.19	n/a
1987	0.29	0.20	n/a
1988	0.30	0.23	n/a
1989	0.30	0.23	n/a
1990	0.31	0.23	0.36
1991	0.31	0.24	n/a
1992	0.31	0.25	n/a
1993	0.33	0.27	0.38
1994	0.32	0.30	n/a
1995	0.34	0.28	0.41
1996	0.32	0.29	0.39

Sources: Rural – SSB (2000b: 18; 2004: 36). Urban – 1978–95 Bramall (2001); 1996 – Chang (2002: 337). Overall – 1980, 1990, 1993 and 1995–96 Bramall (2001).

high by the standards of much of Latin America or sub-Saharan Africa. However, this reflects an overly sanguine view of the survey data from which the Ginis have been computed. In fact, there is little doubt that the surveys were biased, because they excluded migrants, a large proportion of the illiterate population and many of the new rich, as well as making inadequate allowance for differences in the value of imputed rent from housing (Bramall 2001).

One response to the limitations of the official data by scholars has been to estimate revised Gini coefficients which attempt to correct for the limitations of the official SSB figures.[17] Adelman and Sunding (1987), and the World Bank (1997c) have made such revisions, but the most compelling are those derived from the work of Griffin, Zhao Renwei, Li Shi, Khan and Riskin. These latter estimates, which are available for only a handful of years – the first revision dates from 1988 – show a somewhat different picture from the official data. In 1995, for example, these revised estimates show significantly greater inequality (Table 13.5).

Nevertheless, the difference between the revised and the official estimates is quantitative rather than qualitative. A difference of 0.04 in the overall Gini coefficient for 1995 (0.45 compared with 0.41) does not fundamentally alter our assessment of Chinese inequality, not least because even these revised estimates are subject to a number of serious caveats. For example, the revised data make no allowance for the impact of migration to urban areas, which tended to drive up intra-urban inequality because migrants ended up in low-wage jobs.[18] It is therefore entirely possible that the extent of income inequality by the mid-1990s was very much higher than even the revised figures suggest. And some attempts to estimate rural inequality independently of the SSB came up with a Gini of 0.40 for as early as 1984, a figure well above the official Gini of 0.26 and arguably much more plausible for a country with such a diverse rural sector (Bramall and Jones 1993: 48).

Causes of the rise in income inequality

The rise in income inequality is not surprising. As China made the transition to a more market-orientated economy, it was inevitable that wage-based inequalities would rise and that this would drive up overall inequality. For many members of the CCP (notably Deng Xiaoping and Zhao Ziyang), the rise in income inequality was functionally necessary to stimulate productivity (thus reducing absolute

Table 13.5. Alternative estimates of the Chinese income distribution, 1978–1995

	Rural Gini	Urban Gini	Overall Gini
1978	0.22	0.17	0.32
1988	0.34	0.23	0.38
1990	n/a	n/a	0.41
1995	0.42	0.33	0.45

Sources: 1978 – Adelman and Sunding (1987: 163); 1988 – Griffin and Zhao (1993: 61); 1990 – World Bank (1997c: 17); 1995 – Khan and Riskin (1998: 237, 242 and 247).

poverty via growth). Moreover, the very fact that Marx himself had said in his *Critique of the Gotha Programme* that inequality was necessary in the early stages of the transition to socialism provided a suitable ideological justification. Those within the Party bent upon adhering to the late Maoist approach were therefore excused of extreme egalitarianism, and this 'left deviationism' was seen as the major mistake to be guarded against in the Dengist era. According to Zhao Ziyang in 1987 (Central Committee 1991: 668):

> The practice of allowing everyone to 'eat from the same big pot,' egalitarianism and jealousy of other people's incomes still constitute the main tendency in income distribution at present. We must continue to tackle these problems both from an ideological perspective and in our practical work.

Uncertainties in relation to the data make it difficult to be sure about the *precise* reasons for the rise in inequality; for example, revised estimates of income inequality are available only for 1988 and later, and not for the early 1980s. However, extensive decomposition analysis (using the Theil coefficient) by the Khan–Riskin team suggests the following. First, the urban–rural income gap widened between 1988 and 1995. However, and second, the rise in income inequality *within* the urban and rural sectors was even greater, and therefore they conclude that rise in inequality was driven primarily by these intra-local factors. The *absolute* level of inequality was massively affected by the urban–rural gap; it contributed about 40 per cent of total inequality in 1988. However, the *change* in inequality was due more to factors in operation within the rural and urban sectors; by 1995, the contribution of the urban-rural gap was down to a third (Riskin *et al.* 2001: 65). All this suggests that inequality in the People's Republic by the mid-1990s was multi-dimensional. Class-based inequality within China's counties and cities was a new and emerging problem, superimposed on the urban–rural differentials inherited from the late Maoist era.

We can look at some of these trends in more detail. As far as inequality within the rural sector is concerned, the main reason for the rise in inequality was a highly unequal distribution of income from wages and the growing contribution of wage income to total income. The (pseudo-) Gini coefficient for this type of income was 0.74 in 1995, far above the overall Gini coefficient of 0.42 (Khan and Riskin 2005: 364).[19] To put this another way, the richest 10 per cent of households received 26 per cent of total income in 1988 but no less than 61 per cent of wage incomes; in 1995, the share of wage income had gone up to 65 per cent. By contrast, the poorest decile received 1.7 per cent of total income but only 0.08 per cent of wage income in 1988 (Riskin *et al.* 2001: 98). These findings reflect the fact that some households were readily able to gain employment in lucrative rural industry, whereas others (lacking human capital or located in geographically disadvantaged areas) had little option but to work on the family farm. Thus residence mattered; *ceteris paribus*, households living in suburban areas had far more chance of gaining access to industrial jobs than households living in mountainous areas (Riskin *et al.* 2001: 100–2). It was not that wage differentials in the non-farm sector were very large – rather that there was great inequality of opportunity of access to industrial employment (Riskin *et al.* 2001: 11). In this respect, China's experience was very different frmo that of Taiwan, where the growth of the non-farm sector promoted growth with equity:

> Compared to Taiwan, the mainland is so much larger, more populous, and more varied in natural and economic conditions, that diffusion of non-agricultural activities over the population is a much slower task that will take much longer to accomplish. (Riskin *et al.* 2001: 11)

By contrast, income from farming remained comparatively equally distributed, but this was wholly insufficient to offset the rising importance of wage income and its unequal distribution.

The upward trend in income differentials was further exacerbated by rising spatial inequality. Figure 13.6 shows the trend in the coefficient of variation for per capita GDP in China's provinces and metropolitan centres. The top line covers the whole sample; the bottom one excludes the urban centres of Shanghai, Beijing, Tianjin and Liaoning. As far as the trend for the whole sample is concerned,

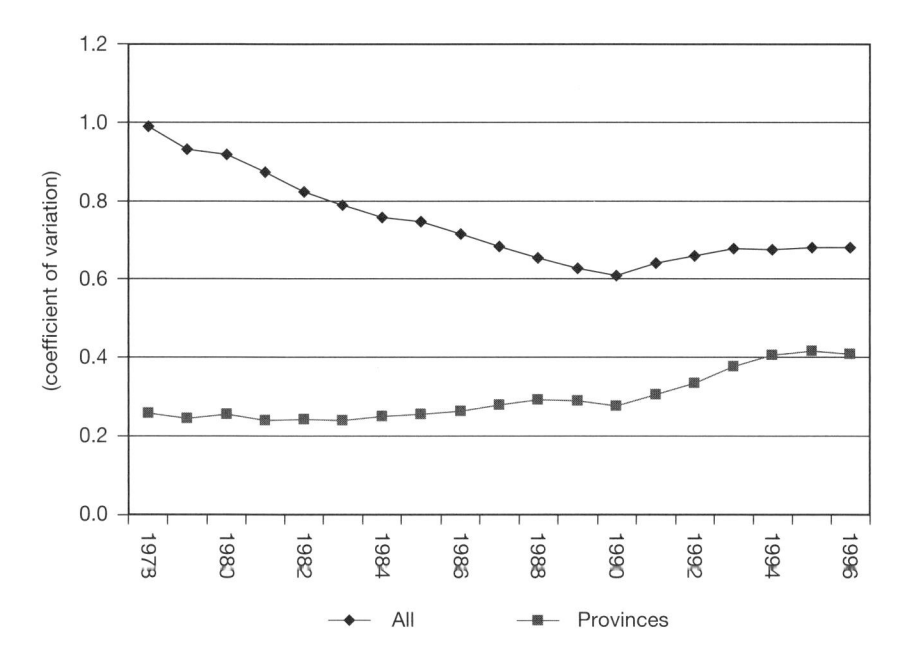

Figure 13.6 Coefficients of variation for per capita GDP at the provincial level, 1978–1996 (Source: SSB (1999).)

Note: The coefficient of variation (CV) is the standard deviation of provincial GDP per capita divided by mean per capita GDP. 'All' covers every one of China's provincial-level municipalities except Tibet, Hainan and Chongqing. The CV labelled 'Provinces' excludes Beijing, Tianjin, Shanghai and Liaoning, the key urban centres. GDP per capita data are at current prices.

the figure shows that the coefficient of variation fell between 1978 and 1990. In essence, this was driven by convergence between the four heavily urbanized centres of Shanghai, Beijing, Tianjin and Liaoning on the one hand (urban China), and the provinces on the other (rural China). In other words, the urban–rural gap actually declined. This reflected a combination of rapid growth in many of the (predominantly rural) provinces and slow growth in the big metropolitan centres which entered the post-Mao era with a relatively high base level of per capita GDP.[20] However, this gap began to open up again after 1990 as controls on Shanghai's growth were lifted, as China became more integrated into the global economy (which favoured the coastal provinces) and because the eastern provinces were able to exploit their geographical advantages in terms of low transport costs, access to large urban markets and ability to attract skilled migrant labour. Nevertheless – and this finding replicates the Riskin *et al.* finding for per capita income mentioned earlier in this section – the contribution of the urban–rural gap declined during the 1980s and early 1990s.

If we look simply at the provinces, the gap remained more or less constant between 1978 and 1990 as rapid agricultural growth helped the poorer regions to make significant strides. However, the slowdown in agricultural growth and the rapid industrialization of the early 1990s in provinces such as Zhejiang, Guangdong and Jiangsu led to a widening thereafter. With fiscal redistribution by central government much less important than it had been in the late Maoist era (Wang and Hu 2001), there were few countervailing forces at work to hold spatial inequality in check.

No discussion of rising income inequality in China would be complete without a mention of corruption.[21] Its scope was very limited in 1978. Of course *guanxi* were important to evade controls and to secure goods in the shortage economy of the 1970s. Nevertheless, late Maoist egalitarianism imposed strict limits on what was possible, especially by way of conspicuous consumption. As Sun (2004: 199) says: 'official privileges were greater in the elitist Soviet Union than in Mao's egalitarian China.' Under Deng Xiaoping, however, corruption spiralled. On the one hand, there was an absence of constraints; China lacked democracy, the rule of law and a free media. To compound the problem, there was little willingness within the CCP to act; many of the chief beneficiaries were the princelings (the sons and daughters of high-ranking Party officials). On the other hand, opportunities expanded. In particular, decentralization empowered local officials; the devolution of power to factory directors gave them unprecedented control over industrial assets, and the two-track pricing policy allowed big rents to be made by buying cheap and selling dear.

Nevertheless, we need to be cautious before concluding that corruption had a major influence on the distribution of income. For one thing (and unsurprisingly), we have no real way of knowing the extent of corruption, because of the limited reach of the household income and expenditure surveys in terms of types of income and households affected. Second, and reluctant though it was, the CCP did act to punish the most serious offenders. Its Disciplinary Inspection Commission was the Party's key instrument; one well-known example of disciplinary action was that taken against Chen Xitong, the Mayor of Beijing, and his son during the mid-1990s.[22] The data (Sun 2004: 47) in fact suggest a steady rise in the number of those disciplined between 1989 and 1996, though whether this reflected an increased propensity to prosecute or an increased incidence of corruption is moot. This did at least something to hold corruption in check, and the abandonment of the two-track pricing system in the 1990s also helped. In other words, the Chinese state was strong enough before 1996 to prevent corruption from becoming uncontrolled.

It is also worth observing that the costs of corruption may not be as great as often alleged. Corruption necessarily involves income redistribution, and this invariably involves a degree of injustice. The Democracy Movement of the late 1980s was motivated as much by anger over corruption as it was by inflation. Furthermore, in so far as resources are wasted in rent-seeking (lobbying government for preferential treatment), there is a clear economic cost (the deadweight loss). However, the overall impact of corruption depends on the use made of the rents. If the beneficiaries use their rents to invest and to promote growth, this may well offset any loss in terms of distribution. In more Marxian language, everything depends upon whether the rents accrue to a rentier class (with its high propensity to consume) or to a capitalist class (with its high propensity to invest). For example, it is well known that corruption was widespread in South Korea and Taiwan in the 1960s and 1970s. However, the main gainers were to be found in the corporate sector, which reinvested heavily and in the process raised the growth rate of GDP to remarkable levels. In other words, income inequality may have been functionally necessary for rapid economic growth in South Korea, and it is arguable that the process was not dissimilar in China. Certainly it is at least possible that the emergence of a dynamic private sector raised the growth rate over and above what it might otherwise have been. Moreover, in so far as corruption took the form of the extraction of resources from the farm sector by local government – which then used the rents to finance the expansion of township and village industry – there may have been real gains from the process. Of course local cadres benefited from this process, but there can be no doubting the rapid pace of expansion of output and employment in the TVE sector in the 1980s and 1990s. Corruption may have generated more inequality, but it may also have led to more rapid growth.

Inequalities in consumption and human development

Whatever the impact of corruption, there is no doubt that income inequalities translated into significant inequalities in consumption. As a result, the China of the mid-1990s had not solved its food problem. The growth of production had given it the *capacity* to resolve the remaining problems, but no more than that. For example, there was still a problem of malnutrition in the countryside; the FAO estimated that there were 146 million people (12 per cent of the population) who were undernourished (FAO 2006b). The 1990 household survey data make this apparent (Table 13.6). Amongst the 66,000 rural households included in the

Table 13.6 Rural daily calorie consumption per capita, 1990

Class	Consumption range (kcals per day)	Number of households	Average calorie consumption (kcals)
1	0–999	597	846
2	1,000–1,499	4,760	1,310
3	1,500–1,999	12,657	1,778
4	2,000–2,499	17,968	2,253
5	2,500–2,999	14,864	2,734
6	3,000–3,499	8,721	3,222
7	3,500–3,999	3,754	3,713
8	4,000–4,499	1,461	4,219
9	4,500 and over	1,409	7,063
All	0–4,500 and over	66,191	2,546

Source: FAO (1993: 296).

Note
These data are derived from the annual SSB survey of income and expenditure. The 1990 survey actually covered 66,478 households so a number have been omitted from the data submitted to the FAO. The survey data are not entirely reliable because they undersample poor households; see Bramall (2001).

survey, average per capita consumption stood at 2,546 kcals per day, which was some 300 kcals higher than the urban average. Yet in 4,760 of these rural households, average consumption was only 1,310 kcals per day, and there were a further 597 households where consumption levels averaged barely 850 kcals. The urban survey also identified significant malnutrition: 410 of the 12,282 urban households sampled recorded per capita consumption of less than 1,000 kcals per day. In these circumstances, it is perhaps not surprising that infant mortality rates rose in some of China's provinces during the 1980s.

The extent of educational inequality also needs to be emphasized. China's urban population in general did well. The ranks of university students were peopled primarily with those born in the cities, and the urban illiteracy rate in 2000 was only 5 per cent. But the rural population did far less well; the illiteracy rate was fully 14 per cent even in 2000.[23] Primary-school completion rates illustrate the scale of the problem. The national average was 92 per cent in 1990–2. However, there was marked regional variation. Whereas completion rates stood at 94 per cent or higher in the three great metropolitan centres, in the Manchurian provinces and along the coast, inland completion rates were much lower. In Sichuan, for example, the figure was only 90 per cent, falling to 84 per cent in Guizhou and only 79 per cent in Jiangxi province (UNDP 1999: 43). Part of the difficulty was the low quality of rural teachers; in the late 1990s, some 43 per cent of urban teachers had a college education compared with only 11 per cent of rural teachers (UNDP 2005: 48). Gender inequalities in education were also marked. Eight per cent of rural males were illiterate in 2000, but the figure was 19 per cent amongst women. Even in the counties around Shanghai, the female illiteracy rate was still 21 per cent, and the rate was 31 per cent in Guizhou, and around 50 per cent on the

Tibetan plateau (RKTJNJ 2005: 57). Considering the pace of GDP growth – and by implication the rise in the potential revenue base of government after 1978 – this was a wretched result.

Conclusion

Having set out the main trends, it is now time to bring the strands together. Can we conclude that overall performance between 1978 and 1996 was much better than during the late Maoist era? How does China's record stand up when placed in international perspective? And to what extent did the economy perform at its potential?

Perhaps the place to start is with the comparative GDP record. On this, as we have seen, China's per capita GDP growth rate was nothing short of spectacular in the twenty years after Mao's death. Table 13.7 merely emphasizes the point by contrasting China's growth record with that of other large developing and middle-income countries, and with the average growth performance of Latin America, East and South Asia and Africa. In all these comparisons, China comes out top, and by some distance. The contrast between the People's Republic (the pioneer of market socialism) and Russia (the exemplar of a country which made a rapid transition to capitalism) is especially illuminating and very much to China's advantage. And the comparison is by no means unfair. Russia may have been handicapped by its overindustrialization as Sachs and Woo (1994) allege, but it also enjoys the great advantages conferred by an abundance of natural resources. The conclusion from all this is very clear: whatever the limitations of the data, there is no gainsaying the fact that China's growth record was remarkable. It is hard to imagine a more eloquent testimony to the effectiveness of market socialism as an instrument for growth promotion.

Table 13.7 China's growth rate in comparative perspective, 1978–1996 (annual growth rates; 1990 prices)

	GDP	*GDP per capita*
China	7.8	6.3
Brazil	2.4	0.5
India	5.3	3.2
Indonesia	6.0	4.0
Nigeria	2.2	–0.4
Russia	–1.8	–1.6
Latin America	2.3	0.3
East Asia	5.7	3.9
Africa	2.2	–0.6

Source: Maddison (2003).

Note
The regional groups here cover 8 large Latin American countries, 16 large East and South Asian countries and 57 African countries. I have used the Maddison data for consistency. The Russia data are for 1990 to 2003; the pre-1990 figures are for the whole of the USSR.

It is also worth noting that China's HDI increased significantly during the transition era. Although educational attainment and longevity improved rather slowly, they did rise. When combined with very big increases in real GDP per head, the inevitable outcome was a very substantial rise in the HDI. The UNDP data here show China's HDI rising from 0.55 in 1980 to 0.68 by 1995, an impressive achievement (UNDP 2003: 242–243). By the mid-1990s, China's human development profile was much closer to that of a middle-income country than to the developing nation implied by its still-low level of GDP per capita. That is, its HDI ranking was considerably better than its per capita GDP ranking (UNDP 2005: 7–8).

For all that, China's HDI record was far short of spectacular between 1978 and the mid-1990s. If we look at some of the larger developing countries, Indonesia did as well as China, and in percentage terms the increase in India's HDI was actually greater. None of this is to say that China's record was poor: it was not. Whereas Russia and South Africa both experienced significant HDI declines, China increased it index by about 24 per cent. But the point is that China's HDI record was not remarkable, even though its rate of GDP growth was so spectacular. More concretely, educational enrolment rates went backwards in the early 19780s, and the rate of improvement in life expectancy was very slow. If we judge life expectancy to be the best single measure of development – the argument outlined in Chapter 1 – we must conclude that China's performance in the Dengist era was distinctly unimpressive.

When we shift the focus to distribution, China did even less well, and this provides one of the most powerful criticisms of the development record of the People's Republic after 1978. To be sure, and as we have seen, absolute (income) poverty in the rural sector fell markedly after 1978. This was no inconsiderable achievement. However, the extent of human poverty in the late 1970s was rather low, and this in turn calls into question the reliability of the estimates of income poverty at the end of the Maoist era.[24] If the base level of rural poverty was much lower than claimed by either the World Bank or the SSB, the supposed achievement in terms of rural poverty reduction after 1978 becomes much less impressive. Moreover, the re-emergence of urban poverty by the mid-1990s calls into question the extent to which the Chinese growth model was capable of generating rapid employment (as opposed to output) growth. In addition, the rise in income inequality was spectacular, being almost certainly more rapid than anywhere else in the world.

Two issues arise here. First, to what extent was rising inequality seen to be undesirable by the Chinese population? The answer here is that it was a cause of concern, and certainly animated popular urban unrest in the late 1980s. However, the survey data from which this sort of conclusion is derived rarely distinguish between the relative importance assigned to absolute poverty as opposed to inequality, so it is hard to be sure whether inequality was the motive force behind social action. Second, and even if inequality provoked unrest, we need to assess the extent to which rising inequality promoted growth – and therefore whether there was a tradeoff between these two development objectives. Here the evidence is hard to interpret. The notion that a fairly high level of inequality is necessary to promote innovation and to ensure high levels of labour productivity is of course well understood, and is common ground between many Marxist and neoclassical scholars. Indeed, as we have seen, the rise in income inequality in China during the 1980s and the early 1990s was justified by Deng Xiaoping and Zhao Ziyang in exactly these terms.

Furthermore, a cursory examination of the evidence certainly supports the idea that inequality was growth-promoting. Low inequality in the late Maoist era was associated with slow growth, and higher inequality between 1978 and 1996 was associated with rapid growth. In reality, however, it is much harder to make the argument. The contrast in growth rates between the Dengist and late Maoist eras was determined by a whole range of factors, of which differing degrees of inequality was only one. And the equalities of the 1970s did not prevent either a marked acceleration in the pace of rural industrial production or the introduction of new high-yielding varieties in agriculture. Moreover, it is far from easy to tease out the post-1978 causal links. Some types of inequality were growth-promoting, but that is hardly true of all types of inequality, especially those associated with the urban–rural and regional income differentials. It is not easy to see how the per capita income gap between (say) rural Jiangsu and rural Guizhou promotes growth in the latter; Guizhou hardly lacked for any incentive to raise income and production. It is equally hard to justify persistent, and perhaps even escalating, discrimination against both women and ethnic minorities in the labour market on functional grounds.

Furthermore, given the key role played by the state in promoting industrialization after 1978, it is not quite clear why the incentives faced by *private* sector agents were so important. Investment rates were very high in the 1980s and 1990s precisely because of the dominance of the state sector, not because of a large private sector motivated by profit-based inequalities. Of course cadres benefited from higher incomes, and therefore were motivated by the opportunity to earn a higher income. However, the prospect of promotion was probably much more important than mere material incentives in driving local government to promote rural industrialization. More generally, too much of the political science and decentralization literature focuses on agency and incentives, rather than capability. A strong case can in fact be made for the notion that the expansion of capability (especially the skills of the workforce) in the late Maoist era was far more important in driving rural industrialization – the really distinctive feature of the Dengist era – than changes in the incentive structure (Bramall 2007). In short, I do not find the argument that greater inequality was functionally necessary for growth very compelling. The fading of the Maoist vision brought China few real benefits, and many tangible costs.

In evaluating post-1978 performance, we also need to take into account the potential of the economy, as argued in Chapter 1. Here the evidence is clear: there is no question that the skill, educational and infrastructural potential of the Chinese economy was vastly greater in 1978 than it had been in 1952 or in 1963. As importantly, the international environment was altogether more benign than it had been during much of the late Maoist era, and this too raised the growth potential of the Chinese economy. Here again, much of the credit must be given to Mao for the way in which the China moved quickly to re-establish relations with the USA in 1972. The result was that China was able to engage in and with the world economy in a way which had not been possible in the 1960s; this allowed the People's Republic to import advanced technology, attract FDI and to exploit the opportunities offered by export markets. In addition, the rapprochement with the USA allowed China to gradually wind down the Third Front programme, which in turn made possible the Readjustment of the 1980s, which allowed scarce investible resources to be shifted away from defence and defence-related metallurgy and machine building to light industry and certain key subsectors of heavy industry. To be sure, the potential threat from the Soviet Union remained, but the USSR was little more than a paper tiger by the mid-1980s. If anything, in fact, the Dengist regime made China's integration with the world economy more difficult by the suppression of the Democracy Movement at Tian'anmen. In short, the Chinese economy did grow quickly after 1978, but the very fact that its potential growth rate was so much higher than it had been in the late Maoist era makes this a much less remarkable achievement than is often claimed. Irrespective of the constellation of policies adopted, the late Maoist economy could not have achieved these rates of growth.

In sum, much of the praise lavished on the market socialist model as implemented by the Dengist regime is undeserved. The growth rate of GDP accelerated – but the favourable inheritance from the Maoist era and the benign international environment made such acceleration all but inevitable. The decline in absolute poverty looks spectacular – but only if we ignore trends in the urban sector and if we exaggerate (as the CCP has consistently done since Mao's death) the extent of rural poverty in the late 1970s. It simply does not make sense to suppose that the vast majority of the rural population could have been living below the absolute poverty line when average life expectancy stood in the mid-sixties. On the debit side of the ledger, the Dengist regime presided over an unparalleled increase in income inequality, and one which brought little demonstrable benefit in terms of more rapid growth. As for the regime's record on human development, the best that can be said is that it was patchy. With GDP growing rapidly, China's dismal record on education and mortality deserves to be castigated. It says much about the literature that it has focused so much on growth and so little on these wider failures.

Notes

1 It is often suggested that Guangdong was little more than a green-field site in 1978, and this is true of places like Shenzhen and Dongguan. But this assessment ignores the impact of both Third Front construction around Shaoguan, and the extensive industrialization which had already taken place across the Pearl river delta by 1978 (Bramall 2007).
2 For example, the partial reform of prices in the 1980s (the dual-track pricing system) created opportunities for the acquisition of very large rents and thus encouraged corruption. Some even concluded that these contradictions would lead to crisis; the title of Chang's book, *The Coming Collapse of China*, says it all.

China's developmental record in the era of Deng Xiaoping   465

3 For some of the literature, see Ren (1997), Rawski (2001), Holz (2003, 2006), Maddison (1998, 2006a, 2006b) and Wu (2006).
4 Pre-1993 service output was adjusted after the 1992 tertiary sector census and therefore the SSB's new data are for the 1993–2004 period only.
5 Note the implication if it were true. If peasant food consumption really did jump from 1,800 to 2,300 kcals in two years, the policy changes of the late 1970s were far more important than decollectivization, which was still in its infancy in 1980. The rise in consumption cannot be attributed to better weather; Kueh's (1995: 299) index shows that the weather of 1980 was little different from that of 1978. It would follow that the combination of collective farming, higher procurement prices, increased fertilizer inputs and high-yielding varieties (discussed in Chapter 7) was remarkably effective, and that decollectivization itself was almost irrelevant for peasant welfare.
6 These official rates are for the population aged fifteen and over. They are misleading because they are calculated as the proportion of illiterates in the *total* population rather than as illiterates as a proportion of the population aged fifteen and over. The true rate of illiteracy in 2000 was 10.3 per cent (RKTJNJ 2005: 54).
7 The actual 2000 figure was only 2.9 per cent (UNDP 2005: 51).
8 For Chinese population issues and the one-child policy, see Banister (1987), Aird (1990) and Scharping (2003)
9 Some of the extensive literature on absolute poverty after 1978 includes OLG (1989), Kuchler (1990), Propaganda Department (1988: ch. 12), World Bank (1992), Riskin (1993a, 1993b), UNDP (1999), UNDP/ILO (2000), Yao (2000), World Bank (2001b), Khan and Riskin (2001), Park and Wang (2001), Riskin and Li (2001), Ravallion and Chen (2004), Asian Development Bank (2004) and UNDP (2005).
10 One study for 1988–95 shows that the effect of rising inequality was to raise the rural poverty rate by 12.9 per cent. This was offset by a 10.3 per cent reduction caused by growth and an unexplained residual which reduced poverty by 5.2 per cent, making for an overall reduction 0f 2.7 per cent (Wei and Gustaffson 1998).
11 For a more general critique of the value of state-led rural industrialization in poverty-stricken areas, see Nyberg and Rozelle (1999)
12 OLG (1989: 1–2) lists 664 counties, of which 327 received state (including 27 pastoral counties and 28 counties located in the Sanxi area of Gansu and Ningxia). This figure of 327 state-funded counties is also given in Kuchler (1990: 131). A figure of 331 centrally funded counties is given by the CCP's Propaganda Office (1988: 176), which includes an additional three centrally funded counties in Hainan (World Bank 1992: 117). Tibetan counties are not included in these lists.
13 Yao's approach is problematic in its uncritical use of official SSB data on per capita incomes and income inequality, and in its attempt at national extrapolation from the experience of three provinces.
14 Work by Meng *et al.* (2005) also shows absolute urban poverty rising between 1986 and 1993, and then stabilizing until the mid-1990s. They argue that this trend occurred despite per capita average income growth because of price rises, the withdrawal of subsidies and rising inequality.
15 For some of the literature on inequality, see Bramall and Jones (1993), World Bank (1997c), Khan *et al.* (1992), Griffin and Zhao (1993), Khan and Riskin (1998), Li and Zhao (1999), Khan and Riskin (2001), Bramall (2001), Riskin *et al.* (2001), Chang (2002), UNDP (1999; 2005), Démurger (2002) and Khan and Riskin (2005).
16 This conclusion is, however, quite sensitive to whether one uses per capita income or expenditure. The data on household expenditure derived from the national accounts show the nominal urban–rural gap rising from 2.9 in 1978 to 3.4 in 1995, though there is considerable year-on-year volatility (the 1996 ratio was 3.1). More importantly, it is also highly sensitive to the definitions of the rural and urban sectors. Chinese practice has been to reclassify many rural citizens as urban in the post-1978 period. As a result,

the rural share in total population declined from 82 per cent in 1978 to only 70 per cent by 1996. In these circumstances, it is hardly surprising that the urban–rural gap did not close. Many rural areas did lift themselves out of poverty and close the gap between themselves and nearby cities by growing rapidly; one can think here of (say) Wuxi city and Wuxi county in Jiangsu province. However, this is not reflected in the data on the urban–rural gap, because successful rural areas were simply reclassified as urban; in fact, this convergence shows up as a reduction in intra-urban inequality. In thinking about the true trajectory of the differential, there is a strong case for using the original definition of a jurisdiction, i.e. its status in 1978. Then the rise of places like Wuxi county would show up – as arguably they should – as a narrowing of the urban–rural differential. I am not claiming here that the urban–rural gap necessarily diminished after 1978; for every successful case of catch-up, there were other cases of relative decline – for example, much of rural northern Jiangsu grew slowly after 1978. Nevertheless, this type of definitional issue is one of the many problems that bedevil simple-minded attempts to argue that 'urban bias' rose or fell in a country during any particular epoch.

17 Studies using these revised data include Khan *et al.* (1992), Griffin and Zhao (1993), Li *et al.* (1998), Khan and Riskin (1998), Li and Zhao (1999), Yang (1999), Riskin *et al.* (2001) and Khan and Riskin (2005).
18 The most recent study (Khan and Riskin 2005) has attempted to correct for this problem by including migrant workers.
19 These pseudo-Ginis measure inequality not just amongst those receiving wage income but for the whole population. In other words, a person with no wage income is classified as having an income of zero for the calculation; the high pseudo-Gini thus has much to do with the fact that a large proportion of the rural population had no wage income at all.
20 These conclusions need to be qualified by the observation that the CVs in Figure 13.6 are for current price GDP per head and therefore take no account of differences in provincial inflation rates. Price indices do exist, but it is not clear that these are very reliable – and in any case rising relative prices in many cases implied a real improvement in the terms of trade of some provinces.
21 Useful discussions of corruption can be found in Kwong (1997), Lü (2000) and Sun (2004). For local taxation and rent-seeking, see Bernstein and Lü (2003).
22 A list of some of the high-ranking officials convicted for corruption before 1992 is given in Sun (2004: 49). Sun also provides lists of office sellers.
23 This and the city rate are true illiteracy rates, i.e. illiterates aged fifteen and over as a percentage of the fifteen-and-over cohort.
24 The life expectancy data derive from the 1982 population census, and, whilst this is not an unimpeachable source, it offers a far more reliable insight into the nature of the economy than the data on income poverty in the late 1970s.

Part 5
The transition to capitalism, 1996–2007

14 Chinese capitalism since 1996

It is not difficult to argue that the death of Deng Xiaoping in February 1997 was a climacteric in Chinese economic policy. His death, one might argue, removed the last check on the growing authority of Jiang Zemin and resulted in the abandonment of the market socialist vision articulated by Deng for so long.[1] Whether one dates the change from the articulation of the policy of radical industrial restructuring (*zhuada fangxiao*) at the 14th Party Congress (1995), the start of the Ninth Five Year Plan period (1996) or from the death of Deng himself, there is little doubt that economic policy changed significantly in the mid-1990s. Most obviously, China has joined the WTO, privatized many of its SOEs and TVEs and abandoned its attempts to control internal labour migration. The rhetoric of socialism may have been retained, but the true goal of the CCP over the last decade has been to effect a rapid transition to a full-blown capitalist economy; the decision to allow private-sector capitalists to become Party members in 2001 at the urging of Jiang Zemin was the most symbolic step.[2]

An alternative reading of the evidence would be that the commitment of the CCP to socialism remains undiminished. Although Jiang moved China in the direction of capitalism, his socialist credentials remain evident from the energy injected into the west China development programme, and continuing state ownership of around 30 per cent of the production of the industrial sector. And the commitment of Hu Jintao, Jiang's successor, is even more apparent. He has, for example, articulated a vision of 'a harmonious society' and the creation – based around (*inter alia*) the abolition of school tuition fees in rural areas – of a new socialist countryside. Moreover, the strategy of breakneck growth has been modified by a new emphasis on energy conservation and on environmental protection. How then can it be fair to argue that China has moved decisively towards the creation of a capitalist economy? This chapter addresses this central question as part of a more general summary of evolving macroeconomic policy after 1996.

Stabilization policy

A central precondition for structural change is macroeconomic stability, and this has been an abiding concern of the CCP leadership throughout the post-1996 period. To that end, the target growth rate has been relatively low, and five-year

470 *Chinese Economic Development*

plans have continued as a framework within which policy objectives could be formulated and realized.

Macroeconomic policy

As we saw in the previous chapter, the Chinese economy at the time of Deng's death was in a relatively healthy state. Zhu Rongji's recentralization of the fiscal system and contractionary monetary policy served to reduce the rate of inflation from about 20 per cent in 1994 to 5 per cent by 1996. A price was paid in the sense that the rate of job creation slowed down and the growth rate of GDP declined. Nevertheless, it was hardly a catastrophic downturn. The growth rate for 1996 was down on the 14 per cent real growth rate achieved in 1992, but the 10 per cent increase recorded was hardly a failure.

The central macroeconomic task for planners during the remainder of the decade and the first years of the new millennium was to ensure that the growth rate remained at around 10 per cent. This conclusion as to the target growth rate was based on the experience of the early 1990s, which suggested that a rate of 14 per cent was unsustainable in that it served to ignite inflation. With that in mind, the investment rate as a share of GDP was held below the 43 per cent recorded in 1993. Only in 2004 did the investment rate return to these dizzy heights, and the result – prices began to rise quite sharply in 2006 and 2007 – seems to confirm the notion that a growth rate of over 10 per cent is simply not sustainable.

The macroeconomic challenge which confronted policymakers in China after 1996 was of course very different from that faced in other parts of Asia, where 1997–8 saw startling falls in GDP caused by capital flight, rising domestic interest rates and a consequent wave of bankruptcy. China avoided these problems for two reasons: controls on the flow of foreign capital were still in place, and China's trade integration with the rest of the world economy was still quite limited. The first ensured that China (like Taiwan) was immune to the financial crisis that engulfed countries like Malaysia and South Korea. China before 1997 had attracted little speculative capital in the first place, and controls prevented large-scale outflows from occurring. The second Dengist legacy ensured that China was largely unaffected by contagion. Precisely because Chinese growth was not export-led, the big falls in GDP across East Asia had only modest effects on the Chinese economy. Only relatively export-orientated Guangdong was hit hard, and even there the pain was far from insupportable. In short, China's limited integration into the world economy has meant that macroeconomic policy-making was comparatively easy even in the late 1990s.

China's success in maintaining a high rate of growth over the last decade is evident from the data (Figure 14.1). There is no sign that the growth rate is slowing; Chinese rates of growth have accelerated over the period since 1999. And if the current pace of convergence between China and the US is maintained, there is every chance that China will become the largest single economy in the world (when measured using purchasing power parity GDP) by 2040. Moreover, it has achieved these rates of growth without very high rates of inflation. Even in

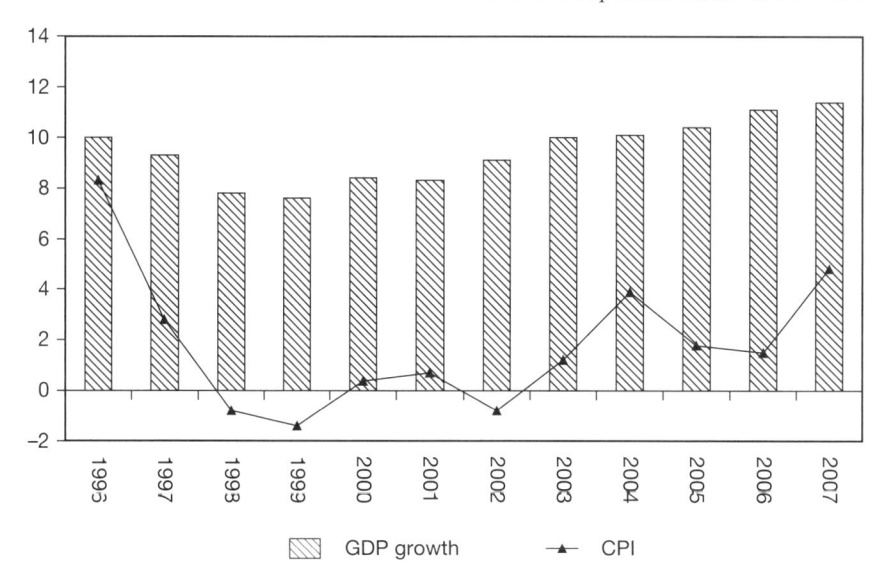

Figure 14.1 Growth of real GDP and the consumer price index, 1996–2007 (Sources: ZGTJNJ (2007: 59 and 309). The figure for 2007 is a preliminary estimate by the SSB.)

2007, when GDP growth reached a peak, the consumer price index rose by only 4.8 per cent.

For all that, policymakers in China and abroad have increasingly viewed growth as unbalanced in the sense that the investment share is too high and the contribution of the service sector too low. According to Hu Jintao (2007):

> We must keep to the new path of industrialization with Chinese characteristics, pursue the policy of boosting domestic demand, particularly consumer demand, and propel three transitions in the mode of economic growth: the transition from relying mainly on investment and export to relying on a well coordinated combination of consumption, investment and export, the transition from secondary industry serving as the major driving force to primary, secondary and tertiary industries jointly driving economic growth, and the transition from relying heavily on increased consumption of material resources to relying mainly on advances in science and technology, improvement in the quality of the workforce and innovation in management.

There is something in this notion that Chinese growth was unbalanced between 1966 and 2008. As far as investment is concerned, there is no doubt that its share in GDP in the decade after 1996 was very high by international standards (World Bank 2007: 218–20). Gross capital formation accounted for 44 per cent of GDP in 2005 (compared to 36 per cent in 1990). By comparison, the average for middle-income countries across the globe was only 27 per cent, and China was well ahead of other large developing economies such as India (33 per cent), Indonesia (22 per cent) and Nigeria (21 per cent). Of course China's high investment rate was one of the reasons for its rapid rate of growth, but it is nevertheless fair to wonder whether it made sense to keep it above (say) 35 per cent. Not only can one argue that investment was increasingly subject to diminishing returns, but also the cost of investment was suppressed consumption – no small consideration for a country which remains relatively poor. It follows from this that China would do better to shift towards productivity-based growth, and, as Hu's speech suggests, this was one of the aims of macroeconomic policy in the years after Deng's death.

Nevertheless, it is far from clear that China would do well to follow this advice. From a theoretical viewpoint, there are good reasons to reject a neoclassical perspective in which the contribution of technical progress can be separated from investment. The neoSchumpeterian view that most technical progress is endogenous and needs to be embodied in new equipment – as a range of economists from Kaldor (1961) and Scott (1989) to De Long and Summers (1991) have suggested – is far more plausible. It follows therefore that there is a real possibility that cuts in the investment share will lead simply to slower technical progress. It is all very well to suggest that China needs to shift towards a more productivity-based growth path in the medium term if growth is to be sustained. However, there is much in the evidence to suggest that Chinese growth has been based around productivity growth ever since the early 1980s precisely because of its high investment rate and growing competition in domestic markets, and therefore that no fundamental change is needed. The very fact than even economists using a neoclassical growth accounting framework (for example Bosworth and Collins 2007) have found that productivity growth has made a big contribution to growth suggests that the notion of a dichotomy between investment- and productivity-based growth is overstated. IMF and World Bank advice to rebalance growth towards consumption may be well intentioned (though we do well to remember that both organizations are financed mainly by the US government, and it is far from obvious that US strategic interests are served by a successful Chinese economy). However, Chinese planners would do well not to respond with alacrity to this sort of suggestion; with growth in excess of 10 per cent the need for drastic action plainly does not exist in the short run.

As for the notion that the service sector is too small, there is again something to this charge. Between 2000 and 2005, for example, the service sector grew less quickly than manufacturing (10 per cent per annum compared to over 11 per cent). Moreover, the share of services in Chinese GDP was only 40 per cent compared with an average of 53 per cent in middle-income countries (World Bank 2007: 190–6). The contrast with India is especially striking given the similarities of the two countries in other respects (notably size and level of development); in India, services accounted for 54 per cent of GDP in 2005.[3] One consequence of this structure of output for China is that the growth of employment – services are of course relatively labour-intensive – is slower than it might be in the short run, thus contributing to China's unemployment problem. Again, however, a good deal of caution is in order. As discussed in Chapter 12, a large manufacturing sector is essential for growth, and it may well be that the push for Chinese deindustrialization is premature. China and India are certainly very different, but it is at least arguable that the large number of English speakers in India makes a development strategy more reliant on IT-intensive services far more sensible than in the Chinese case.

The Five Year Plans

It is commonplace for Western academics to regard Chinese policymakers as having abandoned planning since 1978, and to some extent this is true. The very fact that so much of the economy is subject to market forces makes traditional-style allocation of inputs and outputs across sectors rather meaningless. For exactly this reason, Chinese planning in practice is indicative. Targets are set and the government uses a range of fiscal and financial instruments (primarily taxes and interest rates) to achieve those targets.

Nevertheless, thinking about Chinese development in terms of Five Year Plans is useful because it is evident that economic policy variation occurs across these planning cycles (Table 14.1). Thus the Eighth Five Year Plan (1991–5) marked a sharp deviation from the previous period in that it was an era of very rapid growth which began in 1991. Deng's *nanxun* in 1992 has garnered much attention, but it is evident from the data that the recovery of GDP began in 1991.

The themes of the Ninth Five Year Plan (1996–2000) were very different from those of the Eighth. Instead of growth, the focus was on macroeconomic contraction (to squeeze inflation out of the system) and the wholesale restructuring of the industrial sector under the slogan of *gaizhi* and *zhuada fangxiao*. It is no accident that the key policy announcements were made in 1996, the start of the planning cycle. The Ninth Plan was a very poor period for China's farmers, in contrast to both Eighth and Tenth Plan periods. Wage income (mainly from industry) continued to grow rapidly, but per capita income from farming declined in nominal terms. As for urban China, the impact of the policy of industrial restructuring is painfully

Table 14.1 Variation in growth rates across plan periods

		Rural growth rates		Industrial growth	
		Farm income	Rural wage income	Industrial value-added	Secondary employment
Eighth Plan	1991–5	+25.3	+22.7	+8.7	+2.9
Ninth Plan	1996–2000	–3.3	+11.5	+9.4	–0.1
Tenth Plan	2001–5	+7.0	+10.7	+11.6	+2.8

Sources: ZGTJNJ (2006); SSB (2006c).

Note
Rural growth rates are at current prices. The high inflation rate of the Eighth Plan period means that the absolute data are misleading, but it is the relative rate of farm and rural wage growth that is of interest. Industrial GVA growth rates are at constant prices; industry excludes construction.

apparent in the data on industrial value-added and employment. Value-added growth halved compared with the Eighth Five Year Plan even after adjusting for inflation, and secondary employment growth was almost non-existent, in contrast to the significant rates of growth achieved during the Eighth and Tenth Plans. The Tenth Five Year Plan (2001–5) marked a return to growth promotion. It was recognized that agricultural performance had been poor in the late 1990s, and there was growing concern about the level of urban unemployment. The very fact that WTO entry might lead to further unemployment added more weight to these concerns. The solution to both problems was to accelerate the growth rate, and this is precisely what happened: the growth of farm income, industrial value-added and secondary employment were all well up on the rates during the Ninth Plan.

None of this is to say that important macroeconomic changes did not occur *within* plan periods. The 1994 fiscal recentralization and the programme of macroeconomic contraction introduced by Zhu Rongji in the middle of the Eighth Five Year Plan show that very clearly. Nevertheless, trends during plan periods after 1991 display a degree of coherence which suggests that Chinese macroeconomic planning was by no means dead even in the new millennium. It may not have been the planning of old, but it is evident that the government sought, and to a considerable extent succeeded, to control the pace and pattern of development.

The transition to capitalism

The main theme, however, of economic policy-making after 1996 has not been stabilization policy so much as structural change on an unprecedented scale. Many of the events of the last decade suggest that the Dengist strategy of market socialism has been abandoned and the CCP has instead opted to make the transition to capitalism.

By the late 1980s, many elements of the late Maoist development model had already been jettisoned. Collective farming had long since been abandoned. The hegemony of urban state-owned industry was being challenged by local state-owned enterprises (TVEs) based in the countryside, and by a vibrant private sector. Inequality was spiralling. Any notion that superstructural change was a necessary condition for economic change had long since been abandoned. In so far as this strategy had an ideological underpinning, it was based around the idea of creating a market socialist economy which combined elements of authoritarianism (CCP rule) with state control over key economic sectors and a vibrant market economy.[4]

At the end of the 1980s, however, the doctrine of neoauthoritarianism was becoming increasingly attractive to Chinese intellectuals as an alternative to market socialism. Most of these intellectuals if asked would have styled themselves as neoauthoritarian. That is, they saw a combination of a market-driven economy and an authoritarian state as offering a better path to modernity than the market socialist vision of a mixed economy.[5] The rapid growth of the economy seemingly confirmed the effectiveness of market-led solutions. And the 'chaos' threatened by the demonstrators in Tian'anmen square in 1989 affirmed their conviction that only a strong state stood between them and barbarism. Democracy was a desirable long-run objective, but the basic premise of neoauthoritarianism was that economic change was a necessary condition for political change, thus reversing the late Maoist notion that causality runs as much from the superstructure to base as in the opposite direction. During the early 1990s, this neoauthoritarian doctrine increasingly infiltrated the upper echelons of the Communist Party. For example, Wang Huning (a leading advocate of neoauthoritarianism in the 1980s) became a close adviser to Jiang Zemin. The seeming failure of democracy in Russia and the continuing resilience of Singapore's economy attracted new adherents to the neoauthoritarian cause.

Nevertheless, Chinese praxis in the mid-1990s was arguably still closer to that of market socialism than it was to the neoauthoritarian vision of strong state and free market. The Chinese state was certainly 'strong' enough for it to be classified as neoauthoritarian and the commitment to income equality was admittedly very hollow by then. However, the extent of state ownership in China was still far greater in 1996 than in any of the other East Asian economies, China's commitment to free trade and capital movements remained lukewarm and the internal labour market was still heavily controlled, especially via continuing restrictions on internal labour migration. The drive to create a neoauthoritarian state was seemingly tempered by Deng Xiaoping's commitment to retaining state control over the commanding heights of the economy. Deng's death in February 1997 therefore broke the log-jam because it removed the last check on the neoauthoritarian instincts of Jiang Zemin.

The waning of the market socialist vision

Events since 1996 point towards the conclusion that the aim of policy-making was to create a neoauthoritarian system by maintaining China's strong state, and simultaneously making a thoroughgoing transition to capitalism. One feature of the years after Deng's death was the continuation of the process of price liberalization begun in the late 1970s. In fact, the data suggest that price liberalization was largely complete by 2003. In that year, 87 per cent of producer good sales, 96 per cent of retail sales and 97 per cent of farm commodities were at market prices (OECD 2005: 29). To all intents and purposes, therefore, price determination was by market forces – a characteristic feature of capitalist economies across the globe. Similarly, the rise of the private sector continued. By 2003, private sector companies accounted for 57 per cent of value-added in the non-farm business sector, up from 43 per cent in 1998 (OECD 2005: 81).

Price liberalization and the removal of restrictions on the growth of the private sector were merely a continuation of a policy begun in the early 1980s. However, the same cannot be said of other aspects of the constellation of policies implemented after 1996. There are continuities across the 1996 divide, but we should not underestimate the extent to which the death of Deng Xiaoping was a climacteric in Chinese economic policy-making.

476 Chinese Economic Development

Box 14.1 Key events of the post-1996 era

1995	*zhuada fangxiao* slogan first appears at 5th Plenum of the 14th Party Congress; privatization of small SOEs and TVEs begins in earnest in the autumn
19 February 1997	Death of Deng Xiaoping
July 1997	Asian financial crisis begins in Thailand
September 1997	Jiang Zemin announces decision to cut back the state sector to the 15th Party Congress. Importance of private sector formally recognized Policy of *zhuada fangxiao* re-articulated
April 1999	US and China fail to agree terms for Chinese entry to World Trade Organization
May 1999	Bombing of the Chinese embassy in Belgrade
11 December 2001	Chinese accession to WTO
October 2002	Hu Jintao becomes Party leader in succession to Jiang Zemin
July 2005	*Renminbi* – US dollar exchange rate peg abandoned
March 2007	New property right law passed by the NPC allowing children to inherit wealth made by insider privatizations and fraudulent share dealing

Three new initiatives signalled the end of the Chinese attempt to steer a third way to modernity between national communism and international capitalism. First, the programme of industrial privatization launched initially under the banner of *zhuada fangxiao* ('grasp the large, let go the small') in 1995 and accelerated after September 1997. Whereas industrial policy before 1996 focused on restructuring and liberalization – encouraging, for example, the growth of private and foreign enterprises – policy after 1996 centred around privatization of state-owned industries in the cities and in the countryside. Second, China's accession to the World Trade Organization in December 2001, which heralded the demolition of most of China's remaining tariff and non-tariff barriers to international trade. This was seen as enhancing the impact of privatization by exposing Chinese industrial enterprises to more intense competition. It also served a political purpose: restrictions on the scope for industrial policy implied by WTO membership meant that there was no way back to the market socialist model. Third, and as is discussed in the next section, barriers to internal labour migration were largely removed with a view to reducing the income gap between Chinese regions and ensuring an abundant supply of cheap labour in China's cities.

We have discussed two of these seismic changes already in Chapter 11 (WTO entry) and Chapter 12 (industrial restructuring). Here, therefore, we focus on labour migration.

The growth of internal labour migration

Between the death of Mao and the middle of the 1990s, extensive labour migration occurred between the countryside and China's cities. Some of this was permanent migration (*qianyi*) involving a change in the place of a person's registration (*hukou*).[6] However, an increasing proportion of migrants were temporary, and these made up an increasingly large floating population (*liudong renkou*) across China. It is difficult to be absolutely certain about the size of this floating population because of changing definitions.[7] Nevertheless, most estimates put the number of floaters at around 30 million in the early 1980s, rising to 70 million by the late 1980s and to around 100 million by the end of the 1990s (Chan 2001: 130–1). This growth has continued largely unchecked in recent years.

The 2000 Population Census, undoubtedly the most reliable of any of China's surveys, came up with a figure of no less than 144 million migrants (ZGTJNJ 2002: 102–3). The census data are very revealing (Table 14.2). First, they show that around 79 million of the floaters were long distance migrants; that is, they had migrated across county or provincial borders. This was well up on the figure of 22 million recorded in the 1990 census (Liang and Ma 2004: 470) and demonstrates the extent to which China's population became increasingly mobile as the economy became more market-orientated. Second, the data show clearly that the migration was largely rural to urban and from west to east. Thus the jurisdictions with the largest percentage of floaters were Beijing, Tianjin and Shanghai (the big prosperous urban centres), Zhejiang (where TVEs and private industry had flourished) and Fujian and Guangdong (both of which had attracted abundant FDI). The frontier provinces (Xinjiang, Inner Mongolia and Manchuria), which were still seen as offering opportunities for migrant workers – especially in their resource extraction sectors – also attracted above-average numbers of floaters. Third, the experience of Guangdong stands out. Not only did it attract a large number of floaters, but a disproportionate number of them were long-distance migrants; no less than 15 million of China's 42 million trans-provincial migrants were living in Guangdong in 2000. They were of course attracted to Guangdong's manufacturing industries, especially the dynamic centres of the Pearl river delta in cities such as Dongguan and Shenzhen (Yeung 2001; China Labour Bulletin Research Report 2006).

Nevertheless, although these migrant numbers are large in absolute terms, the rates are still relatively small compared with Europe or North America. It is therefore not surprising that many Western economists were arguing that it was time to remove the remaining residual controls on internal labour migration by the mid-1990s. The World Bank (1997c) was very positive on the benefits to be expected. Knight and Song (1999) argued that Chinese policy had long been characterized by urban bias, and that one feature thereof was the creation of an

Table 14.2 The floating population in 2000

Province	Total floaters	Share in provincial population	Inter-provincial floaters	Share of inter-provincial floaters in national total
	(million)	(per cent)	(million)	(per cent)
Beijing	4.64	33.6	2.46	5.8
Tianjin	2.18	21.8	0.74	1.7
Hebei	4.88	7.2	0.93	2.2
Shanxi	3.72	11.3	0.67	1.6
Nei Menggu	3.83	16.1	0.55	1.3
Liaoning	6.48	15.3	1.05	2.5
Jilin	2.95	10.8	0.31	0.7
Heilongjiang	3.77	10.2	0.39	0.9
Shanghai	5.38	32.1	3.13	7.4
Jiangsu	9.10	12.2	2.54	6.0
Zhejiang	8.60	18.4	3.69	8.7
Anhui	3.56	5.9	0.23	0.5
Fujian	5.91	17.0	2.15	5.1
Jiangxi	3.36	8.1	0.25	0.6
Shandong	7.47	8.2	1.03	2.4
Henan	5.20	5.6	0.48	1.1
Hubei	5.70	9.5	0.61	1.4
Hunan	4.40	6.8	0.35	0.8
Guangdong	25.30	29.3	15.06	35.5
Guangxi	3.23	7.2	0.43	1.0
Hainan	0.98	12.5	0.38	0.9
Chongqing	2.63	8.5	0.40	0.9
Sichuan	6.67	8.0	0.54	1.3
Guizhou	2.42	6.9	0.41	1.0
Yunnan	3.87	9.0	1.16	2.7
Tibet	0.21	8.0	0.11	0.3
Shaanxi	2.37	6.6	0.43	1.0
Gansu	1.56	6.1	0.23	0.5
Qinghai	0.52	10.0	0.12	0.3
Ningxia	0.67	11.9	0.19	0.4
Xinjiang	2.83	14.7	1.41	3.3
Total	144.39	11.4	42.43	100.0

Source: ZGTJNJ (2002: 102–3).

Note
The data here include both intra-county migrants (who were not included in the 1990 census as migrants; they numbered 66 million in 2000) as well as inter-county migrants. For a discussion, see Liang and Ma (2004).

'invisible Great Wall' between urban and rural sectors by means of the erection of barriers to rural–urban migration. Khan and Riskin (2001: 155) also argued in favour of migration, maintaining that the government policy should aim to:

> liberalize control of population movement so as to permit a freer flow of people

in search of economic and social opportunity. We have argued that liberalized policies toward population mobility have helped reduce rural poverty, and we favor furthering this process – including the phasing out of physical restrictions on population movement – to eliminate the inequitable segmentation of the urban labor market and the second class status of rural–urban migrants.

The Chinese government has increasingly heeded these sorts of policy recommendations. Temporary residence permits and identity cards were granted to migrants after 1985, and these allowed them to live legally in urban areas. However, the process went a stage further in the mid-1990s, when local government (at the behest of the CCP) started to award 'blue' *hukou* status to temporary migrants to large cities. So-called because it involved a blue rather than red stamp on the *hukou* card, the blue *hukou* granted a range of rights to migrants in exchange for the payment of a fee to local government. It thus had the effect of integrating migrants further into urban communities, even if discrimination remained (Gaetano and Jacka 2004: 18–20; Dutton 1998; Wong and Huen 1998). It has also become easier to reside in small towns as a result of legislation passed by the State Council in June 1997 and March 2001. In addition, local governments across China have played a key role in helping to export labour, which they have seen as a means towards the end of poverty reduction; the process has been well documented in Anhui province, which has exported large quantities of labour to Shanghai in recent years (Lei 2005).

Nevertheless, there is evidence that these migration-promoting policies have not worked in the sense that there was growing evidence by around 2003/4 of shortages of unskilled labour in the Pearl river delta and in Jiangsu (Inagaki 2006). Guangdong was said to be short of a million workers in 2004, and the deficit in Fujian and Zhejiang was around 2 million; Dongguan alone was predicted to have a shortage of 1 million workers in 2005 (Shao *et al.* 2007: 10). These shortages continued into 2006 and 2007. Given that most scholars believe that there is still a large number of relatively underemployed workers in the countryside, these shortages are widely seen as reflecting labour market failures. More precisely, low wages and discrimination against migrants – such as restrictions on the jobs open to migrants and attempts by local government to limit access to social insurance and public goods – have been seen as discouraging migration (Shao *et al.* 2007). Yet it is not just discrimination. The one-child policy has also played an important role in restricting the supply of young workers. Indeed the very fact that shortages of young female workers are most acute demonstrates very powerfully the discriminatory impact of that policy (Inagaki 2006).

It also needs to be recognized that there is no evidence that the Chinese government is bent upon abolishing the *hukou* system. As Chan and Buckingham (2007) point out, recent changes have had the effect of delegating decisions about migration to local government. And local governments have typically responded by encouraging in-migration by the educated, the wealthy and the skilled, but simultaneously retaining powerful barriers when it comes to in-migration by the poor and the unskilled. For example, by requiring migrants to have worked in the city for two years and to be the owners of a residence before granting *hukou* status, the government of Shijiazhuang has effectively closed the door (Chan and Buckingham 2007: 29).

The intent of central government is clear, such local interference notwithstanding. Controls on labour migration are far less strict than they were even in the early 1990s, and barriers continue to come down. China is still a long way from having created a well-functioning labour market, but it has moved far in that direction. Despite labour shortages in some regions, the scale of migration has increased dramatically over the last decade. And in that the migrants are typically better educated and wealthier than those who do not migrate, the Chinese labour market has many of the features seen in market-orientated OECD economies.

An enduring commitment to socialism?

Much of the evidence discussed earlier in this chapter, and in Chapters 11 and 12, certainly suggests that China has abandoned market socialism. However, even though there is much to suggest that the Chinese leadership is bent upon (and has gone far towards) creating a capitalist economy, some have argued that the true intentions of the CCP are not easily assessed. Dic Lo and Li Guicai (2006: 16), for example, argue that China is still on some form of heterodox trajectory, pointing to 'the fundamental importance which the Chinese state leadership, and the society as a whole, attach to the objective of "constructing a harmonious society"'. What, then, has been the goal of the CCP leadership since 1996?

Official rhetoric and Chinese realities

In answering this question, it is undeniable that Party rhetoric suggests a continuing ideological commitment to socialism; see for example Hu (2007). Moreover, the Eleventh Five Year Plan (2006–10) does seem to have articulated a rather different vision of the Chinese future from those which preceded it, and some have argued that we need to take all this very seriously. According to Lin (2006: 276):

> Although such efforts are still short of being a grand vision of socialism for missing the dimension of democracy, redefining development is nevertheless an honourable and ambitious goal in a country of China's size and in the face of its formidable obstacles. The official statements about readjusting development deserve serious treatment.

Lin certainly has a point. The need to protect China's environment has been recognized, and attempts to calculate green GDP have been made. Restrictions on the inflow of foreign capital and on currency movements remain; in that sense, the globalization of the Chinese economy still has some distance to travel. The policy objective of creating a *xiaokang* (comfortable) standard of living is routinely mentioned, and some efforts have been made to define it in terms of both opulence and human development indicators. Macroeconomic policy emphasis has shifted away from growth and towards redistribution. Much stress has been placed on creating a harmonious society.[8] Perhaps evenly more significantly, the need to develop the rural sector has been stressed repeatedly. Here the aim is to create a 'new socialist countryside' and to solve the *sannong* ('the three rural problems': the problem of agriculture, the problem of rural areas and the problem of the peasantry). This pro-rural vision has been given teeth in the policy announcements of 2006 – the abolition of the agricultural tax and the end of tuition fees for rural children aged between six and fifteen.

All these policy aims were reiterated by Hu Jintao at the start of the 17th Party Congress in October 2007. Few concrete announcements were made, but three aspects of his speech stand out. First, Hu announced that the aim of policy was to quadruple per capita GDP between 2000 and 2020. Although this was more ambitious than the previous aim (which was to increase total GDP by that amount over the same period), it nevertheless implies an annual growth target of only around 6 per cent between 2007 and 2020. Given that the economy was growing by over 10 per cent during 2007, this amounted to an apparent scaling back of China's growth ambitions and by implication a commitment to broader social development. Second, a feature of Hu's speech was a recognition of the environmental implications of rapid growth and the need for conservation. In the introduction to his speech, he even admitted that 'Our economic growth is realized at an excessively high cost of resources and the environment' (Hu 2007). Third, there was not only a recognition that income disparities had widened dramatically, but also a commitment to reducing them:

> A relatively comfortable standard of living has been achieved for the people as a whole, but the trend of a growing gap in income distribution has not been thoroughly reversed, there are still a considerable number of impoverished and low-income people in both urban and rural areas, and it has become more difficult to accommodate the interests of all sides [Section III]. ... We will protect lawful incomes, regulate excessively high incomes and ban illegal gains. We will increase transfer payments, intensify the regulation of incomes through taxation, break business monopolies, create equal opportunities, and overhaul income distribution practices with a view to gradually reversing the growing income disparity [Section VIII].

Nevertheless, it remains to be seen whether any of this rhetoric means very much. For example, it is hard to see how the creation of a 'new socialist countryside' is going to be financed. The same caveat applies to the provision of free tuition to rural children. To be sure, this is not merely posturing. According to Wen Jiabao's *Report on the Work of Government* (March 2007), 'A total of 184 billion *yuan* was allocated by both central and local governments to fund rural compulsory education, enabling us to pay tuition and miscellaneous fees for the 52 million rural students receiving compulsory education throughout the western region and in some areas in the central region ...' during 2006 (Wen 2007). However, it is doubtful that these types of policies will address the underlying

482 Chinese Economic Development

problems. The agricultural tax has long been a very small part of the 'burden' carried by the peasantry, and its abolition will therefore make little difference to peasant incomes. Low enrolment rates in the rural schools certainly have something to do with the cost of education. But at least as big a problem is low demand for education, especially for girls.ABr Wen Jiabao recognized the point. Although the CCP had committed itself to 'completely stop collecting tuition and miscellaneous fees from all rural students receiving compulsory education' in 2007, Wen recognized that this would only 'ease the financial burden of 150 million rural households with children attending primary and middle schools' (Wen 2007). More generally, endemic discrimination by parents against their daughters in the Chinese countryside is the crux of the educational problem, and that is not likely to be addressed by modest subsidies.

Developing western China

Perhaps the clearest sign of the Party's vestigial commitment to some sort of egalitarian vision has been its apparent determination to reduce the regional income gap between eastern and western China.[9]

Figure 14.2 The western region of China, 1997.

Note: This is the official CCP definition of western China. the provincial boundaries are those of 1997 showing Chongqing as a separate municipality.

This certainly had not been the case in the 1980s, when the income gap between the coastal and the interior provinces probably widened. In part this was a consequence of both history and geography interacting with the liberalization of the economy and the decentralization of the fiscal system – which allowed regions well favoured by history and geography to forge ahead. The coastal provinces were certainly favoured by their geography. For one thing, intra-provincial transport costs were very low within the coastal provinces. For another, the great metropolitan centres of Shanghai, Beijing and Hong Kong offered large external economies of scale because they supported both a large pool of skilled labour and offered an immense market to local producers. Perhaps most importantly of all, the eastern provinces were coastal. That reduced long-distance transport costs to other Chinese coastal provinces, but it also gave them easy access to the fast-growing economies along the Pacific Rim, and to the more distant markets of the USA, Australasia and Europe. History too was in their favour. China's railway network was much denser in the eastern provinces than further west, and industrial development before 1949 and under Mao had led to the creation of a skills base and to the establishment of a range of industrial infrastructure. The late Maoist Third Front programme did little more than hold inequalities in check. It could not eliminate them.

However, the widening of spatial income inequalities owed as much to CCP policy as it did to historical legacies and physical geography. For one thing, the fiscal system in operation during the 1980s was characterized by coastal bias. At root, the problems were caused by fiscal decentralization, a process which favoured the more prosperous provinces. Decentralization (*fangquan rangli*) was pioneered in Jiangsu in 1977, where the introduction of *guding bili baogan* (fixed-rate contact) specified that the province was to be allowed to retain 42 per cent of revenue raised over the following four years. The key national reform did not occur until 1980. That year saw a lump-sum system introduced in Guangdong and Fujian and a fixed-rate system (based on the Jiangsu model) put in place in the great metropolitan centres and in Jiangsu itself, while all the remaining provinces operated a system under which specific types of revenue were shared between province and centre (Shirk, 1993: 166–8). The effect of the 1980 reform was to replace a system of *chi daguo fan* (eating out of the same big pot) with that of *fen zao chifan* (eating in separate kitchens) – that is, the provinces were given much greater control over how much revenue they retained and how they allocated it.

Further fiscal reforms followed in sharp succession, and they reinforced regional bias. The 1988 reform, for example, treated fast-growing provinces even more favourably by specifying that a certain proportion of revenue would be handed over to central government but that the contribution rate would be reduced once a target level of revenue had been remitted (Shirk, 1993: 192–3). This *shouru dizeng baogan* system was designed to provide provinces with the incentive to increase revenue by reducing the marginal remittance rate. The system was formalized in the early 1990s. It involved two distinct elements: contracted transfers and earmarked transfers (Wong *et al.* 1995: 90–8) On the one hand, all China's provinces had agreed a fiscal contract which specified that they remitted a certain amount to the centre (rich provinces) or that they received an agreed subsidy (poor provinces). On the other hand, every province received earmarked transfers from central government. Some of these earmarked subsidies were for capital construction. However, it is remarkable that no less than 59 per cent of all earmarked grants took the form of price subsidies. These necessarily benefited affluent, urbanized, areas. As a result, for example, Guangdong's 1990 contracted remittance of 5.2 billion *yuan* was partially offset by an earmarked inflow of 1.24 billion *yuan* (Wong *et al.* 1995: 98).

The net effect of these changes was to reduce the extent of transfers from coastal to interior provinces. The total figure remitted to the centre declined in absolute terms between 1985 and 1990. The seven jurisdictions remitting most to central government (Shanghai, Jiangsu, Liaoning, Tianjin, Shandong, Zhejiang and Beijing) made contracted transfers of 33 billion *yuan* in 1985 but only 28 billion *yuan* in 1990. Looked at over the entire 1978–93 period, the decline was much more steep. Shanghai's surplus of revenue over expenditure fell from 51 per cent of GDP in 1978–80 to only 8.5 per cent in 1991–3. The comparable declines for Beijing and Tianjin were from 26 per cent to 1 and 4 per cent respectively (Wang and Hu, 1999: 190). With less money available to central government, transfers to poor provinces declined. Guizhou's subsidy of 11.7 per cent of GDP in 1978–80 dwindled to only 3.3 per cent by 1991–3 and the decline for Xinjiang was from 24 to 7 per cent. The full details on the five provinces with the biggest (percentage) surplus and the five with the biggest deficit are summarized in Table 14.3. These data show very clearly how some of China's richest areas were able to retain an increasing proportion of tax revenue, thus reducing the ability of central government to transfer funds to poor hinterland areas.

The data given in Table 14.3 undoubtedly need to be qualified in several respects. First, it is unclear whether these official data include financial flows earmarked for military purposes. As all but Guizhou of the poor provinces listed here were frontier provinces, these military flows could well have been significant. Second, and following on from this, it may well be that transfers to poor provinces declined

Table 14.3 Fiscal surpluses as a share of GDP, 1978–1989 (ranked by surplus in 1978)

	1978	1989
Shanghai	52	13
Tianjin	30	3
Beijing	28	3
Liaoning	28	2
Jiangsu	13	3
Yunnan	–9	–5
Guizhou	–13	–6
Ningxia	–20	–15
Nei Menggu	–20	–9
Xinjiang	–25	–10

Sources: by calculation from SSB (1990a; 2005a).

after 1978 because of the termination of the Third Front programme and the ending of the short confrontation with Vietnam. If so, at least part of the decline in subsidies (in particular funds made available for investment in physical capital) represented little welfare loss to their populations. Even declines after 1985 may have reflected continuing fluctuations in military spending. Third, it is hard to believe these data include the full range of flows between provinces, especially (non-military) extra-budgetary transfers and subsidies. Finally, the data exclude loans. In the case of the rich provinces, loans to central government tended to be the norm. The reverse was true for the poorer provinces. But, and notwithstanding these qualifications, it is hard to believe that the official data do not provide at least a qualitatively accurate picture of the pattern of intergovernmental flows over the first decade of the transition era. The very fact that numerous Party officials went on record between 1989 and 1994 to state that central government was becoming increasingly paralyzed by fiscal weakness suggests that there undoubtedly was a crisis caused by the fiscal federalism of the 1980s.

CCP policy also exacerbated regional inequality because its focus was on a coastal development strategy. The Third Front was abandoned and instead emphasis shifted towards the promotion of rapid growth in the provinces along the Pacific seaboard. Still, and despite the creation of four special economic zones in 1979 and 1980, the coastal development strategy was initially very tentative. In no small measure, this was because of the resistance (or at least caution) of Chen Yun. Nevertheless, the documents setting out the Sixth Five Year Plan (1981–5), published in 1983, made clear the intent of the leadership: the continuing development of the Chinese interior was not an end in itself, but should merely serve the purpose of *promoting* economic growth along the coast (Yang, 1997: 83). By the mid-1980s, the rhetoric had softened a little; development in eastern China was to help serve the needs of the interior rather than the reverse.[10] Nevertheless, it was commonplace for CASS economists to put forward the proposition that it was a 'law' of economic development that rapid growth in the coastal region had to precede growth in the interior:

> China's economy can be divided into three major geographic regions: eastern, central and western, and the objective tendency of development is to push from east to west. (Central Committee 1991: 501)

The best-known justification for a pro-coastal strategy was put forward by Wang Jian, who was based at the State Planning Commission. His idea of a grand international cycle (*guoji da xunhuan*) envisaged an initial phase of export growth based upon the labour intensive industries of the coastal region. The export earnings of the coastal region would in turn help to finance capital deepening and the development of the interior in a later phase (Hsu 1991: 9). By 1987, the theory had won favour with Zhao Ziyang, and it was adopted as official Party policy in February 1988. Deng, too, was an ardent supporter.

> The development of the coastal areas is of overriding importance, and the

interior provinces should subordinate themselves to it. When the coastal areas have developed to a certain extent, they will be required to give still more help to the interior. Then the development of the interior provinces will be of overriding importance, and the coastal areas will in turn have to subordinate themselves to it. (Deng 1988: 271–2)

Zhao's fall and the Tian'anmen massacre put a break on the momentum of the coastal development strategy. Moreover, it appears that Deng Xiaoping was himself becoming increasingly concerned by the gap between coast and interior. The spur for this was a belief that the gap in terms of per capita GDP had widened excessively during the 1980s. One obvious way to see this is in terms of the difference in per capita GDP between Guangdong (one of China's richest provinces) and Guizhou (probably the poorest). A simple comparison of per capita GDP between the two (Figure 14.3) appears to show that the ratio widened from around 2 to 1 at the start of the 1980s to over 3 to 1 by the time of the Tian'anmen massacre, a dramatic increase by any standard.

Deng and the CCP were also concerned that regional inequality would interact with ethnic tensions in western China. This held out the possibility of some of fragmentation of the People's Republic itself, and the concerns of the CCP were allayed neither by the close relations between the Dalai Lama and the US administration, nor the collapse of the Soviet Union. Nevertheless, it is unlikely that the creation of breakaway republics is a real concern for the Chinese leadership, not least because the control of the PLA in Xinjiang and Tibet is tight and because the presence of Han settlers in these outposts of empire serves to moderate any separatist push. In practice, the worries of the CCP centred much more on the

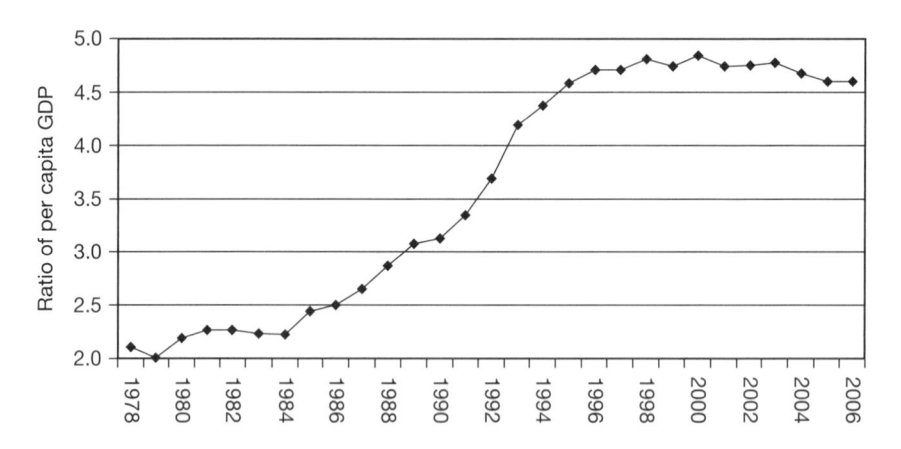

Figure 14.3 The ratio of per capita GDP in Guizhou to per capita GDP in Guangdong (Sources: SSB (2005a); ZGTJNJ (2007: 67 and 106); ZGTJNJ (2006: 63 and 100).)

Note: Data on GDP are at current prices. The population denominator takes no account of the floating population. I discuss some of the limitations of this analysis below.

implications of slow growth in the western provinces for migration. Its abiding fear appears to be a tidal wave of uncontrolled emigration from the west into China's cities, creating enormous social and economic tensions. The best way to prevent such a flood was by means of promoting faster economic growth in the western provinces, thus encouraging migrants to stay put.

Nevertheless, and though Deng was anxious to avoid polarization, he was by no means in favour of egalitarianism. His spring tour of 1992 gave renewed vigour to developing the coastal region, and Deng was at pains to promote the idea of regional comparative advantage (*yindizhuyi*). Certainly he did not see a growing income differential between rich and poor areas as a requiring immediate redistribution via the tax system. Extracts from his speeches of 1992 make this plain:

> If the rich keep getting richer and the poor poorer, polarization will emerge. The socialist system must and can avoid polarization. One way is for the areas that become prosperous first to support the poor ones by paying more taxes or turning in more profits to the state. Of course this should not be done too soon. At present, we don't want to dampen the vitality of the developed areas or encourage the practice of having everyone 'eat from the same big pot'. We should study when to raise this question and how to settle it. I can imagine that the right time might be the end of the century, when our people are living a fairly comfortable life. ... In short, taking the country as a whole, I am confident that we can gradually bridge the gap between coastal and inland areas. (Deng 1992: 362)

> [T]hose areas that are in a position to develop should not be obstructed. Where local conditions permit, development should proceed as fast as possible. There is nothing to worry about so long as we stress efficiency and quality and develop an export-oriented economy. Slow growth equals stagnation and even retrogression. (Deng 1992: 363)

Deng's answer to the regional problem was therefore suitably modest in scope. The solution, he argued, was to 'twin' coastal cities and provinces with western provinces, thereby promoting a transfer of skills and finance. This was called creating *duikou zhiyuan* (sister city relationships). An example was aid from Shenzhen to Guizhou for school building (Wright 2003: 52). To all intents and purposes, this was a strategy which aimed simply to make trickle-down more effective.

By the middle of the 1990s, however, the gap had continued to widen and the rhetoric amongst CCP leaders became increasing shrill.[11] According to Li Peng, the then prime minister, action was imperative:

> We must admit the east-west gap. We must create conditions so that the gap can gradually close. The central government cares very much about this problem and has determined that the West's development is a major issue that must be addressed through policy, funding, and technological support. (Li Peng 1993, cited in Wright 2003: 55)

The Ninth Five Year Plan (1996–2000) gave expression to these concerns. The CCP leadership proposed as the solution to the problem an extension of the open-door policy to encompass the interior and an intensification of Deng's twinning solution, this time under the name of *hengxiang jingji lianxi* (horizontal economic cooperation). Under this arrangement, Beijing was twinned with Inner Mongolia, Shanghai with Yunnan, and the special economic zones with Guizhou. A further policy initiative was the decision to designate Chongqing as a provincial-level municipality in 1997, thus putting it on a par with Beijing, Tianjin and Shanghai. In part this was a way of dealing with the relocation of the population displaced by the Three Gorges dam. As a result, the new municipality is much bigger than Chongqing city and its outlying counties; it also included the poor prefectures of Wanxian to the north-east and Fuling to the south-east. It was hoped that placing all these areas under an administrative jurisdiction which included a large urban centre would make it easier to move displaced peasants into urban jobs. As importantly, however, the new dam would improve navigation along the Yangzi river by increasing its depth. This in turn would allow the Yangzi shipping route to be opened up much further and reduce transport costs. Thus Chongqing would become the hub of development for the entire western region, and it was fitting that it should have municipality status.

Whether the solutions implemented during the Ninth Five Year Plan were successful is moot. Wright (2003: 56) argues that they were not, and he may well be right. Certainly there is no doubt that it is much too early to judge either the impact of the Three Gorges dam or the upgrading of Chongqing to municipality status. Part of the problem is that the only way to measure the benefits generated by the programme is to look at the extent to which the per capita income gap between coast and interior has changed over time, and it is very difficult to track the trajectory of the per capita GDP gap during the 1980s and 1990s. To be sure, Figure 14.3 seems to tell a very clear story. However, there are three problems with these data. First, the Guizhou–Guangdong comparison makes no attempt to adjust for regional price differences. According to the recent analysis offered by Brandt and Holz (2006: 78), this might reduce Guangdong's per capita GDP by around 24 per cent in 2000 relative to Guizhou.[12] Second, the time series data are distorted by the revaluation of GDP following the 2004 Economic Census, which (taken alone) served to widen the gap between the two provinces. This affects the data for 2005 and 2006, and in that sense the series shown in the figure is not consistent. Third (and to some extent offsetting the revaluation of GDP), the data are based upon permanent provincial populations prior to 2005. Taking the floating population into account has the effect of cutting Guizhou's population by around 2 million between 2004 and 2005, whereas Guangdong's population increases by no less than 9 million.

If we take these factors into account, it seems likely that the Guangdong–Guizhou gap was in the order of 2 to 1 at the start of the 1980s, a time when GDP overvaluation, provincial price variation and labour migration was of relatively little import.[13] If we adjust the gap shown in Figure 14.3 for the floating population, use revised official estimates of GDP and accept the Brandt–Holz view of regional price differentials, this rise to around 3.7 to 1 by 2006. But when exactly the increase occurred is moot. It is probable that most of it occurred during the 1990s; Guizhou benefited from the surge of agricultural production in the 1980s, whereas Guangdong gained ground in the 1990s as a result of big inflows of foreign investment and relatively lower rates of price inflation than Guizhou. Out-migration may have benefited Guizhou in absolute terms in the 1990s (though I rather doubt it given that migrants are preponderantly the young and the better educated), but Guangdong almost certainly gained far more from attracting a pool of relatively well-educated workers (at least by the standards of western China) who were willing to work for low wages in the labour intensive industries in the special economic zones and across the Pearl river delta.

Whatever the actual trajectory of regional income differentials, the CCP leadership seems to have concluded by the end of the 1990s that these income gaps could not be allowed to increase any further. This led to the programme of 'Developing the West'. Zhu Rongji set up the Leading Group on Western Development in 1999, which initiated a Develop the West programme (*Xibu da kaifa*); the phrase was seemingly first used by Jiang Zemin in June 1999. This Leading Group was formally placed under the State Council on 16 January 2000 as the Leading Group to Develop the Western Region (*Xibu diqu kaifa lingdao xiaozu*).

As conceived, the Develop the West programme covers the eleven provinces and autonomous regions of western China, though the State Council circular of April 2002 also included the three ethnic prefectures of Xianxi (Hunan province), Enshi (Hubei) and Yanbian (Jilin). The programme drawn up in 2000 envisaged five ways by which development could be promoted (State Council 2002). The first was to increase spending on centrally funded projects. These were primarily infrastructural projects. The most famous is the Qingzang railway linking Qinghai and Tibet (completed in July 2006). Equally important, however, is the east–west natural gas pipeline linking the gas fields in the Tarim basin (Xinjiang) and the Changqing (centred on Jingbian in northern Shaanxi) with Shanghai, which became operational in 2004. Also of great significance is a series of power transmission projects (collectively labelled the east–west power transmission project), which transfer electricity produced at hydrostations on the Jinsha, Lancang and Yellow rivers to eastern China. But spending did not only focus on infrastructure. For example, for every *mu* of cultivated land withdrawn from use, the farmer received a grain subsidy of 150 kg per annum. Furthermore, the central government provided a subsidy of 20 *yuan* for every *mu* of cultivated land converted to forestry or pasture as well as a seedling subsidy of 50 *yuan*. This latter was even classified as infrastructural spending (State Council 2002).

Second, transfer payments to the governments of the provinces of western China were increased. The western provinces were already receiving large fiscal transfer from the centre in the 1990s to cover their budgetary expenditure. These were increased very substantially between 1995 and 2004 as Table 14.4 (covering some of the provinces) shows. These numbers should not be taken too literally. Chinese fiscal data are remarkably opaque, excluding many types of extra-budgetary and

Table 14.4 Budgetary revenue and expenditure in a sample of western provinces (billion yuan)

	1995			2004		
	Revenue	Expenditure	Subsidy	Revenue	Expenditure	Subsidy
Sichuan	12.1	21.2	9.1	38.6	89.5	50.9
Yunnan	9.8	23.5	13.7	26.3	66.4	40.1
Gansu	3.4	8.1	4.7	10.4	35.7	25.3
Xinjiang	3.8	9.6	5.8	15.6	42.1	26.5

Source: SSB (2005a: 853, 921, 1021 and 1123).

Note

Data are in current prices. The all-China consumer price index increased by only 15 per cent in total (not per annum) between 1995 and 2004, so subsidies increased very substantially in real terms over the period. These data cover only local government budgetary revenue. Substantial sums were raised outside the budget by provincial governments.

off-budget revenue and expenditure. Nevertheless, the data probably give a fair indication of the scale in the increase in fiscal transfers.

Three other policies are integral to the Develop the West programme. First, the central government instructed the State Development Bank of China to provide cheap loans and credit for infrastructural projects. The Agricultural Bank of China was also instructed to provide easier credit. Moreover, the restructuring and privatization of SOEs in the western provinces was accelerated and many of them were privatized. There was a perception in China (and amongst Western economists) that the western provinces had been very slow to promote privatization, and therefore efforts were made to accelerate the privatization process after 2000. Third, in an attempt to encourage more FDI into the western region, corporate income tax was reduced to 15 per cent for the period 2001–10.

Many academics continue to be sceptical as to whether any of this will be successful. Lai (2002: 459) argued that 'predatory and wasteful habits, inefficiency, and unfamiliarity with the market and legal norms hinder the building of a favourable investment environment in the west.' This type of allegation has frequently been made, and in fact many Han Chinese scholars offer a discourse that is at best chauvinistic and at worst racist. One example of this is Wang and Bai (1991), but it is a routine for Han Chinese to lament the drunkenness, sloth and incompetence of ethnic minority and other cadres across the western provinces. For writers like Wang and Bai, both subsidies and expenditure on infrastructure will fail because the main problem in the western region is the quality of 'human resources' and the nature of 'socioeconomic relations'. According to them: 'the rural inhabitants of backward regions are clearly characterized by a general lack of entrepreneurial spirit and an excessive adherence to old ways [p. 38]. ... the real problem in China's backward regions ... [is that of] ... reversing the attitude of the local inhabitants towards social wealth and changing their traditional ways of exploiting natural resources' (p. 92). There is no doubt that labour productivity in western China is lower than in the east (Démurger 2002; Hare and West 1999).

It is also fair to say that a number of Western scholars are profoundly sceptical as to whether aid offers much of a solution to the problem of underdevelopment in developing countries.[14] But to jump from this to the conclusion that culture is to blame is a step too far. In fact, the attitude of Han scholars and policymakers is arguably one of the principal obstacles to the development of the western provinces.

However, the main critique of the Develop the West programme is that the only reason the western provinces are being developed is to supply raw materials to the coastal region. In a sense, this is a classic example of imperialism, whereby the metropolitan centre extracts resources from the periphery via a process of unequal exchange in which the west loses its skilled labour and natural resources for a derisory amount of financial recompense. And woven into this 'development of underdevelopment' is a process of colonialism. Han settlers continue to 'flood' into Xinjiang, and Qinghai – historically part of Tibet – is now a Han Chinese province.[15] In short, a discourse of development cloaks a process of exploitation. It remains unclear whether this type of allegation is correct. Many emotive passages have been written about western China. However, the issue awaits a proper scholarly treatment and the results will be very sensitive to assumptions made about the price paid for raw materials exported to other Chinese provinces, and whether this constitutes a process of unequal exchange. It is clear, however, that the apparent enthusiasm manifested by the Chinese government for the development of the western provinces (an enthusiasm reiterated by Hu Jintao) cannot be taken as signifying any clear commitment to egalitarian development.

Assessing policy since 1996

It is true that, even in 2008, the Chinese economy still differs markedly from that of the USA. The extent of state ownership of industry is much greater despite the privatizations of the last decade. And the rhetorical commitment of the CCP to socialism remains undiminished. According to Hu (2007):

> [W]e have adhered to the basic tenets of scientific socialism and in the meantime added to them distinct Chinese characteristics in light of China's conditions and the features of the times. In contemporary China, to stay true to socialism means to keep to the path of socialism with Chinese characteristics.

My own view is that much of this is little more than empty posturing. The Party is of course keen to maintain its hegemony, and mere self-preservation dictates that it should advocate 'social harmony', the creation of 'ladders for social mobility' via free education and a regional development strategy designed to appease indigenous ethnic minorities and Western observers alike. But much of this is a sham. A commitment to the genuinely progressive income taxation needed to ensure social harmony is lacking. It is unlikely that the central government will be able to finance 'free' education; tuition fees may be abolished but the likelihood is that they will be replaced by some other form of tax. As noted earlier, the abolition of the agricultural tax, a much-heralded part of the programme to build a new socialist countryside, is of little significance because it has been only a very small proportion of farm income since the early 1960s.[16] And the western China development programme, ostensibly designed to accelerate the pace of development, is in reality little more than an attempt to make full use of the region's mineral resources and to use it as a dumping ground for the polluting industries of the east.

In view of all this, it is not surprising that a number of the characteristics of Chinese neoauthoritarianism have come in for heavy criticism in the West. For Hutton (2007: 117), for example: 'The Chinese economy and Chinese Communist Party are in an unstable halfway house – an economy that is neither socialist nor properly capitalist.' Beset by social tensions, a lack of democratic pluralism, a failure to create global brands, endemic state predation and growing inefficiency of investment, China's Leninist state, he argues, is certain to collapse unless the Enlightenment institutions developed in the West are adopted.

More importantly, Chinese neoauthoritarianism has been attacked within China itself. Many intellectuals have been blind to the failings of the Chinese state, not least because most of them were making money on the Chinese stock market by exploiting insider knowledge and inadequate legal safeguards. But Chinese liberals have been much less charitable towards the regime, and have published a wide range of critical pieces directed against state corruption, malfeasance and incompetence. The best known of these critiques is He Qinglian's (1998) *Pitfalls of Modernization*, in which she documented a wide range of corrupt practices. Nevertheless, critics like He have largely accepted the desirability of a market economy, and it is in that sense that the term 'liberal' is entirely appropriate as a descriptor for these writers. Much of their criticism has focused on the impossibility of creating such an economy without a well-defined system of property rights. Moreover, very few of China's liberals have taken issue with the notion that an authoritarian state is a necessary condition for growth in the *short* term. Here He Qinglian and Yang Xiaokai are unusual in that they advocate a rapid transition to democracy; in so doing they are the true heirs to the May 4th movement of 1919. But for most, democracy is more in the nature of a long-term aspiration for the People's Republic, and in that sense their perspective is in the neoauthoritarian rather than the liberal tradition.

The late 1990s have also seen the emergence of a group of intellectuals who espoused a return to some form of socialism.[17] The best known is that group of scholars often called the New Left, which includes Cui Zhiyuan, Wang Hui and Wang Shaoguang. These scholars have advocated a more positive appraisal of the Maoist era as well as fiscal reform as a means towards strengthening the Chinese state, which most of them see as an essential condition for modernization.[18] They fear that the CCP might go the same way as its Soviet cousin unless an effective programme of state strengthening can be accomplished.[19] But there are other strands of opinion as well, including neo-Maoists (such as Li Xianyuan and Huang Jisu), and the neostatist He Xin. Li and Huang became famous in 2000 for staging the play *Che Guevara*, which praised revolution and the revolutionary vision of Mao and Che Guevara. He Xin gained notoriety for the support he offered to the Chinese state in suppressing the Democracy Movement, but he has also been a powerful critic of marketization and globalization, arguing that both have adverse implications for welfare, unemployment and living standards. A strong Chinese state is therefore functionally necessary for the realization of He Xin's social market vision (which is based on the German economic model of the 1950s).

Despite their differences, these left-leaning intellectuals have been united in their condemnation of state corruption and its implications for both urban inequality and stability in the countryside, the drift towards capitalism, and in their advocacy of greater state intervention as a solution to China's continuing search for a viable path to modernity. More precisely, the left's critique has focused on three developments since Deng Xiaoping's death: China's entry into the WTO, the mass privatization of state-owned industry and the creation and expansion of the Chinese stock market. As Lin (2006: 268) puts it:

> The reform in effect legitimized much of what socialism stood against in terms of values and practices. Workers, while losing state protection, found no space to organize themselves outside of official trade unions; and farmers remained in a situation of 'taxation without representation'. ... Thus polarization, money fetishism, greed, and corruption poisoned social cohesion. [China] ... became at the same time vulnerable to foreign dependency, private domination, rent seeking, and short term behaviours largely due to state failures.

Nevertheless, the advocates of a return to socialism within China remain handicapped by the narrowness of their vision. The main problem they face is how to deal with the Cultural Revolution, because it is easy for neoliberals to portray that as the inevitable culmination of any programme of mobilizational socialism – and by implication that any form of socialist experimentation is to be avoided. The typical response on the left is simply to avoid the issue and argue that what matters is merely to criticize the current regime (Kipnis 2003). But that does not get the left very far. It is not enough to criticize Chinese capitalism; the real challenge is to outline a viable alternative strategy. One solution to the conundrum is to outline a leftist vision which rejects the Cultural Revolution because of its violence and anarchic quality. Some on the left have taken this approach, advocating in effect a return to Leninism. A more interesting approach – which recognizes that Leninism is a *cul-de-sac* – is that taken by Cui Zhiyuan. He has interpreted the Cultural Revolution as a form of mass democracy, and hence a check on the development of interest groups within the Party; Mao's notion that 'it is right to rebel' thus has much to recommend it in Cui's view. As significantly, Cui has argued that the Cultural Revolution was also an attempt to create workplace democracy (along the lines set out in the Anshan constitution) in which management participated in labour, and this offers a means by which traditional socialist practice can be reinvigorated. Cui's influence within China has admittedly been much circumscribed by his seventeen-year period of residence in the West.[20] Nevertheless, this type of assessment chimes with some of the writings of Western scholars, who have argued that the real failure of the Cultural Revolution was that it did not go far enough.[21] Lin (2006) has also taken a more positive view of the Cultural Revolution:

For all its faults and horrors, the Cultural Revolution in its ideological originality and historicity was as much a democratic revolt against privilege, bureaucracy, and perversions of revolution as it was a mass mobilization opportunistically used for power struggle [p. 170]. ... equally important were the egalitarian and populist drives to reduce the gaps between urban and rural lives and between cadres and ordinary people, and to curtail the rigid sectoral and gender divisions of labor [p. 164].

Lin and Cui in effect argue that, instead of using the army to suppress the Red Guards in 1968, the movement should have been encouraged.

That still leaves open the question of alternatives. Lin argues in favour of what she calls *xiaokang* socialism, which is a programme designed to meet basic meets, develop democracy and promote community – and clearly also a linear descendant of the Cultural Revolution model. For her, a Chinese alternative to traditional state socialism and globalization is eminently feasible. China enjoys the advantages of backwardness, has a tradition of pioneering alternative paths – what was Maoism if not that? – and has the advantage of being a large country and therefore better able to engage with the world economy on its own terms. It is hard to disagree with this analysis. China, almost alone amongst nation-states, can resist the influence of globalization, and it is a prosperous enough country to guarantee income security for its population. The unfolding Chinese tragedy is that its leaders have set their face against such a path.

Notes

1 Jiang represented the 'third generation' of CCP leaders, following Mao and Deng. Officially, he assumed power at the Fourth Plenum of the 13th Central Committee in June 1989 (a chronology reiterated by Hu Jintao at the 17th Congress in October 2007) but in practice his authority was limited until Deng's death.
2 Jiang's justification was framed in terms of his theory of the 'Three Represents' (first articulated in 1998 and accommodated into the 2003 Constitution). The idea here was that the Party represented advanced forces of production, advanced culture and the 'overwhelming' majority of the population. According to this last element in the trinity, the Party came to represent workers, peasants, intellectuals, cadres, soldiers – and capitalists. Where once the Party had been the vanguard of the working class, by 2003 only criminals were excluded from its ranks.
3 For a comparison of China and India, see Wu (2007).
4 A 'strong' state is needed for the implementation of a market socialist model because the state needs to be selective in its industrial policy – that is, it needs to subsidize potentially successful industries, and close down losers (those with a poor productivity record and with limited long-run potential). Advocates of this type of approach, and the closely related 'developmental state' model (Johnson 1985; Chang 2002), have long recognized this. However, the developmental statists typically miss the point that an authoritarian state is not necessary strong; the example of sub-Saharan Africa since 1980 illustrates that rather clearly. More generally, it needs to be recognized that there is no correlation between rates of economic growth and the presence of authoritarian regimes; the international evidence suggests that democracy is usually better for growth (Halperin *et al.* 2005).

5 Amongst Chinese economists, the leading advocates of the neoauthoritarian paradigm in the late 1990s were Dong Fureng, Lin Yifu, Fan Gang and Li Yining. Advocacy of neoauthoritarianism was also of course politically expedient for intellectuals in the aftermath of Tian'anmen because it did not require an attack on Party rule.
 6 For concepts and definitions of migrants, see Chan (2001) and Liang and Ma (2004). The origins of the *hukou* system are discussed in Cheng and Selden (1994). For useful discussions of post-1978 migration patterns, see Bakken (1998), Solinger (1999), West and Zhao (2000), Murphy (2002), Gaetano and Jacka (2004) and Fan (2005). Pre-1978 migration is discussed in Shapiro (2001) and Bernstein (1977).
 7 The authoritative and generally reliable decennial population censuses themselves adopted differing definitions. The 1990 census defined floaters as those living away from their place of registration for more than a year but included only persons living outside their county or city of origin. By contrast, the 2000 census used a six-month cut-off line and included both intra-county and city and inter-county and city migrants (Liang and Ma 2004).
 8 Even under Jiang Zemin, attempts were made to reduce the length of the official working week from forty-eight to forty-four hours in 1996 and to forty hours since 1998 (Lin 2006: 279)
 9 For some of the literature on regional inequality and attempts to Develop the West see Wright (2003), Goodman (2004), Lai (2002), Bao *et al.* (2002), Démurger (2002), Démurger *et al.* (2002) and Yeung and Shen (2004).
10 'Although there should be an order of priority in the economic development of various areas, that does not necessarily mean that development of one area must be postponed pending development of another. The eastern region should take the initiative and consider how to assist the central and western regions to develop' (Central Committee 1991: 501).
11 The writings of Wang Shaoguang and Hu Angang in the mid-1990s (translated in Wang and Hu 1999, 2001) were also influential in redirecting the attention of policymakers to the problems faced by western China.
12 According to their computations, prices increased much more quickly in Guizhou than in Guangdong between 1990 and 2000, such that the cost of a basket of goods fell from being 37 per cent higher in Guangdong in 1990 to being 24 per cent higher by 2000.
13 Even this assumes negligible regional price differences, and that is rather a strong assumption. Prices were set by the state, but variation in (for example) the prices paid by the state for the procurement of grain was still considerable even between provinces as close as Sichuan and Yunnan. On the other hand, the variation in the price of industrial goods in rural areas was fairly small. I know of no systematic study of the net effect of this on provincial costs of living in the early 1980s.
14 For a recent summary of this literature on the impact of aid to LDCs, see Collier (2007). He concludes that aid does have positive effects, perhaps in the order of a growth boost of 1 percentage point per annum, but this is hardly enough to remedy the problem of underdevelopment.
15 The extent of Han settlement can, however, be easily exaggerated. The official data from the 2000 census show that, if we exclude the military presence (and that does make a considerable difference), the Han population of Qinghai was 54 per cent in 2000, and the figures for Xinjiang and Tibet were lower at 41 and only 6 per cent respectively (RKTJNJ 2003: 52).
16 The programme also involves increased investment in health care, rural infrastructure and on supporting farm prices. These goals will no doubt change as the results of the second agricultural census, conducted during 2007, become available.
17 This, and the following, paragraph are heavily based on the work of Zhang (2006).

18 Almost all Chinese intellectuals are nationalists, both out of conviction and from a belief that this is a way to promote stability and hence hold the fragile Chinese state together.
19 Many of the views of the New Left were put forward in the book *China and Globalization: Washington Consensus or Beijing Consensus?* (Huang and Cui 2005). For some of their English-language writings, see Wang C. H. (2003) and Wang H. (2003).
20 For some of Cui's writings in English, see Unger and Cui (1994) and Cui (1997). Liu Kang's writings are also of great interest (Liu 1997, 2004).
21 For some of these ideas, see Dirlik *et al.* (1997).

15 The revolution betrayed?

We saw in the previous chapter that Deng's death in early 1997 led to the abandonment of the market socialist strategy as China embraced the objective of a rapid transition to capitalism. Much state-owned industry has been privatized, China has joined the World Trade Organization and many of the controls on internal labour migration have been removed as a result. By 2008, the Chinese economy was capitalist in all but name.

This change in the development strategy has led to an acceleration in the rate of economic growth. Many of China's human development indicators (such as life expectancy) stagnated between the mid-1980s and the mid-1990s, but they have also improved over the last decade. By the standards of most developing countries, therefore, China's record has been impressive. Nevertheless, these gains have been bought at a high price. Income inequality, fuelled by the privatizations of the late 1990s, is at an all-time high. Levels of public expenditure on health and education lag behind those in many parts of the developed and underdeveloped world. The last decade has seen unprecedented levels of environmental degradation. And urban poverty has increased, driven by rising unemployment. Moreover, the outlook for China is by no means good. It is certain that the growth rate will slow, and it is unlikely that China will ever catch up without fundamental changes to the polity – changes which few in the CCP or across the population in general seem willing to contemplate. It needs more than markets to achieve the goal of modernization.

The growth record

The rate of Chinese GDP growth over the last decade has been impressive. As noted in the previous chapter, a number of Western scholars have questioned the reliability of the Chinese data. Rawski (2001) rightly drew attention to the seemingly contradictory stories told by official GDP data on the one hand, and the energy data on the other. Maddison's estimates of growth are considerably lower than those made by the SSB.[1] And many are frankly sceptical about evidence showing that the Chinese economy continued to grow rapidly during the Asian crisis in 1997–8. It is therefore paradoxical that the Economic Census carried out by the SSB in 2004 (SSB 2006) has had the effect of raising the overall growth rate still further, mainly because the output value of the service sector has been revised upwards for the period since the service sector census of 1992. However, and as noted in the previous chapter, these debates are rather academic. Even the Maddison data, the most pessimistic of those cited in Table 15.1, show an annual per capita growth rate of 6.5 per cent for 1996–2003, which is an impressive rate by almost any standard. If we judge Chinese performance purely on this basis, it is hard to be anything other than very positive, especially as the remarkable rates of advance have now been sustained for more than twenty-five years.

We know that these rates of growth are impressive by Chinese standards. In some ways, in fact, the most remarkable thing about China's experience since the mid-1990s is that the growth rate of GDP has actually accelerated. In a sense this goes far towards providing proof of Marx's fundamental maxim: capitalism may be brutal but it certainly does deliver in terms of economic growth. In the words of the *Communist Manifesto*: 'The bourgeoisie, during its rule of scarce one hundred years, has created more massive and more colossal productive forces than have all preceding generations together. ... what earlier century had even a presentiment that such productive forces slumbered in the lap of social labour' (Marx and Engels 1848: 40–1). More than anything, it is China's accelerating growth that provides the justification for the policies pursued by the CCP since 1996.

For all that, we do well to remember that China's growth rates are hardly unprecedented for a country at its level of development. In Table 15.2, I compare the People's Republic with both Brazil and Indonesia. Per capita GDP stood at about $2,500 in Brazil in 1964, the year in which the military seized power, and the Brazilian miracle came to a halt in 1980 following the second world oil price shock. China achieved Brazil's 1964 level of GDP per head in 1994. In Indonesia's case, the per capita GDP level of $2,500 was achieved in 1990, and it makes sense to see its era of miraculous growth as terminating in 1997, the year of the Asian crisis, swiftly followed by the demise of Suharto.[2]

Given that the starting-point is very much the same in terms of per capita GDP, and given also that Brazil and Indonesia are both 'large' countries by

Table 15.1 Growth of Chinese GDP since 1996 (per cent per annum)

		Prices	GDP	GDP per capita
Maddison	1996–2003	1990	7.4	6.5
SSB	1996–2003	1980 & 1990	8.5	7.6
	1996–2007	1980 & 1990	9.3	8.5

Sources: Maddison (2006b); ZGTJNJ (2007: 59 and 60); SSB (2008).

Note
The SSB data are at comparable prices, i.e. a linked series of data at 1980 and 1990 prices. The translation in ZGTJNJ (2007: 60) suggests constant prices, but the Chinese makes it clear that these are comparable (*kebi jiage*) rather than constant price (*bubian jiage*) data.

Table 15.2 GDP growth rates during economic miracles in large countries

	Year in which per capita GDP of $2500 attained	Subsequent growth rate of GDP (per cent per annum)
Brazil	1964	8.2 (1964–80)
Indonesia	1990	7.6 (1990–7)
China	1994	6.7 (1994–2003)

Source: Maddison (2006b)

Note
Data are at 1990 prices and at purchasing power parity.

world standards, these comparisons are by no means unfair. Of course we cannot normalize for the international environment, but there is no especial bias in that regard. It is therefore particularly interesting that China did no better than either Indonesia or Brazil in terms of real GDP growth. If anything, China's growth rate was slower than in the other two countries. The clear conclusion from this is that there has been a continuing economic miracle since 1996, but China is by no means unique in achieving and sustaining GDP growth of 7 per cent or more.[3]

Environmental damage

The positive effects on welfare resulting from GDP growth in China have been partially offset by the negative effects on welfare which have resulted from the increase in environmental damage that has occurred since 1978.[4] Environmental degradation has been extensive; it is attested to by both the official data, and by the reports carried out by international organizations. The more difficult issue is to assess its significance and what it implies for any assessment of China's overall development record.

The extent of environmental degradation

Emblematic of China's environmental problem is the level of air pollution in many of its cities. The nationally stipulated safe level for particulate matter (PM_{10}) is 100 micrograms per cubic metre.[5] However, many of China's bigger cities routinely suffered from levels of over 200 in the late 1990s (World Bank 2001d: 80–1). Over 100 is commonplace even now. Beijing recorded 141 micrograms in 2005 and Lanzhou, one of the centres of China's chemical industry, recorded 158 (SEPA 2006b: 48). In 2006, the figures were higher: 162 micrograms for Beijing and 192 for Lanzhou (ZGTJNJ 2006: 418). The extent of pollution is higher still in many of China's smaller cities; in fact, Kaifeng's 2004–5 figure was almost 200, the figure exceeded 220 in Linfen and it was over 250 in Panzhihua (World Bank 2007c: xviii). Moreover, although in the larger cities there is some evidence of improvement, this is less so for the smaller cities. Panzhihua provides a clear example of deterioration over the last few years (Figure 15.1).

500 Chinese Economic Development

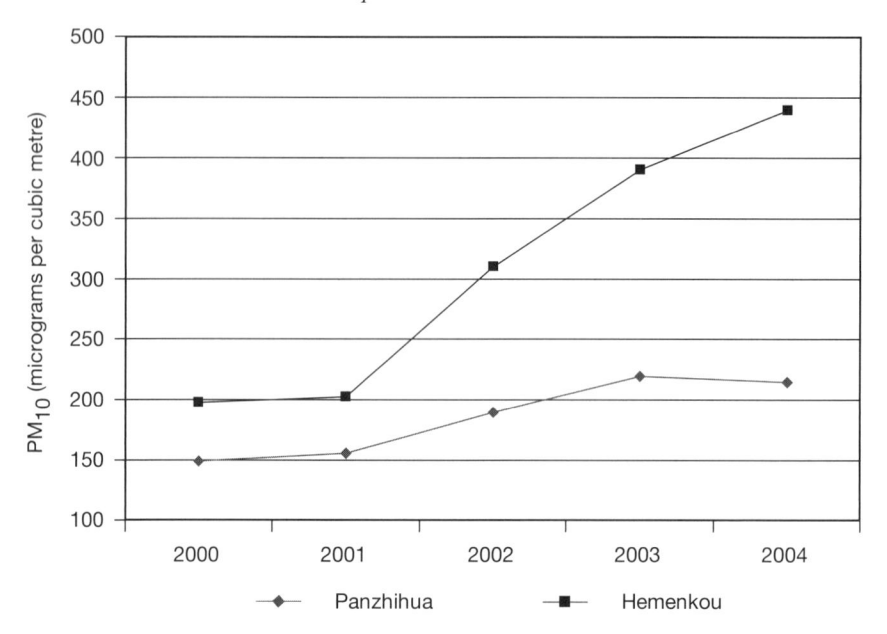

Figure 15.1 Particulate matter concentrations in Panzhihua (Source: Panzhihua City (2005: 62).)

Note: The Panzhihua figure is the average for the whole city. Hemenkou is Panzhihua's most polluted district. For reference, the Shanghai figure for 2005 was 73 mg and that for Paris was 11 mg.

The situation is little better in terms of water quality. Trends in quality are shown in Table 15.3 for the worst polluted of China's river basins during the period since 1991. All three are to be found in northern China, and suffer from high levels of nitrogen, phosphorus, oil and mercury as a result of chemical fertilizer runoff and industrial effluent. The data show the percentage of water rated as grade V or worse, the most polluted grades of water as measured in terms of chemical oxygen demand. Water quality in the Haihe has significantly deteriorated over the period. By contrast, quality in the Liaohe and Yellow river basins has modestly improved, but it remains very low. Part of the problem is overextraction of water for industrial and agricultural purposes. One result of this was that the Yellow river dried up before reaching the sea for 140 days per year on average between 1994 and 1997, compared with only 13 days per year between 1972 and 1976 (Guo 2001: 23).

Poor water quality is not confined to these basins. Quality is generally better in south China, but pollution is in evidence in every river basin. The same is true of China's freshwater lakes; Taihu and Dianchi lakes are both worse than grade V. As for coastal waters, red tides are far from unusual in Bohai (Guo 2001: 39). Even Chinese beauty spots are far from immune from the scourge of pollution; the famous West Lake at Hangzhou is characterized by water of worse than grade V (SEPA 2005: 20–5).

Table 15.3 Water quality in china's most polluted river basins (per cent of river system with water of grade V or worse)

	Haihe	Liaohe	Yellow
1991	40	80	50
1992	48	80	78
1993	47	63	42
1994	45	71	33
1995	65	78	33
1996	57	64	42
1997	48	80	25
1998	62	56	67
1999	50	69	63
2000	68	69	63
2001	75	72	63
2002	79	69	57
2003	66	54	48
2004	57	81	39
2005	56	50	35
Averages			
1991–4	45	74	51
2002–5	65	64	45

Sources: Guo (2001: 12); SEPA (1999; 2000; 2001; 2002; 2003; 2004; 2005; 2006b).

In addition to these general trends, there are many examples of what are best described as environmental disasters in China over the last two decades. The Huai river basin has suffered from massive pollution, much of it caused by effluent from TVEs. For example, the fact that Fuyang had been designated a 'Clean Industry City' did not stop the water running through it from turning black, or many of its citizens being poisoned (Economy 2004: 6–7; Guo 2001). A leak of benzene into the Songhua river in November 2005 cause a major health scare. Linfen (Shanxi province) is one of the most polluted cities on the planet, and had the worst air quality of any city in China according to SEPA reports in 2007; the main reason was coal dust. Much of the Han river turned red in February 2008 because of chemical pollution, and drinking water was badly affected. A massive blue algae plume on Lake Tai caused by sewage and chemical pollutants affected drinking water for millions in the summer of 2007. It is a telling commentary on environmental regulation that this plume has been a regular unchecked event for some years; only the scale of the problem was bigger in 2007. The rapid growth of tourism has led to massive degradation and overcrowding at beauty spots. Yangshuo, the former backpacker haven in Guangxi province, attracted 30,000 tourists in 1986 but that number had grown to 600,000 in 2006 (80 per cent of them were Chinese), causing a sharp reduction in water levels in the Li river. Arsenic in drinking water continues to affect 400,000 people in the Wuyuan area of Inner Mongolia.

These examples highlight the seriousness of the problem even in 2008. Moreover, there is little real evidence that environmental damage is decreasing. As we have seen, water pollution levels in the rivers have at best declined marginally, and, whilst air pollution may be on the wane in the bigger cities, much of that decline has been bought by cities like Beijing and Shanghai 'exporting' their industries to smaller cities in western China. Moreover, China failed to meet ten of the thirteen environmental targets set out in the Tenth Five Year Plan (2000–5). Its biggest failure was in terms of industrial sulphur dioxide emissions, which increased significantly (World Bank 2007c: 1). It is no wonder, then, that both the Eleventh Five Year Plan and Hu's (2007) speech to the 17th Party Congress in October 2007 gave such emphasis to the need to protect and improve the environment. Moreover, Wen Jiabao's (2007) report delivered to the 10th National People's Congress in March 2007 acknowledged some of the failures in 2006:

> However, we fell short of the targets set at the beginning of last year for cutting energy consumption per unit of GDP by about 4% and total discharge of major pollutants by 2%. The main reasons were: Industrial restructuring proceeded slowly, while growth in heavy industry, especially in sectors that are high in energy consumption or are highly polluting, was still overheated. Many backward production facilities that should have been closed down are still in operation. Finally, some local governments and enterprises failed to strictly comply with laws, regulations and standards for energy saving and environmental protection.

It is not surprising that Wen and others have become relatively open about these problems. Environmental damage is hard to hide, and protest against construction work at a local level is now commonplace, much of it covered by the Chinese media. It is an issue that even the CCP cannot ignore, and it has not chosen to do so. For example, four cities were punished (by central government restrictions on spending and urban construction) for flouting environmental regulations: the four were Tangshan in Hebei province, Luliang in Shanxi province, Liupanshui in Guizhou province and Laiwu in Shandong province (*Guardian* 11 January 2007).

Environmental assessment

One way of assessing the direct economic impact of the degradation outlined in the previous section is to classify environmental damage as depreciation. If we then estimate the rate of growth of NDP per person, and include environmental damage within depreciation, there is no doubt that China's per capita NDP growth rate would be below the rate of growth of GDP.

However, what matters in terms of assessing China's record is how it compares with other countries. World Bank (2007d: 180–2) estimates put the damage done by forest depletion, carbon dioxide and particulate matter emissions at 2.8 per cent of Chinese GNI in 2005; the average for low-income countries was 2.4 per cent and it was 1.7 per cent for middle-income countries. These figures do not show China in a terribly favourable light, but the comparisons are problematic; the notion that there was no net forest depletion in Brazil and Indonesia, as the

World Bank estimates suggest, appears unlikely; on this at least, China has quite a good record. It is therefore probably fair to say that the differences between China and other developing countries are more quantitative than qualitative.

More interesting is the two-way comparison between China and India in terms of a number of key indicators. The World Bank estimate of damage in India is 2.6 per cent, little different from China's figure of 2.8 per cent. However, China certainly has something to learn from its Asian rival. In 2004, India used energy more efficiently in absolute terms, producing purchasing power parity GDP to the value of $US5.5 per kilogram of oil used compared with only $US4.4 in China. At least the rate of improvement was much more rapid between 1990 and 2004 in China than it was in India; in China's case, GDP per kilogram more than doubled, whereas in India's case the increase was only around 38 per cent (World Bank 2007a). In some ways, however, this is hardly surprising given that China started from such a low base and is still behind India.

When it comes to the most heavily polluted cities in the world, China is no better, and probably somewhat worse, than India.[6] The Blacksmith Institute put two of China's cities (Linfen and Tianying) in its list of ten most polluted cities, alongside two from India (Sukind and Vapi) in 2007. The World Bank has variously reported that sixteen of the twenty most polluted cities in the world are in China, and twenty of the thirty most polluted. More precisely, the emission of particulate matter exceeded 100 micrograms per cubic metre in Delhi (150), Kolkata (128) Kanpur and Lucknow (both 109), which was on a par with China's most polluted big cities; the 2004 figures for Chongqing, Tianjin and Shenyang were 123, 125 and 101 micrograms respectively (World Bank 2007a). However, as previously noted, these figures for China's biggest cities disguise the extent of particulate matter concentrations in some of the smaller cities such as Linfen (over 200 micrograms) and Panzhihua (250) in 2005 (World Bank 2007c: xviii). Moreover, China does even worse in terms of sulphur and nitrogen dioxide. The figures of 340 and 424 micrograms of sulphur dioxide recorded in Chongqing and Guiyang are far above anything recorded in India (the highest figure there was only 49 micrograms in Calcutta), or anywhere else in the world for that matter; Tehran's 209 micrograms is the closest, barely half the worst Chinese levels. We therefore must conclude that, in international terms, China has a very bad environmental record. Per capita GDP may be higher in China than in India, but it is not obvious that this compensates for China's dismal environmental record.

However, when it comes to historical comparisons, the marginal environmental damage which resulted from a one-*yuan* increase in GDP was almost certainly less after 1978 than it was during the Maoist era. It is difficult to make this type of comparison with any precision, but we can proxy environmental damage by looking at energy used per unit of GDP. In 2004, China produced GDP to the value of $4.4 per kilogram of oil used, compared with only $1.1 per kg in 1978, a remarkable rate of improvement (World Bank 2007a). By this comparison, Maoist China comes off badly; the growth generated by the post-1978 regime had been much more environmentally efficient. Moreover, China's levels of air pollution are far from unusual by world historical standards. Britain, for example, experienced very high levels of coal-related smog before the Clean Air Acts of the 1950s. More generally, the picture is as follows (Rawski 2006: 4):

> [M]any Chinese cities experience levels of air pollution that far exceed today's norms for the advanced economies of East Asia. When compared with historic pollution levels during earlier periods of peak industrialization in Japan, Korea, and the United States, however, these Chinese figures appear routine rather than exceptional.

In other words, the sheer pace of growth made environmental damage inevitable. China's growth was increasingly 'efficient' in environmental terms, but it is the fact that there has been so much of it that is at the heart of China's environmental problem. There is a clear trade-off between growth and environmental protection in poor countries, and China has had to pay the price mandated by rapid growth.

Furthermore, in assessing China's post-1978 environmental record, we also need to recognize that its environmental potential – its ability to achieve growth at low environmental cost – was comparatively limited. There were positive legacies aplenty from the Maoist era, but few of these were in the environmental sphere. To be sure, China had a relatively well-developed railway network, and some of the Maoist experiments with biogas digesters (which used plant products instead of coal to generate methane and hence heat) were fairly successful, even if they did not live up to the claims made by some of their supporters. However, Maoist attempts to promote the use of renewable forms of energy – whether wave, wind or hydro – were virtually non-existent. Nor did Deng's regime inherit an extensive civilian nuclear programme. And the use of natural gas as a source of domestic heating was limited. Perhaps even more importantly, China was constrained by its natural resource endowment in satisfying its energy needs in an environmentally-friendly way. The People's Republic has comparatively little oil; the big finds at Daqing (Heilongjiang) and Shengli (Shandong) had been largely exploited by the 1980s, and the programmes of oil exploration off the Chinese coast and in the western provinces were both expensive and not very successful. As a result, China has been forced to rely on coal, much of which has been of quite low quality (it has a high sulphur content). As result, both acid rain (especially in the south-western provinces) and deaths from indoor air pollution have been significant problems. In short, many of China's post-1978 environmental problems both reflected rapid GDP growth (and were therefore a necessary price to pay) and were in some respects unavoidable given China's natural geography and its inheritance.

We also need to put the health costs of environmental degradation into perspective. The World Bank's (1997d: 19–21) estimates put deaths from urban air pollution at 178,000 and those from indoor air pollution at 111,000 in the early 1990s, with rather fewer deaths from water pollution. According to newspaper reports, its estimate for 2003 (but deleted from its 2007c report because of pressure from the Chinese government) came up with 400,000 deaths from urban air pollution, 300,000 from indoor air pollution and a further 60,000 from low water quality, though this latter did not include deaths from stomach and liver cancers caused by polluted water.[7] The WHO's health profile for China in 2007 came up with not-dissimilar figures – 96,000 deaths from contaminated water (diarrhoea-related deaths only), 381,000 deaths from indoor air pollution and a further 276,000 deaths from outdoor urban air pollution. However, we should note that there were around 1 million deaths a year as a result of smoking in the early 1990s (World Bank 1997d: 19) and over 8 million deaths in total from all causes. In other words, the headline mortality figures because of environmental damage are very high but less striking when we allow for the size of China's population. We should not, therefore, exaggerate the impact of environmental degradation on human health.

For all that, there have been real policy failures in the thirty years since Mao's death, and these have meant that the extent of environmental degradation has been much greater per unit of GDP than it ought to have been. China's environment was bound to deteriorate as a result of the growth of TVEs and continued urban industrial growth. To take the most obvious example: it is hard to justify China's large-scale dam-building projects (McCormack 2001). Not only will they generate very little energy because of the build-up of silt – the problems already associated with the Three Gorges dam have afflicted almost every major dam-building project going back to the Sanmenxia in the 1950s – but they are also causing extensive damage.[8] For example, the construction of a series of dams on the rivers of Yunnan threatens China's relations with other countries. Dam-building on the Lancang (upper Mekong) poses a particular threat to the ecology of the Mekong delta in Vietnam. Some of these dam projects have now been cancelled; the abandonment of the Tiger Leaping Gorge project in 2007 is one example. But much of the damage has already been done.

Other policy failures are less well known. One such is the slow pace at which the Chinese state has promoted the take-up of LPG and natural gas as a means of providing domestic heating. Widespread now in many parts of eastern China, its earlier promotion would have greatly reduced the number of deaths from indoor air pollution. The process would also have accelerated had the government put more effort into developing natural gas production in Xinjiang and Inner Mongolia/Shaanxi at an earlier stage. A second notable failure was the low status the CCP accorded to environmental protection within government. Only in 1988 was the National Environmental Protection Bureau removed from the control of the Ministry of Construction (which routinely expropriated its staff and funds in the 1980s) and placed under the State Council; even then, it acquired ministry status as SEPA only in 1998 (World Bank 2001d: 101). Third, China's decision to abandon attempts to calculate green GDP reflects the very simple fact that they show just how much environmental damage has been done.[9]

In long-run perspective, the greatest mistake over the last few years is the failure to do much to stem the growth of car ownership and traffic pollution. Leaded petrol was banned in July 2000, and China has brought in vehicle emission standards, but there has been no serious attempt to promote alternative forms of urban public transport. Removing cycle lanes in favour of car lanes is as foolish an environmental policy as anyone could imagine; it is hardly offset by attempts to create eco-cities, such as the one mooted for Chongming island in the Yangzi estuary (which will assuredly provide homes only for the very rich). Of course – and not unreasonably – one can point to the fiscal constraints within which the Chinese state is forced to operate and which prevent it from doing more. But the force of this sort of argument is signally weakened by China's hosting of the Olympics in 2008. By any welfare or economic criteria, this type of nationalist project is little short of lunacy. Moreover, China's crass handling of both the security for and the route of the Olympic flame has done it few favours on the international stage; parading the flame through its colony of Tibet was Chinese nationalism at its worst.

Human development

As was the case during the era of market socialism, China's record on human development after 1996 was less impressive than its growth record. Nevertheless, the record was hardly poor.[10]

Admittedly the crude death rate barely changed at all, hovering at around the 6.5 per 1,000 mark over the decade. However, this reflects the growing proportion of old people in the population, which necessarily increases the crude death rate even though age-specific rates have declined. Life expectancy provides a much better indication of mortality, and this measure shows an increase from 68.6 years at birth at the time of the 1990 population census to 71.4 years at the census of 2000. Every one of China's provincial-level units recorded an increase over that decade, and by 2000 no less than twenty-three of the thirty-one administrative units recorded average life expectancy of over seventy years, a remarkable achievement for a country which was still comparatively poor in income terms (ZGTJNJ 2006: 103). Moreover, despite a number of well-publicized cases of contaminated blood being used in hospitals (notably in Henan province), there is no evidence from the (generally reliable) population census data that HIV/AIDS has had an impact remotely comparable to its effects in sub-Saharan Africa.[11]

The trend in mortality is shown in Figure 15.2. It shows that, after the apparent increases of the early 1980s, average life expectancy at birth stagnated between 1987 and 1995 at around sixty-nine years (see Chapter 13). Since the mid-1990s, however, the trend has been upwards. The steep section of the curve after the mid-1990s contrasts sharply with its relatively flat aspect between the mid-1980s and the mid-1990s. As a result, life expectancy by 2005 stood at seventy-two years, three years higher than it had been in the middle of the 1990s.[12]

As for education, the 1993 Educational Reform and Development Programme committed the government to eliminating illiteracy amongst teenagers and guaranteeing nine years of education by 2000. And the trend in educational attainment has been steadily upward since 1990. As Table 15.4 shows, the proportion of the population achieving an upper middle school or university education has climbed steadily. The latter category, for example, shows a rise from 1.4 to 6.2 per cent, and the former an increase from 8 to 13 per cent by 2006. These trends reflect steady increases in enrolment rates. By 2006, 76 per cent of those graduating

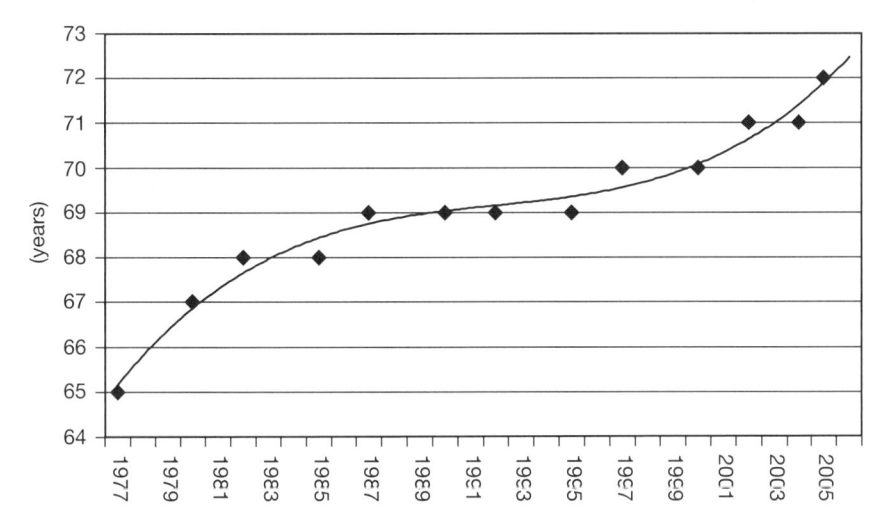

Figure 15.2 Average life expectancy at birth, 1977–2005 (Source: World Bank (2007a).)

Table 15.4 Educational attainment in China (percentage of population aged 6 and over by level of education)

	University	Upper middle school
1990	1	8
1995	2	8
1996	2	9
1997	3	10
1998	3	10
1999	3	10
2000	4	11
2001	4	12
2002	4	12
2003	5	13
2004	5	13
2005	6	12
2006	6	13

Sources: RKTJNJ (2005: 321); ZGTJNJ (2006: 112–13); ZGTJNJ (2007: 118–19).

Note
The residual – the sum of the percentages in each category subtracted from 100 – is the percentage of those aged 6 and over without any schooling. It is not a useful category because few of those aged between 6 and 15 (the years of compulsory education) have been able to complete their education. Published data on Chinese illiteracy are much more useful because they are for population aged 15 and over, but there the rate is calculated using total population as the denominator – which helps the government to understate the true rate of illiteracy. The numbers in this table are themselves derived from an annual 1 per cent sample survey (except for the Census years of 1990 and 2000).

from junior middle school went on to senior middle school, well up on the 50 per cent figure recorded at the end of 1996. Over the same period, the proportion of those going on from primary to junior middle school (though not necessarily completing) apparently rose from 93 to 100 per cent (ZGTJNJ 2007: 799). And education was certainly a route to economic advancement. Of the 215 million people employed in corporations at the end of 2004, 24 per cent were graduates and 34 per cent had a senior middle school education.[13] These ratios are far above the average levels of attainment for the whole population given in Table 15.4.

However, the expansion of education has not been without its problems. For one thing, and because of the rapid increase in the enrolment and graduation of university students, China has increasingly faced considerable difficulties in finding appropriate jobs for its new graduates; in that sense, the Chinese experience has converged on that of India after the divergence of the Maoist era. Whether it makes sense for China to be paying so much attention to its university sector when around 30 per cent of children do not go on to senior middle school is another matter; as Drèze and Sen (2002) point out, China's relative neglect of higher education before 1978 was one of the strengths of the late Maoist model.

Moreover, the targets set out in the 1993 Programme in respect of literacy have not been met. The position was still poor in 2000. The overall illiteracy rate was nearly 9 per cent (14 per cent in rural areas) at the time of the 2000 census, and although many were illiterate elderly people, educational completion rates remained unimpressive in poor areas; some 15 per cent of counties had failed to hit the target even by 2002 (UNDP 2005: 47). After 2000, however, the position actually seems to have deteriorated. The total number of illiterates aged over fifteen rose from 85 million in 2000 (RKTJNJ 2001: 50) to 144 million in 2005 (RKTJNJ 2006: 120). As a result, the overall illiteracy rate was 11 per cent in 2005 (15 per cent in rural areas), significantly up on the 2000 figure of 8.7 per cent. This trend may exaggerate the deterioration because the methodology is not the same in the two surveys; the 2000 data come from a complete census, whereas the 2005 figure is an estimate based on a survey of 1 per cent of the population. Moreover, the increase in the size of China's total population explains part of the rise in total illiteracy.

Nevertheless, there is widespread agreement in policy circles that the illiteracy rate has risen significantly since 2000. In order to address these problems, Wen Jiabao committed the Chinese government in early 2005 to abolishing tuition fees for children going to public schools in rural areas. The policy was reaffirmed in late 2006, when it was announced that fee reductions would be in operation from the spring of 2007 (though it remains to be seen whether the central government proves able to finance such a programme).

In short, although China's record on human development since 1996 is anything but bad, there is considerable evidence that progress has been fitful over the last decade. Life expectancy has improved; so too many aspects of educational attainment. And we do well to remember that China remains well ahead of India, which offers the most relevant comparator. Table 15.5 shows the comparative data for 2004. On every one of these indicators, China is ahead of India, and by some

Table 15.5 Human development levels in China and India, 2004

	China	India
Infant mortality rate (per 1,000)	26.0	62.0
Life expectancy (years at birth)	71.6	63.6
Literacy rate (per cent)	90.9	61.0
Combined gross enrolment rate for primary, secondary and tertiary education (per cent)	70.0	62.0

Source: UNDP (2006).

distance. Despite India's rapid economic growth over the last ten years, China's lead remains considerable.

For all that, there is a real sense that progress on human development has at best been very slow over the last decade. The contrast between the rapid expansion of university education and rising illiteracy rates is especially striking. A country which has generated such rapid economic growth ought to be doing better than this.

Absolute poverty

China's record on poverty reduction is more difficult to fathom, but in the main the record seems to have been better in rural than in urban areas since 1996. Let us consider the two sectors in turn.[14]

Rural poverty

Average income trends in China's poorest provinces seem to point towards an optimistic conclusion about the long-run trajectory of rural poverty. Even in desperately poor Guizhou province, the index of per capita rural income shows a rise of about 42 per cent between 1996 and 2004 (SSB 2005: 907). Chinese statistical data are of course problematic, but it is hard to believe on the basis of this type of data that per capita incomes did not rise significantly in the province. The same seems true of all of China's poorest provinces. If we look at the change in average real per capita income in the six poor provinces of Guizhou, Yunnan, Gansu, Ningxia, Sichuan and Shaanxi, the lowest increase recorded was 42 per cent (Guizhou and Yunnan) and highest was no less than 77 per cent (Sichuan) (SSB 2005).

This optimism is supported by the macrodata on rural poverty. As Table 15.6 shows, the official data show a continuing downward trend in the level of absolute poverty in the countryside. By 2005, the rural total was down to only 24 million (or about 2.5 per cent of the rural population). To be sure, not too much store should be set by the numbers involved because they are very sensitive to the poverty line which is used. We can, for example, contrast official estimates with those made by Ravallion and Chen (2007), which use a more generous definition of what subsistence requires and thereby arrives at a rural poverty rate of over 12 per cent even in 2001. The more important issue is the trend after 1995, and here the evidence

Table 15.6 Official estimates of rural poverty

	Poverty line (yuan)	Poverty rate (per cent of rural population)	Number living in absolute poverty (million)
1995	530	7.1	65
1996	n/a	n/a	n/a
1997	640	5.4	50
1998	635	4.6	42
1999	625	3.7	34
2000	625	3.4	32
2001	630	3.2	29
2002	627	3.0	28
2003	637	3.1	29
2004	668	2.8	26
2005	683	2.5	24

Source: SSB (2006b: 45).

points to a downward trajectory. It is very clear in the official data; the poverty rate falls from 7 per cent in 1995 to 2.5 per cent by 2005. The estimates made by Ravallion and Chen (2007: 10) are a little more opaque; overall poverty rose in 2000. Nevertheless, the overall trend was still downwards, with the rate declining from nearly 15 per cent in 1995 to 8 per cent by 2001. Using the World Bank's $1 per day line, the rate declines from about 20 per cent in the mid-1990s to 16 per cent by 2001 and 10 per cent by 2004 (Chaudhuri and Ravallion 2006: 2).

Nevertheless, China's record on rural poverty needs to be hedged around with qualifications. For one thing, there is strong evidence suggesting that poverty rose in the late 1990s, before falling again in the new millennium (Khan and Riskin 2001; Riskin *et al.* 2001). If we look at trends in the numbers living below the poverty line in some of China's provinces (Figure 15.3), it is evident that not one of these provinces records a monotonic decline in poverty. In all of them, there is a rise in one year or another. And, surprisingly, there was a very substantial rise in poverty in Hunan province over the whole period, even though it is not especially disadvantaged by its geography; indeed Hunan is adjacent to fast-growing Guangdong province, the destination for many of its migrant workers, and one expect some sort of trickle-down to affect Hunan more than most provinces. On the face of it, this evidence suggests that Hunan has suffered backwash, rather than spread, effects – perhaps because of a loss of skilled labour.

However, some caution is in order here before we accept the notion of *increasing* rural poverty after 1996. For one thing, the data in Figure 15.3 do show a trend decline except in the case of Hunan. For another, Khan (2004) and others are more optimistic. On the basis of survey data collected by the Chinese Academy of Social Sciences in 1995 and 2002 for nineteen provinces (the urban part of the survey included urban migrants), absolute rural poverty declined in all except Yunnan and Zhejiang (where the initial level of poverty in 1995 was in any case very low). This owed much to a decline in rural inequality (Khan and Riskin 2005). These

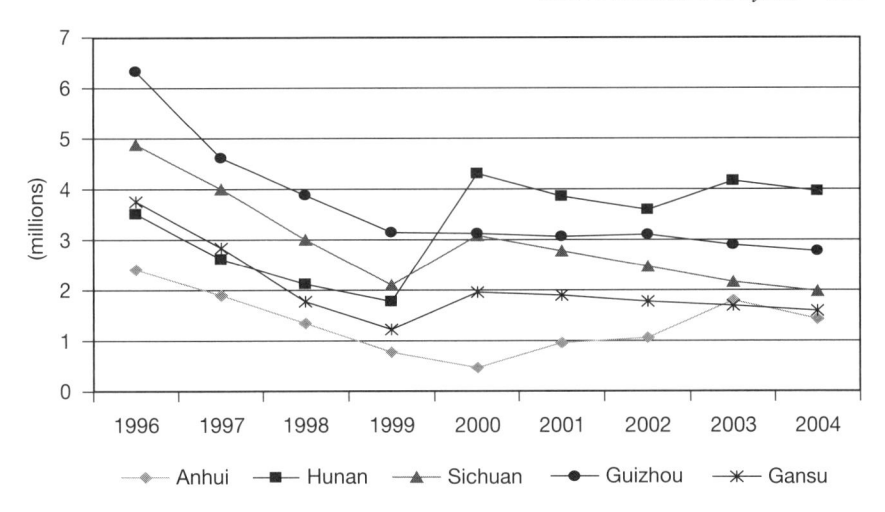

Figure 15.3 Numbers living below the rural poverty line in five provinces, 1996–2004 (Source: SSB (2005).)

Note: The source used here does not give poverty data on all provinces, but the sample is probably indicative of the broad pattern across China.

results also show a very different trend for Hunan, for example, from the SSB data in Figure 15.3. The general conclusion seems to be that Chinese poverty trends are very sensitive to the survey data used, and the way in which the poverty threshold is calculated (see for example Reddy and Miniou 2006).[15] Given these uncertainties, the right conclusion is almost certainly that the pace of reduction was quite slow after 1996, but that there is little proof of any real increase, and certainly not over the entire 1996–2007 period.

Why, then, was the rate of rural poverty decline comparatively slow after 1996? There appear to be four reasons: slower overall growth; a pattern of growth which focused around industrialization and therefore mainly benefited the non-poor; the failure of agricultural output increases to translate into higher rural incomes; and policy failures, in particular an excessive attention to the geographical dimension of poverty.

As far as the first of these four is concerned, there is no doubt that there was a slowdown in Chinese growth in the mid- and late 1990s as a result of the deliberate programme of macroeconomic contraction engineered by Zhu Rongji to reduce inflation. It may therefore be that China needs to achieve a growth rate of over 10 per cent per annum if effective 'trickle-down' is to take place, and to target a growth rate of that sort of magnitude runs the risk that inflation will be ignited. But the clear implication is rather positive: this analysis suggests that the very fast growth achieved in China over the last few years will trickle down in the form of poverty reduction, and that the extent of the decline will be more significant if the high rate of recent growth can be sustained.

A second reason for the modest decline in rural poverty after 1996 is that

Chinese growth is no longer as pro-poor as it was. In the 1980s, GDP growth was driven by the growth of agriculture and the TVE sector, which directly impacted on many farm households. Between 1996 and 2005, however, real agricultural output grew by only 37 per cent, whereas industrial output rose by 142 per cent (ZGTJNJ 2006: 60).

The third – and perhaps the most important – problem for the rural sector is that increases in farm output did not lead to increases in real income in the late 1990s. This is of great significance, because many of China's rural poor are farmers; accordingly, increases in farm income are a *sine qua non* for big falls in rural poverty. However, as Figure 15.4 shows, per capita net farm income rose very slowly over the decade after 1996. Indeed it fell from 976 *yuan* in 1997 to only 834 *yuan* in 2000 and, though it has revived since, its average annual growth rate between 1996 and 2005 was less than 1 per cent a year. By contrast, wage income from employment (mainly in TVEs of one sort or another) increased by nearly 11 per cent per annum and in the process overtook farming as an income source.

This slow growth of farm income reflected not so much any failure of production but rather price trends. Between 1995 and 2000, the prices paid for agricultural products fell by over 20 per cent on average, whereas input prices fell by less than 5 per cent, thus imposing a squeeze on net farm incomes that was only partially offset by rise in productivity. The fall in product prices occurred because of overproduction. Grain output reached no less than 512 million tonnes at its peak in 1998 (well up on the figure of 408 million in 1989), but this served only to depress product prices, in turn leading to a decline in grain output to a trough of 431 million tonnes in 2003 (ZGTJNJ 2006: 480). These trends serve to demonstrate rather clearly that unless some fundamental change in the income elasticity of demand for farm products occurs, drastic action will be needed

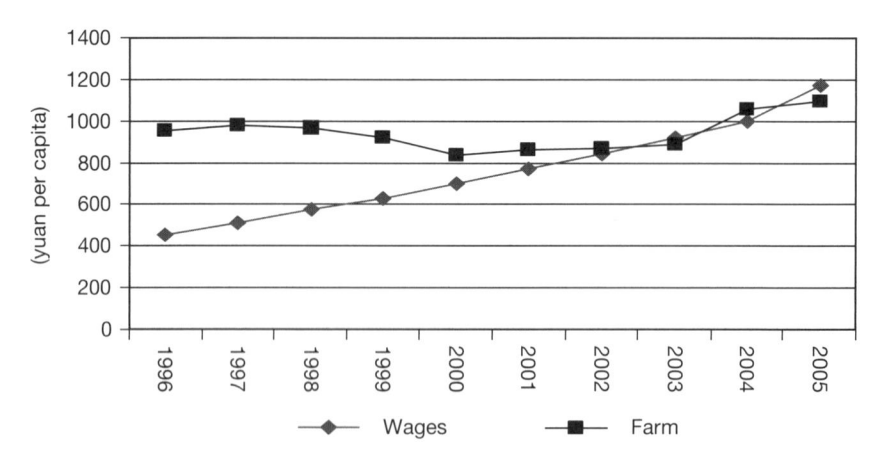

Figure 15.4 The growth of farm and rural income, 1996–2005 (Source: SSB (2006c: 29–32).)

Note: Incomes are in current prices. Farm income here refers to that part of income derived from the family 'business' net of costs of production; it excludes wages earned in farming.

to deal with the problem of low incomes in the farm sector, whether it be a transformation of farm productivity, large subsidies to producers or simply the transfer of the bulk of the farm population into the non-farm sector. The challenge confronting the Chinese state in this respect is almost as great as any it has faced since 1978.[16]

The fourth reason for China's limited success in reducing rural poverty was policy failure. Growth by itself is not enough to solve the rural poverty problem; a more targeted approach is needed. However, Chinese policymakers continue to see rural poverty as geographical in origin; that is, economic geography is hostile to development in many parts of China. Thus the centrepiece of anti-poverty policy has been the provision of aid to the 592 nationally designated poor counties in 2004 (originally so designated in the National 8–7 Poverty Reduction Plan of 1994), all of which received state aid. As Figure 15.5 shows, many of these 592 counties were to be found in the south-west and the north-west, in general in geographically-disadvantaged areas.[17]

But geography was not the only factor at work in China; as Figure 15.5 shows, it is not obvious that adverse geography is the root cause of most of China's remaining rural poverty. After all, most of China's designated poor countries are

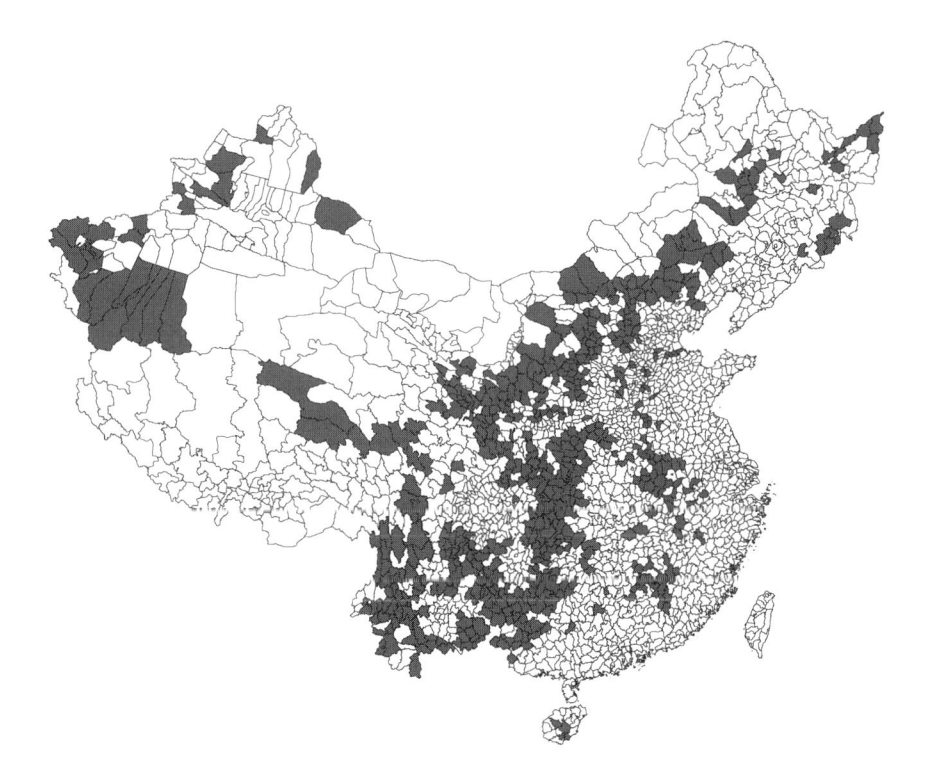

Figure 15.5 Poor counties in China.

Note: These are the counties officially designated poor in 2004.

not to be found in particularly disadvantaged areas. Note, for example, the band of counties in central China, running from southern Shaanxi to Guangxi, areas where geography is not ideal but where it poses far less of an obstacle than in western China. Conversely, many of the western counties are not designated as poor counties at all even though the geographical conditions they face are unremittingly hostile. In other words, low per capita income in many of China's counties is only weakly correlated with geography. To be sure, the counties of Shaanxi and Guangxi are less favoured than the coastal counties but it is far from obvious why geography should be a binding constraint in these counties. Policy failure seems a more likely explanation in many cases. Furthermore, some of the targeted counties are not even poor; their position on the list has as much to do with historical factors (counties which were revolutionary base areas before 1949) and political considerations (the desire to be seen to be appeasing ethnic minorities) as it has to do with absolute poverty reduction.

Second, the problem with the geographical approach is that it is very much a blunt instrument: it ignores both the presence of non-poor living in designated poor counties (who do not need subsidies), and the poor living in non-poor counties (who need, but don't receive, state aid). As has been recognized for some time (Riskin 1993b; Riskin and Li 2001; Zhang *et al.* 2003), many of those living in the designated counties are not poor, whereas many of those who are poor are living outside these designated counties. In fact, of the 26 million people with incomes below the poverty line, only 16.1 million (61 per cent) were living in one or other of the designated counties in 2004 (Nongdiao zonghui 2005). Unsurprisingly, poverty was correlated with farming and low-income status (Asian Development Bank 2004: 42). According to the SSB survey of income in 2005, 11 per cent of poor households were illiterate compared with 7 per cent of the entire rural sample. Only 22 per cent of the income of high-income households came from farming, whereas the proportion was 51 per cent for low-income households (SSB 2006c: 69, 70 and 81). This evidence points very strongly to the conclusion that the elimination of illiteracy and the expansion of the non-farm sector offers one of the best means by which to eliminate continuing absolute poverty in the Chinese countryside.

There is thus considerable force to the view that persistent rural poverty (and the re-emergence of poverty in urban areas) is a product of the transition strategy itself.

> The dominant approach to poverty reflected in government policy towards poor regions views poverty primarily as a result of the lack of reform. By contrast, the new forms of poverty which have arisen in the context of economic transition and marketization may be regarded largely as a consequence of reform processes. (UNDP/ILO 2000: 1)

It is therefore at least arguable that anti-poverty policy in China needs to be partly redirected away from geography and towards other determinants of poverty. The People's Republic has continued to make strides since 1996 towards reducing

The revolution betrayed? 515

rural poverty. However, much more than rapid growth is needed if China is to solve its rural poverty problem.

Urban poverty

As for the urban sector, there is considerable evidence pointing to a rise in poverty in the late 1990s, thus continuing the trend already apparent in the early 1990s and discussed in Chapter 13. The Ravallion–Chen (2007) estimates, for example, show the urban poverty rate rising from 0.6 per cent in 1996 to 1.2 per cent in 1998. A number of other studies point to the same conclusion (Asian Development Bank 2004). Indeed Li and Sato (2006: 132) put the level of urban poverty at no less than 5 per cent of the population, implying an urban poverty headcount of around 20 million people.[18]

The main reasons for the increase in urban poverty are the relatively capital-intensive pattern of growth, and the mass restructuring of state-owned enterprises (leading to unemployment). As Figure 15.6 suggests, the trend in official unemployment has continued to be upward, with the absolute number reaching 8.5 million in 2006. As these data refer only to those made unemployed from SOEs – thus excluding unemployment amongst the self-employed, migrants and even workers in both the collective and TVE sectors – they continue to understate the true level of unemployment.[19]

Welfare payments have mitigated the consequences of rising unemployment; some 2.5 million urban residents received subsidies in 2005, up on the figure of about 1.4 million in 2000 (UNDP 2005: 69; ZGTJNJ 2006: 904). However, the scale of benefits varies considerably; in 1998 the benefit line ranged from 319 *yuan* per month in Shenzhen to 143 *yuan* in Nanchang, with benefits typically being paid only to those with incomes of less than 1,700 *yuan*, which was

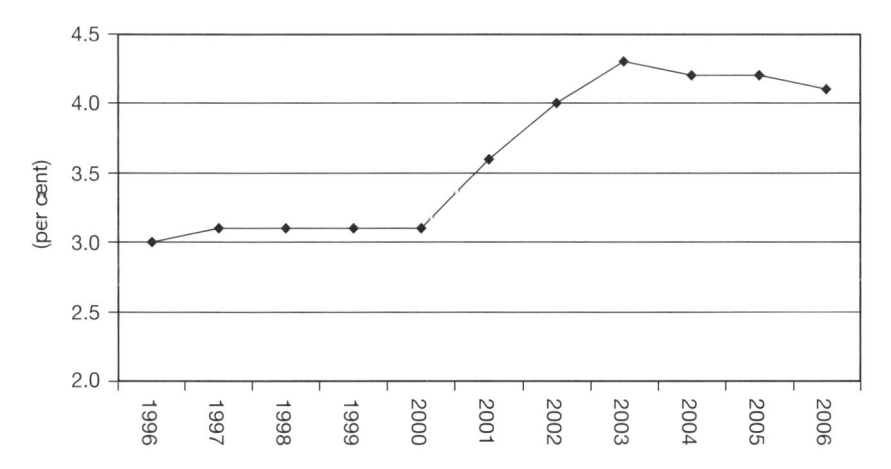

Figure 15.6 Official urban unemployment rates, 1996–2006 (percentage of the urban workforce) (Sources: ZGTJNJ (2007: 127); SSB (2005: 7).)

barely a third of average urban income in 1997 (Asian Development Bank 2004: 86). Recent research on the operation of the urban *dibao* (minimum livelihood guarantee) system suggests that it is efficient in that few of the non-poor receive benefits. However, the scheme covers a remarkably small fraction of the population: in effect, wide coverage is sacrificed for efficiency. As a result, the *dibao* served to reduce the poverty rate barely at all; its effect was to cut the rate, but only from 7.7 to 7.3 per cent of the urban population (Chen *et al.* 2006: 29). In addition, the growth of migration has exacerbated the problem of urban poverty. Migrants on average received an income that was only about 65 per cent of that of urban residents, and this owes much to the difficulties they have in finding employment; they are much more dependent upon income from small business than permanent urban residents. In addition, their access to welfare subsidies is much less than that of official urban residents (Khan and Riskin 2005: 373–5). There is also some evidence that *xiagang* and the unemployment benefit systems have been so badly designed that high replacement rates are discouraging unemployed and laid-off men from looking for work (Giles *et al.* 2006). Unless China grapples with these various issues, urban poverty will remain a significant and probably a growing problem.

In summary, the overall poverty trend across China between 1996 and 2007 appears to have been downwards, mainly because positive trends in the rural sector have probably offset rising urban poverty. As long as economic growth continues along its present trajectory, it is hard to believe that the decline in poverty will not also continue. China thus continues to provide a classic example of the way in which rapid growth serves as an antidote to absolute poverty. A greater emphasis on income redistribution might lead to even faster poverty reduction, but any recommendation along those lines must at least reckon with the possibility that redistribution might undermine the very growth that has led to such big improvements in material living standards for so many of the population. In so far as China has a distributional problem, it centres less on absolute poverty and much more on income inequality.

Inequality

Inequality continued to rise across China after 1996, just as it has during the entire post-Mao era.[20] The official data collected from income surveys show that the trend in Gini coefficient for personal income continued to be upward across the whole economy (Table 15.7). Most Western estimates confirm this trend; Wu and Perloff (2004: 32), for example, have the overall Gini coefficient rising from 0.38 in 1995 to 0.42 in 2001. Ravallion and Chen (2007: 20) suggest that inequality may have declined between 1995 and 1998, but the national Gini rose from 0.4 to 0.45 for the whole period 1996 to 2001, or from 0.35 to 0.39 if an adjustment is made for regional price differences. World Bank estimates put the 2004 Gini at 0.47 and a survey of 7,140 household by the Chinese Academy of Social Science put the Gini at no less than 0.496 in 2006 (*China Daily*, 7 January 2007).

Table 15.7 SSB and other estimates of Chinese income inequality

	Rural Gini	Urban Gini	Overall Gini
1996	0.33	0.29	0.42
1997	0.34	0.30	–
1998	0.34	0.30	0.46
1999	0.34	0.32	0.46
2000	0.35	0.33	0.46
2001	0.36	–	–
2002	0.36	–	–
2003	0.37	–	0.46
2004	0.37	–	0.47
2005	0.38	–	–
2006	0.38	0.33	–

Sources and note
The urban and rural figures are official estimates from Chang (2002: 337); SSB (2006c: 34). The 2006 urban figure is estimated from ZGTJNJ (2007: 348–9). The overall Ginis are from Yusuf and Nabeshima (2006: 9); World Bank (2007: 66).

Decomposition analysis (using Theil coefficients) shows that intersectoral inequality was the largest single contributory factor (41 per cent) to the absolute level of inequality. However, inequality within urban areas exhibited the most dramatic percentage rise between 1990 and 2002, more than doubling over those twelve years (Gill and Kharas 2007: 278).

To be sure, income inequality is an area in which the data, and therefore trends, are very uncertain: the SSB surveys undersample illiterates and the very rich and ignore temporary migrants, as well as understating income from property and subsidies (Bramall 2001). Correcting for these sorts of problems can lead to very different results. Work by Khan and Riskin (2005: 382), for example, has incorporated temporary migrants into the analysis and has measured income from housing more accurately. It shows that the overall Gini coefficient for income (0.45) did not rise at all between 1995 and 2002 because declining rural inequality offset the increase in urban inequality. For all that, it is unclear just how much should be read into the Khan–Riskin conclusion. At the top end of the income scale, the gains from corruption appear to be increasing and there is considerable anecdotal evidence that the incomes of China's newly rich are being understated and undersampled. It is also possible that, whilst Khan and Riskin may have correctly assessed the trend in inequality in the late 1990s (their finding parallels that of Ravallion and Chen for that period), the trend has been dramatically upwards since then as economic growth has accelerated. More importantly, and even if the *trend* may have been only moderately upward, the absolute level of inequality reached in China by 1996, and maintained in the decade thereafter, is very high. Chinese inequality is still some way below that recorded in Brazil (where Gini coefficients of around 0.6 have been the norm for the last two decades), but it is still high by developing country standards.

Inequality and social unrest

Social unrest is of course precipitated by more obvious indicators of socio-economic inequality than by something as abstract as a Gini coefficient. And across a wide range of indicators, inequality in China is plain to see. Take education. In 2005, less than 6 per cent of men were illiterate compared with over 16 per cent of women. Only 11 per cent of women had a senior middle school education, compared with 14 per cent of men (ZGTJNJ 2005: 112–13).[21] The gap between urban and rural areas is also considerable. The average Chinese urban resident had completed 8.5 years of education in 2000, but the average farmer had completed only 5.2 years (Gill and Kharas 2007: 280). The data on mortality also paint a bleak picture of a widening urban–rural divide. In 1990, the rural infant mortality rate was 1.7 times higher than the urban rate. By 2000, however, the ratio had increased to 2.8 to 1, mainly as a result of an absolute rise in female infant mortality in rural areas (Zhang and Kanbur 2005: 197). This was mainly because of the one-child family-planning policy which, combined with Chinese cultural preferences for boys, has resulted in the deliberate neglect and maltreatment of many infant girls. The phenomenon continues to be denied by the Chinese government, but the evidence on survival rates by gender allows of only one interpretation.[22] To compound the problem, the continuing use of ultrasound technology has led to sex-selective abortion and therefore a very biased sex ratio at birth. As Banister says, the underlying problem is a combination of Chinese culture, technological modernization and the one-child policy. In this regard, China has gone backwards since the Maoist era because policy no longer holds in check culturally mandated sex discrimination:

> The traditional custom of female infanticide was in complete or partial abeyance for nearly three decades from the early 1950s until 1978. The infant sex ratios in the census counts of 1953 and 1964 showed no shortage of girls, suggesting that female infanticide was hardly being used then. (Banister 2004: 37)

As for income ratios, the SSB data show that urban incomes doubled in real terms between 1996 and 2005, whereas rural incomes increased by only about 50 per cent. Over the entire 1978–2005 period, the rates of real increase were almost identical, leaving the gap in terms of current income at about 3.2 to 1 in 2005 (ZGTJNJ 2006: 347). However, this gap is hard to interpret because of data problems. Measured urban incomes as reported by the SSB are on the one hand inflated by the exclusion of temporary migrants and by a failure to properly adjust for higher urban price levels. On the other hand, they are understated because of the undersampling of the rich and a failure to account for the range of subsidies paid to the urban but not to the rural population.[23]

In some ways, therefore, the urban–rural gap is better measured in terms of human development.[24] Here the gap is certainly wide across a range of indicators. Illiteracy is one example (Figure 15.7). Here the data for 2004 show a gap of

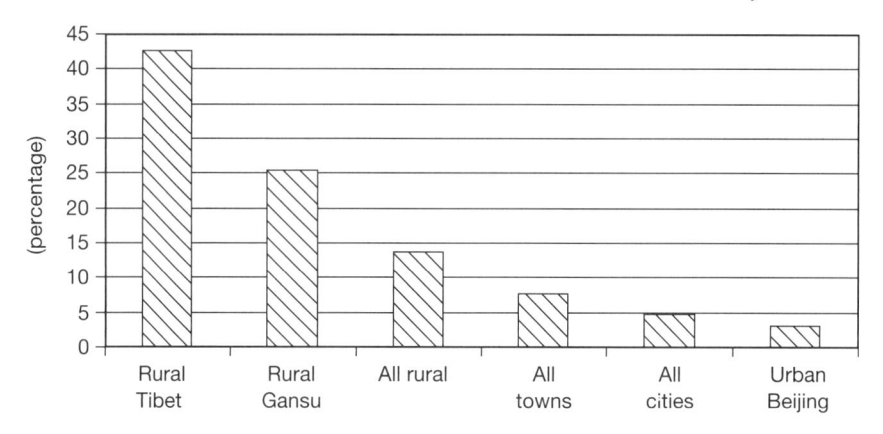

Figure 15.7 Urban–rural illiteracy rates in 2004 (illiteracy rates for the population aged 15 and over) (Source: RKTJNJ (2005: 55–7).)

Note: Data are from the 1 per cent population survey of 2004.

around 3 to 1 between illiteracy rates in China's cities and its countryside. In fact, the gap is even more extreme if we look at the top and bottom end of the scale. In the urban parts of Beijing (Beijing municipality has a number of rural districts under its jurisdiction), the 2004 illiteracy rate was only 3.1 per cent. In rural parts of the north-west province of Gansu, however, the rate was over 25 per cent. Moreover, Gansu was not alone in having a high illiteracy rate; the median rate in the rural part of the ten western provinces was about 20 per cent. To make matters still worse, the criterion used to determine literacy is still the system of 1956 (see Chapter 6) – only 1,500 characters are required in the countryside, whereas it is 2,000 characters in the cities. In other words, illiteracy rates are much higher in the countryside even though it is much easier to be classified as literate than in the cities.[25]

The significance of this inequality is more difficult to assess. There is, for example, a suggestion in some of the literature that the level of tolerance for inequality in Chinese society is quite high (Whyte 2005). Of course there is no doubting the existence of considerable civil unrest across China over the last decade; the absence of both proper democracy and the rule of law combines with inequalities to create an explosive cocktail.[26] By the mid-1990s, peasant protest was commonplace in China's central agricultural provinces (Henan, Hebei, Hubei and Hunan), many of which had experienced slow income growth after 1978. But unrest is well documented almost everywhere in China, whether in inland Sichuan, coastal Guangdong or Anhui.[27] One estimate puts the number of incidents of social unrest as rising from 8,700 in 1993 to 74,000 in 2004 (Shirk 2007: 57) and to 87,000 in 2005 (Bergsten *et al.* 2006: 40).[28]

Such unrest is certainly driven by resentment at the arbitrary exercise of state power by local officials ('local emperors'). This exercise of power takes the form of high rates of taxation – Chen and Wu (2006: 151–5) provide a useful list of the range of taxes levied at a local level – cadre corruption and what was seen as the arbitrary expropriation of land for building and transport purposes. As a result, the burden of rural taxation fell on the poor. As Khan and Riskin (1998: 238–40) show, the share of the poorest 10 per cent of the population in taxation in 1995 was no less than twelve times greater than the decile's share in income, whereas the richest deciles of the population were actually net recipients of transfers. By 2002, the picture had improved somewhat but the burden of rural taxation nevertheless remained highly regressive (Khan and Riskin 2005: 264).[29] They therefore conclude:

> The burden of net rural taxes is largely borne by households who are poor in the rural context and extremely poor in the context of China as a whole. Therefore, a reduction in net taxes on rural households would have a strongly equalizing effect. (Khan and Riskin 1998: 249)

Whether these protests were animated at root by concerns about poverty, rather than by the inequalities created by arbitrary taxation and corruption, is far less clear. However, the very fact that rural poverty has declined – albeit slowly, as we have seen – over the last decade suggests that inequality is the driver. Take for example Anhui province. Per capita real peasant incomes rose by 50 per cent between 1996 and 2005; life expectancy increased by an average of 2.5 years between 1990 and 2000. The number of peasants officially classified as living below the poverty line declined from 2.4 million in 1996 to 1.4 million in 2004 (SSB 2005: 498–9). This suggests a good record on poverty reduction. Nevertheless, as Chen and Wu (2006) have documented, unrest in the Anhui countryside is at a higher level and growing – suggesting that inequality is the main problem.

More generally, it is not that peasants are absolutely poor but rather that they live alongside cadres who enjoy many of the trappings of wealth. Moreover, the source of cadre power lies as much in economic status as it does in any formal monopoly of violence in rural society; it is wealth that makes it possible for rich farmers or rural entrepreneurs to become cadres in the first place. In this way, inequality begets inequality. As Walder (2002) shows, cadre incomes were higher than the average in the countryside by the mid-1990s, and increasingly it was the managers of collective enterprises who were exploiting their high-income status to become cadres and private entrepreneurs.[30] Thus high income allows the affluent to control local government, and that power is then used to consolidate high-income status via corruption and arbitrary taxation. Inequality causes other forms of resentment too. Most obviously, high income allows the rural rich to resist state demands – for example, the strictures of the one-child family policy are easily evaded if one is well off. Such *dingzihu* (nail-like villagers) are inevitably a focus of resentment, as well as a force of inspiration in so far as they are seen as resisting unfair state demands (Li and O'Brien 1996). In short, although poverty is a source of social unrest, income inequality is at least as important. To focus, therefore, on poverty trends – as so much of the economic literature does – is to ignore one of China's key social problems.

Urban centres have not been immune to protest either. Here again both poverty and inequality have been motivating factors. Many of the urban protests have been driven by labour issues, especially low wages and redundancies in the textile sector.[31] This is clearly poverty-driven. However, resentment over low wages and redundancy has been compounded by what is seen as the ability of the rich to buy their way around the law. Cities often levy fines of up to 100,000 *yuan* for violations of the one-child family policy (fines are often charged as multiples of average city income), but this sort of penalty counts as small change for China's growing number of *yuan* millionaires.

The problem of corruption

Corruption has also been a frequent target for protest.[32] It may be growth-promoting in so far as some of the rents created accrue to the more entrepreneurial members of Chinese society, but its social effects are adverse.

Although China's record on corruption is not especially poor by most developing country standards, there is little doubt that its scale has increased since the middle of the 1990s. The rich routinely bribe officials to evade restrictions, whether environmental or birth control; it is easier of course when they are officials themselves. An example of continuing state corruption was the way in which many members of the Politburo, their children and their relatives made vast sums of money by using advance information to convert dollars into *renminbi* before any official announcements was made; the news that the *renminbi* would be revalued was provided to them at an earlier Politburo meeting on 21 July 2005 by Wen Jiabao (Zhang 2006: 80). The misappropriation of social security funds has also benefited a number of government officials, notably Chen Liangyu, the Shanghai Party Secretary. China's National Audit office, in its investigation conducted during the autumn of 2006, estimated that some 7 billion *yuan* had been stolen (CLB 24 November 2006) However, much of the corruption since the late 1990s has been associated with the privatization of SOEs and TVEs, which has usually benefited 'insiders' (i.e. the managers of such companies), who have been able to buy the assets of such companies at very low prices (Sun 2004: 93–6). In addition, it was almost a matter of routine for wealthy Chinese with inside information to manipulate the stock market; rarely has the word 'casino' been better applied. As in the rural sector, corruption has tended to increase urban inequality to levels substantially above those recorded in the official Gini coefficients.

The Chinese state has made some attempt to deal with the most glaring examples of corruption. Chen Xitong, Mayor of Beijing, was jailed in 1998; his son had been convicted in 1997. He Minxu, the deputy-governor of Anhui province, was sacked in November 2006 for accepting bribes. Chen Liangyu, the Shanghai Party Secretary, was sacked in September 2006, though his demise may have had as much to do with Hu's desire to purge those close to Jiang Zemin as to malfeasance *per se*. Some of those who have been engaged in stock market manipulation have also faced the consequences of their actions;

Zhou Zhengyi (allegedly the eleventh-richest man in China at the time) was gaoled for three years; since his release in May 2006, he has been rearrested on charges of fraud and bribery. Zheng Xiaoyu, the head of China's Food and Drug Administration was executed in July 2007; his crime was to allow ineffectual and dangerous products on to the market in return for bribes. Chen Tonghai, the head of Sinopec, resigned in June 2007 and has been investigated for accepting large bribes and for abuse of power.

These high-profile cases notwithstanding, and despite repeated Party-led anti-corruption drives, China's record has probably deteriorated since the mid-1990s. Although indicators of corruption are not very reliable and often simply reflect the prejudices of 'experts', China's record is not improving. For example, the World Bank's estimates of control of corruption show China's rating declining from −0.20 in 1998 to −0.69 in 2005. China is thus well behind the best OECD countries (Finland has a rating of 2.39), and has fallen below India (−0.31). China's record still appears to be better than that of many other poor countries; Bangladesh's rating in 2005 was −1.01 and Ivory Coast achieved −1.23. But the deterioration, whether using World Bank or other indicators, is plain to see.[33] China may not be the most corrupt country in the world, but it has certainly fallen from grace. It is sometimes claimed that greater transparency and a more market-orientated system reduces corruption, but this is offset by the fact that the growth of capitalism has increased exponentially the gains to be made from corruption; many prominently placed Chinese have been unable to resist its lure.

Assessing the impact of labour migration

One of the most obvious characteristics of Chinese society since 1996 has been the growth of labour migration. In many respects, the People's Republic is a country on the move. We therefore need to consider whether this has helped or hindered Chinese development.

Arguments for labour migration

The conventional wisdom is that labour migration between sectors promotes development, an argument first made by Lewis (1954), but subsequently taken up by many neoclassical economists (World Bank 1997c). Migration works by raising economy-wide productivity; it increases the share of the high productivity sector in employment. The impact of migration thus shows up in growth accounting exercises in the form of a higher rate of growth of total factor productivity; see, for example, the estimates of Woo (1998). The initial effect is to raise income inequality, but, as growth proceeds, inequality will fall. Labour inequality thus underpins the Kuznets inverted U hypothesis on the relationship between income inequality and per capita GDP (Fields 1980). Its impact on absolute poverty is argued to be much less ambiguous; modern sector enlargement growth driven by labour migration reduces absolute poverty as poor farmers escape the countryside and find employment in better-paid jobs in the cities.

The theory that underlies the case for labour migration is firmly rooted in a belief that markets work well to promote developmental objectives. Thus the argument for migration has been made on both equity and efficiency grounds. According to Knight and Song (1999: 333):

> Our simulation experiments showed that the migration of labour from the villages that we studied is a powerful mechanism for alleviating poverty and reducing inequality. The effects of such migration are favourable on grounds both of efficiency (raising output and having low opportunity cost) and of equity (disproportionately helping poor households).

The efficiency argument can be represented along the lines of Figure 15.8. LD_R and LD_U represent the demand for labour in the rural and urban sectors respectively. Here w^R and w^U are the respective real wage rates in the rural and urban sectors. If the market had been functioning efficiently (and assuming no difference in average skill levels in urban and rural sectors), the wage rate would have been the same in both urban and rural sectors at E. Any tendency for the urban wage

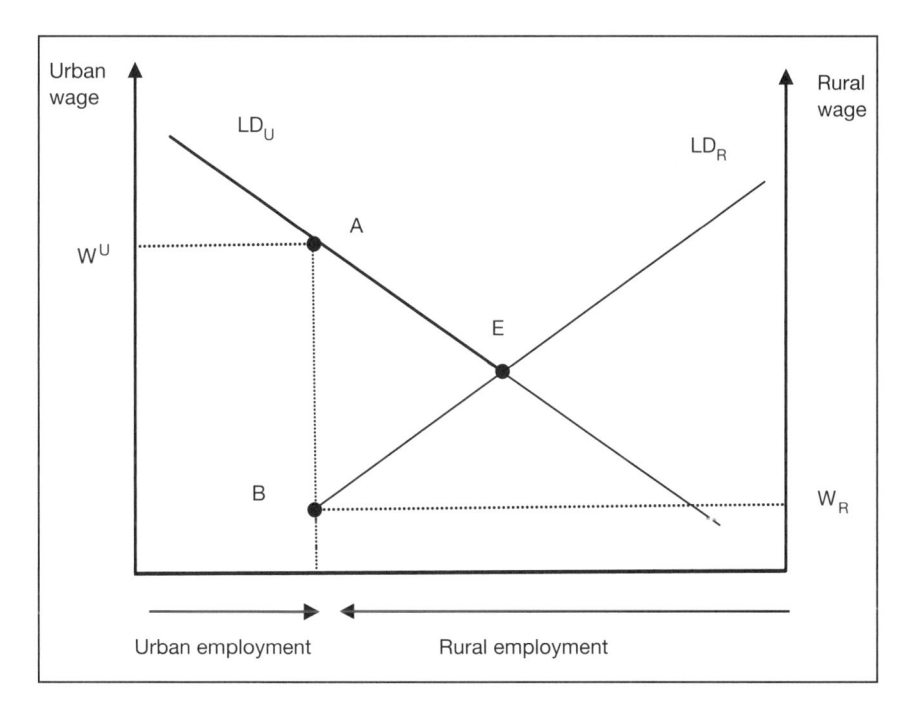

Figure 15.8 Migration and the Chinese labour market.

Note: There are many assumptions here. We assume that labour is paid for its marginal product in both sectors, that marginal productivity was positive but declining and that the urban and rural sectors can be aggregated in this way (it would, for example, be much more realistic to use a three-sector model which distinguishes between agriculture and rural industry).

to rise above the rural wage would have been checked by an immediate influx of rural migrants, which would have driven the urban wage rate back down again to its equilibrium level.

However, because of migration controls, the Chinese labour market was in disequilibrium in the mid-1990s (the argument of course applies even more strongly to China before 1978). More precisely, controls on labour migration meant that the urban wage was much higher than the rural wage. Urban employment was much also lower than it should have been, and profits were much higher; these profits financed the high investment of the late Maoist and post-1978 eras. The high cost of urban labour encouraged firms to employ more capital-intensive technologies instead. In the rural sector, the size of the labour force was far too large, and as a result much of it was underemployed. The direct cost to the economy is shown by the triangle ABE in Figure 15.8 (this is the deadweight loss). Capital movements to some extent compensated for labour restrictions, but China's capital market worked badly because of uncertain property rights and continuing state restrictions on the private sector. In principle, therefore, the removal of residual controls on migration would reduce inefficiency. Greater labour migration would on the one hand reduce the size of the rural labour force and thus push up the rural wage. On the other hand, a greater flow of migrants into China's cities would have depressed the urban wage. In this way, the triangle ABE would gradually become smaller over time.

The distributional arguments for greater labour migration follow on from this analysis. If the effect of migration would be to reduce urban wages and increase rural wages, it would have the effect of reducing the urban–rural gap. For much the same reasons, migration from west to east within China would narrow the gap between the (richer) eastern provinces and the (poor) western provinces. Moreover, it is argued, migration would lead to a big reduction in absolute rural poverty, because, even though migration would depress the average urban wage, migrants would nevertheless benefit because the urban wage would still be higher than the rural wage for the foreseeable future.

Those who advocate migration as a policy solution to the problem of inequality acknowledge that migration has costs. However, the cost-benefit calculus in most of the literature suggests that these costs are much smaller than the benefits in the Chinese case. Indeed for some geographically disadvantaged communities, out-migration may be the only viable solution to the poverty problem. Remittances and return migration can, and do in the Chinese context, alleviate the adverse effects on rural communities of short-term out-migration (Murphy 2002; Zhao 2002). And the way to deal with labour market segmentation in China's cities, it is said, is to improve the way the urban labour market functions, rather than to restrict in-migration.

The costs of migration

Of course there is some truth to the arguments in favour of migration as a means of promoting Chinese development. For example, out-migration may well be the only solution to poverty on the high Himalayan plateau, despite all that this implies for the survival of Tibetan culture.

In general, however, the migration literature is overly sanguine. One problem is that migration replaces one form of inequality (the urban–rural gap) with another, namely greater inequality within urban areas. A central characteristic of the distribution of wages in Chinese cities is that migrant wages are below the urban average, and one reason for this is differences in educational levels. Migrants from rural areas were more highly educated than the rural average, but they were less well-educated than the urban population. For example, Shanghai's floating population was drawn mainly from agriculture in the late 1980s; that was the background of 48 per cent of its floating population in 1988. As a result, the illiteracy rate amongst all migrants was 15 per cent in 1988 compared to the city average of 11 per cent according to the 1990 census (RKTJNJ 1991: 254; Bada chengshi 1990: 232).

However, educational disadvantage was not the only problem, and probably not even the main problem faced by migrants. In Shanghai, for example, only 9 per cent of migrants were illiterate compared to the city average of 8 per cent in 1996 (Li 1996: 13; RKTJNJ 1997: 31). Nevertheless, income inequalities persisted in Shanghai and elsewhere both because migrants lacked skills and because of endemic discrimination. Despite the introduction of the blue *hukou*, the floating population remained inferior in status to permanent urban residents (Amnesty International 2007). The main purpose in granting blue *hukou* was to raise revenue rather than to grant citizenship rights; it thus served to reduce substantially the immediate gains to migration by imposing a large tax on rural to urban migrants. The inferior status of migrants is very evident from the fact that floaters were routinely denied welfare entitlements, access to public education and the right to participate in the political process in the late 1990s (Guo and Iredale 2004; Shao *et al.* 2007; Cai and Wang 2007). This was little handicap to well-off migrants, notably those setting up small businesses. But it placed would-be migrants from poor households at a grave disadvantage, and this was compounded by the overt discrimination in the labour market. In Beijing, for example, a list of 198 types of permitted work was published in February 1998 which sought to push migrants into unpopular and low-paid jobs such as abattoir work, cremation of corpses and mining (SCMP 17 April 1998). The Deputy Party Secretary of Liaoning openly encouraged unemployed workers to 'grab back' the jobs held by migrants (SCMP 15 October 1997). Even 'academic' accounts argued that migrants necessitate high infrastructural spending, cause overcrowding and drain funds out of urban areas and back to the villages (Bada chengshi 1990: 224 and 246). Furthermore, the decision announced by Premier Wen Jiabao in March 2005 (which was to come into effect in early 2007) to exempt rural children aged between six and fifteen from tuition fees does not apply to the children of temporary migrants living in rural areas (CD 13 December 2006). Supposedly illegal schools for migrant workers have been close down and even when migrant children are allowed in, the fees they must pay are typically well above those charged to resident households (Chan and Buckingham 2007: 25).

The extent of discrimination by local governments against temporary migrants and their children shows up clearly in the data. One survey of cities in Jiangsu in 2004 found that 31 per cent of local workers were earning 15,000 *yuan* or more whereas the figure for migrants with a *hukou* outside Jiangsu was only 3.6 per cent; conversely, 25 per cent of migrants had incomes of 5,000 *yuan* or less compared with only 14 per cent of locals (Shao *et al.* 2007: 25). Such inequalities as these reflect both on-the-job discrimination and segmentation, whereby male migrants end up in the construction sector and women as low-paid assembly-line workers or as maids. Of course wage differentials cannot be attributed entirely to discrimination, but a study by Cai and Wang (2007: 22) suggests that over 40 per cent of the differential can be explained in this way. The inferior status of migrants is also evident from their lower level of access to social insurance. In China's large cities during 2005, 64 per cent of urban residents had access to health insurance compared with only 8 per cent of migrants; for pension insurance, the figures were 77 and 9 per cent respectively (Cai and Wang 2007: 24).

Much of this discrimination derives from a notion of native place hierarchy which dates back to long before the 1949 Revolution This phenomenon was commonplace in the pre-1949 labour market; outside workers recruited to the Nantong cotton mills in Jiangsu province during the Republican era were referred to as *chongzi* (worms) (Köll 2003: 97). The arsenals of wartime Chongqing, which initially employed skilled workers who had fled west before the advance of Japanese troops after 1937, tended to discriminate against native Sichuan workers in the early years. Wartime pressures admittedly induced a reduction in segmentation in the arsenals of Chongqing, where initial prejudice against Sichuanese workers broke down in the face of labour shortages and escalating costs (Howard 2004: 83–122). Nevertheless, segmentation offers a useful way to explain the absence of class solidarity amongst the Republican workforce (Honig 1992, 1996; Finnane 1993).

This type of discrimination against geographically defined 'outsiders' – geography thus serves as a basis for discrimination in China in the same way that race does in many other societies – continues in the 1990s. In Shanghai, for example, migrants from Sunan (southern Jiangsu) continue to be treated as inferior to natives but are regarded as infinitely preferable to migrants from Subei (northern Jiangsu) or the even poorer province of Anhui (Honig 1992; Finnane 1993). In Wuxi, discrimination against outsiders was rampant; kinship and patronage appear to have been the key factors in determining access to well-paid jobs (Ma 2000). Localism was also very much the norm in Shenzhen, where place of birth (north or south of the Yangzi river) and the ability to speak Mandarin were basic dividing lines when it came to categorizing workers (Lee 1995: 384–6). Even when migration did take place, wage payments were tied closely to the worker's place of origin. Workers from Sichuan typically occupied the lowest rung in the hierarchy and were usually relegated to jobs in agri-business (Chan *et al.* 1992: 304–7). The labour shortages noted in the previous chapter may well push up the wages of the unskilled, but the wage gap is only likely to close over the medium and longer term.

Nor should the effects of out-migration on rural communities be ignored in any assessment of the impact of migration. Those migrating are typically younger, better educated and more highly skilled than the rural average. In fact, some studies suggest that youth is far more important as a determinant of out-migration than either skill or educational level (Rozelle *et al.* 1999; Mallee 2000). In other words, the effect of migration is to remove a large proportion of the rural working-age population, which in turn hampers the ability of rural communities to maintain agricultural productivity levels and create rural industries. Coupled with the brain drain, the effect of out-migration is to deprive rural areas of the wherewithal for indigenous development, and to skew incomes in favour of those households with few dependents.

The effects of migration are therefore decidedly ambiguous. It may reduce the urban–rural gap, but even here much depends on the effects on the rural communities left behind; there is no certainty that rural incomes will rise post-migration. And even if the income gap does narrow, the overall impact on inequality will be offset by the increase in intra-urban inequality.[34] In effect, one type of inequality is replaced by another.

The response to this in the literature is usually Panglossian: migration problems arise because of ill-functioning or missing markets, and therefore the solution is simply to make markets work better, whether in China or elsewhere.[35] This is clearly influenced by the perceived experience of the USA, deemed to be a successful model precisely because it has 'free' markets. In fact, however, the US amply demonstrates the failure of market-based solutions. Whatever the efficiency of the US labour market, it self-evidently fails on equity grounds; for example, the narrowing of income gaps between states has more to do with the redistributive role played by the federal government than it has to do with labour mobility. In the Chinese case, the empirical literature on the consequences of labour migration is equally unpersuasive. Many of the studies are highly suggestive about the ways in which migration may promote development – Murphy (2002) is a good example – but they are based on very small samples and necessarily tell us little about the likely medium- and long-term consequences. Moreover, to suppose that systemic discrimination can easily be overcome even in the medium term is to fly on little more than a wing and a prayer.

One cannot help but conclude that the advocacy of labour migration by many Chinese policymakers is driven much more by a desire to raise the profits of urban industry, and foreign enterprises invested in China, than by any realistic evaluation of the costs and benefits. And paradoxically, it is not even clear that migration will raise urban profitability. Certainly in-migration will tend to drive down the urban wage by increasing the size of the reserve army of labour, but whether that will boost profitability depends as much upon the impact on consumer demand as it does on costs. Considerations such as these suggest that there is an agenda at work here that is as much about politics and self-aggrandizement as it is about development.

The prospects for sustainable development

What then of China's prospects? Should we be optimistic or pessimistic about the future? Is it likely that China will be able to sustain its rate of economic growth and, more importantly, do better in terms of human development and poverty reduction over the last decade?

The problem of diminishing returns

From a narrowly economic point of view, the answer to this question of sustainability is that the growth rate will slow down over the next decade. For there is no doubt that the pace of growth is threatened by diminishing returns to investment.[36] Chinese growth over the last thirty years has been driven in no small measure by high rates of savings, themselves as much a product of the lack of a proper system of social security as growing affluence. These savings have been mobilized by the Leninist state via state-owned enterprises (both SOEs and TVEs) and the state-controlled banking system to generate exceptionally high rates of investment. This type of growth is all very well, provided a high rate of savings can be maintained and as long as the incremental capital–output ratio remains within acceptable bounds. However, argue Hutton (2007) and others, the limits to investment-led growth are fast being reached in China, and these limits are manifest in the form of sharply diminishing returns to capital. Hutton suggests in effect that China will follow in the footsteps of its Asian cousins unless it adopts the 'soft institutional infrastructure' and 'Enlightenment institutions' of the West which are essential for the technical progress which is the mainspring of capitalist growth.

Most neoclassicals share this diagnosis (although not necessarily the more interventionist solutions proposed by Hutton) It has long been a tenet of their thinking that Chinese growth cannot be sustainable, partly because growth has been driven by capital accumulation (which is subject to diminishing returns in the long run) and partly because much of the measured TFP growth derives from a one-off sectoral reallocation of labour from agriculture to industry. Young (1995) and Krugman (1996), for example, have portrayed the East Asian miracle as built on factor accumulation ('perspiration') rather than technical progress ('inspiration'), and this offers an explanation for the slowdown in growth that has occurred after 1990. China's experience can be thought of in the same way. A paper by Kuijs and Wang (2006: 4) is representative of this type of literature.[37] They find that capital accumulation has played a key role in Chinese growth: indeed the contribution of a rising capital–labour ratio to GDP growth increased from about a third during 1987–93 to well over a half during 1993–2004. This is not sustainable because it implies ever-rising investment levels and because the dominance of industrial productivity growth in the process has widened the productivity gap between the industrial and agricultural sectors. The solution is to rebalance policy by 'reducing subsidies to industry and investment, encouraging the service industry and removing barriers to labour mobility' (Kuijs and Wang 2006: 14). It is an easy step from these theoretical and empirical perspectives to argue that the crash of 1997 in other parts of Asia is a foretaste of what is to come for China.

A variant on this theme is that inefficient resource utilization has led to both a high level of dependency on world markets and to environmental degradation, both of which are threatening the growth process. Inefficient resource utilization means that Chinese growth has become dangerously reliant upon imports of raw materials from the rest of the world; to some extent, therefore, it is becoming 'dependent' upon the world economy. Changes in the world economy, or in the circumstances of African countries supplying many of its primary imports, are therefore potentially very damaging for China. Worse, the growth of Chinese industry has spawned catastrophic levels of pollution and growing water shortages. Acid rain and particulate matter pollute the atmosphere. Most of China's mature forests have been destroyed.

There is undoubtedly something in this sort of analysis. However, it is certainly overstated. As far as the notion of an environmental constraint on growth is concerned, it is hard to see that this will bite anytime soon. As we have seen, the level of environmental degradation is high, but there is little evidence that environmental indicators are getting worse for China as a whole, and in some areas – such as reforestation – there is even improvement. Growing car ownership may change all that, but it is a long way into the future. And whilst water shortages are a problem, they are not yet crippling. Indeed China's south-to-north water transfer projects will help to relieve the worst shortages in the north of the country. As far as dependency on imports is concerned, it seems reasonable to suppose that, provided China maintains a diverse range of suppliers of raw materials, it will remain relatively secure.

Nor do the more narrowly economic arguments about the sustainability of growth suggest imminent collapse. For one thing, although Singapore, South Korea and Taiwan have experienced a slowdown, their growth rate nevertheless remains impressive; there is no sign here of any crash or crisis, suggesting that they have successfully made the transition to innovation-led growth. In fact, their transition has been easier because there has been none to make; Young and others have failed to identify the true extent of technical progress in these economies because of their reliance on a flawed TFP methodology. The reality is that we cannot separate out the effects of productivity growth from those of factor accumulation precisely because technical progress must necessarily be embodied, a point made by Kaldor many years ago. We cannot distinguish shifts in production functions from movements along. As a result, scholars like Young and Krugman have failed to recognize that growth in many of the Asian economies was already partially innovation-based in the 1990s. The same is true of China. One may not believe the estimates of positive TFP growth that are to be found in the literature, but it is hard to believe that China is not experiencing considerable – and perhaps even rapid – technical progress.

There is therefore no reason to expect any collapse in the short run.[38] The efficiency of investment across China is less than one might wish, but there is nothing to suggest that it will drop off quickly – or conversely any reason to doubt that technical progress will accelerate. It could well be that the right comparison is between the China of 1996 and Taiwan and South Korea at the end of the 1950s, rather than between China and East Asia in the early 1990s. Just as Taiwan and South Korea became more open to foreign trade and shook off the worst aspects of crony capitalism at the end of the 1950s, so China's entry into the WTO and the accession of Hu Jintao may push China firmly along the path of sustained growth. To be sure, China's growth will be slower than that achieved by Taiwan and South Korea because its per capita income by 1996 was more than double their levels in 1960, but it is a far cry from this to a prediction of imminent collapse. Chinese growth is certain to slow down as it becomes more prosperous; none of the OECD countries has sustained a growth rate of 10 per cent, or even come close. Accordingly, it is neither controversial nor profound to argue that current Chinese growth cannot be sustained. But a slowdown over a period of twenty or thirty years is very different from an abrupt termination of growth. Moreover, there is little evidence that China is even approaching *la longue durée*. If anything, the evidence suggests that the growth rate is accelerating as the process of modernization continues.

That is not to suggest that slower growth entails no dangers. Given that the Chinese party-state is no longer held together by ideological purpose, it is economic growth – along with a healthy measure of nationalism – that provides the cement which prevents the whole edifice from crumbling. Should a *marked* slowdown in growth occur, the Party will lose the support of both the rural poor, and that of a nascent middle class in urban China (a group which has profited most from the growth of the last ten years). In such circumstances, collapse is all but inevitable. Threats to sustained economic growth therefore need to be taken seriously.

Sustainability: state weakness

Yet the answer to the question of whether Chinese development is sustainable centres on a more fundamental question than growth accounting. The previous section has merely argued that the *potential* for future growth in China remains high, not that China will necessarily be able to live up to its potential.

The crux of the sustainability question is the capacity and intent of the Chinese state. From a neoliberal perspective, a powerful state is necessary to secure property rights and to enforce law relating to property and to the environment. From a heterodox perspective, state strength is necessary if industrial policy is to be effective. From a Marxian point of view, only the state is capable of bringing about the changes to both the Chinese superstructure and to the base that are required for the process of accumulation to continue.

State capacity centres on the balance between its own resources, the power of the localities and the private sector and external constraints. The capacity of central government has certainly diminished, mainly because of the process of fiscal decentralization that has taken place over the last three decades. Nevertheless, although Wang Shaoguang's (Wang and Hu 1999, 2001) argument that the Chinese state was in crisis had some force to it in the early 1990s, the recentralization of the fiscal system engineered by Zhu Rongji has restored much of its capacity. There is no imminent fiscal crisis of the state to be overcome. By the same token, the power of local government has diminished. It has always been possible to defy China's central government, but such deviance does not last long.

Far more serious has been China's decision to reduce its tariff barriers and join the WTO. Of course it may well be that the central government will choose to ignore WTO rules where necessary, and there is no doubt that it will be difficult to enforce the rules of the game on a country which has the military capacity possessed by China. Furthermore, precisely because China remains a poor country, it remains exempt from some of the more stringent conditions imposed by the WTO on richer countries. Nevertheless, it is hard to see how WTO membership is compatible with the pursuit of the sort of selective industrial policy – based around tariffs and subsidies – used to such effect by Japan, Taiwan and South Korea in the late twentieth century. China still has its national champions, but their time may already have passed. There are therefore good reasons to suppose that relentless competition from Western companies will ensure that China's more advanced industrial enterprises will wither and die, and that it will be locked into a development trajectory which depends upon the exploitation of cheap labour. The People's Republic would therefore be well advised to leave the WTO as soon as it can, and thereby regain its policy freedom.

Still more serious is the threat to the state posed by inequality and relative poverty.[39] The emergence of inequality has provided the economic basis for the development of powerful rent-seeking coalitions. This notion that the state has been 'captured' by the capitalist class implies that state policy is inevitably skewed towards serving the needs of these groups – the claims of the few override the needs of the majority.[40] This in turn will provoke a backlash and provide the context for social instability. In a sense, Hu Jintao 'is like the sorcerer, who is no longer able to control the powers of the nether world whom he has called up by his spells' (Marx and Engels 1848: 41).

None of this is fanciful: perhaps the worst facet of contemporary China is the spiralling of *relative* poverty and income inequality. Within the course of two decades, China has become a country riddled with class-based inequalities. To be sure, inequality is in part connected to geography; many parts of western China face a formidable task in raising per capita incomes. Although the decomposition of inequality measures like the Gini or Theil into spatial and intra-local components makes little real sense – the underlying survey data are simply not good enough, though that has not stopped academics from attempting such meaningless computations – it is clear that non-geographical factors are playing a key role in causing inequality.

Nowhere is this more apparent than in the counties of southern Jiangsu. Geography here is not an issue (the land is flat and fertile), yet Gini coefficients for incomes within many counties were well over 0.25 even in the mid-1990s, as those able to gain access to well paid TVE jobs prospered whilst those condemned to life in the farm sector were left further and further behind. This evidence exemplifies a more general truth: much of China's inequality is intra-local and derives from discrimination (on the basis of gender, ethnicity, class and place of origin), educational disadvantage (itself a product of income inequality) and family class background. Unemployment too is causing considerable unrest, and this is potentially dangerous for the regime because many of those threatened or suffering from unemployment are likely to be in the vanguard of any nationwide protest movement. Two obvious groups are former state-sector workers in the

Manchurian provinces and graduates: 1.4 out of the 5 million graduates of 2007 were still unemployed in September (CD 1 November 2007). As Shirk (2007: 52–61) rightly says, this type of unemployment in particular provokes considerable unease amongst the CCP leadership.

Of course it may be that the Chinese government will rise to the challenge to its freedom of action posed by inequality. Certainly it has risen to the challenge when faced by other threats over the last twenty-five years. In any case, China's system of progressive income taxation may do something to mitigate inequality.[41] Only a comparatively small number of people were paying significant levels of tax in the mid-1990s. Even in 2004, the marginal tax rate only reached 20 per cent when wage income reached 74,400 *yuan*, which was over ten times higher than the average urban income from wages (Piketty and Qian 2004: 28). As a result, the personal income tax raised only 209 billion *yuan*, 7 per cent of all government revenue (ZGTJNJ 2006: 287 and 349) However, as the simulation by Piketty and Qian shows, continued rapid economic growth will drag many more of the population into higher income – and therefore higher tax brackets – as the decade wears on. Moreover, the CCP is moving in the direction of making the system more progressive, and making it bite. The threshold at which income tax is payable was raised from 800 to 1,600 *yuan* at the start of 2006, thus exempting many of the urban poor. And in 2007 – for the first time – those earning over 120,000 *yuan* in 2006 are expected to declare their income to the tax authorities. If successfully implemented, these types of policies will certainly go some way towards reducing inequalities, as it has in many Western countries. Optimists like Peerenboom (2007) have perhaps as much justification for their stance as pessimists like Hutton (2007). Whether a government like that of China will countenance the sort of progressive tax system required is more questionable. Indeed compliance is already a problem. At the start of April 2007, the cut-off date for high income declarations, some 1.6 million declarations had been made out of an estimated 7 million high-income earners (*Xinhua* 5 April 2007).

I conclude from all this that the capacity of the Chinese state to act has considerably diminished over the last thirty years, although it is really only over the last decade that private-sector interest groups have become powerful enough to dictate state policy, ironically as a result of state-led privatization. Nevertheless, the Chinese state is far from impotent. The real issue in China is not so much state capacity but its motivation. To this question we now turn.

The cultural constraint

As important as state capacity is its willingness to act. Even if central government is strong, and is able to resist pressure from interest groups at home and abroad, is there any reason to suppose that the Chinese central government will act in such a way as to promote Chinese development?

The rhetoric of Hu Jintao suggests that China's rulers may yet surprise us. Indeed the academic literature is littered with failed attempts to proclaim the coming collapse of China. In one sense, however, there is already compelling evidence that the Chinese state has surrendered. Both the sale of state assets and the decision to join the WTO suggest an abject capitulation to neoliberalism and to sectional interest. The very fact that the Eleventh Five Year Programme accepts rising unemployment does not bode well. And the inability of central government to prevent the continuing use of ultrasound technology to determine the sex of foetuses (which makes possible sex-selective abortion) in China's villages indicates a state which is weak, rather than strong.

Perhaps the most obvious sign of state failure in China's poor record in terms of public spending on health and education. As Table 15.8 indicates, China's level of public spending on education is well below that of many other countries. That it should be behind South Korea and the UK is not surprising given the difference in per capita income, though the very fact that China's population is younger ought to offset that to some extent. But the extent to which China lags behind comparatively poor countries like Costa Rica and Cuba is more surprising. Most startling of all is the comparison with India, which shows that China is well behind. China does little better in terms of public expenditure on health care. Here at least China is well ahead of India, but its record is still far from being impressive. Of course total spending on health and education is much higher than public spending because of large and growing private expenditure. But the figures in Table 15.8 provide a damning commentary on the attitude of the Chinese state to investment in human development, and suggest that the country's future prospects are not very rosy (OECD 2006). To be sure, China's minister of education committed the country to spending 4 per cent of GDP on education by 2010 (CD 1 March 2006), and this has been reiterated since. However, before assuming that this signifies anything, we should recall that China in 1993 committed itself to spending 4 per cent by 2000 – a figure it did not even approach. As Table 15.8 shows, public spending on education in China declined between 1991 and 2002–5 according to the UNDP figures.[42] All this illustrates very clearly the unwillingness of the state to spend on the weak and vulnerable in Chinese society.

Nevertheless, the central issue is not so much whether the state has failed in China over the last decade. Clearly it has. Rather, the question is the extent to

Table 15.8 Public spending on health and education (percentage of GDP)

	Education		Health
	1991	2002–2005	2004
China	2.2	1.9	1.8
South Korea	3.8	4.6	2.9
UK	4.8	5.4	7.0
Cuba	9.7	9.8	5.5
Costa Rica	3.4	4.9	5.1
India	3.7	3.8	0.9
Sri Lanka	3.2	n/a	2.0

Source: UNDP (2007: 294–7).

which the state is in some sense a prisoner of Chinese culture. More precisely there are two questions. First, is Chinese culture inimical to development? Second, is the Chinese state a captive of that culture?

As far as the first question is concerned, it is hard to see that any state can be independent of culture. NeoWeberian analysis implies of course that a state can be autonomous and therefore in some sense 'outside' civil society. However, that sort of state only seems to be possible in a small number of cases, implying that the autonomous state is itself culturally determined: one thinks here of South Korea, Taiwan and Singapore in the late twentieth century. The Maoist state of the 1960s and 1970s can perhaps be seen as a little different. Of course it is arguable that it too was a product of Chinese culture – one cannot imagine a Maoist state ever being accepted in contemporary Europe. Yet the late Maoist state was one of the few regimes that has attempted to change at least some aspects of Chinese culture by means of the sending-down programme and the educational revolution over which it presided. The Maoist example thus suggests that some states may, in some circumstances, be independent of the prevailing national culture, but that these are the exception rather than the rule.

By contrast, the state of Hu Jintao is a pale shadow of its Maoist predecessor in almost every respect. We cannot, therefore, realistically perceive the contemporary Chinese state as outside society. At root, the Chinese state is a mirror of Chinese society and culture. The state no longer sees itself as a vehicle for the transformation of Chinese culture and society via education and superstructural change. Rather, it increasingly reflects cultural predilection: we cannot see the Chinese state as some sort of *deus ex machina* which operates outside the bounds of society. It still has the power to play that sort of transformative role, but the motivation seems to have disappeared amidst a confection of rent-seeking.

That takes us to the second question: is Chinese development promoted by Chinese culture or not? Here Hofstede's (2003) approach to defining culture in terms of five dimensions offers some insight, and the prospects in terms of Hofstede ratings are by no means gloomy. China does well in terms of long-term orientation, and its high power distance index (signifying respect for hierarchy) suggests a great deal of scope for state action centred around propelling growth by means of high rates of savings and investment. To be sure, China rates badly in terms of individualism, which fits in well with a neoclassical discourse of low productivity growth because of a lack of invention. However, even that is far from unambiguous. A relatively hierarchical society like China is likely to be good at the diffusion of technology, and, given that the scope for catch-up growth remains enormous, it is not clear that it matters much if China does poorly in terms of invention.

Whether of course these Hofstede scores really mean very much is moot. Many would argue that China is becoming an increasingly short-term society, as exemplified by the development of a crass consumer culture; and it is hard to see how rampant environmental damage squares with long-term orientation. What is undeniable is that Chinese development is held back by a number of cultural traits, some of which are at least partially captured by Hofstede's five dimensions. The clearest example is Chinese respect for hierarchy and the associated acceptance of inequality (Hofstede's power distance dimension). The result is the pervasive discrimination that afflicts Chinese society. Probably the most obvious demonstration of the problem is gender discrimination, as manifested in persistently high female infant mortality and sex-selective abortion. Banister (2004: 41) eloquently summarizes the situation:

> Neither China's political system nor its economic system is to blame, and further development will not necessarily solve the problem. It is not ignorance, illiteracy or poor education that brings people to abort or dispose of daughters; indeed some evidence shows that a higher educational level is associated with greater daughter loss. The traditional cause of China's shortage of females and the underlying cause today is the son preference endemic in Han Chinese culture. ... Technology has worsened the situation by enabling sex-selective abortion, now added to the arsenal of those wishing to dispose of daughters. China's compulsory family planning policy continues to make the shortage of girls more extreme than it would otherwise be.

This is of course but one type of discrimination. There are many others, particularly that directed against ethnic minorities and the contempt shown by many urban citizens for the countryside and its peoples.[43] In this sort of society, it is hard to see how any egalitarian project can put down proper roots. And that in turn means that the prospects for egalitarian human development are limited.[44]

Nationalism, and how to handle its potential as a unifying force, is also an issue. The Party has promoted nationalism in recent years; the 2008 Olympics and the country's response to the Sichuan earthquake in the same year have both been milked for all they are worth in an attempt to portray these events as an affirmation of all that is heroic and noble in the Chinese nation. However, the chauvinistic response to Tibetan demonstrations, and to the widely-held view in the West that Tibet is a Chinese colony, shows that the Party and nation have much to learn; the refusal to accept that others, including the people of Tibet, have a right to voice their opinion on the subject weakens, rather than strengthens, Chinese claims to the territory. Moreover, many Chinese intellectuals are profoundly ambivalent towards the nationalist agenda; they have often been called 'whateverists' ('whatever China does is wrong, whatever the US does is right') for that reason (Gao 2008: 44). Accordingly, official promotion of the notion that China is about to become a respected Confucian superpower prompts nothing other than derision within the ranks of the Chinese bourgeoisie.

Of course none of these prejudices are innate. They have deep historical roots, and the perceived failure of Maoism – a project in which the governments of Deng and his successors have been deeply implicated – brought to an end any vision of an alternative modernity. Nevertheless, the fact remains that until fundamental change takes place across society, these appalling outcomes will persist. China needs a cultural revolution for all sorts of reasons, and never more so than now. Instead, tawdry Confucian institutes seek to spread this bankrupt culture across the globe; indeed an explicit aim of Hu's (2007) Party Congress speech was to 'enhance the influence of Chinese culture worldwide'. How things have changed. The very name of Confucius was anathema to those who embarked upon the Long March; now it is feted in Zhongnanhai and in the groves of academe in the West. Hu (2007) argued that 'We must have a comprehensive understanding of traditional Chinese culture, keep its essence and discard its dross', but it is clear that only the dross has been retained. The dream of the 1949 Revolution has been well and truly betrayed by those who have inherited the mantle of leadership over the last three decades.

The clearest parallel is between China and Brazil. Brazil enjoyed a period of very rapid economic growth between 1964 and 1980 (Baer 1995). During that period, average per capita GDP growth averaged 8.2 per cent per year, actually higher than the 7.3 per cent recorded by China between 1990 and 2003 according Maddison's estimates. The two countries started from a similar place: per capita GDP in Brazil in 1964 was $2,472, and in China it was $1,871 (Maddison 2006b). Both countries achieved considerable success in terms of absolute poverty reduction, much of it because of labour migration from agriculture to industry and from the countryside to the cities, but many failed to gain very much from this growth (Fields 1980). As a result, both countries experienced a rise in income inequality. In Brazil's case, the Gini rose from about 0.5 in the early 1960s to 0.57 by 1981 (Dornbusch and Edwards 1991: 66–7; Ferreira *et al.* 2006). For China, the rise has been more rapid, though official data suggest that the Chinese Gini in 2004 was only 0.47 (World Bank 2007: 66). But given the doubts about the data, it is likely that true Chinese inequality was considerably greater than this.

Most interesting of all about the comparison is what happened next. In Brazil's case, economic growth has slowed done; it averaged only 2.4 per cent per annum between 1980 and 2003. This slowdown was triggered by Brazil's high levels of external debt, which became a binding constraint in the aftermath of the second oil price shock of 1979 and the subsequent slowdown in growth in the OECD countries. But other long-run factors have played a role, notably the weakness of the Brazilian state in the face of private-sector interest groups. Successive Brazilian governments have resorted to populist policies in an attempt to maintain themselves in office, but have been unable to resolve the fundamental supply-side constraints on the economy which have been manifested in the form of high inflation.[45] And the transition to democracy in 1985 has done little to easy the underlying problems. Successive Brazilian presidents have been unable to resolve the fundamental dilemma of how to reduce absolute poverty without alienating the upper class by means of high rates of taxation, and their ultimate recourse has been to deficit-fuelled growth, which has led to inflation.

Of course China's situation at present is not quite the same as that of Brazil in 1980. It has less external debt, and the supply-side problems are much less acute. Inflationary pressures too are far less acute. Nevertheless, there are eerie parallels. China is increasingly dependent on the world economy for supplies of raw materials, and, though its growth is not export-led, there is no doubt that China has become more dependent on exports as a source of demand over the last decade. Its growth is therefore vulnerable to developments in the world economy, just as Brazil's was. Moreover, as we have seen, Chinese agricultural performance is quite poor. The limits to fertilizer- and water-intensive growth are close to being reached and these constraints may well undermine Chinese growth, just as supply-side bottlenecks in agriculture have constrained Brazil. Finally, cultural acceptance of inequality hampers the freedom of manoeuvre for the Chinese state. It may just be that Brazil holds up to China a picture of its own future.

An assessment of China's development record, 1996–2007

As we have seen in the previous sections, China's development record since Deng Xiaoping's death is patchy. Per capita GDP growth has averaged more than 6 per cent per annum over the last decade even according to the estimates made by Angus Maddison. The proportion of children going on from junior to senior middle schools rose from 50 per cent in 1996 to 76 per cent by 2006. Human development indicators have continued to improve, and China remained comfortably ahead of India on all of these indicators. The trajectory of rural poverty appears to have been downwards, continuing a process begun in 1949. The world's shops have been flooded with China's products. The executives of Western multinationals continue to salivate over the prospects held out to their impoverished imaginations by the size of the Chinese market.

However, there is another side to this coin. For one thing, the data on poverty reduction are by no means uniformly positive. Absolute poverty may have declined somewhat in the countryside over the last decade but this is by no means certain.[46] Some of the data suggest that poverty increased in the late 1990s, and the data on farm income – which fell in absolute terms by a very considerable margin – support that view; it is hard to see a fall in farm income coexisting with a decline in absolute poverty. Even though rural poverty reduction resumed after 2000, that should not blind us to the extent of suffering in the countryside which occurred in the late 1990s. In failing to avoid these sorts of fluctuations, China's government has ill served its rural population. China's urban citizens have fared little better and perhaps worse. Privatization, the restructuring of state enterprises and endemic discrimination against migrants (who have flooded into urban areas in ever-increasing numbers since the mid-1990s) have led to very slow employment growth and hence to the re-emergence of poverty. The urban social security system, lauded for its efficiency in ensuring that the non-poor do not benefit from its largesse, provides little more than derisory support for the indigent.

The record on human development is not especially impressive either. For one thing, rates of illiteracy are on the rise. For another, the progression rate from junior to senior middle school is only now regaining the levels attained in the mid-1970s (Figure 15.9). By this measure, China has made no progress in the thirty years since Mao's death.

Furthermore, high middle-school enrolment rates are not translating into equally high graduation rates even now. In fact, it is a sign of how far China still has to go that only about 11 per cent of the rural workforce had a senior middle school education or better in 2005, a figure which was only marginally higher than the 9.2 per cent figure recorded in 1996 (SSB 2006c: 15). Given that the economy

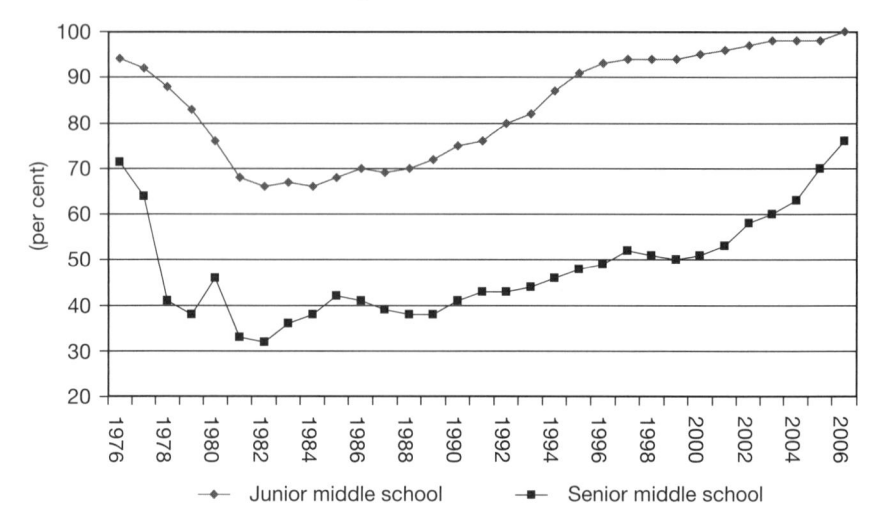

Figure 15.9 Progression rates to junior and senior middle school (percentage graduating from the lower level) (Sources: SSB (2005a: 81–2); ZGTJNJ (2006: 810); ZGTJNJ (2007: 799).)

was growing at around 10 per cent per year during this period, these educational data testify to the very small sums which have been allocated to the educational sector. This indeed was a decade of private affluence amidst public squalor. As Lin (2006: 269) rightly says:

> It is no trivial matter that 1.3 billion people had been largely better off in their standard of living. Such gains. however, were stained and also held back by the negative social consequences of reform – above all the loss in human capital amassed over decades of hard work and arduous struggle.

In two other respects, there are qualifications to China's development record since 1996. For one thing, the potential for development in China over the last decade has been very high. The legacies of Maoism and market socialist development between 1978 and 1996 meant that there was much for Deng's successors to build on. Most obviously there was a large cadre of increasingly skilled labourers available for employment in the state, private and foreign sectors. China's international relations were also favourable; the prospects for rapid trade growth with the EU and the USA were high, and China's capacity to attract FDI had never been so high. The world economy also grew comparatively quickly. The Asian crisis had little effect on China. both because of its capital controls and because few of China's exports went to the Asian region. Only the slow growth of Japan placed a damper on China's prospects. Given these favourable legacies, it is not surprising that China did grow quickly and it is not entirely unreasonable to argue that it should have done better. It is certainly not surprising that the growth rate was faster than it was during the Maoist era.

Second, it is far from obvious that China will be able to sustain its rate of growth. The scope for catch-up is much less now than it was in the 1980s and 1990s, and therefore it is certain that its growth rate will slow down over the next decade. But there are also factors which are in principle under China's control which will ensure that performance is far less good than it might be. There is, for example, a real environmental threat to Chinese growth. The estimates of hydrologists suggest that the aquifers of north China will run dry within thirty years. Levels of air pollution remain very high and will rise sharply as a result of the unchecked growth of car ownership. China is also very short of natural resources, which will make it increasingly dependent upon other countries – and therefore vulnerable. Perhaps more significantly, the Chinese state is much weaker than it was in the mid-1990s because of the decision to join the WTO, and because of privatization (which has immeasurably strengthened private-sector interest groups). Both mean that the scope for industrial policy is much more limited than it was, and therefore the likelihood of successful catch-up with the OECD nations must be low. More generally, the state is constrained by a wider cultural malaise in Chinese society, which continues to mean than discrimination is rife and that high levels of corruption are tolerated. It is this cultural constraint which will be the primary limitation on China's medium-term prospects.

Still, we need to be careful in offering too negative an assessment of China's record and prospects. Its growth rate is phenomenally high and it is not likely to come to a halt soon: such increases in GDP hold out the prospect of a solution to any number of social problems. China's cultural malaise is striking but that too can be changed. Importing Enlightenment values is of course harder than importing technology but it too can happen. Indeed, as China becomes a more prosperous society, it is certain that its values will begin to change. Nothing is certain: the Brazilian *cul-de-sac* looms large. Nevertheless, there is no cause for undue pessimism.

Finally, and coming back to the criteria set out in Chapter 1, the best way to judge a country's development record is in terms of its level of mortality. By this criterion, China has done well since 1996. With a life expectancy of around seventy-two years at birth, the People's Republic is still some way behind the OECD countries and even some middle-income countries. However, we need to remember that China's level of per capita GDP is far below that recorded in Japan and in Scandinavia; China's potential is more limited. It is therefore hardly surprising that China cannot match these countries in terms of mortality; the more relevant comparison is to look at how China is doing relative to countries with a similar level of GDP per head. By that standard, China's record is both impressive and continues to improve. It is all very well to see in Brazil a picture of China's future, but the fact remains that Chinese life expectancy is already higher, even though per capita GDP in Brazil is more than double that in China (World Bank 2007b). The contrast with South Africa is even more striking. South Africa's per capita GDP is also more than double that of China yet life expectancy is nearly twenty years lower. China has come a long way since 1949. The path taken has been chequered, it still has far to go and its prospects are cloudy in several respects. None of that, however, should blind us to its real achievements over the last half century.

Notes

1 Maddison (2006a, 20006b) has in turn come under sustained (albeit not very convincing) attack from Holz (2003, 2006).
2 For a longer comparison we can contrast China during the period 1978–2003 with Indonesia during the full Suharto period (1968–97); the countries attained a per capita GDP level of $1,000 in 1968 (Indonesia) and 1978 (China) respectively, Over these periods, Indonesian GDP grew by 7.4 per cent per annum, exactly the same as in China between 1978 and 2003.
3 The latest ICP estimates of per capita GDP have of course produced rather lower estimates than the Maddison figures (World Bank 2007b). Nevertheless, it is unlikely that these revisions would affect the conclusion very much because all three countries have had their per capita GDP downgraded.
4 For some of the literature, see World Bank (1997d, 2001d, 2007c), Edmonds (1998), Smil (2004), Economy (2004) and Day (2005). For the official view, see the annual *State of the Environment* report published by SEPA (the State Environmental Protection Administration), which it makes available on its website.
5 The World Health Organization stipulates a much more demanding limit of 20 micrograms (World Bank 2007d: 175).
6 For a comparison of environmental damage in China and India, see Winters and Yusuf (2007).
7 In fact, the upper end of the range of mortality implied by the actual report is higher than this (World Bank 2007c: xiii–xiv). Air pollution caused a loss in terms of GDP of up to 3.8 per cent in 2003. If a life is valued at 1 million *yuan* on the basis of willingness to pay for surveys, that implies 514,000 premature air pollution deaths. The 1.9 per cent cost of water pollution implies a further 256,000 deaths. It is not very clear, therefore, that the alleged suppression of the mortality figures has occurred: the report is damning enough as published.
8 SEPA produces an annual bulletin which extols the merits of the Three Gorges dam, but few are fooled by any of this. For an introduction to some of the issues relating to Chinese dam-building, see Dai (1994. 1998), McCormack (2001) and Magee (2006).
9 The preliminary 2004 green GDP report estimated environmental damage around 3.1 per cent of the total. The 2005 data were not published because of disagreements about the provincial rankings that the new estimates provided (Zhang and He 2007).
10 For what it is worth, the human development index shows a rise from 0.69 in 1995 to 0.78 by 2005, no small achievement over such a comparatively short space of time and clear evidence of the progress China has made since the mid-1990s (UNDP 2007: 235).
11 Some 650,000 adults were reported to have HIV/AIDS in China in 2006. This is a very large absolute number, but, as a percentage of the population, it fell far short of the 23 per cent rate recorded in Lesotho and 24 per cent in Botswana. The US rate (0.6 per cent) is also appreciably higher (UNICEF 2007). Underreporting distorts the Chinese figure, but it seems inconceivable (at least if population census data are anything to go by) that the true rate in the People's Republic is remotely comparable to that in sub-Saharan Africa.
12 The rate of improvement would be better but for the poor coverage of China's health insurance schemes. The urban schemes not only are inadequately funded but also usually exclude the unemployed, rural migrants and some private sector enterprises (Duckett 2001).
13 This figure of 215 million workers, which was computed during the course of the First National Economic Census and refers to the situation on 31 December 2004, excludes those living in rural households or who were self-employed in urban areas. Total employment (i.e. the sum of those employed in corporations and the self-employed) in China at the end of 2004 was around 770 million.

14 For some of the literature, see Park and Wang (2001), Khan and Riskin (2001), Riskin *et al.* (2001), Zhang *et al.* (2003), ADB (2004), Khan (2004), Reddy and Minoiu (2006), Ravallion and Chen (2007) and the website of China's Office of the Leading Group for Poverty Reduction (http://en.cpad.gov.cn/).
15 It is certainly arguable that rising health care costs are not properly factored into calculations of real income, and that the true extent of poverty (and its trend) is much worse than these estimates suggest.
16 For a useful discussion of these issues, see Dong *et al.* (2006).
17 The Ministry of Agriculture (MOA) also publishes data on concentrations of rural poverty. Its data for 2004, which are based upon a somewhat different methodology from that used by the SSB, show that there were 25.4 million people living in villages (*cun*) where average income stood at 500 *yuan* or less (compared with the national average of 2,895 *yuan*). Of these 25 million, 11 million lived in either Yunnan and Guizhou provinces in the south-west, 2.6 million in Heilongjiang and 2.3 million in Hunan (Ministry of Agriculture 2005: 328–32). It is a sign of progress, however, that the MOA now produces a list of *cun* and *xiang* rather than the list of counties it produced in the late 1990s (see for example MOA 1999: 400). This suggests at least a growing understanding of the need for a disaggregated approach.
18 Not all studies show this. Meng *et al.* (2005) suggest that urban poverty rose between 1986 and 1993, before stabilizing and then declining between 1996 and 2000.
19 More importantly, these data ignore those workers who were laid off in increasing numbers in the late 1990s.
20 The literature in both English and Chinese is vast and very fast-growing. See for example Khan and Riskin (2001), Riskin *et al.* (2001), Chang (2002), Benjamin *et al.* (2005) and Khan and Riskin (2005).
21 The issue of gender inequality is, however, a complex one. Take life expectancy. Female life expectancy in 2000 for women was seventy-three years, but only seventy years for Chinese men. In this regard, China is little different from other countries, and the raw data on the face of it suggest male disadvantage. But the reality is more complex. For one thing, welfare gains from higher female life expectancy are partly offset by higher female morbidity. For another, the differential in mortality rates for men and women aged under forty in all countries largely explains the overall life-expectancy gap, and this in turn reflects a greater predilection amongst men for risky behaviour (dangerous driving, violence, drinking and smoking). To what extent this predisposition on the part of men is biological and to what extent it is caused by social factors remains a matter for research and debate.
22 For a useful discussion of the Chinese data on mortality, see Banister and Hill (2004).
23 Brandt and Holz (2006) adjust per capita incomes for price differences across provinces. Their data show that the unadjusted urban–rural gap rose from 2.2 to 1 in 1990 to 2.79 in 2000. After price adjustment, the gap increased from 1.78 to 1.99. Both the absolute gap and the rate of increase were therefore less significant when expressed in price-adjusted terms, implying that the urban–rural gap is less of a problem than much of the literature has suggested.
24 However, urban–rural differentials are misleading, because the Chinese authorities are quick to reclassify any successful rural area as urban. That in itself is perfectly reasonable; one indicator of development is urbanization. However, it causes problems when one is making comparisons over time because the sample of urban and rural has changed. The urban–rural gap thus becomes in part a tautology because it is measuring no more than the gap between rich and poor. Any successful rural area is reclassified as urban, and therefore a rich rural area is a contradiction in terms. In the process, the real progress made by formerly poor rural areas by means of industrialization is ignored.
25 Literacy counts obtained in the censuses and in the annual 1 per cent surveys are based upon graduation rates.

26 For some of the literature on peasant protest, see Bernstein and Lü (2003), O'Brien and Li (1996, 2005, 2006) and Chen and Wu (2006). This latter was first published in China as *Zhongguo nongmin diaocha* (*An Investigation into the Chinese Peasantry*) in late 2003 and was banned by the authorities in early 2004. It nevertheless managed to sell around 7 million copies in one form or other.
27 See the compelling account of unrest in the Anhui counties of Lixin, Guzhen, Funan, Linquan and Lingbi offered in Chen and Wu (2006).
28 These are incidents involving 100 persons or more. There is some evidence that a crackdown has led to a reduction in the last two years, but questions remain over whether the falls reported are true (Tanner 2007).
29 That said, one wonders about the reliability of the survey data here. According to Khan and Riskin (2005: 364), net taxation amounted to only 2.6 per cent of rural incomes in 2002. This seems a remarkably low figure given both the anecdotal and local survey data suggesting a heavy burden of taxation and what we know about the extent of peasant protest. Of course it is possible that protest is animated by perceptions, and that the 'burden' of the peasantry is caused more by a combination of low product prices, high input prices and taxation than it is by taxation alone. Still, the suspicion remains that the extent of taxation is underestimated in the Khan and Riskin survey.
30 'by the second decade of reform, new village leaders were recruited very heavily from among collective enterprise managers' (Walder 2002: 371).
31 A useful source of material is the Hong Kong-based *China Labour Bulletin*.
32 For some of the literature on corruption in China, see Lu (2000), Sun (2004) and Yang (2004). A list of high-level officials found guilty in the period between 1992 and 2003 is given in Sun (2004: 50). Hu Angang (2002: 49) has estimated that the cost of corruption in China was around 14 to 15 per cent of GDP in 1999–2001.
33 These World Bank estimates are on a range from +2.5 (low corruption) to −2.5 (high corruption). Data are from the Bank's website (http://www.govindicators.org).
34 It is not even clear that the regional effects are positive. That sort of analysis of the effects of migration assumes that there are decreasing returns to labour inputs, and hence reduced labour supply increases productivity and wages. However, if one assumes that there are pervasive externalities generated by industrial clustering (along the lines suggest by Marshall and by Krugman), the conclusion could easily be reversed. In fact, some studies suggest that migration to coastal provinces interacts with inward investment to widen the regional gap. This is because spillover effects via remittances and return migration are too weak to offset the effects of increasing returns in FDI centres caused by the migration of the young and the educated (Fu 2004).
35 So, for example, discrimination will lead to a lower supply of workers and hence force firms to adopt non-discriminatory recruitment practices and compensation schemes. Markets will thus deal with the problem of discrimination if only they are allowed to work properly.
36 And perhaps because of labour shortages, which were being encountered in Guangdong as early as 2004; according to one report, the shortage amounted to as many as 2 million workers (FT 3 November 2004). These shortages led to a relaxation of the one-child population policy in the province in 2007. Whether any of this will affect growth is moot. By forcing Guangdong employers to pay higher wages and to invest in new technology, labour shortages will probably raise morale and labour productivity.
37 Another pessimistic account is that offered by Prasad and Rajan (2006).
38 Of course Chinese growth may slow abruptly because of developments in the world economy. Brazil (as we will see below) was blown off course by the second oil price shock of 1979, and Indonesia was badly affected by the Asian financial crisis of 1997–8, which led to the fall of Suharto. China has become much more integrated into the world economy over the last decade, and is therefore much more vulnerable than it was in the

mid-1990s. For all that, China is hardly the sort of small open economy that is most vulnerable to crisis.
39 I have discussed the relationship between inequality and state strength in more detail in Bramall (2000).
40 I reject here the pluralist conception that interest groups are forced within a capitalist society to compete with each other and are therefore unable to influence government policy to any significant degree. Competition within interest groups exists, but it is a mistake to overlook the way in which these groups are united by their class status.
41 Labour shortages will have the same effect unless the skill premium increases even more quickly.
42 There are some question marks about the reliability of these data. The shares cited by the UNDP may be internationally comparable, but it is worth noting that Chinese official data show state educational spending falling from 2.7 per cent of GDP in 1992 to 2.3 per cent in 1995 – but *rising* to 2.8 per cent by 2005 (ZGTJNJ 2007: 57 and 812). There is therefore no evidence here of a collapse in educational spending in China, though the key point remains – state spending in the People's Republic on education is rather low by world standards.
43 A typical manifestation of this bias is the way one is deemed literate with knowledge of only 1,500 characters in the countryside, whereas 2,000 are required in the cities.
44 One implication of this analysis is that democracy offers no real solution to the Chinese problem. If culture is the key constraint upon development, it follows the extension of democracy will make the Chinese state even more of a puppet than it already is. India is a more attractive model for other countries than China for its vibrant democracy. However, India's poor record on health and education – especially its provision in these areas for the mass of the Indian population – demonstrates rather clearly the limitations of the Indian model of development. Again, cultural factors may be at the root of the so-called Hindu equilibrium.
45 For a useful discussion of the economic effects of Latin American populism, see Dornbusch and Edwards (1991).
46 Much depends upon whether rising health care costs are fully included in the cost of living index. If they are, a case certainly can be made for rising absolute poverty in some parts of rural China.

16 Summary and conclusions

I conclude by summarizing the arguments laid out, and the evidence discussed, in this book. Chapter 1 outlines the criteria that I believe we should use in assessing China's development record. Although GDP per head is the orthodox metric, the case for giving ultimate priority to life expectancy appears to me to be overwhelming. The chapter also concludes that inequality matters, but that the Gini coefficient is far too blunt an instrument. Some types of inequality 'matter' far more than others, and of these it is class-based inequality which is most likely to undermine the modernization project. As for the point of comparison, it is suggested in Chapter 1 that we should judge short-run economic performance against some counterfactual notion of potential. In addition, however, we cannot consider a development strategy to be a success unless it builds long-run economic capacity and hence ensures the sustainability of growth and the enhancement of life expectancy.

The level of development attained during the last years of the Republican period is the subject of Chapter 2. It shows that levels of human development were abject. Life expectancy was exceptionally low, and the kindest thing that can be said about the educational system is that it was in its infancy. Contact with the West had helped to bring about a technological transformation of sorts in the Treaty Port economy. However, the absorption – still more so the diffusion – of new technology was hampered by an obscurantist culture and an obstructionist state. There was no Chinese equivalent to the European Enlightenment, and that was crucial; for in the final instance, it was the vitality of English culture that led to the development of a capitalist class and hence to the first Industrial Revolution. The absence of both in China during the Qing and Republican eras ensured that there was no Chinese counterpart to that revolution before 1949.

As much as anything, the absence of a progressive landlord class ensured that the growth of the modern sector was constrained by the poor performance of Chinese agriculture. Dismal is perhaps too strong a word to apply to agricultural performance; Rawski has certainly argued as much. But one is hard put to portray agriculture as an engine of growth in the 1930s. Moreover, slow agricultural productivity growth went hand-in-hand with high levels of inequality; Chinese landlords were neither technologically progressive nor socially benign. The Chinese economy of 1949 was not without its possibilities; size alone brought with it a vast population and a substantial inheritance of natural resources. And some of the problems were undoubtedly a legacy of the Japanese invasion and the civil war, rather than the product of a deep-seated malaise. But the state capacity needed to exploit these opportunities and to break out of China's low-level equilibrium trap was signally lacking in the half century before 1949.

Chapter 3 considers the early Maoist era, defined here to mean the period between 1949 and 1955. I argue that these were wasted years. To be sure, the Chinese economy did not perform badly. Recovery from the trough of 1949 was rapid, and life expectancy increased apace in the early 1950s. Moreover, the land reform of 1947–53 did much to raise the living standards of the poorest members of the Chinese population. Nevertheless, short-run economic performance was far from exceptional. The mortality rate remained high, and education was underdeveloped. Per capita GDP even by the mid-1950s had barely surpassed the 1937 peak. Poor agricultural performance remained the fundamental problem. For although output and productivity both rose, the growth rate was not sufficient to keep pace with the demands of the burgeoning industrial sector. The small-scale peasant farming which was the legacy of land reform was simply not up to the task of generating agricultural modernization; even though the rich peasant economy had been deliberately preserved in order to promote growth, agricultural performance remained sluggish. Worse still, little was done during the early 1950s to expand the long-run productive capacity of the rural economy. The investment rate was modest, but perhaps more importantly the Party turned its face against early collectivization; had it been implemented immediately after land reform, the labour force could have been mobilized far more effectively for infrastructural purposes, which would in turn have laid the foundations for higher agricultural yields (via the expansion of irrigation) and hence for more rapid long-run growth.

The period of the Great Leap Forward, the subject of Chapter 4, was one of unmitigated disaster. To be sure, poor weather played a bigger role in the collapse of output during the Great Famine than is generally recognized. At root, however, the fall in food production was a policy failure. It stemmed from a premature attempt to force the development of iron and steel production in the countryside, which served only to divert labour out of the farming sector and cut both sown area and farm yields in the process. In conjunction with a range of distributional failures (the planning system virtually collapsed during 1959–61 in the face of mass migration and output overreporting), labour shortages brought about the worst famine in human history. We will never know its true extent, nor the number of lives it blighted in so many different ways. But its mortality toll can scarcely have been less than 30 million excess deaths, mainly in the provinces of Sichuan, Anhui and Guizhou. Only the abandonment of the worst excesses of the Leap, the restoration of good weather and timely imports of wheat from Canada brought the Great Famine to an end. By then however, much of the reservoir of goodwill enjoyed by the Party in the aftermath of is revolutionary triumph of 1949 had dissipated.

Chapter 5 outlines the strategy of development which was pursued between 1963 and 1978, a period which I call late Maoism. During these years, Mao abandoned economic determinism, and in so doing broke with the Soviet Union in thought as well as deed. Mao's grand design was to remake the superstructure of Chinese society and its economic base at the same time. In emphasizing the importance of superstructural change in this way, Mao made his own distinctive contribution to the evolution of Marxist thought. Late Maoism focused in particular on the reconstruction of the Chinese educational system, which in practical terms meant both the expansion of rural education and the re-education of Chinese urban youth by means of their enforced relocation to the countryside. It also involved a number of concrete economic policies – in particular collective farming and rural industrialization – which aimed to raise living standards in the countryside and hence put an end to the great divide between urban and rural China. Out of all this were born the Socialist Education Movement in 1963 and, far more importantly, the Cultural Revolution (1966–8).

During the Cultural Revolution, Chinese urban society was torn apart, and many of its cultural artefacts destroyed. Few tears were shed for either the objects, or their owners, in the countryside; for rural China, these were golden years during which educational provision expanded apace and the foundations of industrialization were laid. Nevertheless, Mao put an end to the process of urban destruction in 1968 by despatching the architects – the Red Guards – to the countryside to mend their ways and to help modernize rural society. The years after 1968 were less destructive in many ways, but this was an era of disillusionment, especially in urban China. Sporadic violence and purges continued. More significantly, Lin Biao – Mao's chosen successor and the man who presided over the restoration of order to China's streets in 1968 – died in a plane crash in 1971 which followed an attempted coup, and thereafter elite Chinese politics was characterized by a struggle over the succession. Yet we do well to recognize that the late Maoist modernization programme continued. Indeed, and violence notwithstanding, even the urban population had never had it so good. Unemployment was virtually non-existent, and poverty had been all but eliminated by relatively generous wages and by a raft of subsidies to the urban population. In the countryside, the programme of rural transformation proceeded apace during the 1970s. Many of the ambitious irrigation projects begun during the early 1960s were completed, leading to unparalleled increases in yields. Rural industry started to develop quickly, and by 1978 was on the verge of take-off. And perhaps most remarkable of all, the majority of rural children were going to primary and junior middle school for the first time.

The transformation of the educational system, which led to these remarkable results, is the subject of Chapter 6. The educational system was avowedly elitist in the 1950s and early 1960s. Its purpose was to provide a small minority of the Chinese population with a high-quality education, and to provide some minimal level of teaching to the rest. In practical terms, this meant that primary and middle-school education expanded at a glacial pace. In addition, the educational system was failing by the mid-1960s, in that only a small fraction of those graduating from senior middle school were able to go on to university. Worse, competition for university places was fundamentally unequal; the children of workers and cadres were simply unable to compete against the children of the old elite, who benefited from their parents' cultural capital despite the redistribution of income that had taken place in the 1950s. The failure of the system to meet these aspirations goes far towards explaining the violence of the student movement during the Cultural Revolution.

The Cultural Revolution paved the way for the wholesale restructuring of the educational system. Schools and universities initially closed as their student populations took to the street. Gradually, however, the new system took shape. Students were expected to combine study with manual work. A rapid expansion of primary and middle-school education was launched in the countryside. Gilded urban youth were despatched to the countryside to work alongside and learn from the peasantry, and to provide the teachers necessary for the expansion of the rural middle-school system. The exam system was abandoned, and in the process the cultural capital of the old elite was rendered worthless, as access to university education came to depend upon virtue (meaning service to the Revolution) rather than examination marks. Taken as a whole, the evidence suggests that this attempt to remake the Chinese superstructure was remarkably successful. Entrenched attitudes were of course hard to change; and it is fair to say that the quality (at least as conventionally measured) of China's system of urban education declined. However, that decline was more than offset by reduced educational differentials, both within urban areas and – much more importantly – between the cities and the countryside. Moreover, the educational revolution in the countryside transformed rural health and paved the way for the industrialization of the 1970s and 1980s.

The expansion of rural education was presided over by China's communes, the lynchpin of the system of collective farming. The system is discussed in Chapter 7. Collectivization was central to the late Maoist development strategy. One of its purposes was to raise agricultural output and yields by mobilizing the labour force to carry out infrastructure construction, and in particular the expansion of the irrigation system. In the long run, it was hoped that this mobilization would, via farmland consolidation, promote mechanization and allow the release of agricultural labour by raising labour productivity. The second motivation behind the drive for collectivization was a desire to reduce income inequality. And so it proved: collectivization broke the link between income and asset ownership by taking land into public ownership. After 1956, incomes therefore depended upon virtue and work done, rather than the amount of land and capital that was owned. In addition, collectivization would make possible the provision of a range of public goods – health, education and social security.

Chinese collectives were relatively successful in reducing income inequality; by the end of the 1970s, the rural Gini coefficient was extremely low. Furthermore, literacy rates and life expectancy were much higher than they had been in the mid-1950s. However, the late Maoist strategy was less successful in raising agricultural output and yields; at best, per capita agricultural output grew slowly between the late 1950s and the late 1970s. Part of the reason was that collectivization failed to resolve the incentive problem that plagues the operation of large-scale farming across the world in situations where labour is the main input. Nevertheless, collective incentive problems were only part of the reason for slow agricultural growth. More important were the constraints within which the rural sector operated. For one thing, China had reached its arable frontier by the late 1950s; only in Heilongjiang province was there real scope for further increases in cultivated area. For another thing, and more importantly, defence industrialization deprived the farm sector of the inputs (especially chemical fertilizer) it needed to introduce the Green Revolution package. Defence industrialization also dictated that the internal terms of trend were biased against agriculture throughout the late Maoist era. As a result, many types of farm production were simply not profitable in the late 1970s. This incentive problem was every bit as severe as anything posed by collective organization itself.

The reasons for, and the implications of, defence industrialization are outlined in Chapter 8 as a part of a more general discussion of the late Maoist rural industrialization programme. This programme was one of the most distinctive features of the late Maoist development strategy, and signalled a clear break with the orthodox Soviet preoccupation with urban industrialization. Its most important component was the Third Front, the vast programme of defence industrialization initiated after 1964 in response to perceived American, and later Soviet, threats. In essence this was a programme of rural industrialization; it focused on the creation of new industries on green-field sites like Panzhihua in western China as well as in the interiors of coastal provinces like Guangdong. After 1968, the Front merged with a more general programme of rural industrialization led by county governments, by communes and by brigades across the whole of China. The result of this industrialization programme was the creation of an extensive industrial capacity in western China in particular and in the Chinese countryside in general.

In many respects, however, the Third Front was a failure. Most of the industrial enterprises so created were inefficient when judged by the usual metrics of short-run profitability and productivity. Third Front industries were never called upon to fulfil their military function, and therefore the programme was rather pointless when viewed with the benefit of hindsight. Moreover, Front enterprises left few long-run legacies precisely because many of them were located far from the centres of Chinese population (and hence incurred crippling transport costs). And a considerable proportion of the industries established in western China in the late Maoist era were focused on lumber and mineral extraction, and hence generated few of the dynamic economies of scale associated with manufacturing, the only basis for an efficient and sustainable industrial sector. For all that, it would be a mistake to view late Maoist rural industrialization as a failure. The truth is that it was a vast programme of learning-by-doing in which a significant proportion of an untutored Chinese peasantry entered the factory gates, and in the process acquired a range of skills and competencies which were to provide the basis for the meteoric pace of rural industrialization in the post-Mao years. The programme should be judged on the basis of whether it expanded China's long-run industrial potential, not in terms of short-run profits and productivity. By that long-run calculus, the rural industrialization programme was highly successful.

Chapter 9 brings together the themes discussed in the preceding four chapters and proffers a more general evaluation of the late Maoist development strategy. I suggest there that the strategy failed to live up to the hopes of the CCP. For one thing, per capita output growth was slower than in the East Asian NICs and in Japan during their economic miracles. For another, real levels of per capita consumption barely rose at all during the 1960s and 1970s. Industrialization and population growth wrought considerable environmental damage to China's fragile landscape. Extensive rural poverty persisted at the end of the 1970s. And the urban–rural income gap widened, rather than diminished.

For all that, the late Maoist era was a remarkable one. Living standards in rural areas were transformed by improvements in health care, and by the introduction of near-universal middle-school education. The inequalities of the past were banished by collective ownership of the means of production, by the suppression of private industry and commerce and by the creation of a social security net. More importantly, the productive potential of the rural economy was vastly enhanced by the expansion of water conservancy schemes, by the acquisition of skills in the burgeoning rural industrial sector and by the introduction of new, high-yielding seed varieties. *Xiafang* and Third Front programmes may have been unpopular with those who were transferred to live in urban areas, but they too helped to lay the foundations for future rural advance. By the end of the 1970s, the Chinese countryside was poised on the verge of industrial and agricultural revolutions driven by rural industries and by green revolution technology. Within China's cities, the transformation was equally remarkable. The power and status of the old intellectual and professional elite had been swept away; parents with cultural capital were an impediment to social mobility, and instead the status of worker was something to be craved. By the late 1970s, inequalities within China's cities were probably as narrow as anywhere else in the world.

Moreover, once the constraints upon Chinese economic potential during the late Maoist period are laid bare, its record seems remarkable. Had the People's Republic not been isolated, the Third Front programme would not have been necessary and significantly large sums would have been available for spending on health, education, infrastructure and civilian industry. In a very real sense, therefore, high living standards were crowded out by the defence expenditure required to meet the threat posed by American colonial ambition. Still, one should not overemphasize this line of argument. To be sure, the potential of the Chinese economy was limited by external constraints. However, China's international isolation was in part self-inflicted; a more subtle and less ideological foreign policy might have done a better job of ensuring military security, and at a lower economic cost. 'Might' is of course the operative word; Cold War intransigence would not have been so easily overcome, and there is no doubt that there was a strong body of opinion in the US only too willing to see China bombed back to the Stone Age in company with North Vietnam. Nevertheless, the strongest argument for the late Maoist development strategy is not so much that actual performance lived up to its isolation-constrained potential, but that it was so successful in expanding the long-run productive capability of the Chinese economy. In a very real sense, Mao Zedong is the father of China's contemporary economic miracle.

Chapter 10 moves the story on to the post-1978 era, and outlines the unfolding of macroeconomic policy between the death of Mao, and Deng Xiaoping's death in early 1997. It focuses on two of the main policy changes of the 1980s: agricultural decollectivization and the drift towards market determination of prices. I suggest that we should view this period as an attempt to combine planning and markets, and that the epithet market socialism describes it very well. It was not intended during the Readjustment period of 1978–82 that the programme of dismantling Maoism would proceed so far. However, many of the most radical of the early reforms (establishing special economic zones and allowing private farming) were deemed to be the most successful, and as a result the cause of *gaige kaifang* (reform and opening up) gathered momentum. Nevertheless, China's journey during the years of Deng Xiaoping was towards the grail of market socialism, rather than towards the goal of capitalism. The People's Republic, in contrast to the Soviet Union, did not privatize state-owned industry. Prices were liberalized, and new firms, whether privately owned or established by foreigners, were allowed to be set up. The result was that the Chinese economy of 1996 was characterized by a high degree of competition even though the bulk of the industrial sector remained firmly under the control of the state.

The conventional wisdom has it that the rather limited nature of reform in China meant that it was the foreign sector which transformed the Chinese economy during the 1980s and 1990s. As a result – so it is argued – of an avalanche of new technology and foreign direct investment, and an unprecedented surge in exports, the drag on growth imposed by a failing state industrial sector proved not to be very serious. The impact of this process of *gaige kaifang* is the subject matter of Chapter 11, and there is some truth in the notion that opening up had a transformative effect. The Chinese economy has never been more open than it has become in the first years of the new century. Chinese exports have stocked the retail outlets of the West. New technology from abroad has helped to raise productivity in Chinese industry. Migrant workers have flocked from the Chinese interior to find work on the streets of China's fast-growing coastal cities. The very landscape of Guangdong has been transformed by interaction with the foreigners on green-field sites like Shenzhen and Dongguan.

The reality of the open door is more prosaic. For one thing, the policy properly dates from 1971: Mao was much less hostile to foreign trade than has often been suggested. Moreover, China's integration into the world economy even now is far more limited than is generally believed. In fact, much of the Chinese interior has been barely touched by foreign trade and it has received precious little foreign direct investment. The coastal provinces may have been transformed (though few of those living in the mountainous areas within Guangdong province would agree), but not so the Chinese interior. Migrant workers have flooded into Guangdong and China's metropolitan centres, and their remittances have served to reduce absolute poverty in the western provinces. But technological spillovers have been very limited, and the rapid reduction in poverty that occurred across China in the 1980s had far more to do with the transformation of agriculture and rural industrialization than with the open door. In fact, the effect of joining the WTO may even have been to increase poverty; some of the literature certainly suggests as much. All in all, therefore, we do far better to think of the Chinese economic miracle as being made in China rather than in the workshops and shopping malls of the West.

Chapter 12 focuses on the primary engine of growth: China's industrial sector. Here, the Chinese government pursued a strategy which in effect amounted to mimicking the industrial policy approach adopted in the late twentieth century in Japan, Taiwan and South Korea. To that end, China abandoned the late Maoist 'plan ideological' approach in which development was seen as requiring the whole of the industrial sector to be in state hands. Instead, entry by private and foreign companies was welcomed in the hope that the increase in competition so generated would invigorate the state sector. This strategy was complemented by price reform designed to provide profit-based incentives to SOE managers, and by attempts to improve SOE governance by transferring greater power and autonomy to factory directors. China also sought to improve the performance of SOEs by shifting state investment away from heavy industry and the Third Front and towards civilian light industry instead. To be sure, the profit rate declined (given intensified competition, it could hardly have done anything else), and the record on productivity, though better than in the late Maoist era, was not outstanding. But set against this is the fact that the pre-1996 Chinese industrial sector expanded rapidly, mainly because of the creation of new companies in the countryside by township and village governments. It was this industrial expansion which made possible sustained increases in GDP, full employment and a reduction in rural poverty. The contrast with the Soviet Union is sharp, and it testifies to the effectiveness of China's industrial strategy under Deng Xiaoping.

Industrial policy has continued since 1996, its most obvious manifestation being the attempt by the Chinese government to create some 120 globally competitive enterprise groups or national champions. It is evident that these are modelled on the South Korean *chaebols*. Nevertheless, it is clear that China has abandoned its market socialist vision since Deng's death, and instead moved quickly to create a capitalist economy. Emblematic of this shift has been the implementation of the *zhuada fangxiao* programme, which has led to the wholesale closure of great swathes of Chinese industrial enterprises, whether TVEs or urban state- and collectively owned enterprises, in an attempt to raise productivity levels and to create a modern industrial sector. It is too early to judge whether this will be successful, but the auguries are not good. Profit rates have revived, the national champions are performing well and total factor productivity growth continues. However, the revival in profits has more to do with rising world oil prices than anything else; the methodological basis of TFP studies is so suspect that almost any results can be obtained; and the fact of the matter is that the (subsidized) national champions are doing no better than other (unsubsidized) industrial enterprises. Moreover, the growth of rent-seeking coalitions (itself encouraged by wealth transfers via insider privatization) and the surrender of policy autonomy as a result of WTO membership mean that it will be increasingly difficult for the Chinese government to maintain SOE performance. The Chinese state in this sense is becoming increasingly soft and therefore less able to perform the sort of periodic SOE restructuring that is the hallmark of a successful industrial policy model. However, the most powerful indictment of China's post-1996 industrial strategy is that the CCP has lost sight of the essential point: that an efficient industry sector in a poor country is not one with world-best productivity levels. If only that was required, a couple of oil refineries would suffice. A truly efficient industrial sector is one which is capable of ensuring full employment, both directly and indirectly. By that criterion, as persistent unemployment so eloquently testifies, China has failed.

Chapter 13 assesses economic performance in the Dengist era. My conclusion is that the record is far less good than usually believed. True, the rate of growth of GDP has been exceptional by international and historical standards: it is the contrast between the growth rate achieved after 1978, and during the late Maoist era, which is the most striking achievement of the Dengist regime. Yet this achievement is signally lessened by the fact that China's growth potential was far greater in the 1980s and 1990s than it had been in the early 1960s. China's improved relations with the USA meant that there was much greater scope for international trade, and the reformers inherited both a backlog of new agricultural technologies and an array of favourable legacies (infrastructural, educational and skills). Without these legacies, there is no question that China's growth would have been slower after 1978.

Moreover, the record of the Dengist regime was poor in many other spheres. Life expectancy, the best single measure of development, increased only modestly; reductions in child mortality were offset by increased female infant mortality, which reflected the interaction of the one-child family policy and Chinese prejudice against infant girls. Income inequality soared, especially within the cities and the countryside as a new class system emerged; productivity may have increased in the workplace, but it was driven by fear rather than hope. Educational enrolment rates actually fell significantly in the countryside as the failed educational model of the 1950s reasserted itself and the urban elites sought to put peasants back in their place. University enrolments increased, but the expansion of the tertiary sector was bought at the expense of the rural poor and disadvantaged. Even China's greatest apparent achievement in the years of Deng – the reduction in rural poverty – is far less good than it appears when viewed through an official lens. The 1978 data exaggerate the true extent of poverty at the end of the Maoist era, and in so far as poverty declined after 1978, the decline was concentrated in the years up to 1984. Since then, progress has been fitful, with a modest decline in rural poverty offset to some extent by the re-emergence of urban poverty.

I discuss the way in which Chinese economic policy has changed since Deng's death in early 1997 in Chapter 14. In some respects, Jiang Zemin and Hu Jintao seem to have adhered to some of the precepts of socialism. China continues to implement state-led industrial policy along the lines pioneered in South Korea and Japan, and the state sector still produces around 30 per cent of industrial output even in 2008. The Develop the West programme signals an enduring commitment to closing regional income inequalities. The regime's commitment to providing free tuition in rural schools, its bid to create a 'new socialist countryside' and the environmental targets embedded in the Eleventh Five Year Programme – for no longer does China have five year plans – suggests that CCP does not seek to create a fully-fledged capitalist economy.

To my mind, this represents a fundamental misreading of Chinese economic policy-making since 1996. To be sure, the rhetoric of socialism remains and the brand of capitalism which China has established is better described as state capitalism than anything else; state intervention continues to pervade every corner of Chinese society. In reality, however, the language of socialism is being using to cloak the creation of a capitalist system as vicious and malevolent as anything that has been seen across the globe. Phrases such as a 'harmonious society' and a 'new socialist countryside' are no more than words. China's urban elite has no intention of giving up its riches to the peasantry, and no desire to satisfy anything other than the basic needs of the workforce it requires to produce the wealth from which to finance its burgeoning consumption. Enriched by the privatizations of the late 1990s, a new capitalist class has emerged, and it has entrenched its position by undermining the state whether at home (by resisting the creation of a proper system of taxation) or abroad (by presiding over China's lemming-like entry to the WTO, and thereby its surrender to the dictates of global capitalism).

Nevertheless, the central question remains: Chinese capitalism is unpalatable in many of its manifestations, but has it served to increase the well-being of the population over the last decade? This is the subject-matter of Chapter 15. There I argue that there can be no denying the vitality of Chinese capitalism. The growth record of the People's Republic since 1996 has been impressive, and the prophets of doom – for whom the demise of China is around the next corner – continue to be confounded. Nevertheless, it is important to recognize that China's growth record is by no means unique. Brazil did better during its economic miracle between 1964 and 1980, and Indonesia likewise under Suharto between 1968 and 1997. Both were ultimately blown off course by events in the world economy, and the same may happen to China. Any suggestion, therefore, of Chinese exceptionalism is not supported by the evidence. In other respects, China has fared indifferently since 1996. Environmental degradation has been pervasive, and there is little sign of any real improvement; its cities are now amongst the most polluted places on the planet and much of its water has been poisoned by chemical fertilizer and industrial effluent. Urban poverty has risen and inequality has spiralled to very high levels. Even the pace of poverty reduction in the countryside has slowed down.

We should not exaggerate these woes. China's record on life expectancy over the last decade has been better than in the 1980s, and the absolute levels reached – seventy for men and seventy-three for women – are extraordinary for a country which still has such a low level of per capita income. The Chinese environment may have been heavily polluted, but it is not showing up in any obvious way in terms of average life expectancy or morbidity; tobacco is a far more important contributor factor to mortality. And rapid growth and technical advance brings with it potential solutions to a range of a problems.

Nevertheless, the portents are not good. China's central problem is that the state is much weaker than it was a decade ago. It has suffered a loss of economic sovereignty as a result of the decision to enter the WTO. As significantly, the privatizations of the late 1990s have strengthened private sector interest groups at the expense of central government. The result of both these developments is that the state is far less able to conduct industrial policy – by which I mean the systematic and sustained reallocation of resources from slow-growing to dynamic sectors – than it was under Deng Xiaoping. That makes it very unlikely that China's industrial sector will ever be able to catch up. None of this is to suggest that China is on the verge of collapse: it is not. But the Chinese state is much weaker than it was, and that has led to significant dimming of China's development prospects.

Yet more important than state weakness is a growing cultural malaise. Traditional Chinese culture has reasserted itself, in the form of endemic discrimination against women, the naked exploitation of China's colonies (Xinjiang and Tibet) and the increasingly contemptuous attitude of metropolitan elites towards the countryside and migrant workers. The Chinese educational system, most obviously in the guise of the rapid expansion of the tertiary sector, favours the desires of the few rather than the needs of the many. Many of these cultural traits was suppressed and even attacked during the Cultural Revolution and during the 1970s. Excessive female infant mortality had been all but eliminated; industrial policy was designed to promote the development of the west of China, rather to exploit it; the educational system was meritocratic in word and in deed. And the sending-down programme did something to put a halt to metropolitan disdain for the countryside.

Much, therefore, has changed since the late Maoist era. Some of it has been for the good: nobody can deny the rapid increase in material living standards that has been achieved since 1978, and which has continued since 1996. Yet China's dismal record on the environment, the unequal distribution of income, power and privilege, and its chequered progress on human development reflect a growing reassertion of all that is worst in Chinese culture. Collapse is unlikely any time soon, but unless fundamental and far-reaching cultural change takes place, the Brazilian *cul-de-sac* – endemic inequality, environmental destruction and stagnating levels of human development – looms large on the horizon. Cultural change is not impossible: men make their own history. But China has far to go if it is to catch up. If it is to do so, it needs to blend the positive aspects of its Maoist heritage with the more open and economically liberal structures of the post-1978 era. Its leap into the arms of authoritarian capitalism is a mistake, and one from which China will find it hard to recover.

Bibliography

Acemoglu, A., Johnson, S. and Robinson, J. A. (2001). 'The Colonial Origins of Comparative Development.' *American Economic Review*, 91 (5): 1369–401.
Acemoglu, A., Johnson, S. and Robinson, J. A. (2002). 'Reversal of Fortune.' *Quarterly Journal of Economics*, 117: 1231–94.
Acemoglu, A., Johnson, S. and Robinson, J. A. (2003). 'An African Success Story: Botswana.' In Rodrik, D. (ed.) (2003) *In Search of Prosperity*. Princeton: Princeton University Press.
Adelman, I. and Sunding, D. (1987). 'Economic Policy and Income Distribution in China.' *Journal of Comparative Economics*, 11 (3): 444–61.
Aird, J. S. (1990). *Slaughter of the Innocents*. Washington: AEI Press.
Akhand, H. and Gupta, K. (2005). *Economic Development in Pacific Asia*. London: Routledge.
Alesina, A. and Rodrik, D. (1994). 'Distributive Politics and Economic Growth.' *Quarterly Journal of Economics*, 109 (2): 465–90.
Alesina, A. and Spolaore, E. (2003). *The Size of Nations*. Cambridge, MA: MIT Press.
Allen, R. C. (1992). *Enclosure and the Yeoman*. Oxford: Clarendon Press.
Allen, R. C. (1999). 'Tracking the Agricultural Revolution in England.' *Economic History Review*, 52: 209–35.
Allen, R. C. (2003). *Farm to Factory*. Princeton: Princeton University Press.
Althusser, L. (1969/1990). *For Marx*. London: Verso.
Althusser, L. and Balibar, E. (1968/1997). *Reading Capital*. London: Verso.
Amnesty International (2007). 'Internal Migrants: Discrimination and Abuse – The Human Cost of an Economic Miracle.' London: Amnesty.
Amsden, A. H. (1989). *Asia's New Giant*. Oxford: Oxford University Press.
Anand, S. and Kanbur, R. (1993). 'Inequality and Development: A Critique.' *Journal of Development Economics*, 41 (1): 19–43.
Anand, S. and Ravallion, M. (1993). 'Human Development in Poor Countries.' *Journal of Economic Perspectives*, 7 (1): 133–50.
Andreas, J. (2002). 'Battling over Political and Cultural Power during the Chinese Cultural Revolution.' *Theory and Society*, 31 (4): 463–519.
Arrigo, L. G. (1986). 'Landownership Concentration in China.' *Modern China*, 12 (3): 259–60.
Arrow, K. (1962). 'The Economic Implications of Learning by Doing.' *Review of Economic Studies*, 29: 155–73.
Ash, R. F. (1988). 'The Evolution of Agricultural Policy.' *China Quarterly*, 116: 529–55.

Ash, R. F. (ed.) (1998). *Agricultural Development in China, 1949–1989: The Collected Papers of Kenneth R. Walker.* Oxford: Oxford University Press.

Ash, R. F. (2006). 'Squeezing the Peasants: Grain Extraction, Food Consumption and Rural Living Standards in Mao's China.' *China Quarterly,* 188: 959–98.

Asian Development Bank (2004). *Poverty Profile of the People's Republic of China.* Manila: Asian Development Bank.

Atkinson, A. B. (1995). *Income Distribution in OECD Countries.* Paris: OECD.

Bachman, D. (2001). 'Defence Industrialization in Guangdong.' *China Quarterly,* 166: 273–304.

Bada chengshi zhengfu diaoyan jigou lianhe ketizu (Government Joint Research Group for Eight Major Cities) (1990). *Zhongguo da chengshi renkou yu shehui fazhan* (Population and Social Development in Chinese Metropolises). Beijing: Zhongguo chengshi jingji shehui chubanshe.

Baer, W. (1995). *The Brazilian Economy,* fourth edition. London: Praeger.

Bain, I. (1993). *Agricultural Reform in Taiwan.* Hong Kong: Chinese University Press.

Bairoch, P. (1993). *Economics and World History: Myths and Paradoxes.* London: Harvester.

Bakken, B. (1998). *Migration in China.* Copenhagen: Nordic Institute of Asian Studies.

Bakken, B. (2002). 'Review of Seeberg, *The Rhetoric and Reality of Mass Education in Mao's China.*' *International Sociology,* 17 (1): 140–2.

Banister, J. (1987). *China's Changing Population.* Stanford: Stanford University Press.

Banister, J. (1992). 'Demographic Aspects of Poverty in China.' World Bank Working Paper for World Bank (ed.). *China: Strategies for Reducing Poverty in the 1990s.* Washington, DC: World Bank.

Banister, J. (1998). 'Population, Public Health and the Environment in China.' *China Quarterly,* 156: 986–1015.

Banister, J. (2004). 'Shortage of Girls in China Today.' *Journal of Population Research,* 21 (1): 19–45.

Banister, J. (2005). *Manufacturing Employment and Compensation in China.* US Bureau of Labour Statistics. At http://www.bls.gov/opub/mlr (accessed 6 May 2007).

Banister, J. and Hill, K. (2004). 'Mortality in China, 1964–2000.' *Population Studies,* 58 (1): 55–75.

Banister, J. and Zhang, X. B. (2005). 'China, Economic Development and Mortality Decline.' *World Development,* 33 (1): 21–41.

Bao, S. M., Chang, G. H., Sachs, J. D. and Woo, W. T. (2002). 'Geographic Factors and China's Regional Development under Market Reforms, 1978–1998.' *China Economic Review,* 13: 89–111.

Barclay, G. W., Coale, A. J., Stoto, M. and Trussell, J. (1976): 'A Reassessment of the Demography of Traditional Rural China.' *Population Index,* 42 (4): 603–35.

Bardhan, P. (2006). 'Globalization and Rural Poverty.' *World Development* 34 (8): 1393–404.

Barro, R. J. (1997). *Determinants of Economic Growth.* Cambridge, MA: MIT Press.

Barro, R. J. and Sala-i-Martin, X. (1995). *Economic Growth.* New York: McGraw Hill.

Bates, R. H. (1989). *Beyond the Miracle of the Market.* Cambridge: Cambridge University Press.

Baum, R. (1969). 'Revolution and Reaction in the Chinese Countryside.' *China Quarterly,* 38: 92–119.

Baum, R. and Teiwes, F. C. (1968). *Ssu-ch'ing: The Socialist Education Movement of 1962–1966.* Berkeley: University of California Press.

Becker, J. (1996). *Hungry Ghosts: China's Secret Famine.* London: John Murray.

Bell, L. S. (1999). *One Industry, Two Chinas*. Stanford: Stanford University Press.
Benjamin, D. and Brandt, L. (1997). 'Land, Factor Markets, and Inequality in Rural China: Historical Evidence.' *Explorations in Economic History*, 34: 460–94.
Benjamin, D., Brandt, L. and Giles, J. (2005). 'The Evolution of Income Inequality in Rural China.' *Economic Development and Cultural Change*, 53 (4): 769–824.
Bergère, Marie-Claire (1989a). *The Golden Age of the Chinese Bourgeoisie*. Cambridge: Cambridge University Press.
Bergère, Marie-Claire (1989b). 'The Consequences of the Post First World War Depression for the China Treaty-Port Economy.' In Brown, I. (ed.) (1989) *The Economies of Africa and Asia in the Inter-war Depression*. London: Routledge.
Bergsten, C. F., Gill, B., Lardy, N. R. and Mitchell, D. (2006). *China: The Balance Sheet*. New York: Public Affairs.
Bernstein, T. P. (1977). *Up to the Mountains and Down to the Villages*. New Haven: Yale University Press.
Bernstein, T. P. (1984). 'Stalinism, Famine and Chinese Peasants.' *Theory and Society*, 13 (3): 339–77.
Bernstein, T. P. (2006). 'Mao Zedong and the Famine of 1959–1960.' *China Quarterly*, 186: 421–45.
Bernstein, T. P. and Lü, X. B. (2003). *Taxation without Representation in Contemporary Rural China*. Cambridge: Cambridge University Press.
Berry, A. R. and Cline, W. R. (1979). *Agrarian Structure and Productivity in Developing Countries*. Baltimore: Johns Hopkins University Press.
Bhaduri, A. (1973). 'A Study in Agricultural Backwardness under Semi-Feudalism.' *Economic Journal*, 83: 120–37.
Bhaduri, A. (1977). 'On the Formation of Usurious Interest Rates.' *Cambridge Journal of Economics*, 1 (1): 341–52.
Bhagwati, J. (1993). *India in Transition*. Oxford: Clarendon Press.
Bhagwati, J. (2004). *In Defense of Globalization*. Oxford: Oxford University Press.
Bhattasali, D., Li, S. T. and Martin, W. (eds) (2004). *China and the WTO*. Oxford: Oxford University Press.
Bianco, L. (1971). *Origins of the Chinese Revolution, 1915–1949*. Stanford: Stanford University Press.
Bils, M. and Klenow, P. J. (2000). 'Does Schooling Cause Growth?' *American Economic Review*, 90 (5): 1160–83.
Blanchard, O. and Giavazzi, F. (2006). 'Rebalancing Growth in China: A Three-Handed Approach.' *China and the World Economy*, 14 (4): 1–20.
Blanchflower, D. G. and Oswald, A. (2005). 'Happiness and the Human Development Index.' *Australian Economic Review*, 38 (3): 307–18.
Blank, R. (2006). 'A Review of the Labour Market Discussion in the 2006 Economic Report of the President.' *Journal of Economic Literature*, XLIV (3): 669–73.
Blecher, M. (1976). 'Income Distribution in Small Rural Chinese Communities.' *China Quarterly*, 68: 797–816.
Blecher, M. and Shue, V. (1996). *Tethered Deer*. Stanford: Stanford University Press.
Blomstrom, M. and Kokko, A. (1998). 'Multinational Corporations and Spillovers.' *Journal of Economic Surveys*, 12 (2): 1–31.
Bohr, P. R. (1972). *Famine in China and the Missionary*. Cambridge, MA: Harvard University Press.
Borensztein, E., De Gregorio, J. and Lee, J. W. (1998). 'How Does Foreign Direct Investment Affect Economic Growth?' *Journal of International Economics*, 45: 115–35.

Bosworth, B. P. and Collins, S. M. (2003). 'The Empirics of Growth: An Update.' *Brookings Papers on Economic Activities*, 2: 113–206.
Bosworth, B. P. and Collins, S. M. (2007). *Accounting for Growth: Comparing China and India*. At http://www.brookings.edu (accessed 11 May 2007)
Bottomore, T. (ed.) (1991). *A Dictionary of Marxist Thought*, second edition. Oxford: Blackwell.
Bourdieu, P. and Passeron, J. C. (1977). *Reproduction in Education, Society, and Culture*. London: Sage.
Bowman, M. J. and Anderson, C. A. (1963). 'Concerning the Role of Education in Development'. In Geertz, C. (ed.) (1963) *Old Societies and New States*. New York: Free Press.
Bramall, C. (1992). 'Chinese Economic Growth between the Wars.' *China Quarterly*, 131: 784–91.
Bramall, C. (1993). *In Praise of Maoist Economic Planning*. Oxford: Oxford University Press.
Bramall, C. (1995). 'Origins of the Agricultural "Miracle": Some Evidence from Sichuan.' *China Quarterly*, 143: 731–55.
Bramall, C. (1997). 'Living Standards in Prewar Japan and Maoist China.' *Cambridge Journal of Economics*, 21 (4): 551–570.
Bramall, C. (2000a). *Sources of Chinese Economic Growth, 1978–1996*. Oxford: Oxford University Press.
Bramall, C. (2000b). 'Inequality, Land Reform and Agricultural Growth in China, 1952–1955.' *Journal of Peasant Studies*, 27 (3): 30–54.
Bramall, C. (2001). 'The Quality of China's Household Income Surveys.' *China Quarterly*, 167: 689–705.
Bramall, C. (2004). 'Chinese Land Reform in Long-Run Perspective and in the Wider East Asian Context.' *Journal of Agrarian Change*, 4 (1 & 2): 107–41.
Bramall, C. (2006). 'The Last of the Romantics? Maoist Economic Development in Retrospect.' *China Quarterly*, 187: 686–92.
Bramall, C. (2007). *The Industrialization of Rural China*. Oxford: Oxford University Press.
Bramall, C. and Jones, M. E. (1993). 'Rural Income Inequality in China since 1978.' *Journal of Peasant Studies*, 21 (1): 41–70.
Brandt, L. and Holz, C. (2006). 'Spatial Price Differences in China.' *Economic Development and Cultural Change*, 55 (1): 43–86.
Brandt, L. and Sands, B. (1992). 'Land Concentration and Income Distribution in Republican China.' In Rawski, T. G. and Li. L. M. (eds) (1992) *Chinese History in Economic Perspective*. Berkeley: University of California Press.
Brandt, L. L. (1989). *Commercialization and Agricultural Development*. Cambridge: Cambridge University Press.
Brandt, L. L. (1997). 'Reflections on China's Late 19th and Early 20th-Century Economy.' *China Quarterly*, 150: 282–308.
Brandt, L. L., Huang, J. K., Li, G. and Rozelle, S. (2002). 'Land Rights in China.' *China Journal*, 40 (1): 67–97.
Bray, F. (1986). *The Rice Economies*. Oxford: Basil Blackwell.
Brean, D. J. S. (ed.) (1998). *Taxation in Modern China*. London: Routledge.
Brenner, R. (1986). 'The Social Basis of Economic Development.' In Roemer, J. (ed.) (1986) *Analytical Marxism*. Cambridge: Cambridge University Press.
Brenner, R. (1994). *Merchants and Revolution*. Cambridge: Cambridge University Press.
Brenner, R. and Isett, C. (2002). 'England's Divergence from China's Yangzi Delta.' *Journal of Asian Studies*, 61 (3): 609–62.

Broaded, C. M. (1983). 'Higher Education Policy Changes and Stratification in China.' *China Quarterly*, 93: 125–37.
Brömmelhörster, J. and Frankenstein, J. (1997). *Mixed Motives, Uncertain Outcomes: Defence Industry Conversion in China*. London: Lynne Rienner.
Brown, I. (ed.) (1989). *The Economies of Africa and Asia in the Inter-war Depression*. London: Routledge.
Brown, L. (1995). *Who Will Feed China?* New York: Norton.
Brun, J. F., Combes, J. L. and Renard, M. F. (2002). 'Are There Spillover Effects between Coastal and Noncoastal Regions in China?' *China Economic Review*, 13: 161–9.
Brunnschweiler, C. (2008). 'Cursing the Blessings? Natural Resource Abundance, Institutions, and Economic Growth.' *World Development*, 36 (3): 399–419.
Buck, J. L. (1937). *Land Utilization in China*. Oxford: Oxford University Press.
Buck, J. L. (1943). 'An Agricultural Survey of Szechwan Province.' Reprinted in Buck, J. L. (1980) *Three Essays on Chinese Farm Economy*. London: Garland.
Buck, J. L. (1947). 'Some Basic Agricultural Problems of China.' Reprinted in Buck, J. L. (1980) *Three Essays on Chinese Farm Economy*. London: Garland.
Buck, J. L. (1980). *Three Essays on Chinese Farm Economy*. London: Garland.
Byres, T. J. (1979). 'Of Neo-Populist Pipe Dreams: Daedalus in the Third World and the Myth of Urban Bias.' *Journal of Peasant Studies*, 6 (2): 210–44.
Cai, F. (2005). *Zhongguo renkou yu laodong wenti baogao* (Report on China's Population and Labour Force Problem). Beijing: Shehui kexue wenshu chubanshe.
Cai, F. and Wang, D. W. (2007). 'Impacts of Internal Migration on Economic Growth and Urban Development in China.' *CASS Working Paper*. At http://iple.cass.cn/show_News.asp?id=13183 (accessed 18 November 2007).
Campbell, C. (1997). 'Public Health Efforts in China before 1949 and Their Effects on Mortality.' *Social Science History*, 21 (2): 179–218.
Canning, D. (2006). 'The Economics of HIV/AIDS in Low-Income Countries.' *Journal of Economic Perspectives*, 20 (3): 121–42.
Cao, Y. Z., Qian Y. Y. and Weingast, B. (1999). 'From Federalism, Chinese Style to Privatization, Chinese Style.' *Economics of Transition*, 7 (1): 103–31.
Carter, C. (1999). 'Institutional Reform and Agricultural Productivity Growth in China.' In Findlay, C. and Watson, A. (eds) (1999) *Food Security and Economic Reform*. Basingstoke: Macmillan.
Carter, C. (2001). 'China's Trade Integration and Impacts of Factor Markets.' In OECD (2001) *China's Agriculture in the International Trading System*. Paris: OECD.
Carter, C. and Rozelle, S. (2001). 'Will China Become a Major Force in World Food Markets?' *Review of Agricultural Economics*, 23 (2): 319–31.
Cartler, C. (2002). 'Origins and Evolution of a Geographical Idea: The Macroregion in China.' *Modern China*, 28 (1): 79–142.
Carver, T. (ed.) (1996). *Marx: Later Political Writings*. Cambridge: Cambridge University Press.
CD – *China Daily*.
Central Committee (1954). *Constitution of the People's Republic of China*. Beijing: Foreign Languages Press.
Central Committee (1981). 'On Questions of Party History.' In Liu, S. N. and Wu, Q. G. (1986) *China's Socialist Economy*. Beijing: Beijing Review Press.
Central Committee (1991). *Major Documents of the People's Republic of China*. Beijing: Foreign Languages Press.
Chai, J. C. H. (1998). *China – Transition to a Market Economy*. Oxford: Clarendon Press.

Chan, A. (2001). *Mao's Crusade*. Oxford: Oxford University Press.
Chan, A., Rosen, S. and Unger, J. (1980). 'Students and Class Warfare.' *China Quarterly*, 83: 397–446.
Chan, A., Unger, J. and Madsen, R. (1992). *Chen Village*. Berkeley: University of California Press.
Chan, K. W. (2001). 'Recent Migration in China.' *Asian Perspective*, 25 (4): 127–55.
Chan, K. W. and Buckingham, W. (2007). 'Is China Abolishing the *Hukou* System?' At http://faculty.washington.edu/kwchan/AbolishHukou-final.pdf (accessed 22 June 2008).
Chan, T. M. H. (1989). 'China's Price Reform in the 1980s.' In Cheng, J. Y. S. (ed.) (1989) *China – Modernization in the 1980s*. Hong Kong: Chinese University Press.
Chan, T. M. H. (1991). 'The Policy of Opening and Special Economic Zones.' In Kuan, H. C. and Brosseau, M. (eds) (1991) *China Review*. Hong Kong: Chinese University Press.
Chan, T. M. H., Tracy, N. and Zhu, W. H. (1999). *China's Export Miracle*. Basingstoke: Macmillan.
Chang, C. C. (1936). 'Rural Economy.' In Woodhead, H. G. W. (ed.) (1936) *The China Yearbook 1936*. Shanghai: Commercial Press.
Chang, G. G. (2001). *The Coming Collapse of China*. London: Random House.
Chang, G. H. (2002). 'The Cause and Cure of China's Widening Income Disparity.' *China Economic Review*, 13: 335–40.
Chang, G. H. and Shao, Q. (2004). 'How Much is the Chinese Currency Undervalued?' *China Economic Review*, 15: 366–371.
Chang, G. H. and Wen, G. Z. J. (1997). 'Communal Dining and the Chinese Famine of 1958–61.' *Economic Development and Cultural Change*, 46 (1): 1–34.
Chang, H-J. (2002). *Kicking Away the Ladder*. London: Anthem.
Chang, J. (1991). *Wild Swans*. London: HarperCollins.
Chang, J. and Halliday, J. (2005). *Mao: The Unknown Story*. London: Jonathan Cape.
Chao, K. (1977). *The Development of Cotton Textile Production in China*. Cambridge, MA: Harvard University Press.
Chao, K. (1983). *The Economic Development of Manchuria*. Michigan: University of Michigan Press.
Chaudhuri, S. and Ravallion, M. (2006). 'Partially Awakened Giants: Uneven Growth in China and India.' World Bank Working Paper WPS 4069.Washington, DC: World bank
Cheek, T. and Saich, T. (1997). *New Perspectives on State Socialism in China*. Armonk: M. E. Sharpe.
Chen, D. L. (2003). *Sanxian jianshe* (Third Front Construction). Beijing: Zhonggong zhongyang dangxiao chubanshe.
Chen, G. D. and Wu, C. T. (2006). *Will the Boat Sink the Water?* London: Public Affairs.
Chen, J. S., Campbell, T. C., Li, J. Y. and Peto, R. (1990). *Diet, Life-Style, and Mortality in China*. Oxford: Oxford University Press.
Chen, K., Jefferson, G. H., Rawski, T., Wang, H. C. and Zheng, Y. X. (1988a). 'New Estimates of Fixed Investment and Capital Stock for Chinese State Industry.' *China Quarterly*, 114: 243–66.
Chen, K., Wang, H. C., Zheng, Y. X., Jefferson, G. H. and Rawski, T. G. (1988b). 'Productivity Change in Chinese Industry, 1953–85.' *Journal of Comparative Economics*, 12 (4): 570–91.
Chen, L. Y. and Buckwell, A. (1991). *Chinese Grain Economy and Policy*. Oxford: CAB International.

Chen, S. H. and Ravallion, M. (2004). 'Welfare Impacts of China's Accession to the WTO.' In Bhattasali, D., Li, S. T. and Martin, W. (eds) (2004) *China and the WTO*. Oxford: Oxford University Press.

Chen, S. H., Ravallion, M. and Wang, Y. J. (2006). '*Dibao*: A Guaranteed Minimum Income in Urban China?' World Bank Working Paper WPS 3805. Washington, DC: World Bank.

Cheng, N. (1986). *Life and Death in Shanghai*. London: Collins.

Cheng, T. J. and Selden, M. (1994). 'The Origins and Social Consequences of China's Hukou System.' *China Quarterly*, 139: 644–68.

Cheng, Y. S. and Lo, D. (2002). 'Explaining the Financial Performance of China's Industrial Enterprises.' *China Quarterly*, 170: 413–40.

Cheung, K. Y and Lin, P. (2004). 'Spillover Effects of FDI on Innovation in China.' *China Economic Review*, 15: 25–44.

Chevrier, Y. (1990). 'Micropolitics and the Factory Director Responsibility System, 1984–1987.' In Davis, D. and Vogel, E. F. (eds) (1990) *Chinese Society on the Eve of Tiananmen*. Cambridge, MA: Harvard University Press.

China Handbook Committee (1984). *China Handbook – Economy*. Beijing: Foreign Languages Press.

China Labour Bulletin Research Report (2006). 'Falling through the Floor: Migrant Women Workers' Quest for Decent Work in Dongguan, China.' At http://www.china-labour.org.hk/ (accessed 1 December 2006).

Chinn, D. L. (1980). 'Cooperative Farming in North China.' *Quarterly Journal of Economics*, XCIV (2): 279–99.

Chow, G. (2002). *China's Economic Transformation*. Oxford: Blackwell.

Chung, J. H. (2000). *Central Control and Local Discretion in China*. Oxford: Oxford University Press.

CLB – *China Labour Bulletin*. At http://www.china-labour.org.hk/public/main.

Cohen, S. F. (1971/1980). *Bukharin and the Bolshevik Revolution*. Oxford: Oxford University Press.

Collier, P. (2007). *The Bottom Billion*. Oxford: Oxford University Press.

Collier, P. and Gunning, W. (1999). 'Explaining African Growth Performance.' *Journal of Economic Literature*, XXXVII (1): 64–111.

Conquest, R. (1986). *The Harvest of Sorrow*. London: Arrow.

Cornia, G. A. (1985). 'Farm Size, Land Yields and the Agricultural Production Function.' *World Development*, 13 (4): 513–34.

Cowell, F. A. (1995). *Measuring Inequality*, second edition. London: Harvester Wheatsheaf.

Crafts, N. F. R. (1985). *British Economic Growth during the Industrial Revolution*. Oxford: Oxford University Press.

Crespo, N. and Fontoura, M. P. (2007). 'Determinant Factors of FDI Spillovers.' *World Development*, 35 (3): 410–25.

Crook, I. and Crook, D. (1966). *The First Years of Yangyi Commune*. London: Routledge and Kegan Paul.

Crook, I. and Crook, D. (1979). *Mass Movement in a Chinese Village*. London: Routledge and Kegan Paul.

Cui, Z. Y. (1997). 'Privatization and the Consolidation of Democratic Regimes.' *Journal of International Affairs*, 50 (2). At http://www.questia.com (accessed 5 January 2007).

Cutler, D., Deaton, A. and Lleras-Muney, A. (2006). 'The Determinants of Mortality.' *Journal of Economic Perspectives*, 20 (3): 97–120.

Dai, Q. (1994). *Yangtze! Yangtze!* London: Earthscan.
Dai, Q. (ed.) (1998). *The River Dragon Has Come!* Armonk: M. E. Sharpe.
Daly, H. E., and Cobb, J. B. (1994). *For the Common Good*, second edition. London: Beacon Press.
Dasgupta, P. and Ray, D. (1986). 'Inequality as a Determinant of Malnutrition and Unemployment Theory.' *Economic Journal*, 96: 1011–34.
Dasgupta, S. and Singh, A. (2006). 'Manufacturing, Services and Premature Deindustrialization in Developing Countries.' Centre for Business Research Working Paper no. 327. Cambridge: Centre for Business Research.
David, P. (1985). 'Clio and the Economics of QWERTY.' *American Economic Review*, 75: 332–7.
Davies, R. W., Harrison, M. and Wheatcroft, S. G. (1994). *The Economic Transformation of the Soviet Union, 1913–1945*. Cambridge: Cambridge University Press.
Davis, M. (2001). *Late Victorian Holocausts*. London: Verso.
Day, K. A. (ed.) (2005). *China's Environment and the Challenge of Sustainable Development*. Armonk: M E Sharpe.
Deacon, R. and Norman, C. S. (2004).'Is the Environmental Kuznets curve an Empirical Regularity?' UCSB Department of Economics Working Paper. At http://repositories.cdlib.org/cgi/viewcontent.cgi?article=1174&context=ucsbecon (accessed 17 January 2008).
Deininger, K. and Squire, L. (1998). 'New Ways of Looking at Old Issues: Inequality and Growth.' *Journal of Development Economics*, 57 (2): 259–87.
De Long, J. B. and Summers, L. H. (1991). 'Equipment Investment and Economic Growth.' *Quarterly Journal of Economics*, 106 (2): 445–502.
Démurger, S. (2002). 'China's Regional Development.' In OECD (2002) *China in the World Economy – The Domestic Policy Challenges*. Paris: OECD.
Démurger, S., Sachs, J. D., Woo, W. T., Bao, S. M. and Chang, G. (2002). 'The Relative Contribution of Location and Preferential Policies in China's Regional Development.' *China Economic Review*, 13: 444–65.
Deng, X. P. (1978a). 'Hold High the Banner of Mao Zedong Thought and Adhere to the Principle of Seeking Truth from Facts.' In Deng, X. P. (1995) *Selected Works of Deng Xiaoping*, vol. II. Beijing: Foreign Languages Press.
Deng, X. P. (1978b). 'Carry Out the Policy of Opening to the Outside World and Learn Advanced Science and Technology from Other Countries.' In Deng, X. P. (1995) *Selected Works of Deng Xiaoping*, vol. II. Beijing: Foreign Languages Press.
Deng, X. P. (1984). 'Building Socialism with Chinese Characteristics.' In Deng, X. P. (1994) *Selected Works of Deng Xiaoping*, vol. III. Beijing: Foreign Languages Press.
Deng, X. P. (1985). 'There is No Fundamental Contradiction between Socialism and a Market Economy.' In Deng, X. P. (1994) *Selected Works of Deng Xiaoping*, vol. III. Beijing: Foreign Languages Press.
Deng, X. P. (1987). 'We Shall Speed Up Reform.' In Deng, X. P. (1994) *Selected Works of Deng Xiaoping*, vol. III. Beijing: Foreign Languages Press.
Deng, X. P. (1988). 'We Must Rationalize Prices and Accelerate the Reform.' In Deng, X. P. (1994) *Selected Works of Deng Xiaoping*, vol. III. Beijing: Foreign Languages Press.
Deng, X. P. (1990). 'Seize the Opportunity to Develop the Economy.' In Deng, X. P. (1994) *Selected Works of Deng Xiaoping*, vol. III. Beijing: Foreign Languages Press.
Deng, X. P. (1992). 'Excerpts from Talks Given in Wuchang, Shenzhen, Zhuhai and Shanghai.' In Deng, X. P. (1994) *Selected Works of Deng Xiaoping*, vol. III. Beijing: Foreign Languages Press.

Deng, X. P. (1994). *Selected Works of Deng Xiaoping*, vol. III. Beijing: Foreign Languages Press.

Deng, X. P. (1995). *Selected Works of Deng Xiaoping*, vol. II. Beijing: Foreign Languages Press.

Deng, Z. and Treiman, D. J. (1997). 'The Impact of the Cultural Revolution on Trends in Educational Attainment in the People's Republic of China.' *American Journal of Sociology*, 103 (2): 391–428.

Dernberger, R. F. (1975). 'The Role of the Foreigner in China's Economic Development.' In Perkins, D. H. (ed.) (1975) *China's Modern Economy in Historical Perspective*. Stanford: Stanford University Press.

Diao, X. S., Fan, S. G. and Zhang, X. B. (2003). 'China's WTO Accession.' *Journal of Comparative Economics*, 31 (2): 332–51.

Dirlik, A., Healy, P. and Knight, N. (eds) (1997). *Critical Perspectives on Mao Zedong's Thought*. Atlantic Highlands, NJ: Humanities Press.

Dollar, D. and Kraay, A. (2002). 'Growth is Good for the Poor.' *Journal of Economic Growth*, 7 (3): 195–225.

Dollar, D. and Kraay, A. (2004). 'Trade, Growth and Poverty.' *Economic Journal*, 114: F22–F49.

Dong, X. Y., Song, S. F. and Zhang, X. B. (eds) (2006). *China's Agricultural Development*. Aldershot: Ashgate.

Donnithorne, A. (1967). *China's Economic System*. London: Allen and Unwin.

Donnithorne, A. (1984). 'Sichuan's Agriculture: Depression and Revival.' *Australian Journal of Chinese Affairs*, 12: 59–86.

Dornbusch, R. and Edwards, S. (eds) (1991). *The Macroeconomics of Populism in Latin America*. Chicago: University of Chicago Press.

Drèze, J. and Sen, A. (2002). *India: Development and Participation*, second edition. Oxford: Oxford University Press.

Du, R. S. (1996). *Zhongguo de tudi gaige* (Land Reform in China). Beijing: Dangdai Zhongguo chubanshe.

Duckett, J. (2001). 'Political Interests and the Implementation of China's Urban Health Insurance Reform.' *Social Policy and Administration*, 35 (3): 290–306.

Dutton, M. (1998). *Streetlife China*. Cambridge: Cambridge University Press.

Dyer, G. (2004). 'Redistributive Land Reform.' *Journal of Agrarian Change*, 4 (1 & 2): 45–72.

Easterly, W. (2001). *The Elusive Quest for Growth*. Cambridge, MA: MIT Press.

Easterly, W. and Levine, R. (1997). 'Africa's Growth Tragedy.' *Quarterly Journal of Economics*, 112 (4): 1203–50.

Eastman, L. E. (1988). *Family, Fields and Ancestors*. Oxford: Oxford University Press.

Eckstein, A. (1964). 'Sino-Soviet Economic Relations.' In Cowan, C. D. (ed.) (1964) *The Economic Development of China and Japan*. London: Allen and Unwin.

Economy, E. (2004). *The River Runs Black*. Ithaca: Cornell University Press.

Edmonds, R. L. (ed.) (1998). 'China's Environment.' *China Quarterly*, 156: 725–1041.

Ellman, M. (1979). *Socialist Planning*. Cambridge: Cambridge University Press.

Elster, J. (1986). *An Introduction to Karl Marx*. Cambridge: Cambridge University Press.

Elvin, M. (1973). *The Pattern of the Chinese Past*. Stanford: Stanford University Press.

Elvin, M. (2004). *The Retreat of the Elephants: An Environmental History of China*. New Haven: Yale University Press.

Elvin, M. and Liu T. J. (eds) (1997). *Sediments of Time*. Cambridge: Cambridge University Press.

Endicott, S. (1988). *Red Earth*. London: I. B. Tauris
Esherick, J. W. (1981). 'Number Games.' *Modern China*, 7 (4): 387–411.
Esherick, J. W., Pickowicz, P. G. and Walder, A. G. (2006). *The Chinese Cultural Revolution as History*. Stanford: Stanford University Press.
Evans, D. B. (2004). 'Alternative Perspective on Communicable Diseases.' In Lomborg, B. (ed.) *Global Crises, Global Solutions*. Cambridge: Cambridge University Press.
Eyferth, J. (2003). 'De-industrialization in the Chinese Countryside.' *China Quarterly*, 173: 53–73.
Fan, C. C. (2005). 'Interprovincial Migration, Population Redistribution and Regional Development in China.' *Professional Geographer*, 57 (2): 295–311.
Fan, S. G. and Zhang, X. B. (2006). 'Production and Productivity Growth in Chinese Agriculture.' In Dong, X. Y., Song, S. F. and Zhang, X. B. (eds) (2006) *China's Agricultural Development*. Aldershot: Ashgate.
FAO – Food and Agriculture Organization (1993). *Compendium of Food Consumption Statistics from Household Surveys in Developing Countries*, vol. I, *Asia*. Rome: FAO.
FAO – Food and Agriculture Organization (2006a). *Food Balance Sheets*. At http://faostat.fao.org (accessed 30 August 2006).
FAO – Food and Agriculture Organization (2006b). *Food Security Statistics – China*. At http://www.fao.org/faostat/food security (accessed 30 August 2006).
FAO – Food and Agriculture Organization (2007). *ProdSTAT*. At http://faostat.fao.org (accessed 2 March 2007).
Federico, G. (2005). *Feeding the World*. Princeton: Princeton University Press.
Fei, X. T. (1983). *Chinese Village Close-up*. Beijing: New World Press.
Ferreira, F. H. G., Leite, P. G. and Litchfield, J. A. (2006). 'The Rise and Fall of Brazilian Inequality: 1981–2004.' World Bank Working Paper WPS 3867. Washington, DC: World Bank. At http://econ. worldbank.org. (accessed 17 July 2007).
Feuerwerker, A. (1970). 'Handicraft and Manufactured Cotton Textiles in China, 1871–1910.' *Journal of Economic History*, XXX (2): 338–78.
Feuerwerker, A. (1977). *Economic Trends in the Republic of China, 1912–49*. Ann Arbor: University of Michigan, Michigan Papers in Chinese Studies no. 31.
Fewsmith, J. (1994). *Dilemmas of Reform in China*. Armonk: M. E. Sharpe.
Fewsmith, J. (2001). *China since Tiananmen*. Cambridge: Cambridge University Press.
Field, R. M. (1992). 'China's Industrial Performance since 1978.' *China Quarterly*, 131: 577–607.
Fields, G. S. (1980). *Poverty, Inequality and Development*. Cambridge: Cambridge University Press.
Fields, G. S. (2001). *Distribution and Development*. Cambridge, MA: MIT Press.
Findlay, C. and Watson, A. (eds) (1999). *Food Security and Economic Reform*. Basingstoke: Macmillan.
Finnane, A. (1993). 'The Origins of Prejudice.' *Comparative Studies in Society and History*, 35 (2): 211–38.
Fishlow, A. (1965). *American Railroads and the Transformation of the Antebellum Economy*. Cambridge, MA: Harvard University Press.
Florio, M. (2004). *The Great Divestiture*. Cambridge, MA: MIT Press.
Floud, R. C. and Harris, B. (1997). 'Health, Height, and Welfare: Britain, 1700–1980.' In Steckel, R. H. and Floud, R. (eds) (1997) *Height and Welfare during Industrialization*. Chicago: University of Chicago Press.
Floud, R. C., Wachter, K. W. and Gregory, A. (1990). *Health, Height and History*. Cambridge: Cambridge University Press.

Fogel, R. (1964). *Railroads and American Economic Growth*. Baltimore: Johns Hopkins.
Folta, P. (1992). *From Swords to Plowshares? Defence Industry Reform in the PRC*. Boulder: Westview.
Foot, R. (1995). *The Practice of Power*. Oxford: Clarendon Press.
Friedman, E., Pickowicz, P. G. and Selden, M. (1991). *Chinese Village, Socialist State*. New Haven: Yale University Press.
FT – *Financial Times* (London).
Fu, X. L. (2004). 'Limited Linkages from Growth Engines and Regional Disparities in China.' *Journal of Comparative Economics*, 32 (1): 148–64.
Fukuyama, F. (1995). *Trust*. New York: Free Press.
Gaetano, A. M. and Jacka, T. (eds) (2004). *On the Move*. New York: Columbia University Press.
Gao, A. H. (2000). *To the Edge of the Sky*. London: Viking.
Gao, M. B. (1999). *Gao Village*. London: Hurst and Company.
Gao, M. B. (2008). *The Battle for China's Past*. London: Pluto Press.
Gao, T. (2005). 'Labor Quality and the Location of FDI: Evidence from China.' *China Economic Review*, 16: 274–92.
Garnaut, R. (1999). 'Food Security in China.' In Kalirajan, K. P. and Wu, Y. R. (eds) (1999) *Productivity and Growth in Chinese Agriculture*. Basingstoke: Macmillan.
Garnaut, R., Guo, S. T. and Ma, G. N. (1996). *The Third Revolution in the Chinese Countryside*. Cambridge: Cambridge University Press.
Garnaut, R. and Song, L. G. (eds) (2003). *China's Third Economic Transformation: The Rise of the Private Economy*. London: Routledge.
Garnaut, R., Song L. G., Tenev, S. and Yao, Y. (2005). *China's Ownership Transformation*. Washington, DC: World Bank.
GDFZ – Guangdong sheng tongjiju (Guangdong Statistical Bureau) (1990). *Guangdong sheng guomin jingji he shehui fazhan tongji ziliao 1949–89* (Statistical Materials on the Economic and Social Development of Guangdong). Guangzhou: Guangdong tongji chubanshe.
GDTJNJ – Guangdong tongjiju (Guangdong Statistical Bureau) (2003). *Guangdong tongji nianjian 2003* (Guangdong Statistical Yearbook 2003). Beijing: Zhongguo tongji chubanshe.
Ghose, A. K. (2005). *Employment in China*. Geneva: ILO. At http://www.ilo.org/ (accessed 6 May 2007).
Giles, J., Park, A. and Cai, F. (2006). 'Reemployment of Dislocated Workers in Urban China.' *Journal of Comparative Economics*, 34 (3): 582–607.
Giles, J., Park, A. and Wang, M. Y. (2007). 'The Great Proletarian Cultural Revolution, Disruptions to Education, and Returns to Schooling in Urban China.' At http://www.internationalpolicy.umich.edu/edts/ (accessed 25 August 2007).
Giles, J., Park, A. and Zhang, J. W. (2005). 'What is China's True Unemployment Rate?' *China Economic Review*, 16 (2): 149–70.
Gill, I. and Kharas, H. (2007). *An East Asian Renaissance*. Washington, DC: World Bank.
Glyn, A. (2006). *Capitalism Unleashed*. Oxford: Oxford University Press.
Goldstein, M. (2006). 'Renminbi controversies.' *Cato Journal*, 26 (2): 251–66.
Goldstein, M. and Lardy, N. (2005). 'China's Role in the Revived Bretton Woods System: A Case of Mistaken Identity.' *Institute for International Economics Working Paper*, 5 (2): 1–20.
Goldstein, M. and Lardy, N. R. (2006). 'China's Exchange Rate Dilemma.' *American Economic Review* (Papers and Proceedings), 96 (2): 422–6.

Goodman, D. S. G. (ed.) (2004). *China's Campaign to 'Open Up to the West': National, Provincial-level and Local Perspective.* Cambridge: Cambridge University Press.
Görg, H. and Greenaway, D. (2004). 'Much Ado about Nothing? Do Domestic Firms Really Benefit from Foreign Direct Investment?' *World Bank Research Observer*, 19 (2): 171–97.
Gray, J. (2006). 'Mao in Perspective.' *China Quarterly*, 187: 659–79.
Greenhalgh, S. and Winckler, E. A. (2005). *Governing China's Population.* Stanford: Stanford University Press.
Gregory, P. R. (1982). *Russian National Income, 1885–1913.* Cambridge: Cambridge University Press.
Gregory, P. R. and Stuart, R. C. (1974). *Soviet Economic Structure and Performance.* New York: Harper and Row.
Griffin, K. (1984). *Institutional Reform and Economic Development in the Chinese Countryside.* Basingstoke: Macmillan.
Griffin, K., Khan, A. R. and Ickowitz, A. (2002). 'Poverty and the Distribution of Land.' *Journal of Agrarian Change*, 2 (3): 279–330.
Griffin, K. and Saith, A. (1982). 'The Pattern of Income Inequality in Rural China.' *Oxford Economic Papers*, 34 (1): 172–206.
Griffin, K. and Zhao, R. W. (ed.) (1993). *The Distribution of Income in China.* Basingstoke: Macmillan.
Guest, P, and Sutherland, P. (2006). 'How Has China's National Team of Enterprise Groups Performed?' At http://www.tcd.ie/Economics/TEP/2006_papers/TEP8.pdf (accessed 20 May 2007).
Guo, F. and Iredale, R. (2004). 'The Impact of *Hukou* Status in Migrants' Employment.' *International Migration Review*, 38 (2): 709–31.
Guo, X. M. (2001). 'New Countermeasures for Water Pollution Control in China.' Washington, DC: World Bank (background report for World Bank 2001d).
GYWSN – Zhongguo tongjiju (State Statistical Bureau) (ed.) (2000). *Zhongguo gongye jiaotong nengyuan wushinian tongji ziliao huibian* (Collection of Statistical Materials on Chinese Industry, Transport and Energy over the Last Fifty Years). Beijing: Zhongguo tongji chubanshe.
Halperin, M. A., Siegle, J. T. and Weinstein, M. M. (2005). *The Democracy Advantage.* New York: Routledge.
Han, D. P. (2000). *The Unknown Cultural Revolution.* New York: Garland Publishing.
Han D. P. (2001). 'The Impact of the Cultural Revolution on Rural Education and Economic Development.' *Modern China*, 27 (1): 59–90.
Han, Z. R. and Feng, Y. F. (1992). *Xin Zhongguo nongchanpin jiage sishinian* (Agricultural Product Prices over the Forty Years of New China). Beijing: Shuili dianli chubanshe.
Hannum, E. (1999). 'Political Change and the Urban–Rural Gap in Basic Education in China, 1949–1990.' *Comparative Education Review*, 43 (2): 193–211.
Hansen, M. H. (1999). 'The Call of Mao or Money? Han Chinese Settlers on China's South-Western Borders.' China Quarterly, 158: 394–413.
Hanushek, E. A. and Kimko, D. D. (2000). 'Schooling, Labour-Force Quality and the Growth of Nations.' *American Economic Review*, 90 (5):1184–208.
Haq, M. (1995). *Reflections on Human Development.* Oxford: Oxford University Press.
Hare, D. and West, L. (1999). 'Spatial Patterns in China's Rural Industrial Growth and Prospects for the Alleviation of Regional Income Inequality.' *Journal of Comparative Economics*, 27 (3): 475–97.

Hart-Landsberg, M. (1993). *The Rush to Development*. New York: Monthly Review Press.
Hart-Landsberg, M. and Burkett, P. (2005). *China and Socialism*. New York: Monthly Review Press.
Hawke, G. R. (1970). *Railways and Economic Growth in England and Wales, 1840–1870*. Oxford: Oxford University Press.
Hawthorn, G. (ed.) (1987). *The Standard of Living*. Cambridge: Cambridge University Press.
He, K. (ed.) (2004). *Zhongguo de xiangzhen qiye* (China's Township and Village Enterprises). Beijing: Zhongguo nongye chubanshe.
He, Q. L. (1998). *Xiandaihua de xianjing* (Pitfalls of Modernization). Beijing: Jinri chubanshe.
Healy, P. (1997). 'A Paragon of Marxist Orthodoxy.' In Dirlik, A., Healy, P. and Knight, N. (eds) (1997) *Critical Perspectives on Mao Zedong's Thought*. Atlantic Highlands, NJ: Humanities Press.
Heberer, T. (2007). *Doing Business in Rural China*. Seattle: University of Washington Press.
Hertel, T. W. and Winters, L. A. (2006). *Poverty and the WTO*. London: Palgrave Macmillan.
Heston, A. and Summers, R. (1996). 'International Price and Quantity Comparisons.' *American Economic Review* (Papers and Proceedings), 86 (2): 20–4.
Hinton, W. (1966). *Fanshen*. New York: Monthly Review Press.
Hinton, W. (1972). *Hundred Day War: The Cultural Revolution at Tsinghua University*. New York: Monthly Review Press.
Hinton, W. (1983). *Shenfan*. New York: Random House.
Hinton, W. (1990). *The Privatization of China*. London: Earthscan.
Hinton, W. (2006). *Through a Glass Darkly*. New York: Monthly Review Press.
HJTJNJ – Zhongguo guojia tongjiju (State Statistical Bureau) (1996). *Heilongjiang tongji nianjian 1996* (Heilongjiang Statistical Yearbook). Beijing: Zhongguo tongji chubanshe.
HNNY – Hunan nongxueyuan (Hunan Agricultural Research Institute) (ed.) (1959). *Hunan nongye* (Agriculture in Hunan). Beijing: Gaodeng jiaoyu chubanshe.
Ho, D. D. (2006). 'To Protect and Preserve.' In Esherick, J. W., Pickowicz, P. G. and Walder, A. G. (2006) *The Chinese Cultural Revolution as History*. Stanford: Stanford University Press.
Ho, P. (2003). 'Mao's War against Nature? The Environmental Impact of the Grain-First Campaign in China.' China Journal, 50: 37–59.
Hofstede, G. (2003). Culture's Consequences, second edition. Beverly Hills, CA: Sage.
Holz, C. A. (2003). 'Fast, Clear and Accurate: How Reliable Are Chinese Output and Economic Growth Statistics?' *China Quarterly*, 173: 122–63.
Holz, C. A. (2006). 'China's Reform Period Economic Growth: How Reliable Are Angus Maddison's Estimates?' *Review of Income and Wealth*, 52 (1): 85–119.
Honda, G. (1997). 'Differential Structure, Differential Health: Industrialization in Japan, 1868–1940.' In Steckel, R. H. and Floud, R. (eds) (1997) *Height and Welfare during Industrialization*. Chicago: University of Chicago Press.
Honig, E. (1992). *Creating Chinese Ethnicity: Subei People in Shanghai, 1850–1980*. New Haven: Yale University Press.
Honig, E. (1996). 'Native Place and the Making of Chinese Ethnicity.' In Hershatter, G., Honig, E., Lipman, J. and Stross, R. (eds) *Remapping China*. Stanford: Stanford University Press.

Hou, C. M. (1965). *Foreign Investment and Economic Development in China, 1840–1937.* Cambridge, MA: Harvard University Press.

Howard, J. H. (2004). *Workers at War.* Stanford: Stanford University Press.

Howe, C. and Walker, K. R. (1989). *The Foundations of the Chinese Planned Economy.* Basingstoke: Macmillan.

Hsu, R. C. (1991). *Economic Theories in China, 1979–1988.* Cambridge: Cambridge University Press.

Hsueh, T. T. and Li, Q. (1999). *China's National Income, 1952–1995.* Boulder, CO: Westview.

Hu, A. and Jefferson, G. H. (2002). 'FDI Impact and Spillover: Evidence from China's Electronic and Textile Industries.' *World Economy*, 25 (8): 1063–76

Hu, A. G. (2002). 'Public Exposure of Economic Losses Resulting from Corruption.' *China and the World Economy*, 4: 44–9.

Hu, H. Y. (1987). *Zhongguo renkou – Shanghai fence* (China's Population – Shanghai). Beijing: Zhongguo caizheng jingji chubanshe.

Hu, J. T. (2007). 'Speech at the 17th Party Congress.' At http://news.xinhuanet.com/english/2007–10/24/ (accessed 7 November 2007).

Hua, S., Zhang. X. J. and Luo, X. P. (1993). *China: From Revolution to Reform.* Basingstoke: Macmillan.

Huang, J. (2000). *Factionalism in Chinese Communist Politics.* Cambridge: Cambridge University Press.

Huang, J. K., Rozelle, S. and Chang, M. (2004). 'The Nature of Distortions to Agricultural Incentives in China.' In Bhattasali, D., Li, S. T. and Martin, W. (eds) (2004) *China and the WTO.* Oxford: Oxford University Press.

Huang, J. K., Rozelle, S. and Rosegrant, M. W. (1999). 'China's Food Economy to the Twenty-First Century.' *Economic Development and Cultural Change*, 47 (4): 737–66.

Huang, J. K., Rozelle, S. and Wang, H. L. (2006). 'Fostering or Stripping Rural China.' *The Developing Economies*, XLIV (1): 1–26.

Huang, P. (1985). *The Peasant Economy and Social Change in North China.* Stanford: Stanford University Press.

Huang, P. (1990). *The Peasant Family and Rural Development in the Yangzi Delta, 1350–1988.* Stanford: Stanford University Press.

Huang, P. (2002) 'Development or Involution in Eighteenth-Century Britain and China.' *Journal of Asian Studies*, 61 (2): 501–38.

Huang, P. and Cui, Z. Y. (2005). *Zhongguo yu quanqiuhua: huashengdun gongshi haishi Beijing gongshi* (China and Globalization: Washington Consensus or Beijing Consensus?). Beijing: Shehui kexue wenxian chubanshe.

Huenemann, R. W. (1984). *The Dragon and the Iron Horse.* Cambridge, MA: Harvard University Press.

Hunter, H. and Szyrmer, J. M. (1992). *Faulty Foundations.* Princeton: Princeton University Press.

Hussain, A. (1989). 'Science and Technology in the Chinese Countryside.' In Simon, D. F. and Goldman, M. (eds) (1989) *Science and Technology in Post-Mao China.* Cambridge, MA: Harvard University Press.

Hutton, W. (2007). *The Writing on the Wall.* London: Little, Brown.

Ianchovichina, E. and Martin, W. (2004). 'Economic Impacts of China's Accession to the WTO.' In Bhattasali, D., Li, S. T. and Martin, W. (eds) (2004) *China and the WTO.* Oxford: Oxford University Press.

Imai, K. I. (2003). *Beyond Market Socialism.* Tokyo: Institute of Developing Economies.

Inagaki, H. (2006). 'South China's Labour Shortage.' Mizuho Research Paper no. 9. At http://www.mizuho-ri.co.jp (accessed 18 November 2007).

IRRI (International Rice Research Institute) (2007). *Area Planted to Hybrid Rice in the People's Republic of China.* At http://www.irri.org/science/ricestat/ (accessed 10 March 2007).

Ishikawa, S. (1967). 'Resource Flow between Agriculture and Industry – The Chinese Experience.' *The Developing Economies*, 5 (1): 3–49.

Ishikawa, S. (1987). 'Sino-Japanese Economic Cooperation.' *China Quarterly*, 109: 1–21.

Ishikawa, S. (1988). 'Patterns and Processes of Intersectoral Resource Flows.' In Ranis, G. and Schultz, T. P. (eds) *The State of Development Economics.* Oxford: Blackwell.

Islam, N. and Dai, E. B. (2007). *Alternative Estimates of TFP Growth in China.* At http://www.icsead.or.jp (accessed 11 May 20007).

Jameson, F. (1991). *Postmodernism, or the Cultural Logic of Late Capitalism.* London: Verso.

Japan Statistical Association (1987). *Historical Statistics of Japan*, vol. I. Tokyo: Japan Statistical Association.

Jefferson, G., Hu, A. G. Z., Guan, X. J. and Yu, X. Y. (2003). 'Ownership, Performance, and Innovation in China's Large and Medium-Sized Industrial Enterprise Sector.' *China Economic Review*, 14: 89–113.

Jefferson, G. H. (1990). 'China's Iron and Steel Industry.' *Journal of Development Economics*, 33: 329–55.

Jefferson, G. H., Rawski, T. G., Wang, L. and Zheng, Y. X. (2000). 'Ownership, Productivity Change and Financial Performance in Chinese Industry.' *Journal of Comparative Economics,* 28 (4): 786–813.

Jefferson, G. H. and Singh, I. (1999). *Enterprise Reform in China.* Oxford: Oxford University Press.

Jefferson, G. H. and Su, J. (2006). 'Privatization and Restructuring in China.' *Journal of Comparative Economics*, 26 (1): 146–66.

Jiang, H. (1999). *The Ordos Plateau of China.* New York: United Nations University Press.

Jiang, Y. R. and Ashley, D. (2000). *Mao's Children in the New China.* London: New York.

Jiang, Z. M. (1997). 'Report to the Fifteenth Party Congress.' At http://chinadaily.co.cn (accessed 22 September 1997).

Johnson, C. A. (1962). *Peasant Nationalism and Communist Power.* Stanford: Stanford University Press.

Johnson, C. A. (1985). *MITI and the Japanese Miracle.* Stanford: Stanford University Press.

Johnson, S., Svendsen, M. and Zhang, X. Y. (1998). 'Changes in System Performance in Two Chinese Irrigation Systems as a Result of Organizational Reforms.' *Irrigation and Drainage Systems*, 12 (4): 289–309.

Jones, F. (2007). *The Effects of Taxes and Benefits on Household Income, 2005/2006.* At http://www.statistics.gov.uk (accessed 12 February 2008).

Joseph, W. A., Wong, C. P. W. and Zweig, D. (eds) (1991). *New Perspectives on the Cultural Revolution.* Cambridge, MA: Harvard University Press.

JSTJNJ – Jiangsu tongjiju (Jiangsu Statistical Bureau) (various years). *Jiangsu tongji nianjian 2002, 2003 and 2005* (Jiangsu Statistical Yearbook). Beijing: Zhongguo tongji chubanshe.

JSZ – (2000) *Jiangsu sheng zhi: Jiaoyu zhi* (Jiangsu Provincial Records: Educational Records), vol. II. Nanjing: Jiangsu guji chubanshe.

Judd, E. R. (1992). 'Land Divided, Land United.' *China Quarterly*, 130: 338–56.
Kahneman, D. and Krueger, A. B. (2006). 'Developments in the Measurement of Subjective Well-Being.' *Journal of Economic Perspectives*, 20 (1): 3–24.
Kaldor, N. (1961). 'Capital Accumulation and Economic Growth.' In Targetti, F. and Thirlwall, A. P. (eds) (1989). *The Essential Kaldor*. London: Duckworth.
Kaldor, N. (1966). 'Causes of the Slow Rate of Economic Growth in the United Kingdom.' In Targetti, F. and Thirlwall, A. P. (eds) (1989). *The Essential Kaldor*. London: Duckworth.
Kaldor, N. (1970). 'The Case for Regional Policies.' *Scottish Journal of Political Economy*, 17 (3): 337–48.
Kalirajan, K. P. and Wu, Y. R. (eds) (1999). *Productivity and Growth in Chinese Agriculture*. Basingstoke: Macmillan.
Kampen, T. (2000). *Mao Zedong, Zhou Enlai and the Evolution of the Chinese Communist Leadership*. Copenhagen: Nordic Institute of Asian Studies.
Kaplan, E. A. and Sprinker, M. (eds) (1993). *The Althusserian Legacy*. London: Verso.
Kapp, R. A. (1973). *Szechwan and the Chinese Republic*. New Haven: Yale University Press.
Karshenas, M. (1995). *Industrialization and Agricultural Surplus*. Oxford: Oxford University Press.
Kelley, A. C. (1991). 'The Human Development Index: Handle with Care.' *Population and Development Review*, 17 (2): 315–24.
Kelliher, D. (1992). *Peasant Power in China*. New Haven: Yale University Press.
Keynes, J. M. (1924/1971). *A Tract on Monetary Reform*. London: Macmillan
Keynes, J. M. (1933/1982). *The Collected Writings*, vol. XXI. London: Macmillan.
Keynes, J. M. (1936/1973). *The General Theory of Interest, Money and Employment*. London: Macmillan.
Khan, A. R. (2004). *Growth, Inequality and Poverty in China*. Geneva: ILO.
Khan, A. R., Griffin, K., Riskin, C. and Zhao, R. W. (1992). 'Household Income and Its Distribution in China.' *China Quarterly*, 132: 1029–61.
Khan, A. R. and Riskin, C. (1998). 'Income and Inequality in China.' *China Quarterly*, 154: 221–53.
Khan, A. R. and Riskin, C. (2001). *Inequality and Poverty in China in the Age of Globalization*. Oxford: Oxford University Press.
Khan, A. R. and Riskin, C. (2005). 'China's Household Income and Its Distribution, 1995 and 2002.' *China Quarterly*, 182: 356–84.
Khan, M. H. (2004). 'Power, Property Rights and the Issue of Land Reform.' *Journal of Agrarian Change*, 4 (1 & 2): 73–106.
Khan, M. H. and Jomo, K. S. (eds) (2000). *Rents, Rent-Seeking and Economic Development*. Cambridge: Cambridge University Press.
Kipnis, A. (2003). 'Neo-Leftists versus Neo-Liberals.' *Journal of Intercultural Studies*, 24 (3): 239–51.
Kirby, W. C. (1990). 'Continuity and Change in Modern China: Economic Planning on the Mainland and on Taiwan, 1943–58.' *Australian Journal of Chinese Affairs*, 24: 121–41.
Kleinberg, R. (1990). *China's Opening to the Outside World*. Boulder: Westview.
Knight, J. and Song, L. N. (1999). *The Rural–Urban Divide*. Oxford: Oxford University Press.
Kojima, R. (1988). 'Agricultural Organisation: New Forms, New Contradictions.' *China Quarterly*, 116: 706–35.

Köll, E. (2003). *From Cotton Mill to Business Empire.* Cambridge, MA: Harvard University Press.
Kornai, J. (1992). *The Socialist System.* Oxford: Clarendon Press.
Krugman, P. (1991). *Geography and Trade.* Cambridge, MA: MIT Press.
Krugman, P. (1993a). 'Protection in Developing Countries.' In Dornbusch, R. (ed.) (1993) *Policymaking in the Open Economy.* Oxford: Oxford University Press.
Krugman, P. (1993b). 'The Current Case for Industrial Policy.' In Salvatore, D. (ed.) (1993) *Protectionism and World Welfare.* Cambridge: Cambridge University Press.
Krugman, P. (1994). *The Age of Diminished Expectations.* Cambridge, MA: MIT Press.
Krugman, P. (1996). *Pop Internationalism.* Cambridge, MA: MIT Press.
Krusekopf, C. C. (2002). 'Diversity in Land-Tenure Arrangements under the Household Responsibility System in China.' *China Economic Review*, 13: 297–312.
Kuchler, J. (1990). 'On the Establishment of a Poverty-Oriented Rural Development Policy in China.' In Delman, J., Ostergaard, C. S. and Christiansen, F. (eds) *Remaking Peasant China.* Aarhus: Aarhus University Press.
Kueh, Y. Y. (1995). *Agricultural Instability in China, 1931–1991.* Oxford: Clarendon Press.
Kuijs, L. and Wang, T. (2006). 'China's Pattern of Growth.' *China and the World Economy*, 14 (1): 1–14.
Kung, J. K. S. (1994). 'Egalitarianism, Subsistence Provision and Work Incentives in China's Agricultural Collectives.' *World Development*, 22 (2): 175–87.
Kung, J. K. S. (1995). 'Equal Entitlements versus Tenure Security under a Regime of Collective Property Rights.' *Journal of Comparative Economics*, 21 (2): 82–111.
Kunshan xian zhi (Kunshan County Records) (1990). Shanghai: Shanghai renmin chubanshe.
Kuznets, S. (1955). 'Economic Growth and Income Inequality.' *American Economic Review*, 45 (1): 1–28.
Kuznets, S. (1963). 'Distribution of Income by Size.' *Economic Development and Cultural Change*, 11 (2): 1–80.
Kwong, J. (1979). 'The Educational Experiment of the Great Leap Forward, 1958–59.' *Comparative Education Review*, 23 (3): 443–55.
Kwong, J. (1983). 'Is Everyone Equal before the System of Grades: Social Background and Opportunities in China.' *British Journal of Sociology*, 34 (1): 93–108.
Kwong, J. (1997). *The Political Economy of Corruption in China.* Armonk: M. E. Sharpe.
Lai, H. Y. H. (2002). 'China's Western Development Programme.' *Modern China,* 28 (4): 432–66.
Lal, D. (1998). *Unintended Consequences.* Cambridge, MA: MIT Press.
Lall, S. (2001). 'Competitiveness Indices and Developing Countries.' *World Development*, 29 (9): 1501–25.
Lall, S. and Albaladejo, M. (2004). 'China's Competitive Performance.' *World Development*, 32 (9): 1441–66.
Lancieri, E. (1990). 'Purchasing Power Parities and Phase IV of the International Comparison Project.' *World Development*, 18 (1): 29–48.
Landes, D. (2006). 'Why Europe and the West? Why Not China?' *Journal of Economic Perspectives*, 20 (2): 3–22.
Lardy, N. R. (1978). *Economic Growth and Distribution in China.* Cambridge: Cambridge University Press.
Lardy, N. (1984). 'Consumption and Living Standards in China, 1978–1983.' *China Quarterly*, 100: 849–65.

Lardy, N. R. (1987). 'Economic Recovery and the First Five Year Plan.' In MacFarquhar, R. and Fairbank, J. K. (eds) (1987) *The Cambridge History of China*, vol. XIV, part 1. Cambridge: Cambridge University Press.

Lardy, N. R. (1989). 'Dilemmas in the Pattern of Resource Allocation in China, 1978–1985.' In Nee, V. and Stark, D. (eds) (1989) *Remaking the Economic Institutions of Socialism*. Stanford: Stanford University Press.

Lardy, N. R. (1992). *Foreign Trade and Economic Reform in China, 1978–1990*. Cambridge: Cambridge University Press.

Lardy, N. R. (2002). *Integrating China into the Global Economy*. Washington, DC: Brookings.

Lardy, N. R. and Lieberthal, K. (1983). *Chen Yun's Strategy for China's Development*. Armonk: M. E. Sharpe.

Larrain, J. (1991). 'Base and Superstructure.' In Bottomore, T. (ed.) (1991) *A Dictionary of Marxist Thought*, second edition. Oxford: Blackwell.

Latham, A. L. J. and Neal, L. (1983). 'The International Market in Rice and Wheat, 1868–1914.' *Economic History Review*, 36 (3): 260–80.

Lavely, W. R. (1984). 'The Rural Chinese Fertility Transition: A Report from Shifang Xian, Sichuan.' *Population Studies*, 38 (3): 365–84.

Lavely, W., Xiao, Z. Y., Li, B. H. and Freedman, R. (1990). 'The Rise in Female Education in China: National and Regional Patterns.' *China Quarterly*, 121: 61–93.

Law, K. Y. (2003). *The Chinese Cultural Revolution Reconsidered*. Basingstoke: Palgrave Macmillan.

Lawrence, R. and Slaughter, M. (1993), 'Trade and US Wages.' In Brainard, W. C. and Perry, G. L. (eds) (1993) *Brookings Papers on Economic Activity*: 2. Washington, DC: Brookings.

Layard, R. (2005). *Happiness*. London: Penguin.

LDTJ – Zhongguo guojia tongjiju (Chinese State Statistical Bureau) (various years). *Zhongguo laodong tongji nianjian 1997, 2003 and 2005* (Chinese Labour Statistical Yearbook). Beijing: Zhongguo tongji chubanshe.

Lee, C. K. (1995). 'Engendering the Worlds of Labor.' *American Sociological Review*, 60 (3): 378–97.

Lee, J. Z. and Wang, F. (1999). *One Quarter of Humanity*. Cambridge, MA: Harvard University Press.

Lei, G. (2005). 'The State Connection in China's Rural–Urban Migration.' *International Migration Review*, 39 (2): 354–80.

Leeming, F. (1985). *Rural China Today*. London: Longman.

Lenin, V. I. (1919). 'Report on Work in the Countryside.' At http://www.marxists.org/archive/lenin/works/1919/rcp8th/06.htm (accessed 22 June 2008).

Lenin, V. I. (1923/1966). 'On Cooperation.' In *Collected Works of V. I. Lenin*, vol. XXXIII. Moscow: Foreign Languages Publishing House.

Lewis, W. A. (1954). 'Economic Development with Unlimited Supplies of Labour.' *Manchester School of Economic and Social Studies*, 22: 139–91.

Li, B. K. (1985). 'Guanyu jiandaocha dingliang fenxi de jige wenti' (Several Issues Concerning the Analysis of the Determination of the Price Scissors). In He, H. S. (ed.) (1985) *Nongye jingji luncong* (Collected Essays on the Agricultural Economy). Beijing: Nongye chubanshe.

Li, C. (1959). *Zhonghua renmin gongheguo nongye shui shigao* (A History of the Agricultural Tax in the People's Republic of China). Beijing: Caizheng chubanshe.

Li, C. X. (2003). *Mao's Last Dancer*. London: Fusion.

Li, H. B., Liu, P. W., Ma, N and Zhang, J. S. (2005). 'Does Education Pay in Urban China? Estimating Returns to Education Using Twins.' Chinese University of Hong Kong, Department of Economics Discussion Paper. At http://www.econ.cuhk.edu.hk/~discusspaper/00013.pdf (accessed 17 December 2007).

Li, H. B. and Rozelle, S. (2000). 'Saving or Stripping Rural Industry: An Analysis of Privatization and Efficiency in China.' *Agricultural Economics*, 23: 241–52.

Li, H. B. and Rozelle, S. (2004). 'Insider Privatization with a Tail: The Screening Contract and Performance of Privatized Firms in Rural China.' *Journal of Development Economics*, 75: 1–26.

Li, H. Y. (2006). *Mao and the Economic Stalinization of China, 1948–1953*. Lanham: Rowman and Littlefield.

Li, L. J. and O'Brien, K. (1996). 'Villagers and Popular Resistance in Contemporary China.' *Modern China*, 22 (1): 28–61.

Li, L. M. (2007). *Fighting Famine in North China*. Stanford: Stanford University Press.

Li, R. S. (1996). 'Dui dangqian woguo liudong renkou de renshi he sikao' (Reflections on China's Current Floating Population). *Renkou Yanjiu* (Population Research), 20 (1): 10–15.

Li, S. and Sato, H. (eds) (2006). *Unemployment, Inequality and Poverty in Urban China*. Abingdon: Routledge.

Li, S. and Zhao, R. W. (1999). 'Zhongguo jumin shouru fenpei zaiyanjiu' (The Chinese Income Distribution Revisited). *Jingji Yanjiu* (*Economic Research*), 4: 3–17.

Li, S., Zhao, R. W. and Zhang, P. (1998). 'Zhongguo jingji zhuanxing yu shouru fenpei biandong' (China's Economic Transition and Changes in the Income Distribution). *Jingji Yanjiu* (Economic Research), 4: 42–51.

Li, X. Q. (2006). 'The Economic and Political Impact of the Vietnam War on China.' In Roberts, P. M. (ed.) (2006) *Behind the Bamboo Curtain*. Stanford: Stanford University Press.

Li, X. Y., Liu, X. M. and Parker, D. (2001). 'Foreign Direct Investment and Productivity Spillovers in the Chinese Manufacturing Sector.' *Economic Systems*, 25: 305–21.

Li, Y. N. (1990). 'Dynamic Equilibrium in Socialist Economic Reform.' In Nolan, P. and Dong, F. R. (eds) (1990) *The Chinese Economy and Its Future*. Cambridge: Polity.

Li, Z. S. (1996). *The Private Life of Chairman Mao*. London: Arrow.

Liang, W. S. (1982). 'Balanced Development of Industry and Agriculture.' In Xu, D. X. (ed.) (1982) *China's Search for Economic Growth*. Beijing: New World Press.

Liang, Z. and Ma, Z. D. (2004). 'China's Floating Population: New Evidence from the 2000 Census.' *Population and Development Review*, 30 (3): 467–88.

Lin, A. H. Y. (1997). *The Rural Economy of Guangdong 1870–1937*. London: Macmillan.

Lin, B. (1966). 'Why a Cultural Revolution?' In Schoenhals, M. (ed.) (1996) *China's Cultural Revolution, 1966–1969*. Armonk: M. E. Sharpe.

Lin, C. (2006). *The Transformation of Chinese Socialism*. Durham: Duke University Press.

Lin, J. Y. (1990). 'Collectivization and China's Agricultural Crisis in 1959–1961.' *Journal of Political Economy*, 98 (6): 1228–52.

Lin, J. Y. and Yang, D. T. (2000). 'Food Availability, Entitlements and the Chinese Famine of 1959–61.' *Economic Journal*, 110: 136–58.

Lin, J. Y. F. (1992). 'Rural Reforms and Agricultural Growth in China.' *American Economic Review*, 82 (1): 34–51.

Lin, J. Y. F., Cai, F. and Li, Z. (2003). *The China Miracle*. Hong Kong: The Chinese University Press.

Lin, J. Y. F. and Wen, G. Z. J. (1995). 'China's Regional Grain Self-Sufficiency Policy and Its Effect on Land Productivity.' *Journal of Comparative Economics*, 21 (2): 187–206.
Lipton, M. 1977. *Why Poor People Stay Poor*. London: Temple Smith.
Little, D. (1989). *Understanding Peasant China*. New Haven: Yale University Press.
Little, I. M. D. (1982). *Economic Development*. New York: Basic Books.
Liu, H. K. (1988). *Zhongguo renkou – Sichuan fence* (China's Population – Sichuan). Beijing: Zhongguo caizheng jingji chubanshe.
Liu, K. (1997). 'The Legacy of Mao and Althusser.' In Dirlik, A., Healy, P. and Knight, N. (eds) (1997) *Critical Perspectives on Mao Zedong's Thought*. Atlantic Highlands, NJ: Humanities Press International.
Liu, K. (2004). *Globalization and Cultural Trends in China*. Honolulu: University of Hawaii Press.
Liu, M. Q. (1991a). 'Work Incentives and Labour Allocation on China's Communes.' Unpublished DPhil thesis, University of Oxford.
Liu, M. Q. (1991b). 'Intersectoral Labor Allocation on China's Communes.' *Journal of Comparative Economics*, 15 (4): 602–26.
Liu, M. Q. (1994): 'Commune, Responsibility System and China's Agriculture.' In Fan, Q. M. and Nolan, P. (eds) (1994) *China's Economic Reforms*. Basingstoke: Macmillan.
Liu, M. Q., Liu, T-G. and Wu, Z. P. (1998). 'Farmland Consolidation in Mainland China and Taiwan', unpublished ms.
Liu, S. N. and Wu, Q. G. (1986). *China's Socialist Economy*. Beijing: Beijing Review Press.
Liu, S. Q. (1956). 'The Political Report of the Central Committee of the Communist Party of China to the Eighth National Congress of the Communist Party of China.' At http://www.marxists.org/subject/china/documents/cpc/8th_congress.htm (accessed 8 January 2008).
Liu, T. C. and Yeh, K. C. (1965). *The Economy of the Chinese Mainland*. Princeton: Princeton University Press.
Liu, Z. Q. (2002). 'Foreign Direct Investment and Technology Spillover.' *Journal of Comparative Economics,* 30: 579–602.
Lo, D. (1997). *Market and Institutional Regulation in Chinese Industrialization, 1978–94*. London: Macmillan.
Lo, D. (1999). 'Reappraising the Performance of China's State-Owned Industrial Enterprises, 1980–1996.' *Cambridge Journal of Economics*, 23: 693–718.
Lo, D. and Li. G. C. (2006). 'China's Economic Growth, 1978–2005.' SOAS: Department of Economics Working Paper. At http://www.soas.ac.uk/economics/research/workingpapers/ (accessed 21 June 2008).
Lu, R. J. (1992). *Dangdai Zhongguo de Anhui* (China Today: Anhui). Beijing: Dangdai Zhongguo chubanshe.
Lü, X. B. (2000). *Cadre and Corruption*. Stanford: Stanford University Press.
Lucas, R. E. (1988). 'On the Mechanics of Economic Development.' *Journal of Monetary Economics*, 22: 3–42.
Luo, H. X. (1985). *Economic Changes in Rural China*. Beijing: New World Press.
Luxemburg, R. (1918). *The Russian Revolution*. At http://www.marxists.org/archive/luxemburg/1918/russian-revolution/index.htm (accessed 27 December 2006).
Lyons, T. P. (1991). 'Interprovincial Disparities in China: Output and Consumption, 1952-87.' *Economic Development and Cultural Change*, 39 (3): 471–506.
Lyons, T. P. (1994). *Poverty and Growth in a South China County*. New York: East Asia Program, Cornell University.

Ma, B. (1995). *Blood Red Sunset*. London: Penguin.
Ma, D. B. (2006). 'Shanghai–Based Industrialization in the Early Twentieth Century.' At http://www.lse.ac.uk/collections/economicHistory/GEHN/GEHNworkingpapers.htm (accessed 1.8.07).
Ma, X. D. (2000). 'Insider and Outsider Community Strategies toward Migrant Workers.' In West, L. A. and Zhao, Y. H. (eds) (2000) *Rural Labor Flows in China*. Berkeley: University of California Press.
MacFarquhar, R. (1983). *The Origins of the Cultural Revolution: The Great Leap Forward*. New York: Columbia University Press.
MacFarquhar, R. (1997). *The Origins of the Cultural Revolution: The Coming of the Cataclysm, 1961–66*. New York: Columbia University Press.
MacFarquhar, R., Cheek, T. and Wu, E. (eds) (1989). *The Secret Speeches of Chairman Mao*. Cambridge, MA: Harvard University Press.
MacFarquhar, R. and Schoenhals, M. (2006). *Mao's Last Revolution*. Cambridge, MA: Harvard University Press.
Machin, S. and Vignoles, A. (2005). *What's the Good of Education?* Princeton: Princeton University Press.
Maddison, A. (1998). *Chinese Economic Performance in the Long Run*. Paris: OECD.
Maddison, A. (2001). *The World Economy: A Millennial Perspective*. Paris: OECD.
Maddison, A. (2003). *The World Economy: Historical Statistics*. Paris: OECD
Maddison, A. (2006a). 'Do Official Statistics Exaggerate China's GDP Growth?' *Review of Income and Wealth*, 52 (1):121–6.
Maddison, A. (2006b). 'World Population, GDP and Per Capita GDP, 1–2003 AD.' At http://www.ggdc.net/Maddison (accessed 30 August 2006).
Magee, D. (2006). 'Powershed Politics: Yunnan Hydropower under Great Western Development.' China Quarterly, 185: 23–41.
Mako, W. P. and Zhang, C. L. (2003). *Management of China's State-Owned Enterprise Portfolio*. Beijing: World Bank.
Mallee, H. (2000). 'Agricultural Labor and Rural Population Mobility.' In West, L. A. and Zhao, Y. H. (eds) (2000) *Rural Labor Flows in China*. Berkeley: University of California Press.
Mao, Z. D. (1930). 'Oppose Book Worship.' At http://www.marxists.org/ reference/archive/mao (accessed 20 August 2007).
Mao, Z. D. (1937a). 'On Contradiction.' In Mao, D. Z. (1971) *Selected Readings from the Works of Mao Tsetung*. Beijing: Foreign Languages Press.
Mao, Z. D. (1937b). 'On Practice.' In Mao, Z. D. (1971) *Selected Readings from the Works of Mao Tsetung*. Beijing: Foreign Languages Press.
Mao, Z. D. (1950). 'Fight for a Fundamental Turn for the Better in the Nation's Financial and Economic Situation.' In *Selected Works of Mao Zedong*, vol. V (1977). Beijing: Foreign Languages Press
Mao, Z. D. (1954). 'On the Draft Constitution of the People's Republic of China.' At http://www.marxists.org/reference/archive/mao (accessed 20 December 2007).
Mao, Z. D. (1955). 'On the Question of Agricultural Cooperation.' In Mao (1971) *Selected Readings from the Works of Mao Tsetung*. Beijing: Foreign Languages Press.
Mao, Z. D. (1956). 'On the Ten Great Relationships.' In Maoist Documentation Project, *Long Live Mao Zedong Thought*. At http://www.maoism.org/msw (accessed 12 July 2006).
Mao, Z. D. (1957). 'On the Correct Handling of Contradictions among the People.' In Mao, D. Z. (1971) *Selected Readings from the Works of Mao Tsetung*. Beijing: Foreign Languages Press.

Mao (1961). 'Reading Notes on the Soviet Text *Political Economy.*' At http://www.marxists.org/reference/archive/mao/ (accessed 20 August 2007).
Mao, Z. D. (1964). 'Talk on the Third Five Year Plan.' In Howe, C. and Walker, K. R. (1989) *The Foundations of the Chinese Planned Economy.* Basingstoke: Macmillan.
Mao, Z. D. (1966). 'Notes on the Report of Further Improving the Army's Agricultural Work by the Rear Service Department of the Military Commission.' At http://www.marxists.org/reference/archive/mao (accessed 20 August 2007).
Mao, Z. D. (1968). 'Directives Regarding the Cultural Revolution.' At http://www.marxists.org/ reference/archive/mao (accessed 20 August 2007).
Mao, Z. D. (1971). *Selected Readings from the Works of Mao Tsetung.* Beijing: Foreign Languages Press.
Mao, Z. D. (1977). *A Critique of Soviet Economics.* New York: Monthly Review Press.
Marks, R. B. (1998). *Tigers, Rice, Silk and Silt.* Cambridge: Cambridge University Press.
Marx, K. (1852). *The Eighteenth Brumaire of Louis Bonaparte.* In Carver, T. (ed.) (1996) *Marx: Later Political Writings.* Cambridge: Cambridge University Press.
Marx, K. (1859). *A Contribution to the Critique of Political Economy.* At http://www.marxists.org/archive/marx/index.htm (accessed 6 August 2007).
Marx, K. (1875). *Critique of the Gotha Programme.* In Carver, T. (ed.) (1996) *Marx: Later Political Writings.* Cambridge: Cambridge University Press.
Marx, K. (1881). 'First Draft of Letter to Vera Zasulich.' At http://www.marxists.org/archive/marx/works/1894/peasant-question/index.htm#works (accessed 8 January 2008).
Marx, K. and Engels, F. (1848/1998). *The Communist Manifesto.* London: Verso.
Matsuda, Y. (1990). 'Survey Systems and Sampling Designs of Chinese Household Surveys, 1952–1987.' *The Developing Economies,* XXVIII (3): 329–52.
McCloskey, D. N. (1987). *Econometric History.* Basingstoke: Macmillan.
McCloskey, D. N. (1970). 'Did Victorian Britain Fail?' *Economic History Review,* 23: 446–59.
McCormack, G. (2001). 'Water Margins: Competing Paradigms in China.' *Critical Asian Studies,* 33 (1): 5–30.
Meng, X., Gregory, R. and Wang, Y. J. (2005). 'Poverty, Inequality and Growth in Urban China, 1986–2000.' *Journal of Comparative Economics,* 33 (4): 710–29.
Min, A. (1984). *Red Azalea.* New York: Pantheon.
Ministry of Information. (1945). *The China Handbook 1937–43.* London: Chinese Ministry of Information.
Ministry of Information. (1947). *The China Handbook 1939–45.* London: Chinese Ministry of Information.
Misra, K. (1998). *From Post-Maoism to Post-Marxism.* London: Routledge.
Mo, Y. R. (1987). *Jiangsu xiangzhen gongye fazhan shi* (A History of the Development of Township and Village Industry in Jiangsu). Nanjing: Nanjing gongxueyuan chubanshe.
MOA – Nongye bu (Ministry of Agriculture). (1981).'1977 zhi 1979 quanguo qiongxian qingkuang' (Poor Counties in China, 1977–1979). *Xinhua Yuebao* (*New China Monthly*), 2: 117–20.
MOA – Nongye bu (Ministry of Agriculture). (1989). *Zhongguo nongcun jingji tongji daquan 1949–1986* (Complete Statistics on China's Rural Economy). Beijing: Nongye chubanshe.
MOA – Nongye bu (Ministry of Agriculture). (2004). *Zhongguo nongye fazhan baogao 2004* (Report on the Development of Chinese Agriculture). Beijing: Nongye chubanshe.

MOA – Nongye bu (Ministry of Agriculture) (various years). *Zhongguo nongye nianjian 1999, 2005* (Chinese Agricultural Yearbook). Beijing: Nongye chubanshe.
MOH – Weisheng bu (Ministry of Health). (2003). *Zhongguo weisheng tongji gaiyao 2003* (Statistical Outline of Chinese Health). At www.moh.gov. cn (accessed 28 January 2004).
MOLSS – Laodong he shehui baozhang bu (Ministry of Labour and Social Security). (2007). *Laodong he baozhang shiye fazhan tongji baogao* (Statistical Report on the Development of the Labour Force and Social Security, 2007). At www.molss/gov/cn (accessed 7 May 2007).
Moore, B. (1967). *Social Origins of Dictatorship and Democracy*. London: Penguin.
Morishima, M. (1982). *Why Has Japan Succeeded?* Cambridge: Cambridge University Press.
Mosk, C. (1996). *Making Health Work*. Berkeley: University of California Press.
Murphey, R. (1970). *The Treaty Ports and China's Modernization*. Ann Arbor: University of Michigan Papers in Chinese Studies, no. 7.
Murphy, R. (2002). *How Migrant Labor is Changing Rural China*. Cambridge: Cambridge University Press.
Murphy. R. (2006). *Domestic Migrant Remittances in China*. New York: United Nations.
Myers, R. H. (1970). *The Chinese Peasant Economy*. Cambridge, MA: Harvard University Press.
Myers, R. H. (1989). 'The World Depression and the Chinese Economy, 1930–36.' In Brown, I. (ed.) (1989) *The Economies of Africa and Asia in the Inter-war Depression*. London: Routledge.
Myers, R. H. and Peattie, M. R. (1984). *The Japanese Colonial Empire, 1895–1945*. Princeton: Princeton University Press.
Myrdal, G. (1957). *Economic Theory and Under-developed Regions*. London: Duckworth.
Nakagane, K. (1989). 'Intersectoral Resource Flows in China Revisited.' *The Developing Economies*, XXVII (2): 146–73.
NARB (National Agricultural Research Bureau) (1934). *Crop Reporting in China in 1933*. Nanjing: Ministry of Industry.
NARB (National Agricultural Research Bureau) (1936). *Crop Reporting in China in 1934*. Nanjing: Ministry of Industry.
Naughton, B. (1988). 'The Third Front.' *China Quarterly*, 115: 351–86.
Naughton, B. (1995). *Growing Out of the Plan*. Cambridge: Cambridge University Press.
Naughton, B. (1997). 'China's Emergence and Prospects as a Trading Nation.' In Brainard, W. C. and Perry, G. L. (eds) *Brookings Papers on Economic Activity*, 1996:2. Washington, DC. Brookings Institute.
NCGY – Zhongguo tongjiju (State Statistical Bureau) (1989). *Zhongguo fenxian nongcun jingji tongji gaiyao 1980–1987* (An Outline of Rural Economic Statistics by County in China). Beijing: Zhongguo tongji chubanshe.
NCGY – Zhongguo tongjiju (State Statistical Bureau) (1992). *Zhongguo fenxian nongcun jingji tongji gaiyao 1990* (An Outline of Rural Economic Statistics by County in China). Beijing: Zhongguo tongji chubanshe.
Ng, S. H., Ip, O. and Zeng, H. W. (1998). 'Development of the Pearl River Delta: Labour and Employment.' In Cheng, J. Y. S. (ed.) (1998) *The Guangdong Development Model*. Hong Kong: City University of Hong Kong Press.
Nguyen, T., Cheng, E. and Findlay, C. (1996). 'Land Fragmentation and Farm Productivity in China in the 1990s.' *China Economic Review*, 7 (2): 169–80.

Nickum, J. E. (1978). 'Labour Accumulation in Rural China and Its Role since the Cultural Revolution.' *Cambridge Journal of Economics*, 2 (3): 273–86.
Nickum, J. E. (1990a). *Irrigation in the People's Republic of China*. Washington, DC: International Food Policy Research Institute.
Nickum, J. E. (1990b). 'Volatile Waters: Is China's Irrigation in Decline?' In Tso, T. C. (ed.) (1990) *Agricultural Reform and Development in China*. Washington, DC: Ideals.
Nickum, J. E. (1995). *Dam Lies and Other Statistics: Taking the Measure of Irrigation in China, 1931–1991*. Honolulu: East-West Center.
Nolan, P. (1976). 'Collectivisation in China: Some Comparisons with the USSR.' *Journal of Peasant Studies*, 3 (2): 192–220.
Nolan, P. (1988). *The Political Economy of Collective Farms*. Cambridge: Polity.
Nolan, P. (1993a). 'The Causation and Prevention of Famines: A Critique of A. K. Sen.' *Journal of Peasant Studies*, 21 (1): 1–28.
Nolan, P. (1993b). *State and Market in the Chinese Economy*. London: Macmillan.
Nolan, P. (1995). *China's Rise, Russia's Fall*. London: Macmillan.
Nolan, P. (2001). *China and the Global Business Revolution*. Houndmills:Palgrave.
Nolan, P. and Dong, F. R. (eds) (1990). *Market Forces in China*. London: Zed Books.
Nolan, Peter (2002). 'China and the Global Business Revolution.' *Cambridge Journal of Economics*, 26: 119–37.
Nongcun xiaozu – Nongcun diaocha lingdao xiaozu bangongshi (Office of the Leading Rural Survey Group) (ed.) (1986). *Quanguo nongcun shehui jingji dianxing diaocha* (A Typical Example Survey of China's Rural Economy and Society), vol. VII. Beijing: unpublished.
Nongdiao zongdui (Rural Survey Team) (2005). 'Guojia fupin zhongdian xian nongcun juedui pinkun renkou 16.13 million' (16.13 Million of the Rural Population Living in Absolute Poverty Are to be Found in State-Designated Poor Counties). At http://www.sannong.com (accessed 10 August 2007).
Noorbakhsh, F. (1998). 'A Modified Human Development Index.' *World Development*, 26 (3): 517–28.
Notestein, F. W. and Chao, C. M. (1937). 'Population.' In Buck, J. L. (1937) *Land Utilization in China*. Oxford: Oxford University Press.
Nove, A. and Nutti, M. (eds) (1972). *The Economics of Socialism*. Harmondsworth: Penguin.
NSO (National Statistical Office of Korea). *Korean Statistical Data*. At www.nso.go.kr (accessed 31 May 2006).
Nyberg, A. and Rozelle, S. (1999). *Accelerating China's Rural Transformation*. Washington, DC: World Bank.
O'Brien, K. and Li, L. J. (1996). 'Villagers and Popular Resistance in Contemporary China.' *Modern China*, 22 (1): 28–61.
O'Brien, K. and Li, L. J. (2005). 'Popular Contention and Its Impact in Rural China.' *Comparative Political Studies*, 38 (3): 235–59.
O'Brien, K. and Li, L. J. (eds) (2006). *Rightful Resistance in Rural China*. Cambridge: Cambridge University Press.
OECD (1997). *Agricultural Policies in China*. Paris: OECD.
OECD (2000). *OECD Economic Outlook*, no. 68 (December). Paris: OECD.
OECD (2001). *China's Agriculture in the International Trading System*. Paris: OECD.
OECD (2002a). *China in the World Economy*. Paris: OECD.
OECD (2002b). *Agricultural Policies in China after WTO Accession*. Paris: OECD.
OECD (2005). *OECD Economic Surveys – China*. Paris: OECD.

OECD (2006). *Challenges for China's Public Spending*. Paris: OECD.
Offer, A. (2006). *The Challenge of Affluence*. Oxford: Oxford University Press.
Oi, J. C. (1989). *State and Peasant in Contemporary China*. Berkeley: University of California Press.
Oi, J. C. (1992). 'Fiscal Reform and the Economic Foundations of Local State Corporatism in China.' *World Politics,* 45 (1): 99–126.
Oi, J. C. (1993). 'Reform and Urban Bias in China.' In Varshney, A. (ed.) (1993) *Beyond Urban Bias*. London: Frank Cass.
Oi, J. C. (1999). *Rural China Takes Off.* Berkeley: California University Press.
Oi, J. C. and Walder, A. (eds) (1999). *Property Rights and Economic Reform in China*. Stanford: Stanford University Press.
OLG – Office of the Leading Group of Economic Development in Poor Areas under the State Council (1989). *Outline of Economic Development in China's Poor Areas*. Beijing: State Council.
Oswald, A. (1997). 'Happiness and Economic Performance.' *Economic Journal,* 107: 1815–31.
Otsuka, K., Liu, D. Q. and Murakami, N. (1998). *Industrial Reform in China*. Oxford: Clarendon Press.
Ozyurt, S. (2007). *Total Factor Productivity Growth in Chinese Industry, 1952–2005*. At http://www.iariw.org/papers/2007/ozyurt.pdf (accessed 14 January 2008).
Panzhihua City (2005). *An Environmental Profile of Panzhihua City*. At http://www.fukuoka.unhabitat.org (accessed 21 January 2008).
Panzhihua tongjiju (Panzhihua Statistical Bureau) (2001). *Panzhihua tongji nianjian 2001* (Panzhihua Statistical Yearbook). Beijing: Zhongguo tongji chubanshe.
Parish, W. L. (1984). 'Destratification in China.' In Watson, J. L. (ed.) (1984) *Class and Social Stratification in Post-Revolution China*. Cambridge: Cambridge University Press.
Park, A. and Wang, S. G. (2001). 'China's Poverty Statistics.' *China Economic Review,* 12: 384–98.
Patnaik, U. (2002). 'On Famine and Measuring "Famine Deaths".' In Patel, S., Bagchi, J. and Raj, K. (eds) (2002) *Thinking Social Science in India*. London: Sage.
Pepper, S. (1996). *Radicalism and Education Reform in 20th Century China*. Cambridge: Cambridge University Press.
Perkins, D. H. (1969). *Agricultural Development in China 1368–1968*. Edinburgh: Edinburgh University Press.
Perkins, D. H. and Yusuf, S. (1984). *Rural Development in China*. London: Johns Hopkins University Press.
Peerenboom, R. (2007). *China Modernizes*. Oxford: Oxford University Press.
Persson, T. and Tabellini, G. (1994). 'Is Inequality Harmful for Growth?' *American Economic Review,* 84 (3): 600–21.
Peterson, G. (1994a). 'State Literary Ideologies and the Transformation of Rural China.' *Australian Journal of Chinese Affairs,* 32: 95–120.
Peterson, G. (1994b). 'The Struggle for Literacy in Post-Revolutionary Rural Guangdong.' *China Quarterly,* 140: 926–43.
Piazza, A. (1986). *Food Consumption and Nutritional Status in the PRC*. Boulder, CO: Westview.
Piketty, T. and Qian, N. (2004). 'Income Inequality and Progressive Income Taxation in China and India, 1986–2010.' CEPR Discussion Paper at http://papers.ssrn.com/sol3/papers.cfm?abstract_id=922116 (accessed 22 June 2008).

Pomeranz, K. (2000). *The Great Divergence*. Princeton: Princeton University Press.
Poncet, S. (2003). 'Measuring Chinese Domestic and International Integration.' *China Economic Review*, 14: 1–21.
Popkin, S. L. (1979). *The Rational Peasant*. Berkeley: University of California Press.
Potter, S. H. and Potter, J. M. (1990). *China's Peasants*. Cambridge: Cambridge University Press.
Prasad, E. S. (2004). 'China's Growth and Integration into the World Economy.' IMF Occasional Paper no. 232. Washington, DC: International Monetary Fund.
Prasad, E. S. and Rajan, R. G. (2006). 'Modernizing China's Growth Paradigm.' *American Economic Review* (Papers and Proceedings), 96 (2): 331–6.
Pritchett, L. (2001). 'Where Has All the Education Gone?' *World Bank Economic Observer*, 15 (3): 367–91.
Pritchett, L. and Summers, L. H. (1996). 'Wealthier is Happier.' *Journal of Human Resources*, 31 (4): 841–68.
Propaganda Office – Zhonggong zhongyang xuanchuanbu xuanchuanju (Propaganda Office of the Central Committee's Department of Propaganda) (1988). *Jidang Zhongguo nongcun de biange* (The Transformation Surging across Rural China). Beijing: Guangming ribao chubanshe.
Psacharopoulos, G. (2006). 'World Bank Policy on Education.' *International Journal of Educational Development*, 26: 329–38.
Putnam, R. D. (2000). *Bowling Alone*. New York: Simon & Schuster.
Putterman, L. (1990). 'Effort, Productivity and Incentives in a 1970s Chinese People's Commune.' *Journal of Comparative Economics*, 14 (1): 88–105.
Putterman, L. (1993). *Continuity and Change in China's Rural Development*. Oxford: Oxford University Press.
Putterman, L. (1997). 'On the Past and Future of China's Township and Village-Owned Enterprises.' *World Development*, 25 (10): 1639–55.
Putterman, L. and Chiacu, A. F. (1994). 'Elasticities and Factor Weights for Agricultural Growth Accounting.' *China Economic Review*, 5 (2): 191–204.
Qin, H. L. (1995). *Ninth Heaven, Ninth Hell*. New York: Barricade.
Qu, G. P. and Li, J. C. (1994). *Population and the Environment in China*. Boulder: Lynne Rienner.
Ranis, G., Stewart, F. and Ramirez, A. (2000). 'Economic Growth and Human Development.' *World Development*, 28 (2): 197–219.
Ravallion, M. (2006). 'Looking Beyond the Averages in the Trade and Poverty Debate.' *World Development*, 34 (8): 1374–92.
Ravallion, M. and Chen, S. H. (2007). 'China's Uneven Progress against Poverty.' *Journal of Development Economics*, 82 (1): 1–42.
Ravallion, M. and van de Walle, D. (2001). 'Breaking Up the Collective Farm: Welfare Outcomes of Vietnam's Massive Land Privatization.' World Bank Working Paper no. 2710. Washington, DC: World Bank.
Rawls, J. (1972). *A Theory of Justice*. Cambridge, MA: Harvard University Press
Rawski, T. G. (1989). *Economic Growth in Prewar China*. Berkeley: University of California Press.
Rawski, T. G. (2001). 'What is Happening to China's GDP Statistics?' *China Economic Review*, 12: 347–54.
Rawski, T. G. (2006). 'Urban Air Quality in China: Historical and Comparative Perspectives.' At http://www.industrystudies.pitt.edu/papers/China_urban_air_quality_TGR.pdf (accessed 10 January 2008).

Rawski, T. G. and Li, L. (eds) (1992). *Chinese History in Economic Perspective.* Berkeley: University of California Press.

Rawski, T. G. and Mead, R. W. (1998). 'On the Trail of China's Phantom Farmers.' *World Development,* 26 (5): 767–81.

Ray, D. (1998). *Development Economics.* Princeton: Princeton University Press.

Reardon, L. C. (2002). *The Reluctant Dragon.* Seattle: University of Washington Press.

Reddy, S. (2007). 'Death in China.' *New Left Review,* 45: 49–66.

Reddy, S. and Minoiu, C. (2006). 'Chinese Poverty: Assessing the Impact of Alternative Assumptions.' UNDP Working Paper no. 25. At http://www.undp-povertycentre.org/newsletters/WorkingPaper25.pdf (accessed 22 June 2008).

Ren, R. (1997). *China's Economic Performance in International Perspective.* Paris: OECD.

Reynolds, B. L. (1981). 'Changes in the Standard of Living of Shanghai Industrial Workers, 1930–75.' In Howe, C. (ed.) (1981) *Shanghai.* Cambridge: Cambridge University Press.

Richardson, P. (1999). *Economic Change in China, 1800–1950.* Cambridge: Cambridge University Press.

Riskin, C. (1971). 'Small Industry and the Chinese Model of Development.' *China Quarterly,* 46: 245–73.

Riskin, C. (1975). 'Surplus and Stagnation in Modern China.' In Perkins, D. H. (ed.) (1975) *China's Modern Economy in Historical Perspective.* Stanford: Stanford University Press.

Riskin, C. (1978). 'China's Rural Industries.' *China Quarterly,* 73: 77–98.

Riskin, C. (1987). *China's Political Economy.* Oxford: Oxford University Press.

Riskin, C. (1993a). 'Income Distribution and Poverty in Rural China.' In Griffin, K. and Zhao, R. W. (eds) (1993) *The Distribution of Income in China.* Basingstoke: Macmillan.

Riskin, C. (1993b). 'Poverty in China's Countryside.' In Bardhan, P., Datta-Chaudhuri, M. and Krishnan, T. N. (eds) (1993) *Development and Change.* Bombay: Oxford University Press.

Riskin, C. and Li, S. (2001). 'Chinese Rural Poverty Inside and Outside the Poor Regions.' In Riskin, C., Zhao, R. W. and Li, S. (eds) (2001) *China's Retreat from Equality.* Armonk: M. E. Sharpe.

Riskin, C., Zhao, R. W. and Li, S. (eds) (2001). *China's Retreat from Equality.* Armonk: M. E. Sharpe.

RKNJ – Zhongguo shehui kexueyuan renkou yanjiusuo (Population Research Institute of the Chinese Academy of Social Sciences) (ed.) (various years). *Zhongguo renkou nianjian 1985, 1992* (Chinese Population Yearbook). Beijing: Jingji guanli chubanshe.

RKTJNJ – Zhongguo guojia tongjiju (Chinese State Statistical Bureau) (various years). *Zhongguo renkou tongji nianjian 1988, 1991, 1993, 1998, 2001, 2003, 2005 and 2006* (Chinese Population Statistics Yearbook). Beijing: Zhongguo tongji chubanshe.

Rock, M. T. and Bonnett, H. (2004). 'The Comparative Politics of Corruption.' *World Development,* 32 (6): 999–1017.

Rodrik, D. (1995). 'Getting Interventions Right: How South Korea and Taiwan Grew Rich.' *Economic Policy,* 20: 53–101.

Rodrik, D. (ed.) (2003). *In Search of Prosperity.* Princeton: Princeton University Press.

Rodrik, D. (2006a). 'Goodbye Washington Consensus, Hello Washington Consensus.' *Journal of Economic Literature,* XLIV (4): 973–87.

Rodrik, D. (2006b). 'What's So Special about China's Exports?' *China and the World Economy,* 14 (5): 1–19.

Roemer, J. E. (1994). *A Future for Socialism.* London: Verso.

Roemer, J. E. (1996). *Equal Shares*. London: Verso.
Rojas, R. (1968). 'Decision Concerning the Great Proletarian Cultural Revolution.' At http://www.rojasdatabank.org/16points.htm (accessed 4 December 2006).
Roll, C. R. (1980). *The Distribution of Rural Incomes in China*. London: Garland.
Romer, P. M. (1986): 'Increasing Returns and Long-Run Growth.' *Journal of Political Economy*, 94 (5): 1002–37.
Romer, P. M. (1990). 'Endogenous Technological Change.' *Journal of Political Economy*, 98 (5): S71–S102.
Ross, H. (2005). *China Country Report*. Paris: UNESCO. At http://www.unesco.org (accessed 20 August 2007).
Ross, L. (1988). *Environmental Policy in China*. Indianapolis: Indiana University Press.
Rowe, W. T. (1984). *Hankow: Commerce and Society in a Chinese City, 1796–1889*. Stanford: Stanford University Press.
Rowthorn, R. E. and Wells, J. R. (1987). *De-Industrialization and Foreign Trade*. Cambridge: Cambridge University Press.
Rozelle, S. and Huang, J. K. (2006). 'China's Rural Economy and the Path to a Modern Industrial State.' In Dong, X. Y., Song, S. F. and Zhang, X. B. (eds) (2006) *China's Agricultural Development*. Aldershot: Ashgate.
Rozelle, S., Li, G., Shen, M. G., Hughart, A. and Giles, J. (1999). 'Leaving China's Farms.' *China Quarterly*, 158: 367–93.
Ruf, G. A. (1998). *Cadres and Kin*. Stanford: Stanford University Press.
Sachs, J. and Woo, W. T. (1994). 'Structural Factors in the Economic Reforms of China, Eastern Europe, and the Former Soviet Union.' *Economic Policy*, 18: 101–46.
Sachs, J. D. (2005). *The End of Poverty*. London: Allen Lane.
Sachs, J. D. and Gallup, J. L. (2001). 'The Economic Burden of Malaria.' *American Journal of Tropical Medicine and Hygiene*, 64 (1 & 2): 85–96.
Sachs, J. D., McArthur, J. W., Schmidt-Traub, G., Kruk, M., Bahadur, C., Faye, M. and McCord, G. (2004). 'Ending Africa's Poverty Trap.' *Brookings Economic Papers*, 2004 (1): 117–240.
Sachs, J. D. and Shatz, H. J. (1994). 'Trade and Jobs in US Manufacturing.' In Brainard, W. C. and Perry, G. L. (eds) *Brookings Economic Papers*, 1: 1–84.
Sands, B. and Myers, R. H. (1986). 'The Spatial Approach to Chinese History.' *Journal of Asian Studies*, 45: 721–43.
Sands, B. and Myers, R. H. (1990). 'Economics and Macroregions.' *Journal of Asian Studies*, 49 (2): 344–6.
Sang, Y. (2006). *China Candid*. Berkeley: University of California Press.
Scharping, T. (2003). *Birth Control in China 1949–2000*. London: RoutledgeCurzon.
Schran, P. (1969). *The Development of Chinese Agriculture, 1950–1959*. Chicago: University of Illinois Press.
Schran, P. (1978). 'China's Demographic Evolution 1850–1913 Reconsidered.' *China Quarterly*, 75: 639–46.
Schoenhals, M. (1991). 'The 1978 Truth Criterion Controversy.' *China Quarterly*, 126: 243–68.
Schoenhals, M. (ed.) (1996). *China's Cultural Revolution, 1966–1969*. Armonk: M. E. Sharpe.
SCMP – *South China Morning Post*, Hong Kong.
Scott, J. (1976). *The Moral Economy of the Peasant*. New Haven: Yale University Press.
Scott, M. F. G. (1989). *A New View of Economic Growth*. Oxford: Clarendon Press.

SCTJNJ – Sichuan sheng tongjiju (Sichuan sheng Statistical Bureau) (various years). *Sichuan tongji nianjian 1990, 2006* (Sichuan Statistical Yearbook). Beijing: Zhongguo tongji chubanshe.
SCZL – Sichuan gongye qiye zonglan bianji weiyuanhui (Editorial Committee for A Summary Account of Sichuan's Industrial Enterprises) (ed.) (1990). *Sichuan gongye qiye zonglan* (A Summary Account of Sichuan's Industrial Enterprises). Beijing: Zhongguo tongji chubanshe.
Seeberg, V. (2000). *The Rhetoric and Reality of Mass Education in Mao's China*. Lampeter: Edwin Mellen.
Selden, M. (1988). *The Political Economy of Chinese Socialism*. Armonk: M. E. Sharpe.
Selden, M. (ed.) (1979). *The People's Republic of China – A Documentary History*. New York: Monthly Review Press.
Sen, A. K. (1966). 'Labour Allocation in a Cooperative Enterprise.' *Review of Economic Studies*, 33 (4): 361–71.
Sen, A. K. (1981). 'Public Action and the Quality of Life in Developing Countries.' *Oxford Bulletin of Economics and Statistics*, 43 (4): 287–319.
Sen, A. K. (1983). 'Development: Which Way Now?' *Economic Journal*, 93: 745–62.
Sen, A. K. (1985). *Commodities and Capabilities*. Amsterdam: North-Holland.
Sen, A, K. (1988). 'The Concept of Development.' In Chenery, H. and Srinivasan, T. N. (eds) (1988) *Handbook of Development Economics*, vol. I. Amsterdam: North-Holland.
Sen, A. K. (1989). 'Food and Freedom.' *World Development*, 17 (6): 769–81.
Sen, A. K. (1998). 'Mortality as an Indicator of Economic Success and Failure.' *Economic Journal*, 108: 1–25.
Sen, A. K. (1999). *Development as Freedom*. Oxford: Oxford University Press.
SEPA (State Environmental Protection Administration) (1999; 2000; 2001; 2002; 2003; 2004; 2005; 2006a). *The State of the Environment 1999–2006*. At http://english.sepa.gov.cn (accessed 20 January 2008).
SEPA (2006b). *Zhongguo huanjing tongji nianjian* (China Environmental Statistical Yearbook). Beijing: Zhongguo tongji chubanshe.
Seybolt, P. J. (1971). 'The Yenan Revolution in Mass Education.' *China Quarterly*, 48: 641–69.
Shambaugh, D. (ed.) (1982). 'Zhao Ziyang's "Sichuan Experiment".' *Chinese Law and Government*, XV (1): 5–35.
Shambaugh, D. (2002). *Modernizing China's Military*. Berkeley: University of California Press.
Shanin, T. (1986). 'Introduction.' In Chayanov, A. V. *The Theory of Peasant Economy*. Madison: University of Wisconsin Press.
Shao, S. J., Nielsen, I., Nyland, C., Smyth, R., Zhang, M. Q. and Zhu, C. J. H. (2007). 'Migrants as Homo Economicus.' *China Information*, 21 (7): 7–41.
Shapiro, J. (2001). *Mao's War against Nature*. Cambridge: Cambridge University Press.
Shen, Y. M. and Tong, C. Z. (1992). *Zhongguo renkou qianyi* (Population Migration in China). Beijing: Zhongguo tongji chubanshe.
Sheng, Y. M. (1993). *Intersectoral Resource Flows and China's Economic Development.* Basingstoke: Macmillan.
Shirk, S. L. (1982). *Competitive Comrades*. Berkeley: University of California Press.
Shirk, S. L. (1984). 'The Decline of Virtuocracy in China.' In Watson, J. L. (ed.) (1984) *Class and Social Stratification in Post-Revolution China*. Cambridge: Cambridge University Press.

Shirk, S. L. (1993). *The Political Logic of Economic Reform in China.* Berkeley: University of California Press.
Shirk, S. L. (2007). *China: Fragile Superpower.* Oxford: Oxford University Press.
Shue, V. (1980). *Peasant China in Transition.* Berkeley: University of California Press.
Shue, V. (1988). *The Reach of the State.* Stanford: Stanford University Press.
Sichuan nongcun yanjiuzu – Zhonggong Sichuan sheng wei nongcun jingji shehui fazhan zhanlue yanjiuzu (Research Group for the CCP's Sichuan Committee on the Development Strategy for Rural Economy and Society) (ed.) (1986). *Sichuan nongcun jintian he mingtian* (Rural Sichuan Today and Tomorrow). Chengdu: Sichuan kexue jishu chubanshe.
Sicular, T. (1988). 'Agricultural Planning and Pricing in the Post-Mao Period.' *China Quarterly*, 116: 671–705.
Sicular, T. (ed.) (1989). *Food Price Policy in Asia.* Ithaca: Cornell University Press.
Singh, A. (1977). 'UK Industry and the World Economy: A Case of Deindustrialisation?' *Cambridge Journal of Economics*, 1: 113–36.
Singh, A. and Zammit, A. (2006). 'Corporate Governance, Crony Capitalism and Economic Crisis.' Centre for Business Research Working Paper no. 329. Cambridge: Centre for Business Research.
Siu, H. F. (1989). *Agents and Victims in South China.* New Haven: Yale University Press.
Skinner, G. W. (ed.) (1977). *The City in Late Imperial China.* Stanford: Stanford University Press.
Skinner, G. W. (1999). 'Chinese Cities: The Difference a Century Makes.' In Hamilton, G. G. (ed.) (1999) *Cosmopolitan Capitalists.* Seattle: University of Washington Press.
Smil, V. (1984). *The Bad Earth.* New York: M. E. Sharpe.
Smil, V. (2004). *China's Past, China's Future.* London: RoutledgeCurzon.
Smith, R. (1997). 'Creative Destruction: Capitalist Development and China's Environment.' New Left Review, 222: 3–42.
Solinger, D. (1999). *Contesting Citizenship in Urban China.* Berkeley: University of California Press.
Srinivasan, T. N. (1994). 'Human Development: A New Paradigm or Reinvention of the Wheel?' *American Economic Review* (Papers and Proceedings), 84 (2): 238–43.
SSB – Chinese State Statistical Bureau (1959). *Ten Great Years.* Beijing: Foreign Languages Press.
SSB – Zhongguo guojia tongjiju (Chinese State Statistical Bureau) (1985). *Zhongguo gongye jingji tongji ziliao 1949–1984* (Economic Statistics on Chinese Industry). Beijing: Zhongguo tongji chubanshe.
SSB – Zhongguo guojia tongjiju (Chinese State Statistical Bureau) (1990a). *Quanguo gesheng zizhiqu zhixiashi lishi tongji ziliao huibian* (Historical Statistics for China's Provinces, Autonomous Regions and Municipalities). Beijing: Zhongguo tongji chubanshe.
SSB – Zhongguo guojia tongjiju (Chinese State Statistical Bureau) (1990b). *Zhongguo gongye jingji tongji nianjian* (Yearbook of Economic Statistics on Chinese Industry*).* Beijing: Zhongguo tongji chubanshe.
SSB – Zhongguo guojia tongjiju (Chinese State Statistical Bureau) (1997). *Zhongguo guonei shengchanzhi hesuan lishi ziliao* (Historical Data on Chinese GDP). Beijing: Zhongguo tongji chubanshe.

SSB – Zhongguo guojia tongjiju (Chinese State Statistical Bureau) (1999). *Xin Zhongguo wushinian tongji ziliao huibian* (Collection of Statistical Material on Fifty Years of New China). Beijing: Zhongguo tongji chubanshe.
SSB – Zhongguo guojia tongjiju (Chinese State Statistical Bureau) (2000a). *Xin Zhongguo wushinian nongye tongji ziliao* (Fifty Years of Statistical Materials on Chinese Agriculture). Beijing: Zhongguo tongji chubanshe.
SSB – Zhongguo guojia tongjiju (Chinese State Statistical Bureau) (2000b). *Zhongguo nongcun zhumin diaocha nianjian 2000* (Chinese Rural Household Survey 2000). Beijing: Zhongguo tongji chubanshe.
SSB – Zhongguo guojia tongjiju (Chinese State Statistical Bureau) (2003a). *Zhongguo nongcun pinkun jiance baogao 2003* (Chinese Rural Poverty Monitoring Report). Beijing: Zhongguo tongji chubanshe.
SSB – Zhongguo guojia tongjiju (Chinese State Statistical Bureau) (2003b). *Zhongguo nongcun zhuhu diaocha nianjian 2003* (Chinese Rural Household Survey Yearbook). Beijing: Zhongguo tongji chubanshe).
SSB – Zhongguo guojia tongjiju (Chinese State Statistical Bureau) (2004). *Zhongguo nongcun zhuhu diaocha nianjian 2004* (Chinese Rural Household Survey Yearbook). Beijing: Zhongguo tongji chubanshe).
SSB – Zhongguo guojia tongjiju (Chinese State Statistical Bureau) (2005a). *Xin Zhongguo wushiwunian tongji ziliao huibian 1949–2004* (Collection of Statistical Materials on 55 Years of New China). Beijing: Zhongguo tongji chubanshe.
SSB – Zhongguo guojia tongjiju (Chinese State Statistical Bureau) (2005b). *Zhongguo nongcun tongji nianjian 2005* (Chinese Rural Statistical Yearbook). Beijing: Zhongguo tongji chubanshe.
SSB – Zhongguo guojia tongjiju (Chinese State Statistical Bureau) (2006a) 'Announcement of Revised Historical Data on Chinese GDP.' At http://www.stats.gov.cn/ (accessed 16 January 2006).
SSB – Zhongguo guojia tongjiju (Chinese State Statistical Bureau) (2006b). 'Statistical Communiqué on China's Economic and Social Development in 2005.' At http://www.stats.gov.cn/ (accessed 23 September 2006).
SSB – Zhongguo guojia tongjiju (Chinese State Statistical Bureau) (2006c). *Zhongguo nongcun zhumin diaocha nianjian 2006* (Chinese Rural Household Survey 2006). Beijing: Zhongguo tongji chubanshe.
SSB – Zhongguo guojia tongjiju (Chinese State Statistical Bureau) (2006d). *Zhongguo huanjing tongji nianjian 2006* (Chinese Environmental Statistics Yearbook). Beijing: Zhongguo tongji chubanshe.
SSB – Zhongguo guojia tongjiju (Chinese State Statistical Bureau) (2007). 'Statistical Communiqué on China's Economic and Social Development in 2006.' At http://www.stats.gov.cn/ (accessed 6 May 2007).
SSB – Zhongguo guojia tongjiju (Chinese State Statistical Bureau) (2008). 'The National Economy Maintained a Steady and Fast Growth in 2007'. At http://www.stats.gov.cn/ (accessed 27 January 2008).
State Council (1991). *Major Figures of the Fourth National Population Census of China*. Beijing: Zhongguo tongji chubanshe.
State Council (2002). *Suggestions on the Implementation of Policies and Measures Pertaining to the Development of the Western Region*. At http://www.westchina.gov.cn/english (accessed 5 April 2007).
Steckel, R. H. and Floud, R. (eds) (1997). *Height and Welfare during Industrialization*. Chicago: University of Chicago Press.

Steinfeld, E. (1998). *Forging Reform in China.* Cambridge: Cambridge University Press.
Stiglitz, J. E. (1994). *Whither Socialism?* Cambridge, MA: MIT Press.
Stiglitz, J. E. (2002). *Globalization and Its Discontents.* London: Allen Lane.
Stone, B. (1988a). 'Developments in Agricultural Technology.' *China Quarterly,* 116: 767–822.
Stone, B. (1988b). 'Relative Prices in the People's Republic of China.' In Mellor, J. W. and Ahmed, R. (eds) (1988) *Agricultural Price Policy for Developing Countries.* Baltimore: Johns Hopkins University Press.
Streeten, P. (1981). *First Things First.* Oxford: Oxford University Press.
Streeten, P. (1994). 'Human Development: Means and Ends.' *American Economic Review* (Papers and Proceedings), 84 (2): 232–7.
Stross, R. E. (1986). *The Stubborn Earth.* Berkeley: University of California Press.
Studwell, J. (2002). *The China Dream.* London: Profile Books
Su, X. (1980). *Woguo nongye de shehuizhuyi gaizhao* (The Socialist Transformation of Agriculture in China). Beijing: Renmin chubanshe.
Su, X. (1982). 'Zerenzhi yu nongcun jitisuozhi jingji de fazhan' (The Responsibility System and the Development of Collectivized Agriculture in Rural Areas). *Jingji yanjiu,* 11: 3–9.
Su, Y. (2006). 'Mass Killings in the Cultural Revolution.' In Esherick, J. W., Pickowicz, P. G. and Walder, A. G. (eds) (2006) *The Chinese Cultural Revolution as History.* Stanford: Stanford University Press.
Sun, Y. (1995). *The Chinese Reassessment of Socialism 1976–1992.* Princeton: Princeton University Press.
Sun, Y. (2004). *Corruption and Market in Contemporary China.* Ithaca: Cornell University Press.
Tan, S. H., Heerink, N., Kuyvvenhoven, A. and Qu, F. T. (2006). 'Impact of Land Fragmentation on Rice Producers' Technical Efficiency in Southeast China.' In Dong, X. Y., Song, S. F. and Zhang, X. B. (eds) (2006) *China's Agricultural Development.* Aldershot: Ashgate.
Tang, A. M. (1984). *An Analytical and Empirical Investigation of Agriculture in Mainalnd China, 1953–1980.* Taipei: Ching-hua Institution for Economic Research.
Tanner, M., S. (2007). 'Can China Contain Unrest? Six Questions Seeking One Answer.' At http://www.brookings.edu/cnaps/northeast-asia-commentary.aspx (accessed 17 November 2007).
Tanzi, V. and Chu, K. Y. (ed.) (1998). *Income Distribution and High-Quality Growth.* Cambridge, MA: MIT Press.
Targetti, F. and Thirlwall, A. P. (eds) (1989). *The Essential Kaldor.* London: Duckworth.
Tawney, R. H. (1926/1938). *Religion and the Rise of Capitalism.* London: Penguin.
Tawney, R. H. (1931). *Equality.* London: George Allen and Unwin.
Tawney, R. H. (1932). *Land and Labour in China.* London: George Allen and Unwin.
Teiwes, F. C. (1993). *Politics and Purges in China,* second edition. Armonk: M.E. Sharpe.
Teiwes, F. C. and Sun, W. (eds) (1993). *The Politics of Agricultural Cooperativization in China.* Armonk: M. E. Sharpe.
Teiwes, F. C. and Sun, W. (1996). *The Tragedy of Lin Biao.* London: Hurst and Co.
Teiwes, F. C. and Sun, W. (1999). *China's Road to Disaster.* Armonk: M. E. Sharpe.
Teiwes, F. C. and Sun, W. (2007). *The End of the Maoist Era.* Armonk: M. E. Sharpe.
Thompson, E. R. (2003). 'Technology Transfer to China by Hong Kong's Cross-Border Garment Firms.' *The Developing Economies,* 41 (1): 88–111.

Todaro, M. P. and Smith, S. C. (2006). *Economic Development*, ninth edition. Boston MA: Addison Wesley.

Treiman, D. J. (2002). *The Growth and Determinants of Literacy in China*. At http://repositories.cdlib.org/ccpr/olwp/ccpr-005-02/ (accessed 25 August 2007).

Tsou, T., Blecher, M. and Meisner, M. (1979). 'Organization, Growth, and Equality in Xiyang County: A Survey of Fourteen Brigades in Seven Communes.' *Modern China*, 5 (1): 3–39 and 5 (2): 139–85.

Tsui, K. Y. (1991). 'China's Regional Inequality, 1952–1985.' *Journal of Comparative Economics*, 15: 1–21.

UNAIDS/WHO (2007). 'AIDS Epidemic Update 2007.' At http://www.unaids.org (accessed 10 February 2008).

UNDP (United Nations Development Programme) (various years). *Human Development Report 1990, 2003, and 2006*. Oxford: Oxford University Press.

UNDP (2000). *China Human Development Report 1999*. Oxford: Oxford University Press.

UNDP (2002). *China Human Development Report 2002*. Oxford: Oxford University Press.

UNDP (2005). *China Human Development Report 2005*. Beijing: UNDP.

UNDP (2007). *Human Development Report 2007*. Basingstoke: Palgrave Macmillan.

UNDP/ILO (2000). *Policies for Poverty Reduction in China*. Geneva: United Nations.

Unger, J. (1980). 'Bending the School Ladder: The Failure of Chinese Educational Reform in the 1960s.' *Comparative Education Review*, 24 (2): 221–37.

Unger, J. (1982). *Education under Mao*. New York: Columbia University Press.

Unger, J. (1984). 'The Class System in Rural China.' In Watson, J. L. (ed.) (1984) *Class and Social Stratification in Post-Revolution China*. Cambridge: Cambridge University Press.

Unger, J. (2002). *The Transformation of Rural China*. Armonk: M. E. Sharpe.

Unger, J. (2007). 'The Cultural Revolution at the Grass Roots.' *China Journal*, 57: 109–37.

Unger, R. M. and Cui, Z. Y. (1994). 'China in the Russian Mirror.' *New Left Review*, first series, 208: 78–87.

UNICEF (2007). *The State of the World's Children 2007*. At http://www.unicef.org/ (accessed 26 January 2007).

Veeck, G., Pannell, C. W., Smith, C, J. and Huang, Y. Q. (2007). *China's Geography*. Lanham, MD: Rowman and Littlefield.

Veeck, G. and Wang, S. H. (2000). 'Challenges to Family Farming in China.' *Geographical Review*, 90 (1): 57–82.

Vermeer, E. B. (1977). *Water Conservancy and Irrigation in China*. The Hague: Leiden University Press.

Vermeer, E. B. (1982). 'Income Differentials in Rural China.' *China Quarterly*, 89: 1–33.

Vermeer, E. B. (1997). 'Decollectivization and Functional Change in Irrigation Management in China.' In OECD (1997) *Agricultural Policies in China*. Paris: OECD.

Vittinghoff, N. (2005). 'Jiang Qing and Nora.' In Leutner, M. and Spakowski, N. (eds) (2005) *Women in China: The Republican Period in Historical Perspective*. Berlin: LIT Verlag.

Vogel, E. F. (1989). *One Step Ahead in China*. Cambridge, MA: Harvard University Press.

Wade, R. (1990). *Governing the Market*. Princeton: Princeton University Press.

Wagner, D. B. (1995). 'The Traditional Chinese Iron Industry and Its Modern Fate.' *Chinese Science*, 12: 138–61.
Walder, A. G. (2002). 'Income Determination and Market Opportunity in Rural China, 1978–1996.' *Journal of Comparative Economics*, 30 (2): 354–75.
Walder, A. G. and Yang, S. (2003). 'The Cultural Revolution in the Countryside.' *China Quarterly*, 173: 74–99.
Walker, K. R. (1966). 'Collectivisation in Retrospect: The "Socialist High Tide" of Autumn 1955–Spring 1965.' *China Quarterly*, 26: 1–43.
Walker, K. R. (1968). 'The Organization of Agricultural Production.' In Galenson, W. and Liu, T-C. (eds) (1968) *Economic Trends in Communist China*. Chicago: Aldine.
Walker, K. R. (1984). *Food Grain Procurement and Consumption in China*. Cambridge: Cambridge University Press.
Wan, G. H. and Cheng, E. (2001). 'Effects of Land Fragmentation and Returns to Scale in the Chinese Farming Sector.' *Applied Economics*, 33 (2): 183–94.
Wang, C. H. (2003). *One China, Many Paths*. London: Verso.
Wang, G. W. (1955). 'Basic Tasks of China's First Five Year Plan.' In Howe, C. and Walker, K. R. (eds) (1989) *The Foundations of the Chinese Planned Economy*. Basingstoke: Macmillan.
Wang, H. (2003). *China's New Order*. Cambridge, MA: Harvard University Press.
Wang, H. (2006). 'Depoliticized Politics.' *New Left Review*, second series, 41: 29–46.
Wang, H. B. (1994). *Xin Zhongguo gongye jingji shi 1949–1957* (A History of New China's Industrial Economy). Beijing: Jingji guanli chubanshe.
Wang, H. C. (1993). 'Deforestation and Desiccation in China: A Preliminary Study.' At http://www.library.utoronto.ca/pcs/state/chinaeco/forest.htm (accessed 15 January 2008).
Wang, L. X. (1988). 'Mao's Legacy in Anhui', *Kunlun*, 6, December, trans. in Joint Publications Research Service (1989) *China Report – Agriculture*, CAR-89-079: 1–65. Washington, DC: Government Printing Office.
Wang, M. K. (2000). *China's Economic Transformation over Twenty Years*. Beijing: Foreign Languages Press.
Wang, S. G. and Hu, A. G. (1999). *The Political Economy of Uneven Development*. Armonk: M. E. Sharpe.
Wang, S. G. and Hu, A. G. (2001). *The Chinese Economy in Crisis*. Armonk: M. E. Sharpe.
Wang, X. Q. and Bai, N. (1991). *The Poverty of Plenty*. Basingstoke: Macmillan.
Wang, Y. R. (2004). *Zengzhang fazhan yu bianqian* (Growth, Development and Change). Beijing: Zhongguo wuzi chubanshe.
Watson, A. (1984). 'Agriculture Looks for "Shoes that Fit"; The Production Responsibility System and Its Implications.' In Maxwell, N. and McFarlane, B. (eds) (1984) *China's Changed Road to Development*. Oxford: Pergamon Press.
Watson, A. (1989). 'Investment Issues in the Chinese Countryside.' *Australian Journal of Chinese Affairs*, 22: 85–128.
Watson, J. L. (ed.) (1984). *Class and Social Stratification in Post-Revolution China*. Cambridge: Cambridge University Press.
Weber, M. (1905/1976). *The Protestant Ethic and the Spirit of Capitalism*. London: George Allen and Unwin.
Wei, Y. H. D. (2000). *Regional Development in China*. London: Routledge.
Wei, Y. H. D. and Kim, S. W. (2002). 'Widening Inter-County Inequality in Jiangsu Province, China, 1950–1995.' *Journal of Development Studies*, 38 (6): 142–61.
Wei, Z. and Gustaffson, B. (1998). 'Zhongguo zhuanxing shiqi de pinkun biandong fenxi'

(An Analysis of Changes in Poverty during the Transition in China). *Jingji yanjiu (Economic Research)*, 11: 64–68.

Wen, G. Z. J. (1993). 'Total Factor Productivity Change in China's Farming Sector, 1952–1989.' *Economic Development and Cultural Change*, 42 (1): 1–42.

Wen, J. B. (2007). *Report on the Work of Government 2007*. At http://english.gov.cn/official/workreports.htm (accessed 12 November 2007).

West, L. A. and Zhao, Y. H. (eds) (2000). *Rural Labor Flows in China*. Berkeley: University of California.

White, T. (2006). *China's Longest Campaign: Birth Planning in the People's Republic, 1949–2005*. Ithaca: Cornell University Press.

Whiting, S. H. (2001). *Power and Wealth in Rural China*. Cambridge: Cambridge University Press.

Whyte, M. K. (1975). 'Inequality and Stratification in China.' *China Quarterly*, 64: 684–711.

Whyte, M. K. (2005). 'Popular Attitudes toward Income Inequality in China.' Unpublished ms.

Whyte, M. K. and Parish, W. L. (1984). *Urban Life in Contemporary China*. Chicago: University of Chicago Press.

Wilkinson, R. (2005). *The Impact of Inequality*. New York: The New Press.

Winters, L. A. and Yusuf, S. (2007). *Dancing with Giants*. Washington, DC: World Bank.

Wolff, R. D. and Resnick, S. A. (1987). *Economics: Marxian versus Neoclassical*. Baltimore: Johns Hopkins University Press.

Wong, C. P. W. (1991). 'The Maoist Model Reconsidered.' In Joseph, W.A., Wong, C. P. W. and Zweig, D. (eds) (1991) *New Perspectives on the Cultural Revolution*. Cambridge, MA: Harvard University Press.

Wong, C. P. W., Heady, C. and Woo, W. T. (1995). *Fiscal Management and Economic Reform in the People's Republic of China*. Oxford: Oxford University Press.

Wong, L. and Huen, W. P. (1998). 'Reforming the Household Registration System.' *International Migration Review*, 32 (4): 974–94.

Woo, W. T. (1998). 'Chinese Economic Growth.' In M. Fouquin and F. Lemoine (eds) (1998) *The Chinese Economy*. London: Economica.

Woo, W. T. and Bao, S. M. (2003). *China – Case Study in Human Development Progress towards the Millennium Development Goals at the Subnational Level*. At http://hdr.undp.or/publications/papers.cfm (accessed 3 June 2004).

Wood, A. (1994). *North–South Trade, Employment and Inequality*. Oxford: Oxford University Press.

Wood, E. M. (1991). *The Pristine Culture of Capitalism*. London: Verso.

Woods, R. (1992). *The Population of Britain in the Nineteenth Century*. Basingstoke: Macmillan.

World Bank (1989). *India – Poverty, Employment and Social Services*. Washington, DC: World Bank.

World Bank (1990a). *World Development Report 1990*. Oxford: Oxford University Press.

World Bank (1990b). *China – Between Plan and Market*. Washington, DC: World Bank.

World Bank (1992). *China – Strategies for Reducing Poverty in the 1990s*. Washington, DC: World Bank.

World Bank (1994). *China – Foreign Trade Reform*. Washington, DC: World Bank.

World Bank (1996). 'Poverty in China. What Do the Numbers Say?' Background note. Washington, DC: World Bank.

World Bank (1997a). *China 2020*. Washington, DC: World Bank.
World Bank (1997b). *China Engaged*. Washington, DC: World Bank.
World Bank (1997c). *Sharing Rising Incomes*. Washington, DC: World Bank.
World Bank (1997d). *Clear Water, Blue Sky*. Washington, DC: World Bank.
World Bank (1998). *World Development Report 1998*. Oxford: Oxford University Press.
World Bank (2001a). *World Development Indicators 2001*. Washington, DC: World Bank.
World Bank (2001b). *China – Overcoming Rural Poverty*. Washington, DC: World Bank.
World Bank (2001c). *World Development Report 2000/2001*. New York: Oxford University.
World Bank (2001d). *China – Air, Land and Water*. Washington, DC: World Bank.
World Bank (2005). *World Development Indicators 2005*. Washington, DC: World Bank.
World Bank (2007a). *World Development Indicators 2007* (CD-ROM version*)*. Washington, DC: World Bank.
World Bank (2007b). *2005 International Comparison Project*. At http://www.worldbank.org (accessed 10 January 2008).
World Bank (2007c). 'Costs of Pollution in China' (draft). Washington, DC: World Bank.
World Bank (2007d). *World Development Indicators 2007* (paper version). Washington, DC: World Bank.
Wright, D. B. (2003). *The Promise of the Revolution*. New York: Rowman and Littlefield.
Wright, T. (2000). 'Distant Thunder: The Regional Economies of Southwest China and the Impact of the Great Depression.' *Modern Asian Studies*, 34 (3): 697–738.
Wright, T. (2006). 'The Performance of China's Industrial Enterprises.' *China Information*, XX: 165–99.
Wright, T. (2007). 'The Manchurian Economy and the 1930s World Depression.' *Modern Asian Studies*, 41 (5): 1073–112.
Wrigley, E. A. and Schofield, R. S. (1981). *The Population History of England, 1541–1871*. Cambridge: Cambridge University Press.
Wu, H. X. (2001). 'China's Comparative Labour Productivity Performance in Manufacturing, 1952–1997.' *China Economic Review*, 12: 162–89.
Wu, H. X. (2006). 'The Chinese GDP Growth Rate Puzzle.' Tokyo: Hitotsubashi University Research Unit for Statistical Analysis in Social Sciences. At http://hi–stat.ier.hit-u.ac.jp/ (accessed 7 September 2006).
Wu, J. L. (2005). *Understanding and Interpreting Chinese Economic Reform*. Mason: Thomson.
Wu J. X. (1989). 'The New Authoritarianism: An Express Train toward Democracy by Building Markets.' *Chinese Sociology and Anthropology*, 23(2): 36–45.
Wu, N. K. (1993). *A Single Tear*. London: Hodder and Stoughton.
Wu, X. G. and Treiman, D. J. (2004a). *Inequality and Equality under Socialism: Occupational Mobility in Contemporary China*. At http://repositories.cdlib.org/ ccpr/olwp/ccpr-005-02/ (accessed 1 September 2007).
Wu, X. G. and Treiman, D. J. (2004b). 'The Household Registration System and Social Stratification in China, 1955–1996.' *Demography*, 41 (2): 363–84.
Wu, X. M. and Perloff, J. M. (2005). 'China's Income Distribution, 1985–2001.' At http://are.berkeley.edu/~perloff/PDF/china.pdf (accessed 22 June 2008).
Wu, Y. R. (2007). 'Service Sector Growth in China and India: A Comparison.' *China: An International Journal*, 5 (1): 137–54.
Wu, Z. P., Liu, M. Q. and Davis, J. (2005). Land Consolidation and Productivity in Chinese Hosuehold Crop Production.' *China Economic Review*, 16 (1): 28–49.

Wushan xian zhi (Wushan County Records) (1991). Chengdu: Sichuan renmin chubanshe.
WZTJNJ – Wenzhou tongjijiju (Wenzhou Statistical Bureau) (2001). *Wenzhou tongji nianjian 2001* (Wenzhou Statistical Yearbook). Beijing: Zhongguo tongji chubanshe.
Xia, Y. F. (2006). 'China's Elite Politics and Sino-American Rapprochement, January 1969–February 1972.' *Journal of Cold War Studies*, 8 (4): 3–28.
Xinhua (New China News Agency). At http://www.news.xinhuanet.com.
Xu, D. X. (1982). *China's Search for Economic Growth*. Beijing: New World Press.
Xu, D. X. and Wu C. M. (eds). (2000). *Chinese Capitalism, 1522–1840*. Basingstoke: Macmillan.
Xu, X. W. (1988). 'The Struggle of the Handicraft Cotton Industry against Machine Textiles in China.' *Modern China*, 14(1): 31–50.
Xue, M. Q. (1981). *China's Socialist Economy*. Beijing: Foreign Language Press.
XZNJ – Zhongguo xiangzhen qiye nianjian bianji weiyuanhui (Editorial Committee for the Chinese Township and Village Enterprise Yearbook) (1989). *Zhongguo xiangzhen qiye nianjian 1978–1987* (Chinese Township and Village Enterprise Yearbook 1978–1987). Beijing: Zhongguo nongye chubanshe.
Yabuki, S. (1995). *China's New Political Economy*, first edition. Boulder: Westview.
Yan, R. Z., Gong, D. G., Zhou, Z. X. and Bi, B. D. (1990). 'Zhongguo gongnongye chanpin jiage jiandaocha de xianzhuang fazhan qushi yu duice' (The Current Situation, Development Trends and Solutions to the Scissors Differential between Agriculture and Industry in China). *Jingji yanjiu* (*Economic Research*), 2: 64–70.
Yang, B. (1998). *Deng: A Political Biography*. Armonk: M. E. Sharpe.
Yang, D. L. (1996). *Calamity and Reform in China*. Stanford: Stanford University Press.
Yang, D. L. (1997). 'Surviving the Great Leap Famine: The Struggle over Rural Policy, 1958–1962.' In Cheek, T. and Saich, T. (eds) (1997) *New Perspectives on State Socialism in China*. Armonk: M. E. Sharpe..
Yang, D. L. (2004). *Remaking the Chinese Leviathan*. Stanford: Stanford University Press.
Yang, D. T. (1999). 'Urban-Biased Policies and Rising Income Inequality in China.' *American Economic Review* (Papers and Proceedings), 89 (2): 306–10.
Yang, R. (1997). *Spider Eaters*. Berkeley: University of California Press.
Yao, S. J. (2000). 'Economic Development and Poverty Reduction in China over 20 Years of Reforms.' *Economic Development and Cultural Change*, 48 (3): 447–74.
Yeh, K. C. (1968). 'Capital Formation.' In Eckstein, A., Galenson, W. and Liu, T. C. (eds) (1968) *Economic Trends in Communist China*. Edinburgh: Edinburgh University Press.
Yeh, K. C. (1973). 'Agricultural Policies and Performance.' In Wu, Y. L. (ed.) (1973) *China – A Handbook*. Newton Abbot: David and Charles.
Yeh, K. C. (1979). 'China's National Income, 1931–36.' In Hou, C. M. and Yu, T. S. (eds) (1979) *Modern Chinese Economic History*. Seattle: University of Washington Press.
Yeh, K. C. (1984). 'Macroeconomic Changes in the Chinese Economy during the Readjustment.' *China Quarterly*, 100: 691–716.
Yeung, G. (2001). *Foreign Investment and Socio-Economic Development in China: The Case of Dongguan*. London: Palgrave.
Yeung, Y. M. and Shen, J. F. (eds) (2004). *Developing China's West*. Hong Kong: Chinese University of Hong Kong.
Yi, S. (1998). 'The World's Most Catastrophic Dam Failures.' In Dai, Q. (ed.) (1998) *The River Dragon Has Come!* Armonk: M. E. Sharpe.
Yokoi, Y. (1990). 'Plant and Technology Contracts and the Changing Pattern of Economic Interdependence between China and Japan.' *China Quarterly*, 124: 694–713.

Young, A. (1995). 'The Tyranny of Numbers.' *Quarterly Journal of Economics*, 110 (3): 641–80.
Yue, W. (1990). *Dangdai Zhongguo de tongji shiye* (China Today: Statistics). Beijing: Zhongguo shehui kexue chubanshe.
Yusuf, S. and Nabeshima, K. (2006). *China's Development Priorities*. Washington, DC: World Bank.
Yusuf, S., Nabeshima, K. and Perkins, D. H. (2006). *Under New Ownership: Privatizing China's State-Owned Enterprises*. Washington, DC: World Bank.
ZGJYNJ (1984). *Zhongguo jiaoyu nianjian 1949–1981* (Chinese Educational Yearbook). Beijing: Zhongguo renmin chubanshe.
ZGTJNJ – Zhongguo guojia tongjiju (Chinese State Statistical Bureau) (various years). *Zhongguo tongji nianjian 1981, 1983, 1984, 1993, 1994, 2000, 2001, 2002, 2005, 2006 and 2007* (Chinese Statistical Yearbook). Beijing: Zhongguo tongji chubanshe.
Zhang, C. and He, Q (2007). 'Waiting for Greener GDP.' *The Economic Observer* (28 March 2007). At http://www.eeo.com.cn/ens/finance_investment/2007/03/28/51776.html (accessed 28 March 2007).
Zhang, H. (1987). *Zhongguo xiaofei jiegou xue* (Studies on the Structure of Chinese Consumption). Beijing: Jingji kexue chubanshe.
Zhang, J. S., Liu, P. W. and Yung, L. (2007). 'The Cultural Revolution and Returns to Schooling in China.' *Journal of Development Economics*, 84: 631–37.
Zhang, L. X., Huang, J. K. and Rozelle, S. (2003). 'China's War on Poverty.' *Journal of Chinese Economic and Business Studies*, 1 (3): 301–17.
Zhang, Q. and Felmingham, B. (2002). 'The Role of FDI, Exports and Spillover Effects in the Regional Development of China.' *Journal of Development Studies*, 38 (2): 157–78.
Zhang, X. B. and Kanbur, R. (2005). 'Spatial Inequality in Education and Health Care in China.' *China Economic Review*, 16: 189–204.
Zhang, Y. B. (2006). 'Liberal and Socialist Visions in Post-Deng China.' Unpublished doctoral dissertation, Sheffield University.
Zhang, Y. Q. (2000). 'Deforestation and Forest Transition.' In Palo, M. and Vanhanen, H. (eds) (2000) *World Forests from Deforestation to Transition*. Dordrecht: Kluwer.
Zhang. Z. Y. (1988). *Zhongguo jiage jieshou yanjiu* (Research on the Structure of China's Prices). Taiyuan: Shanxi renmin chubanshe.
Zhao, Y. H. (2002). 'Causes and Consequences of Return Migration.' *Journal of Comparative Economics*, 30 (2): 376–94.
Zhao, Z. Y. (1987). 'Advance along the Road of Socialism with Chinese Characteristics.' In Central Committee (1991) *Major Documents of the People's Republic of China*. Beijing: Foreign Languages Press.
Zheng, X. M. (2006). 'Passion, Reflection and Survival.' In Esherick, J. W., Pickowicz, P. G. and Walder, A. G. (eds) (2006) *The Chinese Cultural Revolution as History*. Stanford: Stanford University Press.
Zheng, Y. (1996). *Scarlet Memorial*. Boulder: Westview.
Zheng, Y. L. and Gao, B. H. (1987). *Zhongguo renkou – Anhui fence* (China's Population – Anhui). Beijing: Zhongguo caizheng jingji chubanshe.
Zhongguo shehui kexueyuan (1992). *Zhonghua renmin gongheguo jingji dang'an ziliao xuanpian: Nongcun jingji tizhi juan 1949–1952* (Selected Archival Materials on the Chinese Economy: Rural Economic System Volume). Beijing: Shehui kexue wenshu chubanshe.
Zhongguo shehui kexueyuan (1998). *Zhonghua renmin gongheguo jingji dang'an ziliao xuanpian: Nongcun jingji tizhi juan 1953–1957* (Selected Archival Materials on the

Chinese Economy: Rural Economic System Volume). Beijing: Shehui kexue wenshu chubanshe.

Zhou, X. G., Moen, P. and Tuma, N. B. (1998). 'Educational Stratification in Urban China: 1949–94.' *Sociology of Education*, 71 (3): 199–222.

Zhou, K. X. (1996). *How the Farmers Changed China.* Boulder: Westview.

Zhu, L. and Jiang, Z. (1993). 'From Brigade to Village Community.' *Cambridge Journal of Economics*, 17 (4): 441–62.

ZJJ – Zhejiang juan bianji weiyuanhui (Zhejiang Volume Editorial Committee) (1997). *Zhongguo nongye quanshu – Zhejiang juan* (A Compendium of Chinese Agriculture – Zhejiang Volume). Beijing: Zhongguo nongye chubanshe.

ZJTJNJ – Zhejiang tongjiju (Zhejiang Statistical Bureau) (various years). *Zhejiang tongji nianjian 2002, 2003 and 2005* (Zhejiang Statistical Yearbook). Beijing: Zhongguo tongji chubanshe.

ZSDSWY – Zhonggong Shandong sheng wei yanjiushi (Research Office of the Shandong Committee of the Chinese Communist Party) (1989). *Shandong sishinian* (Forty Years of Shandong). Jinan: Shandong renmin chubanshe.

ZSSWY – Zhonggong Sichuan sheng wei yanjiushi (Research Unit of the Sichuan Committee of the CCP) (ed.) (1984). *Sichuan sheng qing* (Conditions in Sichuan). Chengdu: Sichuan renmin chubanshe.

Index

Africa, sub-Saharan: and Chinese colonialism 380; and trade with China 380; geographical obstacles to development in 31; HIV/AIDS in 9, 506, 540; infant mortality in 31; life expectancy in 9

agricultural performance: before 1949 49, 51–53; early Maoist 96–98, 123; in Great Leap Forward 123, 130–131, 136; late Maoist 226–236; post-1978 226–236, 250, 339–341

agricultural policy: during early Maoism 93–99, 121; during Great Leap Forward 121; during Late Maoism 213–260 *passim*; after 1978 250–254, 337–339, 345–348

agriculture: arable frontier and 243–245; chemical fertilizer and 112–113, 247, 252; collective action problems and 345; contribution to GDP of 52, 55, 304–305; definitional and data problems for 45, 52–53, 97, 101, 116, 228- 229, 357; economies of scale and 52, 96–97, 215, 220–221, 240–241, 342–343; employment in 56, 130; exports and 214; 'five guarantee' households and 259; fiscal policy and 347–348; Forty Articles on 120, 122; 'grain first' policy and 248–249; Green Revolution and 221–222, 249, 251–252, 341–342; imports and 213–216, 343; institutions and 215, 337–339; inverse relationship in 97–98, 220, 240, 343; investment and 221, 348; labour accumulation in 224–226; labour release and 222–223, 234–235, 258, 341; land ownership and 68–69, 94–96, 121; liberalization of 337; mechanization 99, 112–113, 122, 219–220, 222–223; modern inputs in 341–342; multiple cropping 244–245; mutual aid in 95–96; parcellization and 215–216, 222, 342–343; poverty reduction and 447, 511–512; prices and 245–246, 332; productivity and 97–98, 220, 229–236, 257, 258; profitability and 247, 252; property rights in 343–345; rents in 69; sidelines 217; spatial inequality and 304–305; state and 345–348; subsidies for 347; tariffs and 358; taxation of 481; tractor use in 342; triple cropping in 245, 357; weather and 132, 141, 339; *see also* collective farms; cotton; decollectivization; grain; high- yielding varieties; irrigation; land; sannong; technical progress; wool

aid 40, 491

Althusser, L. xxi, 27; on Maoism 288; on the superstructure 148; theory 171

Amsden A. 24; and industrialization by learning 399

Anhui province; chemical fertilizer use in; decollectivization in 135, 337, 338; mortality rates during Great Famine 126–128; poverty in 520; relative GDP per capita in 138–139; rural protest in 519–520, 542

anthropometric measures 41; and Chinese heights 293–294

Anti-Rightist movement (1957) 125

Asian crisis (1997) 470; and impact on East Asian growth 528–529

banks: Grameen 259–260

base, economic: in Marxist theory xxi–xxii, xxv, 80–83, 152; culture and 27

Beijing: education in 519; life expectancy in 57

Index 595

Brazil: comparisons with China and 536–537; income inequality in 517, 536
British mission: burning of 161–162
British Industrial Revolution: agriculture and 222–223, 232; causes of 51, 273; comparison with Qing China and 50; food security in 284; foreign trade during 284; growth rates during 24–25; labour release and 222–223, 232, 273; legacies of 35
Bukharin N. 83
Buck, J. L. 78–79, 223–224

calorie: intake 127–128, 140–141, 293–294, 440–441, 460; requirements 132, 293
Canada: grain imports from 214
capabilities approach 7–11
capitalism: Anglo-Saxon versus Rheinish 328
capital market failure 399–400
capital stock: inherited 35
catch-up growth 24–25, 33–37, 416–417
chemical fertilizer: and econometric studies 254–255; and internal terms of trade 247; imports 363, 365; production of 247–248, 254, 318, 363, 365; role of 112–113, 247, 251; usage of 341
Chengdu: development of 62, 74
Chen Yonggui: elevation to Politburo 306; purged 325
Chen Yun: admiration for early Maoist strategy 327–328; and *fanmaojin* 122–23; and foreign leap forward 167–168; and Great Leap Forward 139
Chinese Communist Party (CCP): in 1949 79; corruption within 458–459, 520, 521–522; membership levels 306; post-1978 326, 356, 357; response to Great Famine 133–134; Third Plenum of 1978 and 169, 325–326; verdict on Maoism 287, 326
Chinese development record: during Republican era 44–53; during early Maoism 111–114; during late Maoism 286–321 *passim;* during market socialism 435–496 *passim*; during 1996–2007 537–539
Chongqing municipality: Chengdu and 62; Third Front and 283; wartime industrialization in 53, 66–67; worker discrimination in 526
class: and education 181, 204–208; and inequality 19–20, 531–532; and missing markets 358; and urban bias 42; composition at Qinghua university 187; structure in rural China 94–95, 106–108
climacterics in development xxiv, 352
coal: industry profitability 348, 359; in Shanxi 66; lack of in Sunan 50–51; pollution from 504; prices 285, 332, 348–349
coastal development strategy 485–485
collective farming: and causes of Great Famine 128–130, 135; canteens in 125, 129–130, 135; debates on 85, 95–96, 98–99, 106–108, 219–220, 257; during late Maoism 155–156, 213–260 *passim;* education and 237; exit rights and 128–130; features of 216–218; 'five guarantee' households 259, group contracting and 251; health care and 237; 'high tide' (1955) 107–109, 121; HYVs and 221; incentives in 125, 150, 217–218, 232–233, 240–243; income distribution in 236–239; introduction of 98–99, 108, 113, 121, 123; irrigation and 224–226; labour mobilization and 223–224, 232; mechanization and 219–220, 222; performance of 226–236; private plots and 217, 236; scale advantages of 215–216, 220; shirking in 232–233, 240–243; social security and 237, 259; structure of 155–156, 216–217; theoretical arguments 218–226, 240–243; workpoints and 217–218, 237, 241–242, 256; *see also* decollectivization; agriculture; terms of trade
colonialism, in western China 490–491
communes *see* collective farming
communism: and Marxian theory 80–83; socialism and 41; poverty and 9
competitiveness 396
Confucianism: and growth 27; and Chinese soft power 535–536
consumption: during 1930s 293; during the 1950s 89, 93, 102–103; during Great Famine 127–129; during Maoist era 293–294; during 1978–1996 440–441; goods production 335; of food 104, 128–129, 140, 293–294
cooperatives 95–96, 116; and exit rights 128, 130
country size: impact on growth of 30–31; in development comparisons 26

corruption: dual-track pricing system and 350; impact on growth in Taiwan and South Korea and 459; income inequality and 20, 458–459, 520; international comparisons of 522; privatization and 521; post-1978 20, 350, 458–459, 520–522

Costa Rica 39–40

cotton industry; deindustrialization and 46; hand-weaving and 46; modern factories and 46–47

Cuba: development path 24, 39; life expectancy in 9

cultural capital: and Bourdieu 211; and education 19, 169, 181, 204–208; and inequality 305–306

Cultural Revolution (1966–68): aims of 149–150; at Qinghua university 159, 173; causes of 158–160; cannibalism during 147, 288; CCP verdict on 287; course of 158–163; deaths during 288; destruction and 160, 314–315; education during 146, 187–199; effects in rural China 162; literature on 170, 171, 288, 493; Mao on 314–315; PLA and 162, 163; production and 161–162; re-interpretations of 493; Socialist Education Movement and 158, 171, 173; street fighting and 146; superstructural change and 149–150; *see also* Maoism; Red Guards

culture: as an obstacle to development in China 532–537; British Industrial Revolution and 51; economic growth and 26–27; East Asian 27; Hofstede scores and 534–535; sustainability of growth and 492, 532–537; western China and 490–491; *see also* Confucianism

cyclical fluctuations in output: during mid-1980s 354; during 1988–90 352; during early 1990s 353; during late 1990s 353, 473; during Asian crisis (1997) 470; post-1996 469–473; under market socialism (1978–96) 441–442; stabilization policy and 469–474

Daqing oilfield 364

data problems: agriculture and 45, 52–53, 97, 101, 116, 228–229, 320, 357; economic census (2004) and 438, 424–425; export share in GDP and 381–382; GDP and xxiii, 45, 73, 101, 272, 393, 437–438; grain consumption and 320; Great Famine mortality and 126, 132; income inequality and 298–299, 454–455; industry and 272, 355; infant mortality rates and 297–298; investment 115; literacy and 177, 184, 195–197, 211–212; Maddison GDP and 5, 44–45, 54, 85, 119, 291–292, 438- 439; poverty and 311; size of state sector and 355; state spending and 543; urban-rural gap and 465–466, 541

data problems for: Cultural Revolution 290; Great Leap Forward 134, 290; late Maoist era 289–291

Dazhai production brigade: abandonment of 'learning from Dazhai' 333; and Chen Yonggui 306; incentive system 150, 161–162, 218, 242; production record of 248; under Hua Guofeng 167

debt, international

decollectivization of agriculture: and growth rates 339–341; as 'spontaneous' process 358; costs of 339, 341–343; during early 1960s 135; during early 1980s 228–229, 250–253, 337–341; econometrics of 253–254; fable of 250–253; incentives and 233; labour release and 234–235; process and pace of 250–251, 337–339, 358; regional variations in 135, 338–339; responsibility system 338

defence: industrialization in China 88, 262, 265–270, 271; *see also* Third Front

deforestation 312

deindustrialization: caused by Chinese exports 361; in China 46, 387; in India 46

democracy: and famine avoidance 134; prospects for 475, 492–493, 543; Singapore and 401; Tian'anmen massacre and 352; *see also* neo-authoritarianism

Dengist era *see* market socialism

Deng Xiaoping: abandonment of Maoism and xxv, 325–327; assumes power 168–169; CCP verdict on Maoism and 287; death of xxv-xxvi, 469; development strategy and xxv-xxvi, 329–331, 352–353; during late Maoist era 166, 168–169, 287; *fanmaojin* 122–123 and; ignorance of Marxism and 168; Jiang Zemin and 475; land reform and 94; Mao and 115, 166, 168; on

coastal development strategy 485–486; on education 195, 201; on foreign trade 365–366, 372; on inequality 336, 487; on market socialism 336, 352–353; on open door policy 372, 485–486; on Practice 168–169; on price reform 351; on rural industry 407; on special economic zones and neglect of Shanghai 333; on work-study 201; role in Great Leap Forward 94, 139, 140, 287; southern tour of 331, 352–353; Tian'anmen massacre and 352; 'two assessments' of education and 195
Deng Zihui 99, 115, 135
depression, world, during the 1930s 63, 73
determinism xxi, 152; over-determinism 148–149
development: anthropometric measures of 41; capability measures of 3, 7–11; constraints for China 112, 317; fluctuations and 4; happiness and 3, 27; international comparisons and 3, 315–317, 461–463; historical comparisons and 3, 24–26, 315; opulence measures of 3, 5–7; missing markets and 358; models of 39–40, 327–329; relative to potential 4, 27–37, 36, 112, 317–318, 463–464, 538; success and 4–5; *see also* Chinese development record; human development; sustainable development
developmental state 494
dibao system 516
Dongguan: migration to 378–379; open door and 376, 384
droughts 132
dual track pricing system 350, 414

education: before 1949 56–57, 175–176; curriculum 181, 184, 190–191; during the Cultural Revolution 160, 162, 187–199; early Maoist 104–105, 113, 175–187; fees 481–482, 508, 525; equity and 184–187, 202–208, 210, 460; gender gap and 193–194, 209, 460, 518; graduation rates and 191–192, 460, 506–508, 537–538; GDP growth and 199–202, 209–210, 212; international comparisons of 57, 196–197; keypoint (*zhongdian*) schools and 176, 195, 211; late Maoist 174–212 *passim*, 237, 305–306; length of schooling and 190; literature on 174, 211; Maoist critique of 180–181; migrants and 525; *minban* schools and 175–176, 177, 188; Ministry of 196; *pinyin* and 194; primary 178–179, 182, 186, 189–190, 191–192, 200; provincial inequalities in 200–201, 204, 296–297, 307; quality 195–199, 202; returns to 36–37, 198, 212, 237; spending on 443, 533; 'two assessments' and (1971) 180, 195; university 150–51, 159–160, 173, 182, 508; work-study and 176, 177, 187, 190–191, 201; *xiafang* and 164, 189; *see also* literacy rates; Red Guards; schools
educational enrolment rates: during Republican era 175–176; during early 1950s 104–105, 176; during 1949–1965 178–180, 182–184; during mid-1960s 185–187, during 1962–1978 191–192, 200; during 1978–1996 442–443; post-1996 506–508, 537–538; provinces 186
education, rural: bias against 105, 181, 184, 198, 305–306; expansion of 164, 188–190, 237; quality of 187–188, 198, 519; tuition fees 481–482
education, secondary (middle school): Republican era 57; in Yan'an 175–176; early Maoist 104, 176; Great Leap Forward 180, 182–184; late Maoist 160, 189, 192–193, 197–198, 203; post 1978 198, 442–443, 508, 537–538
education system: early Maoist 175–177; late Maoist 187–191
efficiency: agricultural 97–98, 220, 229–236, 257, 258, 344; definitions of 262, 395, 397; educational 191–202, 211; industrial 271–278, 397; under-industrialization and 272–274
employment *see* labour
energy: gasfields and 489; natural gas 505; oilfields and 504; power transmission projects and 489; prices 332; *see also* coal; oil
environmental problems: agriculture and 248; cars and 505–506; dam building and 505; deforestation 312; during Republican era and earlier 313; during late Maoist era 311–314; during post-1996 era 499–506; GDP and 313–314, 505; green GDP 505; growth constraints and 529, 539; Hu Jintao on 481; mortality and 540; regulation and 505; rivers and 501, 505; Wen Jiabao on 502; *see also* pollution

ethnic minorities, and fragmentation effects 31
exchange rate: depreciation 368, 370–371; equilibrium 371, 392; pressure for appreciation of 371–372
export-led growth: in China 276, 361, 372–389
exports: agricultural 100, 131, 362; FDI and 367; composition of 365–366; depreciation and 368, 370–371; from Guangdong 374; from Zhejiang; to Soviet Union 100, 131; *see also* open door
export shares in GDP: at official exchange rates 360, 370; at purchasing power parity 381–382

famine: before 1949 139; causes 128–134; in Ukraine 38, 85, 121; *see also* Great Famine
farm size: and collective farming 96–97, 220–221; post-1978 342–343, 344; Republican era 52, 71, 220
Feldman model 115
female infant mortality 444–445; *see also* mortality; life expectancy
feudalism 81
finance: market failure and 399–400
fiscal decentralization: in 1950s 124; in the late Maoist era 270, 277; post-1978 276–277, 353, 483–485
fiscal policy 333, 353–354
and agriculture 347–348, 519–520
fiscal recentralization 353
'five guarantee' households 259
'five small industries' 269–270
Five Year Plans: First (1953–57) 88–89, 93, 110, 113–114, 262; Second (1958–62) 125–126; Third (1966–70) 172, 265; Fifth (1976–80) 167; Sixth (1981–85) 485; Eighth (1991–95) 473–474; Ninth (1996–2000) 473–474, 488; Tenth (2001–05) 473–474; Eleventh Programme (2006–10) 480–481, 533
flooding: in 1954 108
food consumption: and price reform 350; during early Maoism 104; during the Great Famine 127–128, 132, 140; during late Maoism 293–294, 320; during market socialism 440–441
food security 213–216, 284, 343
foreign direct investment (FDI): enclaves of 384; exports and 367, 376; imports and 383–385; in Dongguan 376, 384; in Fujian 276, 367; in Guangdong 276, 367, 375; in Guizhou 375; in Special Economic Zones 367, 376; in Wenzhou 276; in western China; migration and 377–379; Republican era 46–47; spatial pattern of 276, 367; spillovers 276, 368, 382–385; technical progress and 385–386; volume in 1980s 276, 336, 367; volume in 1990s 370, 376–377
foreign leap forward 167–168; imports and 365
foreign trade: and growth 361–362; and job creation 387; and security 214–215; and shares in European GDP 374; and unemployment 387; impact on Guangdong and Fujian of 375; in 1930s 45–46; in early 1950s 99–100; in grain 213–215; in late Maoist era 153, 166; provincial variations in 373–374; with Europe 362, 364; with Japan 363–364; with Soviet Union 362; with USA 363; *see also* exports; imports; Open Door
foreign trade policy: 1949–1971 362–363; 1971–1978 363–366; 1978–1996 366–368; post-1996 369–372
Four Modernizations 136, 317
Fujian province: poverty in 321
functionings 8

gaige kaifang: strategy 327; *see also* market socialism
gaizhi see zhuada fangxiao
Gang of Four: arrest and trial of 166, 168, 319, 325; role of 166
Gansu province: education in 186, 519; GDP per capita in 75; industry in 304; investment in 280; nuclear programme in 281; poverty in xxiii, 309–310
gender: illiteracy rates and 193–194, 209, 460; income inequality and 19–20; infant mortality rates and 444–445, 518, 535; life expectancy and 295, 445, 541
geography: physical 58–60; Skinner and 60–62
government *see* state
gradualism 325: and development choices in early 1980s 327–329; in China 435–436
grain: chemical fertilizer and 247; definition of 256; environmental damage and 312–313; foreign trade in 131, 213–215, 343, 374; 'grain

first' policy 248–249, 312–313; prices 245–247, 252–253, 332; procurements 131, 133, 141, 249, 320; production 97–98, 131–133, 135, 227–228, 341; profits 247, 252; sown area 130, 245, 249, 251–252; trade (*maoyiliang*) 141, 256

grain yields: and HYVs 221; in China 52, 97, 116, 122, 130, 132, 230–231; international comparisons of 230–231

Great Famine (1958–1962): causes of 128–134; educational impact 177; mortality in 126–128, 139, 140; recovery from 134–136; spatial variation during xxiv, 126–128

Great Leap Forward: and early Maoism xxiv, 118–124; and educational policy 177; end of 120, 134; first officially mentioned 120; rural industry and 263–265; strategy 125–126

Green Revolution 221–222, 260

gross domestic product: as a measure of inequality 300; conceptual issues and 5–6; data problems xxiii, 45, 73, 101, 272, 291, 381–382, 437–438

export share in 381–382; purchasing power parity and 7, 381–382, 393, 470; structure of 56, 272–273; *see also* growth rates

gross domestic product levels: at the beginning of the 1950s 54; in Qing China 50; in Republican era China xxiii, 44–45; in Maoist era 291–292; projected 470

growth accounting: technical progress and 472; *see also* catch-up; total factor productivity

growth theory: balance and 124, 471; catch-up and 24–25, 33–37, 416–417; culture and 26–27; diminishing returns to investment and 528–530; education and 199–202. 212; ethnic fragmentation and 31; fluctuations 37–38; geography and 31 32, 60 62; human capital and 36–37; import-led 389–390; inequality and 20, 462–463; initial conditions and 33–37; infrastructure and 34–35; isolation and 25–26, 28–29; investment and 472, 528–530; Kaldor and 34, 35; land-locked countries and 32; learning-by-doing and 24, 37, 199–200, 385–386; natural resources and 32–33; path dependency and 33; potential 27–37; poverty and 388, 511; technical progress and 24–25, 472; endogenous 33–34; neoclassical 472, 528; *see also* catch-up; cyclical fluctuations; education; export-led growth; industrialization

growth rates of GDP: and constant price sets 291–292; comparisons with China; poverty reduction and 511; sustainability of 492–494, 539; *see also* agriculture; industrial

growth rate comparisons: with East Asia 315–316; with EEFSU 439–440; with world economy 461, 499; India 316

growth rates during: Republican era 44–45, 51–53; early Maoism 101–103, 315; Great Leap Forward 131, 136; late Maoism 291–292, 315–316; Readjustment era 334–335; market socialism 334–335, 351, 353, 437–440, 461; post-1996 era 470–471, 473, 497–499, 511

Guangdong province: Asian crisis and 470; education and growth in 200; FDI in 276, 376; fiscal treatment of 276–277, 483, 484; foreign trade of 373–374, 376–377, 383, 470; GDP per head compared with Guizhou 486, 488–489; irrigation in 318; trade with Hong Kong 373–374; *see also* special economic zones

Guangxi province: and street fighting in Nanning 146; cannibalism in 288

Guizhou province: and poverty xxiii, 309–310; decollectivization process in 339; GDP per head compared with Guangdong 486, 488–489; education in 186; foreign trade of 373–374, 383; investment in 281

Guomindang (Kuomintang, KMT): defeat of 79; five year plans of 86–87

Hainan island: becomes province and SEZ 367

Han Chinese chauvinism 490–491, 535

happiness: as a measure of development 13–14; Chinese levels of 14

health care: development and 42; HIV/AIDS and 506; in China 103–104, 295–296, 446

heights; *see* anthropometrics

Heilongjiang province: and *xiafang* 164, 165; cultivated area in 111,

243; decollectivization in 339; grain production in 131; *see also* Manchuria

Henan province: and cannibalism during Great Leap 127; HIV/AIDS in 506

high level equilibrium trap 48–49

high-yielding varieties (HYVs) 153, 156, 221; and decollectivization 251–252, 254; development of 385

HIV/AIDS in China 506, 540

Hua Guofeng xxiv, 167–168: and foreign leap forward 167–168, 173; 'retired' 325, 356

Hu Jintao: and inequality 531; 'harmonious society' and 469; 'new socialist countryside' and 469, 481; on balanced growth 471; on development strategy 480–482; on environmental problems 481; on socialism 491; on soft power and Confucianism 535–536; western China and xxiii

Hu Yaobang: and price reform 349, 350–351; purge of 351, 352

human capital *see* education

human development: happiness and 14; HDI and 11–13, 42; in China; *see also* education; life expectancy

human development in China: and international comparisons 12–13, 56–58, 462, 508–509; spatial inequalities in 67–68, 186, 201, 205, 296–297, 306–307, 445, 460, 519; during 1978–1996 442–446, 462; during early Maoism 103–105; during late Maoism 174–212 *passim*, 294–298; post-1996 506–509, 537–538

Hunan province: education and growth in 200; life expectancy in 297; living standards in 103; poverty in 510–511

Hundred Flowers 124, 171

imperialism: Han Chinese 380, 490–491; in China 45–51; in India 46

imports: and sustainability of growth 528–529; country of origin and 362–364, 380; chemical fertilizer 247–248, 363, 365; during 1970s 364, 365; FDI 384; foreign leap forward 365; grain 213, 343, 346; Republican era 46, 63, 213; raw material 361, 380; Soviet Union and 99–100, 362; tariffs and 354; tariffs and cuts in 368, 370, 375; tariffs on agricultural products 358; Treaty Ports and 51, 63; *see also* foreign trade; oil

income inequality: Brazil and 517; causes of 455–459, 517–522; class and 531–532; collective farms and 236–239; consequences 462–463, 518–521; corruption and 20, 458–459, 517, 521–522; data problems and 298–299, 455, 517; education and 19, 160; equality of opportunity and 19; ethnic minorities and 19; foreign trade and 389; gender and 19–20; geography and 21, 483, 531; Gini coefficient and 16–18, 22, 42–43, 105; growth and 20, 462–463; incentives and 19, 21, 232–233, 456, 462–464; Japan and 18; Kuznets hypothesis and 18, 522; land ownership and 344–345; land reform and 20–21, 105–109; literature on 465, 466; Marx and 20, 456; measurement of 15–22; migration and 522–527; mortality and 21; revolutions and 21; rural 68–72, 236–239, 454–456, 517; rural industry and 456–457; social mobility and 18, 43, 160; South Korea and 18; subsidies and 299, 350; urban 454–456, 517, 525; urban-rural gap and 15, 39, 278–282, 299–302, 454, 465–466, 473, 519, 522–525, 541; Zhao Ziyang on 456; *see also* spatial inequality; western China

income inequality in China: before 1949 68–72; between coast and interior 15, 65, 137, 153–154; compared with other countries 16–17; during the early Maoist era 105–111, 236; during the Great Leap Forward 136–139; during late Maoist era 236–239, 298–305; during 1978–1996 17, 454–461, 462–463; post-1996 516–522

India: and heavy industry 87; development prospects and xxii, 27, 316; development record compared with China 26, 288, 296, 316–317; educational policy compared with China 209, 443; Green Revolution in 221–222; Hindu equilibrium in 27; industrialization strategy of 43

industrial: catch-up in China 416–417, 430; census (1933) 45; competition and profits 420; contribution to GDP growth of 302–304; data problems concerning 272; employment 55, 93, 272–274, 426–429; enterprise scale 404; damage to the environment 312; governance

412–415; investment 91–92, 333–334; liberalization 332, 355; location 65–67, 110, 265–269, 278–282, 403; mergers 420–424; national champions 421; nationalization of 89–91, 120–121; overseas ownership 45–46, 91; ownership structure 412; privatization 332, 355, 408, 413–414, 420–424, 475; productivity 402–403, 415–416; profits 348, 401–402, 415, 419–420; shares in output and employment 272–273, 355; structure of production 87–89, 331, 333–334; unemployment 426–429; *see also* rural industry; state-owned industry; Third Front; total factor productivity; individual industries

industrial development: compared with Britain 273; early Maoist 87–91, 110; international comparisons 272–273; Republican era 46–47, 65–66, 87–88; late Maoist 261–285 *passim*

industrial efficiency: definition of 397; late Maoist era 401–404; market socialist era 1978–1996 415–418; post-1996 425, 429–430

industrial growth: early Maoist 91–93; late Maoist 261–274; market socialist era 418–419; post-1996 425–426

industrialization: defence and 88–89, 265–269, 399; heavy versus light industry and 43, 87–89, 99–100, 124, 262–265, 331, 333–334, 409; income inequality and 302–303; late Maoist legacies and 274–278, 385–386; neoauthoritarianism and 328–329, 474–475, 491–494; primary commodities and 43; Third Front and 265–268; under-industrialization and 272–274, 427–429; *see also* rural industry

industrialization strategies: in East Asia 88–89, 398–399; Stalinism and 113, 117

industrial policy in China: early Maoist 88–89; Great Leap Forward and 263–265; late Maoist 262–270

industrial policy in China post-1978: defence cuts and 410–411; governance and 412–415; liberalization and 411–412; Readjustment and 331, 333–334, 409–411; *zhuada fangxiao* and 420–424

industrialization theories: competitiveness and 396–397; defence and 88–89, 399; heavy industry and 43, 87–89, 115; industrial policy and 397–401; learning by doing and 397; productivity and 396–397; Stalinism and 398; state and 397–401; 'textiles first' and 87, 399; Washington consensus and 398

inequality: origins of Red Guard movement and 160–161, 165, 173, 305; consumption after 1978 and 459–460; education and 184–187, 202–208, 460–461, 518–519; human development and 306–308, 518–519; land ownership and 68–69, 105–109; mortality rates in the USA and 23; status and 305–306, 521; urban-rural educational progression and 203–204, 305–306; *see also* income inequality

infant mortality *see* mortality

inflation: and Democracy movement (1989) 441; rates 53, 71, 349–351, 441–442, 470–471

infrastructure projects 489

Inner Mongolia (Nei Menggu): and over-grazing 312; and *xiafang* 165; industrialization in 281–282

interest rates 71–72, 236

internal trade: barriers to 387; liberalization of 337; Republican era 61–62, 63

intersectoral resource flows: in the Maoist era 245–247, 260; post-1978 347–348, 357

investment: allocation between light and heavy industry 327, 331, 333–334, 398-399; diminishing returns and 528–530; growth and 382, 528–529; in state-owned industry 91–92; international comparisons of rates of 471–472; measurement of 115; spatial inequality and 278–281; *see also* industrialization

investment rates: during early Maoism 91–92, 103, 113, 115; during Great Leap Forward 122, 125; during late Maoism 156–157, 167–168, 280–281; 1978–1996 327, 382; post-1996 470, 471–472

irrigation: after 1978 341–342; and collective farming 224–226, 318; and HYVs 113, 225–226, 250, 318, 341–342; definitions of 225; failures 224, 257, 341–342; in the 1950s 112–113; expansion of 224–226, 250, 318 iron *see* steel production

Japan: agriculture in 222; and colonies 38; cotton mills in China and 47; growth in 25; land consolidation schemes in 343; literacy rates 57; relations with China and 363–364, 391
Jiang Qing: and Mao 319; during Cultural Revolution 158, 171; early life 171
Jiangsu province: education in 57, 199; fiscal decentralization and 483, 484; foreign trade and 276, 373–374, 376–377; inequality in 531; migration within 62; Republican era development in 65; rural industrialization in 281–282; spatial inequality in 321; *see also* Sunan; Wuxi; Yangzi delta
Jiangxi province: Dazhai system in 218, 242
Jiang Zemin: policy agenda of 494; public ownership and 423; WTO entry and 369–370; succeeds Deng Xiaoping 469
Johnson, Chalmers 398–399
Jiuquan 266

Kaldor N.: growth and 34; on manufacturing 35, 395
Kerala 9, 209
Keynes J. M.: and lifestyle 39; on FDI and national finance 30; on savings 39; on stock markets 400; on the long run 43
Khrushchev, N. 119, 123, 133
Korea, South: development record of 11, 102; industrialization strategy 88; Japanese colonialism and 38; land reform in 21
Korean war 54, 88; and Sino-US relations 317
Krugman, P.: on geography and inequality 21–22, 281; on productivity 28, 396
Kuznets curve: and the environment 314

labour: accumulation in agriculture 56, 222–226, 318; employed in industry 273–274, 406, 426–429; mobility 18, 43; service sector employment and 427–428, 472–473; shortages in coastal provinces 479; surplus 52, 223–224, 258; *see also* Lewis model; migration; unemployment
land: contracts 344; cultivated area of 111, 243–245, 260; law (2007) 358, 419; ownership 68–69, 71, 343–345; productivity 230–231; sales 107
land reform 79, 94–96, 105–109; and food security 215; in ethnic minority areas 116
learning by doing: and growth 24, 37, 199–200, 385–386, 397; and industrial development 55, 201–202, 264, 269, 274–278, 283; and open door 385–386; during Maoist era 318–319, 385–386; during the Great Leap Forward 264
Lei Feng 172
Lenin: and agriculture 91, 106, 117, 215; and Chayanov 117; and Marxist theory 83; and mechanization of agriculture 219–220
Lewis model 55, 232; and migration 522
Liaoning: investment in 281; *see also* Manchuria
liberalization of private sector controls; in agriculture 328–330, 337; in industry 328–330, 332, 355, 475; *see also* privatization
life expectancy: and poverty estimates in late 1970s 311; as a measure of development 8, 38; food consumption and 294; gender differences 295, 445; in China compared with other countries 10, 298, 446; limitations of as a measure of development 9–11; Preston curve and 9; provincial patterns of 296–297, 306–307, 445
life expectancy levels: in Republican era China 57; during early 1950s 104; during Maoist era 294–298; post-1978 443–446, 506–507
Lin Biao: and Korean war 54; death of 166; during late 1960s 114, 163; generalship 79, 114; ill-health 163; on aims of Cultural Revolution 149–150
Li Peng: on east-west income gap in China 487–488
literacy rates: and Bowman-Anderson criterion for development 37; and *pinyin* 194; international comparisons of 57, 196–197
literacy rates in China: and Twelve Year Programme for Agricultural Development 122, 177; early 1950s 176; gender differences in 193–194, 209, 519; late Maoist 195–197, 209–210, 296; long run trend 179–180, 193–194; measurement of 177, 184, 195–197, 211–212, 519; provincial

variation in 200–201, 205, 460; post-1978 443, 460, 508–509; Republican era 56–57; urban-rural gap in 518–519
Liupanshui: and Third Front 261, 266, 267
Liu Shaoqi: and educational policy 177, 178, 180, 183; and *fanmaojin* 122–123; and start of Cultural Revolution 158–159; and land reform 95; daughter of 173; Great Leap Forward and 118, 134–135, 140; on industrial location 263; on rural industry 263
livestock: and 'grain first' 249, 312; and land reform 96, 107; slaughter of 123
Lushan Plenum (1959) 120, 134
Luxemburg, R. 151

Ma Yinchu 320
macroeconomic policy: during market socialism 333–335, 351–355; efficiency and 397; post-1996 470–473; unemployment and 396–397; *see also* five year plans
macro-regions 60–62
Maddison, A.: GDP estimates of 5, 44–45, 54, 85, 119, 291–292, 497–498, 540
malaria 156
Malthus 50, 244, 320
Manchuria xxiii, 38, 64, 73; border clashes and 159; industrialization and 110, 281–282; open door policy and 383; Third Front and 265; WTO and 388; decollectivization in 339; literacy rates in 296–297; poverty and agriculture in 449; unemployment in 428
Mao Zedong: CCP verdict on 287; egalitarianism and 153; *fanmaojin* ('oppose rash advance') and 122–123; First Five Year Plan and 93; Great Famine and 133–134; Great Leap Forward and 119–124; Hundred Flowers and 124; literature on 286; Liu Shaoqi and 135, 140, 154; Marxist theory and xxi–xxii, 119, 147–150, 152–155; material incentives and 150; on Book Worship 181; on collective farming 98–99, 119–123, 215–216; on Contradiction 93, 120, 124, 147–148, 177, 263; on counter-revolutionaries 289; on defence 265; on education 180–181; on effects of the Cultural Revolution 314–315; on industrialization 262–263, 265; on international trade 256; on land reform 94–95; on Panzhihua 268; on polarization in the countryside 106; on rural industry 263, 269; on the Ten Great Relationships 93, 111, 120, 124, 137, 153–154, 263, 265; on transition to socialism 85–86, 119; on work-study 187; on *xiafang* 163; superstructural change and xxi, 147–150; trade with USA and 363; 'walking on two legs' and 263
Maoist era: and Stalinism 154, 286; and the Holocaust 286–289; data issues 289–291; deaths 126–128, 139, 140, 288, 295; education in 174–212 *passim*; egalitarianism 94–96, 105–111, 184–187, 278–282; foreign trade and 362–366; growth *see* growth rates; history of the victors and 286–289; literature on xxii, 170, 171, 284, 286–289; *see also* Great Leap Forward; Cultural Revolution; Third Front
Maoist era, development record xxii–xxiii; 1949–1955 111–114; 1955–1963 139; 1963–1978 286–321 *passim*
Maoist era, development strategies xxi–xxii; and First Five Year Plan 79–87; and Great Leap Forward 118–125; and late Maoism 145–173, 261–270
Maoist era, early (1949–1963) xxv, 79–141 *passim;* retrospective assessments of 327–328
Maoist era, late (1963–1978) xxv, 145–321 *passim;* initial phase (1963–66) 146, 158; Cultural Revolution phase (1966–68) 145–147, 158–163; Army phase (1968–71) 146, 163–166; disillusion phase (1971–76) 146, 166–167; struggle for succession phase (1976–78) 146, 167–169
Maoist legacies: and post-1978 growth 274–278, 318–319, 436–437
market socialism (1978–1996) xxvi, 325–359 *passim;* assessments of 435–437; and collapse of Soviet Union 352; as development model 329, 336, 356, 435–436; Deng Xiaoping on 336; economic policy chronology for 330; evolution of 329–355, 352; Maoist legacies and 436–437; potential and 463–464
market socialism, development record during 435–466 *passim*; and absolute

poverty 446–453; and consumption trends 440–441; and cyclical fluctuations 441–442; and education 442–443; and GDP growth 437–440, 461; and human development 442–446, 462; and income inequality 454–461, 462–463; and mortality 443–446; and rural poverty 447–452; and urban poverty 452–453

market socialism, phases of: Readjustment (1978–1982) 331–335; decollectivization and the road to Tian'anmen (1982–1991) 335–339, 348–352; southern tour and last hurrah (1991–1996) 352–355

markets: and market socialism 329; and price determination 348–349; capital 524, 399–400; factor 70–71; failure of 399–401; labour 69, 524–525; land 344; migration and 522–527; missing 358; rental 69, 71; stock 354, 399–400, 414–415, 521

Marx, K.: on capitalism 498; on class struggle 82; on primitive Russian communes (*obshchina*) 114, 257; on inequality 20, 81, 531; on Qing China 50; on role of the superstructure 148, 171; on transition to socialism 82; theory of history and 80–83, 326

material product *see* net domestic material product

migration: case for 379, 477–479, 522–524; costs of 524–527; definitions of 495; discrimination and 62, 479–480, 525–526; effects of 522–527; floating population and 477, 495; *hukou* system and 204, 479–480, 525; inequality measurement and 455, 517; literature on 495; *litu bu lixiang* 448; open door and 377–379; Republican era 62, 526; remittances and 379; return 379, 382–383; rural industry and 448; theory and 523–524, 542; Three Gorges dam and 488; Tibet and 491, 524–525; urban incomes and 516, 525; urban poverty and 453, 515–516; *see also* sending-down

migration destinations: countryside 163–166; Guangdong 378–379, 477; post-1978 477–478; Sunan 62; Xinjiang 378

migration, scale of: Republican era 62, 526; Maoist era 163–164; post-1978 377–379, 477–480

modes of production 80–81

mortality: and HIV/AIDS 10; during the late Maoist era 288, 289, 294–298; during early 1950s 104; during the Great Famine 126–128, 138, 140; during land reform 95; post-1978 443–446, 506–507; *see also* life expectancy

mortality, infant 58, 104, 126; in western China 308; late Maoist 306–308; long run trends 297–298; post-1978 444–445; urban-rural gap in 309

national champions 421

nationalism 535–536; and Olympics 506, 535

natural disasters: before 1949; data problems in assessing 132; in the Maoist era 132; *see also* drought; famine; flooding

Nei Menggu province *see* Inner Mongolia

neo-authoritarianism 328–329, 474–475, 492

net domestic material product: and GDP 6, 41, 291, 437

New Democracy 114–115

New Economic Policy: in the USSR 83–84, 117, 118, 327; in China 118, 327–328; *see also* transition

New Left in China 288, 328, 492–493; Cultural Revolution and 493; socialism and 493; WTO and 369

Ningxia province: and poverty xxiii

Norway: human development in 12; income inequality in 16

nuclear programme 281, 393

oil: Daqing and 364, 504; exports 364, 365–366; imports 380; fields 504

Old Left 327–328, 356–357

one child population policy 479, 518, 535; cadre evasion of 521

open door (post-1978): adverse effects of 386–389, 390; Chinese interior and 368, 383, 390; coastal cities and 367–368; migration and 377–379; poverty and 383, 386–389; provincial capitals and 368; resumption of relations with USA and 366; special economic zones and 367; spillover effects 377–378, 379, 382–385, 393; state policy and 366–368; *see also* World Trade

Index 605

Organization
open door, impact on growth of 372–389, 463–464; in the 1980s 373–375; after 1992 375–380
over-determinism xxi–xxii
ownership: of farmland 155–156; of industry xxvi, 120–121; *see also* privatization

Panzhihua: and Third Front 261, 266–269, 281, 284; mineral resources at 268; pollution at 269, 499–500; steel industry 269
Pearl river delta: industry and 285; migration and 276, 378–379, 477
Peng Dehuai 133–134
People's Liberation Army (PLA) 79, 88; and Red Guards 162–163
planning *see* five year plans
pollution: acid rain 504; air 500–501; cars and 505–506, 529; coal and 504; compared with India 503; health costs 504–505, 540; historical comparisons of 503–504; mortality and 504–505, 540; urban 503–504; water 501–502
population: age structure of 444; census (2000) and 477; during Great Famine 126–128, 138–139; one child policy and 477, 535; sex-selective abortion and 535; urban 163; *see also* migration; mortality
population growth: before 1949 45, 50; during Maoist era 138, 156–157, 243–244, 320; post-1978 444–445
poverty: absolute 22–23, 321, 446–453, 509–516, 541; communism and 9, 70; EU definition of 22; geography and 451–452, 513–514; human 23–24, 308; lines 447, 510; list of poor counties and 309, 450–451, 465, 513; literature on 465; measurement of 22–24, 311, 321, 447–448, 451–452, 510; Office of the Leading Group on Reduction of 450; open door policy and 386–387; policy failures and 513–514; price reform and 452–453; provincial trends after 1996 510–511; relative 22–23; rural 71–72, 447–452, 509–515; rural industrialization and 448–449; urban 452–453, 515–516
poverty trends in China: during the 1950s 107–108, 111; during late Maoist era 308–311, 321; during the late 1970s 309–310; during 1978–1996 446–453; in western provinces xxiii–xxiv, 64–65, 450–452, 509; on the north China plain 65, 310; post-1996 509–516, 537
prices: dual track system of 350; GDP estimates and 291–292; poverty and farm prices 512–513; reform of relative structure of 331–332, 348–352, 354, 359, 475; regional differences in 393, 488–489, 495, 541; seasonal variation in 72; *see also* inflation; terms of trade
price setting: theory of 348–349, 359
privatization: in agriculture 343–345; of industry 332, 355, 408, 413–414, 420–424, 475
productivity: internal terms of trade and 246–247; labour 232–235, 257, 402–403, 417, western China and 490–491; *see also* efficiency; growth accounting; total factor productivity
productivity, agricultural: Maoist 229–236; post-1978 341–343
productivity, industrial: Maoist era 269, 271, 283; post-1978 402–403, 415–417
property rights: in agriculture 344–345

Qing dynasty: famines 139; state during 50; under-development during 49–50
Qinghai province: infant mortality in 308

railways: in the 1950s 110; late Maoist construction and 266, 318; Republican era 48, 63; social savings and 34–35; Tibet-Qinghai 489; Third Front and 34, 266
rainfall 60–61, 224; *see also* weather; drought
Readjustment (1978–82) 328, 331–335, 409–411
Red Guards 159–162, background of 160–161, 165, 173, 305; cultural destruction and 160; Mao and 151; *xiafang* and 146, 163–165, 189, 206
reform era *see* market socialism
remittances from migrants 379, 393
rental markets 69
Republican era: agriculture 51–53, 223–224; data problems and xxiii, 44–45, 52–53; discrimination against migrants in 526; education 56–57, 175, 193–194; famines 139; growth 44–45; inequality in 62–72; industry 46–47, 65–67, 87–88; underdevelopment

606 *Index*

in 54–56; transport 48, 63; world depression and 63, 73
responsibility system *see* decollectivization
revolution, Chinese (1949): causes of 21; completion of 79
rich peasants 94–95, 106–108
rubber industry 100, 312
rural industry 261–285 *passim*, 404–407; commune and brigade 269–271, 333, 405–406; definition of 284; efficiency of 271–274, 264, 271, 274–275; employment in 405–406; fiscal decentralization and 276–277; geography and 449; growth of xxi; human capital and 385; inequality and 300–301; labour force in 234, 270; learning-by-doing and 264, 269, 271, 274–278, 318–319; literature on 274–277, 284; local government and 275–276, 383, 449; location of 281–282, 448–449; Maoist legacies and 274–278; path dependency and 275, 303–305; poverty and 448–449, 512–514; privatization 275–278, 414, 423; productivity in 271, 405; restructuring of 333–334, 423; return migration and 382–383; state ownership and 355; TVEs and 275, 404–407; under Mao 153, 234, 261–285 *passim*, 304–305; Vietnam and 277
rural industry during: Great Leap Forward 125, 130, 263–265; late Maoist era 270–271, 278; Readjustment 333–334, 405–406; post-1978 era 404–407
rural modernization: education and 188–190, 469, 481–482; late Maoist 152–154, 164, 237, 259, 318; prices and 512–513; *sannong* and 481; taxation and 481, 482; under Hu Jintao 469, 481–482; *see also* walking on two legs
rural modernization and intersectoral resource flows: in the Maoist era 245–247, 260; post-1978 347–348
rural protests 519–521
Russia: development in 55–56; GDP growth after 1990 439–440; life expectancy in 9; pre-1917 54–55; revolution in 82–83; transition to capitalism 325, 440; *see also* Soviet Union

sannong (three rural problems) 481
Saudi Arabia 9

savings rates 39
schools: expansion of 188; re-opening of 162; *see also* education
self-reliance 153, 363; *see also* foreign trade
Sen, A. K.: and poverty 9; capability approach of 3, 4, 7–8; on collective farms 240; on democracy 134; on famine 132
sending-down movement *see xiafang*
service sector: contribution to GDP growth 472–473
Shanghai: discrimination against migrants in 526; educational enrolments in 186; exports from 377; fiscal treatment of 484; geography and 66; Great Famine and 129; industrialization in 46–47, 65, 75, 303–304; increasing returns and 281; living standards in 103; population growth in 301–302; Republican era development in 46–47, 65, 75; Pudong and 367–368; special economic zones and 333, 367–368; *xiafang* and 164, 302
Shaoguan: and Third Front 267, 464
Shaanxi province: 1928–30 famine in 139
Shandong province: and famine of 1876–79 139; and mortality during Great Famine 127; and *xiafang* 164; education in 105, 117, 189; poverty in during late 1970s 311
Shanxi province 50, 66, 117; and famine of 1876–79
Shenzhen special economic zone: creation of 332–333, 367; discrimination against migrants in 527; state investment in 333
Shiyan: and Third Front 266
Sichuan province: agriculture in 128, 131, 223, 252, 337; communal canteens in 130; Dazhai system in 242; development in 62, 63, 87–88; decollectivization in 251, 339; deforestation in 312; discrimination in 526; drought in 141; exports to USSR 131, 362; famine in 126–128, 129, 130; foreign trade after 1978 and 373; food consumption in 128, 132, 293; grain procurements in 131, 141, 249; industrialization in 304; investment in 280; poverty in xxiii, 309; relative GDP per capita in 138–139; remittances from migrants 379; slavery in 84, 114; spatial inequality in 321; Third Front and 266–268; *see also* Chengdu;

Chongqing; Panzhihua
silk industry 47
Singapore 157; authoritarianism in 401
Skinner, W. 44, 60–62, 74
slavery 81, 84
social formation 80–82
socialism: abandonment of xxvi, 326–327, 352, 480–482; communism and 80–81; New Left and 493; re-thinking of in China 493–494; transition to 55–56, 80–83, 118–124, 219–220; *see also* market socialism
Socialist Education Movement xxiv, 145, 151, 158, 171
social mobility 18, 43, 160, 305–306
social security: *dibao* system of 526; 'five guarantee' households 259; fund misappropriation and 521; migrants and 526
Soviet Union: and the Third Front 265; relations with China and 53–54, 79, 99–100, 133, 156, 262, 265, 317; collapse of xxiii, 29, 352; collectivization in 113, 121, 219–220; development level of 55–56, 83; growth rates in 6, 83–84, 439–440; industrialization strategy in 43, 87, 113; investment rate in 38, 156–157; isolation and 28–30; productivity growth in 29; revolution in 56; split with China and 133; transition 325
spatial inequality xiii, 21, 39; agriculture and 304–305; geography and 21, 483; educational attainment and 200–201, 204, 296–297; Ten Great Relationships and 137, 153–154; twinning policy and 487–488; *see also* coastal development strategy; western China
spatial inequality during: the 1930s 62–63; 1952–3 63–68; 1950s 109–111; Great Leap Forward 136–139; late Maoism 153–154, 239, 278–282, 296–297, 300–305, 321; 1978–1996 457–458; post-1996 482–491, 513, 519
special economic zones: and Shanghai 333; creation of 332–333, 367; 1973 plan for 166
Sri Lanka: development record of 9, 10
stabilization policy *see* cyclical fluctuations in output
Stalin, J.: and transition in the Soviet Union 83–84; Korean war and 53–54; 'was Stalin really necessary?' 113, 117

state-owned enterprises: efficiency of 401–404, 415–418, 435, 437; governance 412–415; investment in 333–334; output share xxi, 355, 420–424; ownership levels in 120–121; privatization of xxvi, 332, 355, 420–424, 437; productivity in 269, 271, 402–403; profitability in 401–402; restructuring of 332, 407–418, 420–424
state spending 167–168, 333; on education and health 533–534, 543; on poverty reduction 449–450
State Statistical Bureau (National Bureau of Statistics) 116–117, 290, 438
state weakness: and growth prospects 530–532
steel production: at Panzhihua 267–269; during Great Leap Forward 125, 130, 135, 264
stock market 354, 414–415; as casino 400, 521; manipulation of 521
Sunan 50–51; obstacles to in-migration in 62; rural industrialization in 275, 449; *see also* Yangzi delta
superstructure xxi–xxii, xxv, 80–83, 474; and changes in during the Cultural Revolution 150–152; and Maoist thought 147–150, 152–155
surplus: above subsistence 49, 50; labour 52, 223–224, 258
sustainable development 527–537; cultural obstacles and 532–537; diminishing returns to investment and 528–530; environmental threat to 539; state weakness and 530–532

Taiwan: development record of 40, 102; inequality in 457; land consolidation schemes in 343, 346; land reform in 21; Japanese colonialism and 38
tariffs 354; cuts in 368, 370, 375; on agricultural products 358
taxation: agricultural 481; income 532; industrial 418; rural protest and 519–521
Tawney, R. H.: on causes of rural unrest 70; on rural indebtedness 71–72; on rural poverty 68
technical progress: agriculture and 153, 156, 221–223, 247–248, 254, 385; before 1949 48–49; during Great Leap Forward 264; growth and 24–25, 528–529; industry and 264, 416–417;

irrigation and 221, 252; open door spillover effects and 377–378, 379, 382–385; technology transfers and 99–100, 153, 221, 416–417; USSR and 28–29
terms of trade, internal: and education 204; farm output and 245–247, 252–253, 346–347; theoretical issues and 245–246, 260; Third Front and 153, 247; trends during Maoist era 246, 252–253; trends post-1978 332, 346–347
terms of trade, external: and agriculture 343, 346
textile industry: expansion of 46–47, 88, 92, 333
'textiles first' 87–89
Third Front 265–269; beginning of xxiv, 173, 265–266; effects of 274–282, 304, 317; efficiency 269, 271, 283, 403–404; end of 333, 485, 410–411; inequality and 278–282; in Guangdong 267, 268; in Sichuan 266–268; in Gansu 266–267; legacies 35, 274–278, 282–283, 403–404, 410–411; literature on 284, 317; 'little' 267; rationale for 262, 265–266; spatial inequality and 300–305
Tian'anmen massacre (1989) 326, 352
Tianjin: industrial development in 87
Tianshui: and Third Front 267
Tibet: culture and 490–491; geographical obstacles to development in 32; Han colonialism and 491, 535; migration and 491, 524–525; railway and 489
total factor productivity growth: East Asia and 398, 528–529; estimates of 235–236; industrial 429–430, 416–417; Maoist agriculture and 235–236, 258; post-1978 agriculture and 235–236; theoretical issues and 528–529
township and village enterprises *see* rural industry
trade *see* foreign trade; exports; imports; internal trade
transition: and China-Russia comparisons 435–436; Maoist legacies and 436–437; Marxian theory of 80–83, 119, 326; technical progress and 28; Ukraine and 38; *see also* market socialism
transition to capitalism in China after 1978: debates on 326–329, 435–437; literature on 356; process of 329–356, 469–496 *passim*

transition to socialism: in China 82–87, 98–99, 118–124; in Soviet Union 55–56, 83–85
transport costs 61, 63, 343; and imports 387

unemployment 426–429; Chinese exports and 361; graduates and 508, 532; in neoclassical models 396–397; threat to growth of 531; urban 426–429, 453, 515–516
United Kingdom: capital market failure in 400; deindustrialization in 361, 400; industrial development of 273; labour release and 222–223; life expectancy in 295; *see also* British Industrial Revolution
United States of America: deindustrialization in 361, 400; low wages in 400; military threat to China and 99, 214–215, 265, 317, 464; Nixon's China visit and 166, 363; *renminbi* exchange rate and 371; trade with China and 363–364; WTO negotiations and 369–370
urban bias: and migration 477–478; in China 279–280, 287; theory 15
USSR *see* Soviet Union

Vietnam: agriculture in 226, 345; industrial policy and 401; US involvement and 136, 152, 265, 317; war with China and 169; land law in 345

'walking on two legs' 145, 152–153, 263, 286–287; and spatial inequality 278–282; in education 177, 184
war: benefits from 35; industrialization during 53; Korean 54, 102
Washington consensus
weather: and decollectivization 252–253, 339, 465; and the Great Famine 132, 141
Wen Jiabao: and migrant tuition fees 525; on rural education 481–482, 508
Wenzhou: rural industrialization in 275–276; growth of private industry in 332, 413
western China: development strategy for xxiii, 482–491; fiscal transfers and 489–490; industry and 403; infrastructure projects in 489; *see also* Third Front

World Trade Organization: and Chinese liberals 392; Chinese entry and 369–370, 476; impact of 387–388, 530–531
Wuxi (Jiangsu): industrialization in 46, 47, 267

xiafang (sending down) 162–166, 189, 206; and environmental damage 312–313
Xinjiang province (East Turkestan): human development in 296–297; infant mortality in 308

Yan'an 53, 151; education in 175–176
Yangzi delta: and open door 385–386, 390; economic development in xxiv, 50, 73
Yunnan province: and *xiafang* 165; environmental damage in 312; poverty in xxiii; rural industry in 448

Zhao Ziyang: and agricultural liberalization 337; and coastal development strategy 485–486; and neo-authoritarianism 328–329; and open door 368; and price reform 351; in Sichuan 252, 337; on inequality; on primary stage of socialism 326–327; purge of 326, 352
Zhou Enlai: and Cultural Revolution 160; and *fanmaojin* 122–123; and Four Modernizations 136, 317; and Great Famine 139; and import substitution 166
Zhejiang province: education and growth in 199; exports and 276; consumption levels in 102–103; industrialization in 281–282; land ownership in 106; rural industry in 448; *see also* Wenzhou
zhuada fangxiao 420–424, 476
Zhu Rongji: fiscal policy and 353, 470; fiscal recentralization and 353, 474; WTO entry and 369–370

eBooks – at www.eBookstore.tandf.co.uk

A library at your fingertips!

eBooks are electronic versions of printed books. You can store them on your PC/laptop or browse them online.

They have advantages for anyone needing rapid access to a wide variety of published, copyright information.

eBooks can help your research by enabling you to bookmark chapters, annotate text and use instant searches to find specific words or phrases. Several eBook files would fit on even a small laptop or PDA.

NEW: Save money by eSubscribing: cheap, online access to any eBook for as long as you need it.

Annual subscription packages

We now offer special low-cost bulk subscriptions to packages of eBooks in certain subject areas. These are available to libraries or to individuals.

For more information please contact webmaster.ebooks@tandf.co.uk

We're continually developing the eBook concept, so keep up to date by visiting the website.

www.eBookstore.tandf.co.uk